Arguing about Gods

In this book, Graham Oppy examines contemporary arguments for and against the existence of God. He shows that none of these arguments is powerful enough to change the minds of reasonable participants in debates on the question of the existence of God. His conclusion is supported by detailed analyses of the contemporary arguments, as well as by the development of a theory about the purpose of arguments, and the criteria that should be used in judging whether or not arguments are successful. Oppy discusses the work of a wide array of philosophers, including Anselm, Aquinas, Descartes, Locke, Leibniz, Kant, Hume, and, more recently, Plantinga, Dembski, White, Dawkins, Bergman, Gale, and Pruss.

Graham Oppy is Associate Dean of Research in the Faculty of Arts at Monash University. He is the author of *Ontological Arguments and Belief in God* and *Philosophical Perspectives on Infinity*. He is an Associate Editor of the *Australasian Journal of Philosophy*, and he serves on the editorial boards of *Philo, Philosopher's Compass, Religious Studies*, and *Sophia*.

Arguing about Gods

GRAHAM OPPY
Monash University

CAMBRIDGE UNIVERSITY PRESS

CAMBRIDGE UNIVERSITY PRESS
Cambridge, New York, Melbourne, Madrid, Cape Town, Singapore,
São Paulo, Delhi, Dubai, Tokyo

Cambridge University Press
32 Avenue of the Americas, New York, NY 10013-2473, USA

www.cambridge.org
Information on this title: www.cambridge.org/9780521122641

First published 2006
This digitally printed version 2009

A catalog record for this publication is available from the British Library

Library of Congress Cataloging in Publication data
Oppy, Graham Robert.
Arguing about gods / Graham Oppy.
p.   cm.
Includes bibliographical references and index.
ISBN 0-521-86386-4 (hardback)
1. God – Proof.   I. Title.
BT103.O67   2006
212′.1 – dc22   2005037369

ISBN 978-0-521-86386-5 Hardback
ISBN 978-0-521-12264-1 Paperback

In memory of my father,
Edmund Thomas (Ted) Oppy
December 15, 1929–May 31, 1999

Contents

Contents

Preface

As I indicated in the preface to my book *Philosophical Perspectives on Infinity* (2006), this work on arguments about the existence of orthodoxly conceived monotheistic gods was initially intended to form part of a larger work under the title *God and Infinity*. However, while there are places in which I do appeal to my earlier work on infinity – and while there are also places where I try to note the ways in which considerations about the infinite have a differential impact on arguments about the existence of orthodoxly conceived monotheistic gods – I think that it is fair to say that the finished work is more in the nature of an interim summary of my views on arguments about the existence of orthodoxly conceived monotheistic gods.

There are various reasons why this work is only an interim summary. *First*, there are ways in which my views about the topics discussed in this book have changed over time; I see no reason why there will not be further changes in the future. *Second*, the nature of the subject ensures that there are many important topics that bear directly on the assessment of arguments about the existence of orthodoxly conceived monotheistic gods, but about which nothing is said in this book. While I would like to have given an encyclopedic discussion of the subject, it is doubtful that I would have found either publisher or readers if I had tried to do so. *Third*, I have no doubt that there will be interesting new formulations of arguments about the existence of orthodoxly conceived monotheistic gods that appear in the near future – and those new formulations may have important consequences for the chief claims that are defended in the present book. *Fourth*, there is another part of the projected larger work – on the topic of the properties that are typically assigned to orthodoxly conceived monotheistic gods – that forms a companion to the present work but that is not yet ready for publication. Some of the material that one might have thought ought to be discussed in the present work will actually turn up in that other volume, when it finally sees the light of day.

Acknowledgments

Monash University supported the writing of this book in various ways, not least by employing me as a member of its academic staff and by providing me with sufficient time to pursue my research interests. In 2002 and again in 2003, I received generous Monash Research Fund grants that enabled me to make substantial progress on the manuscript. Then, in the first half of 2004, I was granted a sabbatical, during which I was able to devote myself full-time to the completion of this work (together with the completion of *Philosophical Perspectives on Infinity*). I am very grateful for the support that I have received from my colleagues at Monash, from within the School of Philosophy and Bioethics, from within the Faculty of Arts more widely, and from within the university community as a whole.

I have discussed the material in this book with more people than I can remember. I apologise in advance to anyone whose name ought to be on the following list, but who has been omitted: Jeremy Aarons, Mike Almeida, Dirk Baltzly, John Bigelow, John Bishop, David Braddon-Mitchell, John A. Burgess, Stephen Coleman, David Dowe, Robert Dunn, Peter Forrest, John Fox, Richard Gale, Steve Gardner, Karen Green, Alan Hájek, John Hawthorne, Allen Hazen, Lloyd Humberstone, Edward Khamara, Bruce Langtry, David Lewis, John Maher, Behan McCulloch, Peter Menzies, Yujin Nagasawa, Daniel Nolan, Camille Oppy, Alex Pruss, David Simpson, Quentin Smith, Richard Swinburne, Aubrey Townsend, Nick Trakakis, Suzanne Uniacke, Brian Weatherson, and Ed Zalta.

As always, there are some people who deserve special thanks. In particular, I note that there has never been a time – until now – during the lives of my children in which I have not been working on the material that appears in this book (and its companion volumes). Big thanks, then, to Camille, Gilbert, Calvin, and Alfie: I'm sure we'll find other ways to pass the time.

This book contains some material that has been published elsewhere. In particular: section 1.2 is taken from Oppy (2002d); section 1.3 is a very lightly edited version of Oppy (1994); section 1.4 is a very lightly edited version of

Oppy (2004c); section 2.1 is a very lightly edited version of Oppy (2001a); section 2.2 is an initial draft of Oppy (1997b); section 2.3 is taken from Oppy (1996a); section 2.4 contains some material taken from Oppy (1996c); section 3.9 includes a lightly edited version of Oppy (1997c); section 4.1 is a lightly edited version of Oppy (2002c); section 4.3 contains some material taken from (2004d); section 4.4 is a lightly edited version of Oppy (1996b); section 6.2 is a lightly edited version of Oppy (2004a); section 6.3 is a lightly edited version of Almeida and Oppy (2003); and section 6.4 is a lightly edited version of Nagasawa, Oppy, and Trakakis (2004). The remaining sections of the book, including most of section 2.4, almost all of chapter 3, section 4.2, section 4.3, all of chapter 5, section 6.1, all of chapter 7, and all of the various Introductions and Conclusions, are entirely new.

I am grateful to Ashgate Publishing for kind permission to reprint material from my "Some Questions about 'The Hartle-Hawking Cosmology'," *Sophia* 36, no. 1 (1997): 84–95; from my "Reply to Langtry," *Sophia* 40, no. 1 (2001): 73–80; and from my "Review of *God and Design*, edited by Neil Manson," *Sophia* 43, no. 1 (2003): 127–31.

I am grateful to Blackwell Publishing for kind permission to reprint material from my "Gödelian Ontological Arguments," *Analysis* 56, no. 4 (1996): 226–30.

I am grateful to the Hegeler Institute for kind permission to reprint material from my "Pantheism, Quantification, and Mereology," *Monist* 80, no. 2 (1997): 320–36, copyright © 1997, *The Monist: An International Journal of General Philosophical Inquiry*.

I am grateful to Dr. Ward E. Jones, the editor of *Philosophical Papers*, for kind permission to reprint material from my "Salvation in Heaven?" *Philosophical Papers* 33, no. 1 (2004): 97–119; and I am also grateful to my co-authors, Yujin Nagasawa and Nick Trakakis, for their similarly kind permission to reprint this material.

I am grateful to Springer Science + Business Media for kind permission to reprint material from my "Weak Agnosticism Defended," *International Journal for Philosophy of Religion* 36 (1994): 147–67; from my "Hume and the Argument for Biological Design," *Biology and Philosophy* 11, no. 4 (1996): 519–34; and from my "Arguments from Moral Evil," *International Journal for Philosophy of Religion* 56 (2004): 59–87.

I am grateful to the Taylor and Francis Group for kind permission to reprint material from my "Sceptical Theism and the Evidential Argument from Evil," *Australasian Journal of Philosophy* 81, no. 4 (2003): 496–516; and I am also grateful to my co-author, Michael J. Almeida, for his similarly kind permission to reprint this material.

I am grateful to Ed Zalta for kind permission to reprint material from my "Ontological Arguments," *The Stanford Encyclopedia of Philosophy*, Fall 2005 edition, Edward N. Zalta (ed.), http://plato.stanford.edu/archives/fall2005/entries/ontological-arguments.

I am grateful to Quentin Smith, and to the Center for Inquiry, for kind permission to reprint material from my "Arguing about the *Kalām* Cosmological Argument," *Philo* 5, no. 1 (2002): 34–61; and from my "Paley's Argument for Design," *Philo* 5, no. 2 (2002): 41–53.

Finally, I am grateful to ATF Press for kind permission to reprint material from my "God, God* and God'," which first appeared in A. Fisher and H. Ramsay (eds.), *Faith and Reason: Friends or Foes in the New Millenium?* (Hindmarsh: ATF Press, 2004), pp. 171–86.

Last, but not least, thank you to the production team who helped to turn my manuscript into a book. In particular, Beatrice Rehl and Stephanie Sakson have done a sterling job in pushing this project through to completion, as they did in the case of *Philosophical Perspectives on Infinity*.

Introduction

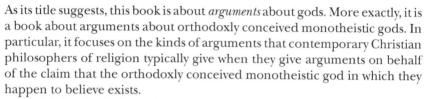

As its title suggests, this book is about *arguments* about gods. More exactly, it is a book about arguments about orthodoxly conceived monotheistic gods. In particular, it focuses on the kinds of arguments that contemporary Christian philosophers of religion typically give when they give arguments on behalf of the claim that the orthodoxly conceived monotheistic god in which they happen to believe exists.

In this book, I take it for granted that there is nothing incoherent – doxastically impossible – in the idea that our universe was created *ex nihilo* by an omnipotent, omniscient, perfectly good being. I propose to consider this question further in a companion volume that is currently incomplete; however, I do not propose there to defend the view that there is something incoherent – doxastically impossible – in the idea that our universe was created *ex nihilo* by an omnipotent, omniscient, perfectly good being.

The main thesis that I wish to defend in the present book is that there are no *successful* arguments about the existence of orthodoxly conceived monotheistic gods – that is, no arguments that ought to persuade those who have reasonable views about the existence of orthodoxly conceived monotheistic gods to change their minds. Since I also contend that there is a very wide range of reasonable views about the existence of orthodoxly conceived monotheistic gods that it is possible for reasonable people to maintain, I take it that the main thesis that I wish to defend is denied by many contemporary philosophers. If the argument of my book is successful, then at least some of those philosophers will be led to change their minds about some things.

The division of the material in the book is, in some ways, quite conventional: there is a chapter on ontological arguments, a chapter on cosmological arguments, a chapter on teleological arguments, a chapter on Pascal's wager, a chapter on arguments from evil, and a chapter on other arguments. Book-ending these chapters, there is an introductory discussion of relevant issues and a concluding discussion that revisits some of the matters raised in the introductory discussion. However, there is not much material in this book that can be found in other books that cover more or less the same territory.

In chapter 1, after some brief remarks about taxonomies of arguments about orthodoxly conceived monotheistic gods, there are three related topics that are discussed. The first of these topics concerns the nature of arguments and argumentation, and the connections that obtain between successful argumentation and reasonable believing. In this section, I sketch my views about rationality and rational belief revision, arguments, rational argumentation amongst rational agents, and the bearing of our departures from perfect rationality on each of the aforementioned topics. The second topic taken up in the first chapter concerns the tenability of agnosticism. Here, I argue that there is no reason at all to suppose that there cannot be reasonable agnostics, that is, reasonable people who suspend judgment on the question of whether there are orthodoxly conceived monotheistic gods. The third topic taken up in the first chapter concerns the bearing of the construction of cases for the existence of unorthodoxly conceived monotheistic gods – for example, perfectly evil monotheistic gods – on the reasonableness of belief in orthodoxly conceived monotheistic gods. Here, I try to defend the view that, while non-theists can reasonably judge that the case for a given unorthodoxly conceived monotheistic god is no less strong than the case for any orthodoxly conceived monotheistic god, theists can reasonably judge that this is not so.

In chapter 2, the discussion of ontological arguments takes for granted the material that is contained in my earlier book on this topic: Oppy (1995c). In the first section of this chapter, I criticise the 'general objection to ontological arguments' that I presented in my earlier book; I no longer believe that this 'general objection' has any teeth. In the second section of this chapter, I discuss a category of ontological arguments – mereological ontological arguments – that received almost no attention in Oppy (1995c). In the third section of this chapter, I provide a slightly more extensive discussion of Gödel's ontological argument than is to be found in Oppy (1995c). In particular, I defend the claim that there is an application of Gaunilo's famous 'lost island' criticism of St. Anselm's ontological argument that can be applied to one version of Gödel's ontological argument. Finally, in the fourth section of this chapter, I provide a careful examination of the arguments of Chambers (2000), and respond to some criticisms of Oppy (1995c) that are made in that work.

The discussion of cosmological arguments that occurs in chapter 3 has several parts. First, I have included some discussion of historically important cosmological arguments in the work of Aquinas, Descartes, and Leibniz. Next, I turn my attention to contemporary defences of cosmological arguments in the work of Bob Meyer, Robert Koons, Richard Gale and Alex

Pruss, and William Lane Craig. Finally, I consider the novel atheological cosmological argument that is defended by Quentin Smith. Since there are many cosmological arguments that are not considered in this discussion, it is important that I note here that I consider these to be the best arguments of this kind that have been advanced thus far. Given that none of these arguments is successful, there is very good reason to think that no cosmological argument that has been advanced hitherto is successful.

In chapter 4, I begin with a reconsideration of Paley's argument for design. I argue that this argument has been misunderstood by almost everyone who has commented on it in the past fifty years. Moreover, I claim that, when the argument is properly understood, it is readily seen to be deficient. Finally – and importantly – I claim that there is no reason to suppose that Michael Behe's recent revival of Paley's argument avoids the criticisms that are sufficient to sink Paley's argument. After a fairly careful discussion of Behe's work, I move on to consider the recent enthusiasm for 'cosmic fine-tuning' arguments for design. Following Manson (2003), I distinguish several different variants of this type of argument, and then argue that none of the variants that I consider is successful. Again, it is important that I note here that I take it that I have examined the best arguments of this kind that have thus far been propounded. Finally, I turn to a discussion of Hume's famous critique of arguments for design in his *Dialogues Concerning Natural Religion*. I'm a big fan of Hume's *Dialogues*; so it should come as no surprise that I defend the claim that it is a mistake to suppose that the various arguments for intelligent design can be shown to be unsuccessful without any appeal to the kinds of philosophical considerations that make an appearance in Hume's *Dialogues*.

Chapter 5 is a brief discussion of Pascal's wager argument. I think that it is pretty obvious that this argument has nothing going for it; nonetheless, it is not hard to find contemporary philosophers who disagree. I list a dozen or so considerations, each of which seems to me to be sufficient to establish that Pascal's wager argument is unsuccessful or, at any rate, to establish that there are large classes of non-theists who are quite properly unmoved by the argument.

In chapter 6, I turn my attention to arguments from evil. As I note at the outset, I am quite happy to allow that there are no successful arguments from evil. However, there are many contemporary philosophers of religion who are prepared to take some arguments for the existence of orthodoxly conceived monotheistic gods seriously while off-handedly dismissing arguments from evil. I claim that this is a mistake. There is perhaps more to be learned from a reconsideration of Mackie's 'logical' argument from evil than there is to be learned from a close examination of cosmological arguments – or so I am prepared to contend. At the very least, 'logical' arguments from evil are in no worse shape than any of the positive arguments that can be advanced on behalf of the existence of orthodoxly conceived monotheistic gods. Moreover, it is equally a mistake to suppose that currently popular 'sceptical theist' critiques of evidential arguments from evil establish that there is something wrong with the rationality of those who make the kinds of judgments that are required for endorsement of the premises of those arguments. I am happy enough to grant that those judgments are not rationally required; but I deny that sceptical theists have shown that those judgments are rationally impermissible. Finally, I think that it is a mistake to suppose that one can get a satisfactory response to arguments from evil merely by appealing to the claim that there is a paradisiacal afterlife that at least some of us will enjoy. If you are serious about 'defending' the claim that there is no inconsistency amongst the various propositions that make up the traditional 'problem of evil', then you cannot hope to mount this 'defence' by appealing to other controversial propositions that you happen to accept.

The arguments that are discussed in chapter 7 are quite diverse. I consider arguments from *authority*, that is, arguments from consensus, historical tradition, expert testimony, and scripture; arguments from *religious experience*, focussing in particular on the argument of Swinburne (1979); arguments from *morality*, that is, arguments from objective values, virtue, happiness, scripture, justice, the costs of irreligion, heavenly reward, conscience, convergence, and practical reason; arguments from *miracles*; arguments from *consciousness*, focussing again on Swinburne (1979); and arguments from *puzzling phenomena*, that is, arguments from providence, efficacy of prayer, mathematical knowledge, the nature of Jesus, unbelief, mystery, information, and beauty. In this section, some of the arguments that are considered are not even *prima facie* plausible; however, almost all of them have at least some contemporary defenders.

Finally, in chapter 8, there is a brief discussion of the contrasting views of Clifford and James on the ethics of belief. I defend the view that, while both Clifford and James are strictly speaking mistaken in the claims that they advance, there is something in the ballpark of Clifford's famous Principle that ought to be accepted: *it is, indeed, irrational, always, everywhere, and for anyone, to believe anything that is not appropriately proportioned to the reasons and evidence that are possessed by that one.* But this version of Clifford's Principle has no interesting consequences for the discussion of arguments about the existence of orthodoxly conceived monotheistic gods; rather, it coheres nicely with the claim that there are no successful arguments about the existence of orthodoxly conceived monotheistic gods.

As I make clear at various places in the text, I view the argument of this book as a work in progress. I am very firmly of the belief that there are no supernatural entities of any kind; *a fortiori*, I am very firmly of the belief that there are no orthodoxly conceived monotheistic gods. I am also pretty firmly of the belief that, even by quite strict standards, those who believe in the existence of orthodoxly conceived monotheistic gods need not thereby manifest some kind of failure of rationality. If I cannot find a satisfactory way to put these two beliefs together, then it will certainly be the latter that falls by the wayside; but I see no reason for thinking that it is not possible consistently – and, indeed, reasonably – to hang on to both beliefs.

1

Preliminary Considerations

There are four preliminary topics that I wish to take up in this first chapter. The first topic is the question of how best to provide a taxonomy of arguments about the existence of orthodoxly conceived monotheistic gods. Here, I am happy to follow the more or less *ad hoc* system of classification that has grown up around Kant's classification of theoretical arguments into the ontological, the cosmological, and the teleological. Since I think that each argument should be treated on its merits, I don't care how the arguments are grouped together; what really matters is that no arguments should be neglected.

The second topic is the question of how best to think about the virtues of arguments. When should we say that an argument for a given conclusion is a successful argument? I defend the view that, in circumstances in which it is well known that there has been perennial controversy about a given claim, a successful argument on behalf of that claim has to be one that ought to persuade all of those who have hitherto failed to accept that claim to change their minds. While this view sets the bar very high, there are, I think, good reasons for preferring it to views that would have one saying that there are successful arguments for conclusions that one does not oneself accept.

The third topic is the question of the tenability of agnosticism. There are many people who have supposed that sensible, thoughtful, reflective, well-informed people cannot be agnostics: the only alternatives are (some kind of) theism and atheism. I think that this supposition is mistaken: if one supposes – as I do – that there can be sensible, thoughtful, reflective, well-informed people who are theists, and that there can be sensible, thoughtful, reflective, well-informed people who are atheists, then it is perhaps not very surprising that one can also maintain that there are sensible, thoughtful, reflective, well-informed people who are agnostics, that is, who suspend belief on the question of whether there is an orthodoxly conceived monotheistic god.

The fourth preliminary topic is the question of the alleged existence of cases for alternatives to orthodoxly conceived monotheistic gods that are no less strong than the case for orthodoxly conceived monotheistic gods themselves, for example, the alleged existence of a case for belief in an omnipotent, omniscient, and perfectly evil creator of the world that relies on 'parallels' to the various arguments that are standardly offered on behalf of belief in an orthodoxly conceived monotheistic god. Here, I argue that the existence of these 'parallel cases' does not provide the materials for a successful argument against the existence of orthodoxly conceived monotheistic gods, even though those who do not accept that there is an orthodoxly conceived monotheistic god may be perfectly justified in maintaining that the cases are, indeed, entirely parallel.

1.1. ARGUMENTS ABOUT THE EXISTENCE OF MONOTHEISTIC GODS

There are many different kinds of arguments that have been offered for and against the existence of monotheistic gods – and, indeed, for the existence of non-monotheistic gods as well, though we shall not be concerned here with any of these arguments. Attempts to classify – exhaustively and exclusively – all of these arguments for and against the existence of monotheistic gods are apt to end in frustration. Nonetheless, I shall attempt to provide a rough survey here, using traditional – Kantian – labels for classes of arguments that, in some sense, seem to be naturally collected together. Part of the point of the exercise is to test the Kantian system of labelling when it is extended to cover both argument for, and arguments against, the existence of monotheistic gods.

There are some arguments for and against the existence of monotheistic gods that proceed more or less *a priori*. In particular, there are **ontological** arguments that start from definitions, or claims about the contents of conceptions or ideas, or claims about what is conceivable or logically possible, or allegedly analytic claims about the concept of existence, or the like, and – without the addition of further premises that are not claimed to be knowable *a priori* – draw conclusions about the existence or non-existence of monotheistic gods. On this characterisation, arguments to the conclusion that a postulated divine attribute is incoherent, or that a postulated tuple of divine attributes are jointly inconsistent, are classified as ontological arguments. If this consequence is deemed unhappy, then one ought to distinguish between ontological arguments for and against the existence of monotheistic gods and non-ontological *a priori* arguments against the existence of monotheistic gods. When thinking about ontological arguments, it is important not to lose sight of the fact that, for more or less any ontological argument in favour of the existence of a given monotheistic god, there are typically closely related ontological arguments against the existence of that god. One of the most important questions to be raised in the context of discussions of ontological arguments concerns the significance of the existence of these 'parodies' of ontological arguments for the existence of monotheistic gods.

There are many kinds of arguments for and against the existence of monotheistic gods that draw upon claims that are allegedly supported by *a posteriori* evidence. In some cases, the claims in question are alleged to be synthetic *a priori*, and hence distinct in kind from the key analytic *a priori* premises in ontological arguments. However – even setting aside Quinean scruples about the alleged distinction between claims that are synthetic *a priori* and claims that are analytic *a priori* – it seems doubtful that we shall go too far wrong if we suppose that the various kinds of arguments that we are about to describe are properly said to be *a posteriori* (evidential) arguments for and against the existence of monotheistic gods.

I shall suppose that **cosmological** arguments for and against the existence of monotheistic gods are arguments with key premises that advert to very general structural features of the universe and/or our ways of theorising about the universe – temporal structure, modal structure, causal structure, explanatory structure, intelligible structure, axiological structure, and the like – of which it is not plausible to claim that we have an exhaustive (analytic) *a priori* knowledge. Since I think that mereology is (analytic) *a priori*, I suppose that any argument for or against the existence of monotheistic gods that appeals only to very general mereological principles is properly classified as an ontological argument. Some might suppose that modality is similarly (analytic) *a priori*, and hence that arguments for or against the existence of monotheistic gods that appeal only to very general modal principles ought also be classified as ontological arguments. However, since I know of no such arguments for or against the existence of monotheistic gods, I think that nothing hangs on this decision. One consideration that will be important in our discussion of cosmological arguments for the existence of monotheistic gods is that these arguments very often involve claims about the impossibility of certain kinds of infinite regresses (in the general structural features under consideration). Nonetheless, I doubt that it should be built into the analysis of cosmological arguments that all arguments of this kind must have a premise of this sort.

I shall suppose that **teleological** arguments for and against the existence of monotheistic gods are arguments with key premises that appeal to particular (contingent) features of the world that are alleged to be *prima facie* plausible instances of intelligent design. Typical teleological arguments for or against the existence of monotheistic gods advert to particular cosmogonic, physical, chemical, biological, psychological, or social features of the world. Many arguments that are classified as teleological arguments under the above proposal are classified as minor evidential arguments by other philosophers. While it may be plausible to claim that the strongest teleological arguments are those that appeal to certain cosmogonic or biological features of the universe, it is not clear why this consideration should lead us to suppose that arguments from consciousness, or the existence of language, or the existence of politically structured societies, and the like, should not also be classified as teleological arguments. Since our discussion shall focus on arguments about cosmogonic and biological features of the universe, it won't really matter to us how this issue is resolved.

Even if we suppose that the class of teleological arguments is fairly broadly defined, it seems that there are many evidential arguments left over – and it also seems reasonable to say that these are **minor evidential arguments**. Among the many different kinds of arguments that can be assigned to this category, we might include arguments from various kinds of authorities, such as scripture, bodies of religious believers, common consent, religious leaders, and the like; arguments from religious experience and revelation; arguments from alleged miracles; and so forth. Since the distinction between cosmological arguments, teleological arguments, and minor evidential arguments is not very clear, the most important point on which to insist is that any evidential argument that is not classified as either cosmological or teleological must be classified as a minor evidential argument, so that no argument is overlooked.

Many people have supposed that there is a category of **moral arguments** for and against the existence of monotheistic deities. The evidential arguments that fall into this alleged category can also be assigned to one of the categories that we have already distinguished. If we focus on the alleged fact that our world has a fundamental moral structure, then we might take ourselves to be concerned with cosmological moral arguments. If we focus, instead, on facts about the allegedly providential distribution of goods and rights in human societies, or on alleged facts about the existence of conscience and a sense of right and wrong in human agents, then we might suppose that we are concerned with teleological moral arguments. If we focus on considerations about the mismatch between happiness and desert in this life, or on the allegedly greater happiness of believers, or the like, then we might suppose that we are dealing with minor evidential arguments. Of course, if there are non-evidential moral arguments, then these must be assigned to different categories.

The classification of **arguments from evil** is also problematic given the categories that we have established thus far. Perhaps the most satisfying suggestion is to assign all of the arguments from evil to the class of teleological moral arguments: these arguments are, after all, concerned with the distribution of goods and rights in our universe. Since some – but not all – arguments from evil are standardly said to be evidential arguments from evil, it might be thought that there is a *prima facie* difficulty that arises for this proposed classification. However, the distinction between **logical arguments from evil** and **evidential arguments from evil** turns merely on the question of whether the claim that evil exists – or that such and such kinds of evil exist, or that such and such quantities of evil exist, or that such and such particular evils have occurred, or the like – is logically inconsistent with the claim that given monotheistic gods exist, or whether that claim merely lowers the probability – or makes it implausible to believe, or somehow undercuts the justification for believing – that given monotheistic gods exist. Of course, even if we are happy to classify arguments from evil as teleological moral arguments, we may nonetheless want to give a quite separate treatment of particular cosmogonic or biological arguments for the existence of given monotheistic gods, and particular arguments from evil against the existence of given monotheistic gods. Moreover, if we suppose that arguments from evil are teleological moral arguments, then we shall doubtless suppose that there are other arguments against the existence of given monotheistic gods – for example, arguments from divine hiddenness, arguments from non-belief, and the like – that should also be classified as teleological moral arguments.

Apart from *a priori* and evidential arguments for and against the existence of monotheistic gods, there are also various kinds of **non-evidential arguments** for and against the existence of monotheistic gods. Arguments that we might include in this general category include the various versions of Pascal's wager, James's arguments on behalf of the will to believe, the many variants of Kant's prudential moral argument, and so forth.

It is sometimes said that, apart from the various kinds of arguments that we have mentioned so far, there are also **cumulative arguments** that somehow combine these arguments into more powerful meta-arguments (or cases) for and against the existence of monotheistic gods. While this is doubtless so, there are pitfalls that we must be careful to avoid.

If we have two valid arguments, each of which entails the conclusion that a particular monotheistic god exists, then we can form a disjunctive argument that also entails the same conclusion. More generally, if we have a large collection of valid arguments, each of which entails the conclusion that a particular monotheistic god exists, then we can form a multiply disjunctive argument that also entails that same conclusion. However, it should not be supposed that a 'cumulative' argument that is formed in this way is guaranteed to be a better argument than the individual arguments with which we began (even if we are properly entitled to the claim that the arguments with which we are working are all valid). For, on the one hand, if all of the arguments are defective on grounds other than those of validity – for example, because they have false premises, or because they are question-begging – then the cumulative argument will also be defective. But, on the other hand, if even one of the arguments with which we began is not defective on any other grounds, then *it* is a cogent argument for its conclusion, and the cumulative argument is plainly worse (since longer and more convoluted). So, at the very least, we have good reason to be suspicious of talk about a cumulative case for the claim that a given monotheistic god does – or does not – exist that is based upon a collection of (allegedly) valid arguments for the claim that the god in question does – or does not – exist.

Of course, the argument of the preceding paragraph is not meant to cast doubt on the obviously correct claim that one can set out a derivation of a conclusion in which there are lemmas, that is, derivations of sub-conclusions that are appealed to in the derivation of the final conclusion. But – despite the appearance of occasional claims to the contrary – it should not be supposed that separate (valid) arguments for or against the existence of a given monotheistic god ever stand in this kind of relationship to one another. The premises in a valid argument may well stand in need of further support before it is plausible to claim that one has a cogent argument for the conclusion in question; but whatever form those supporting arguments take, they cannot be valid arguments that have the conclusion of the original argument as their conclusion.

Talk about a cumulative case makes much more sense if we suppose that we are dealing with 'probabilistic' – or 'inductive', or 'evidential' – arguments, in which the premises provide 'probabilistic' – or 'inductive', or 'evidential' – support for their conclusions. A proposition can be more probable given $p\&q$, than it is given either p alone or q alone. Given that the existence of a given monotheistic god is made more probable – to degree D_1 – by evidence E_1, and that the existence of that monotheistic god is made more probable – to degree D_2 – by evidence E_2, it *may* be that the existence of that monotheistic god is made more probable – to degree D_3, where $D_3 > D_2$ and $D_3 > D_1$ – by evidence $(E_1 \& E_2)$. However, once we start talking about accumulating evidence in this sense, it seems to me that the only interesting question to consider is how a given proposition stands in the light of *all* of the relevant available evidence. That a given proposition is probable given a carefully selected part of the total relevant evidence is not an interesting result. But – at the very least – this makes it very hard to be sure that one has succeeded in setting out a good probabilistic argument for any hotly disputed conclusion. We shall return to these grounds for scepticism about probabilistic arguments for perennially controversial doctrines in subsequent chapters.

1.2. ARGUMENTS

In the following parts of this section, I shall make some preliminary comments about the nature of arguments and argumentation, and about the connection that obtains between argumentation and reasonable believing. It seems to me that these topics need much more careful consideration than they are typically afforded in discussions of arguments for and against the existence of monotheistic gods. Even so, I am conscious that the following discussion is capable of improvement in many different ways.

It seems to me that a full account of what makes for a *successful* argument requires at least the following: (1) an account of rationality and rational belief revision; (2) an account of arguments; (3) an account of rational argumentation amongst rational agents; and (4) an account of the difficulties that arise as a result of the fact that we are not perfectly rational agents. Plainly, this is no small task; and I cannot pretend that I shall do justice to this topic here. Nonetheless, I propose to sketch my answer to the question of what we should suppose is required of a successful argument; I shall make use of this answer when we come to consider various arguments for belief in monotheistic gods in subsequent chapters.

1.2.1. Rationality and Rational Belief Revision

It seems to me to be plausible to think that reasonable people can disagree. Indeed, it seems to me to be more or less platitudinous that there are propositions that p such that some reasonable people believe that p, some reasonable people believe that not p, and other reasonable people are agnostic or indifferent in one way or another. Moreover, it would be wrong to think that, where there is disagreement about the truth of some proposition that p, all but one of the parties to the disagreement must be manifesting irrationality with respect to the subject matter at hand. That is, it seems to me to be more or less platitudinous that there are propositions that p such that some reasonable people act reasonably in believing that p, other reasonable people act reasonably in believing that not p, and other reasonable people act reasonably in being agnostic or indifferent in one way or another.

Of course, some of the actual disagreements among reasonable people can be traced to irrationalities: sometimes reasonable people do have 'blind spots' where irrationality creeps in. Moreover, there is a substantial body of psychological research that suggests that our 'reasonableness' is actually quite imperfect – that is, even at the best of times, we are prone to all kinds of lapses from ideal rationality (especially when it comes to statistical and probabilistic reasoning). However, there are at least two other sources of disagreements among reasonable people that are equally significant. One is that we all have different bodies of evidence – we draw on different bodies of information – that we obtain in all manner of different ways. Even if – perhaps *per impossibile* – we were perfectly rational, it would still be possible for us to disagree provided only that each of us had different partial bodies of evidence. Moreover, even if we were perfectly rational, and had accessed the same full body of evidence, it might still be possible for us to disagree provided that we accessed the evidence in differing orders (and provided that our finite capacities ensured that we could not 'store' – or access – the full body of evidence all at once). The other source of disagreement among reasonable people is that there is no one set of 'priors' that any reasonable person must have. Again – though I admit that this is slightly more controversial – it seems to me that, even if we were perfectly rational, it would be possible for us to disagree simply because we have differing 'priors' (and this would remain true even if we accessed the same full body of evidence in the same order). Of course, in saying this, I am not committing myself to the claim that there are no substantive constraints on 'priors' – it may be that there are quite severe constraints on reasonable sets of 'priors'; however, I am claiming that I can see no reason at all for thinking that there is a unique set of 'priors' that any reasonable person must have on pain of conviction of irrationality.

The above remarks seem to me to fit naturally into a *neo*-Quinean picture of the web of belief.[1] At any time, a person has a network of beliefs that are connected together in various ways. Under the impact of evidence, the person will be disposed to revise his or her beliefs in various ways. If rational, then he or she will be disposed to revise his or her beliefs in accordance with the canons of belief revision (whatever those happen to be – it is not part of my present brief to elaborate any substantial account of the content of those canons). Perhaps, for any given reasonable person in any given state, there is a unique rational revision that he or she ought to make to his or her beliefs under the impact of a given piece of evidence; perhaps not. Even if there is a unique rational revision to be made (for any person in any state given any evidence), there is no reason to think that there is bound to be convergence of belief given similar (or identical) evidential inputs. (If there is no unique rational revision to be made in the envisaged circumstances, then the prospects for convergence are even dimmer. However, I am pre-pared to suppose that there are unique rational revisions.) I see no reason at all why it could not be that a single piece of evidence leads you to believe that p and me to believe that not p, even though we both act with perfect rationality. And even if that claim is too strong, it seems pretty clear that what one ought to come to believe under the impact of any given evidence depends upon what one already believes.

My earlier talk about 'priors' was meant to suggest a Bayesian conception of belief revision. However, it was also intended to be deliberately ambiguous between 'prior probability' and 'prior belief'. It is a crucial part of the picture that I am sketching that all assessment of evidence takes place against an

---

[1] It is important to emphasise that the picture is only neo-Quinean. In particular, it should be stressed that the picture that I have sketched is not incompatible with the further claims that some beliefs are non-negotiable and unrevisable, that some beliefs have contents that are analytic and true *a priori*. Moreover, it is not incompatible with the suggestion that the canons of belief revision – or at least some aspects of those canons – and other framework features of the picture are also somehow *a priori* (e.g., because they are conceptual bedrock, or because there is some legitimate way in which they can be justified by self-application, or whatever). It would take us too far afield to try to investigate the question of just *how* Quinean the picture ought to be.

already existing background of beliefs, so that there can be no question of one's 'examining' all of one's beliefs at once. The crucial questions about reasonable belief revision thus turn out to be questions about coherence with beliefs that one already has. Moreover it seems psychologically reasonable to conjecture that there are bound to be 'environmental' influences on the network of beliefs that one comes to hold (one's belief system is in part caused by one's upbringing, etc.). However, there is no room for the thought that one might 'make over' one's system of belief, throwing out those beliefs that have 'mere causes' and preserving those for which one has 'reasons' – for every belief stands or falls by coherence with the rest, and the environmental influences have an impact on the network as a whole. Of course, it could be that considerations of coherence lead you to revise families of belief – for example, belief in Santa Claus ceases to cohere with the rest of a child's body of beliefs, and is replaced (in part) by beliefs about Santa Claus stories and the like – and that this process of revision leads one to hold that certain beliefs were merely 'caused' – 'I only believed in Santa Claus because my parents inculcated the belief in me'. But this process of labelling can only proceed *ex post facto*: in order to judge that some of one's beliefs are 'merely caused', one must already have reached a state in which one is giving them up. (There is a first-person/third-person asymmetry here: I may be perfectly well entitled, or even obliged, to judge that some of your beliefs are 'merely caused', particularly if they manifest a sufficiently deeply rooted disagreement between us.)

Plainly, there is much more to be said about the nature of reasonable belief. However, the last remaining thing that will be important for what follows is to note that nothing in the account that I have given is inconsistent with the idea that the aim of belief is truth, and the further idea that truth is a non-epistemic, non-relative notion. Nor, indeed, is anything in this account inconsistent with the idea that justification and warrant can be external matters, that is, matters that have more to do with how an agent is connected to the world than with how things are inside the agent's head. All that is being insisted on is that there is an important sense in which reasonable people must be amenable to reason, where "amenability to reason" is a matter of how things are inside the agent's head. If you are going to argue with someone – that is, to present an argument to them, or to engage in genuine argument with them – then you need to suppose that they are reasonable in this sense; but it is perfectly consistent with this assumption of rationality that you suppose that many of that person's beliefs are not warranted or justified, let alone true, because they are not appropriately connected to how things are outside that person's head. (Of course, it is a controversial question whether we should be externalists about warrant and justification. I think that nothing in what follows turns on how we choose to answer that question; in any case, I do not propose to try to pursue that issue here.)

1.2.2. Arguments and Their Role in Belief Revision

I take it that the proper function of arguments is to bring about reasonable belief revision: the aim of my argument for the conclusion that p is to bring you to reasonable acceptance of that conclusion. Of course, there are all kinds of other things that can be done with arguments – I may seek to dazzle you with my brilliance, or entertain you with my logical facility, or . . . – and there are all kinds of other ways in which I may try to bring you to (reasonable) acceptance of the conclusion that p – I may tell you a story that illustrates its truth, or show you some evidence, or. . . . However, the crucial point is that the *telos* of argumentation is bound up with reasonable belief revision.

Given this much, what shall we take to be the characteristics of a good (or successful) argument? Perhaps this seems easy: a good argument is one that succeeds – or perhaps would or ought to succeed – in bringing about reasonable belief revision in reasonable targets. The most successful argument would be one that succeeds – or perhaps would or ought to succeed – in persuading any reasonable person to accept its conclusion; good, but less successful arguments would be ones that succeed – or perhaps would or ought to succeed – in persuading a non-zero percentage of reasonable people to accept their conclusions. However, as we shall now see, there are here many difficulties that lie just below the surface.

Some arguments are deductively valid (or, in some cases, mistakenly supposed to be deductively valid). In this case, what the argument establishes – or purports to establish – is that it is a logical error to accept all of the premises of the argument, and yet to reject the conclusion of the argument: no reasonable person can accept all of the premises, and yet also reject the conclusion. Other arguments – including those that appear to rely upon induction, or inference to the best explanation, and the like – are typically not supposed to be deductively valid. In this case, what is typically supposed is that the argument establishes – or, at any rate, purports to establish – that it is reasonable – perhaps even most reasonable – to accept the conclusion of the argument on the basis of the premises. (If it is most reasonable to accept the conclusion on the basis of the premises, then it seems, again, that no reasonable person can accept all of the premises and yet also reject the conclusion.)

In both kinds of arguments, there are various kinds of things that can go wrong. For instance, in both kinds of cases, one can be mistaken about the kind of support that the premises actually lend to the conclusion. As we noted before, people are far from perfect performers of deductive reasoning, statistical reasoning, probabilistic reasoning, and the like. While it is perhaps dangerous to suppose that these kinds of errors are very widespread, it seems to me that it is highly plausible to suppose that at least some of the arguments that we shall go on to examine do indeed suffer from defects of this kind. However, given the *telos* of argumentation, there is another kind of difficulty that arises in the assessment of the merits of an argument, concerning the acceptability of the premises of the argument. If a reasonable person need not accept all of the premises of an argument, then that argument does not give all reasonable people a reason to accept its conclusion. If a reasonable person ought not to accept all of the premises of an argument, then that argument cannot give any reasonable people a reason to accept its conclusion. Hence, in determining the merit of an otherwise acceptable argument, we *always* need to ask whether reasonable people may, or must, accept all of the premises of the argument. If the argument has no premises – as may be the case, for example, in *reductio* arguments – then this is not a substantive requirement; otherwise, it is.

Even if an argument is in good inferential standing and possessed of acceptable premises, there are still things that can go awry. In particular, arguments that are circular or question-begging, or that presuppose what they are supposed to establish, or the like, are plainly not good arguments. No theist can suppose that the argument "An orthodoxly conceived monotheistic god exists, therefore an orthodoxly conceived monotheistic god exists", or the argument "Either $2 + 2 = 5$ or an orthodoxly conceived monotheistic god exists; it is not the case that $2 + 2 = 5$; therefore, an orthodoxly conceived monotheistic god exists", is a good argument even though, in each case, the argument is classically valid and possessed of premises that the theist supposes to be true. Of course, it is not an easy matter to say exactly what the fault is that is intended to be picked out by the labels "circular", "question-begging", "assumes what it sets out to prove", and the like. However, I think that what I shall have to say in the next section will suffice for the purposes of the current work.

There are many further questions about arguments that I have ducked in the foregoing discussion. In particular, it is worth noting that I haven't said anything about how arguments are identified, that is, about the question of when we should say that we have two different arguments rather than one argument presented in two different forms. One difficulty here is that there are two quite different ways in which one might think about arguments. On the one hand, we might suppose that an argument is identified simply by a collection of propositions, one of which is identified as the conclusion of the argument, and the others of which are identified as the premises. On the other hand, we might think that an argument is identified by a particular derivation of a conclusion from a bunch of premises (so that there can be many arguments with the same premises and conclusions, but which rely on different rules of inference, and travel by different sequences of inferential steps). For present purposes, it seems to me that no harm can come from choosing to work with the first conception; moreover, I think that this is the way in which those who discuss arguments about the existence of God typically think about the identity conditions for arguments. One importance consequence to note is that, where subsidiary arguments for premises in a target argument are introduced, what happens is that a new argument – with different premises – is then brought up for consideration. In general, the move of introducing supporting arguments is a tacit concession that the original argument was not successful.

1.2.3. Rational Argumentative Interchanges between Rational Agents

Suppose that a rational agent A wants to bring a rational agent B to accept the proposition that p. There are two cases to consider. *First*, it might be the case that B has no opinion about whether that p (and even, perhaps, holds no beliefs that are relevant to that question). In that case, any good argument – that is, any argument in which there is sufficient genuine transmission of truth or acceptability from premises to conclusion – that takes as premises things that B already accepts – at least once the premises have been propounded – will be an argument that succeeds in giving B a reason to accept the conclusion that p (and will lead to B's acquisition of a suitable family of beliefs). Moreover, any argument that fails to have the properties just adverted to – that is, any argument that is not good, or that proceeds from premises that B does not accept – will not be an argument that succeeds in giving B a reason to accept the conclusion that p. To repeat this last point: an argument that takes as premises propositions that those to whom the argument is directed do not accept is a failure, and those to whom it is directed are perfectly correct in saying so.

Second, it might be the case that B has already considered the question of whether p, and that B either rejects the claim that p, or else that B suspends judgment about this matter. In either case, given the presumed rationality of B, it is bound to be the case that B has numerous related beliefs that support either the rejection of that claim that p or the suspension of judgment about whether p. So, in this case, what is going to be required, in order to persuade B that p, is a good argument – that is, an argument in which there is sufficient genuine transmission of truth or acceptability from premises to conclusion – that takes as premises things that B believes, and to which B is more strongly committed than B is to the previously mentioned supporting beliefs. (Of course, as in the previous case, these premises can appeal to things that B has not hitherto considered, provided that B is then disposed to accept them.) When presented with an argument that meets these requirements, B will undergo a revision of beliefs in such a way as to take on the belief that p, and various other beliefs as well. Again, as in the first case, an argument that fails to have all of the properties adverted to – that is, an argument that is not good, or that proceeds from premises that B does not accept, or that proceeds from premises to which B is less strongly attached than B is to beliefs that support either rejection of the claim that p or else suspension of judgment whether *p* – simply fails to be an argument that gives B reason to accept the conclusion that *p*.

It is a consequence of the above discussion that it is not easy for one rational person to persuade another rational person who already holds an opinion on a given matter to revise that opinion. Of course, if the proponent of the argument has new evidence that is produced in the course of the argument – and if it is reasonable for the target of the argument to accept that it is new evidence – then persuasion to change of view can be relatively straightforward. But in that kind of case, it is the acquisition of the new evidence that is really doing all of the important work: a *perfectly* rational agent would only need to be presented with the new evidence – without the supporting argumentative dress – in order to be led to make the appropriate revisions in belief. And in cases where there is no new evidence in the premises, it is almost impossible for an argument to be successful, at least in the case of *perfectly* rational agents. Where agents are less than perfectly rational, it may be that there are unnoticed implications of beliefs that, once drawn to their attention, will lead them to belief revision of a desired kind; but a successful argument for the claim that *p* must be one that leads to adoption of the belief that *p*, and not merely to some revision or other in the beliefs of the target of the argument. I think that these consequences of the above account are not unwelcome; it is a commonplace that philosophers almost never change their beliefs about important propositions as a result of the arguments of others, even though the behaviour of philosophers with respect to these beliefs is about as rational as human behaviour ever gets to be.

1.2.4. Handling Departures from Perfect Rationality

At least sometimes, people who refuse to accept the conclusion of an argument that is presented to them are merely manifesting irrationality; so a measure of the worth of an argument can't be taken directly from the rate of success that the argument has in persuading those who did not previously accept the conclusion of the argument to change their minds. Nonetheless, it is surely the case that, if there are many people who do not accept the claim that *p*, and if almost none of those people is persuaded to change his or her mind when presented with a given argument for the conclusion that *p*, then it would take an enormously strong supporting argument – concerning the lack of rationality of all of those people – in order to overthrow the conclusion that the argument in question is plainly no good.

We can also think about these matters in the following way. Suppose that person A wishes to persuade other people to accept the conclusion that *p*. A has an argument that is presented to some people who do not accept the conclusion that. p, and the argument turns out to be entirely unsuccessful: none of the people in question is persuaded to take on the belief that *p* as a result of hearing the argument. A has two options: either A can conclude that the people in question are not rational; or else A can conclude that the argument is a failure. If A concludes that the people in question are not rational, then there is no point in persisting with the attempt to champion *any* argument for the conclusion that *p*. (If A supposes that people who do not believe that *p* are, *ipso facto*, irrational – and, in particular, that such people are *ipso facto* irrational when it comes to the question of whether that *p* – then it is a pointless and empty performance to go on producing arguments with the conclusion that *p*, since there is no possible target for those arguments.) On the other hand, if A concludes that the argument is a failure, then it is up to A to look for a *new* argument for the conclusion that *p*, or to give up on the attempt to use arguments to persuade others to accept the conclusion that *p*; but what A cannot do is to go on insisting that the argument in question is a good one.

Perhaps it might be replied that the above discussion makes the mistake of assuming that there is only *one* thing that arguments are for. Sure, an argument for the conclusion that *p* that does not meet the exacting standards described will not – and ought not to – be able to persuade people to change their minds about whether that *p*; but that doesn't mean that it might not have some other use. Such as? Well, one thing that many so-called arguments do is to exhibit logical relations between propositions; surely it can be useful to exhibit justificatory relations between beliefs, in order to improve our systems of belief. (Think, for example, of the role that systematic proof plays in mathematics. Many of these proofs are plainly not designed in order to persuade cognisers of the proofs of the truth of their conclusions.) Perhaps this point can be conceded in general; however, it seems to me that argument in philosophy – and, in particular, arguments about the existence of an orthodoxly conceived monotheistic god – almost never have this kind of rationale. If we ask about what really plays the role of justifying belief in an orthodoxly conceived monotheistic god in typical believers, we can be quite sure that it is almost *never* the implicational relations that hold between the proposition that an orthodoxly conceived monotheistic god exists and the kinds of propositions that turn up as premises in standard arguments for the existence of an orthodoxly conceived monotheistic god. While there is more to be said on this issue, I think that it is pretty clear that this suggestion about a different use for arguments won't apply in the case in which we are interested; and more generally, I think that it is actually pretty hard to think of anything else that arguments are for.[2] While noting that there is room for

---

[2] Perhaps this overstates matters a bit. For example, it might be that there are non-combative uses for arguments – or, at any rate, derivations – in attempts to exhibit justificatory structures in given collections of beliefs, etc. However, what is of most interest to non-theists is the combative use of arguments for the existence of monotheistic gods, and, there, the standard for success is the one that I have described.

further thought on this matter, I think that there is good reason to proceed under the assumption that the account of argument and argumentation that has been developed in the present section of this book is more or less correct.

1.3. SOME CONSIDERATIONS ABOUT AGNOSTICISM

Agnosticism has had some bad press in recent years. Nonetheless, I think that agnosticism can be so formulated that it is no less philosophically respectable than theism and atheism. This is not a mere philosophical exercise; for, as it happens, the formulated position is – I think – one to which I once subscribed. I include a qualification here since it may be more accurate to say that I have always subscribed to *fallibilist atheism* – but more of that anon.

In the current section, I begin by distinguishing between two different kinds of agnosticism. On the one hand, there is **strong agnosticism**, that is, the view that is sustained by the thesis that it is *obligatory* for reasonable persons to suspend judgement on the question of the existence of an orthodoxly conceived monotheistic god. And, on the other hand, there is **weak agnosticism**, that is, the view that is sustained by the thesis that it is *permissible* for reasonable persons to suspend judgement on the question of the existence of an orthodoxly conceived monotheistic god.

Strong agnosticism is characteristically defended by appeal to the apparent lack of good independent evidential support for the claim that an orthodoxly conceived monotheistic god exists. Underlying this appeal there is typically an epistemological principle that resembles the following: *in circumstances in which the available evidence no more – and no less – supports* p *than it supports logically incompatible hypotheses* $p_1, \ldots, pn, \ldots$, *one ought to suspend judgement between all of the hypotheses* p, $p_1, \ldots, pn, \ldots$. Moreover, also underlying this appeal there is typically a further principle, along the following lines: *it is possible to characterise a suitable notion of evidential support that does not rely upon a relativisation to background assumptions or theories.* In the next two parts of this section, I propose: (i) to sketch the best case that I can make for strong agnosticism; and then (ii) to argue that the case fails because the two kinds of principles required for strong agnosticism cannot be plausibly conjoined.

Weak agnosticism is, I think, best defended *via* an appeal to a principle of doxastic conservatism, along the following lines: *one is rationally justified in continuing to believe that* p *unless one comes to possess positive reason to cease to do so.* In the third and fourth parts of this section, I attempt to make a case for weak agnosticism, and to defend this case against objections. Since the strength of this case depends upon the underlying principle of doxastic conservatism, I shall also provide some assessment of the merits of this kind of approach to epistemology.

1.3.1. The Case for Strong Agnosticism

The strong agnostic claims that it is not rational to believe in the existence of the orthodoxly conceived monotheistic god of traditional Western theism, that is, the unique, personal, omniscient, omnipotent, omnibenevolent, eternal creator *ex nihilo* of the universe. However, unlike some atheists, the strong agnostic does not believe either (i) that talk of such an orthodoxly conceived monotheistic god is meaningless or incoherent, or (ii) that the concept of such an orthodoxly conceived monotheistic god is inconsistent or incoherent, or (iii) that the existence of such an orthodoxly conceived monotheistic god is ruled out by evidence that is available to all, for example, the amounts and kinds of evils in the world. Of course, the strong agnostic might be prepared to concede that it is epistemically possible that one of these atheistic claims is correct; but she holds that there is not yet conclusive reason to believe any one of them. Moreover, unlike other atheists, the strong agnostic does not subscribe to the principle that, *in the absence of any positive evidence for the existence of* x*'s, one is rationally required to believe that there are no* x*'s*. Even though the strong agnostic contends that there is currently available no good evidence for the existence of an orthodoxly conceived monotheistic god, she holds that what is rationally required is merely refusal to assent either to the claim that an orthodoxly conceived monotheistic god exists or to the claim that an orthodoxly conceived monotheistic god does not exist.

A case for strong agnosticism can be constructed as follows: It seems reasonable to allow that it is at least doxastically possible that the universe was created by one or more beings – that is, it is not obvious that this is a claim that can simply be ruled out *a priori*, or on the basis of uncontroversial evidence. So, suppose that the universe *was* created by one or more beings. What is it reasonable to believe about such beings on the basis of the available evidence, – that is, on the basis of what we know, or can reasonably believe, about the universe?

It seems that it would be quite rash to suppose that such beings must be omnipotent and omniscient. True, such beings would surely have powers and knowledge that we do not have. In particular, if they created the universe *ex nihilo*, then they have powers that it is impossible for us to have. But what reason is there to suppose that they can do anything that it is logically possible for them to do, and that they know everything that it is logically possible for them to know? Is there any reason to suppose that one would need to know everything that it is logically possible for one to know in order for one to be able to create a universe such as ours? For instance, should we suppose that the creators of the world must know everything about transfinite arithmetic? This is surely an entirely open question. Similarly, is there any reason to suppose that one would need to be able to do everything that it is logically possible for one to do in order for one to be able to create a world such as ours? Should we suppose that the creators of our universe were able to create uncountably many similar worlds? Or should we suppose that this world is the only world that they had in them? Again, this looks like an entirely open question.

It also seems that it would be very rash to suppose that such beings are omnibenevolent. Even if – as many theists have argued – the amounts and kinds of evil in the world are compatible with the existence of an omnibenevolent deity, it is not at all clear that this evidence does not point more strongly towards creators with an entirely different moral character. At the very least, it seems that it is no less plausible to suppose that the creators of the world have morally indifferent characters, or to suppose that the creators of the world are themselves morally evil – things might get pretty dull in whatever realm they inhabit; and what need our suffering be to them? Of course, in the latter case, there will be problems about the amounts and kinds of good in the world, but, even in the case in which the creators in question are omnimalevolent, it is hard to suppose that there is any more difficulty than there is for the traditional theists who attempts to deal with the problems of evil.

Similar sceptical doubts can be raised about the number, eternity, and personality of these beings. However, the upshot of this inquiry is surely already clear: the available evidence certainly seems to allow many different doxastically possible creators. Perhaps it might be objected that there is evidence that has not been taken into account – for example, the evidence of religious experience, religious authority, revelation, and scripture. However, none of this is 'available evidence', that is, evidence that will be recognised as such by theist and non-theist alike. To determine whether the evidence supports the claim that an orthodoxly conceived monotheistic god exists, we must set aside anything that could only be claimed as evidence for the existence of this orthodoxly conceived monotheistic god by those who already believe that this orthodoxly conceived monotheistic god does in fact exist. Thus, for example, one could only suppose that the Bible provides evidence of the existence of this particular orthodoxly conceived monotheistic god if one already believes that this orthodoxly conceived monotheistic god exists; one who believed, say, that the world was created by a malevolent creature would suppose that the Bible is evidence of the cunning of this being.[3]

---

[3] There is a sense in which everyone can admit that religious experiences occur: for people do report having experiences that they take to be perceptions of God. But then, won't the acceptance of some kind of principle of credulity require one to regard these reports as *prima facie* evidence that such people have veridical perceptions of God? No. The reported content of these experiences is compatible with ever so many hypotheses about the nature of the creators of the world, including hypotheses involving neglectful or deceptive creators,

But if the conclusion of the preceding paragraph is correct, then, even for those who believe that the universe has creators, a question arises, namely: in which of the possible creators ought one to believe? One might take the view that all one ought to believe is that there are creators, and leave it at that. But to take this view is to fail to believe in an orthodoxly conceived monotheistic god, or in any of the other doxastically possible alternatives. Moreover, this view is manifestly insufficient to sustain a religious outlook on life. At this point in the argument, it is an open question whether the creators deserve our thanks. One might be delighted with one's life no thanks to them – so one's own happiness isn't sufficient to answer the question of which attitude one ought to take. In any case, even to believe that there are creators is to believe too much – for it is compatible with all the evidence we possess that the universe is uncreated. And indeed, to the extent that we feel impelled to believe in creators, it seems that we shall be equally impelled to believe in creators of those creators, and so on. If we are prepared to allow that this regress halts somewhere, then it is hard to see how we could rule out the possibility that it halts right at the beginning, that is, with an uncreated universe.

Recently, there has been a revival of interest in teleological arguments that begin with the claim that the occurrence of life in the universe depended upon the utterly unlikely concurrence of a number of improbable events and specific values of universal parameters.[4] Doesn't this data show that it is much more reasonable to suppose that the universe is the outcome of creative intelligence? No. We don't know much about the contours of broadly logical, that is, metaphysical, space – contours that, of course, can be discovered only *a posteriori* – but it seems highly implausible to suppose that ours is the only kind of universe that could support intelligent moral agents. Moreover, although we can conjecture that, as we move along certain axes in logical space, we find only universes that do not contain human beings, we can't even be sure – given enough parameters and initial events – that our local region of logical space isn't densely populated with universes that contain human beings. And, finally, we have little idea what kinds of intelligent moral

and hypotheses on which there are no creators. Hence, all that a reasonable principle of credulity could require is that one accept that such people do have experiences with the reported content; that these people take the content of these experiences to be experiences of a particular deity should not provide one with *any* reason to suppose that the experiences really are of that deity. Indeed, more strongly, one could not take these experiences to be of a particular deity unless one had come to believe in the existence of that deity. (It should also be noted that principles of credulity must be carefully constrained: reports of experiences of alien spacecraft landing in suburban backyards surely should not be taken to constitute even *prima facie* evidence that there have been alien spacecraft landing in suburban backyards.) For more on this topic, see section 7.2 below.

4 See, e.g., Leslie (1985). Leslie has discussed these issues in numerous other publications.

agents there might be other than human beings, nor much idea about the conditions under which they might flourish. So: Even if we are inclined to think that our existence is an incredible stroke of luck, the postulation of creators cannot be guaranteed to explain that luck. For it would seem to be equally a matter of incredible luck that they were disposed to create our universe rather than one of the possible alternatives. Moreover – and more importantly – we have no idea whether ours is the only universe, and hence don't know whether it is appropriate to think that our existence is an incredible stroke of luck. Maybe there are a vast number of uncreated worlds, but ours is the only one that contains intelligent moral agents. Or maybe there are a vast number of worlds that were created by hopelessly incompetent deities. And so on. Once again, it seems that suspension of judgement is the only reasonable course.

So, in sum: the available evidence no more supports the belief that an orthodoxly conceived monotheistic god exists than it supports belief in numerous incompatible hypotheses. But in such circumstances, it cannot be rational to believe that an orthodoxly conceived monotheistic god exists. On the other hand, there seems to be no obvious way of deciding whether it is more likely that the universe was created than that it was not created – though see section 1.3.4 below for a discussion of one argument that might be thought to do the trick. Since the total evidence fails to support any one hypothesis more than its competitors, the only rational course is to suspend judgement. Because it seems reasonable to think that there are many ways in which the world could be uncreated, we may suppose that we are here considering *all* of the doxastically possible hypotheses concerning the origins of the universe.

This completes the case offered on behalf of the strong agnostic for the view that: *it is neither rational to believe that an orthodoxly conceived monotheistic god exists, nor to believe that an orthodoxly conceived monotheistic god does not exist.* The case for the second part of this claim may seem very weak; after all, if one is prepared to assume that the available hypotheses are all equally likely, then it seems that one is obliged to say that the probability that any particular one of them is true is almost infinitesimally small. And, in that case, isn't it really true that one disbelieves the hypothesis that an orthodoxly conceived monotheistic god exists? No; the lottery paradox shows that this can't be right. In a lottery with infinitely many tickets, there is only an infinitesimal chance that any particular ticket will win. Nonetheless, if I believe of each ticket that it won't win, then I shall be obliged to conclude that no ticket will win – that is, I will be obliged to believe something false. What goes for hypotheses about lottery tickets goes for cosmological hypotheses too: for any particular hypotheses among those countenanced above, I should think that it is doxastically very unlikely that the hypothesis is true; but, nonetheless, I should not believe that it *is* false.

1.3.2. Why the Case Fails

There are some obvious lines of response to the outlined argument for strong agnosticism. I shall discuss three related responses; the combined effect of these three responses is, I think, fatal.

(i) The appeals to simplicity and Ockham's Razor
The strong agnostic claims that there is no reason to prefer the hypothesis that an orthodoxly conceived monotheistic god exists to numerous logically incompatible hypotheses – and, more strongly, that there is no reason to prefer any hypothesis about the causal origins of the universe to any other. However, it might be suggested by theists that this claim overlooks one significant consideration that underwrites the choice of belief in an orthodoxly conceived monotheistic god, namely, that the hypothesis that an orthodoxly conceived monotheistic god exists is the *simplest* hypothesis that explains the data, and that this is a reason for supposing that it is more likely to be true.[5] And, similarly, it might be suggested by atheists that the strong agnostic's claim overlooks the importance of a version of Ockham's Razor according to which, in circumstances in which one lacks any evidence for an *a posteriori* existence proposition, one has sufficient grounds to believe the negation of that proposition.[6]

There are various replies available to the strong agnostic. *First*, in response to the theist, she can observe that it is far from clear that the hypothesis that an orthodoxly conceived monotheistic god exists is the simplest hypothesis. On the one hand, some hypotheses that hold that the universe is uncreated seem no less simple.[7] And, on the other hand, it is not clear that the hypothesis that an orthodoxly conceived monotheistic god exists is simpler than, say, one of the numerous hypotheses involving a quite powerful – but not omniscient, quite knowledgeable – but not omnipotent, morally indifferent deity. How is one to decide whether it is simpler to suppose that there is an omniscient orthodoxly conceived monotheistic god or to suppose that the creators have some – perhaps hard to specify – properties that fall short of omniscience? Surely, the fact that the properties in question might presently be "hard to specify" does not show, *ipso facto*, that the hypotheses in question are more complex – for, in that case, our criterion of simplicity depends upon the vagaries of current notation. Yet presumably "likelihood of truth" ought not to be tied to current notation in this way. Of course, it is not here denied that there are good pragmatic reasons for using a criterion tied to the vagaries of current notation in selecting hypotheses, for example, in the sciences. However, it will be insisted that these reasons have nothing to do

---

[5] This line of defence is inspired by the work of Richard Swinburne. See, for example, Swinburne (1979: 53–7).
[6] See McLaughlin (1984).
[7] This point has been well argued in Mackie (1982: 100–1).

with truth; indeed, it will be said that we use simplicity to choose between hypotheses precisely when we recognise that the available evidence does not allow us to discriminate between them in terms of likelihood of truth.

Perhaps the theist might reply that the simplicity of the hypothesis provides a pragmatic reason for adopting the hypothesis that an orthodoxly conceived monotheistic god exists. However, it is hard to see that this could be an overwhelming practical reason. For suppose we ask: what reason could we have for wanting to choose between the competing hypotheses in question? If our reason is that we think that a correct choice will be rewarded, then surely practical reason will be on the side of refusing to choose. For, no matter what our choice is, there are possible creators who will reward us for making it, possible creators who will be indifferent to our making it, possible creators who will punish us for making it, and so on. The only reasonable response seems to be to forget about the whole matter, and to concentrate on something that is much more tractable, namely, one's conduct in one's present life. And if it is objected – as it would have been by Pascal – that one's present life will go best if one chooses to believe in an orthodoxly conceived monotheistic god, quite independently of whether there is an orthodoxly conceived monotheistic god, then the correct thing to say is simply that this is not credible. If there is no orthodoxly conceived monotheistic god, then any use that is made of the mistaken belief that an orthodoxly conceived monotheistic god exists will surely involve costs that could be avoided without giving up any of the benefits accrued. Perhaps the theist might respond with an appeal to Pascal's wager. But – as I have argued elsewhere[8] – the strong agnostic can reasonably contend that there are infinitely many possible creators. Consequently, even if one thinks that the apparatus of decision theory can be correctly applied in cases in which there are infinite utilities, one will find that the value of the wager on an orthodoxly conceived monotheistic god can be trumped by other considerations. And, in any case, there are many other deities whose existence would ensure an equally good outcome. So there is no escape here.

Perhaps, despite the forgoing arguments, the theist will insist that the decision to "forget about the whole matter" involves a choice that reason cannot guarantee to be correct. If it is all right to wager this way, why would it be wrong to wager on belief in an orthodoxly conceived monotheistic god? Well, on the one hand, the decision to "forget about the whole matter" is the only non-arbitrary decision to be made in the circumstances. When theoretical reason recognises that it has next to no chance of obtaining the truth, then it opts to avoid falsehood – compare the corresponding case of the lottery. And, on the other hand, there are practical reasons in favour of "forgetting about the whole matter". For, if the argument advanced by the strong agnostic is cogent, then we are all members of a community that is

---

[8] Oppy (1990), for further discussion, see chapter 5 of the present book.

in the predicament that it cannot answer certain "ultimate questions" about its life. In these circumstances, surely what we owe to ourselves and to each other is to make that part of our lives of which we are certain – and which may be the whole of our lives – as good as possible. That end will be hindered if individuals make different wagers on the question of religious belief, as our history shows; and there is reason to suppose that it won't be furthered even in the unlikely event that we can all agree to wager on the same deity. To do anything other than "forget about the whole matter" is to give up certain goods for utterly uncertain returns. In other words: the expected value of the sceptical wager is greater than the expected value of the wager on an orthodoxly conceived monotheistic god!

Second, in response to the atheist, the strong agnostic can insist that the principle to which the atheist appeals – namely, that in circumstances in which one lacks any evidence for an *a posteriori* existence proposition, one has sufficient grounds to believe the negation of that proposition – is also refuted by the lottery paradox; this, by the way, explains why the two objections were grouped together. The problem is that, in some circumstances in which one lacks evidence, one will lack evidence for every relevant *a posteriori* existence proposition – but one will also know that some relevant *a posteriori* existence proposition(s) must be true. Thus, for example, although there is no good reason to think that there are currently intelligent beings inhabiting the fifth planet of the Vega system, the correct view to have is simply that this claim is *very* unlikely to be true.[9]

I conclude that the strong agnostic can reasonably insist that straightforward appeals to simplicity and Ockham's Razor do not defeat the case constructed in the first section of this chapter. Theoretical reason cares nothing about such considerations, since it is primarily concerned with truth; and practical reason must respond to other considerations that swamp the force of such appeals.

(ii) The Threat of Global Scepticism

A second line of response to the argument of the strong agnostic is to suggest that it proves too much. The strong agnostic relies on the claim that, when confronted with hypotheses between which the available evidence will not decide, one ought to withhold belief from each of those hypotheses. But surely this will be fatal to belief in other minds, belief in the external world,

---

[9] McLaughlin (1984) writes: "'A three-headed hippogriff is alive and well right now on the fifth planet of the Vega system.' If I followed this claim with the frank admission that I had no grounds at all for it, you might be inclined to reject it out of hand (p. 198)". The strong agnostic concedes that the admission that one has no grounds for one's assertion would remove any reason for others to accept what one says – but this is not to concede that it gives those others reason positively to disbelieve it. Of course, the others might well have good independent reasons for thinking that the claim in question is *very* unlikely to be true – but that is a different issue.

belief in the reality of the past, belief that the future will be like the past, belief in scientific theories, and so on. For, in all these cases, it is plausible to suggest that there is no *evidence* that supports the commonly held views against sceptical alternatives. Consider, for example, the case of belief in scientific theories. Suppose that it turns out that there are genuinely conflicting total scientific theories that account equally well for all the evidence available to us. In that case, the considerations adduced by the strong agnostic in support of her agnosticism suggest that one ought not to believe of any particular such theory that it is true.[10]

Perhaps the strong agnostic can dig in her heels. One person's *modus ponens* is another person's *modus tollens*. Why not insist that, in the circumstances envisaged, there would be no point in arbitrarily believing of one of these theories that it is the one true theory. Since the theories are *ex hypothesi* equally empirically adequate, we should use whichever one is most convenient for practical application, chosen according to the circumstances in question. And, beyond that, we lose nothing if we simply admit our ignorance. Note, by the way, that the strong agnostic need not here take a stand on one important dispute between realists and anti-realists. It may be that there is only one possible empirically adequate total scientific theory, formulable in many different notations. However, it may also be that – among the genuinely conflicting total scientific theories that account equally well for all of the evidence available to us – the one true theory is distinguished only by facts that are inaccessible to us. All that the strong agnostic needs is the concession that there is now no good reason to believe that the former alternative obtains. So there is no threat to the strong agnostic argument here. And nor is there any threat from actual – as opposed to ideal – science, for it is simply not the case that we have good reason to believe that we have ever been confronted with genuinely competing, empirically adequate, theories. The historical record suggests that we have little reason to believe that any of our theories is empirically adequate – though it does suggest that there is good reason to suppose that later theories are more empirically adequate than their predecessors. So we don't have reason to believe that our scientific theories are true, even though we have the best possible reasons for accepting them, that is, for relying on them in making predictions, giving explanations, and so on.

Perhaps this response is not acceptable; clearly, there is room for much further debate. But, in any case, no similar moves are plausible in the remaining cases. While there is not universal agreement that there is something wrong with constructive empiricism – and other less than robustly realist accounts of scientific theories – there is more or less universal agreement that there is something wrong with scepticism about the external world,

---

[10] This line of response is inspired by the early writings of Alvin Plantinga. See, esp., Plantinga (1967).

other minds, induction, and the past. Of course, there is little consensus about exactly where such sceptics go wrong; but it does seem plausible to think that such scepticism should be rationally avoidable. Certainly, if the strong agnostic is saddled with the claims that one ought to suspend judgement on the question of whether there are other minds, that one ought to suspend judgement on the question of whether the world was created just five minutes ago, that one ought to suspend judgement on the question of whether heavy objects will fall towards the centre of the earth tomorrow, and that one ought to suspend judgement on the question of whether there really are chairs, tables, and wombats, then this is good reason to think that there is something wrong with strong agnosticism. But how could the strong agnostic avoid the objectionable claims?

Perhaps like this: It is clear that there are cases – such as lotteries – in which the type of argument deployed by the strong agnostic is correct. In other words, in *some* cases in which one is confronted by a range of hypotheses between which no available considerations can decide, the reasonable thing to do is to suspend judgement. This suggests that if the sceptical conclusions are to be avoided, there must be "available considerations" that decide in favour of, for example, the hypothesis that there really are chairs, tables, and wombats. But what could these considerations be? Well, one feature of all the sceptical hypotheses is that if one is to accept them, then one must suppose that one is very special. On sceptical hypotheses about other minds, one supposes that one is utterly different in kind from other apparent people. On sceptical hypotheses about the existence of chairs, tables, and wombats, one supposes that great pains have been taken to deceive one – and, hence, one also supposes that one is utterly different in kind from other apparent people. On sceptical hypotheses about the similarity between past and future, one supposes that the time in which one's own life takes place involves a special sort of discontinuity. And on sceptical hypotheses about the reality of the past, one supposes that part of one's own life has a special status in the apparent chronicle of history. Now, the proposal that the strong agnostic wishes to make is that it is partly constitutive of reasonable belief that one does not hold beliefs that require one to suppose that one is special in the way that the sceptical hypotheses require one to believe that one is special. Moreover, this proposal does serve to draw a line between the argument defended by the strong agnostic and the sceptical conclusions; one makes no assumption that one is special – in the way required by sceptical hypotheses – in adopting any of the alternatives to the traditional theistic hypothesis – and so the proposal does eliminate sceptical arguments while leaving the agnostic argument untouched.

Of course, there is an obvious problem with this line of defence, namely, that the strong agnostic seems to have given up the idea that the only court of appeal in deciding between the truth of competing hypotheses is the available evidence. Why should hypotheses that require that one is special be rejected if this consideration has no bearing on the truth or falsity of those hypotheses? And if it is constitutive of rationality that one should reject such hypotheses, then why can't the opponents of the strong agnostic insist that it is also constitutive of rationality to be moved by considerations of simplicity? Perhaps it can be conceded that there is an available position, that is, the view that, the alleged constitutive principle apart, the only thing to which one can appeal in deciding between hypotheses is the available evidence – but it is hard to see how the position could be motivated. And if the position can't be suitably motivated, then it seems that the argument of the strong agnostic fails. However, there may still be a plausible response available to the strong agnostic, namely, to insist that it is simply obvious that the case of cosmological hypotheses is relevantly like the case of a lottery, but relevantly unlike the cases of implausible scepticism, even though it is remarkably hard to say what these relevant respects are. To show that the argument of the strong agnostic is wrong, an opponent needs similarly to distinguish the case of the lottery from the sceptical cases, and then to show that cosmological hypotheses fall on the side of the sceptical cases. Even though the argument of the strong agnostic is incomplete, it surely presents a challenge that theists and atheists are obliged to meet.

(iii) The Rationality of Ungrounded Beliefs
A third line of response can be taken to begin from a denial of the claim that there is still a remaining challenge for theists and atheists. To fend off the sceptical arguments, the strong agnostic either appeals to a principle that is claimed to be partly constitutive of rational belief, or else simply insists that cosmological hypotheses are relevantly like lotteries. But in neither case does the strong agnostic offer any evidence in support of these claims. Moreover, it is hard to see what form such evidence could take. But, in that case, it seems that the strong agnostic will need to insist that either the principle or the claim – or both – is *cognitively basic* – that is, that there is nothing further that is suitably independent to which one could appeal in order to defend them. But if this is right, then why shouldn't a traditional theist claim that belief in the existence of an orthodoxly conceived monotheistic god can be cognitively basic – that is, unsupported by any independent evidence, and yet perfectly justified, perhaps because supported by non-independent grounds?

   Perhaps the strong agnostic might object that there are obvious differences between the suggested status of the principle to which she appeals and the suggested status of belief in an orthodoxly conceived monotheistic god. In particular, the principle to which the strong agnostic appeals is intended to be a requirement on right reason; but the belief to which the theist appeals is only claimed to be rationally permitted; that is, the theist is not making the surely ill-advised attempt to claim that belief in an orthodoxly conceived monotheistic god is rationally required even though there is not the slightest evidence to support that belief. Perhaps, then, it might be suggested that cognitively basic beliefs and principles must be ones that can reasonably be thought to be obligatory. More exactly: if one holds that a certain principle or belief is cognitively basic, then one must hold that any reasonable person in the same broad kind of doxastic situation in which one finds oneself would also adopt that belief or principle.

This claim has been denied.[11] However, the strong agnostic might well doubt that the denial is reasonable. For consider. If one allows that certain beliefs or principles are cognitively basic, and yet also allows that it is equally permissible to adopt conflicting basic beliefs or principles, then surely there is nothing to sustain one's own choice of beliefs and principles. If one genuinely allows that it is equally permissible to adopt alternative basic beliefs or principles, then surely one must hold that one's own basic beliefs and principles are entirely arbitrary. But no one can think that her basic beliefs and principles are arbitrary; for that is to throw reason to the winds. In particular, one must think that one's basic beliefs are true, and that one's basic principles are conducive to the formation of true beliefs. But basic beliefs selected arbitrarily from amongst beliefs most of which are false will almost certainly be false, and basic principles selected arbitrarily from amongst principles most of which are not conducive to the formation of true beliefs almost certainly will not be conducive to the formation of true beliefs. No one can reasonably think that her basic beliefs and principles have been arbitrarily selected.[12]

One possible response to this objection is to claim that there can be theists who recognise no alternatives to their cognitively basic belief in an orthodoxly conceived monotheistic god: surely, if there are any such people, it is rational for them to believe in an orthodoxly conceived monotheistic god. This point can be conceded; but only because it is irrelevant. Such people, if there are any, are not sufficiently well informed; they do not possess relevant information about at least doxastically possible alternatives to belief in an orthodoxly conceived monotheistic god. However, if they did possess that information, they would cease to be rational if they continued to maintain that belief in an orthodoxly conceived monotheistic god is cognitively basic. The aim of the strong agnostic is to argue that no one who is fully appraised of the arguments developed by the strong agnostic can reasonably believe in an orthodoxly conceived monotheistic god; hence, people who are simply ignorant of the relevant considerations cannot constitute counter-examples.

---

[11] See, e.g., Plantinga (1983: 77) and Wolterstorff (1983: 176ff.).

[12] The strong agnostic should probably add a qualification here. If one were first-personally dissociated from certain beliefs, then it might be possible for one to think that those beliefs had been arbitrarily selected. Moreover, there might be a thin sense of "rational" in which such beliefs could nonetheless be rational. However, the crucial point would still remain: One could not give unreserved first-personal endorsement to such beliefs. In a suitably thick sense of "rational", beliefs that cannot be first-personally endorsed are not rational.

And, of course, the same point applies to people who are unable to understand the arguments, or who wilfully refuse to consider them, and so on. People who lack reasoning skills, or who refuse to use the skills they have, cannot constitute counter-examples to the claims of the strong agnostic.[13]

Another possible response is to suggest that there can be theists who recognise no *legitimate* alternatives to their cognitively basic belief in an orthodoxly conceived monotheistic god. The idea here is that, *from within the religious life*, belief in an orthodoxly conceived monotheistic god can be seen to be well grounded. Given the appropriate religious background, there are conditions and circumstances that "call forth" belief in an orthodoxly conceived monotheistic god, that is, conditions and circumstances in which, on this view, a believer will be correctly disposed to say: an orthodoxly conceived monotheistic god is speaking to me; an orthodoxly conceived monotheistic god has created all this; an orthodoxly conceived monotheistic god forgives me; and so on.[14] Of course, the theist recognises that there are many other possible stances that share this "self-justifying" status[15]; so there is no suggestion that the grounds in question might be available even to those who do not believe. But, it will be said, while it is true that there are no reasonable or evidential considerations that will take one from an initially sceptical position to belief, and while it is also true that the grounds for religious belief – drawn from revelation, religious experience, and scripture – are not suitably available to non-believers, nonetheless this is simply irrelevant to the question of whether theistic belief is rational. What matters is that, in the light of the evidence as she construes it, the theist's belief that an orthodoxly conceived monotheistic god exists is manifestly rational. Since the theist is not in the position of the non-believer, she does not share his doxastic problem – and, indeed, need take no account of it.

The strong agnostic may object that this attitude is indefensible. Surely, if it is conceded that belief in an orthodoxly conceived monotheistic god is just one among many possible views that shares all of the doxastic virtues of belief in an orthodoxly conceived monotheistic god, then the maintenance of any one of those views must be entirely arbitrary. And, in that case, it cannot be rational to persist with any one of them. If there is no

---

[13] Wolterstorff (1983) makes much of the points dismissed in this paragraph; see, esp., p. 155.
[14] See, e.g., Alston (1983: 104–5).
[15] Consider, for example, belief in a morally deficient deity, god*, who doesn't care for us much at all – there are other worlds that she created that she likes much better – but who nonetheless presents herself to people in the guise of an omnibenevolent being. On this view – which might well seem better able than orthodox theism to explain the amounts and kinds of evils in the world – conditions and circumstances will call forth certain beliefs: god* is speaking to me; god* has created all this; god* is trying to convince me that she cares for me; and so on. From within this view, belief in god* will seem to be just as well grounded as belief in an orthodoxly conceived monotheistic god seems from the viewpoint of the orthodox theist.

viewpoint-independent consideration – that is, consideration that is common to the range of views – that favours the adoption of one of the views, and yet it is conceded that no view is in any way doxastically superior to any other, then it really is unreasonable to adopt any one of those views. After all, in adopting a particular view, one must suppose that that view has the fundamental merit of being true. But if there is no further doxastic virtue that the view has, then what reason can there be for thinking that it is the one that is true? Indeed, wouldn't the adoption of one of these views – for example, belief in an orthodoxly conceived monotheistic god – be just like the adoption of one of the sceptical hypotheses discussed earlier in that it requires an inappropriate belief that one is "special"?

I think that the strong agnostic is only partly right here. It is true that, according to the epistemological picture under discussion, doxastic agents are required to think that they are doxastically special in the following sense: any rational agent should concede that there are no suitably independent external considerations that show that her view is superior to rationally permissible alternatives. However, there is nothing wrong with this consequence of the picture – for the only genuine alternative to the picture is, as the opponents of the strong agnostic earlier insisted, an untenable scepticism. That there are alternatives to one's own views that are, in a suitably external sense, doxastically just as good does not give one any reason to think that the views that one has are probably false. A rational agent will persist with the views that she has until she is shown that she can *improve* her view by changing it.

Why then does the position of the strong agnostic have intuitive appeal? I think this is so because of a confusion between rules of dialectical debate and doxastic principles. In debate, and hence in philosophical argument, the only considerations to which *useful* appeal can be made are those that are acceptable to all participants. Hence, if one supposed that the project of philosophy is to justify the view that one holds in debate, then one would need to suppose that such justification would proceed from principles agreed to by all reasonable persons. But that just shows that this is a bad conception of the project of philosophy. For it is simply misguided to think that any world-view can be defended in this way by appeal to purely external considerations.[16]

Of course, it should now be clear why I said that strong agnosticism fails because the two kinds of principles upon which it relies cannot be plausibly conjoined. On the one hand, the principle that *in circumstances in which the*

---

[16] Perhaps an opponent might dig in her heels, and insist that her world is the only reasonable world-view. Even if she were right, this would be a pointless thing to say; her opponents would surely feel themselves equally entitled to make the same kind of claim about themselves. Two possibilities seem to arise: (i) the parties to the debate simply agree to differ, but each insists in her heart that she alone is *rational*; (ii) the parties agree to differ, but each alone insists that she is *right* (or *more nearly right*). To me, it seems clear that the second outcome is preferable.

available evidence no more – and no less – supports p *than it supports logically incompatible hypotheses* p$_1$, . . . , pn, . . . , *one ought to suspend judgement between all of the hypotheses* p, p$_1$, . . . , *pn*, . . . , is clearly correct if "the available evidence" is taken to include internal considerations, but also clearly incorrect if "the available evidence" is taken to include only external considerations. But, on the other hand, this is just to deny the second required principle, namely, that *it is possible to characterise a suitable notion of evidential support that does not rely upon a relativisation to background assumptions – theories, points of view.*

In sum: strong agnosticism fails because it does not respect the tenets of methodological conservatism. There cannot be an obligation on reasonable persons to believe only what is required by suitably independent evidence – for, under this obligation, subjects would not be able to believe all kinds of things that it is quite clear they ought to believe. Moreover, there is no way for the strong agnostic *suitably* to motivate her response to the threats posed by various kinds of scepticism and by the possibility of appeals to simplicity and Ockham's Razor – for, once the demand for external *evidential* motivation lapses, the plausibility of the claim that these responses are externally motivated simply evaporates.

1.3.3. Retreat to Weak Agnosticism

Given that the strong agnosticism fails, one attracted to an agnostic position should retreat to weak agnosticism. Moreover, the reason given for the failure of strong agnosticism suggests that this retreat should be easily accomplished – for, given the precepts of methodological conservatism to which the opponents of the strong agnostic appealed, it is surely plausible to think that there are no suitably external considerations that must lead a reasonable weak agnostic to give up her position. However, this will be so only if the precepts of methodological conservatism are acceptable – so we shall now turn our attention to them.

The epistemological precepts under consideration are forcefully enunciated and defended by Harman (1986). The most important principle is the *Principle of Conservatism: One is justified in continuing fully to accept something in the absence of special reason not to.* An important subsidiary tenet is that one should subscribe to the *Principle of Positive Undermining* – namely, that *one should stop believing that* p *whenever one positively believes one's reasons for believing that* p *are no good* – but not to the *Principle of Negative Undermining* – namely, that *one should stop believing that* p *whenever one does not associate one's belief in* p *with an adequate justification, either intrinsic or extrinsic.* There are yet further principles – for example, *The Principle of Clutter Avoidance* and *The Interest Condition* – that form important planks in the theory, but these will not concern us here. This approach to epistemology has numerous merits, not least that it serves to defuse debates about various previously

controversial issues – for example, debates about various kinds of philosophical scepticism. However, rather than emphasise these merits, I shall
instead consider some potential difficulties.

Initially, the most plausible objection to this approach to epistemology
lies in the suggestion that it conflates "internal" and "external" justification.
Thus, for example, Price (1988: 38–9) claims that Harman fails to distinguish between "an 'external' justification of a principle or habit of belief
revision that aims to show that it is somehow useful or appropriate to conform to a certain rule; and an 'internal' justification that aims to provide
the kind of reason to which an agent could actually appeal in support of
an application of the principle in question." Price then goes on to observe
that "[Harman's Principle of Conservatism] is plausible only if 'justified' is
taken in the external sense. Thus if we have always believed in the existence
of Ralph (the Great One), our continuing to do so may well exemplify a useful habit of conservatism, painfully acquired in the evolution of the species.
But when we encounter someone who believes instead in Stella (the Great
One), and hence feel the need to justify our faith, our long and unblemished
record gives us no reason to keep it."

Various responses to this objection may be viable; I think that what should
be resisted is the suggestion that, when one encounters an apparently reasonable person who holds a position that contradicts the position that one
espouses, one *thereby* incurs an obligation to find suitably external justificatory reasons that support one's own position. Of course, one ought to have
a – possibly causal – story about how the other person has gone wrong – perhaps they were mislead by false testimony even though they were perfectly
justified in accepting that testimony, and so on – but there is no reason
to think that this story should seem anything other than question-begging
to the one with the conflicting view. Recall how difficult it has proved to
find non-question-begging defences for induction. That suitably external
defences seem to be unavailable does not give any of us the slightest reason
to give up our inductive practices. To persist with one's belief in Ralph, one
does not need to find reasons that would lead the previously uncommitted
to believe in Ralph and not in Stella; rather, all one needs is a differential
causal explanation of how the believers in Stella came to have those false
beliefs – compare the strategy, available to theists, that ascribes the error of
atheists and agnostics to the effects of sin. Of course, one can't merely say:
"I subscribe to the Principle of Conservatism, so I have a sufficient reason to
continue to believe in Ralph." But one can say: "Because I subscribe to the
Principle of Conservatism, I hold that it is sufficient for me to find 'internal' reasons – that is, reasons that, from an external standpoint, may seem
to be entirely question-begging – in order to justify my continued belief in
Ralph rather than Stella." One does not need to suppose that one's reasons
are available to other points of view in order to continue to accept them as
reasons.

On the basis of this rather brief discussion, I conclude that Harman's epistemological proto-theory – that is clearly closely related to the views of those theists who appeal to the proper basicality or proper unarguedness of religious beliefs – is a very promising platform for the support of weak agnosticism. Of course, more would need to be said to persuade the unconvinced; but it is beyond the brief of the present section to try to do so. And in any case, by the lights of the underlying epistemological theory, there may not be any point in pressing on with an attempt to persuade the unconvinced. Such people should read this section as an argument for a conditional thesis, namely, that by the lights of the presupposed epistemology, weak agnosticism is a defensible position.

Even those who are prepared to countenance or espouse the underlying epistemology may feel that there remains a pressing objection of principle, namely, that weak agnosticism is inconsistent in its treatment of sceptical religious hypotheses and other sceptical hypotheses. If the weak agnostic is not prepared to accept or reject the many conflicting hypotheses about the cosmological origins of the universe, why isn't she similarly prepared neither to accept nor reject conflicting hypotheses about the age of the universe, or the nature of the external world? Isn't this simply an inconsistency on her part? Not at all. There is no good methodological precept that says that a rational person will have a definite opinion about everything; indeed, it seems plausible to suppose that, for any reasonable person, there will be many controversial questions about which she simply suspends judgement. And in those cases, one correct way to represent her epistemic state is to claim that she is unable to decide between a range of competing hypotheses. Of course, there may be costs to explicit suspensions of judgement, in the form of the complexity of the representations involved; but these costs are traded against what will seem to be improved prospects of avoiding error, and so on.

1.3.4. Some Objections Considered

Despite the argument of the preceding section, there are some objections to weak agnosticism that remain to be discussed. In particular, there are three objections that suggest that weak agnosticism is actually inconsistent or, strictly speaking, unbelievable. I shall consider these objections in turn.

(i) The Deistic Alternative

There is an argument, inspired by an argument that Forrest (1982) uses against David Lewis's modal realism, that suggests that it is more reasonable to believe that there are creators than it is to believe that the world is uncreated. Of course, the purported upshot of this argument is only that the weak agnostic should retreat to *deism* – that is, it is not suggested that this argument could motivate a shift to theism: *Corresponding to any uncreated world, there are infinitely many created worlds, each with a different creator. Consequently, the odds are infinitely in favour of the hypothesis that our world is created; it is almost vanishingly unlikely that our world was not created. So we ought to believe that the world has creators.*

Lewis (1986: 119–21) has suggested one way to respond to the above argument, namely, to claim that it can be paralleled to its discredit. On one way of partitioning the integers, there are infinitely many non-prime numbers for each prime number. Consequently – following the above argument – if an integer is chosen at random I ought to believe that it is non-prime. However, on another way of partitioning the integers, there are infinitely many prime numbers corresponding to each non-prime number. Consequently – following the above argument – if a number is chosen at random, I ought to believe that it is prime. So, I have two equally good arguments that lead to the conclusion that, if a number is chosen at random, I ought to believe both that it will be prime and that it will be non-prime. Clearly, then, both arguments are to be rejected, along with the argument that purports to make trouble for agnosticism.

Lewis's objection refutes the argument that I initially gave: the only probabilistic arguments that one can make about infinite cases are ones in which one has no relevant choices to make about the partitioning of the probability space.[17] However, suppose that I had argued as follows: *I have no idea whether or not the world that we actually inhabit was created. However, there are infinitely many worlds that differ from it at most in that they have creators, different from the creators, if any, that it actually has – and there is only one world that differs from it at most in having no creators. So, among the relevant possibilities, there are infinitely many worlds that have creators, and only one that is uncreated. Consequently, there is next to no chance that the world that we actually inhabit is uncreated.* In this case, Lewis's response is not available. This argument is solely about the actual world and worlds relevantly like it, not about all the possible worlds that there are. Consequently, there is no partition that can be gerrymandered

---

[17] Consider the following case, which I owe to David Lewis: A fair die is to be tossed infinitely many times. You are to be assigned one toss; you are then to estimate the chance that it is a six. Why should you not reason as follows: *Whichever toss I am allotted, the chance that I shall get a six is one-sixth. So I know already that the chance that I get a six is one-sixth.* Answer: No reason at all. The choice of a partition of the probability space must respect the fact that you will first be assigned a toss. Partitions that combine outcomes from different tosses are irrelevant, since they fail to respect this fact. However, in the arguments about prime numbers and creators, there is no relevant fact that only one of the partitions manages to respect.

Perhaps it might be objected that the argument about prime numbers fails to take into account the way in which we grasp the natural numbers, namely, according to the standard ordering: 1, 2, 3.... Isn't this a reason for saying that, really, we ought to think it vanishingly unlikely that a number chosen at random will be prime? No: if – *per impossibile* – a natural number really were chosen at random – say, by an omnipotent and omniscient deity – then the argument given by Lewis would be correct.

by a Cantorian argument. So if this argument is to be defeated, some other response is required.

The new argument requires the assumption that there is only one way in which a world such as ours could be uncreated. But – as I noted earlier – an agnostic will not be prepared to grant this assumption. She will say that, for all she has good reason to believe, there may be infinitely many different ways in which an uncreated world can arise. Perhaps worlds are created in pairs, or triples, or quadruples, and so on. Perhaps worlds are randomly distributed – like raisins in a plum-pudding – throughout some higher-dimensional space in which they arise as the result of some acausal process which occurs in that space. And so on. Since the agnostic sees no reason to think that it is no more likely that the world is uncreated than it is that the world was created according to one particular hypothesis about that act of creation, she has no reason to accept the modified version of Forrest's argument.[18] Agnostics can reasonably resist deism.

(ii) Proofs and Other Evidence
There are theists and atheists who will continue to insist that weak agnosticism is unreasonable because the existence – or non-existence – of an orthodoxly conceived monotheistic god can be demonstrated by arguments that appeal only to uncontroversial evidence. Thus, for example, there are theists who maintain that there are rationally compelling ontological, and/or cosmological, and/or teleological, and/or moral, and/or other arguments that establish the conclusion that an orthodoxly conceived monotheistic god exists; and there are atheists who maintain that there are rationally compelling ontological, and/or moral, and/or other arguments that establish the conclusion that an orthodoxly conceived monotheistic god does not exist.

---

[18] It may be worth noting that Lewis can make a similar response to Forrest's. Forrest's argument is as follows: *There are infinitely many worlds that differ from the actual world at most in that they have epiphenomenal stuff in some places and not in others, but only one world that differs from the actual world at most in that there is no epiphenomenal stuff anywhere. So we should believe that it is overwhelmingly likely that our world contains epiphenomenal stuff.* Now, Lewis allows that, for all he knows, there may be qualitatively indistinguishable worlds. But, if there are infinitely many worlds that are qualitatively indistinguishable from a world that differs at most from the actual world in that it has no epiphenomenal stuff, then Forrest's argument won't work. So Lewis can say: Sure, for all we know, there might be epiphenomenal stuff; but then again, there might be infinitely many worlds that are qualitatively indistinguishable from a world that differs at most from the actual world in that it has no epiphenomenal stuff. There is no obligation to accept the premise that is required by Forrest's argument. (Note, by the way, that it simply does *not* follow from this response that a modal realist *ought* to believe either that there is epiphenomenal stuff or else that there are infinitely many worlds that are qualitatively indistinguishable from a world that differs at most from the actual world in that it has no epiphenomenal stuff anywhere.)

I think that such theists and atheists are mistaken. While they may be entirely within their rights to suppose that the arguments that they defend are *sound*, I do not think that they have any reason to suppose that their arguments are *rationally compelling*, that is, that they provide reasonable opponents with compelling internal reasons to change their views. Of course, some will find this contention controversial – but perhaps the subsequent chapters of this book will help to make it appear plausible. Setting that promissory note aside, perhaps it is worth making the following point. It surely should be granted that, at least *prima facie*, there can be reasonable theists, atheists, and agnostics – for, after all, there are undeniably sensitive, thoughtful, and intelligent people who fall into all three camps. Of course, it could conceivably turn out that, for example, there can be reasonable agnostics only in that undemanding sense of "reasonable" in which reasonable persons can hold unobviously contradictory, or unobviously unnecessarily complex, or unobviously unnecessarily explanatorily weak views, and so on. But it seems to me to be clearly absurd to suppose that there are currently available arguments that should show, to the satisfaction of all, that members of two of the camps have views that are unobviously contradictory, or unobviously unnecessarily complex, or unobviously explanatorily weak, and so on. Members of each of the camps may have causal hypotheses that explain how their opponents come to possess false views; but these hypotheses ought not do anything to impugn the rationality of the maintenance of those views.

(iii) The Problem of Other Attitudes
Some people may be inclined to object that weak agnosticism is unlivable. Could one really carry on the projects of a normal life if one were not prepared to rule out, for example, the hypothesis that the world is the product of a malevolent deity? Wouldn't doubts about the value and meaning of life cripple one's ordinary conduct?

I don't see why. Earlier, I had my strong agnostic claim that the only reasonable thing to do in the face of such worries is to forget about them. This seems right. It is a psychological question – a matter of temperament – that decides whether one could be a weak agnostic. Why shouldn't one think that value is there to be created or pursued regardless of the truth of cosmological hypotheses? Perhaps there will be a nice or nasty surprise later on; and perhaps not. Perhaps there is *much* more to the universe than meets the non-metaphysical, non-theological eye; but, then again, perhaps not. What good could possibly be served by worrying about these possibilities now?

Perhaps this response is unconvincing. Certainly, I concede that more should be said. Perhaps, when that more is said, I shall have been forced to allow that weak agnostics must shift their ground to a fallibilist atheism – that is, to a position that treats the alternative cosmological hypotheses as definitely ruled out, but that leaves room for a higher-order concession of the possibility of epistemic error – compare the "paradox of the preface". However, for now, it certainly *seems* to me that weak agnosticism remains a livable option. In any case, I turn now to consider the suggestion that the case for strong agnosticism can be adopted to make a compelling argument for the rejection of theism, quite apart from the question of the positive doxastic stance that is mandated by that rejection.

1.4. PARALLEL CASES FOR 'ALTERNATIVE' DEITIES

One family of challenges to theistic belief derives from considerations concerning the claim that there is an omnipotent, omniscient, eternal, perfectly free, *perfectly evil* sole creator of the universe *ex nihilo.*[19] These challenges begin with the claim that a case can be made for the existence of this being – call it god* – that "parallels" the case that can be made for the existence of an of an orthodoxly conceived monotheistic god. (Perhaps one might think that it would be more accurate to say that the claim is that the case for the existence of god* is just as good or bad as the case for the existence of an orthodoxly conceived monotheistic god, and that part of the case for god* is contrived simply by mimicking or paralleling the case for an orthodoxly conceived monotheistic god. For, *prima facie* at least, it seems that there are extra wrinkles that are needed in the case of god* to construct arguments from scripture, or revelation, or religious experience, or religious authority, and so on. However, proponents of the challenges to theism that are under consideration ought to reply that the kinds of 'evidence' adverted to here are equally well explained on the hypothesis that an orthodoxly conceived monotheistic god exists – where the explanation goes via an orthodoxly conceived monotheistic god's good intentions to help us – and on the hypothesis that god* exists – where the explanation goes via god*'s evil intentions to harm us. I shall suppose that we should allow this generous construal of the notion of a 'parallel' case, and that no harm will follow from this concession.)

One kind of response to this family of challenges on behalf of theistic belief would be to deny that the mimicking *arguments* are genuinely parallel, for example, to claim that the ontological or cosmological or teleological or some such . . . argument for an orthodoxly conceived monotheistic god is stronger than the corresponding argument for god*, or that the problem of evil is a weaker argument against an orthodoxly conceived monotheistic god than the problem of good is against god*. It seems to

[19] See, e.g., Madden and Hare (1968), Cahn (1976), Stein (1990), New (1993), Daniels (1997). Also, cf. discussions of 'the Perverse God' in the literature on Pascal's wager (for references, see Jordan (1994b)), and discussions of a-being than-which-none-worse-can-be-conceived in the literature on ontological arguments (for references, see Oppy (1995c)).

me that the kind of response looks *prima facie* rather unpromising; in any case, I propose to proceed under the *pro tem* assumption that this kind of response won't work. (Those who disagree with my judgement here should for now take me to conducting a 'conditional' investigation: what can be said in response to these kinds of challenges to theistic belief if one concedes that the mimicking arguments for god* do genuinely parallel the traditional arguments for an orthodoxly conceived monotheistic god?) Instead, I shall focus attention on a line of response that aims to establish that there are reasons for thinking that the concept of god* is incoherent in a way in which the concept of an orthodoxly conceived monotheistic god is not. In particular, I shall consider the suggestion that the notion of an omniscient and perfectly evil being can be shown to be incoherent in ways that tend not at all to establish that the notion of an omniscient and perfectly good being is incoherent. If this suggestion is correct, then – other things being equal (as the proponents of the objection hold that they are!) – it seems that the hypothesis that an orthodoxly conceived monotheistic god exists is clearly to be preferred to the hypothesis that god* exists.

I propose to argue that, even if these counterarguments do establish that the hypothesis that an orthodoxly conceived monotheistic god exists is clearly to be preferred to the hypothesis that god* exists, this is not enough to show that theists are home free – for there are many other alternative gods for whom 'parallel' cases could be constructed, and for which this particular counterargument is ineffective. I shall then go on to consider the consequences of this claim for the status of the debate between theists and their opponents. (I shall also argue that there are serious questions to be raised about the counterarguments against god*. However, I shall not place too much emphasis on these questions in this section.) To get to these considerations, some preliminary scene setting is required.

1.4.1. Preliminary Remarks

For the purposes of this section, I shall suppose that *theists* are those who are committed to the claim that there is an omnipotent, omniscient, eternal, perfectly free, perfectly good, sole creator of the universe *ex nihilo*. Moreover, I shall suppose that an equivalent statement of this first supposition is that *theists* are those who are committed to the claim that an orthodoxly conceived monotheistic god exists.[20] Some people who choose to call themselves 'theists' may wish to vary the defining description that I have used here; however, provided that we agree that an orthodoxly conceived monotheistic

---

[20] This assumption is pretty clearly false. However, it is true that very many of those who suppose that there is an orthodoxly conceived monotheistic god do suppose that there is an omnipotent, omniscient, eternal, perfectly free, perfectly good, sole creator of the world *ex nihilo*.

god is at least omnipotent, omniscient, and perfectly good – and that no other being has any of these properties – this disagreement will not affect any of the subsequent discussion.

At a first stab, we might suggest that to believe a proposition is to assign it a probability strictly greater than 50 percent; that to disbelieve a proposition is to assign it a probability strictly less than 50 percent; and that to suspend judgement on a proposition is to assign it a probability of exactly 50 percent. However, it is unrealistic to suppose that we always assign perfectly precise numerical probabilities to propositions. Suppose instead that the probability that one assigns to a proposition is vague over an interval (p, q).[21] Then a second stab would be this: to believe a proposition is to take p strictly greater than 50 percent; to disbelieve a proposition is to take q strictly less than 50 percent; and to suspend judgement on a proposition is to take p less than or equal to 50 percent, and q greater than or equal 50 percent. No doubt there is room for further refinement.[22] However, supposing that this second stab will be adequate for our purposes, we shall have: a *theist* assigns a probability to the claim that an orthodoxly conceived monotheistic god exists that is vague over an interval that is bounded below by 50 percent; an *atheist* assigns a probability to the claim that an orthodoxly conceived monotheistic god exists that is vague over an interval that is bounded above by 50 percent; and an *agnostic* assigns a probability to the claim that an orthodoxly conceived monotheistic god exists that is vague over an interval that includes 50 percent. (Clearly, there is at least one other category, namely, those who assign no probability to the claim that an orthodoxly conceived monotheistic god exists. For want of a better term, I shall call such persons *innocents*.)

Following the discussion earlier in this chapter, I shall assume that the primary purpose of arguments is to change minds. That is, I shall suppose that the primary purpose of theistic arguments is to convert atheists, agnostics, and innocents to theism. (Likewise, the primary purpose of atheistic arguments is to convert theists, agnostics, and innocents to atheism; and the primary purpose of agnostic arguments is to convert theists, atheists, and innocents to agnosticism. I take it that there can be no innocent arguments. I shall henceforth concentrate on the theistic case – but the same

---

[21] No doubt we do sometimes assign precise probabilities to propositions. We can represent these precise assignments by degenerate intervals (r, r).

[22] Note that the view outlined in the main text has the resources to accommodate intuitions about 'leanings' – e.g., the interval (10, 51) represents agnosticism leaning towards atheism. Note, too, that it isn't obvious why one should want to say that (47, 49) represents agnosticism – it seems at least equally plausible to claim that it represents tentative atheism. Finally, note that the fact that adoption of the view outlined in the main text entails that belief is not closed under conjunction is arguably a welcome consequence (in view of problems *such as* the lottery paradox and the paradox of the preface). Despite all this, the view is still subject to difficulties – particularly with respect to questions about the logical closure of belief – but not ones that will have an impact on the current discussion.

considerations will apply, *mutatis mutandis*, to agnosticism and atheism.)
A really successful theistic argument would be one that required anyone,
on pain of irrationality, to become a theist. However, any argument that
required some reasonable people to revise up the bounds of probability
that they assign to the proposition that an orthodoxly conceived monotheistic god exists would count as having some degree of success. (An argument
that forces a revision up of the bounds of probability is one that forces a revision from vagueness over the interval (p, q) to vagueness over the interval
(p', q'), where either p' is greater than p, or q' is greater than q, or both.)[23]
    In our assessment of arguments, we suppose that the targets of the argu-
ments are rational belief-revisers, that is, we suppose that the targets of the
arguments are disposed to revise or update their beliefs in accordance with
the canons of rational belief revision. Of course, exactly what these canons
are is a matter of considerable dispute. (For example, Bayesians hold that
updating must proceed by way of conditionalisation.) And an even more
controversial question is whether there are further constraints to be placed
upon reasonable sets of belief. (For example, some Bayesians hold that reasonable sets of beliefs are regular, that is, do not assign probabilities vague
over the degenerate intervals (0, 0) and (1, 1) to anything other than *a
priori*, necessary, analytic falsehoods and *a priori*, necessary, analytic truths,
respectively. However, Bayesians are characteristically loath to add much
in the way of constraints on prior probabilities.) For my purposes, I shall
suppose that we do not need to worry about further constraints on sets of
beliefs: if a person who is disposed to revise or update his or her beliefs in
accordance with the canons of belief revision has an unreasonable set of
beliefs, then there are considerations that can be presented to him or her
that will force a revision or update of beliefs (in ways that remove the unrea-
sonableness). Of course, there is bound to be some idealisation here: actual
people are reasonable to a greater or lesser extent at different times, and
reasonableness is perhaps only one amongst several desiderata that actual
belief sets aim to satisfy. So we idealise the targets of the arguments in some
ways: we demand that they care about the reasonableness of their beliefs
(at least with respect to the questions at issue), and so on. However, we are

---

[23] Of course, there are further distinctions that could be drawn here. The strongest successful
    argument would require everyone to assign probability (1, 1) to the claim that there is an
    orthodoxly conceived monotheistic god. (Some proponents of ontological arguments have
    thought that their arguments did this.) Perhaps the weakest successful argument would be
    one that required some reasonable persons to revise up ever so slightly one of the bounds on
    the interval that represents their doxastic attitude towards the probability that an orthodoxly
    conceived monotheistic god exists. (Of course, being a weakly successful argument in this
    sense might not be much of a recommendation of an argument – particularly if we don't
    insist on much in the way of constraints on reasonable prior probabilities.) And there is a
    wide range of possibilities in between. It is beyond our current concerns to pursue this kind
    of taxonomy here.

also bound to use the actual judgements of what we take to be reasonable people – including, no doubt, ourselves – as a guide to the responses of our 'ideal' reasonable agents (for what else could we use?).

Various potential pitfalls loom. Sometimes when you disagree with me, I take this as evidence that you are subject to failings of rationality. Other times, when you disagree with me, I just say that this is one of those things about which reasonable people can differ. It is hard to say how we draw the line between these kinds of cases. I am inclined to think that, at least *pro tem*, it should be conceded that there can be reasonable atheists, agnostics, theists, and innocents (even under certain kinds of idealisations). Certainly, my own experience suggests to me that clever, thoughtful, and insightful reasonable people can belong to any of these categories. At any rate, I shall begin by supposing that one should think that the dialectical situation is something like this: reasonable theists present arguments for the existence of an orthodoxly conceived monotheistic god to reasonable non-theists, who then offer the parallel arguments involving god* in reply. All parties to the debate are presumed to be dispositionally rational, that is, disposed to revise their beliefs in accordance with the canons of belief revision. We shall perhaps need to rethink this conception of the dialectical situation later on. But for now, we can turn our attention to the details of the arguments given by the participants in the debate.

1.4.2. What the 'Parallel Cases' Might Show

Various recent authors have contended that there are difficulties for theism that arise from consideration of the claim that god* – an omnipotent, omniscient, eternal, perfectly free, *perfectly evil* sole creator of the universe *ex nihilo* – exists. These alleged difficulties are of at least two quite different kinds that need to be carefully distinguished.

One suggestion is that there is an argument *against* belief in an orthodoxly conceived monotheistic god – that is, an argument against theism – that can be based upon consideration of god*. Roughly, this argument goes as follows: There is no more reason to believe in an orthodoxly conceived monotheistic god than there is to believe in god*. (Every consideration that can be adduced in favour of an orthodoxly conceived monotheistic god counts equally in favour of god*; and every consideration that can be adduced against an orthodoxly conceived monotheistic god counts equally against god*.) But in circumstances in which there is no more nor less reason to believe in an orthodoxly conceived monotheistic god than there is to believe in god*, it would be positively irrational to believe in an orthodoxly conceived monotheistic god. So it is wrong to believe in an orthodoxly conceived monotheistic god – there ought to be no theists.

Another suggestion is that there is a *reply* to theistic arguments for belief in an orthodoxly conceived monotheistic god that can be based upon consideration of god*. Roughly, this reply goes as follows: Every argument for an orthodoxly conceived monotheistic god can be paralleled by an equally compelling argument for god*. So no one who is not already a theist has any more reason to believe in an orthodoxly conceived monotheistic god then they do to believe in god*. But, in these circumstances, it would be irrational to come to believe in an orthodoxly conceived monotheistic god on the basis of theistic arguments. So no non-theists should be persuaded by theistic arguments to change their minds and come to believe in an orthodoxly conceived monotheistic god.

Since god* is typically invoked by non-theists in discussions in which they are replying to theistic arguments, there is often uncertainty about just what the arguments involving god* are intended to establish. After all, one very good way to reply to your argument for the conclusion that p is to provide a compelling argument that not p. So, even though it would suffice for the purposes of replying to theistic arguments to show that non-theists ought not to be persuaded by theistic arguments to change their minds and come to believe in an orthodoxly conceived monotheistic god, it would also be (more than) enough for these purposes to show that there ought not to be any theists. In any case, even if actual debates sometimes involve confusion about these issues, the theoretical points are clear enough: there are two quite different contexts in which arguments involving god* appear – and different considerations must be appealed to in the assessment of these arguments in these different contexts.

Having noted these two different uses to which non-theists might put arguments involving god*, I shall now put this distinction aside. (It would only needlessly complicate the discussion to try to take it into account here.) However, we shall return to it later.

1.4.3. The Importance of Moral Knowledge

In the face of the challenges raised by god*, one might be tempted to argue in something like the following way. Suppose we grant that there is such a thing as moral knowledge (and hence that there is such a thing as moral belief, properly so-called). Suppose we grant further that there is a necessary connection between moral belief and motivation – moral beliefs are necessarily motivating in such a way that one can believe that an action is good or right only if one is inclined to do or to approve that action, other things being equal. Then it seems that we have the basis for an argument that there can be no such being as god*. On the one hand, god* is supposed to be omniscient. Hence, in particular, if there is moral knowledge, then god* knows – and hence believes – every moral truth. But then, if moral beliefs are necessarily connected to motivation, it follows that god* is motivated to pursue the good and the right – and that is inconsistent with the claim that god* is perfectly evil.

An argument that bears some resemblance to the one just given is provided by Daniels (1997). Daniels argues in the following way: It is a conceptual truth that everyone most wants what is good – and hence it is also a conceptual truth that everyone most shuns what is bad. But it follows from this that no one can knowingly do what is bad – and from this it follows that god* cannot exist.

Daniels's argument is subject to some immediate difficulties. In particular, it seems that there are many different ways of understanding the claim that everyone most wants what is good; but it is far from clear that there are ways of understanding this claim on which it is both true and yet also entails that god* cannot exist. First, there are questions about how to understand 'most wants' – does the claim concern the strength of first-order desires, or the content of all-things-considered desires, or the content of interests objectively conceived (so that one can be completely oblivious to what it is that one 'most wants')? Second, there are questions about how to understand 'good' – does the claim concern what is good by one's own lights ('what seems to one to be good', 'what seems to one to be good now'), or what is good by some more objective standard ('what is good from the standpoint of eternity')? Putting together these claims in different ways yields statements of quite different standing, ranging all the way from ostensible tautologies – 'what one wants most now all things considered is what one wants most now all things considered' – to obvious falsehoods – 'what one most strongly desires is (and must always be) what is good from the standpoint of eternity'.

To get an objection to the existence of god*, it seems that what Daniels needs is the claim that 'what one desires, all things considered, is (and must always be) what is good from the standpoint of eternity'. After all, if the requirement of perfect goodness is to have any bite, it must require conformity to some kind of objective standard (I am not perfectly good just because I always do what is good by my lights!). But mundane considerations about weakness of will and our moral failings show immediately that it is not true that what we desire, all things considered, is (and must always be) what is good from the standpoint of eternity. Perhaps there is some further difficulty with the idea that there might be a being that always desired, all things considered, that which is worst from the standpoint of eternity – but it is not at all obvious what this difficulty is (and there seems to be no way of repairing Daniels' argument in order to demonstrate it). Henceforth, then, I shall concentrate on the argument from moral cognitivism that I outlined above.

1.4.4. Objections to Moral Knowledge

The argument against god* presented at the beginning of the previous section has some controversial premises. Not everyone agrees that there is moral knowledge, moral truth, and moral belief. (Some philosophers have held that knowledge does not entail belief. Given this implausible claim, and the further implausible claim that it is only moral belief, and not moral knowledge, that is essentially motivating, one could claim that the argument is invalid – god* might be omniscient and yet have no moral beliefs! Other philosophers have held – on independent grounds whose nature need not concern us here – that god* has no beliefs at all. Again, one might try to use this view to undermine the argument against god* while not disputing the truth of the premises of the argument. However, it seems to me that, if one is disposed to think that moral beliefs are essentially motivating, then one ought also to think that moral knowledge is essentially motivating, even if one holds that knowledge does not entail belief. At any rate, it seems to me that the prospects for this kind of reply to the argument against god* are not very bright.)

Famously, Humeans deny that there can be essentially motivating beliefs – it is desires that are essentially motivating states, but beliefs and desires are distinct existences – and hence they either deny that moral beliefs are essentially motivating, or else they deny that there is any such thing as moral belief (properly so-called). If one accepts that moral beliefs are not essentially motivating, then the argument against god* collapses – why shouldn't god* prefer the destruction of the world to the scratching of his little finger, even though he knows perfectly well that this is wrong? And if one accepts that there is no such thing as moral belief (properly so-called), then of course there is no such thing as moral knowledge (properly so-called) – and hence there is no reason why there should not be an omniscient yet completely immoral being.

There are other routes to the claim that there is no (such thing as) moral knowledge. It is a commonplace that many philosophers have been error-theorists or non-cognitivists about moral discourse. If there are no moral propositions or properties – or if there are moral properties and propositions, but the properties are necessarily uninstantiated and the propositions are necessarily false – then there can be no question of moral knowledge. If what we take to be expression of moral knowledge is merely the expression or projection of our emotions or desires or preferences, then there is no truth-apt content to ground talk of moral truth and moral knowledge. From a number of currently occupied and often-defended standpoints in meta-ethics, the argument against god* is plainly mistaken.

Of course, these meta-ethical questions are enormously controversial. If the point of the arguments involving god* is to persuade theists to change their minds, then that argument can be sustained only if these controversial views can also be defended. (It seems plausible to me to think that theists are unlikely to be error-theorists or non-cognitivists about ethics. Perhaps, indeed, we have here an argument that they ought not to be error-theorists or non-cognitivists about ethics.) On the other hand, if the point of these arguments is simply to respond to theistic arguments for the existence of an orthodoxly conceived monotheistic god, then the controversial status of these views is less pressing. (If one is firmly persuaded of the correctness of an error-theoretical or non-cognitivist treatment of ethics, why shouldn't one rely on this persuasion in replying to arguments for the existence of an orthodoxly conceived monotheistic god?) Perhaps it would be nice to have a response that relied on less controversial assumptions, but it seems perfectly satisfactory nonetheless.

1.4.5. Other Alternatives

The argument involving god* is only one of a family of arguments (or challenges) that can be made to theism. Suppose we accept – on the basis of the argument given above, together with our allegiance to moral cognitivism – that there can be no such being as god*. There are still other beings that raise problems for theism. Consider, for example, god'. God' is a being who is as much like an orthodoxly conceived monotheistic god as can be, except that god' is perfectly evil. Given the concessions just made, god' is neither omniscient nor omnipotent – there is moral knowledge that god' does not possess, and moral actions that god' is unable to perform. (Perhaps there are moral questions that god' is unable to answer. Whether or not this is so depends on tricky questions about the supervenience of the moral on the non-moral that I shall not consider here.) Nonetheless, god' is *very* powerful and *very* knowledgeable – and so the question arises whether there is a substantially stronger case to be made for the existence of god' than there is to be made for the existence of an orthodoxly conceived monotheistic god.

It seems to me to be plausible to suggest that the case for god' that parallels the traditional case for an orthodoxly conceived monotheistic god is about as good as the corresponding parallel case for god*. Given the concessions that we have made concerning moral cognitivism, it seems plausible to claim that god' is a perfectly evil being (a being than which none more evil can be consistently conceived). Consequently, it seems clear that we can develop parallels to familiar ontological, cosmological, and teleological arguments for an orthodoxly conceived monotheistic god. In the case of other familiar theistic arguments – moral arguments, arguments from religious experience, arguments from scripture, arguments from testimony to religious miracles, and so on – the arguments are not so much 'parallel' arguments as they are competing arguments of comparable cogency. (So, for example, if there really is religious experience as of a perfectly good and orthodoxly conceived monotheistic god, this is just the kind of deception in which you would expect a perfectly evil being to engage.) There are many details to be argued over here – just as in the case of the arguments for god* – but I shall proceed under the assumption that the case for god′ is pretty much as good as the case for god*.

Perhaps there is some 'flaw' in the case for god′ that resembles the difficulty that moral cognitivism raises for god*. It seems doubtful that non-theists who wish to run the kind of line that is being pursued here ought to be very concerned about this possibility. After all – as Hume observed in his *Dialogues Concerning Natural Religion* – there are clearly many, many alternative hypotheses that one could formulate about the attributes of a sole creator of the universe (especially if we allow that a 'sole creator' can be a committee, or a body corporate, or the like). For many of these conceptions, one can construct a case that parallels – or at least robustly competes with – the traditional case for an orthodoxly conceived monotheistic god. So, even if the case for god′ fails, there are plenty of standbys waiting in the wings. (Perhaps you might think that it is obvious that the case for these standbys cannot be as strong as the case for god* or god′. However, we haven't yet seen what kind of objection might be made to the case for god′; as things stand – contrary to what one might have initially expected – the case for god′ might be stronger than the case for god*. Perhaps there are other gods out there for which the case is stronger still.) And in any case, we have yet to see whether there is any comparable objection to the case for god′.

1.4.6. An Alternative Line of Defence

Once god′ and his ilk appear on the horizon, one might wonder whether it was such a good idea to pursue the moral cognitivism objection to god*. If there is to be a defence of an orthodoxly conceived monotheistic god against the proliferating alternatives, it seems likely that it will not proceed piecemeal. (Of course, there might be a mixed strategy – knock out virtually all of the alternatives with a general argument, and then mop up the very small number of recalcitrant cases that remain. However, I shall start from the optimistic standpoint that supposes that there is a pure general strategy that can succeed.)

What kind of general defence might there be? I suspect that the best bet at this point is to invoke some kinds of considerations concerning simplicity, or opposition to scepticism, or insistence on believability, or the like. The hypothesis that an orthodoxly conceived monotheistic god exists is simpler than the hypothesis that any of the alternative gods exists, and this is a reason to prefer it to them, other things being equal (as they apparently are!). The hypothesis that one of the alternative gods exists is a kind of sceptical hypothesis that is doxastically parasitic on the hypothesis that an orthodoxly conceived monotheistic god exists. (Whenever one has an explanation or theory, one can cook up alternative explanations or theories that 'work' equally well. Consequently, one can avoid scepticism only if one is prepared to accept that these cooked-up theories and explanations can be set aside.) The hypothesis that an orthodoxly conceived monotheistic god exists is a live and believable hypothesis, unlike the hypotheses concerning the alternative gods; since no one could take these alternatives seriously, we are warranted in setting them aside. And so on.

Of course, the above list of considerations is rather heterogeneous: it may be that god* is not ruled out by the simplicity test even though it is ruled out by the others. Moreover, none of the considerations has been developed in any detail. (There are notoriously difficult questions about criteria for simplicity, criteria for determining when explanations and theories have been gerrymandered, reasons for thinking that unbelievability is a good ground for ruling out hypotheses, and so on.) However, I shall suppose that we have enough to be going on with.

1.4.7. Why Theists Suppose That the 'Cases' Diverge

At this point, I think that we need to recall the two different uses to which non-theists might put arguments involving god*, god', and their ilk. Suppose, first, that non-theists are interested only in defending themselves against theistic arguments, that is, they have no (immediate) interest in persuading theists to give up their belief in an orthodoxly conceived monotheistic god. In this case, it seems to me, it is clear that the invocation of god*, god' and so on, does make prosecution of the theistic case much more difficult. On the one hand, a much more substantial burden is incurred if one undertakes to persuade non-theists to give up on ethical non-cognitivism (and other ostensibly acceptable philosophical views that must be advanced in order to construct arguments to defeat particular alternative gods). And, on the other hand, the claims about simplicity, gerrymandering, and so on, seem unlikely to have much force since, in an important sense, simplicity and the appearance of gerrymandering are very much in the eye of the beholder. (More exactly, judgements about simplicity, gerrymandering, and so on, are sensitive to what else it is that one believes.) It seems to me, at any rate, that the claims about an orthodoxly conceived monotheistic god, god*, god', and many other gods besides, are pretty much on a par as far as simplicity, absence of gerrymander, and believability are concerned – and it also seems to me that most reasonable non-theists are likely to agree.

(Perhaps a useful point of comparison here is with what I shall call 'tools for prognostication'. It seems to me that hypotheses about the possibility of predicting the future using tea leaves, crystal balls, sheep entrails, the constellations of the heavens, the writings of prophets, the utterances of trees, and so on are pretty much on a par as far as simplicity, absence of gerrymander, and believability are concerned. Adverting to these various different tools for prognostication is one good move to make in defending oneself against the arguments of someone who wishes to argue that one – but only one – of these tools yields reliable information about the future. Of course, one might well point out that this move is parasitic on the further assumption that there is no good evidence for – nor plausible mechanism that could be used to explain how one comes by – knowledge of the future (via the listed mechanisms). But exactly the same point can be made by non-theists against theists: by the lights of non-theists, there is no good evidence for – nor plausible mechanism that could be used to explain how one comes by – knowledge of an orthodoxly conceived monotheistic god. It seems entirely natural to think that one who is disposed to claim that there is no good evidence for the existence of an orthodoxly conceived monotheistic god will also be disposed to say that one might as well believe in god*, or god′, or some other unorthodoxly conceived nontheistic god, given the available evidence. While these two claims are distinct, there is a clear sense in which they fit naturally together.)

Suppose, on the other hand, that proponents of the arguments involving god*, god′ and their ilk are interested in attacking theists, that is, in trying to persuade theists to give up their theism. Then it is much less clear that the invocation of god*, god′, and their ilk adds substantially to the attack. After all, reasonable belief in an orthodoxly conceived monotheistic god will fit into a network of beliefs that are very likely to conspire to produce the judgement that the hypothesis that an orthodoxly conceived monotheistic god exists is simpler, less gerrymandered, and more believable than the hypotheses about the existence of alternative gods. At any rate, it seems to me that I have more reason to trust the verdicts of those theists whom I deem to be reasonable – that is, more reason to suppose that the fact that these people make those judgements shows that those judgements can reasonably be made by reasonable people – than I have to insist that reasonable theists take on my judgements about the simplicity, and so on, of various hypotheses. (Moreover, I can note that those who are disposed to believe in an orthodoxly conceived monotheistic god given the available evidence will naturally judge that it is much more plausible to suppose that an orthodoxly conceived monotheistic god exists given the available evidence than it is to suppose that god*, or god′, or some other unorthodoxly conceived monotheistic god exists given the available evidence.)

By this point, readers are bound to have noticed that I have now committed myself to the claim that theists will not (and indeed ought not to) concede that the case for an orthodoxly conceived monotheistic god can be paralleled by the case for god*, or god′, or . . . , if what is meant by this is that they have no more reason to believe in an orthodoxly conceived monotheistic god than there is reason to believe in alternative gods given the available evidence. By the lights of theists, 'the case for an orthodoxly conceived monotheistic god' must seem much superior to the case for alternative gods – else, they would not be theists. So the *prima facie* appearances to which I alluded at the beginning of this section are deceptive – there is a clear sense in which reasonable theists can and must deny that the case for god*, god', and so on, is as good as the case for an orthodoxly conceived monotheistic god.

1.4.8. A Final Comment

There are many problems here. The main one that we are now confronting is how to think about the epistemological and dialectical context in which the arguments under consideration are to be located. It is perhaps natural to think in the following way. A representative reasonable theist presents the case for believing in an orthodoxly conceived monotheistic god to a representative reasonable non-theist. The non-theist responds by providing a parallel to the case just provided but which supports the existence of some alternative deity: god*, or god', or.... The theist then is faced with the challenge of finding some difference between the case for an orthodoxly conceived monotheistic god and the cases for the alternative gods.

I suggest that one ought to be very suspicious about this talk of 'the case for an orthodoxly conceived monotheistic god'. In the case of many things that we believe, the grounds that we have for those beliefs far outrun our abilities to articulate those grounds. (For example, it seems that it is no requirement of rationality that one ought to be able to recall the grounds for any belief that one has come to hold.[24]) Moreover, even in cases in which this is not so, it is often the case that the process of articulation could be extended indefinitely (there is always more that could be said). Consequently, talk about 'the case for an orthodoxly conceived monotheistic god' too readily leads to confusion of epistemological and dialectical ('dialogical'?) questions that ought to be kept distinct.

I conclude – albeit tentatively (and without in any way supposing that the forgoing constitutes either an adequate discussion or defence) – that it may well be the case that theism and non-theism are both reasonable responses to the evidence that people have, and yet that any case that theists put forward for the existence of an orthodoxly conceived monotheistic god can be 'paralleled' by cases for the existence of other gods about which: (i) theists reasonably judge that the cases are not genuinely parallel (but often for reasons that they have not yet, and perhaps that they shall never have, successfully articulated); and (ii) non-theists reasonably judge that

---

[24] See, e.g., Harman (1986) for further discussion of this kind of consideration.

the cases are genuinely parallel (where this judgement is typically a natural expression of – or companion to – their view that there is insufficient evidence for belief in the existence of an orthodoxly conceived monotheistic god).[25]

[25] Two points in particular that need further work: (1) I do not think that my line of argument could be adapted to defend the reasonableness of belief in any hypothesis (e.g., I do not think that reasonable and suitably informed persons can believe in astrology). My judgement, that there are reasonable theists whose belief in God is reasonable, is crucial to my argument. (2) There is a distinction between descriptive and normative conceptions of 'reasonableness' that might have important consequences for my argument. (Why suppose that my intuitions about the reasonableness of my friends have any normative significance?) I hope to consider these issues elsewhere.

2

Ontological Arguments

In Oppy (1995c), I divided the ontological arguments that I examined into six classes: (i) definitional arguments, (ii) conceptual arguments, (iii) modal arguments, (iv) 'Meinongian' arguments, (v) experiential arguments, and (vi) 'Hegelian' arguments. While I claimed neither that this taxonomy is mutually exclusive nor that it is exhaustive, I did note that I knew of no purely *a priori* argument for the existence of an orthodoxly conceived monotheistic god that did not belong to at least one of these categories. For each of these categories of argument, I exhibited arguments from that class and gave a detailed account of what I took to be shortcomings of the exhibited arguments. Moreover, I gave a fairly carefully qualified argument for the conclusion that there could not be a successful ontological argument that belonged to any of the six classes that I had identified. Finally, among other things, I provided an account of the use of parodies in the discussion of ontological arguments.

Since I wrote that earlier book, I have come to have some further misgivings about the general objection to ontological arguments, that is, the 'carefully qualified' argument for the conclusion that there could not be a successful ontological argument that belonged to any of the six classes of ontological arguments that I had identified. Furthermore, I have come to think that there are various ways in which the discussion in that earlier book is seriously incomplete. First, there is a class of ontological arguments – the mereological ontological arguments – whose existence is acknowledged only in passing (see the discussion at p. 262) and which deserves more extensive discussion. Second, the discussion of Gödel's ontological argument (at pp. 224–5) is very compressed and admits of profitable expansion. Finally, my discussion of parodies of ontological arguments has been criticised – by Chambers (2000) – in a way that invites response. The aim of the present chapter is to carry out these tasks, beginning with the reconsideration of the 'general objection' to ontological arguments that I presented in Oppy (1995c).[1]

2.1. MY 'GENERAL OBJECTION' RECONSIDERED

As I noted above, I have come to have doubts about the 'general objection' to ontological arguments presented in Oppy (1995c). Since Langtry (1999) provides a critical discussion of this general objection, it will be useful to begin by considering what he has to say against it. While I am no longer sure that that general objection is correctly expressed in my book – and, indeed, while I am no longer confident that there is such a general objection to be given – I also think that Langtry's criticisms of that objection are not quite right. Consequently, what I propose to do here is the following: first, to rehearse briefly the general objection to ontological arguments given in my book; second, to briefly recapitulate Langtry's criticisms of this general

---

[1] Among the comments of those who reviewed Oppy (1995c), the most puzzling to me are the claims in Gale (1998) that the argument of that book commits me to some kind of 'Wittgensteinian fideism'. I take it that 'Wittgensteinian fideism' is something like the view that claims are always made from within 'language games', that whether or not a claim can be correctly asserted depends upon the 'language game' within which it is asserted, and that there is no 'external' standpoint from which it is possible to criticise the assertions that belong to a particular 'language game'. A 'Wittgensteinian fideist' in philosophy of religion will claim that the assertion that a given monotheistic god exists is 'internal' to the 'language game' to which talk of that monotheistic god belongs, and hence that it is beyond criticism or defence by philosophical argumentation. I think that it is obvious that there is no commitment to any claims that even remotely resemble 'Wittgensteinian fideism' in Oppy (1995c). While it is true that my primary aim is to establish the conclusion – with which I hope that all philosophers of religion might be persuaded to agree – that there are no *dialectically effective* ontological arguments, i.e., arguments of such a kind that those who do not already accept the conclusions of those arguments ought to be brought to accept those conclusions when they are presented with the arguments, on pain of conviction of some kind of irrationality or other cognitive failing, there is no obvious connection between 'Wittgensteinian fideism' and this kind of concern with the dialectical efficacy of arguments. As I explained in chapter 1 of the present work, I am inclined to a kind of pluralism about reasonable belief: there are various reasons why it seems right to me to suppose that not all agreement can be traced back to irrationality or other dramatic cognitive failings of that kind. However, that kind of pluralism about reasonable belief is not inconsistent with hostility towards 'Wittgensteinian fideism', for which I certainly carry no brief: just because there can be 'reasonable disagreement' about some propositions, it does not follow that there can be 'reasonable disagreement' about all; and neither does it follow that the claims of any given 'language game' are immune to 'external' scrutiny. Moreover – and perhaps more important – there is no reason to suppose that pluralism about reasonable belief is somehow inconsistent with a robust metaphysical realism: it is perfectly possible for someone to have a 'reasonable belief' that is nonetheless false. I hold that it is simply true that there are no monotheistic gods, nor, indeed, supernatural entities of any kind. However, I do not see why – as Gale seems to suppose – I cannot also hold that not all of those who disagree with me on this matter are thereby convicted of some kind of irrationality, or other dramatic cognitive failing of that ilk.

objection; third, to explain why I think that Langtry's criticisms are ineffective; and fourth, to air some doubts of my own about the argument that I originally defended.

2.1.1. The General Objection Rehearsed

Consider a putative ontological argument $P_1, \ldots, P_n \therefore C$. The conclusion of this argument contains some vocabulary whose use – in the way in which it is used in the conclusion of the argument – brings with it ontological commitment to an orthodoxly conceived monotheistic god. Perhaps, for example, the name 'God' has an ontologically committing occurrence – as in the sentence 'God exists'. Or, perhaps, the definite description 'the greatest conceivable being' has an ontologically committing occurrence – as in the sentence 'The greatest conceivable being exists'. Or, perhaps, the indefinite description 'a being than which none greater can be conceived' has an ontologically committing occurrence – as in the sentence 'A being than which none greater can be conceived exists'. Or, perhaps, there is a quantifier expression whose domain is required to include an orthodoxly conceived monotheistic god in its range, as in the sentence 'There is an omnipotent, omniscient, omnibenevolent sole creator of the universe'. And so forth: there are many different kinds of expressions that can be used to incur ontological commitment; some such expression must be used in an ontologically committing way in the conclusion of our argument.

But now consider the premises of the argument. Clearly, the conjunction of the premises must incur an ontological commitment to an orthodoxly conceived monotheistic god (or else the argument will not even be valid). Yet if the premises involve expressions – names, definite descriptions, quantified noun phrases, and the like – whose use incurs an ontological commitment to an orthodoxly conceived monotheistic god, then it seems that opponents of the argument will be able to object to the argument on the grounds that it begs the question. Suppose, for example, that the argument goes like this: 'God is the creator of the universe. Therefore God exists'. An even moderately alert opponent of the argument will point out that, on any construal on which this is a valid argument, the first premise clearly presupposes what the argument sets out to prove.

Perhaps one might think to reply to this argument that it could be the case that there are occurrences of expressions inside the scope of protective operators that prevent the incurring of the ontological commitments of the kind in question, but without harming the validity of the argument. Suppose, for example, that we amend the argument that we gave previously, so that it reads: 'According to my definition, God is the creator of the universe. Therefore God exists'. Unfortunately, in this case, it is clear that the inclusion of the protective operator – while it does, indeed, undo the problematic ontological commitment – undermines the validity of the argument. And this point seems to be perfectly general: no matter which protective operators are used, if they really are able to cancel the problematic ontological commitments, then it will no longer be the case that the argument is valid.

So the proponent of any given ontological argument is faced with a dilemma: how can one hope to formulate the argument in a way that is valid but not question-begging? Use any vocabulary that brings with it an ontological commitment to an orthodoxly conceived monotheistic god in the premises, and the argument is question-begging; clothe ontologically committing uses of this kind of vocabulary with protective operators, and the argument ceases to be valid.

2.1.2. Langtry's Response to My General Objection

Langtry claims that there is a strategy that is open to proponents of ontological arguments, but that the general objection fails to recognise. Suppose, for example, that the following is a non-redundant premise in an ontological argument: 'It is impossible that anything prevents the existence of God'. If we were to replace this premise with the claim that 'According to such-and-such definition, it is impossible that anything prevents the existence of God', then the validity of the argument will be disrupted: all that we will be able to conclude is that, according to the given definition, an orthodoxly conceived monotheistic god exists. But, says Langtry, this is not the only option open to the proponent of the argument: why not instead replace the premise with the claim that 'If God exists, then it is impossible that anything prevents the existence of God'? (Strictly, Langtry suggests replacement with the claim 'If the description "God" is satisfied by an existing individual, then it is impossible that anything prevents the existence of God'. However, the semantic ascent here is either inadequate or unnecessary: either an orthodoxly conceived monotheistic god's existence is just a matter of the name 'God' being satisfied by an existing individual – in which case we might as well stick with the shorter conditional – or else there could be something other than an orthodoxly conceived monotheistic god that satisfies the name (just as there can be, and are, many people in South America who are called 'Jesus') – in which case only the shorter conditional gives the claim that is required.) Isn't this an alternative suggestion that evades the twin forks of the general objection?

2.1.3. Discussion of Langtry's Response to My General Objection

Well, no. 'If God exists, then . . . ' is just another kind of protective operator that can be used to disown ontological commitment – or, at any rate, so the most plausible reading of this suggestion would conclude. And, as Langtry himself concedes, it would have just the same kind of disastrous consequence: all that we will be able to conclude, given the new premise, is that if an orthodoxly conceived monotheistic god exists, then an orthodoxly conceived monotheistic god exists – and that it is hardly the startling result that we set out to prove. Langtry seems to suppose – on the basis of the discussion of particular kinds of ontological arguments in earlier chapters of the book – that the general objection supposes that protective operators are bound to be of the 'according to such-and-such theory...' kind. And, from the standpoint of that supposition, his objection makes good sense. But a careful reading of p. 115 of Oppy (1995c) shows that operators of the 'according to such-and-such theory...' kind are merely examples drawn from a much wider category of intensional operators. Given that conditionals of the form 'If God exists, then...' incur no ontological commitment to God, then the use of these conditionals fits the general characterisation of 'intensional operators', as that characterisation is intended in the general objection.

Perhaps it might be replied that the above suggestion relies upon a rather implausible conception of conditionals. Suppose, for example, that we treat claims of the form 'If God exists, then...' as material conditionals, that is, as equivalent to disjunctions of the form 'Either God does not exist, or...'. Since claims of this form can be true if there is no orthodoxly conceived monotheistic god, we don't want to say that they involve an ontological commitment to an orthodoxly conceived monotheistic god. But, on the other hand, it is hard to see what contribution a claim of this form could make to an argument *for* the existence of an orthodoxly conceived monotheistic god in which there are no other uses of the name 'God' that are ontologically committing. As we noted before, the conjunction of the premises in the argument must incur an ontological commitment to an orthodoxly conceived monotheistic god if the argument is to be valid; since this premise does not incur such a commitment, there are only two options: either there are some other premises that alone or together incur the commitment – in which case we can simply forget about the conditional premise and focus on those other premises – or there are some other premises that do not alone incur the commitment but that, in conjunction with the conditional premise, do incur the commitment. But how could premises that together incur no ontological commitment to an orthodoxly conceived monotheistic god – which do not entail that an orthodoxly conceived monotheistic god exists – be made to incur that commitment by the additional conjunction of a premise of the form 'Either God does not exist or...'? If $\{P_1, \ldots, P_n\}$ does not entail G, then neither does $\{P_1, \ldots, P_n, \sim G \vee D\}$.

In his discussion, Langtry writes: "Suppose that [the claim that if God exists, then it is impossible that anything prevent the existence of God] follows from some metaphysical theory T, and is acceptable only to people who hold T. People advancing the... argument hope that some atheists and agnostics hold T. There is no general reason why atheists and agnostics should not hold T, since the content of [the claim that if God exists, then it is impossible that anything prevent the existence of God] does not commit one to the existence of God. If the agnostics and atheists also hold [some other claim], and are brought to agree that [these two claims] jointly entail that God exists, then the . . . argument will be dialectically effective. The atheists and agnostics will not be able to avoid theism by saying that their agreement to [these claims] committed them only to the conclusion 'According to *T*, God exists'"(149). But, on the one hand, as we have just seen, if the two claims jointly entail that an orthodoxly conceived monotheistic god exists, then so does the other claim alone – and it is hard to see what reason there is for supposing that reasonable atheists and agnostics will be committed to any such claim. On the other hand, if the two claims do not in fact entail that an orthodoxly conceived monotheistic god exists – even though some atheists and agnostics mistakenly think that it does – then it is simply not the case that what we have here is a 'dialectically effective argument' (in the sense in which this expression is used in my book). So, in fact, there is no problem of the kind that Langtry finds for the general objection to ontological arguments that I proposed.

2.1.4. Other Worries about My General Objection

Even if you agree with me that Langtry's response to the general objection to ontological arguments is unsuccessful, you may still be inclined to object that the general objection proves too much. I shall consider four separate lines of thought, each of which is intended to establish a conclusion of this kind.

1. *First*, it might be thought that the general objection could be run against any deductive argument, no matter what conclusion it has. If the conclusion of the argument $P_1, \ldots, P_n \therefore C$ is controversial, then objectors to the argument will claim that the argument is invalid, or that one of the premises is unacceptable, or that the conclusion of the argument should actually be understood in such a way that it turns out to be benign and acceptable to all, and yet this is just the burden of the general objection. Surely, we don't want to say that there is a general objection to the use of deductive arguments in controversial areas of philosophy!

2. *Second*, it might be thought that the general objection could be run against any deductive argument that has an existential conclusion. If the existence claim that is the conclusion of the argument $P_1, \ldots,$ $P_n \therefore C$ is controversial, then objectors to the argument will claim that the argument is invalid, or that one of the premises is unacceptable, or that the conclusion of the argument should actually be understood in such a way that it turns out to be benign and acceptable to all, and yet this is the burden of the general objection. Surely, we don't

want to say that there is a general objection to the use of deductive arguments for existential conclusions in areas of philosophy in which there is disagreement about ontology!

3. *Third*, it might be thought that there are straightforward cases of arguments that show that the general objection is mistaken even in the case of classical propositional logic. Consider, for example, the following argument: "Either it is raining, or God exists. Either it is not raining, or God exists. Hence, God exists". In this argument, neither of the occurrences of the name 'God' in the premises is ontologically committing; in each case, the premise could be true in circumstances in which no orthodoxly conceived monotheistic god exists. Nonetheless, it seems clear that no one should think that an argument that fits this pattern is any good; if the general objection does not work in this case, then it seems clear that it fails as a general objection to ontological arguments.

4. *Fourth*, it might be thought that there are clearly kinds of arguments that avoid the strategy of the general objection, even if that strategy escapes the first three objections that I have considered. Suppose, for example, that one were to argue in the following way: 'According to such-and-such a story, God exists. What the story says is true. Therefore God exists'. More formally, we might represent this argument in the following way: 'According to such-and-such a story, God exists. For any proposition that p, if according to the story it is the case that p, then it is the case that p. Therefore God exists'. Of course, no one is likely to think that an argument that fits this pattern is any good – but the question is whether the general objection provides a good reason for rejecting arguments of this kind. Plausibly, the answer is 'No!' In this argument, there doesn't seem to be any particular bit of referential apparatus in the premises that incurs the commitment to an orthodoxly conceived monotheistic god: in the first premise, the occurrence of 'God' lies within the scope of protective operators; and, in the second premise, the only obvious commitment is to the propositions that lie in the domain of the propositional quantifier.

I think that some of these objections can be met. The strategy of the general objection is to focus on the referential apparatus that is used in the premises of ontological arguments. Deductive arguments can be used in cases in which there is no disagreement about ontology, that is, no disagreement about what kinds of things there are, what kinds of properties are instantiated, and so forth. In those cases, the general objection gives no reason at all to be suspicious of those uses of deductive arguments: it's only in cases where there is dispute about ontology that the considerations of the general objection are supposed to get a grip (cf. 118n7). So the first of the above objections fails: there is no general objection to the use of deductive

arguments in philosophy that can be generated from the kinds of considerations that are appealed to in the formulation of the general objection to
ontological arguments.

The suggestion that the general objection might extend to other areas
in which there is ontological dispute seems to me to be not obviously unacceptable. Remember that the objection is supposed to work only in the
case of ontological arguments, that is, in the case of arguments all of whose
premises are – reasonably alleged to be? – knowable *a priori*. Where there is
sufficient disagreement about ontology, it seems not implausible to suppose
that this disagreement will not be susceptible of resolution on purely *a priori*
grounds. Suppose, for example, that I am a fictionalist about numbers. It
would be absurd to think that I ought to be persuaded to give up my fiction-
alism by the observation that there are prime numbers between 10 and 20 –
and for just the reason that is suggested by the general objection in the case
of ontological arguments: all that a fictionalist will accept is that, according
to the mathematical fiction, there are prime numbers between 10 and 20.
However, even if the above suggestion is not implausible, it is not clear to me
that it is correct. In particular, I suspect that the mereological ontological
argument described in Oppy (1997b) – and below – does not fall to the
general objection; and, if that's right, then the general objection does not
succeed in ruling out all *a priori* arguments for ontological conclusions.

The claim that arguments with disjunctive premises can make problems
for the general objection seems to me to be reasonably easy to meet, provided
that one is prepared to adopt fairly liberal standards for the identification
of arguments. Suppose that one were given the following argument: 'God
exists; either it is raining or it is not raining; therefore, God exists'. Clearly,
the general objection will apply in this case: the word 'God' appears with
an ontologically committing use in the first premise. But this argument is a
fairly trivial reformulation of the argument that was supposed to be making
trouble. So the suggestion would be to allow for 'trivial reformulation' of
arguments in considering the question of whether the general objection
applies to a given argument. Of course, that leaves the question of what
exactly should be allowed to count as 'trivial reformulation': given that the
premises entail that an orthodoxly conceived monotheistic god exists, it will
always be possible to 'reformulate' the premises so that this claim is num-
bered among them. Perhaps there is some way of taking this idea further;
however, since I have already indicated that I don't think that the general
objection works, I do not propose to try to do this.

The final worry seems to me to be impossible to surmount. Even if there
were no other worries that confronted the general objection, it now seems
to me that there are going to be forms of arguments that escape worries
about the use of 'referential apparatus' of the kinds that were originally
considered. Perhaps it might be said that there can be no plausible *a priori*
arguments of the type in question; but it seems to me to be clearly an open

question whether there are other forms of argument that escape the worries that take centre stage in the general objection, and yet that can have as their conclusion the claim that an orthodoxly conceived monotheistic god exists. Moreover, as I noted above, it seems plausible to think that my mereological ontological argument is a case in point (though it is clearly a contentious matter whether one should think that the proper conclusion of the argument is that an orthodoxly conceived monotheistic god exists).

Having said all this, it is perhaps worth pointing out that the statement of the general argument in Oppy (1995c) is heavily qualified. It was something of an afterthought – an attempt to generalise a pattern that seemed to emerge from the particular criticisms of the different kinds of arguments that I had characterised and investigated – and I did not intend to rest much weight upon it. That I now have even more reasons to be suspicious of it seems to me not to undermine the value of the rest of the material in the book. What seems right to me is this: that no ontological argument that has been thus far produced evades a three-pronged criticism: either it has plainly question-begging premises; or it is invalid; or it establishes the existence of something uncontroversial (that can reasonably be taken to have no religious significance, e.g., the physical universe). But much the same thing seems to me to be true about other deductive arguments for the existence of an orthodoxly conceived monotheistic god, for example, cosmological arguments and teleological arguments: either they are invalid; or they have plainly question-begging premises; or they establish the existence of something that can reasonably be taken to have no religious significance. Perhaps there is a question about the extent to which the premises in the other arguments are merely false and not also plainly question-begging; but, given the kind of account of begging the question that I favoured in Oppy (1995c) – and that I am still inclined to defend – it is not clear to me that I could take this line.

In sum: even if the general objection is right, it is not well motivated by the observations that led me to formulate it. More importantly, I no longer think that the general objection is right: there is no way I can see of patching the general objection to make it watertight. It still seems to me to be more or less inconceivable – on the basis of the currently available arguments at least – that there is a successful ontological argument. But the only evidence that I can point to in support of this contention is the clear failure of all of the kinds of ontological arguments that have hitherto been produced.

2.1.5. One Last Comment

Langtry is puzzled by my suggestion that one might want to consider the interpretation of ontological arguments in which implicit protective operators are inserted, particularly given the fact that these inserted operators upset the validity of the arguments. "Why would the theist in this context think it worth discussing a definition or theory that the theist realises that atheists and agnostics all reject?" However, it is important to recall that there is an independent motivation behind the suggestion that ontological arguments typically admit of several different readings, which derives from the classic discussion of *Proslogion II* in Lewis (1970). If it is plausible to suppose that there are typically several different readings of ontological arguments between which it is easy to slide, then we have an explanation of why it is that theists have occasionally been attracted by the thought that ontological arguments are successful proofs of the existence of an orthodoxly conceived monotheistic god. On Lewis's – admittedly controversial – interpretation of *Proslogion II*, there are two different readings of the argument, one of which is invalid, the other of which has a question-begging premise, and between which it is not implausible that one might fail to distinguish. In my book, I suggested that Lewis's strategy can be extended to apply to a great variety of ontological arguments, and that it does give a plausible explanation of the attractiveness of those arguments.

Even if this response to Langtry is deemed unsuccessful, there is an even more important – and, in my view, more substantial – reason for objecting to the general objection on the grounds that it provides an unsatisfactory understanding of what the theist is doing when she advances an ontological argument with a premise that contains vocabulary whose use requires an ontological commitment to an orthodoxly conceived monotheistic god. Whatever the theist may be thinking, the crucial point is that a satisfactory ontological argument cannot contain any referential apparatus whose use in the premises brings with it an ontological commitment to an orthodoxly conceived monotheistic god. If the theist advances an argument that does contain such referential apparatus, then it is clear that atheists and agnostics will reject those premises; at best, they will accept them only under the scope of protective operators that ward off the problematic commitment (but that also serve to disrupt the validity of the arguments). If the theist wishes to replace the problematic premise with something else that does not incur the problematic commitment, then the theist is free to do so; but the effect of this is to produce a new argument, and until the new argument is actually given, there is no reason at all to think that there is a successful argument to be had. Moreover – as we pointed out in the previous paragraph – it won't do to acknowledge the problem half-heartedly, for example, by adding 'def.' as an annotation to the argument, while actually sliding backwards and forwards between the initial question-begging interpretation on which the argument is valid, and the amended non-question-begging interpretation on which the argument is simply invalid. Where a theist advances a premise that contains referential vocabulary whose use brings with it an ontological commitment to an orthodoxly conceived monotheistic god, the non-theist will accept the premise only if it is prefixed with an operator that cancels that commitment – and, in all actual cases, the addition of the operator is sufficient to disrupt the validity of the original argument (assuming that it was, indeed, valid).

2.2. MEREOLOGICAL ONTOLOGICAL ARGUMENTS

Mereological ontological arguments are – as the name suggests – ontological arguments that draw on the resources of mereology, that is, the theory of the part-whole relation. In the following discussion, I begin by presenting a paradigmatic mereological ontological argument. Next, I present what I take to be a 'minimal' reason for supposing that this argument is not successful.

2.2.1. A Mereological Ontological Argument

I shall suppose that the following is a paradigmatic instance of a mereological ontological argument:

1. I exist. (Premise, contingent *a priori*)
2. (Hence) Some – that is, least one – thing exists. (From 1)
3. Whenever some things exist, there is some thing of which they are all parts. (Premise, from mereology)
4. (Hence) There is exactly one thing of which every thing is a part. (From 2, 3)
5. The unique thing of which every thing is a part is God. (Definition)
6. (Hence) God exists. (From 4, 5)

The status of premise 1 is controversial: friends of two-dimensional modal logic (and others) will be reluctant to grant that the proposition that I exist is both contingent and knowable *a priori* (even by me). Instead, they will insist that all that I know *a priori* is that the sentence "I exist" expresses some true proposition or other when I token it. But, of course, even that will suffice for the purposes of the argument. Provided that I know *a priori* that the sentence "I exist" expresses some true singular proposition or other – that is, some proposition or other that contains an individual – then I have an *a priori* guarantee that there are some individuals, and so I am entitled to assert 2. Of course, it will remain true that there are some people who refuse to accept 2: consider, for example, those ontological nihilists who think that the proper logical form of every sentence can be given in a feature-placing language.[2] However, many people will be prepared to grant that we can

---

[2] See, e.g., O'Leary-Hawthorne and Cortens (1995).

know *a priori* that there are at least some individuals – and that is enough to sustain interest in our argument to this point.[3]

The status of premise 3 is also controversial: there are various reasons why one might be inclined to reject it. However, it is important to be clear about exactly what the premise says. Note, in particular, that it does not say that, whenever some things exist, there is some thing that is the mereological sum of those things. Rather, what it says is that, whenever some things exist, there is some thing of which all of those things are parts – that is, the thing completely overlaps each of the parts, but the parts together need not completely overlap the thing. Of course, given the mereological claim about sums, the weaker claim follows, so friends of unrestricted mereological composition will certainly be happy with 3. But one could subscribe to 3 on independent grounds: one might think, for example, that it is just impossible for there to be two things that are not both parts of a single, more inclusive thing. Again, there will be people who are not prepared to accept 3. But, for now, it seems reasonable to suppose that there will be lots of people who are quite happy with it. (We shall have more to say about 3 later.)

The inference of 4 from 3 looks distinctly suspicious. Indeed, it seems to have the form of the quantifier-exchange fallacy that moves from ∀∃ to ∃∀. However, we can patch this. What we need to suppose is that we can talk unrestrictedly about every thing. Now, consider *all* things. If premise 3 is correct, then it does indeed follow that there is some thing of which every thing is a part. (By 'part', I mean 'proper or improper part', of course.) Moreover, it is then extremely plausible to suggest that there can be only one such thing: in order to deny this, one would need to deny the uniqueness of composition (a course that is possible but, at least *prima facie*, quite unattractive). Of course, some people will not be happy with the claim that we can talk unrestrictedly about every thing. Among the reasons that might be given for this unhappiness, perhaps the most important is the suggestion that unrestricted quantification leads to paradox. However, it is important to bear in mind that we are talking about quantification over individuals here. Whether one supposes that there are finitely many, or countably many, or continuum many, or Beth-2 many, or even proper class many individuals, it is hard to see how any contradiction can arise from this assumption. Of course, there are other objections that one might make to the totality assumption. However, it again seems reasonable to suppose that there will be lots of people who are quite happy with it. (Once more, we shall return to this assumption later.)

---

[3] Also, it might be possible to develop a related argument within the framework of ontological nihilism. For, presumably, the sentence 'I exist' will translate into a sentence that is contingent *a priori* and that entails the translation of the sentence 'Some things exist'. Of course, mereological pantheism would also need to be reconceived – as, indeed, would mereology. I leave all of this as an exercise for ontological nihilists (if such there be).

On the basis of the above considerations, it seems reasonable to suggest that there will be lots of people – including lots of people who do not count themselves as having any kinds of religious beliefs – who will be happy with the argument to 4. Or, perhaps better, there will be lots of people – including lots of people who do not count themselves as having any kinds of religious beliefs – who will be prepared to accept the following argument at least as far as 5:

1. I exist. (Premise, contingent *a priori*)
2. Some things – that is, at least one – exist. (From 1)
3. If some things exist, then there are some things that are all of the things that exist. (Premise, from the meaning of 'all'.)
4. Whenever some things exist, there is some thing of which they are all parts. (Premise, from mereology)
5. There is exactly one thing of which every thing is a part. (From[4] 3, 4)
6. The unique thing of which every thing is a part is God. (Definition)
7. Hence God exists. (From 5, 6)

In other words, there will be lots of people who are happy to allow – on more or less *a priori* grounds – that there is exactly one thing of which every thing is a part. So, for these people, the important question will be whether the thing of which every thing is a part deserves to be called 'God'. If this thing does deserve the name, then a certain kind of monotheism is vindicated; if this thing does not deserve the name, then – presumably – this kind of monotheism is simply a mistake.[5]

2.2.2. Is the Sum of All Things Properly Called 'God'?

Before we can decide whether the thing of which every thing is a part deserves to be called 'God', we need to know more about the attributes of this thing. Even if our mereological ontological argument is successful, it doesn't give us much information about the thing of which every thing is a part (nor about its parts). Moreover, it is clear that opinion here will divide widely according to prior metaphysical conviction.

---

[4] Strictly speaking, the axiom of uniqueness of composition is also required to get to 5 from 3 and 4. Cf. the discussion in section 2.2.5 below.

[5] One should distinguish between *distributive pantheism* – the view that each thing is divine – and *collective pantheism* – the view that the thing of which all things are parts is divine. Moreover, when considering collective pantheism, one should distinguish between *mereological collective pantheism* – the view that the thing of which all things are parts is just the mereological sum of all its proper parts – and *non-mereological collective pantheism* – the view that the thing of which all things are parts is something over and above the mereological sum of all its proper parts. Throughout this section, the topic of discussion is collective pantheism – and, in particular, mereological collective pantheism.

Consider physicalists, that is, those who suppose that there is exactly one physical universe, which has none but physical parts. These people will suppose that the thing of which every thing is a part is the physical universe. (I assume, of course, that these physicalists suppose that there are no non-physical individuals.)

Consider modal realists, that is, those who suppose that there are many possible worlds.[6] These people will suppose that the thing of which every thing is a part is the mereological sum of the possible worlds. (I assume, of course, that these modal realists suppose that there are no individuals that are not overlapped completely by the sum of possible worlds.)

Consider Platonists, that is, those who suppose that, amongst the things that there are, there are non-spatio-temporal individuals laid up in Plato's heaven. These people will suppose that all of these individuals number among the parts of the thing of which every thing is a part.

And so on.[7] Some of these views seem to lead to better candidates for the name 'God' than others. However, in order to make progress on this question, we need to think some more about what a decent deserver of that name should be like.

In some respects, the result is bound to be heterodox. However we proceed, we are not going to arrive at a personal creator. But that is as it should be: monotheists of the kind under consideration here typically do not suppose that there is a personal creator. Moreover, there are ways of recovering many other parts of religious orthodoxy. Consider the modal realist view mentioned above. Everything that can be done is done by some part of the thing of which every thing is a part – so there is a sense in which this being is omnipotent. Everything that can be known is known by some part of the thing of which every thing is a part – so there is a sense in which this being is omniscient. Every possible virtue is possessed by some part of the thing of which every thing is a part – so there is a sense in which this being is omnibenevolent. (Not quite the traditional sense, of course. After all, every possible vice is also possessed by some part of the thing of which everything is a part – so, in the same kind of sense, this being is omnimalevolent. Moreover, this remains true even if lots of apparently possible evil worlds are deemed impossible.) Every thing is located in the thing of which every thing is a part – so there is a sense in which this being is omnipresent. Provided that one is prepared to allow temporal parts into one's ontology, one can also get a sense in which the thing of which every thing is a part is omnitemporal. And so on. (Perhaps you could even make a case for the claim that the sum of possible worlds is a being than which no greater can be conceived; after all, on this view, there is no greater being to have conceptions of!)

---

[6] For more about modal realism, see Lewis (1986).

[7] Another view that deserves mention in this connection is that kind of physicalism that is committed to the many-worlds interpretation of quantum mechanics. On this view, the thing of which all things are parts is (of course) the mereological sum of all of the many worlds.

Perhaps it is worth noting that similar points can be made about the physicalist view mentioned above. Everything that is done is done by some part of the thing of which every thing is a part – so there is a sense in which this being is omnipotent. Everything that is known is known by some part of the thing of which every thing is a part – so there is a sense in which this being is omniscient. Every virtue that is possesses is possessed by some part of the thing of which every thing is a part – so there is a sense in which this being is omnibenevolent. (Not quite the traditional sense, of course. After all, every vice that is possessed is also possessed by some part of the thing of which everything is a part – so, in the same kind of sense, this being is omnimalevolent.) Every thing is located in the thing of which every thing is a part – so there is a sense in which this being is omnipresent. And so on. (Perhaps you could even make a case for the claim that the physical world is a being than which no greater can be conceived; after all, on this view, there is no greater being to have conceptions of!)[8]

These kinds of considerations about the attributes of the thing of which every thing is a part do not speak to the most important issue. Somehow or other, the appropriateness of the application of the name 'God' to an object depends upon (i) whether or not it is appropriate to take up typical religious attitudes towards that object; and perhaps also on (ii) whether or not that object could properly be seen as the focus of one of the well-known organised religions. Of course, it isn't easy to say what the typical religious attitudes are; but, amongst them, there should surely be some kind of awe and also some kind of dependence and gratitude. Awe is easy: it is natural to think that our physicalists would be in awe of the physical thing of which all other things are parts. (Such awe may not be mandatory; however, it would surely be widespread.) But if that's all we are talking about – something on the order of an aesthetic response to a spectacular landscape – then it just seems wrong to say that there is anything of religious significance here. To deserve the appellation 'religious' there must be more: feelings of dependence and gratitude (or other responses on which the machinations of organised religion can get a grip). But there is no reason to think that these responses will be appropriate for the kinds of things of which all other things are parts mentioned above. Indeed, it would just be a mistake to respond to the physical universe – or the sum of possible worlds – with responses that are appropriately directed only towards persons. (There are, of course, senses in which one might have feelings of dependence upon, and gratitude towards, the thing of which every thing

---

[8] It will be natural to object that omniscience, omnipotence, etc. should not be given the radically extensional understanding that our physicalists provide. This is a fair point; however, it is also worth noting that omniscience, omnipotence, and so on, are sometimes understood in the non-modal way that we have indicated: most powerful (or, at least, than which there is none more powerful), most knowing (or, at least, than which there is none more knowing), and so on.

is a part. First, *dependence*: clearly, your continued existence depends upon
its continued existence – if it goes out of existence, then so do you. Second,
gratitude: given the first point, there is clearly some sense in which you should
be grateful that the thing of which every thing is a part has not gone out of
existence. Of course, the important point to make is that these are not the
'religious' responses to which reference was made above. Even though it is
hard to articulate precisely, there is clearly a good sense in which the kinds
of dependence and gratitude that it would be appropriate to have are not
religious.)

No doubt, the conclusion of this discussion was obvious from the beginning. Even if we are as concessive as we can be about the claim that there
is one thing of which every thing is a part, our mereological ontological
argument is bound to lack probative force. You can call my physicalists
'monotheists' if you like – after all, the word can be yours to do with as you
please – but it won't follow that these people have religious beliefs (in any
ordinary sense of the word 'religious belief'). Likewise for our modal realists
and Platonists. Of course, it remains at least a doxastic possibility that the
thing of which every thing is a part is a being with religious significance –
that all depends on what the thing of which every thing is a part turns out
to be. But we aren't going to learn anything about this from our ontological
argument (or from any other ontological argument, either). If our physicalists and modal realists and Platonists are wrong about the nature of the
thing of which every thing is a part, then it could turn out that their beliefs
about this thing ought to be religious – but, as things stand, there is no
reason to think that it is in fact the case that beliefs about the thing of which
every thing is a part ought to be religious (in the sense gestured at above).

2.2.3. Revising the Taxonomy of Oppy (1995c)

The objection of the previous section might be thought of as a minimal
objection to our mereological ontological argument. As we noted, it is certainly possible to contest some of the metaphysical assumptions that the
argument requires. However, the argument can be firmly resisted even if all
of these assumptions are allowed to stand. Consequently, the sensible thing
to do is to adopt this line of resistance, since it costs so little in terms of
theoretical commitments.

This approach is consistent with the general approach to ontological
arguments that I advocated in Oppy (1995c). However, as I noted – at least
inter alia – above, the main line of argument in that work suggests that the
best known and most often defended ontological arguments are vulnerable
to the following minimal criticism: these arguments have one reading on
which they are invalid, and another reading on which they are question-
begging, that is, require assumptions that non-theists can reasonably reject,
at least for all that the ontological arguments in question show.

The identification of mereological ontological arguments – given only the briefest of treatments in my book[9] – suggests that this general criticism is not quite right. For, in many cases, the best known and most often defended ontological arguments may also have a third reading on which they are neither question-begging nor invalid, but on which the entity whose existence they establish is a being of no religious significance. Consider, for example, the following argument:

1. I conceive of a being than which no greater can be conceived. (Premise)
2. (Hence) A being than which no greater can be conceived exists. (From 1, by a familiar argument that I shan't reproduce here.)
3. (Hence) God exists.

The question to ask about this argument is how to construe expressions of the form "I conceive of X". Clearly, there is a "relational" sense in which a sentence of this form can only be true if X exists; and there is another "non-relational" sense in which a sentence of this form can be true whether or not X exists. If "I conceive of X" is meant to be construed in the latter "non-relational" way, then an opponent of the above ontological argument should insist that the argument is invalid. (I omit further details, since they are not relevant to the point I wish to make here.) On the other hand, if "I conceive of X" is meant to be construed in the former, "relational" way, then the opponent of the argument has a choice: either deny that X exists – which is tantamount to claiming that the argument is question-begging – or else accept that X exists, but deny that X is a being that has any religious significance. (As noted above, in the case in question, our modal realist could claim that the being than which no greater can be conceived is just the mereological sum of all possible worlds, a being that is in no sense a good deserver of the name 'God'.)[10]

2.2.4. A Remark about the Interpretation of Anselm's *Proslogion*

One way of restating the conclusion of our minimal criticism of mereological ontological arguments in section I is that they do not provide an interesting or informative mode of presentation of the being whose existence they purport to establish. There are many metaphysical perspectives from which one can accept the claim that there is a thing that has every thing as a part – but many of these seem to have nothing at all to do with religious belief.

---

[9] See p. 262.
[10] If I were revising my book, I would certainly add mereological ontological arguments to my taxonomy, and devote a chapter to their discussion. However, this addition would not make any substantive difference to the criticisms of ontological arguments that I develop there.

A similar point can be made concerning a debate about the interpretation of St. Anselm's *Proslogion*. Some people hold that the existence of an orthodoxly conceived monotheistic god is established by the end of Part II; others hold that the existence of an orthodoxly conceived monotheistic god is not established until the end of Part III; and yet others hold that the existence of an orthodoxly conceived monotheistic god is not established until the end of the entire work, or at any rate the end of Part XXIII. However, all agree that the existence of a being than which no greater can be conceived is established by the end of Part II – and they also all agree that the being than which no greater can be conceived is an orthodoxly conceived monotheistic god. So the point of disagreement is just about whether a mode of presentation has been found that makes it clear that the being whose existence has been established is an orthodoxly conceived monotheistic god.

Our discussion of mereological ontological arguments suggests that there may be some point to this debate – compare the dismissive remarks in my book.[11] For – to use the same example again – it might be that our modal realists can agree that there is a unique being than which no greater can be conceived; and, if that is right, then there is reason to think that the existence of an orthodoxly conceived monotheistic god has not been established by the end of Part II. (Of course, theists should agree that the being whose existence is established by the end of Part II is an orthodoxly conceived monotheistic god; but they should not think that the argument will persuade non-theists of the truth of the claim that the sentence 'God exists' expresses a truth.) Naturally, there are reasons why one might be sceptical about the claim that I have just made: one might doubt that 'greater than' should be cashed out in mereological terms; one might doubt that our modal realists are really entitled to analyse conceivability in terms of possibility; and so on. However, the point I want to make is just this: there will be some people who will (apparently) reasonably think that the argument of *Proslogion II* is sound, but that the being whose existence it establishes is not a being of any religious significance.

(It is also worth thinking a little more about the expression 'being than which no greater can be conceived'. It is at least possible to take this expression to exhibit the same 'relational' / 'non-relational' ambiguity that was discussed above in connection with the expression 'I conceive of X'. In one sense, the greatest being – if there is such – is the being than which no greater can be conceived. For our modal realists, and under plausible assumptions about the mereological nature of greatness, this being is just the sum of possible worlds. So, on the 'relational' reading, the being than which no greater can be conceived just is the sum of possible worlds. Since some traditional theistic conceptions talk about 'the sum of all possibilities',

---

[11] See pp. 208–9.

it is not obvious that we should think that these considerations are entirely irrelevant to traditional theistic argumentation.)

2.2.5. Other Premises Reconsidered

Many people will feel that the minimal criticism of mereological ontological arguments for which I have argued can be supplemented with much stronger criticisms. In particular, there will be many people who will think that premises 3 and 4 of the revised version of the argument will not stand up to scrutiny. So perhaps it will be a good idea to close with a slightly closer look at these premises.

Premise 3 says that if some things exist, then there are some things that are all of the things that exist. Why might one be disposed to reject this claim? Apart from the worries about 'total' entities mentioned in the introduction, the most likely suggestion is that considerations from ordinary language suggest that quantification is always restricted quantification: there is no sense to be made of the suggestion that there can be unrestricted quantification. In my view, one only has to state this claim in order to see how implausible it is. Consider the claim that everything is self-identical. Surely, the most natural way to understand the quantifier here is to take it to be unrestricted: absolutely every single thing without exception is identical to itself. But when we quantify unrestrictedly, we quantify over absolutely all the things there are; and, if we can quantify over all the things there are, then there are some things such that they are all the things there are. (Perhaps my counterargument is question-begging. Too bad. The claim that, if there are some things, then there are some things that are all the things there are strikes me as a very good candidate for a claim that is both analytic and *a priori*. It is often hard to find good arguments for primitive claims of this sort.)

I suppose that some people will hold that 'exists' is ambiguous: it has different senses in different discourses. On this view, to say that chairs and numbers exist will be, strictly speaking, nonsensical. For while according to number discourse, it is analytic that there are numbers, and according to chair discourse, it is analytic that there are chairs, there is no discourse in which one can say that there are both chairs and numbers (and hence in which one can ask whether there are chairs, and whether there are numbers).[12] However, against this kind of Carnapian position, I want to side with Quine: 'exists' is univocal, and there is a single language in which all claims about existence can be assessed.[13] Of course, I'm not offering an argument here; rather, I have identified one class of people who will not be disposed to

---

[12] The *locus classicus* for this view is Carnap (1956). See also Price (1992).
[13] See Quine (1953) for Quine's arguments.

accept Premise 3. As I have already hinted, I think that this view is extreme; moreover, I expect that only something equally extreme will suffice for the rejection of Premise 3.

Premise 4 is – at least *prima facie* – much more problematic. Premise 4 says that whenever some things exist, there is some thing of which they are all parts. But there seem to be lots of views on which this claim is mistaken. Suppose, for example, that you think that there are non-spatio-temporal individuals (such as numbers). Suppose further that you are not a friend of unrestricted mereological composition. Then it might well seem natural to you to claim that there are lots of pairs of things that are not both parts of some more inclusive thing, for example, my heart and the number 2. Of course, if you are a friend of unrestricted mereological composition, then you get Premise 4 for free: but, otherwise, it seems that the acceptability of Premise 4 will depend upon prior metaphysical conviction about what there is.[14]

Curiously, the kind of thought that typically motivates opposition to unrestricted mereological composition – namely, that deservers of the appellation 'thing' must have some kind of 'inner unity' that is not bequeathed by mere mereological composition – is an intuition that is shared by many monotheists. One of the key religious intuitions is that there is – or, indeed, that there must be – some kind of 'inner unity' to things. Consequently, there is some reason to think that Premise 4 of our mereological ontological argument cannot properly be motivated by an appeal to unrestricted mereological composition: the principle of unrestricted mereological composition doesn't capture – and, indeed, is plausibly at odds with – one of the principle intuitions of many monotheists.

Even amongst those who are prepared to accept unrestricted mereological composition, there may be some who are prepared to deny (the standard mereological axiom of) uniqueness of composition. For instance, there are those who think that there is a relation of constitution that is not mereological in nature: the statue and the lump of clay from which the statue is constituted are distinct, even though they have the same clay-ey parts. However, this example isn't enough to motivate rejection of uniqueness of composition; for, in this example, the relation of constitution is not symmetrical – the clay constitutes the statue, but the statue does not constitute the clay. Consequently, the statue has parts – for example, the left-hand part of the statue and the right-hand part of the statue – that the clay does not (remember that we are supposing that the statue is distinct from the clay from which it is constituted). To deny uniqueness of composition on these kinds of grounds, one needs to find a case in which the relation of constitution is symmetrical: for then one could hold that there are two distinct

---

[14] For some other arguments that might plausibly be taken as objections to the idea that there is one thing of which all other things are parts, see van Fraassen (1995).

entities that have exactly the same parts. It is not easy to think of a plausible example of this, however.

In sum, then: there are various views that will lead one to reject the mereological ontological argument for the existence of the thing of which all things are parts. I doubt that there are arguments that will persuade people who hold these views to change their minds. However, there are also many people who will accept the argument for the existence of the thing of which all things are parts. Some of these people will be monotheists – but if they are, it will be for reasons that the mereological ontological argument does not make apparent.

2.2.6. Dessert

Many formulations of mereology include the null part, that is, the thing that is part of every thing. (The inclusion of the null part bestows a nice symmetry on the resulting theory.) This fact provides the means to include a discussion of 'the devil' in our theory – provided, of course, that we are prepared to identify 'the devil' with the null part. Of course, this suggestion doesn't make much sense from the standpoint of orthodox theism – the devil is not merely the contrary or opposite of an orthodoxly conceived monotheistic god – but it is important to remember that pantheism already stands at a considerable remove from orthodoxy.[15] Moreover, we can see that 'the devil' will have lots of interesting properties once the identification with the null part is made. (For instance, since 'the devil' is part of every thing, there is a good sense in which 'the devil' is omnipresent. Moreover – as noted above – 'the devil' turns out to be the exact opposite – the dual – of the thing of which every thing is a part. Given the attitudes that our monotheist supposes are appropriate for the thing of which every thing is a part, it seems natural to think that our monotheist will suppose that contrary attitudes are appropriate for 'the devil'. And so on.)

As I mentioned above, not all mereologists accept the existence of the null part. Those who do not, and who provide reasons for rejecting the null part, can be taken to be providing reasons for rejecting 'the devil' (under the proposed identification). However, I shan't bother to labour this point here.[16]

---

[15] Similar points can be made about discussions of the being than which no lesser can be conceived, the being than which no worse can be conceived, etc. Even if these beings have nothing to do with the devil – as traditionally conceived – they are of interest in their own right in the discussion of parodies of ontological arguments. Cf. Oppy (1995c: 182).

[16] I am indebted to Daniel Nolan for discussion of the material presented in this section. In particular, the idea that one might identify the null part with 'the devil' is his. (Perhaps he will produce a more elaborate discussion of this idea elsewhere.)

2.3. GÖDEL'S ONTOLOGICAL ARGUMENT

There is a small, but steadily growing, literature on the ontological arguments that Gödel developed in his notebooks, but that did not appear in print until well after his death. These arguments have been discussed, annotated, and amended by various leading logicians; the upshot is a family of arguments with impeccable logical credentials. (Interested readers are referred to Sobel (1987, 2004), Anderson (1990), Adams (1995), and Hazen (1999) for the history of these arguments and for the scholarly annotations and emendations.) Here, I shall give a brief presentation of the version of the argument that is developed by Anderson, and then make some comments on that version. This discussion follows the presentation and discussion in Oppy (1995c, 2000c).

Definition 1: *x* is *God-like* iff *x* has as essential properties those and only those properties that are positive.

Definition 2: *A* is an *essence* of *x* iff for every property *B*, *x* has *B* necessarily iff *A* entails *B*.

Definition 3: x *necessarily exists* iff every essence of *x* is necessarily exemplified.

Axiom 1: If a property is positive, then its negation is not positive.

Axiom 2: Any property entailed by – that is, strictly implied by – a positive property is positive.

Axiom 3: The property of being God-like is positive.

Axiom 4: If a property is positive, then it is necessarily positive.

Axiom 5: Necessary existence is positive.

Axiom 6: For any property *P*, if *P* is positive, then being necessarily *P* is positive.

Theorem 1: If a property is positive, then it is consistent, that is, possibly exemplified.

Corollary 1: The property of being God-like is consistent.

Theorem 2: If something is God-like, then the property of being God-like is an essence of that thing.

Theorem 3: Necessarily, the property of being God-like is exemplified.

Given a sufficiently generous conception of properties, and granted the acceptability of the underlying modal logic, the listed theorems do follow from the axioms. (This point was argued in detail by Dana Scott, in unpublished lecture notes that circulated for many years. It is also made by Sobel, Anderson, and Adams.) So, criticisms of the argument are bound to focus on the axioms, or on the other assumptions that are required in order to construct the proof.

Some philosophers have denied the acceptability of the underlying modal logic. And some philosophers have rejected generous conceptions of properties in favour of sparse conceptions according to which only some predicates express properties. But suppose that we adopt neither of these avenues of potential criticism of the proof. What else might we say against it?

One important point to note is that no definition of the notion of "positive property" is supplied with the proof. At most, the various axioms that involve this concept can be taken to provide a partial implicit definition. If we suppose that the "positive properties" form a set, then the axioms provide us with the following information about this set:

1. If a property belongs to the set, then its negation does not belong to the set.
2. The set is closed under entailment.
3. The property of having as essential properties just those properties that are in the set is itself a member of the set.
4. The set has exactly the same members in all possible worlds.
5. The property of necessary existence is in the set.
6. If a property is in the set, then the property of having that property necessarily is also in the set.

On Gödel's theoretical assumptions, we can show that any set that conforms to (1)–(6) is such that the property of having as essential properties just those properties that are in that set is exemplified. Gödel wants us to conclude that there is just one intuitive, theologically interesting set of properties that is such that the property of having as essential properties just the properties in that set is exemplified. But, on the one hand, what reason do we have to think that there is any theologically interesting set of properties that conforms to the Gödelian specification? And, on the other hand, what reason do we have to deny that, if there is one set of theologically interesting set of properties that conforms to the Gödelian specification, then there are many theologically threatening sets of properties that also conform to that specification?

In particular, there is some reason to think that the Gödelian ontological argument goes through just as well – or just as badly – with respect to other sets of properties (and in ways that are damaging to the original argument). Suppose that there is some set of independent properties $\{I, G_1, G_2, \ldots\}$ that can be used to generate the set of positive properties by closure under entailment and "necessitation". ("Independence" means: no one of the properties in the set is entailed by all the rest. "Necessitation" means: if P is in the set, then so is necessarily having P. I is the property of having as essential properties just those properties that are in the set. G_1, $G_2, \ldots$ are further properties, of which we require at least two.) Consider any proper subset of the set $\{G_1, G_2, \ldots\} - \{H_1, H_2, \ldots\}$, say, and define a new generating set $\{I^*, H_1, H_2, \ldots\}$, in which I^* is the property of having as essential properties just those properties that are in the newly generated set. A "proof" parallel to that offered by Gödel "establishes" that there is a being that has as essential properties just those properties in this new set. If there are as few as seven independent properties in the original generating set, then we shall be able to establish the existence of 720 distinct 'God-like' creatures by the kind of argument that Gödel offers. (The creatures are distinct because each has a different set of essential properties.)

Even if the above considerations are sufficient to cast doubt on the credentials of Gödel's 'proof', they do not pinpoint where the 'proof' goes wrong. If we accept that the role of Axioms 1, 2, 4, and 6 is really just to constrain the notion of 'positive Property' in the right way – or, in other words, if we suppose that Axioms 1, 2, 4, and 6 are "analytic truths" about 'positive properties' – then there is good reason for opponents of the "proof" to be sceptical about Axioms 3 and 5. Kant would not have been happy with Axiom 5; and there is at least some reason to think that whether the property of being God-like is "positive" ought to depend upon whether or not there is a God-like being.

2.4. ON THAT THAN WHICH NO WORSE CAN BE CONCEIVED

Timothy Chambers (2000) claims that I am mistaken in holding that a certain parody of St. Anselm's *Proslogion* argument is "innocuous" (and he also claims that Philip Devine is mistaken in holding that a different parody of that argument is "redundant").[17] In this section, I propose to examine Chambers's claims to critical scrutiny, beginning with a fairly careful presentation of the arguments that he gives on behalf of his opinions.

2.4.1. St. Anselm's Argument and Parodies Thereof

Chambers discusses the following arguments.[18]

Anselm's Argument

1. There is, in the understanding at least, a being than which no greater being can be thought.

---

[17] Chambers cites Devine (1975: 257–8) as the location of Devine's endorsement of the "Redundancy Thesis", and Oppy (1995c: 183) as the location of my endorsement of the "Innocuity Thesis". I think that a careful reading shows that I did not actually endorse the "Innocuity Thesis" in that earlier book; all I claimed is that it is *not clear* that the parody in question poses a serious challenge to St. Anselm. Whether Devine actually endorses the "Redundancy Thesis" in his article depends upon what, exactly, the "Redundancy Thesis" is taken to be: the interpretation upon which I eventually settle is not one that Devine (1975) explicitly endorses. ("Innocuity Thesis" is barbarous; however, I shall stick with it, since it is the expression that Chambers introduces.)

[18] I have made some minor emendations to Chambers's formulation of some of these arguments; however, nothing turns on these emendations. I have also chosen to use "worse" throughout as the converse of "greater"; Chambers sometimes uses "lesser" instead. It is, I think, easier to understand what is intended in the various parodies than it is to find words in natural language that give precise expression to that intention.

2. If it is even in the understanding alone, it can be thought to be in reality as well.
3. Which would be greater.
4. (Therefore) There exists, both in the understanding and in reality, a being than which no greater being can be thought.

Gaunilo's Parody

1. There is, in the understanding at least, an island than which no greater island can be thought.
2. If it is even in the understanding alone, it can be thought to be in reality as well.
3. Which would be greater.
4. (Therefore) There exists, both in the understanding and in reality, an island than which no greater island can be thought.

The Devil Corollary

1. There is, in the understanding at least, a being than which no worse being can be thought.
2. If it is even in the understanding alone, it can be thought to be in reality also.
3. Which would be still worse.
4. (Therefore) There exists, both in the understanding and in reality, a being than which no worse being can be thought.

The No-Devil Corollary

1. There is, in the understanding at least, a being than which no worse being can be thought.
2. If it exists in the understanding and in reality, it can be thought to exist in the understanding alone.
3. Which would be still worse.
4. (Therefore) There does not exist in reality a being than which no worse being can be thought.

The Extreme No-Devil Corollary

1. Suppose there is, in the understanding at least, a being than which no worse being can be thought.
2. If it exists in the understanding, then it is possible that it not exist in the understanding.
3. Which would be still worse.
4. (Therefore) There does not exist in the understanding a being than which no worse being can be thought.

Chambers argues: (1) that the Devil Corollary is a more powerful challenge to Anselm's Argument than is Gaunilo's Parody, because the Devil Corollary "proves resilient in the face of objections which dispose of Gaunilo's

Parody";[19] and (2) that the No-Devil Corollary is far from an innocuous challenge to Anselm's Argument because it "underwrites" the Extreme No-Devil Corollary, and the Extreme No-Devil Corollary "threatens Anselm's Argument at its very foundations".

At least initially, it might seem puzzling that Chambers defends both of these claims, that is, both (1) and (2). After all, the Devil Corollary requires the assumption that it is worse if a being than which no worse being can be thought exists in both reality and the understanding rather than in the understanding alone; whereas the No-Devil Corollary requires the assumption that it is worse if a being than which no worse being can be thought exists in the understanding alone rather than in both reality and the understanding. Consequently, there is at least *prima facie* reason to suppose that one cannot claim that *both* the Devil Corollary and the No-Devil Corollary are successful parodies of Anselm's Argument. However, I take it that this initial puzzlement is resolved by the recognition that Chambers does not suppose that the Devil Corollary is a successful parody of Anselm's Argument: while it is more successful than Gaunilo's Parody, it ultimately fails to establish that Anselm's Argument is unsound. On the other hand, it does seem that he supposes that the No-Devil Argument gives rise to a strong challenge to Anselm's Argument that may indeed succeed in establishing that Anselm's argument is unsound.[20]

2.4.2. Assumptions upon Which St. Anselm Allegedly Relies

Chambers identifies numerous assumptions upon which, he claims, the various arguments presented above rely.[21] I shall list these assumptions here for future reference; I shall also comment on some of them and suggest minor amendments to others. First, there is an initial round of assumptions that Chambers claims are required if Anselm's Argument is to have any chance of succeeding:

1. **DOMAIN AUGMENTATION**: The domain over which our quantifiers range is not limited merely to objects that 'really exist'; specifically, we

---

[19] Chambers also says that the "Redundancy Thesis" that is rejected in (1) *holds* that an apt reply to Gaunilo should likewise dispose of the Devil Corollary, and *entails* that the Devil Corollary is sound only if Gaunilo's Parody is likewise sound.

[20] An alternative resolution of the initial puzzlement would be given by the claim that "worse" is to be interpreted differently in the two arguments. While I take this suggestion sufficiently seriously to allow that there might be only *prima facie* reason to suppose that one cannot claim that both the Devil Corollary and the No-Devil Corollary are successful parodies of Anselm's Argument, I do not think that it is the view that Chambers adopts.

[21] The status of these assumptions is interesting. Given that we are examining parodies of arguments, it is a nice question whether these assumptions should be explicitly built into the arguments under consideration (at least in those cases where it is not plausible to claim that they are already implicitly present).

augment the domain to include intentional entities, or, in Anselm's (translated) words, 'objects existing in the understanding'.[22]

2. **DOMAIN RESTRICTION**: Unlike some domains that countenance 'objects of thought' (e.g., Meinong's), the present domain does not contain any element bearing contradictory properties.[23]

3. **EXISTENCE PREDICATION**: We treat expressions of the form 'x exists in agent A's understanding' and 'x exists in reality' as predicates (denoted by '$U_A x$' and 'Rx', respectively).[24]

4. **LOGIC OF EXISTENCE PREDICATES**: The predicates '$U_A x$' and 'Rx' receive like logical treatment as other predicates in our deductive system. These predicates are also mutually consistent – it is possible, that is, for an element of the domain to instantiate both predicates.

5. **CONTINGENCY OF GREATNESS**: The greatness of an object might have been different from what it, in fact, is.

6. **GREATNESS AND EXISTENCE**: Some items' greatness is, in part, a function of whether they exist merely in the understanding or whether they also exist in reality. In particular, a being than which no greater being can be thought is greater if it exists both in reality and in the understanding than if it exists merely in the understanding.[25]

---

[22] This assumption, in its original formulation, is naturally taken to entail that each item in the domain is either a "really existent object" or an "intentional entity", or both. However, understood this way, the Domain Assumption immediately rules out the Extreme No-Devil Corollary. Moreover, Chambers's gloss on Anselm's Argument seems to involve commitments to merely possible objects and merely possible worlds – yet it is not clear that these belong to either of the mentioned categories. (Part of the difficulty is that it isn't clear whether the relevant domain of intentional entities includes just those entities that are thought of by the Fool, or just those entities that are thought of by some really existing thing, or just those entities that are thought of by some possible being in some possible world, or some other collection of entities.)

[23] In this assumption, we really need some explanation of what it is for properties to be "contradictory". A natural thought is that properties are "contradictory" if it is not possible for them to be co-instantiated. However, it is not clear how well this thought fits in with the rest of Anselm's theoretical framework. (Consider, e.g., the properties '_ is a pool of water' and '_ is a pool of XYZ'. There is a widely accepted view according to which these properties cannot be co-instantiated; nonetheless, it does not seem obviously right to say that these properties are contradictory: at the very least, there is no reason why rational beings must be able to tell *a priori* that these properties cannot be co-instantiated. I shall not try to pursue these kinds of considerations here.)

[24] Chambers says that the first two assumptions concern the *objects of discourse*, whereas the next few assumptions concern the *predicates and relations of discourse*. However, the only predicates and relations that Chambers takes up are *existence* and *greatness*: there is no discussion of other predicates and relations that are possessed by the objects of discourse. In the last section of this chapter, I shall suggest that this is a serious shortcoming in Chambers's presentation.

[25] I have made some slight alterations to Chambers's formulation of this assumption; nothing of substance turns on these alterations. I have made similarly slight alterations to Chambers's formulations of the next two assumptions as well.

7. **HYPOSTASIS OF MEANING**: If a person understands an expression 'M' – where 'M' has the syntax of a referring expression, for example, a proper name, a definite description, and so on – then there exists in that person's understanding a thing that answers to the understood expression.[26]

8. **INTERPRETATION OF 'GREATEST POSSIBLE BEING'**: The sentence 'There is a being than which no greater being can be thought' has the canonical formulation: there is a being, x, in the understanding that is such that the greatness of x is m, and it is not possible that there is a being y that is such that the greatness of y is n and $n > m$.[27]

Second, there is a pair of assumptions, either of which – according to Chambers – constitutes a plausible reason for rejecting Gaunilo's Parody[28]:

9. **SPECIALISED GREATNESS**: For any sortal predicate S – distinct from the catch-all predicate '$\_$ is a being' – there exists a distinct function for any item x's greatness as an S, $g(x, S)$. Moreover, for a pair of S's, y and z, it is possible that y is a greater being than z – $g(y) > g(z)$ – even though z is at least as great an S as y – $g(z, S) \geq g(y, S)$. Finally, for a great many predicates S, the value of $g(x, S)$ does not vary with the existence in reality, or non-existence in reality, of x.

10. **RIDER TO HYPOSTASIS OF MEANING**: The application of the assumption that to every understood referring expression there corresponds an object from the domain is to be restricted to referring expressions that are meant to be understood to "contain" only properties that belong necessarily to their common subject.

Third, there is a round of assumptions that – according to Chambers – are required if the Devil Corollary is to be a genuine parallel to Anselm's Argument[29]:

---

[26] A full dress presentation of this assumption would be complicated. Note that, if a person understands an indefinite description – 'an M', say – or an instantiable predicate – '$\_$ is an M', say – then I take it that Anselm will want to say that there are Ms in that person's understanding. So 'referring expression' needs to be given a fairly charitable interpretation.

[27] Chambers's formulation of this assumption seems to me to be unfortunate: why should we suppose that the greatness of beings must be finite? However, nothing important turns on the correction of this blemish (at least, not for the purposes of the present section).

[28] Actually, as we shall see, Chambers equivocates on the status of these assumptions. Initially, he claims that they are merely "*prima facie* apt for disposing of Gaunilo's Parody". But, by the conclusion, they are "objections that dispose of Gaunilo's Lost Island".

[29] It would be neater, I think, to generalise the assumption of Contingency of Greatness and the assumption about Greatness and Existence in Anselm's Argument: we could say, for instance, that the Value of an object is contingent, and that that Value depends upon the domains to which the object belongs. Then there would be no further assumptions to make when we turn to the Devil's Corollary. However, I have followed Chambers's exposition because nothing much hangs on the adoption of this suggestion.

11. **CONTINGENCY OF 'EVILNESS'**: The 'evilness' of an object might have been different from what it in fact is.
12. **'EVILNESS' AND EXISTENCE**: Some items' 'evilness' is, in part, a function of whether they exist in the understanding or whether they also exist in reality. In particular, a being than which no worse being can be thought is worse if it exists both in reality and in the understanding than if it exists merely in the understanding.
13. **INTERPRETATION OF 'WORST POSSIBLE BEING'**: The sentence 'There is a being than which no worse being can be thought' has the canonical formulation: there is a being, x, in the understanding, which is such that the 'evilness' of x is m, and it is not possible that there is a being y that is such that the 'evilness' of y is n, where $n > m$.

Finally, there is a pair of assumptions – 'augmentations' of the Greatness and Existence Assumption – either of which, according to Chambers, constitutes a plausible reason for rejecting the Devil Corollary:

14. **AXIOLOGICAL GREATNESS OF EXISTENCE**: A being than which no greater being can be thought that exists both in reality and in the understanding is a greater being than a being than which no greater can be thought that exists only in the understanding *because* for x to be a greater being than y is just for x to be more morally perfect than y, and existence is a perfection, that is, good in itself.
15. **ONTOLOGICAL GREATNESS OF EXISTENCE**: A being than which no greater being can be thought that exists both in reality and in the understanding is a greater being than a being than which no greater being can be thought that exists only in the understanding *because* for x to be a greater being than y is just for x to be "more real" than y, and any item that exists both in reality and in the understanding is "more real" than if the item exists in the understanding alone.

2.4.3. Chambers against the "Redundancy" Thesis

Chambers's argument against the "Redundancy Thesis" goes as follows: There is a pair of canonical strategies, either of which is apt – or perhaps merely *prima facie* apt – for disposing of Gaunilo's Parody, but neither of which is apt – or even *prima facie* apt – for disposing of the Devil Corollary. Hence, since the "Redundancy Thesis" holds that an apt reply to Gaunilo should dispose of the Devil Corollary, it follows that the "Redundancy Thesis" is mistaken.

There are several reasons for caution in accepting this argument. An obvious starting point is the slippage between "being *prima facie* apt" and "being apt" for disposing of Gaunilo's Parody. Which is it to be? If we take the more cautious view that the canonical strategies may be no more than *prima facie* apt for disposing of Gaunilo's Strategy, then it seems doubtful that we are entitled to reject the claim that the Devil Corollary is redundant. For suppose that the canonical strategies are *no more than prima facie* apt for disposing of Gaunilo's strategy, that is, that neither of them turns out to be a sustainable objection to Gaunilo's Argument. Then, clearly enough, Chambers has given us no reason at all to think that the Devil Corollary is not redundant. At best, on this cautious approach, the most that Chambers is entitled to conclude is that the Devil Corollary may not be redundant: there are reasons for thinking that the "Redundancy Thesis" may not be correct.

The obvious alternative would be to take the less cautious approach, that is, to insist that the canonical strategies do, in fact, succeed in disposing of Gaunilo's strategy, even though they do not succeed in disposing of the Devil Corollary. However, as we have already noted, Chambers himself is wary of taking this approach. Moreover, I think that there is good reason for this caution.

On the one hand, it seems to me that the assumption of Specialised Greatness does not obviously have the consequences that Chambers takes it to have. Suppose that he is right about the predicate "__ is an island". Nonetheless, we can manufacture a predicate "__ is an island-being", and insist that island-beings are greater if they exist than if they do not. Existence may make no difference to the existence of islands *qua* islands; but, by stipulation, it does make a difference to the existence of island-beings *qua* island-beings. Of course, we don't need to assume at the outset that any actual islands are island-beings; until we run through Gaunilo's Parody, we might even suppose that there are no island-beings, that is, things that are just like islands except that existence is a great-making property for them. If the assumption of Specialised Greatness is apt for disposing of Gaunilo's Parody, a very small adjustment returns a very similar parody that is not apt for disposal in the same way.[30]

On the other hand, the second strategy that Chambers offers seems to me to be hardly in any better shape. True enough, one might contest the idea that there is a greatest conceivable island: for any island, no matter how great, we can conceive one still greater. But exactly the same point can be made about beings in general: for any being, no matter how great, one can conceive one still greater. Chambers argues that, whereas the greatness of an island *must* vary directly with some quantity that is necessarily finite, but not necessarily bounded above – the number of coconut trees, say – the greatness of beings in general is not subject to the same kind of

---

[30] Perhaps it is worth noting here that many people have contested the idea that existence is a great-making property for beings *qua* beings and yet not a great-making property for, say, islands *qua* islands. Why *should* the Fool think that the Specialised Greatness assumption is true?

constraint. But, on the one hand, it is not obvious that the claim about islands is correct: after all, the greatest conceivable island will be neither too large, nor too densely populated with coconut trees! And, on the other hand, we need to be given reasons why the same kind of point does not apply in the case of beings in general: why *should* we think that the greatness of beings *qua* beings is relevantly different from the greatness of islands *qua* islands?

For the above reasons, it seems to me that the less cautious approach is not defensible, or, at any rate, has not yet been given a satisfactory defence. It is controversial whether there are telling objections to Gaunilo's Parody that are not also telling objections to the Devil Corollary. So – again – the most that we conclude is that the "Redundancy Thesis" is controversial. (Perhaps it is worth noting here that Chambers also fails to address the question of whether there are telling objections to the Devil Corollary that are not also telling objections to Gaunilo's Parody. If, for example, there is good reason to think that it is worse if that being than which no worse being can be thought exists only in the understanding alone, then there is a good objection to the Devil Corollary that is not a good objection to Gaunilo's Parody. Of course, even if this point were correct, it would not necessarily count in favour of the "Redundancy Thesis", but it would suggest a note of caution about the way in which Chambers presents his argument: if the Devil Corollary is knocked over sufficiently easily by *other* considerations, then it is not clear that we should think of it as a non-redundant alternative to Gaunilo's Parody.)

Even if I am right that Chambers's argument against the "Redundancy Thesis" is not entirely compelling, I should stress that I have not claimed that the "Redundancy Thesis" is correct. Indeed, there is a sense in which some versions of "Redundancy Thesis" are surely mistaken. Recall that the key expression in Anselm's Argument is "that being than which no greater being can be thought". A partial analysis of this expression yields the schema: "that F than which no G'er F can be thought". One family of parodies of the argument – of which Gaunilo's Parody is an instance – works with the schema: "that F than which no greater F can be thought". But another family of parodies of the argument – of which the No Devil Argument is an instance – works with the schema: "that being than which no G'er being can be thought". Since it is plausible to think that quite different issues can arise in connection with these two rather different schemas, it is plausible to think that there is a sense in which the No-Devil Argument may not be redundant: it may raise issues that are raised by no instance of the family of parodies to which Gaunilo's Parody belongs. At the very least, there is nothing in the considerations raised above that serves to show that no further issues arise in connection with parodies that work with the schema: "that being than which no G'er being can be thought" than arise with parodies that work with the schema: "that F than which no greater F can be thought".

On the other hand, even if the point raised in the previous paragraph is conceded, it remains the case that it could be that the family of parodies to which Gaunilo's Parody belongs raises more pressing worries for the proponent of Anselm's Argument than does the family of parodies to which the Devil objection belongs. To determine which is the more pressing objection, we need to make a complete survey of all of the considerations that are raised by each, and then to find some way of weighting the relative strengths of these considerations. Until the task is done, there is no way of determining whether there are any *telling* objections that arise only in connection with the Devil objection.

2.4.4. Chambers against the "Innocuity" Thesis

Chambers's argument against the "Innocuity Thesis" goes as follows: The core contention of the "Innocuity Thesis" is that the following claim is no cause for Anselmian alarm:

1. If Anselm's Argument is sound, then so is the No-Devil Corollary. But the following assumptions are all assumptions that the Anselmian ought to accept:
2. If we understand the expression 'that being than which no greater being can be thought', then we also understand the expression 'that being than which no worse being can be thought'.
3. If the No-Devil Corollary is sound, then the Extreme No-Devil Corollary is also sound.
4. If the Extreme No-Devil Corollary is sound, then there does not exist in the understanding that being than which no worse being can be thought.
5. If we understand the expression 'that being than which no worse being can be thought', then there does exist in the understanding that being than which no worse being can be thought.

Moreover, (1)–(5) together entail:

C* If Anselm's Argument is sound, then we do not understand the expression 'that being than which no greater being can be thought'.

And yet the Anselmian is committed to:

6. If Anselm's argument is sound, then we do understand the expression 'that being than which no greater being can be thought'

So, finally, since (C*) and (6) together entail that Anselm's argument is not sound, the position of the Anselmian has been reduced to absurdity.

   Chambers claims that the above argument – which involves only the "innocent-seeming" assumptions (2)–(5) – establishes that the "Innocuity Thesis" is mistaken: "The No Devil Corollary, if accepted as a valid corollary of Anselm's turn of thought, turns out to underwrite a further argument which threatens Anselm's Argument at its very foundation: the intelligibility of the notion of 'a being than which no greater being can be thought'. So much for the Innocuity Thesis!" However, Chambers also notes that it is open to the Anselmian to try to pinpoint a "faulty assumption" among (1)–(6); that is, he does not conclude that what he has given is a definitive proof that Anselm's Argument is unsound.

In fact, I think that the Anselmian does not have to look very far to find a contestable premise here: there are various reasons why (3) – that is, the claim that, if the No-Devil Corollary is sound, then the Extreme No-Devil Corollary is also sound – ought not to be accepted by defenders of Anselm's Argument.

The first and most obvious point is that, if one accepts that the No-Devil Corollary is sound, then, *a fortiori*, one accepts that the conclusion of the Extreme No-Devil Corollary is not true, and hence one accepts that the Extreme No-Devil Corollary is not sound. (The first premise of the No-Devil Corollary is the negation of the conclusion of the Extreme No-Devil Corollary.) Since this establishes beyond all doubt that (3) is false, no one – not even an Anselmian – has any reason to think that Chambers's argument provides so much as a *prime facie* reason for holding that Anselm's Argument is unsound.

A second point that seems worth noting is that the Extreme No-Devil Corollary does not share the same form as Anselm's Argument (and all of the other parodies under consideration). On the one hand, the Extreme No-Devil Corollary is a *reductio ad absurdum*, in which the first premise is merely assumed for the sake of the *reductio*; on the other hand, Anselm's Argument is a categorical derivation of the conclusion from the stated premises (so that the allegedly parallel first premise is asserted to be true in Anselm's Argument). Furthermore, the second premise in the Extreme No-Devil Corollary replaces talk in the consequent – of the second premise in Anselm's Argument and all of the other parodies under consideration – about what "can be thought" with talk about what "is possible". For both of these reasons, the Extreme No-Devil Corollary is not a parody of Anselm's Argument in the strict sense: it is not an argument that can be obtained from Anselm's Argument merely by the uniform substitution of "non-logical" vocabulary. Given the difficulties in determining the precise logical form of Anselm's Argument, there are serious questions to be asked about purported "parodies" that do not conform to this very strict requirement.

A third reason for an Anselmian to be suspicious of the Extreme No-Devil Corollary is that it seems to flout the assumption about Domain Augmentation that Chambers claims is required if Anselm's argument is to have any chance of succeeding. Of course, Anselm's Argument would go through just as well if there are things that belong to some further domain, that is, they exist, but neither in the understanding nor in reality. But an Anselmian should not be happy with the idea that a thing of this kind might be greater than that being than which no greater being can be thought – and yet it is hard to see how this claim can be ruled out if we allow that there is a further domain of the kind in question. (True enough, in *Proslogion 15*, Anselm goes on to say that God is something greater than can be thought; but, however this further claim is to be understood, it must be in a way that is compatible with the claim that that being than which no greater being can be thought exists in the understanding of the Fool.[31])

Even if I am right that Chambers's argument against the "Innocuity Thesis" is mistaken, it remains open that the conclusion of his argument is true: there may be an argument that goes by way of something other than the Extreme No-Devil Corollary that shows that the No-Devil Corollary is not the harmless corollary of Anselm's Argument that some people have taken it to be. However, at the very least, there remains work to be done to establish that this is the case. (From the symmetry of the case, it seems to me to be natural to think that someone who accepts Anselm's Argument will also accept the No-Devil Corollary. That Anselm himself accepts the No-Devil Corollary is perhaps evidence for the naturalness of this thought. However, it is clear that – for all that we have good reason to believe – this *prima facie* case could easily be overturned.)

2.4.5. What Is the Point of These Parodies?

The discussion of the previous two sections is not entirely satisfactory. The problem is that we have made no attempt to tie Chambers's talk about "redundancy" and "innocuity" to a serious account of exactly what it is that Gaunilo's Parody is supposed to achieve.

I take it that the aim of the Anselmian is to construct an argument that, by the lights of the Fool, gives the Fool all-things-considered reason to believe that a being than which no greater being can be thought exists (in reality). Consequently, I take it that what Gaunilo's Parody is intended to be used to show is that, by the lights of the Fool, Anselm's Argument does not provide the Fool with all-things-considered reason to believe that a being than which no greater being can be thought exists (in reality). If this is right, then it is no part of the intended aim of Gaunilo's Parody that it should be used to show that, by the lights of the Fool, the Fool does not have all-things-considered reason to believe that a being than which no greater being can be thought exists (in reality). Nor, if what I said above is right, is it part of the intended aim of Gaunilo's Parody that it can be used to show that, either by the lights of the Fool, or by the lights of the Anselmian,

---

[31] The considerations about properties that are raised in the last part of the present section may be relevant here.

or by the lights of both: (1) the Fool has all-things-considered reason to believe that no being than which no greater being can be thought exists (in reality); or (2) the Anselmian does not have all-things-considered reason to believe that a being than which no greater being can be thought exists (in reality); or (3) the Anselmian has all-things-considered reason to believe that no being than which no greater being can be thought exists (in reality).[32]

Given what I take to be the intended aim of Gaunilo's Parody, I think that it is plausible to claim that Gaunilo's Parody succeeds in its intended aim iff the following conditions are met: (1) Gaunilo's Parody has the very same "logical" form as Anselm's Argument (so that the one argument is logically valid just in case the other argument is also logically valid);[33] (2) by the lights of the Fool, the premises of Gaunilo's Parody have the same degree of acceptability as the premises of Anselm's Argument; (3) there is no difference in the suppressed premises, and so on – if any – that are required by the two arguments; and (4) Gaunilo's Parody has a conclusion that, by the lights of the Fool, the Fool does not have all-things-considered reason to accept.[34] Of course, the wider aim of Gaunilo's Parody – that is, showing that, by the lights of the Fool, Anselm's Argument does not provide the Fool with all-things-considered reason to believe that a being than which no greater being can be thought exists (in reality) – could be served by any argument that meets the conditions: (1) that, by the lights of the Fool, the argument in question is sound iff Anselm's Argument is sound; and (2) that it has a conclusion that, by the lights of the Fool, the Fool does not have all-things-considered reason to accept. However, it may not be easy to

---

[32] There are, of course, other aims that might be attributed to the Anselmian: perhaps, for example, the Anselmian wants to exhibit some of the "justificatory structure" of the beliefs of those who hold that there is, in reality, a being than which no greater being can be thought. In this particular case, I do not think that the claim is plausible: not even Anselm believed that his argument was an important plank in the foundations upon which his belief in the existence (in reality) of a being than which no greater being can be thought rested. (And nor did Anselm believe that it would perform this function in the case of more nearly ideal cognitive agents than we.) Moreover – though I cannot try to argue for this here – I do not believe that there is any other intended function that it is plausible to attribute to Anselm's Argument.

[33] Given the lack of precision in its formulation, this condition requires sympathetic interpretation. Any argument instantiates many "logical forms" – but there is just one "logical form" that is the right one for the purposes of the intended analysis.

[34] Given (3), (1) is guaranteed if the two arguments have the same "syntactic" form, i.e., if either can be obtained from the other by uniform substitution of nothing but "non-logical" vocabulary. Of course, it is a nice question what we should mean here by "non-logical vocabulary". If "being" counts as a "logical" expression, then Gaunilo's Parody fails to meet the stated requirement; if "greater" counts as a "logical" expression, then the Devil Corollary and the No-Devil Corollary fail to meet the stated requirement. I take it that there is a good intuitive sense in which neither "being" nor "greater" is a "logical" expression.

establish that, by the lights of the Fool, a given argument is sound iff Anselm's Argument is sound *unless* one adopts the strategy of Gaunilo's Parody.

Since the No-Devil Corollary does not meet the very strictest standards that can be set for Gaunilo's Parody – it cannot be obtained from Anselm's Argument by uniform substitution of "non-logical" vocabulary – there is *prima facie* reason for preferring Gaunilo's Parody to it. But, of course, this consideration is nowhere near strong enough to establish that Gaunilo's Parody does everything that any parody could do. And yet *this* is surely what the "Redundancy Thesis" amounts to: that *if any parody can be used to show that, by the lights of the Fool, Anselm's Argument does not provide the Fool with all-things-considered reason to believe that a being than which no greater being can be thought exists (in reality), then Gaunilo's Parody does this.*[35] Similarly, the "Innocuity Thesis" amounts to the following claim: that *the No-Devil Corollary cannot be used to show that, by the lights of the Fool, Anselm's Argument does not provide the Fool with all-things-considered reason to believe that a being than which no greater being can be thought exists (in reality).*

Since it seems to me to be reasonable to suppose that anyone who does not accept that there is a being than which no greater being can be thought will also fail to accept that there is a being than which no worse being can be thought, it seems to me to be reasonable to suppose that the "Innocuity Thesis" is correct. By the lights of the Fool, it isn't true that the No-Devil Corollary has a conclusion that the Fool does not have all-things-considered reason to accept; consequently, the conditions for successful parody are not satisfied by this argument. (Remember that we have already rejected the claim that the No-Devil Corollary is sound iff the Extreme No-Devil Corollary is sound. So there is no hope of resurrection of the "Innocuity Thesis" by that back-door route.)[36]

As I have already indicated in several places, it is harder to know what to say about the "Redundancy Thesis". If we suppose that Anselm's Argument relies upon the Specialised Greatness assumption, then there may be some reason to hold that Gaunilo's Parody does, but the Devil Corollary does not, fall foul of this assumption. However, on the other hand, it seems plausible to claim that Gaunilo's Parody does better than the Devil Corollary in other respects:

---

[35] In note 17, I said that Devine does not defend what I take to be the (more or less) canonical formulation of the "Redundancy Thesis". I can now say why. What Devine is concerned to argue is that, by the lights of the Anselmian: (1) there is just the same reason to reject at least one of the premises of the Devil Corollary as there is to reject at least one of the premises of Gaunilo's Parody; yet (2) while there is reason to reject at least one of the premises in the parodies, there is good reason to accept all of the premises in Anselm's Argument. Even when properly generalised, this is a quite different claim from the claim that is expressed in the "Redundancy Thesis".

[36] If the argument in the present part of this book is acceptable, then the cautious expression in Oppy (1995c) seems well justified: it certainly is *not* clear that the No-Devil Corollary should give concern to proponents of Anselm's Argument.

in particular, by the lights of the Fool, unless existence is interpreted as an *intensifier* – which makes great things greater and "mean" things even worse – the Fool need not have reason to suppose that the third premise of the Devil Corollary is no less acceptable than the third premise of Anselm's Argument. In other words: Gaunilo's Parody plainly does better than the Devil Corollary with respect to the "third round" assumptions that Chambers introduces when he begins to argue against the "Innocuity Thesis".

Suppose that we put together all of the key assumptions that Chambers ends up claiming are needed for Anselm's Argument:

1. Existence (in reality) is a great-maker for beings, but not for islands, and so on.
2. Existence (in reality) is not an intensifier; rather, it is always an increaser of value in beings.
3. Non-existence (in reality) is a worse-maker for beings, but not for islands, and so on.
4. Non-existence (in reality) is not an intensifier; rather, it is always a decreaser of value for beings.

Given that these assumptions are built into Anselm's Argument, both of the potentially damaging parodies that Chambers considers are blocked. However, if the argument that I gave earlier is correct, then Gaunilo's Parody can be repaired to avoid the blockage. (Why shouldn't the Fool suppose that he can understand the expression "island-being than which no greater island-being can be thought" just as well (or ill) as he can understand the expression "being than which no greater being can be thought"?) But it is not at all clear how the Devil Corollary might be similarly rejigged in the face of this difficulty. For this kind of reason, I am *tentatively* inclined to the conclusion that the "Redundancy Thesis" is indeed correct; but I must stress that I am not at all sure that this is right, and I must also admit that I have not given anything remotely approaching a rigorous argument on behalf of this conclusion.[37]

2.4.6. Chambers's Representation of St. Anselm's Argument

Before closing this section, I would like to make some comments about the way in which Chambers translates Anselm's Argument into canonical

---

[37] It is tempting to suppose that the argument of Tooley (1981) – about a solvent than which no greater solvent can be thought and an insoluble substance than which no greater insoluble substance can be thought – improves upon Gaunilo's Parody, since it delivers up an explicit contradiction rather than a mere absurdity. However, this supposition is entirely consistent with the "Redundancy Thesis": for, if Tooley's argument does derive an explicit contradiction, then Gaunilo's Parody yields an absurdity – and an absurdity is all that the Fool requires.

notation. Following Adams (1971), Chambers claims that the argument has the following "logical form":

$$\exists x\{U_F x \;\&\; g(x) = m \;\&\; \sim \Diamond [\exists y (g(y) = n \;\&\; n > m)]\} \tag{1}$$

$$\forall x\{[U_F x \;\&\; g(x) = m \;\&\; \sim \Diamond [\exists y (g(y) = n \;\&\; n > m)]] \rightarrow \Diamond Rx\} \tag{2}$$

$$\forall x\{[U_F x \;\&\; g(x) = m \;\&\; \sim \Diamond [\exists y (g(y) = n \;\&\; n > m)] \;\&\; \sim Rx] \rightarrow \Box (Rx \rightarrow (g(x)$$
$$= n \;\&\; n > m))\} \tag{3}$$

$$\therefore \exists x\{U_F x \;\&\; g(x) = m \;\&\; \sim \Diamond [\exists y (g(y) = n \;\&\; n > m)] \;\&\; Rx\} \tag{4}$$

Read straight, these symbols translate back into English as something like the following:

1. There is something that exists in the understanding and that is such that its greatness cannot be exceeded.
2. Anything that exists in the understanding and that is such that its greatness cannot be exceeded could exist in reality.
3. If something that exists in the understanding and that is such that its greatness cannot be exceeded does not exist in reality, then it is necessarily the case that if it exists in reality it is even greater.
4. (Therefore) There is something that exists both in the understanding and in reality that is such that its greatness cannot be exceeded.

And, at least *prima facie*, this is quite different from Anselm's Argument, that is, from the argument that was displayed at the beginning of this section. In particular, it should be noted that where Anselm's Argument talks about 'a being than which no greater being can be *thought*', this argument talks about 'a being than which no greater being can be *be*'. The effect of this change seems to be to reinterpret "conceivability" – what *can be thought* – in terms of "possibility" – what *can be*. Yet Chambers himself notes that there are reasons for refusing to interpret Anselm's "conceivability" in terms of "logical possibility"; indeed, Chambers seems to be prepared to defend the Extreme No-Devil Corollary against certain objections by appealing to the need to keep "conceivability" and "logical possibility" apart.[38] Getting straight about these matters requires us to go back to the assumptions that lie behind Anselm's proof.

Chambers tells us that Anselm assumes that the domain of objects can be partitioned into two overlapping sub-domains: the objects that exist in reality and the objects that exist in the understanding. However, Chambers tells us nothing about the properties that are possessed by objects that belong to both domains. Suppose, for example, that Anselm himself exists in the

---

[38] In particular see notes 36 and 37.

understanding of the Fool. What properties does Anselm have in the understanding of the Fool? It is certain that Anselm has properties about which the Fool is ignorant; it is hardly any less certain that the Fool takes Anselm to have properties that Anselm does not in fact have. Given these facts, and given that we are prepared to say that an object exists in the Fool's understanding when the Fool has an appropriate conception of that object, it seems clear that we should also be prepared to say that an object possesses certain properties in the Fool's understanding when the Fool's conception of that object is of an appropriate kind. That is, if we are prepared to say that objects exist in the understanding of the Fool, we should also be prepared to say that those objects 'encode' certain properties, namely, those properties that the Fool takes those objects to have. And, of course, for those objects that also exist in reality, we should be prepared to allow that the properties that those objects 'encode' in the Fool's understanding may well be different from the properties that those objects have in reality.[39]

When we now turn to the 'logical form' of Anselm's Argument, we shall need to be careful to invoke the appropriate mode of property possession when we consider objects that exist in the understanding. Plausibly, the first premise of the argument should be rendered as follows:

$$\exists x \{ U_F x \ \& \ \text{Encode}_F (x, \lambda z (g(z) = m \ \& \sim \Diamond [\exists y (g(y) = n \ \& \ n > m)]))\}$$

This formulation captures the point that it is part of the Fool's *conception* that the being in question is a being than which there can be no greater being. The obvious alternative – which might be thought of as a distinct reading of the ambiguous offering made by Chambers – would be:

$$\exists x \{ U_F x \ \& \ \text{Possess}(x, \lambda z (g(z) = m \& \sim \Diamond [\exists y (g(y) = n \ \& \ n > m)]))\}$$

This reading could be true even if the Fool thinks of the entity in question as something that is utterly insignificant, even though the entity in question happens to have the property of being that than which no greater being can be thought. Plainly enough, this is not the premise that Anselm intends to support with an argument by way of the Hypostasis of Meaning assumption.

Given that we adopt this suggestion about the correct rendition of the first premise, there are various options that require scrutiny for the remaining

---

[39] If we think, for example, about the case of fictional objects – objects that exist only in the understanding but not in reality – such as Santa Claus or Sherlock Holmes, we might decide that there is room for further refinement of the theory. In particular, we might decide that even objects that only exist in the understanding can really have properties. For instance, we might want to say that Santa Claus really does *have* the property of existing only in the understanding, even though he *encodes* the property of existing in reality. I shall not try to pursue these subtleties here; however, it is important to emphasise that it is no easy matter to "grant" both the Domain Augmentation assumption and the Logic of Existence Predicates assumption to Anselm.

two premises. In the case of the second premise, we need to choose between at least the following three options:

$$\forall x\{[\,U_F\,x\,\&\,\text{Encode}_F\,(x,\,\lambda z(g(z)=m\,\&\sim\lozenge[\exists y(g(y)=n\,\&\,n>m)]))\,)]\to\lozenge\,Rx\}$$

$$\forall x\{[\,U_F\,x\,\&\,\text{Encode}_F\,(x,\,\lambda z(g(z)=m\,\&\sim\lozenge[\exists y(g(y)=n\,\&\,n>\,m)])))]$$
$$\to\,\text{Encode}_F\,(x,\,\lambda z[\lozenge\,Rz])\}$$

$$\forall x\{[\,U_F\,x\,\&\,\text{Encode}_F\,(x,\,\lambda z(g(z)=\,m\,\&\sim\lozenge[\exists y(g(y)=n\,\&\,n>\,m)])))]$$
$$\to\,\lozenge\text{Encode}_F\,(x,\,\lambda z\,Rz)\}$$

Similarly, in the case of the third premise, we need to choose between at least the following two options (and no doubt others besides):

$$\forall x\{[\,U_F\,x\,\&\,\text{Encode}_F\,(x,\,\lambda z(g(z)\,=\,m\,\&\,\sim\lozenge[\exists y(g(y)\,=\,n\,\&\,n>\,m)]))$$
$$\&\,\text{Encode}_F\,(x,\,\lambda z[\sim\,Rz])]\,\to\,\text{Encode}_F\,(x,\,\lambda z[\square\,(Rz$$
$$\to\,(g(z)\,=\,n\,\&\,n>\,m))])\}$$

$$\forall x\{[\,U_F\,x\,\&\,\text{Encode}_F\,(x,\,\lambda z(g(z)\,=\,m\,\&\,\sim\lozenge[\exists y(g(y)\,=\,n\,\&\,n>\,m)))]$$
$$\&\,\text{Encode}_F\,(x,\,\lambda z[\sim\,Rz])]\,\to\,\square\text{Encode}_F\,(x,\lambda z(Rz$$
$$\to\,(g(z)\,=\,n\,\&\,n>\,m)))\}$$

Without many further assumptions governing the behaviour of 'Encode$_F$', we cannot decide between the alternatives on offer, and neither can we say what might follow from any chosen set of premises. So, even if we grant that Chambers has correctly identified some of the assumptions that lie behind Anselm's Argument, it seems very plausible to hold that it is much harder to arrive at a clear conception of the "logical form" of Anselm's Argument than Chambers supposes. Moreover – particularly once we have seen the complexities into which the discussion descends – we might well be inclined to revisit the question of the choice of implicit assumptions upon which Anselm's Argument depends.[40]

2.4.7. Some Further Reflections on the Validity of St. Anselm's Argument

There is an enormous literature on the material in *Proslogion II–III*. Some commentators deny that St. Anselm tried to put forward any proofs of the existence of God. Even among commentators who agree that St. Anselm

[40] In particular, I think that we should be loath to grant both the Domain Augmentation assumption *and* the Hypostasis of Meaning assumption to Anselm. Talk about "existence in the understanding" should be mere translation of talk about "understanding of referring expressions". So we should insist that the Anselmian state his argument in *these* terms. If he cannot do this, then we have very good *prima facie* reason for thinking that his talk about "existence in the understanding" does not conservatively extend acceptable talk about "understanding of referring expressions". The many issues that arise here will need to be deferred to some other occasion.

intended to prove the existence of God, there is disagreement about where the proof is located. Some commentators claim that the main proof is in *Proslogion II*, and that the rest of the work draws out corollaries of that proof (see, e.g., Charlesworth (1965)). Other commentators claim that the main proof is in *Proslogion III*, and that the proof in *Proslogion II* is merely an inferior first attempt (see, e.g., Malcolm (1960)). Yet other commentators claim that there is a single proof that spans at least *Proslogion II–III* (see, e.g., Campbell (1976)) and, perhaps, the entire work (see, e.g., La Croix (1972)). I shall ignore this aspect of the controversy about the *Proslogion*. Instead, I shall just focus on the question of the analysis of the material in *Proslogion II* on the assumption that there is an independent argument for the existence of God that is given therein.

Here is one translation of the crucial part of *Proslogion II* (due to William Mann (1972: 260–1); alternative translations can be found in Charlesworth (1965), Barnes (1972), Campbell (1976), and elsewhere):

Thus even the fool is convinced that something than which nothing greater can be conceived is in the understanding, since when he hears this, he understands it; and whatever is understood is in the understanding. And certainly that than which a greater cannot be conceived cannot be in the understanding alone. For if it is even in the understanding alone, it can be conceived to exist in reality also, which is greater. Thus if that than which a greater cannot be conceived is in the understanding alone, then that than which a greater cannot be conceived is itself that than which a greater can be conceived. But surely this cannot be. Thus without doubt something than which a greater cannot be conceived exists, both in the understanding and in reality.

There have been many ingenious attempts to find an argument that can be expressed in modern logical formalism, which is logically valid, and which might plausibly be claimed to be the argument that is expressed in this passage. To take a few prime examples, apart from the case of Adams (1971)/Chambers (2000), Barnes (1972) and Oppenheimer and Zalta (1991) have also produced formally valid analyses of the argument in this passage. We begin with a brief presentation of each of these analyses, preceded by a presentation of the formulation of the argument given by Plantinga (1967), and including a presentation of some of the formulations of Lewis (1970).

Plantinga

1. God exists in the understanding but not in reality. (Assumption for *reductio*)
2. Existence in reality is greater than existence in the understanding alone. (Premise)
3. A being having all of God's properties plus existence in reality can be conceived. (Premise)

4. A being having all of God's properties plus existence in reality is greater than God. (From (1) and (2))
5. A being greater than God can be conceived. (From (3) and (4))
6. It is false that a being greater than God can be conceived. (From definition of "God")
7. Hence, it is false that God exists in the understanding but not in reality. (From (1), (5), (6))
8. God exists in the understanding. (Premise, to which even the Fool agrees.)
9. Hence God exists in reality. (From (7), (8))

Barnes

1. The Fool understands the expression "the being than which no greater can be conceived". (Premise)
2. If a person understands an expression "*b*", then *b* is in that person's understanding. (Premise)
3. If a thing is in a person's understanding, then the person can conceive of that thing's existing in reality. (Premise)
4. Each thing that exists in reality is greater than any thing that exists only in the understanding. (Premise)
5. If a person can conceive of something, and that thing entails something else, then the person can also conceive of that other thing. (Premise)
6. If a person can conceive that a specified object has a given property, then that person can conceive that something or other has that property. (Premise)
7. Hence the being than which no greater can be conceived exists in reality. (From (1)–(6), by a complex series of steps here omitted)

Adams (and Chambers)

1. There is a thing *x*, and a magnitude *m*, such that *x* exists in the understanding, *m* is the magnitude of *x*, and it is not possible that there is a thing *y* and a magnitude *n* such that *n* is the magnitude of *y* and *n* > *m*. (Premise)
2. For any thing *x* and magnitude *m*, if *x* exists in the understanding, *m* is the magnitude of *x*, and it is not possible that there is a thing *y* and magnitude *n* such that *n* is the magnitude of *y* and *n* > *m*, then it is possible that *x* exists in reality. (Premise)
3. For any thing *x* and magnitude *m*, if *m* is the magnitude of *x*, and it is not possible that there is a thing *y* and a magnitude *n* such that *n* is the magnitude of *y* and *n* > *m*, and *x* does not exist in reality, then it is not possible that if *x* exists in reality, then there is a

magnitude n such that n is greater than m and n is the magnitude of x. (Premise)

4. (Hence) There is a thing x and a magnitude m such that x exists in the understanding, and x exists in reality, and m is the magnitude of x, and it is not possible that there is a thing y and a magnitude n such that n is the magnitude of y and $n > m$. (From (1)–(3))

Lewis

1. For any understandable being x, there is a world w such that x exists in w. (Premise)
2. For any understandable being x, and for any worlds w and v, if x exists in w, but x does not exist in v, then the greatness of x in w exceeds the greatness of x in v. (Premise)
3. There is an understandable being x such that for no world w and being y does the greatness of y in w exceed the greatness of x in the actual world. (Premise)
4. (Hence) There is a being x existing in the actual world such that for no world w and being y does the greatness of y in w exceed the greatness of x in the actual world. (From (1)–(3))

Lewis also suggests an alternative to (3) that yields a valid argument:

3. There is an understandable being x such that for no worlds v and w and being y does the greatness of y in w exceed the greatness of x in v.

He also suggests two alternatives to (3) – not presented here – that yield invalid arguments. (Of course, there further two alternatives are crucial to Lewis's overall analysis of the passage: essentially, Lewis suggests that Anselm equivocates between an invalid argument with plausible premises and a valid argument with question-begging premises. In this respect, Lewis's analysis is quite different from the other analyses currently under discussion.)

Oppenheimer and Zalta

1. There is (in the understanding) something than which there is no greater. (Premise)
2. (Hence) There is (in the understanding) a unique thing than which there is no greater. (From (1), assuming that the "greater-than" relation is connected)
3. (Hence) There is (in the understanding) something that is the thing than which there is no greater. (From (2), by a theorem about descriptions)
4. (Hence) There is (in the understanding) nothing that is greater than the thing than which there is no greater. (From (3), by another theorem about descriptions)

5. If that thing than which there is no greater does not exist (in reality), then there is (in the understanding) something that is greater than that thing than which there is no greater. (Premise)
6. (Hence) That thing than which there is no greater exists (in reality). (From (4) and (5))
7. (Hence) God exists. (From (6))

Considered as interpretations of the argument presented in the *Proslogion*, these formulations are subject to various kinds of criticisms.

First, the modal interpretations of Lewis (1970) and Adams (1971) don't square very well with the rest of the *Proslogion*: the claim that "being than which no greater can be conceived" should be read as "being than which no greater is possible" would have us render the claim of *Proslogion 15* to be that God is a being greater than any which is possible. And that is surely a bad result.

Second, the Meinongian interpretations of Adams (1971), Barnes (1972), and Oppenheimer and Zalta (1991) produce arguments that, given the principles involved, could easily be much simplified, and that are obviously vulnerable to Gaunilo-type objections.

Consider, for example, the case of Oppenheimer and Zalta. They have Anselm committed to the claim that if anyone can understand the phrase "that than which F", then there is something in the understanding such that F (see their footnote 25); and they also have him committed to the claim that if there is something that is the F-thing, then it – that is, the F-thing – has the property F (see p. 7). Plainly, though, if Anselm is really committed to these principles, then he could hardly fail to be committed to the more general principles: (1) if anyone can understand the phrase "an F", then there is at least one F-thing in the understanding; and (2) if there are some things that are the F-things, then they – that is, the F-things – must have the property F. (It would surely be absurd to claim that Anselm is committed only to the less general principles: what could possibly have justified the restrictions to the special cases?)

But, then, mark the consequences. We all understand the expression "an existent perfect being". So, by the first claim, there is at least one existent perfect being in the understanding. And, by the second claim, any existent perfect being is existent. So, from these two claims combined, there is – in reality – at least one existent perfect being.

This argument gives Anselm everything that he wants, and very much more briefly. (The *Proslogion* goes on and on, trying to establish the properties of that than which no greater can be conceived. How much easier if we can just explicitly build all of the properties that want to "derive" into the initial description.) So, if Anselm really were committed to the principles that Oppenheimer and Zalta appear to attribute to him, it is hard to understand why he didn't give the simpler argument. And, of course, it is also hard to understand why he didn't take Gaunilo's criticism. After all, when it is set out in this way, it is obvious that the argument proves far too much.

Third, some of the arguments have Anselm committed to claims about greatness that do not seem to correspond with what he actually says. The natural reading of the text is that, if two beings are identical save that one exists only in the understanding and the other exists in reality as well, then the latter is greater than the former. But Barnes (1971), for example, has Anselm committed to the much stronger claim that any existing thing is greater than every non-existent thing.

Given these kinds of considerations, it is natural to wonder whether there are better interpretations of *Proslogion II* according to which the argument in question turns out *not* to be logically valid. The following is a modest attempt to provide such an analysis.

We start with the claim that the Fool understands the expression "being than which no greater can be conceived"; that is, even the Fool can entertain the idea or possess the concept of a being than which no greater can be conceived. Now, entertaining this idea or possessing this concept requires the entertainer or possessor to recognise certain relationships that hold between given properties and the idea or concept in question. For example, given that you possess the concept of, or entertain the idea of, a smallest really existent Martian, it follows that you must recognise some kind of connection between the properties of being a Martian, really existing, and being smaller than other really existing Martians, and the concept or idea in question.

Following Anselm, we might say that, since you understand the expression "smallest really existent Martian", there is, in your understanding, at least one smallest really existent Martian. (Or, apparently following Descartes, one might say that real existence is "part of" – or "contained in" – the idea of a smallest really existent Martian.) However, in saying this, it must be understood that we are not actually predicating properties of anything: we aren't supposing that there is something that possesses the properties of being a Martian, really existing, and being no larger than any other Martian. (After all, we can safely suppose, we don't think that any Martians really exist.) In other words, we must be able to have the concept of, or entertain the idea of, a smallest really existing Martian without believing that there really are any smallest Martians. Indeed, more strongly, we must be able to entertain the concept of a smallest really existent Martian – and to recognise that the property of "really existing" is part of this concept – while nonetheless maintaining that there are no smallest existent Martians.

It will be useful to introduce vocabulary to mark the point that is being made here. We could, for instance, distinguish between the properties that are encoded in an idea or concept and the properties that are attributed in positive atomic beliefs that have that idea or concept as an ingredient. The idea "really existent Santa Claus" encodes the property of real existence; but it is perfectly possible to entertain this idea without attributing real existence to Santa Claus, that is, without believing that Santa Claus really exists.

We can then apply this distinction to Anselm's argument. On the one hand, the idea "being than which no greater can be conceived" encodes the property of real existence – this is what the *reductio* argument establishes (if it establishes anything at all). On the other hand, it is perfectly possible to entertain the idea of a being than which no greater can be conceived – and to recognise that this idea encodes the property of real existence – without attributing real existence to a being than which no greater can be conceived, that is, without believing that a being than which no greater can be conceived really exists.

Of course, the argument that Anselm actually presents pays no attention to this distinction between encoding and attributing – that is, between entertaining an idea and holding a belief – and neither does it pay attention to various other niceties. We begin from the point that the Fool entertains the idea of that than which no greater can be conceived (because the Fool understands the words "that than which no greater can be conceived"). From this, we move quickly to the claim that even the Fool is "convinced" – that is, believes – that that than which no greater can be conceived possesses the property of existing in the understanding. And then the *reductio* argument is produced to establish that that than which no greater can be conceived cannot exist only in the understanding but must also possess the property of existing in reality as well (and all mention of the Fool, and what it is that the Fool believes, disappears).

As it stands, this is deeply problematic. How are we supposed to regiment the references to the Fool in the argument? Is the *reductio* argument supposed to tell us something about what even the Fool believes, or ought to believe? Are the earlier references to the Fool supposed to be inessential and eliminable? How are we so much as to understand the claim that even the Fool believes that that than which no greater can be conceived exists in the understanding? And how do we get from the Fool's understanding the words "that than which no greater can be conceived" to his believing that that than which no greater can be conceived possesses the property of existing in the understanding?

Following the earlier line of thought, it seems that the argument might go something like this:

1. (Even) the Fool has the concept of that than which no greater can be conceived.
2. (Hence) (Even) the Fool believes that that than which no greater can be conceived exists in the understanding.

3. No one who believes that that than which no greater can be conceived exists in the understanding can reasonably believe that that than which no greater can be conceived exists only in the understanding.
4. (Hence) (Even) the Fool cannot reasonably deny that that than which no greater can be conceived exists in reality.
5. (Hence) That than which no greater can be conceived exists in reality.

While this argument does not look very compelling, it is plausible to claim that it would have seemed compelling to someone who failed to attend to the distinction that we have drawn between entertaining ideas and holding beliefs, and who was also a bit hazy on the distinction between the vehicles of belief and their contents. When the Fool entertains the concept of that than which no greater can be conceived, he recognises that he is entertaining this concept (i.e., he believes that he is entertaining the concept of that than which no greater can be conceived – or, as we might say, that the concept is in his understanding). Conflating the concept with its object, this gives us the belief that that than which no greater can be conceived possesses the property of existing in the understanding. Now, suppose as hypothesis for reductio that we can reasonably believe that that than which no greater can be conceived possesses the property of existing only in the understanding. Ignoring the distinction between entertaining ideas and holding beliefs, this means that when we entertain the idea of that than which no greater can be conceived, we entertain the idea of a being that exists only in the understanding. But that is absurd: when we entertain the idea of that than which no greater can be conceived, our idea encodes the property of existing in reality. So there is a contradiction, and we can conclude that, in order to be reasonable, we must believe that that than which no greater can be conceived exists in reality. But if any reasonable person must believe that that than which no greater can be conceived exists in reality, then surely it is the case that that than which no greater can be conceived exists in reality. And so we are done.

No doubt this suggestion about the interpretation of Anselm's argument is deficient in various ways. However, the point of including it is illustrative rather than dogmatic. In the literature, there has been great resistance to the idea that the argument that Anselm gives is one that modern logicians would not hesitate to pronounce invalid. But it is very hard to see why there should be this resistance. (Certainly, it is not something for which there is much argument in the literature.) The text of the *Proslogion* is so rough, and so much in need of polishing, that we should not be too quick to dismiss the suggestion that Anselm's argument is rather more like the argument most recently sketched than it is like the logically valid demonstrations provided by commentators such as Barnes, Adams, Chambers, and Oppenheimer and Zalta.

2.5. CONCLUDING REMARKS

Having done my best to update the discussion of Oppy (1995c), I shall close with a brief observation about the bearing of considerations about the infinite on the analysis of ontological arguments.

Plainly enough, there is very little explicit appeal to principles that concern the infinite in ontological arguments. (One exception is the possible explicit appeal to unrestricted mereological composition in mereological ontological arguments.) However, the best known – and perhaps most interesting – historical ontological arguments involve descriptions in which – it might plausibly be supposed – there is implicit appeal to considerations involving the infinite. As we noted in earlier chapters, when one speaks of 'that than which no greater can be conceived', or 'that which is absolutely perfect', or the like, it seems plausible to suppose that one incurs some kind of commitment to the intelligibility of 'completed' infinities. Moreover – if this is right – then it also seems plausible to claim that those who accept arguments of this kind are thereby committed to the existence of at least one 'actual' infinity.

The contention that I have just made is supported by some of the literature that discusses the 'perfect island' objection to St. Anselm's ontological argument(s). Some critics have supposed that 'a being than which no greater being can be conceived' differs from 'an island than which no greater island can be conceived' precisely because, while there can be no 'infinite' island, there can be an 'infinite' being. Regardless of the view that one takes about this objection, it seems clear that the making of this objection supports the contention that considerations about the infinite lurk not too far below the surface in the presentations of the familiar historical ontological arguments.

3

Cosmological Arguments

As I pointed out in the Preface to Oppy (2006), a full discussion of cosmological arguments would need to be very extensive indeed. Even with our focus restricted primarily to considerations about the role of the concept of the infinite in cosmological arguments, we shall need to give a fairly summary treatment of some of the relevant issues.

After some initial considerations about the classification of cosmological arguments – and of the way in which one ought to distinguish between cosmological arguments and teleological arguments – we shall begin with a discussion of the first three of Aquinas' *Five Ways*. Next, we shall consider the cosmological arguments that Descartes defends in *Meditation III* and that Leibniz advances in his essay "On the Ultimate Origination of Things". Then, we shall consider much more recent versions of cosmological arguments involving causation and contingency due to Meyer (1987), Koons (1997), and Gale and Pruss (1999). Finally, before turning to some concluding observations, we consider the recent defence of *kalām* cosmological arguments in the work of Craig (1979a), and the recent construction of an atheological cosmological argument in the work of Smith (1988).

3.1. SOME INITIAL CONSIDERATIONS

There are many different kinds of *a posteriori* arguments for the existence of God. Following Kant, we shall suppose that it is possible to sort many of these arguments into two major classes: the *cosmological* arguments and the *teleological* arguments. At least roughly, we might suppose that cosmological arguments advert to very general structural features of the universe and/or our ways of conceptualising the universe, whereas teleological arguments advert to more particular functional features of the universe and/or our ways of conceptualising the universe. Perhaps this rough characterisation is hopelessly mistaken. No matter: since we shall treat each argument on its merits – that is, without regard to the general class to which it is assigned – the

97

only important consideration is that we should not overlook any plausible *a posteriori* arguments that will not be treated elsewhere.

Again, speaking very roughly, we might suppose that it is characteristic of cosmological arguments that they involve a premise that claims that a certain kind of infinite regress or infinite collection is impossible. While the general structural features of the universe that are adverted to in cosmological arguments vary widely – *temporal* structure, *modal* structure, *causal* structure, *explanatory* structure, *intelligible* structure, *axiological* structure, and so forth – it seems plausible to claim that all of these kinds of arguments typically involve appeal to the claim that there are ways in which these various structures cannot be infinite.

A final characteristic of cosmological arguments is that they typically issue in conclusions that – at least *prima facie* – are only very doubtfully of genuine religious significance. Even if, for example, one can establish that there is an efficient cause for the existence of the visible (physical) universe, it is not at all clear why one should suppose that this efficient cause can be identified with the creative activity of any of the gods whose existence is postulated in extant world religions. At the very best, cosmological arguments are arguments for a conclusion that *might* serve as an important premise in some further argument for the existence of a religiously significant being.

3.2. AQUINAS' FIRST THREE WAYS

As many authors have noted, there are interesting structural similarities among the arguments in at least the first three of Aquinas' Five Ways. Thus, for example, Kenny (1969) claims – roughly – that at the core of each of these Ways, there is an argument with the following structure.

1. The two-place relational predicate 'R' is instantiated – that is, there are a and b such that Rab.
2. R is irreflexive – that is, nothing can stand in this relation to itself.
3. R is transitive – that is, if Rab and Rbc, then Rac.
4. There cannot be a beginningless series of things that stand in the relation R to one another – that is, there cannot be . . . e, f, g such that . . . Ref, Rfg.
5. (Hence) There is a unique thing to which other things stand in the relation R but which does not stand in the relation R to anything.

In the First Way, the relation Rxy is the relation x is changed by y; in the Second Way, the relation Rxy is the relation x is efficiently caused by y; and in the Third Way, the relation Rxy is the relation x owes its necessity to y.[1]

---

[1] Strictly, Kenny claims that, in the Third Way, Rxy is the relation x can cease to exist by turning into y. This seems to me to be a highly contentious rendering of the relation x owes its necessity to y, i.e., of the relation that is explicitly mentioned in the standard translations.

In fact, Kenny claims that the same structure can be discerned in the Fourth Way – where Rxy is the relation x is less noble, less true, or less good than y – and in the Fifth Way – where Rxy is the relation x is directed to a goal by y, where y is higher than x in the scale of cognitive powers. However, it seems to me that there is insufficient textual support for the claim that this structure is present in the arguments of the Fourth Way and the Fifth Way.[2] Moreover, for reasons that will emerge as we proceed, it also seems to me that it is only roughly correct to claim that the precise structure that Kenny describes is to be found in each of the first three Ways. Nonetheless, it is true that there are many affinities among the arguments in each of the first three Ways.

I shall begin with a discussion of the Second Way, and then, after a briefer discussion of the First Way, turn to a similarly extended discussion of the Third Way. I shall leave discussion of the Fourth Way[3] and the Fifth Way[4] to some other occasion.

Second Way: The Second Way is plausibly construed as an argument about efficient causation.[5] With very little alteration to standard translations, we may represent this argument as follows:

1. Some things exist, and their existence is caused.
2. Whatever is caused to exist is caused to exist by another.
3. An infinite regress of causes resulting in the existence of a particular thing is impossible.
4. (Hence) There is a (unique) first cause of existence that is not itself caused to exist.

The most obvious difficulty with this argument is that it is invalid. The strongest conclusion that could be drawn from the three premises is that there are first causes, that is, that there are causes of existence that are not themselves caused to exist. There is nothing in the premises that justifies drawing the conclusion that there is *exactly one* first cause.

Even if the conclusion of this argument were merely that there are first causes of existence, it is not clear that the conclusion would follow from the premises. If we suppose that the causal relation in question is transitive – so

---

[2] In particular, it is worth noting that there is no *explicit* argument against an infinite regress in either the Fourth Way or the Fifth Way. For purposes of taxonomy, I see no obvious reason why the Fourth Way and the Fifth Way should not be classified as teleological arguments – though perhaps it could be contended that 'the gradation observed in things' and 'the guidedness of nature' are both (putative) very general structural features of the universe.

[3] For discussion of the Fourth Way, see, e.g.: Annice (1956), Sanford (1967), Kenny (1969), Ross (1969), Brady (1974), and Urban (1984).

[4] For discussion of the Fifth Way, see, e.g.: Faricy (1957), Harrison (1961), Kenny (1969), and Ross (1969).

[5] For other discussions of the Second Way, see, e.g.: Ross (1969) and Martin (1990).

that, if *a* is a cause of *b*, and *b* is a cause of *c*, then *a* is a cause of *c* – then, by the irreflexivity of the causal relation that is vouchsafed by premise 2, it will follow that there are no circles of causes. However, if we do not suppose that the causal relation is transitive, then there is nothing in the premises to rule out circles of causes, for example, a situation in which *a* causes *b*, *b* causes *c*, and *c* causes *a*.

The third premise in the argument is plainly stronger than necessary: it would be sufficient to suppose that there *is* no infinite regress of causes resulting in the existence of a particular thing. Of course, one might suppose that the only reason that one could have for believing this claim is that there is good reason to accept that there cannot be an infinite regress of causes resulting in the existence of a particular thing. But, whatever view you take about this modal claim, you could hardly suppose that it is more secure than the claim that nothing can be the efficient cause of its own existence. So there is a curious disparity in the modality of the second and third premises in the argument as it is presented.

Taking all of these difficulties into account, we might suppose that the argument is better reformulated as follows:

1. Some things are caused.
2. Things do not cause themselves.
3. There are no circles of causes.
4. There are no infinite regresses of causes.
5. (Hence) There are first causes.
6. There is no more than one first cause.
7. (Hence) There is exactly one first cause.

While this argument is, I think, valid, there are still questions that can be raised about most of the premises. Setting aside worries that one might have about the lack of a satisfying analysis of efficient causation, it seems quite uncontroversial to accept that some things have causes. But, beyond this point, there are many hard questions to face.

It seems to me to be relatively uncontroversial to suppose that nothing can be a *direct* or *unmediated* cause of itself. However, it is far more controversial to suppose that there *cannot* be a – perhaps very large – circle of causes, each of which is an efficient cause for the next. The large literatures on the possibility of time travel and the possibility of circular time attest to the controversial status of the claim that nothing can be an indirect or mediated cause of itself (and/or the claim that there cannot be circles of causes). Perhaps we can argue from the absence of evidence of time travel to the conclusion that there *are* no circles of causes or things that are indirect or mediated causes of themselves. However, at the very least, it should be recognised that the second and third premises are in need of substantial further support.

As I argue in Oppy (2006), it is very doubtful that there is a cogent argument for the conclusion that there *cannot* be an infinite regress of efficient causes – or, at any rate, that there is an argument of this kind that is not question-begging in the current context. Plainly enough, for example, if we suppose that God exists of (broadly) logical necessity, and that there is no (broadly) logically possible world in which there is a physical universe that is not brought into existence by God, then we shall be in a position to conclude that there can be no infinite regress of efficient causes – but, if *this* is our reason for holding that there cannot be an infinite regress of efficient causes, then we shall not then be well placed to rely on the claim that there can be no infinite regress of efficient causes when we come to *argue* for the existence of God. However, once blatantly question-begging considerations are set aside, it is very hard to see how one could construct a cogent argument for the claim that there cannot be an infinite regress of efficient causes. Perhaps one might hope to argue from Big Bang cosmology to the claim that there *is* no infinite regress of efficient causation, but – as we shall go on to argue in connection with the *kalām* syllogism – it seems to be the case both that there can be infinite regresses of efficient causation within Big Bang universes and that efficient causation can extend 'through' the initial singularity in Big Bang universes. If this is right, then it is hard to see how one could hope to mount an *empirical* argument for the claim that there is no infinite regress of efficient causation in our world.

Aquinas does offer an argument on behalf of the key 'infinite regress' premise in the Second Way, recapitulating a similar argument that is given in the First Way. What he says is that, if there were no first cause in a series of causes, then there would be no intermediate causes either, and hence no effect. But this argument is powerless to establish the conclusion that there cannot be an infinite regress of causes: for, if there were an infinite regress of causes, then it would be true that there is no first cause, and yet it could also be true that, if any of the earlier causes were 'eliminated', then the effect would be eliminated as well. (Of course, it isn't really true that the 'elimination' of a cause guarantees the 'elimination' of the effect: it could be, for example, that the cause pre-empts some other process that would give rise to the effect were it not so pre-empted. But, having noted this consideration, there is no harm in setting it aside: the objection to the argument currently under consideration goes through even if causes are – implausibly – supposed to be both necessary and sufficient conditions for their effects.) As many other commentators have noted, there is nothing in the considerations to which Aquinas here appeals that deserves to be treated as a cogent reason for supposing that there cannot be an infinite regress of efficient causes.[6]

---

[6] Perhaps the discussion in the main text is a bit brief. Suppose you think that, if there is an infinite regress of 'causes', then it is only 'conditionally' true that one event causes another. Then, you might say, the assumption that one event 'categorically' – or 'unconditionally' – causes another is, indeed, inconsistent with the assumption that there is an infinite regress of causes (cf. Clark (1988: 373ff.)). Fair enough. However, if you do think this way, then trouble strikes at another point – for what non-question-begging argument can you give for the conclusion that there are categorical causes, in the sense of 'categorical' that is here at issue?

Even if one is not persuaded by the criticisms that have been offered of the other premises in our revised version of the second way, one should surely think twice before supposing that the final premise is suitably uncontroversial to play the role that is required in this argument. Since a first cause is merely an efficient cause that itself has no efficient cause, one might think that anyone who accepts a libertarian conception of freedom is bound to allow that the physical universe is full of first causes: my free decision to write this book is an efficient cause of the existence of this book, but that free decision – according to libertarians about freedom – did not itself have an efficient cause.[7] Moreover, even compatibilists about freedom should demand *evidence* to support the claim that any pair of objects share a common efficient cause of their existence. In standard Big Bang models, there are parts of the universe that are causally isolated from one another: there are chains of efficient causation that trace back to independent "initial" data. Given this fact, there is surely no *empirical* support for the claim that all chains of efficient causation terminate in the same initial efficient cause.

In sum, there are many reasons for thinking that the Second Way is not a persuasive or cogent argument for the conclusion that there is a unique first cause of existence that is not itself caused to exist. Even when Aquinas' argument is repaired so that the conclusion does follow from the provided premises, we find that the premises are highly controversial and, in some cases, entirely lacking in non-question-begging support.

First Way: The First Way is sometimes couched in terms of 'change' and sometimes in terms of 'motion'. I do not think that it matters for our purposes how we choose to render the key term in our version of the argument.[8]

1. Some things are in a process of change.
2. Whatever is in a process of change is being changed by something else.

If it is uncontroversial that some things cause other things, this is only in the sense the some things are conditional causes of other things. The *argument* for an uncaused cause obtains no increase in cogency if the notion of 'cause' is interpreted in the way here suggested.

7 There is some awkwardness in this alleged counterexample, due to the fact that the second way is actually couched in terms of causes of the existence of things. If 'things' is interpreted broadly – to include states of affairs and the like – then it is a straightforward matter to press the objection in the text. But if 'things' is interpreted narrowly – so that it extends to cover only 'individual particulars' – then one might worry that 'decisions' do not fall under the scope of the intended interpretation. However, in this case, the point to note is that the existence of a thing may be explained perfectly well in terms other than the existence of some (other) thing: an efficient cause of the existence of some one thing need not be the existence of some other thing, in this narrow sense of 'thing'. But then there will be ever so many 'first causes', i.e., efficient causes of the existence of some thing that are not themselves the existence of (another) thing.

8 For other discussions of the First Way, see, e.g.: Owens (1952/3), Wallace (1956, 1975), Salamucha (1958), Kenny (1969), and King-Farlow (1975).

3. An infinite regress of changers, each changed by another, is impossible.
4. (Hence) There is a first cause of change, not itself in a process of change.

This argument is subject to many of the same difficulties as the Second Way.

For starters, the argument seems to be plainly invalid: the most that could follow from the premises is that there are first causes of change that are not themselves in a process of change. There is nothing in the premises of this argument that justifies drawing the conclusion that there is a unique first cause of change that is not itself in a process of change. Moreover, as in the case of the second way, there is a modal mismatch between the second and third premises, perhaps most plausibly repaired by weakening the third premise to a claim about the actual world alone.

The second premise – that anything in a process of change is being changed by something else – seems highly controversial. If there are objectively chancy processes, then there are processes of change that are not 'brought about' by anything else. Hence, in particular, if there are libertarian free choices, then there are processes of change that are not 'brought about' by anything else. (When minds are in a process of freely changing, then – *a fortiori* – by libertarian lights, there isn't anything else that is 'bringing about' these changes.) Acceptance of the second premise of this argument not only requires rejection of the plausible claim that there are objectively chancy processes, but also entails rejection of both free will defences against logical arguments from evil and free will theodicies quite generally.

The third premise – revised to be the claim that there is no infinite regress of changers, each changed by another – is also extremely controversial, for the same reasons that the corresponding premise in the second way is extremely controversial. As we noted above, it is hard to see that there is anything in Big Bang cosmology that rules out the existence of an infinite regress of changers, each changed by another, even though it is true in Big Bang cosmology that the physical universe has merely finite age. But, on the other hand, as we also noted above, it is equally difficult to find a cogent *a priori* objection to the existence of physically instantiated infinite regresses that is not blatantly question-begging in the present context.

Third Way: The core of the Third Way appears to have much the same kind of structure as the first two ways.[9] However, there is an interesting – and much discussed – supporting argument for the claim that there are necessarily existent beings that is not paralleled by supporting arguments

[9] For other discussions of the Third Way, see, e.g.: Wright (1951), Owens (1952/3, 1971, 1974), O'Donoghue (1953, 1969), Connolly (1954), Finili (1954), Bobik (1968, 1972), Edwards (1968, 1971, 1973), Durrant (1969), Kenny (1969), Mautner (1969), Ross (1969), Mabey (1971), Prado (1971), Solon (1973), Knasas (1978, 1980), Quinn (1978), Kondoleon (1980), Kelly (1981, 1982), Brown (1982), Mackie (1982), and Martin (1990).

for the claim that there are things in a process of change, or things whose existence has an efficient cause. According to standard translations, the argument of the Third Way is something like this:

1. There are contingent things.
2. If an existent thing is contingent, then there was a time when it did not exist.
3. (Therefore) If every existent thing is contingent, then there was a time when nothing existed.
4. Something that does not exist can be brought into existence only by something that already exists.
5. (Therefore) If there was a time when nothing existed, then nothing exists now.
6. Something exists now.
7. (Therefore) Not every existent being is contingent.
8. A necessary being may or may not owe its necessity to something else.
9. The series of necessary beings that owe their necessity to something else does not regress to infinity.
10. (Therefore) There is a necessary being that does not owe its necessity to something else.

The first difficulty in discussing this argument is to decide how the words 'necessary' and 'contingent' are to be understood. The gloss that Aquinas himself provides is that a being is contingent iff either it is possible for that being to come into existence or it is possible for that being to go out of existence. I take it that what follows from this gloss is that a being is necessary iff it exists at all times in all possible worlds in which it exists at any time, but that it need not be the case that a necessary being exists in all possible worlds. If a necessary being exists at any time in a given possible world, then it exists at all times in that possible world.

Given this understanding of 'contingency', the first premise in the argument seems unproblematic: there are many beings that are 'contingent' in this sense. However, on this understanding of 'contingency', it is very hard to see why we should suppose that the second premise is true: just because it is *possible* that a being came into existence does not entail that, as a matter of fact, it has not always existed (and nor does it entail that, as a matter of fact, the being will go out of existence).

Perhaps one might try arguing in the following way. If there is a possible world in which a being comes into existence, then there is a world in which that being is caused to come into existence. But if there is one possible world in which a being is caused to come into existence, then in every possible world in which that being exists, it is caused to come into existence in exactly the same way, because causal origin is an essential property of any being. I think that the thesis of necessity of origin is too controversial to play the role that would here be required of it; but it would require a very substantial digression to provide a satisfactory treatment of this point.

In any case, there is a more pressing objection to the second premise. On our account of contingency, a being is contingent just in case *either* it is possible that it comes into existence or it is possible that it goes out of existence. Consider, then, a contingent being that cannot come into existence, though it can, of course, go out of existence: if such a being were to exist now, then it could not have failed to exist at any earlier time. There is nothing in our gloss on contingency that rules out the current existence of contingent things that have existed at all prior times.

Even if we do suppose that the second premise is true, it seems that there is good reason to contest the inference from the first two premises to the first interim conclusion at 3. Even if no contingent being exists at all earlier times in our world – that is, no contingent being exists at all times in some initial segment of the history of our world – it does not follow that, if every existent being is contingent, then there was an earlier time at which nothing existed. To obtain this interim conclusion, we would need to add a further premise that rules out an infinite sequence of comings into existence and goings out of existence. Else we can satisfy the demand that no contingent being exists at all times in some initial segment of the history of a world – and the further demand that any contingent being is brought into existence by some change in some other being – in a world in which there are no more than two contingent beings, A and B: just suppose that A's going out of existence brings B into existence, and B's going out of existence brings A into existence. Of course, we don't need to suppose that past time is infinite in order to make this story run: we could fit the infinite series of alternations between A and B into a standard Big Bang structure, provided that the intervals in which A and B exist become shorter and shorter as one approaches the temporal origin. Moreover, even if you don't think that it is possible for there to be intermittent existence of this type, it is clear that, at the very least, you will need to suppose that there have been only finitely many contingently existent beings in order to reach the first interim conclusion at 3.

The next premise in the argument introduces a new round of difficulties. Initially, it may seem plausible to suppose that, if something is to come into existence at a time t, then it must be brought into existence by something that exists at times prior to t. But why should we suppose that it is simply impossible for something to come into existence at a time t without being brought into existence by something that exists at times prior to t? In particular, if we suppose that there can be a first instant of time, t_0, then how can we suppose that those things that come into existence at time t_0 are brought into existence by things that exist at times prior to t_0? We shall return to a more detailed discussion of the claim that everything that begins to exist has a cause of its beginning to exist when we turn to discuss the *kalām* cosmological arguments. For now, I shall merely content myself with the observation that it is very hard to see how to provide this claim with a convincing non-question-begging defence.

Given the discussion to this point, it seems to me that we are well entitled to conclude that Aquinas fails to provide adequate argumentative support for the claim that not every existent being is contingent. However, it may nonetheless be that we can defend this claim – albeit in a way that very probably does serious damage to the overall aim of the argument of the Third Way. Suppose that the spatiotemporal manifold of the actual universe is strongly inextendible. In that case, it is plainly true that the physical universe is itself a necessary existent: there is no possible world in which *it* exists at some times and yet fails to exist at all times. If the physical universe counts as a 'being', then it is very plausible to suppose that, on the account of 'contingency' now in play, the physical universe is a necessarily existent being. If the physical universe counts as a 'being', then not all beings are contingent, on the account of 'contingency' now in play.

Given the assumption that the spatiotemporal manifold of the actual world is strongly inextendible, the claim that a necessary being may owe its necessity to something else clearly relies upon the assumption that how things are in the temporal realm can depend upon how things are in some non-temporal realm. If the existence of the physical universe *depends upon* something else, then – at the very least – there are possible worlds in which there is no physical universe because that something else is different in some way. Moreover, if there is neither space nor time 'beyond' the physical universe, then the 'something else' upon which the existence of the physical universe depends can be neither spatial nor temporal.

But why should we suppose that the existence of the physical universe does depend upon something else? If the existence of the physical universe does not depend upon something else, then, in the sense of 'necessity' now in play, it does seem to follow that there is a necessary being that does not owe its necessity to anything else. Yet, in that case, the conclusion at which we have arrived seems to be one that lacks any kind of religious significance: even the most demanding atheist could agree that the physical universe is a necessary being that does not owe its necessity to anything else, in the sense of 'necessity' here at issue.

Of course, even if one rejects the conclusion for which I have just argued, there are other reasons for finding fault with Aquinas' argument from the claim that not every existent being is contingent to the conclusion that there is a (unique) necessary being that does not owe its necessity to anything else. As in the first two ways, the argument seems plainly invalid: the most that the argument could establish is that there are necessary beings that do not owe their necessity to anything else. Moreover, the premise that rules out an infinite regress of necessary beings, each of which owes its necessity to the next, is plainly in need of further support.

In sum, there are many reasons for thinking that the Third Way is not a persuasive or cogent argument for the conclusion that there is a unique first cause of existence that is not itself caused to exist. Even when Aquinas' argument is repaired so that the conclusion does follow from the provided premises, we find that the premises are highly controversial and, in some cases, entirely lacking in non-question-begging support.

If the analyses that I have presented are well founded, then there is very good reason to think that none of the first three of Aquinas' Five Ways is a persuasive or cogent argument for the conclusion that there is an unchanged changer, or an uncaused caused, or a necessary being that owes its necessity to nothing else. Still less, then, does any of these three arguments provide a reason for believing in the existence of the God of any familiar strand of monotheistic religious thought. There are well-known – and widespread – forms of monotheistic religious thought that do not accept that God is unchanging, or that God is the one and only uncaused cause, or that God is the one and only necessary being that does not owe its necessity to anything else. On many of the conceptions of God that might be adopted, these arguments would provide no support for the existence of God even if – contrary to fact – they were compelling arguments for the existence of unchanged changers, or uncaused causers, or necessary beings that do not owe their necessity to anything else.

3.3. DESCARTES' CAUSAL ARGUMENT

In *Meditation III*, Descartes offers a very curious causal proof of the existence of an orthodoxly conceived monotheistic god.[10] The proof is curious not merely because of the apparatus that it requires, but also because one of the most damaging objections to the proof is noted by Descartes himself in *Meditation IV*, though he does not himself note explicitly that the point for which he argues in *Meditation IV* undermines the proof in *Meditation III*. Some interpreters have supposed that this shows that Descartes didn't seriously mean to endorse the alleged proof in *Meditation III*; I leave it to historians of philosophy continue the debate about whether or not this is really so. (Of course, scepticism about Descartes' support for the *Meditation III* proof extends to scepticism about Descartes' support for many other arguments in the *Meditations*.)

In the first two *Meditations*, Descartes takes it that he has shown that there are propositions that are immune to sceptical doubt. In particular, he takes it that certain first-person judgments – of one's own existence, and about one's

---

[10] For other discussions of the *Meditation III* argument, see, e.g.: Stainsby (1967), Kenny (1968), Norton (1968, 1974, 1978), Dilley (1970), Brewster (1974), Brecher (1976), Elliot and Smith (1978), Stevens (1978), Williams (1978), O'Briant (1979), Armour (1980), Clatterbaugh (1980), Delahunty (1980), Immerwahr (1982), and Flage and Bonnen (1989).

current mental states – are immune to doubt. Moreover, he takes it that he has shown that he is essentially a thinking being, and that minds are radically different kinds of things from bodies. However, even if these conclusions are correct, it does not follow that Descartes' projected reconstruction of all of our knowledge can be carried out. The main problem is that it seems most unlikely that we will be able to deduce propositions about, for example, the state of the external world, from propositions about what is going on in our heads. That it seems to me to be hot now does not entail the conclusion that it is hot now. So how can Descartes hope to reconstruct what we take to be our ordinary knowledge of the world from the indubitable propositions that he has discovered?

At the beginning of *Meditation III*, Descartes declares that 'clear and distinct perception' is a criterion of truth. Then, using this principle, he goes on to argue that there exists an infinitely perfect being that therefore cannot be a deceiver. From this, he concludes that he can rely upon his sense perceptions to establish the nature and existence of a mind-independent external world, provided that he takes care to distinguish what he perceives clearly and distinctly to be true from those of his perceptions that are unclear or indistinct.

Plainly enough, Descartes' refutation of scepticism – and his defence of science – relies crucially on the success of his proof of the existence of an orthodoxly conceived monotheistic god. However, if the proof of the existence of an orthodoxly conceived monotheistic god is to play the role that is assigned to it in the *Meditations*, then it must meet a very high standard indeed. If Descartes is to object to scepticism by claiming – in outline – that *an orthodoxly conceived monotheistic god exists, an orthodoxly conceived monotheistic god is wholly good, a wholly good being would not deceive his creatures, we are an orthodoxly conceived monotheistic god's creatures, hence our senses are reliable and we do know all of the things that we ordinarily take ourselves to know*, then any propositions that Descartes uses as premises in his arguments will need to be indubitable, and any argumentative moves that he makes will also need to be beyond doubt. However, since it would be independently interesting if Descartes managed to prove the existence of an orthodoxly conceived monotheistic god from premises that are merely plausible or likely to be true, we shall not be interested in holding him to the high standards that he sets for himself.

3.3.1. A Rule about Clear and Distinct Perception

Descartes begins by claiming that the procedure by which he arrived at the Cogito reveals that all of the things that we conceive very clearly and distinctly are true. In his view, reflection on the process by which he became convinced of the indubitability of his own existence shows that anything that can be clearly and distinctly conceived must be true.

You might worry that there is some circularity here. In the end, the guarantee that clear and distinct conception delivers truth must reside in the existence of an orthodoxly conceived monotheistic god. If there were a Deceitful Demon, then it might well be that He could bring it about that you clearly and distinctly conceive things that are not true. Yet it is also true that the proof that an orthodoxly conceived monotheistic god exists relies on the principle that what one clearly and distinctly conceives is true. So Descartes' argument is not going to be accepted by someone who thinks that there might be a Deceitful Demon, and who also doubts that everything that one clearly and distinctly conceives is true.

More importantly, it does not seem right to say that reflection on the process by which Descartes became convinced of the indubitability of his own existence shows that anything that can be clearly and distinctly conceived must be true. For the Cogito is a very special kind of thought that arguably owes its indubitability to the self-refuting nature of its denial. Most of the things that we clearly and distinctly conceive – and, in particular, the claims whose truth Descartes himself shall want to deduce from this principle – do not have this character. It is not self-defeating to doubt 'evident' principles of mathematics and metaphysics – at least, not in the same sense in which it is self-defeating to doubt that one exists; so the principle concerning the truth of clear and distinct conceptions does not have the same epistemological status as the Cogito. Nonetheless, it must be conceded that we could hardly have an inquiry at all unless we supposed that clear and distinct conception leads to truth or, at any rate, to reasonable belief. If I think that clear and distinct conceptions are no more likely to be true – or deserving of belief – than unclear and indistinct conceptions, then there seems to be no point in my engaging in any sort of inquiry at all. But, in that case, how can I understand what I am doing when I do engage in such inquiry? Surely I do not suppose that I am just wasting my time?

Even if the principle about the truth of clear and distinct conceptions does not meet the requirements of the *Meditations*, it does seem to be a principle that it would be self-defeating to deny. So it seems reasonable to accept the principle, and to join Descartes in continuing his inquiry. Of course, there is still a problem about the apparent vagueness of talk of 'clarity and distinctness': perhaps the principle seems innocuous only because it has no definite content. However, let us set that kind of sceptical thought aside.

3.3.2. The Origins of Ideas

To establish the background for his proof, Descartes announces a threefold classification of the origins of *ideas*. By the word 'idea', Descartes means a mental entity that is analogous to a picture of an object. That is not to say that Descartes means that ideas are images; rather, it is to say that Descartes thinks that ideas can play a role in thought that is similar to the role that pictures play in the representation of the world. In themselves, ideas are neither true nor false; just as, in themselves, pictures are neither accurate nor inaccurate. But when it is judged that a certain idea corresponds to the way that the world is, then that judgment can be true or false; just as, when a picture is held to be a representation of a particular object or state of affairs or event, then that representation can be more or less accurate.

Furthermore, Descartes holds that ideas are ingredients of all thoughts, or states of consciousness. Perhaps some states of consciousness just involve the occurrence of ideas before the mind, for example, in imagination. But, in many cases, states of consciousness also involve an attitude towards the idea – as in judging, or willing, or fearing, or denying, or approving. Of course, it may be that there is nothing in reality that corresponds to certain ideas, for example, in a case in which one is afraid of a fictional entity such as the bogeyman; however, there will always be an idea – that is, a mental entity – that constitutes the mental object of the fear.

Descartes suggests that there are three possible sources that ideas might have: (i) they can be *innate*, in which case they will have existed in the mind for as long as the mind has existed; or (ii) they can be *adventitious*, in which case they will have been produced in the mind by some external agency; or (iii) they can be *fictitious*, in which case they will be merely the product of the mind's own inventiveness. It is not clear whether Descartes thinks that this system of classification is exclusive and/or exhaustive. However, it is important to note Descartes' insistence that one cannot tell straight off to which class particular ideas belong. In particular, that an idea comes into consciousness involuntarily – apparently as the result of the perception of an external object – is no guarantee that that idea is adventitious; for it might be that there is some faculty in the mind that gives rise to these involuntary ideas or 'sensations'. And our natural inclination to suppose that ideas 'resemble' external objects is also open to suspicion, especially in view of the various sensory illusions to which we may be subject.

3.3.3. A Scholastic Principle

Descartes supposes that it is obvious that the possession of an idea is something that needs a cause. He then adds:

> It is manifest by the natural light of reason that there must be at least as much reality in the efficient and total cause as in its effect: for whence can the effect draw its reality if not from its cause? And how could this cause communicate its reality to its effect, if it did not have it in itself? And hence it follows, not only that nothingness cannot produce anything, but also that the more perfect, that is to say that which contains in itself more reality, cannot be a consequence and dependence of the less perfect.

Concerning this passage, Williams (1978: 135) notes:

It is one of the most striking indications of the historical gap that exists between Descartes' thought and our own, despite the modern reality of much else that he writes, that he can unblinkingly accept this unintuitive and barely comprehensible principle as self-evident in the light of reason.

It must be said that it is not easy to explain what the principle means, let alone to suppose that we can see 'clearly and distinctly' that is must be true.

First of all, Descartes supposes that there are degrees of reality. Among the basic metaphysical categories, there is a series of dependencies: *modes* – non-basic properties – depend on *accidents* – basic properties; and accidents – basic properties – depend on *substances* – particular things. Moreover, within the category of substances, there is a further series of dependencies: created substances are dependent upon an infinite and independent substance, namely, an orthodoxly conceived monotheistic god. For the purposes of *Meditation III*, it is really only the second series of dependencies that matters; moreover, it is relatively clear what Descartes means when he says that an orthodoxly conceived monotheistic god has a higher degree of reality than other substances: he means that an orthodoxly conceived monotheistic god is infinite, independent, and uncreated, whereas other substances are finite, dependent, and created.

Second, Descartes supposes that the notion of degrees of reality applies also to ideas. Making use of pre-existing – and confusing – Scholastic terminology, Descartes distinguishes between the *formal reality* and the *objective reality* of ideas. The *formal reality* of an idea is the degree of reality of the independently existing object that that idea is about or of, supposing that there is such an independently existing object; the formal reality of fictitious ideas is zero, since there is no independently existing object that they are about or of. The objective reality of an idea is the degree of reality of the object of an idea, where the object of an idea is here construed as a sort of thing that might well not exist, for example, a fictitious entity. Roughly – but only roughly – the objective reality of an idea is the degree of reality that the object of that idea would have were it to exist. This is only roughly correct since it seems plausible to suppose that there can be ideas of objects that could not possibly exist, and yet that could be ranked in order of their perfection. However, we shall not need to worry about ways in which the Cartesian distinction might be modified or improved upon.

3.3.4. Constructing the Argument

Next, Descartes puts his Scholastic principle to work. From whence, he asks, does an idea derive its objective reality? Answer: From the formal reality of an independently existing object! Of course, the objective reality of one idea may be derived from the objective reality of other ideas, when new ideas are formed by the combination of old ideas; but such a regress must come to an end. And when the regress does come to an end, we must reach ideas whose objective reality is derived from independently existing objects that have at least as much formal reality.

Now, consider the ideas that I have, that is, the ideas of myself, of other human beings, of animals, of inanimate objects, of angels, and of an orthodoxly conceived monotheistic god. Ideas that represent other human beings, or animals, or angels, may be formed by combining ideas of myself, of material or inanimate things, and of an orthodoxly conceived monotheistic god. Ideas of material or inanimate things combine ideas of substance, number, duration, primary qualities – size, shape – and secondary qualities – colour, sound, heat, and taste. Ideas of substance, duration, and number derive from the idea of myself, since I am a thinking substance that persists through time, and since I can count my own ideas. Ideas of secondary qualities almost certainly arise from my own mind; and perhaps ideas of primary qualities do so as well. So I can account for the objective reality of all my ideas in terms of my own formal reality, provided that I can account for the objective reality of the idea of an orthodoxly conceived monotheistic god.

But how are we to account for the objective reality of the idea of an orthodoxly conceived monotheistic god? I do not formally have the degree of reality that objectively belongs to the idea of an orthodoxly conceived monotheistic god. For an orthodoxly conceived monotheistic god is a substance infinite, independent, all-knowing, all-powerful, and by which I myself – and any other thing that exists, if indeed there is any – have been created. Yet I am finite, dependent, limited in knowledge and power. So the objective reality of the idea of an orthodoxly conceived monotheistic god could not have arisen from my formal reality; rather, there must be an independently existing object that has as much formal reality as the objective reality of my idea of an orthodoxly conceived monotheistic god. But that is just to say that an orthodoxly conceived monotheistic god must exist, since no other object can have as much formal reality as the objective reality of my idea of an orthodoxly conceived monotheistic god.

Roughly, we may schematise the argument as follows:

1. There must be at least as much reality in any efficient and total cause as there is in the effect of that cause. (Scholastic Principle)
2. Nothing can exist (or happen) without a cause. (Further Scholastic Principle)
3. The objective reality of my idea of an orthodoxly conceived monotheistic god has a cause, say, C_1. (From 2)
4. C_1 has as much reality as my idea of an orthodoxly conceived monotheistic god. (From 1)
5. C_1 either has as much objective reality or as much formal reality as the objective reality of my idea of an orthodoxly conceived monotheistic god. (From definitions of *objective* and *formal* reality)

6. If C_1 has as much objective reality as the objective reality of my idea of an orthodoxly conceived monotheistic god, then C_1 is my idea of an orthodoxly conceived monotheistic god. (From definition of the idea of an orthodoxly conceived monotheistic god.)
7. Nothing can be its own cause. (Yet Another Scholastic Principle)
8. C_1 cannot have as much objective reality as the idea of an orthodoxly conceived monotheistic god.
9. C_1 has as much formal reality as the objective reality of my idea of an orthodoxly conceived monotheistic god. (From 5 and 8)
10. If C_1 has as much formal reality as the objective reality of my idea of an orthodoxly conceived monotheistic god, then C_1 is God. (From the definition of the idea of an orthodoxly conceived monotheistic god.)
11. C_1 is an orthodoxly conceived monotheistic god. (From 9 and 10.)

3.3.5. Objections

I shall not address all of the objections that might be lodged against this argument. However, I shall consider two of the objections that seem to be particularly worrisome. (Our earlier discussion of perfection suggests ways that one might question the assumption that the idea of an orthodoxly conceived monotheistic god with which Descartes operates is so much as coherent. But we shall not repeat that earlier discussion here.)

First, there are questions that can be asked about the further Scholastic Principles that are appealed to in this argument. These questions are of two types, namely, (i) questions about the justification that can be given for these principles, and (ii) questions about the consistency of Descartes' appeal to these principles.

As we have already noted, there are various difficulties that arise concerning the justification of the claim that nothing can exist – or happen – without a cause. This claim cannot be defended by appeal to strong principles of sufficient reason – for those strong principles are demonstrably inconsistent. But without the backing of strong principles of sufficient reason, it is quite unclear why we should accept any weak versions of that principle that would suffice to underwrite the claim to which Descartes appeals. Furthermore, despite the fact that we can find (efficient) causes for the existence – or occurrence – of many of the things with which we are acquainted, there are various classes of things for which any such claim is highly controversial. On the one hand, quantum mechanics appears to serve up instances of events that lack efficient causes. On the other hand, on libertarian conceptions of freedom, it seems that free human choices do not have efficient causes. Given these various kinds of objections, it is highly doubtful that Descartes is entitled to the claim that his further Scholastic Principles are true, let alone that they are known to be true by the natural light of reason.

Even setting aside these kinds of considerations, it is also doubtful that Descartes – or any other monotheist – can consistently endorse the

assumption that nothing can exist or happen without a cause. For monotheists almost always suppose that their god exists uncaused. Perhaps it might
be said that there is really no inconsistency here, that what the monotheist
means is that nothing other than an orthodoxly conceived monotheistic
god exists without a cause. But what reason is there to believe this modified
principle? If we are prepared to allow that there can be things that exist
without a cause, then why shouldn't we suppose that the physical universe is
an object that exists uncaused? As many non-theists have noted, arguments
for the existence of God that include a premise to the effect that every object
and event requires a cause are bound to prove too much, because the causal
principle in question can be satisfied only by an infinite causal regress, or a
circle of causes, or the like.

   Second, there is an obvious objection to Descartes' argument in the suggestion that the idea of an orthodoxly conceived monotheistic god is a purely
negative idea that can be obtained from reflection upon one's own limitations. If this suggestion is correct, then it seems that we can give a perfectly
adequate account of the objective reality of the idea of an orthodoxly conceived monotheistic god in terms of the formal reality of ourselves – for,
in that case, the objective reality of the idea of an orthodoxly conceived
monotheistic god differs only in degree but not in kind from the objective
reality of the idea of oneself.

   To meet this objection, Descartes suggests that the idea of an orthodoxly
conceived monotheistic god cannot be a purely negative idea that is obtained
by reflection upon one's own limitations:

> How would it be possible for me to know that I doubt and desire, that is to say, that
> I lack something and am not all perfect, if I did not have in me any idea of a more
> perfect being than myself, by comparison with which I know the deficiencies of my
> nature?

Furthermore, Descartes notes (i) that infinity is not merely a negative conception, since I have an idea of more reality in the infinite being than in
any finite one, and (ii) that the clearness and distinctness of the idea of an
orthodoxly conceived monotheistic god – by comparison with the unclarity
and indistinctness of, for example, the ideas of the secondary qualities – is
evidence that the idea of an orthodoxly conceived monotheistic god did not
arise within me.

   The latter two responses do not seem to be very convincing. Descartes
himself is forced to concede that we do not have an adequate idea of an
orthodoxly conceived monotheistic god as an infinitely perfect being; a
finite mind cannot have a positive apprehension of the infinite. He goes on
to say that, nonetheless, in thinking of an orthodoxly conceived monotheistic god as having in the highest degree whichever perfections I – however
inadequately – know about, as well as others of which I have no distinct conception whatsoever, I have a clearer and more distinct idea of an orthodoxly

conceived monotheistic god than I do of anything else. To me, this sounds extremely dubious: for surely the fact that I cannot have a positive apprehension of the infinite is direct evidence that I do not have a clear and distinct idea of an orthodoxly conceived monotheistic god. At the very least, we need to be told a lot more about what counts as a 'clear and distinct' idea: in the absence of a fairly spectacular story, it seems very likely that Descartes' claim is simply unsupportable.

The first response is also unconvincing, in a way that does enormous damage to Descartes' view. Given that our ideas of perfection and infinity are not adequate, it seems that what we have are merely relative grasps of these notions. That is, we understand that some things are less perfect than others, and that some things have fewer limitations, or limitations to a lesser extent, than do other things – and then, by an act of imagination, we form the merely relative conception of an entity that is more perfect than all other entities, and that is subject to fewer limitations than any other entity. It is easy – though perhaps nonetheless incorrect – to suppose that an entity that is more perfect than all other entities must be an entirely perfect entity, and that an entity that is subject to fewer limitations than any other entity must be an entity that is subject to no limitations. Consequently, it is easy to see how one might arrive at the idea of an entirely perfect entity or an entity that is subject to no limitations, beginning with the merely relative conception of an entity that is more perfect than all other entities and subject to fewer limitations than any other entity, and making a natural – though admittedly not obviously correct – further assumption. But if we can arrive at the idea of an orthodoxly conceived monotheistic god in this perfectly natural way from reflection on our own limitations, then, even if the various Scholastic Principles to which Descartes appeals are correct, there is still no adequate justification for the claim that the objective reality of our idea of an orthodoxly conceived monotheistic god can be due only to the formal reality of an entity that corresponds to that idea.

In sum: (a) Descartes' view of the nature of our idea of an orthodoxly conceived monotheistic god is inconsistent, since he needs to say both that it is not entirely adequate and that it is not merely negative or relative, and (b) there is a very plausible story that can be told about the acquisition or invention of that kind of idea of an orthodoxly conceived monotheistic god that it seems most reasonable to suppose that we have, that needs to make no assumption of the actual existence of an object that corresponds to that idea.

3.3.6. A Related Argument

There is an argument, closely related to the one that we have just been criticising, that occurs towards the end of *Meditation III*. There, Descartes begins his discussion with the following question: *whether I, who have this idea of [an orthodoxly conceived monotheistic god], could exist if there were no [orthodoxly conceived monotheistic god]*? Descartes considers four positive replies that might be made to this question: (i) that one might have created oneself; (ii) that one might have always existed, and hence never have been created by anything; (iii) that one might have been created by lesser beings than an orthodoxly conceived monotheistic god – for example, by one's parents – that were in turn created by lesser beings than an orthodoxly conceived monotheistic god – that is, one's grandparents – and so on, *ad infinitum*; and (iv) that one might have been created by a committee of beings, each of which possesses some of the attributes of an orthodoxly conceived monotheistic god, but none of which possesses all of the attributes of an orthodoxly conceived monotheistic god – and hence none of which actually is an orthodoxly conceived monotheistic god. Descartes argues that none of these replies can be sustained.

Against the *first* suggestion – that is, the suggestion that one might have created oneself – Descartes claims that, if one had created oneself, then one would surely have made oneself an entirely perfect entity, since it would have been easier for one to do this than to make oneself the imperfect entity that one manifestly is. This seems to me to be a most peculiar response. If there is anything that is manifest by the natural light of reason, it is surely that nothing can create itself: no being can bring itself into existence. Rather than speculate about the properties that one would have given oneself if one had created oneself, it seems to me that Descartes would be on much safer ground if he were simply to dismiss this suggestion out of hand.

Against the *second* suggestion – that is, the suggestion that one has always existed – Descartes says:

> It is quite clear and evident to all those who will attentively consider the nature of time, that a substance, in order to be conserved in each moment of its duration, needs the same power and action that would be necessary to produce and create it afresh, if it did not yet exist. . . . It is only necessary therefore for me to ask myself if I possess any power or virtue capable of acting in such a way that I, who exist now, shall exist in the future: for, since I am nothing but a thinking thing . . . if such a power resided in me, indeed I should at the very least be conscious of it; but I am conscious of no such power, and thereby, I know evidently that I depend on some being different from myself.

This response suffers from various difficulties. First, the 'clear and evident' principle is surely not well described. Why shouldn't one who 'attentively considers the nature of time' suppose, instead, that anything that exists will continue to exist unless it is acted upon by a destructive power of the same magnitude as that required to produce and create it? One might suggest that the various conservation principles of contemporary physics provide some support for this alternative claim – but, even without any such further argument, it seems clear that we have been given no good reason to accept the principle upon which Descartes' response relies. Second, it is doubtful that Descartes' response would seem compelling to anyone who thinks that a thinking thing can have unconscious parts, for example, of the kind suggested in Freudian theories of the unconscious. If the 'power and action' that Descartes requires could emanate from such a source, then the causal principle to which he appeals is insufficient to establish that he has not always existed.[11] Third, even setting aside considerations about the unconscious, it is far from obvious that every power possessed by a mind must be available to direct inspection by that mind. Suppose that you set me a difficult mathematical problem, surely, there is no reason to assume that I can tell, just by introspection, whether or not I have the power to solve the problem.

Nonetheless, it seems to me that one does have perfectly good reasons for denying that one has always existed. It is – I think – true that, on solipsistic or idealistic hypotheses, it is quite hard to see why one should not suppose that one has always existed; after all, that assumption is perfectly consistent with all of the evidence from experience that one possesses. Consequently, it is only by setting aside the Cartesian contention that one is essentially only a thinking thing that one is likely to get an adequate response to the claim that one has always existed. But one *should* set this Cartesian contention – and correlative solipsistic and idealistic hypotheses – aside.

Against the *third* suggestion – that is, the suggestion that one has been created by lesser beings than an orthodoxly conceived monotheistic god – Descartes objects that any being that could have created you would also need to have the idea of an orthodoxly conceived monotheistic god, and so would stand no less in need of a further cause that explains why *it* has the idea of an orthodoxly conceived monotheistic god. Moreover, Descartes insists that there could not be merely an infinite regress of such lesser beings, each of which possesses the idea of an orthodoxly conceived monotheistic god, for, even if there were such an infinite regress, there would still be something in need of explanation, namely, why there is any being at all that possesses the idea of an orthodoxly conceived monotheistic god. Since this suggestion stands or falls with the more elaborate argument from the earlier part of *Meditation III*, we need not give any further discussion of it here.

Against the *fourth* suggestion – that is, that one might have been created by a committee of beings, each of which possesses some of the attributes of an orthodoxly conceived monotheistic god, but none of which possesses all of the attributes of an orthodoxly conceived monotheistic god – Descartes objects that *unity*, *simplicity*, and *inseparability* are amongst the perfections

---

[11] Following the lead of Norton (1968), there has been some discussion in the literature of the question of whether Descartes' admission that he might have 'unknown faculties' undermines the argument for the existence of an orthodoxly conceived monotheistic god in *Meditation III*. Plainly enough, the same kinds of issues arise for the possibility that is mentioned in the main text; it may be that, on Descartes' own admission, he cannot rule out the possibility that he has the power to conserve himself in existence.

that are attributed to an orthodoxly conceived monotheistic god by one's idea of an orthodoxly conceived monotheistic god. However, if we suppose that we can form the idea of a being that possesses all perfections by putting together our independent conceptions of the various individual conceptions, then it seems that creation by a committee of beings might well suffice for the purpose at hand. After all, it is not at all plausible to suppose that the ideas of *unity*, *simplicity*, and *inseparability* can be obtained only by way of the idea of an orthodoxly conceived monotheistic god, indeed, these ideas are plainly ones that can be derived by reflection on the knowledge that is obtained in the first two *Meditations*. Unless there is a perfection that could be possessed only by an orthodoxly conceived monotheistic god, and not by anything else – whether member of a committee of creative beings or not – then it seems that Descartes' objection to this suggestion fails. At the very least, some further argument is required to establish that the parts of Descartes' idea of an orthodoxly conceived monotheistic god do not trace back to distinct sources in beings, each of which manifest some – but only some – of the perfections that are combined together in the idea of an orthodoxly conceived monotheistic god.

Apart from the already noted difficulties that face this new Cartesian argument for the claim that only an orthodoxly conceived monotheistic god could be the ultimate source of my idea of an orthodoxly conceived monotheistic god, it is also worth noting that Descartes' argument relies upon the assumption that he has discussed all of the plausible alternatives to the claim that his existence, given that he possesses the idea of an orthodoxly conceived monotheistic god, must be due to creation by an orthodoxly conceived monotheistic god. If, for example, we could suppose that the existence of the physical universe has no explanation, even though my possession of the idea of an orthodoxly conceived monotheistic god is perfectly understandable given the existence of the physical universe, then there would not be so much as *prima facie* reason to suppose that Descartes has a compelling case. But – as we in effect noted in Oppy (2006) – the kind of story told by Lavine (1994) makes it very plausible to suppose that one can give a naturalistic account of the origins of the concept of infinity. Furthermore, once we have a naturalistic account of the origins of the concept of the infinite, we can then easily construct a naturalistic account of the origins of the concept of a being that is infinitely powerful, infinitely wise, infinitely good, and so forth. Given these points, the prospects for rehabilitation of this Cartesian cosmological argument are surely very, very slender indeed.

3.3.7. Concluding Remarks

The argument of *Meditation III* fails. From the point of view of the overall project of the *Meditations*, the argument fails simply because it requires assumptions that are highly dubitable and not, in any sense, recognisable as true by the unaided light of natural reason. However, even from a less demanding standpoint, the argument can be seen to be quite unconvincing: it is easy to explain how we come to have the idea of an orthodoxly conceived monotheistic god without adverting to the actual existence of an orthodoxly conceived monotheistic god.

3.4. LEIBNIZ'S ARGUMENT

In his little essay "On the Ultimate Origination of Things" (1697), Leibniz presents and defends a cosmological argument based on a strong version of the principle of sufficient reason. There is at least some reason to suppose that the argument that Leibniz defends takes something like the following form:

1. There are contingent beings, that is, beings that do not provide a sufficient reason for their own existence.
2. There is a sufficient reason for everything that exists or happens. In particular, for each being, there is a (not necessarily distinct) being that provides a sufficient reason for the existence of that being.
3. A being is necessary iff it is its own sufficient reason.
4. A circle of contingent beings, each of which provides a sufficient reason for the next, requires a sufficient reason for its existence, that is, a sufficient reason for the existence of that circle of contingent beings.
5. A sufficient reason for a circle of contingent beings, each of which provides a sufficient reason for the next, cannot be a member of that circle.
6. An infinite series of contingent beings, each of which provides a sufficient reason for the next, requires a sufficient reason, that is, a sufficient reason for the existence of that infinite series of contingent beings.
7. A sufficient reason for an infinite series of contingent beings, each of which provides a sufficient reason for the next, cannot be a member of that series.
8. (Hence) There is – and, indeed, must be – a necessary being that constitutes the sufficient reason for the existence of contingent beings.

If something like this is the argument that Leibniz means to defend, then it faces various kinds of severe difficulties.

Perhaps the most pressing difficulty is that, at least at first sight, the argument seems to be invalid. Suppose that we follow Leibniz in imagining that the book on the *Elements of Geometry* is eternal, one copy always being made from another. Then, given premises 7 and 8, we shall be obliged to conclude that there is something that explains the eternity of this book: there is a sufficient reason for the infinite series of copies of the *Elements of Geometry*. But there is nothing in the example that demands that the explanation must advert to a necessary being, that is, to something that is its own sufficient reason. Suppose, then, that an explanation can be found in a contingent being. That being may in turn be part of a circle or infinite chain of beings, each of which explains the next, but when we postulate a further being to explain the existence of this circle or chain, we need be no closer to establishing that there is a necessary being. Unless we have some kind of principle of mereological aggregation – for example, that any fusion of beings is itself a being – we can easily describe a model in which all of the premises of the Leibnizian argument are true, and yet in which the conclusion of this argument is false.[12]

Apart from questions concerning the validity of the argument now under discussion, there are obvious questions that arise about the acceptability of some of the premises. As we noted in Oppy (2006), it seems to be incoherent to suppose that there could be anything – being, fact, state of affairs, or whatever – that is its own sufficient reason. Consequently, while the definition of 'necessary being' with which Leibniz works may be unexceptionable, it is also trivial: there can be no necessary beings on Leibniz' account of 'necessary being'. Moreover, as we also argue in Oppy (forthcoming), the principle of sufficient reason that Leibniz enunciates is plainly unacceptably strong: it cannot be the case that there is no brute contingency in the world, if there is contingency at all.

It is, perhaps, instructive to compare the argument that I have attributed to Leibniz with the arguments that I attributed to Aquinas. Aquinas tries to argue from the instantiation of certain explanatory relations – for example, that *a* is an efficient cause of *b* – to the conclusion that there is exactly one unexplained explainer, by way of a key assumption about the impossibility of an infinite regress of explanations. These arguments fail for various reasons, not least that there is no way that their premises can guarantee that there is just one unexplained explainer. Leibniz tries to argue from the instantiation of certain conditional explanatory relations – for example, that *a* is a sufficient reason for *b* provided that there is a sufficient reason for *a* – to the conclusion that there is exactly one self-explaining explainer, by way of a key assumption about the universality of categorical explanatory relations. This argument fails for various reasons, not least that the premises fail to guarantee that there is just one self-explaining explainer. Aquinas' arguments face the difficulty of justifying the claim that there cannot be an infinite regress of explanations; Leibniz' argument faces the difficulty that the principle

---

[12] It isn't clear to me whether Leibniz simply assumes that the world – 'the aggregate of the chain of states or series of things' – is a thing to which the principle of sufficient reason applies, or whether he supposes that the kind of argument that I have attributed to him in the main text establishes that this is so. If Leibniz does assume a strong principle of mereological composition, then there is good reason to suppose that the argument in the main text does not accurately capture the argument that he in fact gives. Nonetheless, some of the further objections that we go on to make clearly apply to the claims that Leibniz makes, quite apart from considerations about principles of mereological composition.

that he appeals to in order to rule out an infinite regress of explanations is too strong to be acceptable. It is an interesting question where one might turn to look for a plausible set of premises that are strong enough to yield the conclusion that there is a unique 'first principle', and yet that are not so strong as to entail that there is no contingency in the world.

Since, as I have hinted at various places, it is controversial whether the argument that I have been discussing ought to be attributed to Leibniz, it will perhaps be useful to close with a discussion of a different argument that has been thought to be contained in the writings bequeathed to us by Leibniz. This argument runs as follows:

1. There is a sufficient reason why everything that is is so and not otherwise. Wherever there is a plurality of logically possible alternatives, there is a sufficient reason why the alternative realised is the one realised.
2. Sufficient reasons are either causes or choices or both.
3. Of any cause, as distinguished from choice, one can always legitimately ask what its cause is.
4. (Hence) Causes cannot be ultimately sufficient reasons. (From 3)
5. The actual universe is not the only (logically) possible universe.
6. (Hence) The sufficient reason for the existence of the actual universe is a choice. (From 1, 2, 4, and 5)
7. Choices are sufficient reasons only insofar as they are rational choices.
8. A choice is rational insofar as it is a choice of the best; and insofar as limitations of power and knowledge are imposed on the chooser, the choice is rational only relative to these limitations and therefore requires further explanation.
9. (Hence) An absolutely rational choice, requiring no further explanation, is a choice of the best, made by a being that is subject to no limitations. (From 7 and 8)
10. (Hence) God exists. (From 6 and 9)

Several features of this argument are of interest.

First, the principle of sufficient reason that is appealed to as the first premise seems to me to be indefensible, for the reasons given in Oppy (2006) I do not believe that any principle as strong as this one can be reasonably accepted.

Second, if we accept that one can always ask for a further cause when one is presented with a cause, then why should we not accept that one can always ask for a further cause or choice when one is presented with a choice? If agent *A* makes choice *C* at time *t* in circumstances *S*, there is at least *prima facie* reason to think that there is always room to ask: why did *A* make *that* choice at that time in those circumstances, rather than some other choice that might have been made instead? Whatever reasons one might have for supposing that choices are not causes, there seems to me to be no prospect of defending the claim that choices differ from causes in being more obviously good candidates for endpoints of demands for explanation.

Third, it is quite unclear why we should suppose that only *rational* choices are sufficient reasons. Given that we have already assumed that choices are not causes, and that all sufficient reasons are either choices or causes, it seems that this assumption will lead to the conclusion that there is no sufficient reason for irrational choices, whence, the principle of sufficient reason adverted to in the first premise is shown to be false. Perhaps one might try insisting that irrational choices are causes, but that response seems both implausible and entirely *ad hoc*. Given that causes are sufficient reasons, it seems quite incredible to suppose that irrational choices are not sufficient reasons.

Fourth, it is quite unclear why choices of the best should be held to require no further explanation, while choices of less than the best do require further explanation. It seems to me that, no matter what choice one makes, there is a plausible candidate explanation of that choice in terms of one's beliefs and preferences. Whether or not one makes a good choice – for example, a choice that has the best outcomes, or that conforms to objective moral prescriptions, or that is the choice that one's fully informed rational self would want for one to choose – depends upon the preferences that one has, and the information that one is able to bring to bear when one weighs up the alternative courses of action that are open to one. Of course, this Humean conception of choice might be contested; but, at the very least, it is worth observing that the denial of this Humean conception of choice is extremely controversial: there is little prospect for claiming that an argument that relies on the denial of this Humean conception of choice is a successful argument for the existence of God.

Fifth, it is quite unclear why we should suppose that a being that is subject to no limitations can make absolutely rational choices, particularly if we grant the assumption that a rational choice is always a choice of the best. Suppose that there is a being, U, that is subject to no limitations. Consider a world w and a time t at which U is to make a choice between possible actions. For simplicity, suppose that there are just two possible actions A and B between which U is to choose. Given that A and B are possible actions, there is a world w' that shares the history of world w to t and in which U chooses to perform A; and there is a world w'' that shares the history of world w to t and in which U chooses to perform B. Since the worlds w' and w'' share the history of world w to t, these are both worlds in which U is subject to no limitations, and in which A and B have the same value that they have in w. Since U chooses A in w', it follows that A is the best option in w, and, in particular, it follows that A is better than B in w; since U chooses B in w'', it follows that B is the best option in w, and, in particular, it follows that B is better than A in w. Contradiction. If there is a being that is subject to no limitations, and if it always does the best, then it cannot be the case that it chooses to do the best, at least on a libertarian conception of choice.

Sixth, as Voltaire famously insisted, it is *prima facie* most implausible to suppose that this is the best of all possible worlds that a perfect and unlimited being could choose to make, given that every feature of the world is ultimately to be explained in terms of a choice that is made by this being. On the assumptions that are made in the above argument, for any state of the world, there is a series of why questions that leads ultimately to the explanation that the world is in that state because the best possible world is one in which the world is in that particular state. While – as we shall see in our discussion of arguments from evil – it might not be utterly implausible to claim that a monotheistic god could do no better than to make the world that we inhabit, it does seem to be massively implausible to suppose that the world that we inhabit is the very best of all possible worlds.

Once again, I do not suppose that anyone should think that the argument that we have been considering is a successful argument for the existence of a monotheistic god.

3.5. MEYER AND THE AXIOM OF CHOICE

Meyer (1987) sets out a cosmological argument that is explicitly intended to update the argument of the Second Way in the light of more sophisticated views about the nature of efficient causation. The argument runs as follows.

(1) There is a universal set V of all items.

(2) V is partially ordered by the relation A of causal anteriority.

(3) Every chain S in the set V has a lower bound under A.

(4) If X is a partially ordered set under a relation R, and every chain S in X has a lower bound under R, then X has a minimal element.

(5) (Hence) There are minimal elements in V under A, and every element in V has a causally anterior minimal element.

(6) V is a directed set under the relation A.

(7) If D is a directed set under a partial order R, and every chain C in D has a lower bound under R, then D has exactly one minimal element.

(8) (Hence) There is exactly one minimal element G in V under A, and G is causally anterior to every element in V.

Before we turn to an analysis of this argument, we need to explain some of the key terms that are used in setting it forth.

Items are whatever it is that efficient causation relates: events, states of affairs, objects, or what have you. While it is a controversial question what exactly it is that efficient causation relates, we don't need to decide this question for the purposes of Meyer's argument. The assumption that there is a set of items might be thought to be controversial; however, as Meyer says, one could reformulate the argument using only the assumption that items form a proper class. The assumption that items form a set is merely a matter of convenience; nothing substantive hangs on it.

The relation A of *causal anteriority* is defined on pairs of items: Axy just in case x is causally anterior to y. For the purposes of Meyer's argument, it is assumed that A is reflexive, transitive, and antisymmetric, so that it constitutes a *partial order*. The assumption of antisymmetry rules out causal loops. The assumption of reflexivity, while holding that each item is causally anterior to itself, does not amount to the assumption that each item causes itself: for only items to which there is nothing that is causally anterior are so much as candidates for being self-caused. Thus, it seems to me that the only thing that is controversial in the second premise is the assumption that causal anteriority is anti-symmetric.

The idea behind the third premise is that, for every causal sequence C, there is an item I that is causally anterior to every item J in C. This is a very strong assumption, but – as Meyer insists – it is not so strong as to obviously beg the main question at issue. One cannot get to the interim conclusions at line 5, from the first three premises alone. If one is prepared to reject the axiom of choice – and hence to reject that version of the axiom of choice that is presented in the fourth premise – then there is no satisfactory way of completing the proof. (Of course, we recall from Oppy (2006) that the fourth premise is just Zorn's Lemma, that is, that it is a well-known formulation of the axiom of choice.)

A set S that is partially ordered under a relation R is *directed* (down) iff, for any two elements J and K in S, there exists an item I that is a lower bound for both J and K. Thus, the premise at line 6 says that any pair of items has a common causal ancestry.

As Meyer points out, one of the advantages of his cosmological argument is that it is uncontroversially valid, whereas the arguments of Aquinas and Leibniz have premises that are insufficient to yield their alleged conclusions, there is no doubt that Meyer's premises do entail that there are first elements under the relation of causal anteriority. Moreover, as Meyer also points out, there is at least some reason to suppose that causal sequences are 'deeply infinitistic' in the way that his formulation allows. "Consider . . . the rolling of a ball across the floor . . . . If we view this situation from the viewpoint of the most casual physics, the ball occupies a succession of points $\langle x_0, y_0 \rangle, \ldots,$ $\langle x_i, y_i \rangle, \ldots$ on an appropriate plane, where x_i and y_i are real numbers. The ball's occupying any of these points is, presumptively, an item in a causal sequence. Yet this ordering is not of the 1, 2, 3 variety. To the contrary, since the real numbers are densely ordered, there is between any two distinct pairs $\langle x_i, y_i \rangle$ and $\langle x_k, y_k \rangle$ a third pair $\langle x_j, y_j \rangle$" (Meyer (1987: 346)). Given recent enthusiasm for *kalām* cosmological arguments – and, in particular, for arguments that deny 'actual' infinities – there is perhaps a little irony in the fact that an argument that explicitly appeals to a 'deeply infinitistic' assumption is an improvement on more traditional formulations of causal cosmological arguments.

Despite the advantages of Meyer's argument, there are some disadvantages that should also be noted. While acceptance of the axiom of choice is plausibly a very small price to pay for securing the validity of a causal cosmological argument, the other difficulties that arise in the arguments of Aquinas and Leibniz persist. In particular, while the axiom of choice can help in securing first elements under the relation of causal anteriority, this axiom provides no help in securing the further requirement that there be exactly one such first element. Given that there is plausibly no good empirical support for the claim that V is a directed set under the relation A, it is hard to see how there could be any satisfying non-question-begging argument in support of this assumption. Moreover – as Meyer himself explicitly acknowledges – there is nothing in the considerations that he presents that provides new reason to suppose that causal anteriority is antisymmetric, or to suppose that for every causal sequence C, there is an item I that is causally anterior to every item J in C (his version of the claim that everything that happens has a cause). As we have already noted, it is very hard to find non-question-begging support for either of these controversial claims.

3.6. KOONS AND CONTINGENCY

Koons (1997, 2001) provides a very interesting new cosmological argument that incorporates features of previous arguments from causation and contingency. One advantage of Koons's formulation is that it involves an explicit statement of the mereological principles, modal principles, and non-monotonic logical principles that provide the theoretical background to the argument.

Koons's argument is framed against the background of a 'modal mereology' of facts. On the one hand, the argument assumes that there is a 'fixed domain of possible facts': the very same facts are possible in each possible world. On the other hand, the argument assumes that facts obey mereological principles of composition: aggregation of facts is a species of conjunction.

The background modal logic for Koons's argument is a quantified version of T. In this logic, we have both the Barcan principle and the converse Barcan principle. Since the Barcan principle and the converse Barcan principle are not plausible in the case of individuals – surely there are possible worlds in which there exist individuals that do not in fact exist, and surely there are possible worlds in which individuals that in fact exist have no existence – this requirement makes it clear that the variables in Koons's argument can range only over facts.

The mereological principles upon which Koons relies are the following:

1_M. x is a part of y iff anything that overlaps x overlaps y.

2_M. If x is a fact of type ϕ, then there is an aggregate or sum of all of the possible facts of type ϕ. $(\exists x \phi(x) \rightarrow (\exists y)(\forall z)(Ozy \leftrightarrow (\exists u)(\phi(u)\&Ouz)))$

3_M. x is identical to y iff x is a part of y and y is a part of x.

4_M. If x is a part of y, then necessarily, if y obtains, x obtains.

Furthermore, Koons introduces the following definition: a fact x is *wholly contingent* iff x obtains and no fact that is part of x obtains necessarily.

Koons's argument also relies upon some fundamental assumptions about causation. While he treats causation as primitive 'for the purposes of this argument', Koons notes that he supposes that causation can be reduced to modality. The principles that Koons assumes are the following three:

1_C. If x causes y, then x and y both obtain.

2_C. If x causes y, then x does not overlap with y.

3_C. Every wholly contingent fact has a cause.

Apart from these assumptions, Koons also claims that causes do not necessitate their effects: 'it is quite possible for C to be in every sense the cause of E, even though it was possible for C to occur without being accompanied by E' (1997: 196). According to Koons, the fact that causes are not sufficient for their effects makes it possible for him to embrace an indeterministic theory of human freedom, while nonetheless maintaining that human choices have causes.

Finally, Koons's argument relies on an assumption about defeasible or non-monotonic reasoning. When we stated principle 3_C above, we didn't make it explicit that we are committing ourselves only to the claim that *normally*, a wholly contingent fact has a cause. The causal principle is a 'default or defeasible' rule: 'any given wholly contingent fact has a cause unless some positive reason can be given for thinking that the fact in question is an exception to the rule' (1997: 197).

With these preliminaries out of the way, we can move on to the argument itself. Koons begins by proving two lemmas.

The first of these lemmas says that all the parts of a necessary fact are themselves necessary. This is proved as follows. Since T is a normal modal logic, it includes the principle that if it is necessary that if A then B, then, if it is necessary that A, it is necessary that B. Moreover, 4_M says that if x is a part of y, then, it is necessary that if y obtains, then x obtains. So we have that, if y is a necessary fact, and x is a part of y, then it is necessary that x obtains.

The second of these initial lemmas says that every contingent fact has a wholly contingent part. This is proved as follows. Suppose that a is a contingent fact. If a is wholly contingent, then a has itself as a wholly contingent part. If a is not wholly contingent, then, by definition, a has a necessary part. So, by 2_M, there is a fact $\hat{y}(y \sqsubseteq a \& \square Oy)$ that consists of the aggregate of all of the necessary parts of a. Since a is contingent, a is not itself part of $\hat{y}(y \sqsubseteq a \& \square Oy)$. Hence, by 1_M, there is a b that overlaps a but that does not overlap $\hat{y}(y \sqsubseteq a \& \square Oy)$. So it follows that there is a part c of a that is not part of $\hat{y}(y \sqsubseteq a \& \square Oy)$. Suppose that d is a part of c. Then d is a part of a, but d does not overlap $\hat{y}(y \sqsubseteq a \& \square Oy)$. So d is not necessary. But d was chosen arbitrarily. So there is no part of c that is necessary. So c is wholly contingent. So a – an arbitrarily chosen contingent fact – has a wholly contingent part.

Let C be the aggregate of all wholly contingent facts. Koons notes that, if there are any wholly contingent facts, then it follows from 2_M that a fact overlaps C iff that fact overlaps a wholly contingent fact.

Koons next proves a third lemma, that if there are any contingent facts, then C is a wholly contingent fact. This is proved as follows. Suppose that there is a contingent fact. Then, by the second lemma, there is a wholly contingent fact, since any contingent fact has a wholly contingent part. To show that C is wholly contingent, we need to show that C has no necessary parts. So, suppose that a is a part of C. Since a is a part of C, a overlaps C. Hence, a overlaps b, where b is a wholly contingent part of C. Since a and b overlap, they have a part d in common. But because b is wholly contingent, this means that d is contingent. By the first lemma, if a were necessary, then d would be necessary. So a is contingent. Hence, an arbitrarily chosen part of C is contingent. Whence C is wholly contingent.

We are almost done. By 3_C and the third lemma, if there are any contingent facts, then C has a cause. Hence, by 2_C, if there are any contingent facts, then C has a cause that does not overlap C. But every contingent fact overlaps C. (Why? Suppose a is a contingent fact. By the second lemma, a has a wholly contingent part, b. But, by 2_M, and the definition of C, b and C overlap.) By 1_C, any cause of C must obtain. So C is caused to obtain by a necessary fact. If there are any contingent facts, then C – the sum of all wholly contingent facts – is caused to obtain by a necessary fact.

Before we move on to consider what might follow from the claim that, if there are any contingent facts, then C – the sum of all wholly contingent facts – is caused to obtain by a necessary fact, we should pause to assess the argument to this point. It seems to me that there are three main ways in which Koons's argument to this point is open to challenge.

First, it seems to me that it is highly controversial to suppose that possible facts obey the mereological principles to which Koons supposes them to be subject. The primary difficulty is not, I think, with the idea that, if a fact is conjunctive, then we may suppose that the conjuncts of the conjunctive fact are parts of that fact – though even here one might have worries about the idea that non-sentential entities could be properly said to have *conjuncts*. Rather, the primary difficulty concerns the relationship between the alleged part-hood relation and entailment. It is presently a fact that I am sitting in my room in the Menzies building typing away at my word processor. What are the factive parts of this fact? Unless we suppose that the factive parts of this fact are whatever facts are entailed by this fact, how can we so much as set about trying to establish what are the factive parts of this fact? (It is not so immediately clear that there is a difficulty in investigating the non-factive parts of a fact. It may seem plausible to suppose that I, and my room, and my word processor, and the Menzies building are all non-factive parts of the fact that I am sitting in my room in the Menzies building typing away at my word processor. But even if this is plausible, it is no help at all in answering the question about the factive parts of this fact, that is, the question about which other facts are part of this fact.)

If we suppose that factive part-hood for facts is explained in terms of entailment, then, of course, Koons's argument collapses, since any necessary fact is then part of each contingent fact. In the face of this threat, it seems to me to be reasonable to ask for a more detailed theory of factive part-hood than has been provided thus far. Of course, it may be that there is such a theory to be had: perhaps, for example, it can be maintained that the fact that I am sitting in my room in the Menzies building typing away at my word processor is an *atomic* fact, and hence one that has no proper parts. However, it seems to me that one needn't be an unreconstructed positivist in order to take the view that the lack of a clear account of factive part-hood undermines the claim that, as it stands, Koons's argument is a convincing argument for the conclusion that, if there are any contingent facts, then C – the sum of all wholly contingent facts – is caused to obtain by a necessary fact.

Second, it seems to me to be highly controversial to suppose that facts are causally related to one another. Koons claims that 'in this context' – that is, in the context of his proof – 'there is no clear reason to distinguish . . . between facts, events, and states of affairs, so long as each of these is thought of as concrete parts of the world' (196). However, against Koons's claim that events are merely 'thick, complex facts', it seems to me that there are fairly strong *prima facie* grounds for supposing that events and facts belong to distinct ontological categories. Indeed, if we consider Koons's examples of alleged 'thick, complex facts' – namely, the death of Caesar and the Civil War – one might wonder how one could suppose that these presumptively complicated events are properly described as thick, complex facts. Consider the fact that Caesar died. If this is a thick, complex fact, then presumably that's because it has many, complicated factive parts. But – to return to our previous worry – what could these many and complicated factive parts be? There is, after all, no evidence of *conjunction* in the claim that Caesar died. It seems right to me to suppose that an event with an apparently atomic description can be thick and complex – no doubt this is true of the Civil War – but it is much less obvious that a fact with an apparently atomic description can be thick and complex, particularly if facts have factive parts in the way that Koons's argument requires. At the very least, we need to be given much more than Koons gives us to be justified in assuming that it is facts rather than events that are the relata of causal relations.[13]

Third, as I have argued elsewhere,[14] it seems to me to be just wrong to suppose that one can satisfactorily defend the role that the claim that every wholly contingent event has a cause has in this argument by suggesting that this claim is a default or defeasible principle of reasoning. Koons (1997: 196) writes:

Even though we have excellent empirical evidence for the generalisation that wholly contingent facts have causes, it is hard to see how any amount of data could settle conclusively the question of whether or not this generalisation admits of exceptions. This is a legitimate worry, but I would response by insisting that, at the very least, our experience warrants adopting the causal principle as a default or defeasible rule. This means that, in the absence of evidence to the contrary, we may infer, about any particular wholly contingent fact, that it has a cause. This is, however, all that is needed for the cosmological argument to be rationally compelling. The burden will be shifted to the agnostic, who must garner evidence of a positive sort for the proposition that the cosmos really is an exception to the rule. Merely pointing out the defeasible nature of the inference does not constitute a cogent rebuttal.

There are many different comments that one might make about these claims, but perhaps the most important is the following. Suppose that C is brought about, that is, suppose that it is a fact that C is brought about. If this fact were necessary, then the obtaining of C would be necessary, contradicting the claim that C is (wholly) contingent. However, if the fact that C is brought about were contingent, then, on Koons's own principles, it would follow that this fact has a part that is wholly contingent. That is, the fact that C and the fact that C is brought about would overlap. But, by 2$_C$, the fact that C is brought about is wholly distinct from the fact that C – if 'causes and effects are separate existences', then the obtaining of C and the causing of C to obtain must be 'separate existences'. So, on Koons's own principles, it seems that we can conclude that C cannot be brought about.

I take it that what this little argument shows is that we cannot accept the generalisation that every contingent fact has a cause *even* as a defeasible or default generalisation in Koons's sense. The *most* that we could be warranted in allowing – all other considerations aside – is that, normally, a wholly contingent fact *other than* C has a cause. But, given this principle, we simply

---

[13] It is worth noting that some of Koons's assumptions appear to be more controversial for events than they appear for facts. Consider, for example, 2$_M$ and 2$_C$. It is not uncontroversial to suppose that, if there are φ events, then there is an event that is the sum of all of the φ events; and neither is it uncontroversial to suppose that if an event C causes an event E, then C and E do not overlap.

[14] See Oppy (1999) and Oppy (2004b). I shall not here repeat the criticisms that I made of Koons's argument in those earlier papers. Nonetheless, I continue to believe that those criticisms are substantially correct.

cannot reach the conclusion that if there are any contingent facts, then C – the sum of all wholly contingent facts – is caused to obtain by a necessary fact.

Even if we did accept that Koons's argument establishes that, if there are any contingent facts, then C – the sum of all wholly contingent facts – is caused to obtain by a necessary fact, it is not clear why we should suppose that this conclusion has any religious significance. If anything, the conclusion of Koons's cosmological argument seems to be even further removed from the claim that an orthodoxly conceived monotheistic god exists than are the conclusions of Aquinas' Five Ways. While Koons does offer further arguments that are intended to show that his proof contributes to the task of establishing that an orthodoxly conceived monotheistic god exists, I do not need to advance further criticisms of those arguments here – for, if the considerations that I have advanced in the present section are correct, then Koons's argument does not even succeed in establishing that we have defeasible reason to suppose that, if there are any contingent facts, then C – the sum of all wholly contingent facts – is caused to obtain by a necessary fact.[15]

3.7. GALE, PRUSS, AND 'WEAK' SUFFICIENT REASON

Gale and Pruss (1999) offer an interesting cosmological argument that they claim improves upon traditional cosmological arguments such as that defended by Leibniz because it relies only upon a 'weak' version of the principle of sufficient reason. Before we can set out this argument, we need to give some definitions and to set out some preliminary assumptions.

Definition 1: A possible world is a maximal compossible conjunction of abstract propositions.

Definition 2: The Big Conjunctive Fact (BCF) for a possible world is the conjunction of all of the propositions that would be true if that world were actual.

Definition 3: The Big Conjunctive Contingent Fact (BCCF) for a possible world is the conjunction of all of the contingent propositions that would be true if the world were actual.

Assumption 1: For any proposition p and any world W, the BCF for W either contains p, or the negation of p, but not both.

Assumption 2: For any proposition F, and any world W, if F is in W's BCF, then there is some possible world W^* and proposition G such that W^*'s BCF contains F, and G, and the proposition that G explains F. (Weak Principle of Sufficient Reason, or W-PSR)

---

[15] I discuss Koons's corollaries in Oppy (1999). Koons (2001) responds to my discussion. I hope to examine Koons's responses to my criticisms on some other occasion.

The proof runs as follows:

1. If F_1 is the BCCF for a world W_1, and F_2 is the BCCF for a world W_2, and $F_1 = F_2$, then $W_1 = W_2$. (By Definition 1 and Definition 3)
2. @ is the BCCF for the actual world. (Definition)
3. For any proposition F, and any world W, if F is in W's BCF, then there is some possible world W^* and proposition G such that W's BCF contains F, and G, and the proposition that G explains F. (W-PSR)
4. (Hence) There is a possible world W' and a proposition # such that the BCF for W' contains @, and #, and the proposition that # explains @. (From 2 and 3)
5. W' = the actual world. (From 1, Definition 1, Definition 2, and Assumption 1. A world's BCF cannot be contained in another world's BCF, since a world's BCF is a maximal proposition. So, if we instantiate for F with a BCF in Assumption 2, it must be that $W = W^*$)
6. (Hence) In the actual world, there is a proposition # such that the BCF for the actual world contains @, #, and the proposition that # explains @.

Gale and Pruss provide many further steps of argumentation that lead to the conclusion that # is a contingent proposition that reports the free intentional action of a necessary being that explains the existence of the actual world's universe. However, here we shall be primarily concerned with the argument for the conclusion at line 6.

Gale and Pruss claim, quite explicitly, that their argument is an improvement on more familiar cosmological arguments because the principle of sufficient reason upon which their argument relies is weaker than the principle of sufficient reason that is invoked in those more familiar arguments. If an argument appeals to the principle that, necessarily, for every proposition that p, if it is the case that p, then there is an explanation of why it is the case that p (S-PSR, the Strong Principle of Sufficient Reason), then, according to Gale and Pruss, that argument 'imposes' on atheistic opponents of theism: 'the strong version of PSR – S-PSR – occupies almost as high an echelon in one's wish book as does the proposition that God exists'. But 'even if our atheistic opponents reject W-PSR, our argument represents an advance over traditional cosmological arguments that had to appeal to S-PSR in that atheists must pay a greater price, run a greater risk of being wrong, for rejecting our argument than a traditional cosmological argument'.

There are at least two different kinds of reasons that one might have for denying that the use of W-PSR – in the framework in which it is deployed by Gale and Pruss – marks any kind of advance over the use of S-PSR.

First, it is not really clear that W-PSR is weaker than S-PSR. Many years ago, Fitch proved that if O is a sentential operator that is veridical (i.e., such that $(\forall p)\,(Op \to p)$) and dissective (i.e., such that $(\forall p)\,(\forall q)\,(O(p\&q) \to p)$, then $(\forall p)\,(p \to \diamond Op) \leftrightarrow (\forall p)\,(p \to Op)$. Since explanation is very plausibly both veridical and dissective, we can prove in any standard modal logic that W-PSR ↔ S-PSR. Since it is plausibly true *a priori* that explanation is both veridical and dissective, it is at the very least true *a priori* that W-PSR is equivalent to S-PSR. Consequently, it can hardly be true that atheists run a greater risk in rejecting W-PSR than they run in rejecting S-PSR: it is true *a priori* that the risk is no greater in the one case than in the other. Moreover, if it is really true that S-PSR occupies an echelon in one's wish book as high as that occupied by the proposition that an orthodoxly conceived monotheistic god exists, then it seems that – on the basis of the noted equivalence – one is surely justified in maintaining that W-PSR occupies an echelon in one's wish book as high as that occupied by the proposition that an orthodoxly conceived monotheistic god exists. But, if that's right, then one could hardly have done worse to offer the following argument instead:

1. Necessarily, for every proposition that p, if it is the case that p, then there is an explanation of why it is the case that p (i.e., there is a proposition q such that q, and q explains p).
2. @ is the BCCF for the actual world.
3. (Hence) In the actual world, there is a proposition # such that the BCF for the actual world contains @, #, and the proposition that # explains @.

The thought that *this* is a convincing proof surely occupies an echelon in anyone's wish book at least as high at that occupied by the proposition that God exists!

Second – making use of the noted logical equivalence between S-PSR and W-PSR – there are at least *prima facie* plausible positive reasons to reject W-PSR. It's not merely that non-theists are perfectly within their rights to refuse to accept S-PSR; rather, there are *prima facie* plausible positive reasons to think that this principle is false.

Davey and Clifton (2001) argue that the assumption that there is a Big Conjunctive Contingent Fact is open to challenge. Roughly, the point that they make is that there are properties of propositions – for example, the property of being contingently true and not containing oneself as a proper conjunct – for which it is demonstrable that there is no conjunction of all of the true propositions that possess any given one of those properties. Given that there are such properties, why are we entitled to the assumption that there is a conjunction of all of the contingently true propositions? Gale and Pruss (2003) suggest that, while they haven't offered a comprehension principle – and so are not committed to the claim that there is a conjunction of all of the true propositions that possess any given property – they are nonetheless entitled to the assumption that properties are innocent until proven otherwise; since it has not been shown that the claim that there is a conjunction of all true contingent propositions leads to contradiction, we have not yet been given reason to suppose that there is no Big Conjunctive Contingent Fact.

For those who are sceptical that it is right to suppose that properties are innocent until proven otherwise, Gale and Pruss offer a further argument. Suppose that one thinks that the only propositions that appear in conjuncts in the BCCF* for a world are taken from the following list:

(a) all true contingent atomic propositions;
(b) a 'that's all' clause that says that any true contingent atomic proposition is one of those mentioned in (a);
(c) all true propositions appearing in the explananda of basic propositions or of conjunctions thereof;
(d) all true basic propositions reporting causal relations;
(e) a 'that's all' clause that says that all the actual explanatory relations supervene on the facts reported in (a), (b), (c), and (d).

Given these assumptions, isn't it plausible to suppose that there is a BCCF* that can play the role that the BCCF plays in the argument that Gale and Pruss initially gave?

I'm not sure. The notions of *conjunction* and *atomicity* upon which Gale and Pruss rely are nowhere adequately explained. In Oppy (2000b), I noted that, despite the claims of Gale and Pruss to the contrary, one might wonder whether the BCCF for a world can differ from the BCF for that world: since a conjunction of a necessary proposition with a contingent proposition is itself contingent, the conjunction of all contingent propositions would 'include' all of the necessary propositions. Gale and Pruss (1999) gestured towards a resolution of this difficulty with the claim that there are no 'truth-functional repetitions' in either the BCF or the BCCF; however, in Oppy (2000b) I urged that it simply isn't clear whether this proposal will suffice to avoid the collapse of BCCF into BCF; and I also noted that, given that Gale and Pruss (1999) say that one proposition 'contains' a second just in case all of the 'conjuncts' of the latter are 'conjuncts' of the former, there is reason to suppose that they have some kind of notion of 'atomic conjunct' in mind. This conjecture is confirmed in Gale and Pruss (2003), where they say explicitly that a world's Big Conjunctive Contingent Fact is a conjunction of atomic propositions, and add that 'a singular positive proposition is atomic iff it either is not further analysable relative to a given language or does not require further analysis for the purpose for which it is being used in some inquiry'. But if the BCCF is a conjunction of atomic propositions, then it seems that the BCCF must be 'contained' in the BCCF* in such a way that the existence of the BCCF* can hardly be more secure than the existence of the BCCF itself.

Suppose that we agree that the standing of the objection from Davey and Clifton (2001) that we are currently considering is uncertain. Nonetheless, there are further reasons for supposing that S-PSR is unacceptable. As Davey and Clifton themselves argue, S-PSR runs counter to modal intuitions that are at least as deeply entrenched as the intuitions about possible explanations that allegedly support S-PSR. Surely, there are some true contingent propositions of which it is true that it is possible that those propositions lack explanations; surely it is possible that there is brute contingency. If it is possible that there is brute – unexplained – contingency, then it follows that S-PSR – and, hence, W-PSR – is false.

In response to the claim that there is stronger intuitive support for the claim that there is brute – unexplained – contingency than there is for W-PSR, Gale and Pruss (2003) offer four different responses. First, they suggest that belief in W-PSR 'coheres better with our proclivity to seek an explanation for any contingently true proposition'. Second, they claim that 'we would not be likely to seek an explanation if we did not believe that it is at least logically possible that there is one'. Third, they claim that, while 'we know what it is like to verify that a given proposition has an explanation . . . we have no idea what it is like to verify that a given proposition has no explanation'. Fourth, they claim that respected scientists such as Einstein exhibit 'deep resistance . . . to the idea that some contingent propositions do not have an explanation'.

None of these suggestions is particularly compelling.

First, there are countless contingently true propositions for which we have no proclivity to seek explanations: the vast majority of true propositions – even amongst those whose truth we recognise – are banal and uninteresting. So there is no proclivity of the kind that Gale and Pruss claim coheres better with W-PSR. Moreover, even if there were such a proclivity, that would hardly be evidence that W-PSR is true: there is no logical or evidential guarantee that believers of falsehoods will not prosper.

Second, it is not obvious that there is anything at all unlikely about seeking for explanations in cases in which one does not believe that it is at least logically possible that there is one. Consider the situation of a mathematician who is unsure whether a given proposition is true – and hence who is unsure whether it is logically possible for there to be a proof of that proposition – but who searches for a proof nonetheless. Since this is an example in which the proposition at issue is known not to be contingent, it is not immediately relevant to W-PSR. But suppose we believe, following Kripke, that there are propositions that are both necessary and only knowable *a priori*. Suppose, further, that p is a proposition about whose status we are in the dark: it might be true and contingent, but equally, it might be false and necessary. In this case, it seems to me that one could perfectly well seek an explanation of the truth of p, while nonetheless recognising that it might not even be logically possible that there is an explanation of why it is that *p*, because it might be that *p* is necessarily false. Perhaps it is plausible to suppose that one won't seek an explanation for *p* unless one believes that it is at least doxastically possible that *p*; but this plausible supposition provides no support for W-PSR. And, in any case, even if it were true that we would not be likely to seek an explanation if we did not believe that it is at least logically possible that there is one, no support for W-PSR would eventuate: there is no logical or evidential guarantee that believers of falsehoods will not prosper.

Third, while it may be right that there is an asymmetry between verifying that a proposition has an explanation and verifying that a proposition has no explanation – and while it might even be true that importance attaches to this asymmetry that does not also attach to the asymmetry between falsifying that a proposition has an explanation and falsifying that a proposition has no explanation – it is quite unclear why we should attach any importance to this point. It seems to me to be plausible to claim that we do know what it is like to find good reasons for thinking that a given proposition has no explanation. Consider, for example, the claim that we have good reason to believe that quantum mechanics commits us to objectively chancy events. There are many interpreters who suppose both that quantum mechanics is a true theory and that it commits us to objectively chancy events. If these interpreters are right, then we do have good reason to believe that there are true propositions – about, say, particular quantum events – that do not have explanations. In general, it seems to me that there is no particularly good reason to care about verification, the more so if 'verification' is given a robust interpretation: if there are good all-things-considered reasons for supposing that some propositions have no explanation, then W-PSR is in serious trouble.

Fourth, it is tempting to respond to the observation that Einstein was deeply resistant to the idea that some contingent events do not have an explanation by saying: I'll match your Einstein with a Bohr, and raise you a Heisenberg, a Feynmann, and a Hawking! However, it is not clear that we need to have recourse to this obvious point about the availability of competing authorities, since it is not clear that Einstein really was deeply resistant to the idea that some contingent propositions do not have explanations. True enough, Einstein didn't like the idea that there are contingent (physical) *events* that lack explanation – but it hardly follows from this that he supposed that there are no contingent *features* of the world that lack explanation.

According to Gale and Pruss, the considerations to which they appeal 'lend credence to the claim that, in the epistemic order, W-PSR is more deeply entrenched than the claim that it is possible that a given contingent proposition has no explanation'. However, in my opinion, this is plainly not so: the considerations to which they appeal lend no more than very weak support to W-PSR, and there are plainly counter-veiling considerations that offer no less support to the denial of W-PSR.[16]

Even if we were to grant that Gale and Pruss have a satisfactory response to the objection from the intuitive possibility of brute contingency, there may yet be other ways in which it is possible to argue that S-PSR is unacceptable. For – as I argue in Oppy (2006) – it may be that there are arguments that suffice to reduce S-PSR to absurdity. Suppose that we do agree that there is a BCCF for the actual world. To what could we possibly appeal in order to explain the obtaining of this proposition? Plainly enough, we can't appeal to a proposition that is not entailed by BCCF; for, *ex hypothesi*, there is no such proposition. Gale and Pruss claim that the obtaining of the BCCF is explained by the proposition that there is a very powerful and intelligent being that freely causes the existence of the actual cosmos, where this contingent proposition is, itself, one of the conjuncts of the BCCF. According to Gale and Pruss, this proposition is a self-explaining proposition. However, as I argue in Oppy (2006), there cannot be self-explaining propositions: the very concept of a self-explaining proposition is incoherent. Of course, if that's right – that is, if it is true that there cannot be self-explaining propositions – then the BCCF cannot have an explanation, and neither S-PSR nor W-PSR can be true. It certainly seems to me that the intuition that there cannot be self-explaining propositions is much more secure than the intuition

---

[16] Gale and Pruss also offer the following "epistemic argument" for the conclusion that it is logically possible that W-PSR applies to the BCCF for the actual world:

1. It is logically necessary that if God exists, there is an explanation for the BCCF of the actual world.
2. It is epistemically possible that God exists.
3. (Hence) It is epistemically possible that there is an explanation for the BCCF of the actual world.
4. (Hence) It is logically possible that there is an explanation for the BCCF of the actual world.

About this argument, Gale and Pruss claim that there cannot be 'a parallel epistemic argument for the proposition that it is logically possible that there is no explanation for the BCCF of the actual world'. But consider the following argument:

1. Necessarily, if there is no intelligent, powerful, necessarily existent creator of the universe, then there is no explanation for the BCCF for the actual world.
2. It is epistemically possible that there is no intelligent, powerful, necessarily existent creator of the universe.
3. (Hence) It is epistemically possible that there is no explanation for the BCCF of the actual world.
4. (Hence) It is logically possible that there is no explanation for the BCCF of the actual world.

Since 1 is one of the key claims that Gale and Pruss argue for in their paper, they are hardly in any position to question it. So their argument from the alleged absence of a parallel justification of the claim that there is no explanation for the BCCF of the actual world fails.

that any contingently true proposition is such that it is logically possible that it has an explanation for its obtaining.

In sum: there are various reasons for supposing that the new cosmological argument that Gale and Pruss defend is not a cogent argument for the conclusion that, in the actual world, there is a proposition # such that the BCF for the actual world contains @, #, and the proposition that # explains @. There are very good reasons for supposing that W-PSR – their key principle of sufficient reason – is false; and there are also serious doubts about the use of other key notions – for example, 'conjunctive proposition' and 'atomic proposition' – in the setting up of the proof.

3.8. CRAIG AND THE *KALĀM* ARGUMENTS

There has been extensive discussion of *kalām* cosmological arguments in recent times.[17] Revival of interest in these arguments is primarily due to the publication of Craig (1979a). In the following discussion, I shall focus primarily on the arguments in Craig (1979a); however, I shall supplement this discussion by reference to later publications wherever this seems to me to be appropriate. While Craig has changed his mind about some of the details and emphases in his views, there is a considerable similarity between the doctrines that have been endorsed in his various publications.

Craig (1979a) claims that the following syllogism is a sound and persuasive proof of the existence of an orthodoxly conceived monotheistic god:

1. Everything that begins to exist has a cause of its existence.
2. The universe began to exist.
3. (Therefore) The universe has a cause of its existence.

In support of the second premise, Craig offers four supporting arguments, two *a priori* and two *a posteriori*. These four supporting arguments are as follows:

1.1. An actual infinite cannot exist.
1.2. An infinite temporal regress of events is an actual infinite.
1.3. (Therefore) An infinite temporal regress of events cannot exist.

2.1. The temporal series of events is a collection formed by successive addition.

---

[17] See, e.g.: Marmura (1957), Hourani (1958), Fakhry (1959), Wolfson (1966, 1976), Goodman (1971), Craig (1979a, 1979b, 1985, 1988, 1991a, 1991b, 1991c, 1992a, 1992b, 1992c, 1993a, 1993b, 1994a, 1994b, 1997a, 1999, 2000, 2003a), Mackie (1982), Wainwright (1982), Sorabji (1983), Conway (1984), Smith (1985, 1987, 1988, 1991 1993a, 1994a, 1995b), Davidson (1987), Goetz (1989), Prevost (1990), Grünbaum (1990, 1991, 1994, 1996, 2000), Oppy (1991, 1995a, 1995b, 1995c, 1996d, 2001b, 2002a, 2002b, 2002c, 2003a), Morriston (1999, 2002a, 2002b), and Oderberg (2002a, 2002b).

2.2. A collection formed by successive addition cannot be an actual infinite.

2.3. (Therefore) The temporal series of events cannot be an actual infinite.

3.1. Scientific observation strongly confirms standard Big Bang cosmology.

3.2. According to standard Big Bang cosmology, the visible universe arose from an initial singularity less than twenty billion years ago.

3.3. (Therefore) The universe began to exist.

4.1. The visible universe is in a state that is far from thermodynamic equilibrium.

4.2. If there were an infinite temporal regress of events, then the visible universe would not be in a state that is far from thermodynamic equilibrium.

4.3. (Therefore) The universe began to exist.

In support of the first premise, Craig offers two supporting arguments, though he also insists that it is not really in need of support: 'it is so intuitively obvious ... that probably no one in his right mind *really* believes it to be false' (141).

5.1. There is overwhelming empirical support – "the strongest support that experience affords" – for the claim that everything that begins to exist has a cause of its existence.

5.2. (Therefore) Everything that begins to exist has a cause of its existence.

6.1. There can be no objects of knowledge unless there are *a priori* categorial structures of thought.

6.2. There are objects of knowledge.

6.3. If there are *a priori* categorial structures of thought, then it is knowable *a priori* that everything that begins to exist has a cause of its existence.

6.4. (Therefore) Everything that begins to exist has a cause of its existence.

I shall begin by discussing the supporting arguments, before turning to a discussion of the standing of the syllogism that Craig identifies with "the *kalām* cosmological argument".

SUB-ARGUMENT 1. Craig offers an extended defence of the first philosophical sub-argument, including extensive defences for each of the two premises of this sub-argument. We shall begin by examining the reasons that Craig offers for accepting each of the premises of this sub-argument.

In defence of the claim that "an actual infinite cannot exist", Craig offers several different kinds of considerations.

First, Craig argues against Platonism in the philosophy of pure mathematics, that is, against the view that mathematical entities exist. In particular, he argues against the view that Platonism affords a tenable interpretation of Cantor's transfinite numbers. The core of his argument is the claim that 'naïve Cantorian set theory gives rise … to irresolvable antinomies' (89), and the allegedly consequential claim that the only tenable responses to this situation are retreat to intuitionism and retreat to a kind of deductivist formalism ("axiomatization").

I think that this argument is very weak. There is good evidence that Cantor did not embrace the *logical* conception of sets that was espoused by Frege and Russell, and that does lead into the labyrinth of paradox; rather, Cantor espoused a *combinatorial* conception of sets that is more or less enshrined in the axioms of ZFC.[18] Moreover, quite apart from the views held by Cantor himself, it is clear that one can – and that many mathematicians do – embrace a Platonist interpretation of the theory of transfinite numbers that is embedded in ZFC. It is a serious mistake to suppose – as Craig does – that Platonists must be wedded to problematic principles of comprehension: there is no reason why Platonists cannot be combinatorialists. Furthermore, there are good reasons not to accept retreat to deductivist formalism: if the line that Craig takes here is seriously pursued, then it surely leads to the claim that classical mathematics should be rejected, and that either some kind of intuitionistic mathematics, or else some kind of finite mathematics, should be accepted in its stead. While this position can be defended, the costs should be noted: on this view, we are committed to the claim that we can form no coherent understanding of the actual infinite. Consequently, when we come to consider an orthodoxly conceived monotheistic god and its attributes, we cannot then say either that an orthodoxly conceived monotheistic god is, or that an orthodoxly conceived monotheistic god's attributes are, actually infinite.

Second, Craig claims that even a 'basic exposition of the Cantorian system itself ought to make it intuitively obvious that it is impossible for an actual infinite to exist in reality' (72). In his view, the "purely conceptual nature" of the Cantorian system is made clear by the nature of transfinite arithmetic (75f.), and, in particular, by the fact that there is no definition of subtraction and division for transfinite cardinals (81). Moreover, this same conclusion is supported by such observations as that there are just as many points in a line as there are in a cube and that there are the same number of points in any lines, and by the "staggering" observation that ε_0 is less than (the limit ordinal that is identified with) $\aleph_1$.

Once again, I think that this argument is very weak. As consideration of Conway's **No** makes clear, there is no reason why one shouldn't have

---

[18] Zermelo-Fraenkel Set Theory with the Axiom of Choice.

subtraction and division of transfinite ordinals and transfinite cardinals, if this is what one's heart is set upon. Of course, the rules for all of the arithmetic operations look different from the rules that apply in familiar finite arithmetic: but, as Conway emphasises, all of the arithmetic operations are defined only once – for all of the Conway numbers – and a little familiarity quickly breeds the view that these operations are natural. Moreover, it is quite unclear why one should suppose that the allegedly counter-intuitive behaviour of the transfinite ordinals and cardinals somehow casts doubt on the idea that the very smallest transfinite cardinals do find application to "the real world", unless one somehow supposes that classical mathematics should be rejected *in toto* and replaced with an acceptable intuitionistic or finite mathematics. If the Cantorian theory of the transfinite numbers is intelligible, then we can suppose that some parts of it find application "in the real world", while nonetheless granting that most of it does not. We can suppose that there are $\aleph_0$ objects, or c spacetime points, without going on to suppose that we can find "real world" applications for much larger Cantorian cardinals.

Third, Craig claims that the kinds of puzzle cases that are discussed in Oppy (2006) show that 'various absurdities would result if an actual infinite were to be instantiated in the real world' (82). As I note in that other work, there are good reasons for claiming that the puzzles to which Craig adverts – primarily Craig's Library and Hilbert's Hotel – actually show no such thing. Apart from the errors that Craig makes in his assessment of the puzzle cases that he discusses, the key point to note is that these puzzle cases simply have no bearing on, for example, the question of whether the world is spatially infinite, or the question of whether the world has an infinite past. At most, it seems that one might suppose that these puzzles show that there cannot be certain kinds of actual infinities; but one could hardly suppose that these puzzles show that there cannot be actual infinities of any kind.

In sum: the defence that Craig offers of the claim that there cannot be an actual infinite is very weak. We should agree that, if one is prepared to reject classical mathematics – and to embrace an intuitionistic or finite alternative – then one will be in a position to deny that there can be actual infinities. However, we have not yet been given any good reason to think that those who accept classical mathematics cannot go on to suppose that there *could be* actual infinities. Moreover, if we do suppose that we have good reason for supposing that there cannot be an actual infinite, then we shall be committed to the claim that there is no sense in which an orthodoxly conceived monotheistic god could be actually infinite; if there is an orthodoxly conceived monotheistic god, then that orthodoxly conceived monotheistic god can know only finitely many things, can perform only finitely many actions, and so forth. And, of course, this worry persists even if we consider ways in which one might argue for the weaker claim that there is no actual infinite; while this weaker claim might be used to support the claim that the past is finite, it also has the consequence that an orthodoxly conceived monotheistic god is actually finite (though perhaps potentially infinite) in every respect.

In defence of the claim that an infinite temporal regress is an actual infinite, Craig begins with the observation that the claim seems 'obvious enough . . . if there has been a sequence composed of an infinite number of events stretching back into the past, then the set of all events would be an actually infinite set' (95). This seems right: an infinite number of events stretching back into the past would form an actually infinite set, as would an infinite number of events stretching into the future. However, Craig claims that an infinite number of events stretching into the future is not an actual infinity, but is rather a merely potential infinity. Consequently, he takes himself to have some work to do to establish that an infinite number of events stretching back into the past is not merely a potential infinity.

First, Craig argues that the past is real in a way that the future is not, because past events have existed: 'they have taken place in the real world, while future events have not since they have not occurred' (96f.). However, it seems to me that, if we are taking tense seriously – that is, if we are rejecting the four-dimensionalist view that is strongly supported by the general theory of relativity – then there is something odd about the way that Craig draws his past/future asymmetry. On the one hand, the past does not exist: while it was the case, it is no longer. On the other hand, the future does not exist: while it will be the case, it is not yet. If there are reasons of the kind that Craig is here countenancing for supposing that the past cannot be infinite, then surely those reasons will carry over to support the contention that the future cannot be infinite. Craig doesn't think that the past is real in the way that the present is: he doesn't suppose that it is possible for there to be travel into the past. Equally, he should be prepared to allow that the future is real in a way in which the past is not: the future is still to come in the real world, while the past is not, since it has already occurred. At the very least, there is plenty of room here for those who are unsympathetic towards actual infinities to conclude that the future must be finite (and then to worry about the consequences of this conclusion for claims about the extent of life after death).

Second, Craig claims that some of the puzzles that are discussed in Oppy (2006) – in particular, the Tristram Shandy puzzle – give us additional reason to suppose that the past series of events cannot be infinite. However, despite Craig's claim that 'the Tristram Shandy story. . .tells us that an actually infinite temporal regress is absurd', I think that the discussion in Oppy (2006) shows that that story establishes no such conclusion. As we noted in that earlier discussion, one might think that there are principles of sufficient reason to which one can appeal in order to support the claim that the past series of events cannot be infinite. However, as I note in Oppy (2006), it is a delicate matter to discover a principle of sufficient reason that is both strong enough to yield the desired conclusion and yet not obviously in need

of additional argumentative support. At the very least, it seems to me that
we have not yet been given any reason at all to suppose that there are non-
question-begging arguments in support of the claim that the past series of
events cannot be infinite.

In sum: while I am happy to grant that an infinite temporal regress is
an actual infinite, I do not think that Craig makes a good case for the
claim that the future series of events can be infinite while the past series
of events cannot be infinite. While one can insist that a word like "actual"
or "real" marks a genuine metaphysical distinction between the past and
the future – "the past is actual while the future is merely potential" – it
seems to me that it is very hard to give non-question-begging content to
this insistence. There are two perspectives – that of the presentist and that
of the four-dimensionalist – from which there is no such distinction to be
drawn. Since presentism and four-dimensionalism are both susceptible of
serious philosophical support, this point alone should suffice to cast doubt
on Craig's claim that his arguments 'will be sufficient to convince most
people that the universe had a beginning' (99).

As Craig himself notes, there is a gap between the conclusion of the first
sub-argument and the second premise of the main argument: perhaps one
might think that, while the series of events in the universe is finite in the
past, the universe itself is infinite in the past: 'the temporal series of events
was preceded by an eternal, quiescent universe, absolutely still' (99). Against
this suggestion, Craig offers two arguments, one *a priori* and one *a posteriori*.
I do not propose to discuss these arguments here. Whether or not they
are cogent, it seems to me to be plausible to suppose that, if the series of
events in the universe is finite in the past, then so too is the universe itself.
Since the first premise of the first sub-argument is so controversial – and
since the considerations that Craig advances on behalf of that premise are
so weak – we may perhaps be excused from considering the remainder of
the argument in any depth.

SUB-ARGUMENT 2. As Craig observes, in effect, the second sub-argument
comes into play only if the first sub-argument fails. If there cannot be an
actual infinite, then, *a fortiori*, the temporal series of events cannot be an
actual infinite. Consequently, we set aside any reasons that we might have
for supposing that there cannot be an actual infinite when we turn to argue
for the premises in this argument. If we tacitly appeal to the claim that
there cannot be an actual infinite in order to support the premises in the
second sub-argument, then we defeat the purpose of propounding this sub-
argument.

On behalf of the first premise of this sub-argument – that is, the claim that
the temporal series of events is a collection formed by successive addition –
Craig observes that it seems "obvious enough". However, as I note in Oppy
(2006), if one supposes that time has the structure of the real numbers
and if one also supposes that there are continuous processes in time, then
one will deny that past events form a *series*, and one will also deny that the

collection of past events fall under a relation of *successive addition*. Since we are here not assuming that there cannot be an actual infinite, and since time is modelled by the real numbers in so many of our most successful scientific theories, it is hard to see what grounds one could have for supposing that it is simply "obvious" that past events constitute a series formed by successive addition. At the very least, it seems to me that we need some very substantial independent argument before we are persuaded to accept this premise.

On behalf of the second premise of this sub-argument – that is, the claim that a collection formed by successive addition cannot be an actual infinite – Craig notes that it is tantamount to the claim that it is impossible to count to infinity. He offers the following illustration of what he takes to be the central difficulty: 'Suppose we imagine a man running through empty space on a path of stone slabs, a path constructed such that when the man's foot strikes the last slab, another appears immediately in front of him. It is clear that, even if the man runs for eternity, he will never run across all of the slabs. For every time his foot strikes the last slab, a new one appears in front of him, *ad infinitum*. The traditional cognomen for this is the impossibility of traversing the infinite.' (104)

In Craig's example, the question is not whether the man can run across all of the slabs, but rather whether he can run across infinitely many slabs. For, if he achieves the latter task and yet not the former, he will still have completed an actual infinite by successive addition. If we suppose that the rate at which the slabs appear is constant, then, in any finite amount of time, only finitely many slabs appear: there is no time at which infinitely many slabs have been crossed. However, if the man runs for an infinite amount of time – that is, if, for each n, there is an nth slab that the man crosses – it is nonetheless true that infinitely many slabs are crossed: there is an actually infinite collection that is formed by successive addition. (Of course, Craig will resist this way of characterising matters: given his view that the future is not real, he will insist that it is at best true that infinitely many slabs will be crossed: the collection that is formed here by successive addition is at best "potentially infinite".)

But what if we suppose that the time lapse between slabs decreases according to a geometric ratio, and that the man is replaced by a bouncing ball whose height of bounce decreases according to the same geometric ratio? If the ball hits the first slab at one minute to twelve, the second slab at $\frac{1}{2}$ minute to twelve, the third slab at $\frac{1}{4}$ minute to twelve, and so on, then the ball can come to rest on a slab at twelve, having made infinitely many bounces on different slabs in the interval between one minute to twelve and twelve. In this example, we have a process – the bouncing of the ball – that plainly does form an actual infinite by successive addition. Consequently, we don't need to challenge Craig's view about the reality of the future in order to reject the second premise of the argument under discussion: there are perfectly ordinary processes that involve formation of an actual infinite by successive addition in not obviously impossible worlds (in which space and time are composed of points, and there are no quantum or thermodynamical effects to rule out the precise application of classical kinematics to the motion of a bouncing ball). Since Craig has – for the purposes of this argument – renounced the claim that there cannot be actual infinities, it is quite unclear what reason we are supposed to have for rejecting this counter-example to the alleged impossibility of forming actual infinities by successive addition.[19]

To strengthen the case for the second premise in this sub-argument, Craig adverts to his discussions of Zeno's paradoxes and the first Kantian antinomy. But, as the discussion in Oppy (2006) makes clear, there is nothing in either Zeno's paradoxes or the first Kantian antinomy to support the claim that a collection formed by successive addition cannot be actually infinite. In his discussion of Zeno's paradoxes, Craig claims that all supertasks are impossible because the completion of a supertask requires the performance of an 'infinitieth' task, that is, a last task immediately before the end state is achieved. Thus, for example, in his examination of Thomson's lamp, Craig writes that: 'in the real world, the state of the lamp [at the end of the manipulations of the switch] . . . is determined by the state of the lamp at the prior instant, which would be the "infinitieth" moment in the series' (180). But, of course, the assumption that there must be an *immediately* prior instant is precisely what proponents of the possibility of this kind of supertask deny: if time is a continuum, then there is no instant that is immediately prior to a given instant.

If anything, the second of Craig's philosophical sub-arguments fares even worse than the first: there is no clear and uncontroversial support to be given to either of the two premises in this argument. While there are views that entail that a temporal series of events cannot be infinite – for example, the view that, as a matter of necessity, there are only finitely many temporal

---

[19] Craig (1979a: 186n12) does say that 'a real ball is never perfectly resilient and so never bounces an infinite number of times before coming to rest'. If this is the claim that, in the actual world, balls are not perfectly resilient, then it seems unexceptionable: there are good thermodynamical – and quantum mechanical – reasons for denying that balls are perfectly resilient. Consequently, there are also good reasons for denying that, in worlds sufficiently like the actual world, balls are perfectly resilient: if you hold fixed enough of the actual laws and the actual boundary conditions, then you will surely have a world in which balls are not perfectly resilient. But nothing that we have said so far rules out acceptance of the claim that there are possible worlds governed by physical laws that are not altogether unlike the laws that obtain in our world, and yet in which balls are perfectly resilient. Moreover, it is precisely a claim of this form that is accepted by defenders of the possibility of supertasks, such as Benacerraf (1962) and Earman and Norton (1996). Despite Craig's numerous assertions that his opponents confuse "real possibilities" with "merely mathematical possibilities", it seems to me that it is rather Craig's insistence on the simple – and under-explained – division between "real possibilities" and "merely mathematical possibilities" that causes him to misrepresent the views of those whom he attacks. Possible worlds governed by laws and boundary conditions that are similar in some – but not all – ways to the laws and boundary conditions that govern the actual world are "real" possible worlds: worlds in which there are concrete, physical objects, and not merely numbers, sets, and other mathematical "abstractions".

atoms – one requires some quite heavy duty metaphysical assumptions in order to adequately support the conclusion of the second philosophical sub-argument. If we suppose, as Craig suggests, that he is looking for arguments that ought to persuade more or less any reasonable person, then it is surely clear that neither of Craig's philosophical sub-arguments comes anywhere near to meeting this standard.

SUB-ARGUMENT 3. Study of the large-scale history and structure of the universe is one of the more speculative branches of physical science. Following Kragh (1996: 6f.), we may suppose that modern scientific cosmology dates from work done in 1917 on global solutions to the field equations of general relativity. From Einstein's initial work until the mid-1960s, there was a substantial division of opinion amongst cosmologists, with many leading figures inclining towards steady-state theories. However, a variety of considerations – including the discovery of the cosmic background radiation by Penzias and Wilson in 1965 – motivated subsequent widespread acceptance of the idea that the visible universe is the result of expansion from an earlier state of much greater density and temperature. Subsequent developments – including the analysis of the COBE data – show that there is a very good fit between standard Big Bang models of the universe and empirical data back to quite early stages in the history of the visible universe. Even allowing for the speculative and volatile nature of scientific cosmology, it seems to me to be plausible to allow that there are non-initial segments of standard Big Bang models that are well confirmed by the empirical data.

Despite the good fit between non-initial segments of standard Big Bang models and empirical data, there are very few cosmologists who suppose that standard Big Bang models are well confirmed over the entire history of the universe. The sticking point, of course, is the account of the very earliest history of the universe. In standard Big Bang models, there is an initial blow-up scalar polynomial singularity, that is, a point at which physical components of the curvature tensor diverge. There are very few theorists who are prepared to allow that this is a true representation of the earliest history of the universe. On a straight interpretation of the FRW models, there is no first moment at which the universe exists, but physical components of the curvature tensor diverge as $t \rightarrow 0$. Since Craig is a vociferous opponent of the actual infinite, he cannot possibly suppose that either of these features of the FRW models corresponds to anything in reality. But then, before we can draw any conclusions about the nature of the very earliest universe, we need to be presented with suitably modified FRW models in which these problematic features have been removed.

The construction of models that give an accurate representation of the very earliest universe is a matter of considerable current research activity. Since it seems plausible to suppose that the very earliest universe is a domain in which quantum mechanical considerations will be important, there is a widely held view that we shall not have our suitably modified FRW models until we understand how to unify quantum mechanics and general relativity in a quantum gravitational theory. But, at the time of writing, there is no reason to suppose that we are at all close to the construction of a satisfying theory of this kind. Consequently, we are in no position to draw any conclusions about the very earliest parts of the universe from the current state of cosmological theorising.

If we are prepared to leave the domain of properly scientific theorising, then we might suppose that – despite the lack of any decent scientific model of the earliest parts of the universe – we can nonetheless conclude from the available scientific data – and, in particular, from the goodness of fit between non-initial segments of standard Big Bang models and that data – that the universe "began to exist". After all, one might suppose, the very use of the terminology "the earliest parts of the universe" is surely an acknowledgment that there was "an absolute beginning of the universe about fifteen billion years ago" (130).

There are at least four reasons to be cautious here.

First, as noted by Earman (1995: 205f.), models of the Big Bang – such as the standard FRW models – are, in themselves, entirely neutral on the question of whether they model "an absolute beginning" of the physical universe. Whether the metric in an FRW model can be extended through the initial singularity depends upon the continuity/differentiability conditions that are placed on that metric. We might follow Geroch and Traschen in demanding that any physically meaningful extension of the metric should be *regular*; in that case, we shall conclude that there is no physically meaningful extension of the metric in a standard FRW model. However, at the very least, it is clear that we need some further justification for the claim that standard Big Bang models do in fact model "an absolute beginning" of the physical universe. Consequently, we are far from having good reason to suppose that not yet developed quantum-gravitational replacements for these standard Big Bang models will model "an absolute beginning" of the *physical* universe.

Second, as also noted by Earman (1995: 207), even if we suppose that there can be no physically meaningful extension of the metric through the initial singularity in standard FRW models, it does not follow that there can be no mathematically meaningful extension of the metric through that singularity. While it might be thought that this point supports the hypothesis that there might be a temporal domain in which God can perform the activities that result in the creation of the universe, it should be noted that this hypothesis also leaves room for the suggestion that there is some other cause for the creation of the universe that is part of an infinite regress of contingent causes. If we suppose that there can be a mathematically meaningful extension of the metric through the initial singularity in an FRW model, and if we suppose that there can be causation in the domain of that extension, then there is nothing in the empirical data that allegedly supports the claim that there is such a singularity to rule out the claim that there is an infinite regress of contingent causes. At the very least, we should be very cautious in our treatment of the claim that we have good reason to suppose that not yet developed quantum-gravitational replacements for standard Big Bang models will model "an absolute beginning" of the *contingent* universe.

Third, as argued by Grünbaum (1991), even if we suppose that there is no meaningful extension of the metric through the initial singularity in standard FRW models, it is a mistake to suppose that there is "an absolute beginning" in these models. If there are no meaningful extensions of the metric through the initial singularity in standard FRW models, then, equally, there are no meaningful extensions of the metric to $t = 0$ in these models. As Earman (1995: 208f.) notes, in the standard Big Bang models, for every time t there is an earlier time t', and the state of the universe at t' is a causal determinant of the state of the universe at t. Thus, it turns out that, even in the standard Big Bang models, there is no "absolute beginning" of the physical universe. Once again, the properties of standard Big Bang models give us no reason at all to suppose that not yet developed quantum-gravitational replacements for these standard Big Bang models will model "an absolute beginning" of the *physical* universe.

Fourth, despite the difficulties that we have noted thus far, one might suppose that there is surely good reason to claim that modern scientific cosmology makes it plausible to claim that the universe is finite in the past: there have been no more than twenty billion years during which the physical universe has existed. Since this seems right, one might then go on to suggest that there is, after all, a perfectly good sense in which modern scientific cosmology supports the claim that the universe began to exist: something begins to exist iff it is finite in the past, whence, since the universe is finite in the past, it follows that the universe began to exist. However, the important point to keep in mind now is whether the first premise of the *kalām* argument is true under this interpretation of "begins to exist": is it true that anything that begins to exists has a cause of its beginning to exist under this interpretation of "begins to exist"? We shall return to this point later.

In view of the considerations that have been adduced here, it seems to me that we should conclude that there is no good reason to suppose that current scientific cosmology supports the contention that there was an "absolute beginning" of the universe about fifteen billion years ago. Given the current state of scientific cosmology, it does seem highly plausible to suppose that the visible universe is no more than twenty billion years old; but there are various reasons why support for this contention does not readily translate into support for the contention that the universe had an "absolute beginning" no more then twenty billion years ago. Unless we accept the claim that something begins to exist iff it is finite in the past, we have no reason to find any merit in the third of Craig's sub-arguments.

SUB-ARGUMENT 4. It would take us very far afield to try to give a proper discussion of the second of Craig's empirical arguments. For the purposes of the current work, it suffices to note that there is no stronger argument for an "absolute beginning" in the thermodynamical considerations to which Craig appeals than there is in contemporary scientific cosmology. At best, the thermodynamical considerations can establish only that the *physical* universe is finite in the past: they cannot establish that there is no infinite regress in the *contingent* universe; and neither can they establish that there was an initial state of the universe at $t = 0$. Unless we accept the claim that something begins to exist iff it is finite in the past, we have no reason to find any merit in the fourth of Craig's sub-arguments.

Before we turn to an examination of the sub-arguments that Craig (1979a) offers in support of the first premise in his *kalām* cosmological argument, it is worth pausing to assess the overall contribution that the first four sub-arguments make in supporting the second premise in the *kalām* cosmological argument. I claim that the two *a priori* arguments are very weak indeed: they give no serious support to the claim that the physical universe began to exist. Moreover, I claim that the two *a posteriori* arguments at best support the claim that the physical universe is finite in the past. If we do not accept the claim that something begins to exist iff it is finite in the past, then we shall conclude that the two *a posteriori* arguments also fail to give substantial support to the claim that the physical universe began to exist.

SUB-ARGUMENT 5. As we have already noted, Craig claims that there is no real need to offer support for the claim that everything that begins to exist has a cause of its existence: the truth of this claim is allegedly so immediately apparent that no sane person could fail to recognise it. Nonetheless, he does go on to say that the claim has overwhelming empirical support: "it is repeatedly confirmed in our experience. Constantly verified and never falsified, the causal proposition can be taken as an empirical generalisation enjoying the strongest support experience affords" (145).

Whether or not we suppose that we are dealing here with an empirical generalisation, we are entitled to ask for clarification of the meaning of the claim whose truth is allegedly so evident that no sane person can reject it. On the one hand, we need to know more about what it takes for something to count as "beginning to exist"; on the other hand, we need to know more about what it takes for something to count as "a cause [of the existence of some thing]".

One might suppose – roughly following Grünbaum (1990) – that an object x begins to exist at a time t just in case: (1) x exists at t; (2) there are times prior to t; and (3) there is no time prior to t at which x exists.[20]

---

[20] In place of (3), Grunbaum actually offers:

(3′) There is a temporal interval (t', t) immediately prior to t at which x does not exist.

Unlike the formulation in the main text, this formulation allows for the possibility of intermittent existents, i.e., objects that come into and go out of existence. It is not clear to me that one ought to allow that this is a possibility. In any case, the question of the possibility

Moreover, one might suppose that an object x begins to exist just in case there is some time t at which x begins to exist. On these assumptions, it does not seem immediately objectionable to claim that anything that begins to exist has a cause of its beginning to exist; and neither does it seem immediately objectionable to suggest that this claim finds strong empirical support. However, of course, it should also be noted that – whether or not we accord any reality to the time $t = 0$ in standard Big Bang models of the universe – it is not true on the current assumptions that the universe – as modelled in standard Big Bang cosmology – began to exist. If we accept this account of what it is for something to begin to exist, then Craig's *kalām* argument is in ruins.

One might suppose – roughly following Craig (1992a) – that an object x begins to exist at a time t just in case: (1) x exists at t; and (2) there is no time prior to t at which x exists. Moreover, again, one might suppose that an object x begins to exist just in case there is some time t at which x begins to exist. On these assumptions, provided that we accord reality to the time $t = 0$ in standard Big Bang models of the universe, it does turn out to be true that the universe – as modelled in standard Big Bang cosmology – begins to exist. However, if we do not accord any reality to the time $t = 0$ in standard Big Bang models of the universe, then, on these assumptions, it is not true that the universe – as modelled in standard Big Bang cosmology – begins to exist. Since – as we have already seen – there is good reason to deny that the time $t = 0$ is accorded any reality in standard Big Bang cosmology, we again have reason to hold that, on this account of what it is for something to begin to exist, Craig's *kalām* argument is in ruins. Moreover, even if we do suppose that we can accord reality to the time $t = 0$ in standard Big Bang models of the universe, we now have to confront the question of whether it is plausible to claim that there is strong empirical support for the universal generalisation that *everything* that begins to exist has a cause for its beginning to exist, on the current construal of "begins to exist". The answer to this question seems plainly to be negative. In experience, we only ever meet with objects whose coming into existence is preceded by times at which those objects do not exist. Nothing in experience bears on the question of the causal antecedents of objects that begin to exist at $t = 0$. So, on the current account of what it is for something to begin to exist, the key premise in Craig's fifth sub-argument should be rejected: it is not true, on this account of what it is for something to begin to exist, that there is "the strongest support that experience affords" for the claim that everything that begins to exist has a cause of its beginning to exist.

of intermittent objects is clearly tangential to the issues that are the primary focus of the present discussion. Those who are concerned about the failure of the subsequent discussion in the main text to address this alleged possibility are free to make the necessary – and straightforward – amendments.

One might suppose that an object x begins to exist at a time t just in case: (1) x exists at all times in some open or closed interval (t, t'); and (2) x exists at no times in any open interval (t'', t). Moreover, again, one might suppose that an object x begins to exist just in case there is some time t at which x begins to exist. On these assumptions, even if we accord no reality to the time $t = 0$ in standard Big Bang models of the universe, it turns out that the universe – as modelled in standard Big Bang cosmology – begins to exist at $t = 0$. However, as presaged by the discussion in the previous paragraph, we now have to face the question of whether it is plausible to claim that there is strong empirical support for the universal generalisation that *everything* that begins to exist has a cause for its beginning to exist, on the current construal of "begins to exist". Once again, it seems to me that the answer to this question is negative. There is nothing in our experience that provides support for the universal generalisation that, if an object x exists at all times in some open or closed interval (t, t'), and at no times in any open interval (t'', t), then there is a cause of the existence of that object in the open or closed intervals (t, t'). In particular, nothing in experience bears on the question of the causal antecedents of objects that – in the sense now at issue – "begin to exist" at $t = 0$. So, once again, on the current account of what it is for something to begin to exist, the key premise in Craig's fifth sub-argument should be rejected: it is not true, on this account of what it is for something to begin to exist, that there is "the strongest support that experience affords" for the claim that everything that begins to exist has a cause of its beginning to exist.

Unless there is some other account of what it is for something to begin to exist that has been overlooked here, it seems to me that we are entitled to conclude – prior to any discussion of the use of the expression "a cause [of the existence of some thing]" – that the fifth of Craig's sub-arguments is extremely weak. While – for all that we have argued so far – there may be senses of "begins to exist" in which there is empirical support for the claim that it is true that everything that begins to exist has a cause of its beginning to exist, those are not senses in which there is any support for the claim that the universe began to exist.

SUB-ARGUMENT 6. Craig (1979a: 148) is ambivalent about the merit of the sixth sub-argument, and with good reason. Even if one accepts the highly controversial neo-Kantian assumption that there can be no objects of knowledge unless there are *a priori* categorial structures of thought, it is utterly unclear why one should suppose that, if there are *a priori* categorial structures of thought, then it is knowable *a priori* that *everything* that begins to exist has a cause of its beginning to exist. In particular, the claim – in itself highly controversial – that there can be rational thought only if there is a causal structure in the world that is reflected in the categorial structure of thought, supplies no evident support for the further claim that the categorial structure in question must accurately reflect the causal structure of the world at or very near to $t = 0$. The reasons that we gave above for rejecting the fifth of Craig's sub-arguments carry over, more or less unchanged, as reasons for rejecting the sixth of his sub-arguments: there is nothing in *our* current experience, or in *our* ways of thinking about the current state of the world, that both provides substantive support for the claim that *everything* that begins to exist has a cause of its existence and yet does not undermine the claim that the universe began to exist.

Even if we are prepared to dismiss the sub-arguments that Craig offers in support of the first premise in his major syllogism, we must still confront his contention that the truth of this premise is so immediately apparent that no sane person could really fail to accept it. There are various comments that one might make about this apparently gratuitous slur on the many thoughtful atheists who have failed to accept that there is a sense of "begin to exist" in which it is true both that the universe began to exist and that everything that begins to exist has a cause of its existence.

First, if one is prepared to accept that conceivability is a good guide to possibility, then it is hard to see how one can deny that it is possible that there be physical universes that have no cause of their existence, since it seems plainly true that it is conceivable that there be physical universes that have no cause of their existence. Of course, as we noted in Oppy (2006), one can deny that conceivability is a good guide to possibility – but then one must be prepared to pay the costs of this denial. Moreover, if one accepts the claim that conceivability is a good guide to possibility, then, at the very least, one has some serious explaining to do if one wishes to maintain that physical universes that have no cause of their existence are merely "logical" – but not "real" – possibilities.[21]

Second, as we have already noted, there are hard questions to be asked about the meaning of the expression "a cause [of the existence of some thing]". Craig (1992a: 235) says clearly that he is here talking about *efficient* causes – and not about material causes, or formal causes, or final causes, or constitutive causes, or the like. Plausibly, then, the claim that we are investigating can be restated as the claim that any event of the coming into existence of a thing is an efficient effect of some other – distinct, independent – event or events.

---

[21] It should be noted that the sense of possibility at issue here is plainly not that "narrow" logical possibility that is constituted by freedom from inconsistency in first-order logic. I take it that, however the notion of "conceivability" is spelt out, it is not conceivable that $2 + 1 = 7$, or that some prime numbers weigh more than Jackie Gleason. Uncaused physical universes are conceivable in a way in which these "narrow" logical possibilities are not. (Cf. Craig (1993b: 2) for the accusation that I conflate "narrow" logical possibility with "broad" logical possibility, i.e., with the kind of possibility that he denies to uncaused physical universes.)

This restatement still leaves open the question of what we should count as a 'thing'. If 'things' include states of affairs, then the claim is plausibly interpreted to be a kind of principle of sufficient reasons: every contingent state of affairs has an efficient cause, or the like. As I argue in Oppy (2006), there is good reason to reject any strong principle of this type; in particular, it is worth noting that no libertarian about freedom can suppose that every contingent state of affairs has an efficient cause. On the other hand, if 'things' are not meant to include states of affairs, but rather are to be limited to 'individual particulars', or the like, then it is worth asking why we should suppose that this more limited principle is worthy of belief when the more extensive principle plainly is not. I see no reason to accept that untutored intuition finds any more merit in the more limited principle than it finds in the more extensive principles; moreover, I see no evident reason why the kinds of arguments that Craig offered should not be taken to support the more extensive principles no less strongly than they support the more limited principle. If there can be contingent states of affairs that have no efficient cause of their coming to obtain, then why can't there be 'individual particulars' that have no efficient cause of their coming into existence?

Third, there are apparently possible cases that might be taken to controvert the claim that every 'individual particular' has an efficient cause of its coming into existence. Suppose, for example, that there is a kind of subatomic particle – an X-particle – that is unstable, and that can decay in one of two ways, but for which it is an objectively chancy matter which type of decay occurs when this kind of particle decays. On the one hand, an X-particle can decay into an α-particle and a γ-particle; on the other hand, an X-particle can decay into a β-particle and a δ-particle. Suppose, now, that a particular X-particle decays into an α-particle and a γ-particle. Is there an efficient cause of the coming into existence of the α-particle in this case? Plainly enough, there is a material cause: the existence of the X-particle is a material cause of the existence of the α-particle. But it might be said that the objectively chancy nature of the decay process yields the result that the existence of the X-particle is not an efficient cause of the existence of the α-particle; and it might be further suggested that there is no other plausible candidate efficient cause for the existence of the α-particle.

I don't say that it is obviously right to assert that, in the case described, there is no efficient cause for the existence of the α-particle. However, I do think that this case makes it clear that, before we can assent to the claim that there is an efficient cause for the coming into existence of any thing, we need to be told a lot more about the analysis of efficient causation. There are many different philosophical theories of efficient causation, and some of those theories allow that, in the case described, there is no efficient cause for the existence of the α-particle. Of course, those theories that allow that, in the case described, there is no efficient cause for the existence of the α-particle may be mistaken; but we need to move beyond the level of appeal to untutored intuition in order to decide whether or not this is really so.

While there is clearly more to be said on this topic, I think that I have already said enough to justify the contention that it is not in the least bit obvious that everything that begins to exist has an efficient cause of its beginning to exist. For all that has been argued so far, it may be that it is nonetheless true that everything that begins to exist has an efficient cause of its beginning to exist – but, at the very least, those who suppose that it is true have much work to do to convince those who do not agree with them.[22]

Conclusion

So far, I have argued: (1) that the two premises in Craig's major *kalām* syllogism receive no adequate support from the sub-arguments that he advances on their behalf, and (2) that there is no good reason to accept Craig's contention that the first premise is so obvious as not to stand in need of any support. On the basis of this prior argumentation, I think that it is reasonable to conclude that Craig's case is unpersuasive: there is nothing in his major syllogism, nor in the supporting arguments that he advances on behalf of the premises in this major syllogism, that should persuade any reasonable person not already convinced of the truth of the conclusion of that syllogism to accept that the universe has a cause of its existence. Of course, this is not to say that there is good reason to reject the claim that the universe has a cause of its existence; and neither is it to say that there are no theists whose belief that the universe has a cause of its existence is reasonable. To argue for either of those contentions would be to engage in a project vastly different from the one that I have undertaken here: for all that I have tried

---

[22] One possible response to this criticism – if it is deemed to be telling – would be to amend the first premise in the *kalām* syllogism to the claim that everything that begins to exist has either an efficient cause or a *material* cause of its beginning to exist. While there is no less support in experience, or in consideration of the Kantian categories, for the claim that everything that begins to exist has a material cause for its beginning to exist – and while there is equally no less support in untutored intuition for this claim – it is plain that one could not argue for the existence of an immaterial God on the basis of this premise. However, it is not clear that the move to the weaker, disjunctive claim improves matters much: for the *kalām* syllogism is not intended to issue in the conclusion that the universe has either an efficient cause or a material cause for its beginning to exist. At the very least, one needs further supporting argument in order to get from the weaker, disjunctive claim to the desired conclusion that the universe has an efficient cause for its beginning to exist. (It is perhaps worth noting that there are various places in which Craig has addressed the question of whether pair production in a quantum mechanical vacuum constitutes violation of the principle that everything that comes into existence has a cause of its coming into existence – see, e.g., Craig (1979: 165) and Craig (1997a: 241). While one can correctly insist that there is a *material* cause for the coming into existence of particles that are produced in this way, it is highly doubtful whether one is entitled to claim that there is an *efficient* cause for this coming into existence.)

to do is to show why one ought not to suppose that Craig's *arguments* are good.

3.9. SMITH'S ATHEOLOGICAL COSMOLOGICAL ARGUMENTS

In a series of publications for the late 1980s, Quentin Smith (1988, 1991, 1993b, 1993c, 1994b, 1995a, 1995b, 1997a, 1997b, 1999, 2000) defends the claim that work in modern scientific cosmology actually supports the conclusion that our universe is not the product of the creative activities of a supernatural agent. There are a number of different particular conclusions for which Smith argues in these works. *First*, Smith argues that Craig's empirical arguments for supernatural creation from the evidence of physical cosmology fail. Of course, I agree with Smith's conclusion on this matter, and I do not propose to evaluate his criticisms of Craig's arguments here. *Second*, Smith argues that work in modern scientific cosmology strongly supports the conclusion that our universe began to exist, but that there was no 'external' cause – and, in particular, no supernatural perfect cause – of its beginning to exist. Despite his rejection of an 'external' cause – and, in particular, a perfect supernatural cause – for the beginning of the universe, Smith does allow that there is an 'internal' cause for the beginning of the universe. *Third*, Smith argues that, if the Hartle-Hawking cosmology were true of our universe, then it would strongly support the claim that our universe is not the product of the creative activities of a supernatural agent.

3.9.1. The Central Argument

The central argument for the alleged inconsistency between Big Bang cosmology and classical theism is presented in Smith (1991: 200f.):

1. If God exists and there is an earliest state E of the universe, then God created E.
2. God is omniscient, omnipotent, and perfectly benevolent.
3. An animate universe is better than an inanimate universe.
4. (Therefore) If God created E, then E is ensured to contain animate creatures or to lead to a subsequent state of the universe that contains animate creatures.
5. There is an earliest state of the universe, and it is the Big Bang singularity.
6. The earliest state of the universe is inanimate.
7. The Big Bang singularity is inherently unpredictable and lawless, and consequently there is no guarantee that it will emit a maximal configuration of particles that will evolve into an animate state of the universe.

8. Therefore, the earliest state of the universe is not ensured to lead to an animate state of the universe.
9. Therefore, God did not create the earliest state of the universe.
10. Therefore, God does not exist.

As Smith himself notes, there are various places where this argument is vulnerable to objection. I shall begin by discussing the four objections considered in Smith (1991), before moving on to other objections that might also be lodged.

A. Unpredictability Does Not Entail Absence of Divine (Fore-)Knowledge
Some monotheists will surely want to object that the (alleged) fact that the Big Bang singularity is inherently unpredictable and lawless does not entail that no monotheistic god can know what will issue from a given initial singularity. In particular, some monotheists will follow the lead of Craig (1991b: 493ff.) in claiming that there are true counterfactuals about what would issue from any given initial singularity, and that a monotheistic god could know these true counterfactuals prior to the decision to create a given initial singularity. Against these Molinists, Smith (1991: 6off.) claims that considerations about the semantics of counterfactuals show that there cannot be true counterfactuals of the kind in question, since there isn't anything that could serve as truth makers for these counterfactuals. In response, Craig (1991b: 493ff.) insists that the counterfactuals in question could be barely true, that is, true, but not in virtue of the obtaining of any categorical state of affairs. As I shall further explain in Oppy (in preparation), it seems to me that this response violates a plausible requirement on truth makers for counterfactuals; I do not believe that there can be 'barely true' counterfactuals of the kind that Craig's response to Smith requires. Given the assumption that it is, indeed, an objectively chancy matter what emerges from a given initial singularity, it seems to me that it is true that not even a monotheistic god can know what will emerge from that singularity at the 'point in the order of creation at which the singularity appears'. Indeed, I would go further: I suspect that I am about as certain that there cannot be 'barely true' counterfactuals of the kind that Craig envisages as Craig is that 'nothing can come into existence uncaused'; and I face just the same kind of difficulty that he faces in trying to argue for something that just seems so evidently to be true. If there were nothing else wrong with Smith's argument, and nothing wrong with Craig's *kalām* argument other than its reliance upon the contested claim that 'nothing can come into existence uncaused', then I would be happy enough to say: these facts *alone* show that, as things stand, *both* arguments are unsuccessful. Against those intelligent, thoughtful philosophers who hold that there can be 'barely true' counterfactuals of the kind that Craig envisages, it is hard to see how one might even begin to construct an argument that there cannot be such counterfactuals: this is a quite fundamental level

of disagreement. Of course, future philosophers *might* make progress on this issue – just as they *might* make progress on the question of the possibility of entities that come into existence uncaused; but there is no question *now* of a resolution to the satisfaction of all intelligent, thoughtful, well-informed inquirers.

B. The Initial Singularity Is a Theoretical Fiction

As Smith (1991: 6off.) notes, some monotheists might wish to deny that there is an initial singular point (or surface) in Big Bang universes. Craig (1991b: 498ff.) suggests that monotheists might claim that "the temporal series is like a series of fractions converging towards zero as a limit: $1/2$, $1/4$, $1/8$, ... Just as there is no first fraction, so there is no first state of the universe." Moreover, according to Craig (1991b: 498), "If such a metaphysical interpretation of the initial singularity is even possible, then [Premise 5] is unsubstantiated, and Smith's anti-theistic argument is undercut." While – as I argued earlier – I agree with Craig's implicit suggestion that there are good reasons to deny that there is an initial singular point (or surface) in Big Bang universes, I do not think that Craig can reasonably claim that these considerations defeat Smith's atheological argument without also conceding that it defeats his own sub-arguments against the possibility of 'actual infinities'. If 'the possibility of this metaphysical interpretation' is sufficient to undermine Smith's atheological argument, then it is also sufficient to undermine Craig's theological argument *wherever* that theological argument relies on the assumption that the temporal series cannot be like a series of fractions converging towards zero as a limit: $1/2$, $1/4$, $1/8$, ... Of course, given the stance that I have already taken in my criticisms of Craig's argument, I take it that the premise in Smith's argument is false: there is no initial singular point (or surface) in Big Bang universes. Consequently, I take it that Smith's atheological cosmological argument fails for this reason *alone*.

C. Intervention Could Ensure an Animate Universe

Even if we have good reason to believe that a Big Bang singularity is inherently unpredictable and lawless, it seems that a monotheist can suppose that it is possible for a monotheistic god to 'intervene' at some point after the moment of creation to ensure that any universe that it creates turns out to be an animate universe. Against the proposal, Smith (1991: 56f) objects that a monotheistic deity would be manifestly *incompetent* if it were required to intervene after the initial creative act in order to realise its intentions for the universe. At best, this response might explain why premise 2 is included as part of Smith's argument; it is only if we make certain assumptions about the perfection of a monotheistic god that we might suppose that such a being could not create a Big Bang universe. But, in fact, it might be questioned whether we do have good reason to suppose that 'intervention' at some point after the moment of creation would reveal incompetence, even on the part of a perfect creator. Craig (1991b: 498ff.) suggests (i) that our ignorance about the goals and intentions of a perfect creator makes it impossible for us to justify a charge of 'inefficiency', and (ii) that there is no reason to suppose that a timeless omnipotent creator will be subject to any constraints of efficiency, since there are no limits to the time and power that it possesses, and hence no reasons for it to husband resources. Smith in Craig and Smith (1993: 239ff.) replies (i) that, since there is not the slightest evidence that there are goods that would be realised by divine intervention at some point after a Big Bang singularity that could not be realised in a direct creation of the thus modified state, the conclusion of his argument is plainly made plausible by its premises; and (ii) that a *perfect* timeless omnipotent creator will have aesthetic reasons to optimise its creative activities: it is intuitively plausible to suppose that it is a lapse from perfection to fail to optimise everything that one does. Craig in Craig and Smith (1993: 265ff.) responds (i) that 'sceptical theism' serves just as well to defeat Smith's argument as it does to defeat Rowe's evidential argument from evil, and (ii) that it is not at all evident that a creative being that intervenes at some point after the creation of a Big Bang singularity has failed to optimise its creative activities, even taking aesthetic considerations into account. I am sympathetic to *both* sides in this dispute. On the one hand, it seems to me that, if you believe that there is a perfect creator of the universe, then – more or less *a fortiori* – you will suppose that, for all you know, a perfect being could intervene in a Big Bang universe that it has already created in order to ensure that that universe is animate. But, on the other hand, it seems to me, if you believe that there is no perfect creator of the universe, then – again, more or less *a fortiori* – you will suppose that considerations about the inaccessibility of the intentions and goals of perfect beings must further diminish the strength of *a posteriori* arguments for the existence of such a creator; and, in particular, you will suppose that the considerations about intervention here dovetail perfectly with one's reasons for supposing that there is no perfect creator of the universe. Given that Craig and Smith disagree about many other related matters, it is more or less inevitable that Craig and Smith disagree about how the probabilities are to be assigned here. While my assignment of probabilities coincides with that of Smith, it seems to me that Craig is perfectly within his doxastic rights to insist on the reasonableness of his assignment of probabilities, given his doxastic lights. I see no reason why reasonable theists need be persuaded of the truth of the premise upon which Smith's atheological argument relies.

D. Why Is Creation of an Animate Universe Required?

As Smith (1993a: 254ff.) observes, some monotheists might claim that their monotheistic god is under no obligation to create an animate universe if, indeed, that god creates any universe at all. To this objection, Smith replies that it is simply inconsistent with the standard conception of a perfect monotheistic god that it fails to have more reason than not to create an animate universe. Craig (1991b: 502f.) claims that there is no reason why it should not be only contingently true that a perfect monotheistic god has more reason than not to create an animate universe. Smith in Craig and Smith (1993: 237) replies that, if a perfect monotheistic god is omnibenevolent, then it is bound to have more reason than not to create an animate universe. Craig in Craig and Smith (1993: 262f.) replies that a perfect monotheistic god need only be contingently omnibenevolent, though, of course, it will be essentially perfectly good. Moreover, if a perfect monotheistic god is triune, then there isn't even *prima facie* reason to suppose that it requires living creatures as the objects of its benevolence: each of the divine persons can will the good of the other two. In this dispute, at least initially, my sympathies lie with Craig. I don't see why one should expect that a perfect being would create an animate universe; indeed – as I argue at length in Oppy (in preparation) – I don't see why one should expect that a perfect being would create *anything at all*. There is at least some *prima facie* reason to suppose that creation must be a blemish on perfection. When Craig in Craig and Smith (1993: 263) writes: 'the wonder of creation is that God should voluntarily and out of no necessity of His own nature graciously choose to create finite persons and invite them into this inner fellowship of the Godhead', it seems to me that he is giving expression to essentially the same kind of point: far from supposing that there is good reason to suppose that a perfect monotheistic god must make an animate universe, there is actually good reason to suppose that a perfect monotheistic god would not make anything else at all.

Apart from the considerations that are picked up in the writings of Smith and Craig on this topic, there are some other reasons that one might have for being suspicious about Smith's atheological cosmological argument. In particular, it seems to me (i) that it is not obviously true that an animate universe is better than an inanimate universe, and (ii) that it is not obviously true that an initial singularity must be 'inherently unpredictable' in the sense that is required by Smith's argument. On the former point, it seems to me that one might justifiably observe that Smith's argument is curiously anthropocentric, in much the same kind of way that the 'cosmic fine tuning' arguments for design are curiously anthropocentric. On the latter point, it seems to me that one might justifiably observe that it is a controversial question whether we do have good reason to suppose that the physical universe is replete with objectively chancy features. If the 'inherent unpredictability' and 'lawlessness' of initial singularities is merely an epistemic – as opposed to ontological – matter, then there is not even *prima facie* reason to suppose that Big Bang cosmology counts against the existence of a perfect monotheistic creator. Since it is still a controversial matter whether we should suppose that the unpredictability of an initial singularity is merely epistemic, it could at best be a controversial matter whether Big Bang cosmology counts against the existence of a perfect monotheistic creator.

In sum, then, there are a number of reasons why it seems to me to be plausible to conclude that Smith's atheological cosmological argument is unsuccessful. *First*, the claim that there cannot be 'barely true' counterfactuals is sufficiently controversial that reliance upon it undermines the claim that Smith's argument is successful (even though, as I noted above, I see no reason at all to doubt that this claim is true). *Second*, it seems to me that there is very good reason to suppose that 'the initial singularity' in Big Bang models of the universe is a theoretical fiction; at the very least, this claim is far too controversial to support the contention that Smith's argument is successful. *Third*, it seems to me that there is insufficient support for the claim that, if there is a perfect creator of our universe, then it could not intervene at some point after the initial singularity in order to ensure an animate universe. *Fourth*, it seems to me that there is insufficient support for the claim that a perfect being is required to create an animate universe; indeed, it seems to me that there is insufficient support for the claim that it is plausible to suppose that a perfect being would create any universe at all. (Of course, this claim suggests a different kind of attack on perfect being theology; however, again, it seems to me that the key claim is too controversial to form the basis of a successful argument.) *Fifth*, it seems to me to be not at all obvious that animate universes are better than inanimate universes, or that the best animate universes are better than the best inanimate universes, or that there are animate universes that are non-arbitrarily better than all inanimate universes, and so forth. *Sixth*, there is room for suspicion about the claim that the 'inherent unpredictability' of initial singularities is not merely epistemic in nature; there is enough uncertainly in the interpretation of quantum mechanics and other key physical theories to allow for withholding of judgment on this matter. Given that Smith's atheological cosmological argument depends upon so many claims that are at best controversial, there is very good reason to deny that that argument is successful.

3.9.2. Self-Causation and Sufficient Reason

As we noted above, in the decade following the publication of the first version of his atheological cosmological argument, Smith has supplemented his discussion with defences of a variety of controversial theses. In Smith (1993b), he defends the claim that, if a mind's creation of a Big Bang singularity could be a causal act, then causation is indefinable. In Smith (1995a), he defends the claim that a beginningless universe has an internal causal explanation, though it has no external causal explanation. In Smith (1995b), he defends the claim that there is a sufficient reason why there are true propositions that entail that some contingent concrete object exists, *given* that space-time necessarily exists and contingently contains a

quantum-mechanical vacuum. In Smith (1997b), he defends the claim that
'The Law of the Simplest Beginning' – that is, the claim that the simplest
possible thing (i.e., an initial singularity) comes into existence in the simplest possible way (i.e., uncaused) – is a brute, contingent truth. In Smith
(1999), he defends the claim that there are three different ways of avoiding
the assumption of an uncaused beginning to the universe without appealing to an external cause, namely, (i) by appeal to a circle of internal causes,
(ii) by appeal to an infinite regress of internal causes, and (iii) by appeal to
'backward' internal causes.

While Smith's work on self-causation and sufficient reason seems to me
to be very interesting, I have doubts about at least some of it.

In particular, it seems to me that there are serious questions to be asked
about 'The Law of the Simplest Beginning'. The claim that it is a 'law' that
the simplest possible thing comes into existence in the simplest possible
way is, at best, highly controversial. Moreover, the suggestions that an initial
singularity is the simplest possible thing and that an uncaused beginning is
the simplest possible way to come into existence seem to me to be very hard
to support. It is not easy to see how 'The Law of the Simplest Beginning'
could be a *natural* law – for what is the domain in which it is intended
to have application? But even those who are not sceptical about the very
idea of natural laws should surely be sceptical about the suggestion that
there are *non-natural* laws that have application to the origins of universes.
It is also hard to see how one could devise uncontroversial metrics for the
complexity of possible things and the complexity of possible ways of coming
into existence. And even if one could devise such metrics, it is hard to see why
one should be confident that initial singularities and uncaused beginnings
will be identified as the simplest possible candidates according to these
metrics. Some theists might be inclined to insist that their monotheistic god
is the simplest possible thing – recall our earlier discussion of the doctrine
of divine simplicity – but it seems to me that one does better simply to refuse
to accept the terms of this discussion.

While there is much more that might be said about Smith's views on
self-causation and sufficient reason, I do not propose to discuss this topic
further here.

3.9.3. Alleged Consequences of 'The Hartle-Hawking Cosmology'

Smith (1994b) claims that 'the Hartle-Hawking cosmology' is inconsistent
with classical theism in a way that redounds to the discredit of classical
theism, and, moreover, that the truth of 'the Hartle-Hawking cosmology'
would undermine reasoned belief in any other varieties of theism that hold
that the universe is created.

I don't think that Smith manages to substantiate these *prima facie* implausible claims. In particular, I do not think that he manages to provide an

intelligible account of what he takes to be the crucial consequence of 'the Hartle-Hawking cosmology' – namely, that there is a probability strictly less than 100 percent and strictly greater than 0 percent of a universe like ours coming into existence *ex nihilo*. The main purpose of this section is to explain why it seems to me that this claim is simply incoherent.

There are other points at which Smith's arguments could be attacked. For example, Markosian (1995) objects to Smith's assumption, that the claim that an orthodoxly conceived monotheistic god wills that a universe with a given initial state exists *entails* the claim that the objective probability of such a universe coming into existence is 100 percent (and similarly to Smith's assumption, that the claim that an orthodoxly conceived monotheistic god wills that Hawking's wave function law obtain *entails* that the objective probability of our universe coming into existence is (say) 95 percent). Markosian's objection relies on the idea that one could evaluate the consequents of these conditionals at times earlier than the times at which the willings in the antecedents occur. However – as we have already had occasion to note, at least *inter alia* – it is quite doubtful that one should allow that there are times of the kind that Markosian's objection requires; and, certainly, Smith himself denies that there can be any such times. In any case, rather than object to the *entailments* that Smith's argument requires, *I* shall focus my attention on the coherence of the objective probabilities that Smith invokes.

There are various other critics – for example, Craig (1997b) and Deltete and Guy (1997) – who have contested the claim that Smith has shown that 'the Hartle-Hawking cosmology' yields a non-trivial *unconditional* probability for the coming into existence of our universe *ex nihilo*, on the grounds that one can interpret the relevant probabilities realistically only if one supposes that there is a prior *physical* state from which the universe evolves, that is, a prior state that is not properly described as 'nothing', and that is also not properly dismissed as a mere mathematical abstraction. It is clear that the line of criticism that I shall pursue is closely related to this one, though I do believe that it is distinct from it.

One might also worry about the way in which Smith formulates the problem. He defines 'classical theism' to be 'the theory that there necessarily exists a disembodied person who is necessarily omniscient, omnipotent and omnibenevolent and necessarily the cause of whatever universe there is' (p. 238). His main claim is that 'the Hartle-Hawking cosmology' is inconsistent with 'classical theism' thus construed. But this claim may be quite uninteresting: for it may be that 'classical theism' is internally inconsistent; and, even if it is not internally inconsistent, it may be that 'classical theism' is trivially inconsistent with 'the Hartle-Hawking cosmology'. (For example, a reading of Smith's definition that has it that there is only one initial state of the universe that an orthodoxly conceived monotheistic god could create – all others being inconsistent with his necessary omnibenevolence – is trivially inconsistent with any theory that assigns non-zero probabilities to non-actual initial states, and may be internally inconsistent as well.) Smith's claim might turn out to be comparatively uninteresting for other reasons. Suppose that most theists would commit themselves to no more than the claim that there is a very good, very wise, and very powerful person who created the universe – and suppose further that there are no compelling reasons for them to shift to stronger positions such as the one outlined by Smith. In that case, the important question will be whether *this* position is inconsistent with 'the Hartle-Hawking cosmology'. (Hawking himself seems to claim that his cosmology makes the hypothesis of any kind of creator otiose; if Smith really means to defend Hawking, then surely it is this claim that he ought to be defending.) However, I don't need to fuss about these details: if I am right to claim that Smith's account of 'the Hartle-Hawking cosmology' is incoherent, then the further details of Smith's argument can be safely ignored.

A. Smith's Argument

To begin, we should hear from Smith:

Hawking's atheistic dreadnaught is a 'wave function of the universe'. The wave function is $\Psi[h_{ij}, \phi]$. Without bothering overly much about technical niceties, we may take ϕ as representing the matter field of the initial state of the universe, roughly, how much matter this state contains and how it is distributed. h_{ij} may be regarded as representing the metrical structure of the initial state of the universe, that is, the sort of curvature possessed by the three dimensional space of this state. Ψ is the amplitude, which is important since the square of the modulus of the amplitude gives a probability, namely, the probability that the universe will begin to exist with the metric h_{ij} and the matter field ϕ. The square of the modulus of the amplitude is $\Psi|[h_{ij}, \phi]|^2$. As Hartle and Hawking say, this gives us the probability 'for the Universe to appear from nothing', specifically, it gives us the unconditional probability that a universe begins to exist with the metric h_{ij} and matter field ϕ.... Hawking's cosmology... implies that it is probable (to a degree less than one) that the universe begins to exist with a non-singular state, namely h_{ij}, ϕ, in accordance with the wave function $\Psi[h_{ij}, \phi]$. (236–7)

This may sound forbiddingly technical; but none of the technicalities will matter. The basic idea divides into two parts: (i) that there is a way of assigning probabilities to possible initial states of universes, and (ii) that these probabilities can be interpreted as unconditional probabilities for the coming into existence *ex nihilo* of universes with those initial states. (Jazzing things up a little, the idea is that there is a wave function, Ψ, the square of the modulus of the amplitude of which gives unconditional probabilities for the coming into existence *ex nihilo* of universes with characteristics determined by the points or regions of the space over which the wave function is defined.)

Two different kinds of objections to these ideas immediately suggest them-selves. First – and most important – it seems that no coherent sense can be given to the idea that an assignment of possibilities of the kind in question *could* be interpreted as an assignment of unconditional probabilities for the coming into existence *ex nihilo* of universes with given initial states. Second, the suggestion that there is a space of (aspects of) initial states of universes over which a wave function can be defined clearly *could* give rise to vari-ous difficulties if one tried to assign some kind of substantival existence to the space in question – but it isn't clear that Smith's argument manages to avoid the attribution of some kind of substantival existence to the space in question. I shall consider these objections in turn.

B. Probabilities?

It is plain that Smith is supposing that the probabilities that are to be assigned to possible initial states of the universe are objective probabilities – that is, they are not measures of epistemic uncertainty and the like, but rather measures of what Lewis calls 'chances'. One might worry about whether there are any such things – cf. Markosian's worries about unconditional probabilities (Markosian (1995: 248)) – but I shall simply set this kind of worry aside. (I think that quantum mechanics requires objective chances, but I don't propose to try to justify this contention here.)

Ordinarily, these objective probabilities must be indexed to worlds and times: events have chances at times in worlds. (For example, there was a 10 percent chance at time t_0 that this radioactive atom would decay within the next 25 seconds.) But – on the assumption that there is now a determi-nate, non-probabilistic fact of the matter about the initial state of the actual universe (and, more generally, on the assumption that for any time from the time of the initial state on there is a determinate, non-probabilistic fact of the matter about the initial state of the actual universe) – these indexed objective probabilities can't be what Smith has in mind. Why? Consider the thought that, at some time t_n, there is a certain objective probability that our world evolved from a given initial state. Given the assumption that there is a determinate, non-probabilistic fact of the matter about the initial state of the universe at any time from the time of the initial state on, this thought must be mistaken: *at any time*, the objective chance that our universe evolved from a given initial state is 1 or 0, depending upon whether or not our universe did evolve from that initial state. Or, more cautiously, *at any time from the initial state of the universe on*, the objective chance that our universe evolved from a given initial state is 1 or 0, depending upon whether or not our uni-verse did evolve from that initial state. If there is a time at which there is a certain objective probability that our world evolve from a given initial state, that time must be a time that precedes the initial state of the universe.

The same point applies if we try to develop Smith's account in the con-text of an ensemble of universes. Consider the thought that we can assign objective probabilities to the existence of universes with given initial states ('the unconditional probability that a universe begins to exist with [given initial conditions]'). Given the assumption that there are now – and at all other times from the times of the relevant initial states on – determinate, non-probabilistic facts of the matter about the existence of universes with given initial states, this thought must be mistaken: for, at any time (except times prior to the initial states of the universes in question), the objective probability that there is a universe with a given initial state is 1 or 0, depending upon whether or not there is such a universe.

Quite generally, we – here, now – must suppose that objective unconditional probabilities about entirely past events and about temporally unconnected events (e.g. – at least on standard assumptions – the existence of other universes) are 1 or 0; or else we must give up the assumption that there are now determinate, non-probabilistic facts of the matter about entirely past events and temporally unconnected events. Since Smith clearly does suppose that there is now a determinate, non-probabilistic fact of the matter about the initial state of the universe, it seems that he does not have the resources to provide a coherent account of the objective probabilities that figure in his argument.

(Talk about 'the initial state of the universe' in this section may seem problematic: surely, we don't need to commit ourselves to the claim that there was a first instant of time, even if we do want to accept that the universe is temporally bounded in the past. Agreed. But this talk is harmless, since we could talk instead about 'some suitably small initial segment of the universe', without needing to make any substantive changes to the argument. Since it is simpler to persist with the fiction that there is a first instant of time, I shall continue to do so – nothing substantial turns on this pretence *here*.)

C. Substantival Space?

The only way out – it seems to me – is for Smith to allow that the space over which the objective probabilities are to be distributed has some kind of independent, determinate, non-probabilistic reality: given just the existence of this space, there are objective probabilities concerning the existence of universes with certain initial states. Or, rather, given just the existence of this space, there are objective probabilities about the *coming into* existence of universes with certain initial states. And in the qualification lies the rub: it is not enough that the space over which the probabilities are distributed is invested with some kind of independent reality, it must also be invested with temporal properties – that is, it must be supposed to be somehow temporally (and causally) antecedent to our universe. In order for there to be objective probabilities about the *coming into* existence of universes with certain initial states, there must be times that precede the coming into existence of the universes in question – and, in order for this to be possible, there must be a temporal space over which the probabilities can be distributed.

Even if the suggestion is coherent – about which more later – it is clearly disastrous for Smith's argument. In particular, if this is the right way to interpret 'the Hartle-Hawking cosmology', then it is clearly *not* the case that it involves 'a Universe appearing from nothing': if the objective probabilities invoked in Smith's interpretation of the model are intelligible, then this is precisely because there are other temporally prior entities upon which the existence of the Universe depends. Yet, if this point is conceded, then classical theism – or, at least, something very much like it – can embrace 'the Hartle-Hawking cosmology' while nonetheless insisting that it was an orthodoxly conceived monotheistic god who created those prior entities.

It should be noted here that, on this kind of account, an orthodoxly conceived monotheistic god would be a cause – perhaps indeed *the* cause – of the universe. If I point a gun at you and arrange for it to be triggered if a certain radioactive particle decays within a certain period of time, and if the particle decays within that period of time leading to your death, then I have caused your death. Smith's argument – in sections 3–5 of his paper – is undermined by, among other things, his failure to consider alternatives in which an orthodoxly conceived monotheistic god creates temporal entities – hence, entities other than laws – which in turn lead to the existence of universes. Moreover, even if all an orthodoxly conceived monotheistic god does is to will that a certain law obtains, and if it is a consequence of that law that there is a 95 percent chance that a universe should arise, and if a universe does arise, then – *pace* Smith – an orthodoxly conceived monotheistic god is the cause of the existence of the universe.

D. Emergence ex nihilo?

Although it is dubious whether it is coherent – let alone consistent with modern physics – to suppose that there are entities or states or spaces that are temporally prior to the universe, it seems plausible to suggest that the informal gloss that Hartle and Hawking place on their 'wave function for the Universe' does commit them to such a supposition. For consider: 'One can interpret the functional integral over all compact four geometries bounded by a given three-geometry as giving the amplitude for that three-geometry to arise from a zero three-geometry, i.e. a single point. In other words, the ground state is the amplitude for the Universe to appear from nothing' (p. 2961).

Even ignoring the fact that a single point is not nothing, it seems very doubtful that this claim about possible interpretations of the functional integral can be correct. In particular, there is the following obvious question: why is it correct (or natural) to interpret the functional integral as giving the amplitude for that geometry to *arise* from a zero geometry; and, more basically, what could be meant by the description 'the amplitude for a three-geometry to *arise* from a zero-geometry'? It is one thing to develop a device that assigns probabilities to three-geometries (of a certain kind); it is quite another to say that this device yields probabilities that are amplitudes for those geometries to *arise* from a zero geometry.

The temporal (and causal) implications of 'arise' are not the only difficulties here. There are, after all, lots of initial states of the universe that get assigned non-zero probabilities. But if the probabilities in question are probabilities for the emergence *ex nihilo* of universes with given initial states, then we have objective probabilities for the emergence of lots of universes distinct from ours. Should we think that some (most, all) of these universes exist? If not, why not? (Note how Smith switches back and forth between talk of probabilities for 'a universe' to emerge from nothing, and talk of probabilities for 'the universe' to emerge from nothing.) Of course, on at least some interpretations of quantum mechanics, ordinary wave functions 'collapse' to unique values under some conditions – but why should there be taken to be this kind of 'collapse' if there isn't any prior state for the collapse to precede from? Unless the emergence of one universe prevents the emergence of any other, then it is hard to understand how there can be mere probabilities for universes to emerge – and yet it is equally hard to understand how 'the Hartle-Hawking cosmology' requires or ensures that the emergence of one universe prevents the emergence of any other. (Remember: the universes 'come from nothing': so it's not as if there is a pre-existing arena that only one universe can occupy.)

In view of these problems, it seems plausible to suggest that one might look for other interpretations of the functional integral. Moreover, it seems that other interpretations should not be hard to come by: for most of the standard interpretations of quantum mechanics, there will be a corresponding interpretation of the functional integral. For example, there will be an interpretation according to which it is an 'eternally' chancy matter what 'the boundary' of the universe is like, since there was no collapse of the wave function on 'the boundary' (this amounts to giving up the assumption that there is now a determinate, non-probabilistic fact of the matter about the initial state of the universe). And there will be an interpretation according to which there are many worlds, only some of which have the same kind of 'boundary' as our world (here, *modulo* problems about cardinality that need to be finessed, the probabilities give the percentages of worlds that have given kinds of 'boundaries'). And so on.

Perhaps there will be insurmountable problems for other attempted interpretations of the functional integral. (I don't have the technical expertise to tell.) If not, then we can be confident that these interpretations will not require the (incoherent) idea that the functional integral yields an amplitude for 'the universe to appear from nothing' – and hence we shall not have any reason (of the kind that Smith provides) to think that the interpretation is incompatible with classical theism. On the other hand, if no other interpretation can be provided, then we can either (i) refuse to give any serious interpretation of the 'probabilities' allegedly defined by the functional integral (while otherwise continuing to endorse 'the Hartle-Hawking cosmology') or – as Smith himself acknowledges – (ii) reject 'the Hartle-Hawking cosmology' as an adequate cosmological theory. Of course, neither of these options poses any particular threat to classical theism.

(It is worth noting that the second of these options – that is, refusing to accept 'the Hartle-Hawking cosmology' – is particularly attractive, to a much greater extent than Smith himself allows; after all, the simple fact is that even most physicists don't think that 'the Hartle-Hawking cosmology' gives a true description of the early universe. Given the state of current investigations into the early universe – a state marked by widespread disagreement even about the vocabulary in which the theory ought to be couched – it is massively implausible to think that a demonstration that classical theism is inconsistent with 'the Hartle-Hawking cosmology' would present any sort of obstacle to current reasonable theistic belief.)

E. Concluding Remarks
In sum, then: there is no reason at all to think that 'the Hartle-Hawking cosmology' has dramatic consequences for classical theism (or for any other kind of religious belief). However, it should not be too quickly concluded that there are no prospects for rehabilitating Smith's argument.

Markosian (1995: 248) suggests, *inter alia*, that if there were an argument from 'the Hartle-Hawking cosmology' to the rejection of classical theism, then there would be an argument from orthodox quantum mechanics – or, indeed, from any other non-deterministic theory that traffics in objective chances – to the rejection of classical theism. The idea, I take it, would be something like this: Consider an allegedly chancy event, for example, the decay of a radioactive particle. Quantum mechanics assigns a certain value, strictly greater than zero and strictly less than one, to the chance that this particle will decay in a given period of time. But if an orthodoxly conceived monotheistic god wills every detail of the world, and if there is, in advance of the event, a fact of the matter about what the particle will do – suppose, for example, that it will decay in the given time – then it seems that quantum mechanics must be wrong – since, under our supposition, the objective chance that the particle will decay is one.

Of course, this is a familiar argument, and one that has nothing at all to do with 'the Hartle-Hawking cosmology'. Moreover, there are various strategies that might be employed in response, for example, one could deny that an orthodoxly conceived monotheistic god wills the outcome of genuinely chancy events, whether or not an orthodoxly conceived monotheistic god knows what these outcomes will be; or one could deny that an orthodoxly conceived monotheistic god so much as knows what the outcomes of genuinely chancy events will be; or one can give an epistemic interpretation to the quantum-mechanical probabilities (factoring out the information that an orthodoxly conceived monotheistic god knows in advance what the outcomes will be); or one can deny that an orthodoxly conceived monotheistic god's knowledge (and/or willing) has any effect on the objectively chancy status of the event; and so on.

3.10. CONCLUDING REMARKS

Even if the discussion to this point does succeed in establishing that the various theistic arguments that I have examined are unconvincing, it is clear that this is only a small part of all that non-theists might hope to claim about these arguments. For all that has been argued here, it could be that there are reformulations of the arguments that have been examined that are convincing. Moreover – and perhaps more plausibly – for all that has been argued here, it could be that there are quite different arguments that draw upon the same kinds of intuitive considerations that are appealed to in the arguments that I have examined, but that do provide convincing support for their conclusions.

Part of the difficulty here is that the task of rejecting these kinds of arguments seems endless: there are many variations on each of the arguments, and each of these variations deserves to be treated on its merits. Of course, non-theists may very plausibly have further beliefs – even world-views – that support the conclusion that no argument of any of these kinds *can* be cogent. But it seems to me to be highly plausible to suppose that there is even more variation amongst the fundamental theoretical commitments of non-theists than there is amongst the fundamental theoretical commitments of theists: for all that non-theists have in common is their rejection of theism. True enough, theism admits of a wide variety of fundamental theoretical commitments – even amongst monotheists, there are many important differences and disagreements – but all theists are united by the fact that they endorse theism: they believe in the existence of supernatural agency, and so forth. In the face of the evident variation in the fundamental theoretical commitments of non-theists, it seems to me that it is prudent to try to do no more than to set out a taxonomy of the range of questions that must be faced, and of the kinds of choices that can be made. If we could all agree on this much, that would at least be a start.

As I note in the preface to Oppy (2006), a full discussion of the theoretical background of cosmological arguments requires a thorough discussion of infinity, time, causation, necessity, sufficient reason, and contemporary cosmology. (Perhaps it requires a thorough discussion of other topics as well.) Here, I can do no more than indicate what the questions are that need to be examined in the course of this discussion.

3.10.1. Infinity

There is a series of questions about infinity that we need to address. First, we need to answer the question of whether the concept of the (numerical) infinite is coherent. Second, if we decide that the concept of the (numerical) infinite is coherent, we need to answer the question of whether the concept of the (numerical) infinite can have any correct application to non-abstract subject matters. Finally, if we decide that the concept of the (numerical) infinite can have application to non-abstract subject matters, we need to answer the question of whether there is reason to suppose that the concept of the (numerical) infinite does have correct application to non-abstract subject matters. (For what it's worth, my own view – argued for in Oppy (2006) – is that the concept of the (numerical) infinite is indeed coherent, that the concept of the (numerical) infinite can have correct application to non-abstract subject matters, and that there are a number of strong – but plainly defeasible – reasons to suppose that the concept of the (numerical) infinite does have correct application to non-abstract subject matters. At present, there is good empirical evidence that the future of our universe is infinite. Moreover, even if we restrict ourselves to the present and past states of our world, it seems to me that there is good reason to hold that there are infinitely many different spatial regions, if not infinitely many different spatial points, and that there is also good reason to hold that the "series of past events" may be infinite even if the universe began with a Big Bang. Finally, it seems to me that it is an open question of whether contingent reality extends beyond the confines of our universe; if it does, then the question of the application of the concept of infinity to contingent reality takes on a very different appearance.)

3.10.2. Time

There are several different kinds of questions that we need to answer in connection with time. First, there are the questions that arise when we ask whether time is a substance. Second, there are the questions that arise when we ask whether the past and/or the future are real. Third, there are the questions that arise when we ask whether time is composed of instants. Fourth, there are the questions that arise when we ask whether time is fundamental, that is, whether time belongs to the supervenience base of the universe. (For what it's worth, a brief summary of my own views on these matters is as follows. While there is good reason to be sceptical about the use of the labels 'substantivalism' and 'relationalism' in connection with theories of time, there is something right about the view that time is a substance: the general theory of relativity provides fairly strong support for the view that the spatiotemporal manifold has an independent existence or reality.

Similar considerations drawn from contemporary physics also support the view that both the past and the future exist, and (hence) that there are true claims about the future that are made true by the future, whether or not they are also made true by how things have been up until the present. In my view, there is good – but plainly defeasible – reason to suppose that time is composed of instants, that is, to suppose that time has the structure of the real numbers: while we presently have no idea how to construct an empirically adequate theory in which time does not have the structure of the real numbers, future physics might well give one reason to reject the contention that time is composed of instants. Finally, it seems to me that it is somewhat uncertain whether time is anything more than a supervenient feature of the universe: the balance of probabilities may favour the view that time is fundamental, but there is considerable speculation amongst contemporary physicists about whether this is really so.)

3.10.3. Causation

There are so many different relevant questions that arise when one turns to the topic of causation that it is hard to know where to begin. First, there are questions about the scope of the concept of causation: should we suppose that all causes are efficient causes, or should we accept further parts of the traditional schedule of "causes"? Second, there are questions about the analysis of causation, on each of the types of causation that we admit. In particular, for example, there are many competing accounts of efficient causation between which one needs to decide: regularity theories, counterfactual theories, network theories, conserved quantity theories, agency theories, and so forth. Third, there are questions about the kinds of efficient causation that one is prepared to countenance: should we suppose that there is an efficient cause for the continued existence of the world that is (at least conceptually) distinct from the efficient causes that explain why states of *this* kind succeed states of *that* kind? Fourth, there are questions about the relata of causal relations: is the relationship of cause and effect primarily a relationship between objects, or events, or facts, or states of affairs, or propositions, or what? Fifth, there are questions about the basic principles that govern each of the distinct kinds of causes that we admit. So, for example, if we suppose that events are the basic causal relata, there is the question of whether we should suppose that every contingent event has an efficient cause. Sixth, there are questions about the bearing of contemporary physical theories on the answers to some of the preceding questions. For example, how should we suppose that quantum mechanics and general relativity bear on the question of whether every contingent event has an efficient cause? Seventh, there are questions about the analysis of determinism, objective chance, and freedom of choice: for example, what are the consequences of analyses of efficient causation – and accounts of basic principles that govern efficient causation – on further claims about determinism, objective chance, and freedom of choice? Eighth, there are questions about the relationship between causation and supervenience: for example, can we allow that there is any such thing as supervenient causation? And there are more important questions about causation that bear on the analysis of cosmological arguments that we have not yet mentioned. (While I have views on all of these questions, I won't try to summarise these views here.)

3.10.4. Necessity

In Oppy (2006), I briefly note most of the important questions that need to be addressed when we turn to a discussion of alethic modality. First, there are questions about the different kinds of modalities that can be distinguished: alethic, epistemic, doxastic, and so forth. Moreover, within each of these broad kinds, there are further important distinctions to be considered: perhaps, for example, we can distinguish among narrowly logical, broadly logical, and metaphysical alethic modalities. Second, there are questions about the logic of the various kinds of modalities that we have distinguished: there are many controversial questions that need to be answered before one settles on any given quantified modal logic. Third, there are hard questions about the semantics of modal discourse and, in particular, about the ontology to which one is committed in making modal claims. Should we suppose that modal discourse commits us to the existence of possible worlds; and, if so, what should we suppose these worlds to be? Fourth, there are equally hard questions about the epistemology of modal discourse and, in particular, about the connections between imagination and alethic modality. Should we suppose that whatever seems to us to be clearly and distinctly conceivable is metaphysically possible? Should we suppose that any "recombination" of the "elements" of the actual world is itself a possible world? (As I have already noted, I have no firm views on many of the key questions about modal ontology and modal epistemology. I'm inclined to reject the claim that there is any clear distinction between 'broadly logical' and 'metaphysical' modality, and to insist that those who think that there is a distinction here are very probably conflating alethic modality with doxastic modality. Consequently, I'm inclined to think that those who insist on connections between alethic modality and conceivability are also very probably conflating alethic modality with some kind of doxastic modality. However, I don't have a developed theory of alethic modality to replace the more or less orthodox conceivability account.)

3.10.5. Sufficient Reason

In Oppy (2006), I provide a fairly cursory account of principles of sufficient reason. Here, it seems to me that it is clear enough what questions should be asked. First, there are questions about the taxonomy of principles of sufficient reason: what different kinds of principles of sufficient reason might be proposed as candidates for belief? Second, there are questions about the analysis of the notion of 'sufficient reason': for instance, should we suppose that sufficient reasons necessitate that for which they are sufficient reasons? Third, there are questions about the reasonableness of endorsing strong principles of sufficient reason: are there, for example, good arguments for the claim that strong principles of sufficient reason are self-undermining? Fourth, there are questions about the utility of weaker principles of sufficient reason: if, for example, we suppose that principles of sufficient reason are merely methodological rules of thumb, then can we seriously suppose that they can be made to carry a substantial metaphysical load? (It may be recalled that I argued that stronger principles of sufficient reason are, indeed, self-undermining, and that acceptable principles of sufficient reason need to be so weak that they are not fit for the purposes to which proponents of cosmological arguments have wished to put principles of sufficient reason.)

3.10.6. Contemporary Cosmology

There are many questions about contemporary cosmology – and contemporary science more generally – that bear on the assessment of cosmological arguments. First, there are questions about the way that we should assess the bearing of empirical evidence upon metaphysical theorising: should we think that *a priori* first philosophy provides us with reason to reject widely accepted scientific theories, or should we suppose that widely accepted scientific theories almost certainly trump allegedly *a priori* first philosophy? Second, there are questions about the interpretation of scientific theories: should we be realists about our scientific theories, or should we give them some kind of non-realist interpretation? And if we are realists about our scientific theories, how do we determine exactly what it is that acceptance of these theories commits us to? For instance, would acceptance of general relativity commit us to the existence of space-time points? Third, if we are to be realists about our scientific theories, there are questions about the standing of particular scientific theories: for example, how confident should we be that quantum mechanics – or general relativity, or orthodox Big Bang cosmology – is true? Fourth, there are questions about the relationship between science and other spheres of inquiry: should we suppose that science fits seamlessly into a single scheme of inquiry, or should we suppose that there are schemes of inquiry – for example, 'common sense' – that are prior to, and more reliable than, science? (Once again – as in the case of causation – I shall not try to summarise my views on these matters, though I do have reasonably considered opinions about almost all of the questions mentioned.)

Given the long schedule of questions that we have just rehearsed, it seems to me to be plausible to suppose that one could be faced with interlocutors who are able to go on giving answers to these questions that do not indicate any evident lapses from rationality, but who disagree greatly with one another on the answers to given questions. On the one hand, I suppose that there can be theists who have answers to all of these questions that, taken together, form a coherent and rationally defensible view of the world. On the other hand, I suppose that there can be non-theists who have answers to all of these questions that, taken together, form a coherent and rationally defensible view of the world. If these suppositions are correct, then we should be very sceptical about claims to the effect that there are successful cosmological arguments that serve to vindicate either theism or atheism. If person A reasonably accepts propositions $p_1, \ldots, p_n$, and person B reasonably accepts propositions $q_1, \ldots, q_m$, where many different subsets of the p_i and q_j are jointly inconsistent, then it will be easy for each of A and B to construct arguments, appealing mostly to premises that the other accepts, but with one or two propositions that they accept but their opponent rejects thrown in, that 'establish' that their opponent's position reduces to absurdity. Before we turn to look at any cosmological arguments – and before we note the various other kinds of difficulties that actually recorded cosmological arguments face – it is highly plausible to suppose that there is not going to be a *short* and *simple* argument that succeeds in establishing either theistic or non-theistic conclusions. But all of the arguments that we have considered here are short and simple: none has the dozens of complex premises that would be required in order to evade the charge that one is simply begging the question on key issues. So we should not be in the least bit surprised to discover that there are many different things that are wrong with the kinds of arguments that we have examined.

4

Teleological Arguments

Although I haven't emphasised this point in my previous discussion, it is plausible to suppose that a full discussion of teleological arguments would also need to be very extensive indeed. As in the earlier discussion of cosmological arguments, I shall need to give a fairly summary treatment of many of the key issues.[1]

The plan of this chapter is as follows. I begin with a discussion of Paley's famous presentation of 'the eighteenth century argument for design' that is set out in his *Natural Theology*, and then move on to a discussion of the updated version of Paley's argument that is defended by Michael Behe. Next, I examine the recent discussion of fine-tuning design arguments, before turning to a discussion of some of the important features of Hume's critique of arguments for design. The last comments in this chapter take up the question of the general bearing of considerations about infinity on arguments for design.

4.1. BIOLOGICAL DESIGN: PALEY

Discussions of Paley's argument typically begin by insisting either that Paley's argument is an argument by analogy or that Paley's argument is best understood as an argument by inference to the best explanation, or perhaps both of these things at once.[2] However, it seems to me that, if we look carefully

---

[1] For other discussions of biological arguments for design, see, e.g.: Taylor (1963), Jack (1964), O'Briant (1967), Plantinga (1967), Swinburne (1968, 1972), Tennant (1969), Pearl (1970), Olding (1971, 1973), Grave (1976), Ruse (1977), Nelson (1978), Doore (1980), Mackie (1982), Dawkins (1986), Glass and Wolfe (1986), Behe (1996a), Dembski (1998), and Manson (2003). For other discussions of fine-tuning arguments for design, see, e.g.: Davis (1987), Leslie (1989), Wilson (1991), Collins (1999, 2003), White (2000), Manson (2000a, 2000b, 2003), McGrew et al. (2001), and Manson and Thrush (2003).

[2] Examples of those who claim that Paley's argument is an argument by analogy include: Martin (1959: 4), Hurlbutt (1965: 171–2), Barbour (1966: 84), Hardy (1975: 28), Gillespie

174

at the considerations that Paley actually presents, then we shall see that his argument is not best characterised in either of these ways. Perhaps it might nonetheless be the case that the best way to understand the overall project of Paley's *Natural Theology*[3] is to suppose that he is advocating an argument by inference to the best explanation – or some other related inductive technique – to the conclusion that an orthodoxly conceived monotheistic god exists; but we shall be in a better position to evaluate this suggestion once we are clearer about the form of the argument that Paley actually uses.

Paley's initial discussion – in which he sets out and defends his argument – may be thought of as having four parts. In the first part, Paley makes some remarks about the inevitability of inference to design in certain cases. In the second part, Paley notes that the inevitability of this inference is quite robust, and survives various kinds of philosophical objections. In the third part, Paley argues that it would make no difference to the inevitability of the inference to design in the cases in question if there were also something analogous to biological reproduction present in these cases. In the fourth and final part, Paley claims that inference to design in the case of the works of nature is no less justified than the 'inevitable inferences' described in the first part of the argument. I shall consider these various parts of Paley's discussion in turn.

4.1.1. The Watchmaker Argument

Famously, Paley begins by arguing that, if we were to find a watch, we would inevitably suppose that the watch had a designer and maker:

In crossing a heath, suppose I pitched my foot against a stone, and were asked how the stone came to be there, I might possibly answer, that, for any thing I knew to the contrary, it had lain there for ever: nor would it perhaps be very easy to shew the absurdity of this answer. But suppose I had found a watch upon the ground, and it should be enquired how the watch happened to be in that place, I should hardly think of the answer which I had before given, that, for any thing I knew, the watch might have always been there. Yet why should not this answer serve for the watch as well as for the stone? Why is it not as admissible in the second case, as in the first? For this reason, and for no other, viz. that, when we come to inspect the watch, we

(1979: 84), Ruse (1979: 70–1), Swinburne (1979: 134–6), Mackie (1982: 133–145), Bowler (1984: 49,117), Leslie (1989: 151), Martin (1990: 125), Davies (1993: 95), Gould (1993: 138–52), Moody (1996: 94), Swinburne (1996: 57–8), Davis (1997: 99), Clack and Clack (1998: 25–6), and many others from many different disciplines. An example of those who claim that Paley's argument is an argument by inference to the best explanation is Sober (1993: 30–1). The lone dissenting voice that I know of – to be discussed right at the end of this chapter – is Matson (1965: 125–31). Perhaps the most egregious of those mentioned above is Barbour, who attributes an argument to Paley that begins: "Just as a person on a desert island, finding a watch whose parts are integrated...".

[3] Paley (1890/1805). All page numbers in the main text are to this work.

perceive (what we could not discover in the stone) that its several parts are framed and put together for a purpose. . . . This mechanism being observed (it requires indeed an examination of the instrument, and perhaps some previous knowledge of the subject, to perceive and understand it; but, being once, as we have said, observed and understood), the inference, we think, is inevitable, that the watch must have had a maker: that there must have existed, at some time and at some place or other, an artificer or artificers who formed it for the purpose which we find it actually to answer; who comprehended its construction, and designed its use. (9–11)

Although it can't be said that Paley's discussion is entirely clear, it seems reasonable to suggest that he supposes that it is the observations (i) that the watch has a principal function, (ii) that various of the parts of the watch have functions, and (iii) that the materials from which the parts are constructed are well suited to the functions that those parts have that lead us to make the inference that the watch has a designer. (For future reference, I shall introduce the label "Paley's Hypothesis" to refer to this claim: *that it is the observations (i) that the watch has a principal function, (ii) that various of the parts of the watch have functions, and (iii) that the materials from which the parts are constructed are well suited to the functions that those parts have that lead us to make the inference that the watch has a designer.*)

Some of Paley's language may suggest that he thinks that when we look at the watch we (can) just see that it is a designed product – 'we perceive that its several parts are framed and put together for a purpose' – but there are at least two reasons why this can't be what he intends: (i) if this were right, there would be no need to speak about 'inference'; and (ii) the discussion would not carry over to the works of nature, since it simply isn't true that we (can) just see that animals and plants are designed products. (At any rate, those of us who are not already persuaded of the truth of the conclusion of the argument for design – and more, besides – do not see any such thing. And that's enough to undermine any argument based on this alternative way of understanding Paley's initial discussion.)

However, if this is right, then there is clearly room for questioning whether Paley has correctly identified the source of our confidence in the 'inference' that a given watch is the product of design. There are at least two difficulties here. On the one hand, it seems highly doubtful that it is considerations about 'function' that play the main role: there are other more immediate things that we see when we inspect the watch that will make the 'inference' to design inevitable. And, on the other hand, it seems highly doubtful that considerations about 'function' could be sufficient to underwrite the 'infer-ence' to design. Let's take these points in turn.

Paley notes, parenthetically, that there may be some role for background knowledge in the discernment of the function of the watch and its parts, and of the suitability of the materials from which the parts are constructed for the functions that they serve. But it is clear that there are other roles that background knowledge could play in the inference to 'design'. For example, we all know that brass does not occur in nature; likewise, we all know that smooth, clear glass is made in factories. Again, we all know that cogwheels do not grow on trees. And so on. Surely, it is this kind of knowledge that makes it inevitable that we shall 'infer' that the watch is the product of intelligent design.[4] (Suppose that the CPU from my desktop computer had fallen through a space-time wormhole, and that Paley had stubbed his toe on it while walking on his favourite heath. I have no doubt that he would have had no trouble identifying the CPU as a product of intelligent design, even though he would not have recognised the materials from which it is made, and even though he would not have been able to guess at the function that it – and almost all of its parts – serve. A similar point could be made for Geiger counters and countless other manufactured objects.)

Suppose, instead, that Paley had come upon a rabbit's heart lying on the common. Given a little background knowledge, he would have recognised that this is something with a proper function, with parts that have proper functions, and with parts whose material constitution is well suited to the functions that those parts play. (Think, for example, of the natural functions of cell membranes, cell nuclei, etc.) Nonetheless, I don't think that there is the slightest reason to suppose that there is anything at all inevitable about the 'inference' from the observed properties of the rabbit's heart to the conclusion that it is the product of intelligent design. (Again, perhaps some people might find this inference 'inevitable'; but it is surely plausible to think that this reaction will not be found in anyone other than those who are already thoroughly convinced that the natural world is the product of intelligent design.)

If the above is correct, then it seems clear that the claim that Paley actually makes in the first part of his initial discussion leaves his overall argument dead in the water. The compelling reasons that we have for supposing that the watch is the product of intelligent design simply do not carry over to reasons for supposing that the natural world is the product of intelligent design. The background knowledge that we have about the production of manufactured materials and components is not paralleled by any comparable knowledge about the production of biological materials and components. And the suggestion that considerations concerning 'function' and 'suitability of materials to function' are sufficient to underwrite the 'inference' is clearly question-begging. What the argument purports to *establish* is that these kinds of considerations alone suffice to underwrite an inference to intelligent design; hence, it cannot rest on the *presupposition* that these kinds of considerations do, in fact, suffice to underwrite that inference.

---

[4] There may be some philosophers who will want to insist that it is an analytic – or necessary, or perhaps even a *priori* – truth that watches are the products of intelligent design (and hence to suggest that my suggestion is no more accurate than was Paley's). However, this consideration is not really to the present point: for we can still ask about what grounds our 'inference' to the conclusion that *this* thing is a watch, and then exactly the same considerations will arise over again.

Even though it will plainly follow that the overall argument that Paley gives is no good, I don't think that this is a reason for rejecting my interpretation of the key claim in the first part of his initial presentation of the argument. Perhaps we can construct a better argument for biological design in terms of inference to the best explanation. But I do not think that any such argument can be read naturally into the text that Paley actually produced. Moreover, it is not particularly relevant that Paley might have happily adopted one of these modern versions of the argument; that can be true even if the argument that Paley actually gives fails in ways in which those modern arguments do not.[5]

4.1.2. Some Objections Addressed

Paley argues that the inference to the conclusion, that the watch must have had a maker, is very robust. On the one hand, our confidence in the inevitability of the conclusion is not shaken even if we are quite ignorant about relevant matters concerning watches and their production. And, on the other hand, other hypotheses that one might offer in competition with the claim about design seem implausible or even downright silly. Let's take these points in turn.

In Paley's view, it would make no difference to the inevitability of the inference if (i) we had never seen watches made; (ii) we had never known anyone capable of making a watch; and (iii) we were utterly incapable of making watches ourselves, or of understanding how they are made. Furthermore, it would make no difference to the inevitability of the inference if the watch did not work properly ('if it sometimes went wrong, or seldom went exactly right'). Finally, it would also make no difference to the inevitability of the inference if there were parts of the watch whose function we could not determine (or even parts for which we can't determine whether or not they have any function). Of course, the points that Paley makes here are perfectly

---

5 Mackie (1982: 144) writes: 'Paley argued that if we found a watch on the ground we should infer that it had been made by an intelligent being. This is true, because we hardly ever find watches except where the supposition of human manufacture is antecedently plausible – on people's wrists, in their pockets, in jeweller's shops, and so on. But if watches were found as commonly on the seashore as shellfish, or as commonly on dry land as insects, this argument would be undermined.' Surely, this isn't right: it's not the relative scarcity of watches in natural environments that makes it reasonable for us to insist that they are products of intelligent design. (Suppose there are more sheets of paper scattered about on dry land than insects: that won't give us any reason to think that sheets of paper are naturally occurring objects.) Moreover, it's not the common location of watches in human environments that makes this insistence reasonable, either. (Suppose that, at some time in the future, nothing but plastic is used for packaging. Suppose further that there are tin cans scattered all over the floors of the oceans and around wilderness areas, but – because of local clean-up campaigns – they are found nowhere else. At that time, it will not become reasonable to suppose that tin cans are naturally occurring objects.)

correct, as far as they go – but I do not think that they go far enough. Clearly, Paley must be supposing that our confidence in the inference relies upon our ability to recognise the functions of the watch and its parts. Otherwise, he would also make the perfectly correct points that (i) it would make no difference to the inevitability of our inference that the watch did not work at all, and (ii) it would make no difference to the inevitability of our inference that we could determine none of the functions of the watch and its parts. (Recall the earlier point about Paley's undoubted ability to recognise that CPUs and Geiger counters are products of intelligent design.) Whatever the standing of this objection, the important point to recognise is that my inter- pretation of the first part of Paley's initial presentation – and, in particular, my attribution of what I have called "Paley's Hypothesis" to Paley – makes good sense of the claims that he makes, and of the claims that he fails to make, at this point.

In Paley's view, it would be absurd to suggest that (i) the parts of the watch might have been framed and organised by chance, or (ii) that there is a natural tendency for materials to assemble themselves into watches, or (iii) that there are natural laws that ensure that there will be watches, or (iv) that we should be agnostic about the design of watches if we don't know much about them. Once more, it seems that the points that Paley makes here are perfectly correct, as far as they go. However, it is worth noting that these arguments don't lend much support to the claim that our confidence in the inference to design relies upon our ability to recognise the functions of the watch and its parts – for these arguments consider only some quite implausible alternative hypotheses about the origins of the watch. Perhaps it might be said that these arguments lend some support to the view that Paley's argument really works by inference to the best explanation (and that what he takes himself to be doing here is to be dismissing the main competing hypotheses to his own). But it seems to me to be much more plausible to suppose that Paley is still asking about *the grounds of our confidence* in the inference to design in the case of the watch – and that he is failing to locate the correct source of that confidence.

4.1.3. An Infinite Regress of Watches?

Paley argues that the inference to the conclusion, that the watch must have had a maker, will also survive the hypothesis that watches produce baby watches, that is, the hypothesis that watches duplicate themselves and that all current watches have arisen from this process of duplication. The core of the third part of his initial discussion is, I think, this:

Arrangement, disposition of parts, subserviency of means to an end, relation of instruments to a use, imply the presence of intelligence and mind. No one, therefore, can rationally believe, that the insensible, inanimate watch, from which the watch before us issued, was the proper cause of the mechanism we so much admire in it; could be truly said to have constructed the instrument, disposed its parts, assigned their office, determined their order, action, and mutual dependency, combined their several motions into one result, and that also a result connected with the utilities of other beings. All these properties, therefore, are as much unaccounted for, as they were before. (20/1)

There are two points to note here. First, Paley more or less explicitly says that function is an infallible sign of intelligent design. Second, he argues that duplication that preserves function does not remove the need for intelligent design. Of course, there is a sense in which the parent watch "constructs the child watch, disposes its parts, assigns their office, etc." However, as Paley in effect claims, if you grant that function is an infallible sign of intelligent design, then the appearance of function in the child watch is not fully explained in the account of the production of that watch by its parent: there is still no explanation of the appearance of function in watches on this account.

Moreover, Paley insists, it is of no avail to run the story further back: no number of previous generations can remove the need to appeal to a designer in order to explain the presence of function in *any* of those generations. If you allow that there is an infinite sequence of previous generations, and no first generation, you might think that you have thereby avoided the need to postulate a designer: the presence of the appearance of design in any given generation is explained by the process of duplication and the appearance of design in the previous generation. But Paley insists that this is not so: function and suitability of constitution to function require design even in this case. Of course, this point could be contested: if this is really a possible case, then it might be thought to constitute a counter-example to Paley's Hypothesis, that is, to the principle upon which Paley's initial discussion relies. However, the important point for our purposes is that there seems to be more evidence here for the interpretation of Paley's discussion that I have proposed: Paley's refusal to take this point makes sense if we suppose that he thinks that it is already established that where there is function and suitability of constitution to function, there is design.

(A question worth asking in connection with this part of Paley's discussion is whether it is really conceivable that watches are the offspring of prior watches. Paley claims that it is clear that our confidence in the 'inevitability' of the inference to design is not diminished when we find that watches reproduce. However, if it turns out that what Paley is asking us to suppose is that watches are animals – and perhaps this will turn out to be 'conceivable' in the relevant sense – then it is not clear that we should remain so confident about the 'inevitability' of the inference in question. I think that what Paley should say is that he is supposing that watches are 'self-replicating machines' – and, of course, since they are 'machines', it will still be the case that these are entities that are the products of intelligent design. (If we manage to colonise the galaxies with self-replicating machines, it will always remain true that those machines – and their descendants, if it turns out that those machines are capable of evolution – are the products of intelligent design.) But if Paley does say this, then it seems pretty clear that it is the insistence that watches are machines – and not the facts about function and suitability of constitution to function – that is now doing all of the work in the inference to design.)

4.1.4. The Argument in Full Dress

In the previous sections of this chapter, I have made various suggestions about the correct interpretation of Paley's initial discussion. Collecting together these suggestions, it seems to me that the basic form of Paley's argument is as follows:

1. There are cases in which the presence of function and suitability of constitution to function makes it inevitable that we infer to intelligent design. (Premise)
2. (Hence) In general, the presence of function and suitability of constitution to function guarantees a role for intelligent design. (From 1)
3. There is function and suitability of constitution to function in the natural world. (Premise)
4. (Hence) The natural world is the product of intelligent design. (From 2 and 3)

This argument is plainly an *a posteriori* argument – since the first premise and the second premise make empirical claims – but it is nonetheless a straightforwardly deductive argument. There is some murkiness involved in the inference to 2, but I do not think that this is a reason for refusing to attribute this argument to Paley.[6] Of course, this argument is not stated explicitly and in so many words, but, again, I don't think that this is a compelling reason for refusing to attribute it to Paley. Note, in particular, that Paley no more explicitly states an argument by analogy or an argument by inference to the best explanation: these interpretations have the same *kind* of status as the proposal that I have just made.

[6] There are ways in which the murkiness might be mitigated. For instance, one might seek to represent Paley's further reasoning in something like the following manner. (1) The inference to intelligent design, in the case of the watch, is inevitable. (2) The inference to intelligent design, in the case of the watch, is correct. (3) The inference to intelligent design, in the case of the watch, is based on the observation of function and suitability of constitution to function. (4) If the inference to intelligent design, in the case of the watch, is both correct and inevitable, then the observations that support that inference must provide a logical guarantee for the correctness of that inference. Hence (5). It must be that, necessarily, where there is function and suitability of constitution to function, there is intelligent design.

What should we say about this argument? Perhaps we might try contesting the move at 2 on the grounds that, even if we find an inference inevitable in certain circumstances, that does not show that the inference is any good, or that it is bound to be correct. However, it seems to me that this is not a particularly powerful objection. Part of what Paley means by saying that the inference is 'inevitable' is just that it is obviously correct: when we see the watch, we ought to infer that it is the product of intelligent design; and, moreover, we are quite entitled to insist that it is necessarily the case that watches are the product of intelligent design. Furthermore, when we look for an explanation of the inevitability of the inference, there seems to be nothing else to which we can appeal: what makes the inference inevitable is some necessary truth – or perhaps necessary truths – that underlie it. But if this is right, then the move from 1 to 2 seems reasonable: if it really is the case that it is the presence of function and suitability of constitution to function that makes the inference to design in the case of the watch *inevitable*, then we should agree that it is *necessarily* the case that where there is function and suitability of constitution to function so too there is intelligent design.

If the move from 1 to 2 survives scrutiny, then the only obvious problem for the argument is 1 itself. And, as I have already argued, it seems pretty clear that 1 is unacceptable because question-begging. True enough, there are cases in which we find an inference to intelligent design inevitable. (There are things that are necessarily products of intelligent design.) But in those cases, it is not the presence of function and suitability of constitution to function that makes the inference inevitable. Rather, as my previous discussion suggests, it is background knowledge about origins – origins of the materials used in manufacture, origins of the arrangement of the parts, and so forth – that makes the inference inevitable in those cases in which is it inevitable. Paley's argument fails because he fails to recognise the real explanation of *why* it is that we shall inevitably infer that things like watches are products of intelligent design.

(It might be suggested that the argument is better formulated by replacing 1 and 2 with the single premise:

(1 + 2) Necessarily, where there is function and suitability of constitution to function, there is intelligent design.

If the argument is formulated in this way, then it is clear that this is the premise that should be contested, and it is also clear opponents of the argument will plausibly be able to allege that the argument is question-begging. However, I prefer the formulation that I gave, because it is clear that the first part of Paley's discussion is meant to support something like this premise, and it is worth asking how the discussion succeeds in doing this. My suggestion, in effect, is that what Paley means to show is that we rely on 2 as an enthymeme in some clearly sound inferences. But if that's right, then surely we have the best of reasons to accept 2 as a premise in an argument for intelligent design.)

4.1.5. Alternative Formulations

As I mentioned initially, discussions of Paley's argument typically suppose either that it is an argument by analogy or that it is an argument by inference to the best explanation. A typical formulation of the argument might go something like this:

1. The natural world contains function and suitability of constitution to function. (Premise)
2. This fact is well explained if we and the world are the product of intelligent design. (Premise)
3. There is no other explanation of this fact that is anywhere near as good. (Premise)
4. (Hence) Probably, we and the world are the product of intelligent design. (From 1, 2, and 3)
5. If we and the world are the product of intelligent design, then we and the world are the work of an orthodoxly conceived monotheistic god. (Premise)
6. If we and the world are the work of an orthodoxly conceived monotheistic god, then an orthodoxly conceived monotheistic god exists. (Premise)
7. Probably, an orthodoxly conceived monotheistic god exists. (From 4, 5, and 6)

Should we think that this argument is *much* better than the one that I attributed to Paley, and that this is a reason for attributing it to him instead? I don't think so. The relevant part of the argument[7] – down to the interim conclusion 4 – seems to me to be not much better than the argument that I attributed to Paley; and, in any case, this attribution doesn't receive much support from the text that Paley produced. To make a case for the first part of this contention, let me begin by reminding you of some of the standard objections to this kind of argument.

First, for reasons that Hume gave – and that we shall soon examine in much greater detail – it isn't clear that the appearance of function and suitability of constitution to function in the natural world is *well explained* if we and the world are the product of intelligent design. Given that there is bound to be function and suitability of constitution to function in the

---

7 It is well known that Hume provided a large number of objections to the fifth premise of this argument. However, for present purposes, we are just focussing on the (sub)argument for intelligent design; the prospects for turning any such (sub)argument into an argument for the existence of an orthodoxly conceived monotheistic god are another matter entirely.

designer, it seems that this cannot be a satisfying route to a *complete* explanation of the appearance of function and suitability of constitution to function
in the natural world. If we must postulate (just as much?) unexplained function and suitability of constitution to function in the designer, then there is
no explanatory progress – and hence, arguably, there is no good explanation
at all.

Second – as we shall again emphasise in subsequent discussion – it is not
clear that there is no other explanation of the appearance of function and
suitability of constitution to function in the natural world that does about
as well as the appeal to intelligent design. To start with, there is evolutionary theory. If it is contested that this provides a decent explanation of the
appearance of function and suitability of constitution to function in the natural world, then there are always the alternative metaphysical hypotheses
countenanced by Hume (and others). Perhaps, for example, the postulation of an ensemble of universes will explain the appearance of function
and suitability of constitution to function in the natural world about as well
as the appeal to intelligent design.

These seem to me to be quite telling objections to the argument sketched
above.[8] Moreover, it seems clear that opponents of the argument can quite
plausibly allege that the conjunction of 2 and 3 is question-begging in the
present context. Perhaps it might be conceded that the objection to Paley's
argument as I construe it is more obviously correct than are the objections
to the argument currently under consideration – but I don't think that there
is all that much to choose between them. And whatever weight charity lends
to the inclination to attribute something like this argument to Paley – as
the argument that he *intended* to give, or would have given if only he'd been
a student of contemporary philosophy – is more than counterbalanced by
the distance that this interpretation must depart from the text that Paley
actually produced.

4.1.6. The Remainder of Paley's *Natural Theology*

Even if it is granted that the discussion to this point has some force, it might
nonetheless be contended that there are reasons for refusing to attribute
the argument in question to Paley. True enough, the argument that I have
outlined seems to fit what he says when he states his argument in the initial
chapters of his book. But those initial chapters occupy only a tiny portion of
the book, a far greater proportion of which is occupied with detailed discussion of the appearance of design in the natural world. If Paley's argument
is as I say it is, then why does he bother to go in for detailed discussion of

---

[8] If you disagree with me about this, no matter. We shall return to a discussion of design
arguments in which there is inference to the best explanation – or the like – in subsequent
sections of the present chapter.

many cases, when a fairly superficial discussion of one case seems to be all that is required?

This is a good question. But it's a good question for the competing interpretations of Paley as well. If Paley's argument were an argument by analogy, or an argument by inference to the best explanation, it seems that the bulk of Paley's book could not make any contribution to the argument. Since Paley divides the early chapters into 'state(ment) of the argument' and 'application of the argument', it seems to me to be plausible to think that the 'watch' argument is over and done with at the end of the statement of the argument. What follows is not meant to add to the strength of the case; rather, it is intended to do something else. Plausibly, I think, it is intended to show just how stupid atheists are: in case after case, it is no less obvious that there is function and suitability of constitution to function in animals than that there are these things in watches and other human artefacts, and yet atheists fail to draw the obvious conclusion![9]

Perhaps it might be said that there is a style of argument – a sort of naïve induction – that might be supported by piling up cases. But what would the conclusion of this argument be? That there is evidence of design in x percent of the world (by mass or volume)? That there is evidence of design in x percent of living species? And if we can be quite sure that, say, the human heart is the product of intelligent design, then what reason could we have to resist the inference to the conclusion that the rest of the human body (and all other plants and animals) are also products of intelligent design? If the eighteenth- and nineteenth-century friends of the argument for design took themselves to be piling up evidence for the existence of an orthodoxly conceived monotheistic god when they participated in the Boyle lectures, the Bridgewater treatises, and the like, it seems to me that this can only have been in the sense that they took themselves to be showing just how stupid atheists are. The evidence for the existence of an orthodoxly conceived monotheistic god is *all around*: almost every creature and organ exhibits more intricate functions and better suitability of constitution to function than the most exquisite productions of human art. But then, why don't atheists infer to design in the former case when they are prepared to infer to design in the latter case just because of the presence of function and suitability of constitution to function?

Having made this case as forcefully as I can, I must admit to some residual disquiet. Paley doesn't explicitly say that he is doing what I take him to be doing in this part of his book. Moreover, after I'd written the first five parts

---

[9] Plausibly, there are also other things going on. For instance, Paley no doubt hopes to establish the *benevolence* of the designer, on the basis of an examination of the details of creation. However, the bare inference to the existence of a designer is not made any stronger by the material that is presented in the rest of the book. To the extent that what follows has any implications for this matter, it can only be for the obviousness of the conclusion for which Paley argues.

of this section, I discovered that something like the interpretation that I have proposed was made once before. If my interpretation is correct, then why wasn't it accepted on the previous occasion on which it was proposed? Since this second point may appear substantial, I shall conclude this section with some further comments on it.

In his 1965 book, *The Existence of God*, Wallace Matson argues that 'the argument for design' should not be interpreted as an argument by analogy; rather, it should be interpreted as a deductive argument that relies on the false premise that, necessarily, where there is function and suitability of constitution to function, there is design. (I've modified Matson's words slightly, to fit the language that I adopted earlier.) Moreover, the placement of a footnote to Paley suggests that Matson thinks that this claim applies in particular to Paley's treatment of the argument. Now, I want no part of Matson's more general claim: there are many different arguments for design, some of which proceed by inference to the best explanation, some of which proceed by analogy, and some of which proceed in the way in which I claim Paley's argument proceeds. Moreover, the considerations that can be urged against these arguments differ from case to case. However, even though Matson's general claim seems to me to be hopelessly overstated, I do agree that his characterisation of the general form of the argument for design applies accurately to the argument that Paley presents in his *Natural Theology*. And I conjecture that the reason why this point was not taken up is that it lies somewhat buried in a discussion that most people, for quite independent reasons, will have taken to be seriously flawed. If Matson has argued his case only in connection with Paley, then I suspect that people would not still be so quick to suppose that the argument that Paley gives is an argument by analogy.

4.1.7. Concluding Remarks

In the preceding parts of this section, I have set out what I take to be the logical structure of Paley's argument for design. I have argued (a) that most commentators have misrepresented the argument that Paley actually gives, and (b) that the argument that Paley actually gives is manifestly a poor one. Even if I am right, these matters are likely to be of interest mainly to historians of ideas. However, there are two ways in which the arguments that I have given are important for contemporary debates.

First – as we shall see in the next section – there *are* people who claim to be modern-day defenders of Paley's *argument*. Given the argument that Paley actually gave, I don't think that anyone should want to claim such a mantle. (Of course, there are also people who say respectful things about Paley's argument; consider, for example, Dawkins' claims about the persuasiveness of Paley's argument prior to Darwin.[10] Again, I don't think that anyone who

---

[10] Dawkins (1986).

recognises the argument that Paley actually gives should want to say any such things.)

Second, and perhaps more important, there are modern versions of what is still essentially Paley's argument. Paley appealed to the biological data that were available in his day. Modern defenders of biological design arguments appeal instead to data from cell biology or biochemistry. But if the core of their argument is the claim that, necessarily, where there is function and suitability of constitution to function there is design, then that claim cannot be supported in the way in which Paley tries to support it. The inevitability of the "inference" to design in the kinds of cases that Paley considers does nothing at all towards supporting the claim that, necessarily, where there is function and suitability of constitution to function, there is design.

4.2. BIOLOGICAL DESIGN: BEHE

The best known recent defence of biological arguments for design is to be found in the work of Michael Behe (1996a, 2001). Behe claims that there are biological systems – in particular, biochemical systems – that provide defeasible evidence for the existence of an intelligent designer of those systems. In this section, I shall provide a fairly detailed examination of some of the arguments that are presented in Behe (2001), beginning with this discussion of the ways in which the argument that he presents differs from the argument that was defended by Paley.

4.2.1. Differences from Paley

According to Behe, there are two important differences between 'modern' arguments for intelligent design and the kind of argument that was defended by Paley. *First,* and most important, Behe claims, the argument that he defends is intended to establish only the existence of intelligent design, and does not attempt to establish that the designer is a monotheistic god. While this restriction in scope means that the argument achieves less, it also means that the argument is more resilient: it is not vulnerable to many of the kinds of objections that Hume made against the kind of argument that Paley defended. *Second,* according to Behe, 'modern' arguments for intelligent design are 'scientific' because they 'depend critically on physical evidence found in nature' and 'can potentially be falsified by other physical evidence'. Moreover, these arguments do not 'rest on any tenet of any particular creed', and neither are they 'deductive arguments from first principles'.

It is not clear that the two features to which Behe draws attention really do distinguish the kind of argument that he presents from the argument that Paley gave. *First,* while it is true that the argument of Paley's *Natural Theology* is intended to establish the existence of a monotheistic god, the part of that text that is standardly identified as 'Paley's argument for design' has as its conclusion just the claim that there is intelligent design. Behe himself allows that the 'modern' argument for biological design may well have 'philosophical and theological implications'; the difference between his work and Paley's is only that Paley attempts both halves of the task whose labour Behe seeks to divide between those who are scientists and those who are philosophers or theologians. *Second*, if it is appropriate to call Behe's argument 'scientific' for the reasons that he gives, then it is no less appropriate to say that Paley's argument is 'scientific' in exactly the same sense: for Paley's argument does not rest on the tenets of any particular creed, does not involve a deductive argument *from first principles*, and does depend critically on physical evidence found in nature, namely, the physical evidence of biological function and of the suitability of biological constitution to biological function. If there is a fundamental difference between the argument that Behe presents and the argument that Paley defends, of the kind that Behe himself attempts to identify, then it lies in the *defeasible* nature of the key premise that Behe assumes – though, of course, those who defend the standard interpretation of Paley's argument will not even concede this much: if Paley's argument is an argument by analogy or an argument by inference to the best explanation, then it contains a key premise that is defeasible in just the way that Behe's key premise is defeasible.

4.2.2. Behe's Argument

Of course, even if the argument in the previous subsection is correct, it should not immediately be concluded that Behe's argument is nothing more than a re-presentation of the argument that Paley originally formulated. For, at least *prima facie*, there is one very significant difference between the argument that Behe presents and the argument that Paley defended: whereas Paley claims that function and suitability of constitution to function are guarantees of intelligent design, Behe claims that 'irreducible complexity ' is a defeasible mark of intelligent design.

In Behe (1996a: 39), Behe says that *a system is irreducibly complex iff it is a single system that is composed of several well-matched, interacting parts that contribute to the basic function, and where the removal of any one of the parts causes the system to effectively cease functioning.* As an intuitive illustration of something that falls under this classification, Behe (2001: 79) offers the example of a simple mechanical mousetrap:

A common mousetrap has several parts, including a wooden platform, a spring with extended ends, a hammer, holding bar, and catch. Now, if the mousetrap is missing the spring, or hammer, or platform, it doesn't catch mice half as well as it used to, or a quarter as well. It simply doesn't catch mice at all. Therefore, it is irreducibly complex. It turns out that irreducibly complex systems are headaches for Darwinian theory, because they are resistant to being produced in the gradual, step-by-step manner that Darwin envisioned.

While we shall have reason to ask questions about Behe's characterisation of 'irreducible complexity', we shall return to this task after we have completed our presentation of Behe's argument for intelligent design. Since Behe does not present his argument in standard form, there may be room for argument about whether the following formulation does justice to his text.[11] Nonetheless, it seems to me that the following is a reasonable encapsulation of the argument that Behe means to defend:

1. There are cases in which the presence of irreducible complexity leads us correctly to infer to intelligent design.
2. (Therefore) In general, the presence of irreducible complexity is a defeasible guarantee of intelligent design.
3. There is irreducible complexity in the natural world.
4. (Therefore) There are elements of the natural world that are the product of intelligent design.

This presentation of the argument makes it clear just how close Behe's argument is to the argument that Paley defended, at least given my (controversial) account of the argument that Paley defended. Moreover, those who dispute my account of Paley's argument can still present Behe's argument in a form that closely parallels their preferred version of Paley's argument. For instance, if you suppose that Paley's argument is best thought of an inference to the best explanation, then you will doubtless suppose that Behe's argument is best thought of as having the following form:

1. The natural world contains irreducible complexity. (Premise)
2. This fact is well explained if we and the world are the product of intelligent design. (Premise)
3. There is no other explanation of this fact that is anywhere near as good. (Premise)
4. (Hence) Probably, we and the world are the product of intelligent design. (From 1, 2, and 3)

Interestingly, Behe (2001: 170) provides evidence that speaks in favour of attributing to him an argument that parallels that argument that I attribute to Paley, that is very similar in kind to the evidence that in fact supports the attribution that I make to Paley. For consider the following:

Every day of our lives we decide, consciously or not, that some things were designed, others not. How do we do that? How do we come to a conclusion of design? To help see how we conclude design, imagine that you are walking with a friend in the

---

[11] Indeed, I think that it is fair to say that Behe's presentation of his argument – at least in Behe (2001) is unnecessarily *opaque*.

woods. Suddenly your friend is pulled up by the ankle by a vine and left dangling in the air. After you cut him down you reconstruct that situation. You see that the vine was tied to a tree limb that was bent down and held by a stake in the ground, the vine was covered by leaves so that you wouldn't notice it, and so on. From the way the parts were arranged you would quickly conclude that this was no accident – this was a designed trap. That is not a religious conclusion, but one based firmly in the physical evidence.

It is clear that the proposal that Behe is here making is that the way that we 'come to a conclusion of design' is by noticing the presence of irreducible complexity: in the case of the trap, it is the 'irreducible complexity' of the arrangement of the parts of the trap that supports the conclusion that your friend's misadventure is no accident. Take away the covering leaves, or the stake, or the knot that attaches the vine to the tree limb, or the tree limb itself, and your friend will – very probably – not end up dangling in the air. So, he claims, it is the detection of 'irreducible complexity' that underwrites 'inferences' to intelligent design, wherever those inferences are made. (Perhaps it is worth noting here that it is very plausible to claim that Behe's hypothesis about how we come to 'conclusions of design' fails in just the same kinds of ways that Paley's hypothesis fails. On the one hand, there are often more immediate features than 'irreducible complexity' that support 'conclusions of design';[12] on the other hand, there are plenty of cases where there is 'irreducible complexity' and yet in which the inference to intelligent design is by no means immediate. I shall say more to substantiate these claims below.)[13]

[12] In particular, this is true of systems that are evidently not 'irreducibly complex' and yet that are nonetheless evidently products of intelligent design. Consider, for example, a lecture theatre that contains removable chairs. The chairs are part of the lecture theatre, and contribute to the functioning of the lecture theatre: remove all of the chairs without replacement, and the lecture theatre no longer functions as a place where students can sit and take notes. But the removal of a single chair – a functioning part of the whole – makes no discernible alteration to the functioning of the lecture theatre. Since the system that consists of the room and the chairs is evidently not 'irreducibly complex', and since that system is no less evidently the product of intelligent design, we can hardly suppose that inferences to intelligent design must be underwritten by detection of the presence of irreducible complexity. (Perhaps there are difficulties that arise in determining when one has a 'single system' and in determining what counts as a 'part' of a single system. But those are difficulties for Behe's definition that *he* has an obligation to confront; it is, after all, his definition.)

[13] Behe (1996a: 192ff.) contains a more extended discussion of 'detection of design'. There, Behe claims that 'for discrete physical systems – if there is not a gradual route to their production – design is evident when a number of separate, interacting components are ordered in such a way as to accomplish a function beyond the individual components'. As with much of Behe's writing, it is frustrating to try to attribute a clear content to this observation. Is he supposing that it must be *evident* that there is not a gradual route to production before it is evident that a discrete physical system is the product of design? Is he supposing that it can be evident that a discrete physical system is the product of design in circumstances in which, while it is not evident, it is nonetheless true that there is no gradual

4.2.3. Some Objections to Behe's Argument

There are many different objections that one might lodge against the argument that I have attributed to Behe. I shall discuss only a handful of those objections here.

First, there are difficulties that are occasioned by Behe's definition of 'irreducible complexity' and, in particular, by his claim that irreducible systems are single systems that are 'composed of several parts'. There are two different ways in which the claim that a system is 'composed of several parts' can be understood: for it might be, on the one hand, that a system is *composed without remainder* of several parts; or it might be, on the other hand, that a system is *composed of several parts, together with various other bits and pieces.*

If we read 'composed of several parts' in accordance with the second interpretation, then Behe's definition of 'irreducible complexity' says that *a system is irreducibly complex iff it is a single system that is composed – but not without remainder – of several well-matched, interacting parts that contribute to the basic function, and where the removal of any one of the parts causes the system to effectively cease functioning.* However, if this is how the account of irreducible complexity is to be understood, then it is quite unclear why we need to make any reference to the intricate biochemical systems that are Behe's stock in trade. For consider me, a single biological system that has many parts. Cut off my head, and I cease functioning. Rip out my heart and I cease functioning. Remove my bowel and I cease functioning. Plainly enough, I am an irreducibly complex system on this second interpretation of Behe's definition – and so, surely, we are right back with the argument that Paley originally developed. On this second reading of irreducible complexity, we should all be immediately disposed to conclude to intelligent design when asked about the provenance of human beings – and yet, of course, it isn't true that intelligent and thoughtful human beings all have this immediate disposition.

If we read 'composed of parts' in accordance with the first interpretation, then Behe's definition of 'irreducible complexity' says that *a system is irreducibly complex iff it is a single system that is composed without remainder of several well-matched, interacting parts that contribute to the basic function, and where the removal of any one of the parts causes the system to effectively cease functioning.* However, if this is how the definition of 'irreducible complexity' is to be understood, then it is far from clear that there is even one example of an 'irreducibly complex' system in nature. For example, in the discussion of

route to the production of that system? And, in any case, what is required for it to be the case that there is a 'gradual route' to the production of a system? Suppose that an automotive assembly line operates very slowly: would that be a 'gradual route' to the production of a car? Setting these kinds of questions aside, I take it that there is nothing in Behe (1996a) that improves on the discussion of 'the design inference' in Behe (2001).

the bacterial flagellum – Behe's favourite example of an irreducibly complex biochemical system – Behe (2001: 79) himself writes:

In the absence of the hook, or the motor, or the propeller, or the drive shaft, or *most* of the 40 different types of proteins that genetic studies have shown to be necessary for the activity or construction of the flagellum, one doesn't get a flagellum that spins half as fast as it used to, or a quarter as fast. Either the flagellum doesn't work, or it doesn't even get constructed in the cell. Like a mousetrap, the flagellum is irreducibly complex. (Emphasis added)

But if – as this passage suggests – *some* of the different types of proteins that are required for the construction and functioning of the flagellum can be removed without causing the system to effectively cease functioning, then the flagellum is not irreducibly complex according to this first interpretation of Behe's definition of 'irreducible complexity'. Of course, there *might* be other examples of systems that are irreducibly complex according to this definition – but the ubiquity of redundancy in nature suggests to me that it is plausible to suppose that it won't be easy to find any such cases.

Since the difficulty here concerns the *analysis* of 'irreducible complexity' – and since it is arguable that we have some pre-analytical understanding of what this term means – it might be claimed that we don't really need to repair the analysis in order to save Behe's argument. I'm not so sure; at any rate, given that 'irreducible complexity' is Behe's technical term, I would like to be given a definition for it that avoids the difficulty that I have been discussing.[14]

Second, it is worth reconsidering the quotation from Darwin that Behe uses to motivate his selection of 'irreducible complexity' as the feature upon which his argument is to turn. Darwin said:

If it could be demonstrated that any complex organ existed that could not possibly have been formed by numerous, successive, slight modifications, my theory would absolutely break down.

Behe claims that, even in principle, it is 'quite difficult' to envisage how the bacterial flagellum could have been formed by numerous, successive, slight modifications. However, it is not clear that this is right. In principle, it doesn't seem too hard to suppose that, as move back through evolutionary history,

---

[14] It is perhaps worth noting that the discussion in Behe (1996a: 39f.) is no help in resolving these questions. In that discussion, Behe identifies 'direct' production of a system with 'continuously improving the initial function, which continues to work by the same mechanism', and claims that no irreducibly complex system can be produced 'directly'. He then goes on to claim that, while irreducibly complex systems might be produced by 'an indirect, circuitous route', the likelihood that this is so plummets as the 'complexity of the interacting system increases', and as we encounter more and more biochemical systems that are irreducibly complex. Hence, by Behe's own admission, it seems that irreducibly complex systems do not fit Darwin's bill: they are not systems for which it can be 'demonstrated that they . . . could not possibly have been formed by numerous, successive, slight modifications'.

we first find earlier versions of the bacterial flagellum that consist of the same number of identifiable components, but in more 'primitive' forms – a slightly different propeller, a slightly different motor, a slightly different hook, a slightly different drive shaft, and so on. There is no difficulty in supposing that these evolutionary ancestors of the present bacterial flagellum deliver less power to the motion of the bacteria to which they belong. Moreover, as we go further back, we may suppose that there is more and more 'global' difference between the ancestral bacterial flagella and the present bacterial flagellum: if each of the components is slightly different, then the sum of the components may be quite different, while nonetheless still recognisably an ancestor of the present bacterial flagellum.

Even if we grant that the present bacterial flagellum is 'irreducibly complex' – that is, such that, if one removes any one of its parts, the whole ceases to function – it is not immediately obvious that the ancestral bacterial flagellum that we have hypothesised must also be 'irreducibly complex'. If we make enough small changes to the parts of the present bacterial flagellum, it is not clear that there is any reason in principle why we should not arrive at an ancestral bacterial flagellum in which it is possible to replace two of the ancestral parts with a single earlier ancestral part without seriously damaging the function that that ancestral bacterial flagellum is required to carry out in the environment that it inhabits. Perhaps, for example, with enough small changes elsewhere, one does not require a clear differentiation between the hook and the propeller; perhaps the differentiation of these two parts can come at a later stage in the evolutionary process. But if this is right, then the (alleged) fact that the bacterial flagellum is 'irreducibly complex' is insufficient to show that it could not have arisen as the result of 'numerous, successive, slight modifications'.[15]

I think that this response is, alone, sufficient to undermine the claim that Behe has found a compelling, *in principle*, objection to Darwin. Even if it is true that there are biological or biochemical systems that are 'irreducibly complex' on either of the readings of Behe's definition of that term, there is no good reason to suppose that an irreducibly complex biological system

---

[15] Behe (1996b) writes:

> An irreducibly complex system cannot be produced directly by numerous, successive, slight modifications of a precursor system, because any precursor to an irreducibly complex system that is missing a part is by definition non-functional. Since natural selection can only choose systems that are already working, then if a biological system cannot be produced gradually, it would have to arise as an integrated unit, in one fell swoop, for natural selection to have anything to act on.

> Clearly, the first sentence in this passage presupposes that a precursor to an irreducibly complex system must itself be irreducibly complex: make a series of slight modifications to a system that is irreducibly complex such that each modification only slightly reduces its function, and the end result is a system that is also irreducibly complex. As I have argued in the text, I see no clear reason to suppose that this is so.

could not arise as the result of 'numerous, successive, slight modifications'. Perhaps – as Behe (2001: 168–9) claims – an examination of the scientific literature shows that 'no one has ever proposed a serious, detailed model for how the flagellum might have arisen in a Darwinian manner, let alone conducted experiments to test such a model'; but even if Behe is right about this, it seems to me that he has failed to provide *any* good reason to suppose that the flagellum 'is a serious candidate to meet Darwin's criterion'. Unless there is good reason to suppose that there is some *in principle* difficulty in the obtaining of irreducibly complex biological systems by 'numerous, successive, slight modifications', it is pointless to complain that we lack a detailed account of the evolution of the bacterial flagellum: for, even if this is so, we have been given no reason to suppose that such an account could not be supplied.[16]

Third, it is worth noting that it is possible to grant to Behe that it is impossible that the bacterial flagellum should have evolved as the result of a series of numerous, successive, slight 'increases', while nonetheless disputing the conclusion that it is impossible that the bacterial flagellum should have evolved as the result of numerous, successive, slight 'modifications'. In the sketch that I gave above, I hypothesised that there might have been a point at which one part became two in an ancestral bacterial flagellum; and this hypothesis might have suggested commitment to an evolutionary account in which there is a gradual increase in the number of parts of what comes to be the current bacterial flagellum. But there is no reason why a Darwinian cannot allow that there can be increases in simplicity and decreases in number of parts as evolutionary time advances. Dawkins (1986) – and various subsequent authors – have suggested the model of an arch. Arches are 'irreducibly complex': remove one brick, from anywhere in the structure, and the entire arch collapses. Nonetheless, arches can be constructed by 'numerous, successive, slight modifications': one builds the arch with additional 'scaffolding', and then removes the scaffolding to leave the free-standing archway. By analogy, then, it is clear that a Darwinian may allow that 'removal of scaffolding' can result in 'irreducible complexity' in biological systems. I do not know whether there is any plausibility to the suggestion that there is 'removal of scaffolding' in the evolutionary history of the bacterial flagellum; however, I cannot see any *in principle* reason why the current

---

[16] Behe (1996a: 165ff.) claims that an extended examination of the relevant literature shows that, not only are there no successful attempts to sketch a plausible history for various irreducibly complex biochemical mechanisms, but that there have been very few attempts to sketch such detailed histories. Supposing that Behe is right about these claims, it seems clear that we should not join him in supposing that 'the theory of Darwinian molecular evolution . . . should perish', but rather that we should suppose that there is currently much that we do not know about the origins of life. There is no a *priori* guarantee that we shall ever have a satisfactory, *detailed* account of the origins of life, even if life did begin as a result of Darwinian molecular evolution.

'irreducible complexity' of the bacterial flagellum might not be explained in these terms.

Fourth, it is worth asking whether Darwin really ought to have been committed to 'numerous, successive, slight modifications' in the sense in which Behe's discussion supposes him to have been. Given Behe's analogy between the bacterial flagellum and an outboard motor, one might be tempted to observe that improvements in outboard motors are necessarily restricted to improvements that arise as the result of the efforts of those who are working on improved outboard motors. Sometimes, developments in quite different areas – for example, materials engineering or aeronautical engineering – can lead to the production of 'improved' engine components to replace the existing components in an outboard motor. In general, improvements to outboard motors do not always need to be invented 'from scratch'; sometimes, they can be borrowed from improvements that have been made elsewhere. If some of the basic 'components' of an ancestral bacterial flagellum could have developed in other biological systems – perhaps as a result of 'numerous successive slight modifications' – and then assembled to form that ancestral bacterial flagellum by a further 'slight modification', then there is another possible pathway that could, in principle, lead to the production of the 'irreducibly complex' bacterial flagellum. Once again, I have no idea whether the suggestion, that the evolutionary history of the bacterial flagellum includes the incorporated 'readymade' parts, is really plausible; but, again, it is hard to see that there is any *a priori*, in principle, objection that can be made against this suggestion.[17]

In view of the above objections, it seems to me to be reasonable to conclude that the argument that I have attributed to Behe is weak: even if it is true that there are biological systems that are 'irreducibly complex' in the sense that they are composed without remainder of parts each of which is indispensable for any level of functioning in the system in question, I see no reason at all why such systems could not evolve as the result of Darwinian evolution. Given the strong, independent evidence in favour of the claim that current organisms are the result of an extremely long chain of Darwinian evolution, we should not suppose that 'irreducible complexity' poses a serious threat to 'evolution by numerous, successive, slight modifications'.[18]

[17] Miller (2003) provides citations to various scientific publications in which it is claimed that there are biological and, indeed, biochemical systems that have – or at any rate, could have – arisen as the result of 'takeover' from previously existing sub-systems that served very different ends. So the claim that I make in the main text overstates things: I do have some reason to believe that part of an account of the evolution of 'irreducibly complex' systems could make reference to the 'takeover' of previously existing sub-systems. However, I don't need to appeal to this fact in order to show that Behe's argument for design is inconclusive.

[18] It is worth noting that Behe (1996a: 5) says that he find the idea of common descent – i.e., the idea that all organisms share a common ancestor – 'fairly convincing', and that he has 'no particular reason to doubt it'. Moreover, Behe (1996a: 39f.) says that, while an irreducibly

4.2.4. Two Cases

A large part of Behe (2001) is taken up with his responses to two objections laid against the arguments of Behe (1996a), by Doolittle (1997) and Miller (1999). These responses turn on the details of the interpretation of Barry Hall's work on the experimental evolution of a lactose-utilising system in *E. coli*, and the work of Bugge et al. on the blood-clotting cascade in mice. I shall make a few brief comments on Behe's discussion of each of these cases.

A. *Blood Clotting*

Doolittle (1997) claims that the work of Bugge et al. shows that the blood clotting cascade is not irreducibly complex, since the elimination of two genes – and the consequent elimination of both plasminogen and fibrinogen – results in mice that have a less sophisticated but nonetheless functional blood-clotting system. As Behe (2001: 83) observes, it seems that Doolittle is wrong on this point: the mice in question do not have a less sophisticated but nonetheless functional blood-clotting system; rather, they have no functional blood-clotting system at all. However, when Behe (2001: 84) goes on to claim that the work of Bugge et al. 'buttresses the case for irreducible complexity . . . [and] shows . . . that the idea of intelligent design is considerably stronger than its detractors would have us believe', it seems to me that he greatly oversteps the conclusions that can be drawn from the failure of Doolittle's argument. As I have already argued, one does not need to dispute the claim that the blood-clotting system is 'irreducibly complex' in order to deny that it is evidence for intelligent design. Perhaps – as Behe suggests – Doolittle's argument shows that Doolittle doesn't have 'a good handle on irreducible complexity'; but it is a very long step from there to the claim that the blood-clotting cascade could not possibly have been the result of Darwinian evolution.[19]

complex system cannot be produced 'directly' – i.e., 'by continuously improving the initial function, which continues to work by the same mechanism' – one cannot definitively rule out the possibility of an indirect, circuitous route. It seems to follow from these two claims that Behe supposes that much of the evolutionary history of current organisms has been 'indirect and circuitous': for, by his account, it seems that he must suppose that wherever it is the case that there is an irreducibly complex system S in an organism O that 'works by the same mechanism' as an irreducibly complex system S' in an organism O', where O is an evolutionary descendent of O', then the evolution of S from S' must have been 'indirect and circuitous'. So, for example, while mammals inherited a nervous system, and a digestive system, and a circulatory system, and so forth, from pre-mammalian ancestors, the mammalian nervous system, and digestive system, and circulatory system, and so forth were not obtained by continuous improving of initial function that worked with the same mechanisms that were found in pre-mammalian ancestors.

[19] Even if Doolittle did manage to show that the blood clotting system is not 'irreducibly complex', Behe could just turn his attention to a different biochemical system. There is no reason to suppose that the argument that Doolittle gives could be duplicated in the case of every putative 'irreducibly complex' biological system. (Perhaps it is worth noting that

B. An 'Evolved' Operon

Miller (1999) claims that Hall's work on the experimental evolution of a lactose-utilising system in *E. coli* shows that Behe is wrong to suppose that complex multipart biochemical systems can arise only as the result of intelligent design, and not as the result of Darwinian evolution. Roughly, what Hall's work shows is that, if a particular gene that codes for part of the lactose-utilising system is deleted, and if certain other conditions are satisfied, then there will be 'adaptive mutation' in other genes to compensate for the deleted gene, and to preserve the operation of the lactose-utilising system. Against Miller, Behe claims that Hall's work 'shows the limits of Darwinism and the need for design', since (i) we do not yet have a good Darwinian account of 'adaptive mutation'; (ii) there is reason to think that no other 'close' mutation in *E. coli* could have preserved the operation of the lactose-utilising system; and (iii) the 'satisfaction of other conditions' requires that the system is artificially supported by intelligent intervention. Given that I have not misrepresented the views of either Miller or Behe, it seems to me that they are both wrong. Hall's work on the results of deleting a particular gene – and thereby removing a part of an 'irreducibly complex' system – seems to me to have no clear consequences at all for the question of whether that system could have *arisen* as a result of Darwinian evolution, since it issues neither in the suggestion of an evolutionary pathway by means of which the system in question might plausibly have evolved, nor in reasons to suppose that there could be no such pathway.[20]

If the above comments are on the right track, then it seems to me that the particular criticisms upon which Behe focuses are, indeed, ineffective. However, it remains an open question whether there are effective scientific criticisms that can be lodged against Behe's work – see, for example, Miller (2003). Moreover, even if the criticisms that Behe addresses are ineffective, it is plainly a mistake to suppose that the failure of these criticisms

Behe (2001: 174) begins by claiming that Doolittle presents the blood-clotting system as a putative counterexample to intelligent design. But it seems clear that all that Doolittle argues is that the blood clotting system is not irreducibly complex. Hence, there is no justification for claiming that Doolittle supposes that the blood clotting system is a putative counterexample to intelligent design. (What would be a 'counterexample to intelligent design'? How could anything wear on its face the claim that nothing is the product of intelligent design? And who could suppose that there is a good inference from the fact that something is not 'irreducibly complex' to the claim that is it not the product of intelligent design?)

[20] Perhaps it is worth noting here that Miller (2003: 296ff.) provides good reason to dispute the claim in Behe (1996a: 185) that "[t]here is no publication in the scientific literature – in prestigious journals, specialty journals, or books – that describes how the molecular evolution of any real, complex, biochemical system either did occur or even might have occurred."

There have been many such publications in the scientific literature. Miller cites 'feasible' accounts of the evolution of the Krebs cycle, the bacterial flagellum, the eukaryotic cilium, and the cytochrome c oxidase proton pump, among others.

somehow bolsters the case for intelligent design. Even 'very competent scientists . . . highly motivated to discredit claims of intelligent design . . . and capable of surveying the entire biomolecular literature for experimental counterexamples' are not guaranteed to choose the best examples with which to make their case.

4.2.5. Falsifiability

The closing paragraphs of Behe (2001) take up various questions about the falsifiability of theories. Behe claims that, whereas the hypothesis of intelligent design is a falsifiable theory, the theory of Darwinian evolution is not. For, while the claim that *no unintelligent process could produce a given system* is falsifiable – via the exhibition of an unintelligent process that is capable of producing the system in question – the claim that *some unintelligent process could produce a given system* can be falsified only by examining all of the 'potentially infinite number of possible unintelligent processes' that might have led to the production of the system. Furthermore, Behe (2001: 179) claims that, in the face of the unfalsifiability of the theory of Darwinian evolution, (i) advocates of that theory should 'try as diligently as possible to positively demonstrate' the truth of the theory, and (ii) the criterion for judgment of the Darwinian theory should be taken to be whether a 'complex organ exists which seems very unlikely to have been produced by numerous, successive, slight modifications, and which is such that no experiments have shown that it or comparable structures can be so produced'.

There are various things that seem to be wrong here.

First, the principle claim of intelligent design theory is that *some* biological systems *are* the product of intelligent design. It need be no part of this claim that the biological systems in question could not be the product of an 'unintelligent' process; indeed, it seems that it would clearly suffice if it were merely true that it is most unlikely that the systems in question are the product of an 'unintelligent' process. Similarly, the principle claim of the Darwinian theory is that *all* biological systems are the product of natural selection. While it follows from this claim that *some* biological systems *could* be the product of an 'unintelligent process', the proponent of the Darwinian theory is clearly committed to the stronger claim about what is actually the case.

Second, in view of the above remarks about the proper characterisation of intelligent design theory and Darwinian theory, it seems that Behe's general approach to the question of falsification will have him saying that intelligent design theory is unfalsifiable – since one can falsify the claim that some biological systems are the product of intelligent design only by examining all biological systems – whereas the Darwinian theory is plainly falsifiable, since it takes only one system that is not the product of natural selection to establish that not all biological systems are the products of natural selection.

If Behe's general approach to the question of falsification can be justified, then it won't have the consequences that he supposes it to have.

Third, however, it seems that Behe's general approach to the question of falsifiability is unsupportable. One cannot assume – as Behe apparently does – that existential claims are unfalsifiable where universal claims are not. How, exactly, could one falsify the claim that all biological systems are the product of intelligent design? What experiments can one perform that will prove beyond any doubt that there is no intelligent designer of the universe? What observations can one make that will decisively falsify the claim that natural history has unfolded according to the specifications of a divine architect?

Fourth, in any case, it seems to me that it is just a mistake to think that science is primarily concerned with proof and irreversible falsification. Scientific reasoning is a very complex enterprise, and it is no straightforward matter to explain how empirical evidence is properly related to the scientific theories that we accept. However, it seems to me that there is something right in the claim that scientific reasoning is tentative, and conjectural, and always open to revision in the light of further information. Given the evidence that we have amassed, the Darwinian theory is far and away the best theory of the evolution of life on earth – but, of course, this is not to say either that the Darwinian theory has been decisively confirmed or that allegedly competing theories – including 'the theory of intelligent design' – have been decisively refuted.

Fifth, Behe's proposed modification to 'the criterion of judgment for the Darwinian theory' raises more questions than it answers. On the one hand, who is to determine whether it 'seems very unlikely' that a given system has been produced by numerous, successive, slight modifications? On the other hand, why should Darwinians be required to provide 'experimental' proof that 'unintelligent' processes can produce particular biochemical systems? Despite Behe's apparent claims to the contrary, it is hard to see why we should suppose that it must be possible to recapitulate evolutionary history in the laboratory, even on the assumption that the Darwinian theory is true. (If it seems reasonable to him to impose such strictures on Darwinians, why shouldn't it seem reasonable to Darwinians to ask him for a laboratory demonstration in which an intelligent agent creates biochemical systems in the kinds of conditions that prevailed at the time that life first arose on earth?)

4.2.6. Concluding Remarks

Overall, it seems to me that the *case* that Behe makes for intelligent design is no stronger than the case that was made by Paley. The use that Behe makes of the appeal to information derived from contemporary biochemistry does nothing to strengthen the argument advanced by Paley in his

Natural Theology. Moreover, as I have already argued, that argument – that is, the traditional argument for biological design that is advanced by Paley – is not a strong argument. Even if we focus our attention on the inference from biological evidence to intelligent design – and refrain from asking any further questions about the qualities of the inferred designer beyond those of intelligence and power – we should not suppose that there is anything in the *arguments* advanced by either Paley or Behe that supports the conclusion that the universe is the result of supernatural planning. Of course, even if this is so, it remains open that the considerations to which Paley and Behe appeal could be reassembled to make a compelling argument for that conclusion. We shall return to consider this matter in section 4.4 below.

4.3. COSMIC FINE-TUNING

So far, the main burden of my argument has been to establish that the *argument* of Paley's *Natural Theology* – and any subsequent *argument* that is clearly descended from the argument of Paley's *Natural Theology* – fails. However, as anyone even remotely acquainted with recent developments in the discussion of arguments for design can observe, there are other versions of arguments for design that are at least *prima facie* far more plausible than the arguments that have been discussed above. On the one hand – as we hinted above, and as we shall see in more detail in the next section – there are other formulations of arguments from biological design that do not fail for the same reasons that Paley's argument fails. On the other hand – as we shall see in the present section – there are arguments that draw on contemporary physical cosmology that raise a whole host of new challenges for those who deny that there are good arguments for the conclusion that our universe is the product of intelligent design.

The basic idea behind the 'cosmic fine-tuning' design arguments is well known. Recent developments in physical cosmology apparently provide reason to suppose that there are various well-defined parameters that help to characterise the universe in which we live that are such that, if they differed even slightly in value from the values that they actually possess, then it would have been impossible for life of any kind to arise in our universe. Moreover, recent developments in physical cosmology also support the contention that our universe is both temporally and spatially finite. Given these developments in physical cosmology, some philosophers and theologians have supposed that it is reasonable to conclude that the 'fine-tuning' of our universe for life is evidence that our universe is the product of intelligent design.

In the following discussion, I shall do the following things. *First*, I shall briefly survey the reasons that we have for supposing that, if certain parameters had taken values only slightly different from the values that they actually take, then there would have been no life in our universe. *Second*, I shall consider the various ways in which an argument for design might be formulated, drawing upon the alleged evidence of cosmic fine-tuning. *Third*, I shall consider some objections to each of the formulations of the arguments for design that has been presented for examination. *Fourth*, I shall discuss the hypothesis that our universe is part of a multiverse, that is, an ensemble of universes, and, in particular, I shall carefully examine the argument of White (2000) on behalf of the conclusion that the alleged evidence of cosmic fine-tuning cannot support the hypothesis that our universe is part of a multiverse.

4.3.1. The Evidence for Fine-Tuning

According to contemporary physical cosmology, the physical universe is characterised by a range of precisely definable parameters: age, mass-energy, entropy, curvature, mass-energy density, temperature, rate of expansion, fine structure constant, mass ratios of fundamental particles, fundamental force strengths, cosmological constant, and so forth. While not all of these parameters are independent, even according to contemporary theories, there is no reason to suppose that subsequent developments in physical cosmology will show that the value of just one – perhaps hitherto unknown – parameter fixes the values of all of the rest or – even more surprisingly – that there are no parameters that require 'fixing' in a truly fundamental theory of everything.

According to well-established contemporary physical cosmology, if one takes a standard model of the physical universe, and makes adjustments to the value assigned to any one of several of the above-mentioned parameters, while holding the values of all of the other parameters fixed at their actual values, one produces a model of a physical universe that is dramatically different, in all manner of ways, from the actual universe that we inhabit.

Consider, for example, the case of gravity. As Collins (2003: 189f.) notes, if the magnitude of gravitational attraction were increased three-thousand-fold, it would clearly be impossible for the kind of life that we observe on earth to evolve – since no land-based creatures could withstand the crushing force, and no 'technologically advanced' creatures such as ourselves could evolve in a water-based environment in which the density of creatures differs hardly at all from the density of their surroundings.

Or consider, for another example, the strong nuclear force. As Collins (2003: 182f.) notes, a 50 percent decrease in the strength of the strong force would undercut the stability of all of the elements essential for carbon-based life, and a 'slightly larger' decrease would eliminate from the universe all elements bar hydrogen. But in a universe in which there is nothing but hydrogen, there plainly won't be any life as we know it; and, moreover, it seems plausible to suppose that there won't be any other kind of life either. Furthermore, as Collins (2003: 183ff.) also notes, there is some – though, as yet, not conclusive – reason to suppose that a 0.5 percent change in the strength of the strong force would be sufficient to destroy almost all of the carbon and oxygen in stars, and hence to prevent the evolution of the carbon-based life forms that we know and love.

According to more controversial – but, nonetheless, well-supported – contemporary physical cosmology, there are cases in which adjustments to the value assigned to parameters have more spectacular effects than those mentioned above. So, for example, a change in the value of the cosmological constant – so that the value of that constant becomes 'significantly' different from zero – would lead either to a universe that almost instantaneously collapses back on itself (in the case that the value is negative) or to a universe that expands so rapidly that it never contains anything more than a very dilute gas of radiation and fundamental particles in an otherwise empty space (in the case that the value is positive). In this case, the consequences of the adjustment to the value of the parameter are more severe than merely the ruling out of life as we know it: it is hard to see how there could be any kind of life in either of the scenarios just described.

While there are questions that can be asked about many of the detailed claims that are made concerning the fine-tuning of particular cosmic parameters – and while it seems to me to be not obviously irrational to suppose that there will be no fine-tuned cosmic parameters in a mature physical cosmology – I propose to proceed to a discussion of the fine-tuning arguments on the assumption that we have pretty secure reasons for supposing that there are cosmic parameters that are 'fine-tuned for life' in the sense hinted at in the preceding discussion. That is, I shall simply take for granted – in the subsequent discussion – that it is true that there are cosmic parameters for our universe that are such that, in universes in which the other cosmic parameters take the same value as they take in the actual universe, but in which the value of the chosen parameter is (sufficiently) different, there is not the slightest chance that life will arise (and hence, in particular, there is not the slightest chance that carbon-based life of the kind that we know and love will arise).

4.3.2. Design Arguments Based on Cosmic Fine-Tuning

As Manson (2003: 5ff.) notes, there are several different types of arguments that can be mounted on the basis of the 'cosmic fine-tuning' of our universe.

First, there are Bayesian arguments for the conclusion that the probability of intelligent design on the fine-tuning data is high. To construct a Bayesian argument of this kind, we might begin by identifying the following propositions:

K_1: If there were so-and-so variation in the value of such-and-such cosmic parameter, then there would be no life in our universe.

E_1: There is life in our universe.
D_1: Our universe is the product of intelligent design.

Given the identification of these propositions, a Bayesian cosmic fine-tuning argument might have something like the following form:

1. $Pr(E_1/K_1 \& \sim D_1)$ is very small.
2. $Pr(E_1/K_1 \& D_1)$ is quite high.
3. $Pr(D_1/K_1)$ is much greater than $Pr(E_1/K_1 \& \sim D_1)$.
4. (Hence) $Pr(D_1/E_1 \& K_1)$ is quite high.[21]

Second, there are *likelihood* arguments for the conclusion that the probability of intelligent design on the fine-tuning data is higher than the probability of any relevant competing hypothesis on the data. While there is some question about how, exactly, to state an argument of this kind, we might suppose that the only relevant alternative to the hypothesis of intelligent design is the hypothesis:

M_1: Our universe is the product of a mindless chance process.

Given this supposition, it seems reasonable to suppose that a likelihood argument for intelligent design on the basis of the fine-tuning data will take something like the following form:

1. $Pr(E_1 \& K_1/D_1) > Pr(E_1 \& K_1/M_1)$.
2. (Hence) We should prefer D_1 to M_1 (at least on the evidence $E_1 \& K_1$).

Third, there are what we might call classical statistical arguments for the conclusion that any hypothesis other than the hypothesis of intelligent design can be rejected (whence it follows that the only acceptable conclusion is that our universe is the product of intelligent design). Craig (2003b) provides a useful example of an argument of this kind:

1. The physical constants and quantities in the Big Bang possess certain values.
2. There is no theory that renders the values of those physical constants and quantities in the Big Bang physically necessary.
3. The values of those physical constants and quantities in the Big Bang are fantastically fine-tuned for the existence of intelligent, carbon-based life.

---

[21] Directly from Bayes' theorem, we have that $Pr(D_1/E_1 \& K_1) = Pr(E_1/D_1 \& K_1) \times Pr(D_1/K_1)/Pr(E_1/K_1)$. So the value of $Pr(D_1/E_1 \& K_1)$ increases as the values of $Pr(E_1/D_1 \& K_1)$ and $Pr(D_1/K_1)$ increase, and as the value of $Pr(E_1/K_1)$ decreases. Moreover, from the definition of conditional probability, we have that $Pr(E_1/K_1) = Pr(E_1/D_1 \& K_1) \times Pr(D_1/K_1) + Pr(E_1/\sim D_1 \& K_1) \times Pr(\sim D_1/K_1)$.

4. The probability of each value, and of all of the values together, occurring by chance is vanishingly small.
5. There is only one universe. (It is 'illicit in the absence of evidence to multiply one's probabilistic resources simply to avert the inference to design'.)
6. The universe has occurred only once.
7. (Hence) The probability that the constants and quantities should have come to possess the values that they do possess as the result of chance or 'sheer accident' is well within the range at which that hypothesis can be rejected (provided that the other conditions that must obtain for the rejection of hypotheses are satisfied). (From 1–6)
8. There is considerable physical information about the conditions that are necessary for intelligent, carbon-based life: information about temperature ranges, constitutive elements, forces, and the like.
9. This physical information is independent of the information concerning the fantastic fine-tuning for the existence of intelligent, carbon-based life mentioned at step 3 above.
10. (Hence) One is warranted in inferring that the physical constants and quantities given in the Big Bang are not the result of chance: we can reject the hypothesis that the constants and quantities came to possess the values that they do possess as the result of chance. (From 7–9)

Craig (2003b) also provides the following formulation of what he takes to be a 'sound and persuasive' teleological argument from 'the fine-tuning of the initial state of the Universe':

1. The fine-tuning of the initial state of the Universe is due either to physical necessity, or to chance, or to intelligent design.
2. The fine-tuning of the initial state of the Universe is due neither to necessity nor to chance.
3. (Hence) The fine-tuning of the initial state of the Universe is due to intelligent design.

While there are quibbles that one might have about the formulation of each of the above arguments, they will suffice for the purposes of our subsequent discussion.

4.3.3. Objections to Arguments from Cosmic Fine-Tuning

Since I'm prepared to own up to being a card-carrying Bayesian, I attach most significance to the first of the three kinds of arguments that are identified in Manson (2003). Nonetheless, I shall try to give all three kinds of arguments a fair run for their money.

A. Bayesian Arguments

As we noted above, the conclusion of a Bayesian 'cosmic fine-tuning' argument for design is something like this: the (subjective) probability that a rational agent assigns to the hypothesis that our universe is the product of intelligent design, conditional upon the fact that our universe is life-supporting despite the fact that the window for life-supporting universes is very small, is quite high. Moreover, as we noted above, the premises of a Bayesian 'cosmic fine-tuning' argument for design include claims such as the following: the (subjective) probability that a rational agent assigns to the hypothesis that our universe is life-supporting, conditional upon that fact that the window for life-supporting universes is very small and the hypothesis that our universe is the product of intelligent design, is very small. Plainly enough, then, the acceptability of these arguments will be undermined if it turns out that there is no way of making sense of the claim that the window for life-supporting universes is very small. But – as argued forcefully by McGrew et al. (2001) – it is not at all clear that we can make sense of the claim that the window for life-supporting universes is very small.

If we are to claim that the window for life-supporting universes is very small – that is, if we are to claim that it is very *unlikely* that our universe should fall into the life-permitting range given merely *a priori* knowable background evidence – then we need to be able to place a probability measure on the space of possible worlds.

One difficulty that we face in constructing such a measure is whether or not we can reasonably appeal to some kind of principle of indifference. Given that we have no reason to suppose that any value of a physical parameter is more likely than any other value of that parameter within the range of possible values that can be taken by that parameter, do we thereby have reason to suppose that each possible value of the parameter in question is equally likely? If we can reasonably appeal to some kind of principle of indifference, then, once we have determined the range of possible values of our parameters, we shall be entitled to assign a uniform probability distribution over those possible values. However, if we cannot reasonably appeal to some kind of principle of indifference, then, even having determined the range of possible values of our parameters, the most that we will be able to do is to assign an uninformative family of probability distributions to our parameters. Given – as I argue in Oppy (2006) – that there are serious difficulties that face that adoption of principles of indifference, and given that it is (consequently) plausible to suppose that ignorance is more properly represented by families of probability distributions – there is reason to be suspicious of the premises in Bayesian 'cosmic fine-tuning' arguments for design on these grounds alone.

If we set aside any scruples that we might have about the principle of indifference – and if we insist (consequently?) that, on any decent conception of epistemic probability, one ought to assign precise probability distributions rather than families of probability distributions – then there are still further obstacles that confront any attempt to make sense of the suggestion that the window for life-supporting universes is very small. For what should we suppose is the range of values that can be taken by the various parameters that are alleged to be fine-tuned for life?

If, on the one hand, we suppose, for example, that the various force strengths can fall anywhere in an interval $[0, \infty]$, then – as we see in Oppy (2006) – there is no way of defining a flat probability distribution over an interval $[0, \infty]$. Or – more exactly – if we want to have a flat 'probability' distribution over an interval $[0, \infty]$, then – as we see in Oppy (2006) – we shall need to suppose that 'probabilities' do not obey the principle of countable additivity. But – as we see in Oppy (2006) – there are various good reasons why probabilities should be countably additive.

If, on the other hand, we suppose, for example, that the various force strengths can fall anywhere in an interval $[0, R]$, where R is an upper limit to the possible force strengths to which it is legitimate to appeal for the purposes of the 'cosmic fine-tuning' argument for design, then we face the apparently intractable problem of justifying the choice of R. Are we to suppose that there is some value R, such that it is *impossible* for the force strengths to exceed that value? (What reason is there to suppose that there is any such value?) If not, what grounds could we possibly have for ignoring all of those possible worlds in which the value of the force strength is greater than R when we compute the probability that the value of a given parameter falls within the life-permitting range? After all, if a proponent of the 'cosmic fine-tuning' argument is free to choose a value of R that suits the purposes of proponents of the argument, why shouldn't an opponent of the 'cosmic fine-tuning' argument be free to insist on a value of R that suits the purposes of opponents of the argument? Given the various other assumptions that proponents of the 'cosmic fine-tuning argument' are required to make, there are choices of R that will yield the result that it is certain that our universe is life-permitting even on the hypothesis that there is no cosmic designer, and there are choices of R that will yield the result that it is more or less certain that our universe is not life-permitting. What suitably independent reason is there to prefer one apparently arbitrary choice to another?

Even if we set aside both scruples about the principle of indifference and worries about the intervals over which the values of the various constants are supposed to vary, there are still further difficulties to be faced by a proponent of a Bayesian 'cosmic fine-tuning' argument for design. In our formulation of the argument, we have not so far fussed much about the fact that there are many different parameters, each of which is allegedly 'fine-tuned' for life. As we have already noted, careful arguments for the 'fine-tuning' of parameters typically derive from models of the universe in which the value of one parameter is allowed to vary while the values of other parameters are held fixed at the values that they actually possess. But if we consider the n-dimensional Cartesian space in which each axis represents an independent parameter that is susceptible of 'fine-tuning', it is not clear that we are entitled to the conclusion that the life-permitting region around the actual universe constitutes a small ball in a much larger region that is not life-permitting. For, while there are arguments that (plausibly) establish that, as one moves away from the actual universe in the direction of one or other of the axes, one 'soon enough' moves into a region that is not life-permitting, these are highly special directions that may not be characteristic of the space as a whole. While it seems to me to be unwise for opponents of 'cosmic fine-tuning' arguments for design to rest very much on this objection, it also seems to me that there is work to be done here by those who suppose that the argument is convincing.

So far, we have been worrying about the first premise in our Bayesian 'cosmic fine-tuning' argument for design, that is, about the claim that the conditional (subjective) probability of life in our universe, given the fact that the window for life-supporting universes is very small and the hypothesis that there is no intelligent designer of our universe, is very small. This is not the only problematic assumption in our Bayesian 'cosmic fine-tuning' argument for design.

The second premise in our Bayesian 'cosmic fine-tuning' argument for design claims that the conditional (subjective) probability of life in our universe, given the fact that the window for life-supporting universes is very small and the hypothesis that there is an intelligent designer of our universe, is quite high. While it might, perhaps, be conceded that the probability adverted to in the second premise is *greater* than the probability that is adverted to in the first premise, it is not immediately obvious to me that the probability adverted to in the second premise should be said to be 'quite high'. Given only the hypothesis that there is an intelligent designer of a universe – and given no further assumptions about the *preferences* of that designer – it is not clear to me that there is very much that one can conclude about the kind of universe that the designer is likely to produce. Moreover, it is not obvious that one can meet this alleged problem by 'bulking up' the hypothesis of design, that is, by adding claims about the preferences of the designer to the hypothesis that there is an intelligent designer, since, at least *prima facie*, it seems plausible to suppose that any such additions will drive down the *a priori* probability that the hypothesis in question is true. At the very least, there is clearly room for careful reflection about the best formulation of the hypothesis that is to play the role of D_1 in our Bayesian 'cosmic fine-tuning' argument for design.

As we, in effect, noted in the previous paragraph, there are serious questions to be raised about the third premise in our Bayesian 'cosmic fine-tuning' argument for design, that is, about the claim that the prior probability that there is an intelligent designer of the universe is 'quite high' (and, in particular, 'much higher' than the conditional probability of the claim that our universe is life-permitting given the fact that the window for life-supporting universes is small and the denial of the hypothesis that there is an intelligent designer of the universe). I do not see any reason to suppose that it is somehow 'contrary to reason' to assign a *very* small prior probability to the hypothesis that our universe is the product of intelligent design.[22] There is nothing in our experience that weighs against the claim that all intelligent designers are physically embodied agents who work with pre-existing physical materials; moreover, there are no details that we can supply to explain how there could be intelligent designers that are not physically embodied agents who work with pre-existing physical materials. Furthermore, we have plenty of evidence that consciousness and intelligence in our universe are reducible to neurological functioning. While these – and other similar – considerations are plausibly taken to be defeasible, it seems to me to be very hard to deny that non-theists can mount a serious defence of the claim that the prior probability that our universe is the product of intelligent design is very low indeed. But no one who reasonably maintains the belief that the prior probability that our universe is the product of intelligent design is very low indeed should be persuaded to change his or her mind about the existence of an intelligent designer for the universe on the basis of a Bayesian 'cosmic fine-tuning' argument for design *even if* he or she holds that there is nothing else wrong with this argument. If you suppose that there is nothing else wrong with a Bayesian 'cosmic fine-tuning' argument for design, then you will plausibly allow that the considerations adduced *raise* the probability of the hypothesis of intelligent design; but it is not clear that any great significance should be attributed to this fact. Apart from anything else, it will surely be equally plausible to allow that the considerations adduced in Bayesian evidential arguments from evil *lower* the probability of the hypothesis of a perfectly good creator, on the assumption that there is nothing else wrong with those arguments. So, on pain of allowing that there are good arguments on both sides of the debate about the existence of a perfect being, it seems that we should turn back with renewed vigour to the question of whether there is anything else wrong with these kinds of Bayesian arguments. And, as I have already argued, it is plausible to claim that there are many other difficulties that confront Bayesian 'cosmic fine-tuning' arguments for design.

B. Likelihood Arguments

The best discussion that I know of likelihood versions of 'cosmic fine-tuning' argument for design – and, indeed, of likelihood versions of arguments for

---

[22] Equally, I see no good reason to suppose that it is somehow contrary to reason to refuse to assign any probability to the hypothesis that our universe is the product of intelligent design. However, I shall not focus on – what I take to be – this special case of agnosticism in my subsequent discussion.

supernatural design more generally – is contained in Sober (2003).[23] As Sober makes clear, the ambition of likelihood arguments for supernatural design is very limited. These arguments do not issue in conclusions about which hypotheses ought to be believed, nor even in conclusions about which hypotheses are probably true. Rather, these arguments simply tell you about 'how the observations at hand discriminate among the hypotheses under consideration'. In my view, this means that there is very little reason to be interested in likelihood versions of 'cosmic fine-tuning' arguments for design, in the context of our present inquiry; for we are interested in arguments in support of the claim that there is an intelligent designer of the universe, and – on Sober's own account – likelihood versions of 'cosmic fine-tuning' arguments for design do not issue in conclusions of this type. However, as Sober points out, there are good reasons to suppose that even the limited ambition of likelihood versions of 'cosmic fine-tuning' arguments for design fails to be realised.

In the case of likelihood arguments for supernatural design in general, the chief criticism that Sober levels against them is that we have no clear way of evaluating $\Pr(E_1 \& K_1 / D_1)$, that is, the likelihood of the hypothesis of design given the observations that we make and the background knowledge to which we can legitimately appeal. Since I have already endorsed this criticism in the case of Bayesian 'cosmic fine-tuning' arguments for design, I shall not return to discuss it further here. Without assumptions about the goals and abilities of an hypothesised designer, it is – as Sober claims[24] – very hard to see how we can make any defensible claims about the kinds of universes that such a designer will probably make.

In the case of likelihood versions of 'cosmic fine-tuning' arguments for design, Sober (2003: 43ff.) claims that there is a second serious problem that sometimes arises, even if we allow that 'the design hypothesis has built into it auxiliary assumptions that suffice for its likelihood to be well defined'. According to Sober, likelihood arguments are prone to undermining by *observational selection effects*: the procedures that are used in obtaining observations can be relevant to the assessment of likelihoods. Initially, given our concession about auxiliary assumptions, one might suppose that

---

[23] Not that I agree with everything that Sober says in that article. In particular, I would take issue with his claim that 'Bayesians think that all hypotheses have probabilities'. Most Bayesians that I know allow that there are many hypotheses to which no (precise) probability is assigned. So the alleged fact to which Sober here points – viz, that it is highly implausible to suppose that all hypotheses have probabilities – is not a good reason for retreating from consideration of probabilities to consideration of likelihoods.

[24] It is worth noting that Sober explicitly acknowledges that many earlier generations of critics of arguments for design have levelled this same criticism against the argument: after mentioning Keynes (1921) and Venn (1866), Sober says that 'the basic idea was formulated by Hume'. I think that this concession doesn't fit very well with the subsequent denial (Sober 2003: 42) that Hume 'dealt a deathblow' to arguments for design.

Pr(Constants are right/Design) > Pr(Constants are right/Chance). However, our observation that the constants are right depends upon the fact that we exist: we could not exist to make the observations that we do if the constants were not right. So, according to Sober, we ought to take this into account. But Pr(Constants are right/Design and we exist)=Pr(Constants are right/Chance and we exist)=1. Hence, in this case, because of the observational selection effect, we have no good reason to suppose that the observation that the constants are right is more probable on the hypothesis of intelligent design than it is on the hypothesis of chance.

Whether or not Sober is right to suppose that likelihood versions of 'cosmic fine-tuning' arguments for intelligent design are undermined by observational selection effects, it is important to note that Sober denies that Bayesian versions of 'cosmic fine-tuning' arguments for intelligent design are (similarly) undermined by observational selection effects. There is no reason to suppose that Pr(Design/Constants are right and we exist) $\neq$ Pr(Design/Constants are right): it is the likelihoods of hypotheses, and not their probabilities, that are vulnerable to observational selection effects (if, indeed, they are thus vulnerable). Since this conclusion appears correct, it seems to me that the debate about observational selection effects fails to touch the most interesting versions of 'cosmic fine-tuning' arguments for intelligent design.

It is not clear to me that likelihood versions of 'cosmic fine-tuning' arguments for intelligent design *are* undermined by observational selection effects. It is true, of course, that likelihood arguments can be undermined by observational selection effects: it can be, for example, that an (implicit) assumption about uniform sampling is undermined by further information about the procedures actually used in order to obtain the observations. So, to use Sober's example, I shouldn't suppose that the hypothesis that all of the fish in the lake are more than ten inches long is more probable than the hypothesis that half of the fish in the lake are more than ten inches long, on the evidence that all of the (many) fish that I caught are more than ten inches long, if the implement that I used for fishing was unable to capture fish that are less than ten inches long. But, even granting this example, why shouldn't I suppose that the hypothesis that the universe is the product of intelligent design is more probable than the hypothesis that the universe is the result of chance, on the evidence that the universe is fine-tuned for life, even given the fact that, if the universe were not fine-tuned for life, I would not be around to observe it? After all, it is not in the least bit obvious that there is an implicit assumption about uniform sampling that is built into the initial argument but that would then be defeated by the further observation that, if the universe were not fine-tuned for life, I would not be around to observe it. Of course, I'm not here arguing that likelihood versions of 'cosmic fine-tuning' arguments for intelligent design are *not* undermined by observational selection effects; the point is just that, on the basis of the considerations that Sober – and others – advance, I cannot see that they are thus undermined.

C. Classical Statistical Arguments

The classical statistical 'cosmic fine tuning' argument for design defended in Craig (2003b) is explicitly constructed as an instance of the 'generic chance elimination argument' that is introduced in Dembski (1998). Consequently, *one* important question for this kind of argument is whether the account of design inferences that is provided in Dembski's work admits of a satisfactory defence.

The main aim of Dembski's work is to describe a procedure for deciding how best to explain a given observation E. It seems to me that the 'explanatory filter' that Dembski defends can be fairly summarised as follows. (Here, I rely on the discussion in Fitelson et al. (1999). As they note, this account of Dembski's 'explanatory filter' may rely on some charitable assumptions about the acceptance and rejection of hypothesised explanations; there are places where it is not easy to determine exactly what Dembski has in mind.)

1. There are three mutually exclusive and exhaustive classes of potential explanations for E: Regularity, Chance, and Design.
2. Regularity is more parsimonious than Chance, and Chance is more parsimonious than Design. Consequently, evaluation proceeds by starting at the top of the list, and moving downwards until you reach an explanation that you can accept.
3. If E has high probability, then you should accept Regularity; else, you should move on.
4. If Chance assigns E a sufficiently low probability and E is 'specified', then you should reject Chance and move on; else, you should accept Chance.
5. If you have rejected both Regularity and Chance, then you should accept Design.

There are many different and important difficulties that face this attempt to explain 'inferences to design'.

First, it is not clear what types of explanations belong to the categories of Regularity, Chance, and Design. Thus, for example, Dembski gives conflicting accounts of Regularity at different places in the book. Moreover, it seems that each of these categories contains explanations that have never been considered, and that perhaps may never be considered, perhaps because no human being is capable of grasping them. When, for example, the 'explanatory filter' rules out Regularity, it is supposed to be ruling out the very possibility that there is an explanation of E in terms of necessity, or law, or high probability causes, or whatever. (Consequently, one wonders whether, at step 2, Craig's argument really conforms to Dembski's prescription: how does one get from the observation that *no known* theory renders the values of

the relevant parameters necessary to the conclusion that there *is* no theory
that has this result?)

Second, it is not at all clear why we should be entitled to say that the
category of Regularity explanations is more 'parsimonious' than the category of Chance explanations, or that the category of Chance explanations
is more 'parsimonious' than the category of Design explanations. On the
one hand, it is not clear that there is any clear conception of 'parsimony'
that will deliver the ranking of categories that Dembski describes. And, on
the other hand, it seems that, however the notion of 'parsimony' is to be
understood, it is not the right notion to be invoking at this point. After all, it
is well known from the literature on model selection that there is a delicate
trade-off between 'simplicity' and 'goodness of fit' that must be negotiated
in the choice of models, and – I would argue – in the choice of individual
hypotheses or explanations as well. Depending on the case at hand, it seems
that any type of explanation – whether Regularity, or Chance, or Design –
could turn out to be the most 'parsimonious'.

Third, it is quite unclear how the notion of 'probability' is to be understood
in the criteria that are used to assess Regularity, Chance, and Design. As
Fitelson et al. emphasise, it is easy enough to work out the likelihoods of
hypotheses given an observation E; but likelihoods are insufficient to warrant
rejection of hypotheses outright. (What likelihoods tell you, at best, is that
one hypothesis should be preferred to another, given just the observation E
that is currently under consideration.) I would suggest that this talk about
'probability' can be well explained in Bayesian terms; but, in that case, there
is no getting away from the need to consider the prior probabilities that
are assigned to hypotheses. However, if Dembski is talking about neither
likelihoods nor Bayesian posterior probabilities, then it seems to me to be
utterly unclear what he means when he uses the word 'probability' in this
context.

Fourth, there are various difficulties that confront the suggestion that
Chance can be eliminated if E is 'specified' and Chance assigns it a 'sufficiently small' probability. Dembski has quite a lot to say about 'specification', but – as Fitelson et al. (1999) argue in detail – it seems doubtful
that his account conforms to intuitive judgments about the circumstances
in which 'chance' hypotheses should be accepted and rejected, no matter
how the interpretation of 'sufficiently small probability' is resolved. Moreover, Dembski's account of 'sufficiently small probability' also has various
counter-intuitive consequences. According to Dembski (1998: 183ff.), the
probability of E is sufficiently small (relative to a set of probabilistic resources
Ω) iff the probability of E_Ω conditional on the chance hypothesis is strictly
less than a half, where E_Ω is an 'event' that occurs iff the original event
E 'occurs at least once in the probabilistic resources that are relevant to
the occurrence of E'. If – as Fitelson et al. seem to suppose – the notion
of 'probabilistic resource' is to be understood in frequentist terms, then

this definition has evidently absurd consequences. However, if the notion of 'probabilistic resource' is not to be understood in frequentist terms, then how are we to make sense of it at all?

Fifth, there are difficulties that arise when we consider the application of Dembski's explanatory filter to conjunctive and disjunctive hypotheses. Given the way that Dembski has assembled his explanatory filter, it is plain that there will be cases in which conjunctive and disjunctive hypotheses get assigned to one class, even though the conjuncts and disjuncts in those hypotheses are not all assigned to that class (and, indeed, in some cases, are all assigned to some other class). If an event E is the mereological sum of disjoint events E_i, then it might turn out that the filter says that each of the E_i should be explained in terms of Regularity, while E itself should be explained in terms of Chance. Perhaps there is nothing objectionable about this kind of outcome; but, at the very least, one would like to be given some reasons for supposing that it is not objectionable.

In sum, it seems to me that there are many good reasons to deny that Dembski's 'explanatory filter' provides an infallible template for inferences to design. Apart from the various points of detail that have been mentioned above – and other points of detail that have not been mentioned at all – the most important problem to note is that there is no reason at all to suppose that one can rule out all of the hypotheses that belong to Regularity and Chance without ever pausing to compare them with the hypotheses that belong to Design. Before we begin, we know that, for any observation E, we can frame design hypotheses that have greater *likelihood* than any chance hypotheses, given this observation or evidence. But it may nonetheless be the case that, on this observation or evidence, there is no design hypothesis that has greater *probability* than any of a number of chance hypotheses. Unless we examine particular hypotheses – particular theories – of Regularity, Chance, and Design, there is not even the remotest prospect that we can choose among these categories in seeking an explanation for a given observation.

Apart from difficulties that arise from the embedding of Craig's argument in Dembski's explanatory framework, there are other difficulties that face his classical statistical 'cosmic fine-tuning' argument for design. For instance, as we noted in connection with Bayesian 'cosmic fine-tuning' arguments for design, it is very hard to explain how it can be true that 'the probability that the constants and quantities should have come to possess the values that they do as the result of sheer chance is vanishingly small', since it seems impossible to place an appropriately justified probability measure on the space of possible universes. However, in what follows, I merely want to take up the question of whether Craig's argument really does meet the conditions that Dembski (1998) lays down for inferences to design.

According to Dembski (1998: 144), before one can determine whether a pattern is suitable to eliminate chance, one needs to have all of the following items in place: (1) a collection of events E, (ii) a descriptive language D,

(iii) an event e ∈ E, (iv) a pattern d whose correspondence * maps D to E, (v) a chance hypothesis H, (vi) a probability measure p, where p(e/H) is the likelihood of e given H, (vi) side information I, and (vii) a bounded complexity measure $\Phi = (\varphi, \lambda)$, where $\varphi(d, I)$ is the difficulty of formulating d given I, and λ fixes the level of complexity at which formulating such patterns is feasible.

One very important point to note here is that Dembski's generic chance elimination argument applies only to events, that is, to 'actual or possible occurrences in space and time' (72). As Dembski himself notes, 'one cannot submit an object to the Explanatory Filter' (73): his generic chance elimination argument requires events as the data on which it works. Moreover, while Dembski himself claims that 'we can submit the event that produces an object to the Explanatory Filter . . . [and in that way] assign probabilities to objects by assigning probabilities to the events that produced the objects' (73), it is worth noting at the outset that, on Dembski's own account, there will be no assigning probabilities to 'unproduced' objects such as universes that have no cause for their existence; and neither will there be any assigning of probabilities to states of the universe that obtain at all times at which the universe exists. If one assumes that there are no *events* that are prior to our fine-tuned universe, then there is no way that one can use Dembski's theoretical apparatus to 'eliminate the chance hypothesis'. If one supposes that the values of the various 'fine-tuned' constants are the same at all times at which the universe exists, then, again, there is no way that one can use Dembski's theoretical apparatus to 'eliminate the chance hypothesis' – for the generic chance elimination argument does not work with states of objects.

Craig suggests that we take, as the first step in the argument, '[one's learning] that the physical constants and quantities given in the Big Bang possess certain values'. Now, true enough, there is an event here, namely, a process in which some learning occurs. But that event is not the one for which Craig seeks to 'eliminate the chance hypothesis'. Rather, as the rest of Craig's argument makes clear, the 'event' for which he seeks to 'eliminate the chance hypothesis' is 'that the physical constants and quantities in the Big Bang possess certain values': but this 'event' is really a state of affairs, and hence – as I have just noted – lies outside the reach of Dembski's generic chance elimination argument, on Dembski's own account of how that argument is supposed to work. Moreover, while Craig might suppose that there is an event – the coming into existence of a universe in which the physical constants and quantities have certain values' – that can be used to bring this state of affairs within the reach of Dembski's generic chance elimination argument, there is no reason at all why Craig's opponents should be prepared to concede that there was any such event. If the sum of contingent events and processes coincides with the spatiotemporal universe, then there is no 'event' or 'process' of the universe's 'coming into existence from nothing': even if there is an initial state of the universe, there is no event that brings about that state, and neither is there any event in which that state 'comes about'.

Setting aside worries about the starting point of Craig's argument, there are other ways in which one might worry about whether it is really a good instance of Dembski's generic chance elimination argument. In the second premise – the ruling out of 'Regularity' – Craig claims that, since there is no theory that would render the values of the various constants and quantities 'physically necessary', there can be no explanation in terms of 'regularity'. According to Dembski (1998), a 'regularity' is an event 'that will (almost) always happen' (36), or an event that is 'highly probable' (38). As I read Dembski, there is no requirement that the high probability in question has anything to do with *physics*: while he gives examples in which regularities are due to natural laws (38) or to 'reducibility' to natural laws (53), the category of 'regularities' is supposed to pick up all 'high probability events'. So, for example, if one supposes that it is more or less certain that a perfect being will make a fine-tuned physical universe, then the event of the bringing about of a fine-tuned physical universe by a perfect being is an instance of regularity. Since Dembski *defines* 'design' as the absence of either regularity or chance – and notes explicitly that it has nothing at all to do with the presence of intelligence – it seems to me that, if Craig were really following the template that Dembski sets out, then he must be supposing at this point that it is *not* highly likely that the kind of perfect being in which he believes will make a fine-tuned universe. But, in that case, one wonders what use he thinks he will be able to make of his final conclusion.

Another point that Dembski (1998) takes great pains to emphasise in his presentation of the generic chance elimination argument is that one has to 'do the math' – see, for example, the repeated exhortations on p. 228. In themselves, unsupported assertions about 'small' – or even 'fantastically small' – probabilities are no use at all: in order to 'make the design inference' one must be able to show that the relevant saturated probability is less than 0.5. Craig asserts that the probabilities that arise in the case of fine-tuning are 'fantastically small' – and concludes that they are 'well within the bounds needed to eliminate chance' – but it is not at all clear that this is so. True enough, the famous Penrose calculation yields a number that is well below Dembski's 'universal probability bound'; but that calculation depends upon various theoretical assumptions that might be questioned. And, as far as I know, there are no other 'fine-tuning' probabilities that come anywhere near Dembski's 'universal probability bound'. But, if that's right – and if Craig isn't resting his whole case on the Penrose calculation – then, by Dembski's lights, there is a lot of mathematical detail that is missing from Craig's argument. By itself, the calculation of a small probability means nothing; one needs to have a demonstration that the relevant saturated probability is less than 0.5. (Of course, the exhortation to 'do the math' brings us back to the question of how to fix a probability distribution on the space of possible universes.

While Dembski's examples seem to make tacit appeal to maximum entropy priors and the like, those examples are all of finite spaces – so I do not think that Dembski gives us any guidance at all about how to 'do the maths' in the kind of application that Craig wants to make.)

In view of the above considerations, it seems to me that we should not be too quick in supposing that Dembski's theoretical framework can be adapted to produce an argument from fine-tuning of the kind that Craig advances. When these considerations are added to the worries that one might have about Dembski's theoretical framework, and the independent reasons that one might have for questioning some of the premises in Craig's argument from fine-tuning, it seems to me that one has more than enough reason to claim that this argument is not successful.

4.3.4. The 'Many Universes' Hypothesis

A number of philosophers have defended the claim that the cosmic fine-tuning data provide more support for the claim that there are 'many universes' than it provides for the claim that our universe is the product of intelligent design. Many other philosophers have supposed that the key question to be answered in connection with the fine-tuning data is whether that data provides more support for the claim that our universe is the product of intelligent design than they provide for the hypothesis that there are 'many universes'. But, very recently, a growing number of philosophers have defended the view that the cosmic fine-tuning data simply cannot provide *any* support for the claim that there are 'many universes': there is something like 'the inverse gambler's fallacy ' at work in the minds of those who suppose otherwise.

The case for the claim that the cosmic fine-tuning data provide support for the claim that there are 'many universes' is made very forcefully in Leslie (1989). The basic idea is very simple. If we suppose that there are 'many universes' in which the 'fine-tuned' properties vary uniformly, then we shall suppose that it is more or less inevitable that there are 'universes' that are hospitable to life. Consequently, it seems that our discovery of the apparent cosmic 'fine tuning' might be taken to be evidence that there are 'many universes' rather than evidence that there is an intelligent designer who selected those 'fine-tuned' values so as to bring about a life-permitting universe. For, that there should be a universe in which there is life is much more likely if there are 'many universes' than if there is just one universe, given that the properties that are apparently fine-tuned for life really do vary uniformly across 'universes'.

In my opinion, the most carefully worked out *objection* to the suggestion that the many-universe hypothesis is supported by the fine-tuning data appears in White (2000). In the rest of this section, I propose to subject White's arguments to close scrutiny, to see (a) whether he manages to establish that the alleged cosmic fine-tuning provides no reason at all to suppose that there are many universes, and (b) whether his arguments can be adapted to establish that the alleged cosmic fine-tuning provides more support for the hypothesis of intelligent design than it does for the hypothesis that there are many universes.

White examines "the two main lines of reasoning" that are intended to establish that the fact that our universe is fine-tuned for life provides some reason for thinking that there are universes other than our own. The first line of reasoning takes a probabilistic approach to confirmation, according to which confirmation is raising of probability. The second line of reasoning develops the thought that, even if many universes would not render the fine-tuning of our universe more probable, they would make it less surprising (and this is a reason for thinking that there are universes other than our own). According to White, neither of these lines of reasoning is successful. I shall examine only the first line of reasoning here.

The Probabilistic Argument

I shall suppose that White is right to claim that, within the context of a probabilistic approach to confirmation, evidence E confirms an hypothesis H, given background knowledge K iff $\Pr(H/E\&K) > \Pr(H/K)$. Consequently, I shall also suppose that the following theorems of the probability calculus may prove useful in our discussion:

1. $\Pr(H/E\&K) > \Pr(H/K)$ iff $\Pr(E/H\&K) > \Pr(E/{\sim}H\&K)$
2. $\Pr(H/E\&K)=\Pr(H/K)$ iff $\Pr(E/H\&K)=\Pr(E/{\sim}H\&K)$

The argument that White develops is intended to show that, given this way of understanding confirmation, the fine-tuning evidence provides no support at all for the hypothesis that there are many universes.

White's argument, for the conclusion that the existence of many universes would not make the fine-tuning of our universe probable, begins with the 'simplifying assumption' that we can partition the space of possible outcomes of a big bang into a finite set of equally probable boundary conditions. While this assumption is hardly innocuous, there is surely no danger in following out White's argument to see where this assumption leads. If it turns out that White's argument is otherwise unexceptionable, then perhaps we shall have reason to revisit this assumption; on the other hand, if White's argument fails even when this assumption is granted, then we shall be able to conclude that it is unlikely that there is any successful variant of White's argument.

So, suppose that we can partition the space of possible outcomes of a big bang into a finite set of equally probable boundary conditions $\{T_1,\ldots,T_n\}$. Let α be our universe, and let T_1 be the unique configuration that is necessary to permit life to evolve. Each actual universe instantiates a unique T_i.

Let m be the number of universes that actually exist. Consider the following three propositions:

(E) α is life permitting.
(E') Some universe is life-permitting.
(M) m is large.

On the one hand $\Pr(E'/M) > \Pr(E'/{\sim}M)$, that is, the probability that there are life-permitting universes is higher if there are many universes than if there are few. On the other hand, $\Pr(E/M)=\Pr(E/{\sim}M)$, that is, the probability that our universe is life-permitting is no different if there are many universes than if there are few. Why?

E is just the claim that α instantiates T_1, and the probability of this is just $1/n$, regardless of how many other universes there are, since α's initial conditions and constants are selected randomly from a set of n equally probable alternatives, a selection that is independent of the existence of other universes. The events that give rise to universes are not causally related in such a way that the outcome of one renders the outcome of another more or less probable. They are like independent rolls of a die. (261/2)

But, since E entails E', when we take all of our relevant evidence into account, we see that that evidence does not raise the probability that there are many universes, that is, it is not in any sense evidence for the existence of many universes.

A Difficulty about Background Knowledge

One immediately obvious problem with White's argument is that it does not make use of the official account of confirmation that we introduced in our introductory remarks. In those remarks, a role is given to background knowledge – evidence confirms hypotheses *given background knowledge* – and yet there is no mention of background knowledge in White's argument.

This is not a trivial point. Suppose, for example, that I include the fact that I am alive in my background knowledge. Then $\Pr(\alpha$ is life-permitting$/K) = 1$. Hence, neither E nor E' confirms the hypothesis that α is life-permitting given this background knowledge. To get around this difficulty, it seems that we shall need to restrict K to necessarily true propositions that are knowable *a priori*, that is, to propositions that are true in every possible world, and that can be known to be true independently of any evidence. Given that we have no *other* evidence, it seems reasonable to claim that E' confirms the hypothesis that there are many universes, for the reason that White gives. That is $\Pr(E'/M\&k) > \Pr(E'/{\sim}M\&k)$, where k is restricted to *a priori* knowable necessary truths.

Of course, one might have cause to wonder at the significance of the claim that $\Pr(E/M\&k) > \Pr(E/\sim M\&k)$, even given that this claim is borne out, on the current construal of background evidence. By the results mentioned in the introductory section, we would have that $\Pr(M/E\&k) > \Pr(M/k)$ – that is, the probability that there are many universes is greater on the additional evidence that some universe is life-permitting than it is on necessary and *a priori* background evidence alone – but what should we then conclude? Clearly, we don't have an argument here that the probability of M is raised when all of our relevant evidence is taken into account. (And, for exactly the same reason, we don't have a parallel argument to the conclusion that the probability that there is an intelligent designer of our universe is raised when all of the relevant evidence is taken into account.)

It is tempting to conclude at this point that, if there is a decent confirmation theoretical argument from the fine-tuning data to the conclusion that there are many universes, it can't be the argument that White criticises. However, let us put this thought aside, and continue with our examination of White's argument.

An Assumption about Names

A crucial claim in White's argument for the conclusion that E does not confirm M is his claim that $\Pr(E/k){=}1/n$. It will repay us to consider some remarks that he makes in attempting to justify this claim. (Remember to keep in mind that the background evidence k is restricted to claims that are both necessary and knowable *a priori*.)

In footnote 6, he writes:

The name 'α' is to be understood as rigidly designating the universe that happens to be ours. Of course, in one sense, a universe can't be ours unless it is life permitting. But the universe which happens actually to be ours, namely α, might not have been ours, or anyone's. It had a slim chance of containing life at all.

Earlier, in the main text, he says: 'The inhabitability of our universe depends on ... arbitrary, contingent features.'

But, now, let's ask about the *essential* properties of α. Are the boundary conditions of α merely 'arbitrary and contingent' features of it, or are they essential properties that it possesses in every possible world in which it exists? (Note that the answer to this question is not determined by the observation that the description "the universe which happens to be ours" fixes the reference of "α". While it *may* be knowable *a priori* that α is our universe, it by no means follows from this that it is a necessary truth that α is our universe.) We consider the two cases in turn.

1. Suppose we say that the boundary conditions are merely 'arbitrary and contingent' features of α. Then, in order to properly model the situation – following the lead that White provides in establishing the initial model – it

seems to me that we should suppose that there are equiprobable universe haecceities $\beta_1, \ldots, \beta_m$. Furthermore, we should suppose that there are $m \times n$ different equiprobable possible universes that can exist across the various possible worlds. (This claim is arrived at by a straightforward consideration of all of the different combinations of the β_i and the T_j that can be made.) Of course, at any given possible world, there can be no more than m universes (since there are only m haecceities, and these are what individuate universes).

Now, if we calculate the probability that α ($=\beta_1$, say) is life-permitting, then that probability does increase as the number of universes that exist increases. For:

Pr(α is life permitting at w/k)
= Pr(α exists at w and is life permitting at w/k)
= Pr(α exists at w/k) $\times$ $1/n$

On the assumption that universes are selected uniformly (without replacement) from amongst the β_i, we have that:

If one universe is selected, Pr(α exists at w/k) = $1/m$
If m universes are selected, Pr(α exists at w/k) = 1

So, if only one universe is selected, then Pr(α is life permitting at w/k)= $1/m \times n$; and if m universes are selected, Pr(α is life permitting at w/k)= $1/n$. Hence Pr(E/M&k) > Pr(E/~M&k), which is just what we required to show.

2. Suppose, on the other hand, that we say that the boundary conditions are essential features of α. In this case, it seems to me that we should say that the probability that α exists depends upon how many universes there are; and we should also say that the probability that α is life-permitting, given that it exists, is 1.

If we make the assumption that there can be no more than one universe instantiating each of the T_j – an assumption that we might justify by appeal to a principle concerning the identity of indiscernibles – then we can say that:

If there is only one universe in w, then Pr(α is life-permitting at w/k)= $1/n$
If there are n universes in w, then Pr(α is life-permitting at w/k)=1.

So, as before, Pr(E/M&k) > Pr(E/~M&k), which is what the claim that apparent fines-tuning supports the many universe hypothesis requires.

Hence, no matter how we think about the modal status of the boundary conditions that our universe possesses, it is not true that the probability that our universe is life-permitting has a value that is independent of the number of universes that there are. Given that we are restricting our background knowledge to *a priori* knowable necessary truths, it does indeed seem to be the case that $Pr(E/M\&k) > Pr(E/\sim M\&k)$, just as the proponent of the many-universe hypothesis maintains.

Recourse to Objective Chances?
Even if the argument to this point is acceptable, one might well think that one only need make small changes to White's argument in order to repair the damage. In particular, one might think that White would do better to invoke "objective chances" in place of the "subjective probabilities" that have figured in the arguments thus far.

Let's turn again to the first of the scenarios discussed in the previous section. Suppose that the boundary conditions are "arbitrary and contingent". Suppose, further, that one or more of the universe haecceities is instantiated. Finally, suppose that, after a period of time – that is, after the universes already exist – the boundary conditions are uniformly assigned to the universes. Now, consider our universe – β_1, say – at a time at which it already exists, but before the boundary conditions are assigned to it. Surely – given the assumptions that White makes, and that we are still supposing to be in force – it is true that, at that time, $Ch(\beta_1$ supports life at @)$=1/n$. (Here, "@" rigidly designates the actual world, i.e., the totality of all the things that actually exists, including all of the universes that there are; and "Ch" indicates that what is at issue is an objective chance.) And then, give the Principal Principle, we should be able to conclude that $Pr(\alpha$ supports life at @$/K_t) = 1/n$, where K_t is a complete characterisation of the world prior to t.

Even if it is true that $Pr(\alpha$ supports life at @$/M\&K_t)=1/n = Pr(\alpha$ supports life at @$/\sim M\&K_t)$, while $Pr($some universe supports life at @$/M\&K_t) > Pr($some universe supports life at @$/\sim M\&K_t)$, it is not clear why we should think that the truth of this claim is cause for concern for those who claim that the fine-tuning data are evidence that there are many universes. In particular, it is worth asking what is so special about K_t. Granted, perhaps, a proponent of the many-universe hypothesis cannot argue that $Pr(E/M\&K_t) > Pr(E/\sim M\&K_t)$. But this alone is not sufficient to show that there is not some other K_o for which $Pr(E/M\&K_o) > Pr(E/\sim M\&K_o)$. We have already seen that we can make a plausible case that $Pr(E/M\&k) > Pr(E/\sim M\&k)$: why isn't this sufficient to discharge the argumentative burden that falls upon the proponent of the many-universe hypothesis?

Perhaps there are replies that can be made at this point. Certainly, if we allow the various assumptions that we have made to get to where we are now, then there is clearly a question about whether we *can* construct a good confirmation theoretic argument for the claim that the fine-tuning data provide probabilistic support – confirmation – for the hypothesis that there are many universes. However, before we turn to pursue this argument further, I want now to turn to the question of the bearing of the foregoing discussion on the question of whether the fine-tuning data provide evidence that confirm the claim that there is an intelligent designer of the universe.

A Different Target

While the target of White (2000) is those who claim that the fine-tuning data provide evidence that there are many universes, it is important not to lose sight of the fact that the hypothesis that there are many universes is typically offered as a competitor to the hypothesis that the universe is the product of intelligent design. There are many philosophers who argue for no more than the conditional claim that the alleged fact that the boundary conditions of our universe are fine-tuned for life is no better evidence for the existence of an intelligent designer of our universe than it is for the existence of many universes. We have seen that the attempt to argue that the alleged fact that the boundary conditions of our universe are fine-tuned for life provides no evidence for the existence of many universes may succeed in one case, namely, that in which those boundary conditions are fixed by an objectively chancy process at some time after the beginning of the universe. However – as I shall now proceed to argue – if this is a case in which apparent fine-tuning is no evidence for many universes, then it is also a case in which apparent fine-tuning is no evidence for intelligent design.

Suppose that the history of our universe is filled with objectively chancy events. Suppose further that D_N is a complete characterisation of the world up until now. Clearly, $Pr(D_N/K_t)$ will be very small indeed; but this does not give us the slightest reason to be dissatisfied with the claim that history is replete with objectively chancy events. So long as we have good reason to hold that there are objectively chancy events, then we are bound to accept that the present state of the world is massively improbable given only the evidence available at much earlier states of the world. While it is not obviously inconsistent with the assumptions that we have made that there is an intelligent designer who set up the universe in such a way that it would be an objectively chancy matter whether life subsequently develops in that universe, there is nothing in the fact that life does develop in a universe of this kind to support the contention that the universe is the product of intelligent design. After all, it is built into the specification of the case that we are considering that the values of the 'fine-tuned' constants are assigned as the result of an objectively chancy event; hence, *a fortiori*, the assignment of those values is not, itself, the result of intelligent oversight.

In short: while – as I allowed at the end of the previous section – there may be cases in which it is true that one cannot make a good inference from fine-tuning data to the existence of many universes using the argument that White considers, it turns out that in those cases one cannot make the analogous inference from that same fine-tuning data to the existence of an intelligent designer. Even before we consider other replies that might be made on behalf of the proponent of the inference to the existence of many universes, we can see that White's argument, if successful at all, must prove too much for the purposes of proponents of arguments for design.

The Inverse Gambler's Fallacy

Hacking (1987) suggests that the inference to 'many universes' on the basis of the cosmic fine-tuning data is fallacious in the same kind of way that the inference in what he calls 'the inverse gambler's fallacy' is fallacious. Consider a gambler who is asked, 'Has this pair of dice been rolled before?' and who asks to see the dice rolled before he makes a judgment. When the dice come up double-six, our gambler concludes that the dice have probably been rolled several times before, since it is so unlikely that they would land double-six on a single roll. According to Hacking – and White – this inference is just like the inference to the conclusion that there are 'many universes' on the basis of the observation that it is very unlikely that the Big Bang produce a life-permitting universe in a single shot. Given the stochastic independence of the rolls of the dice, it is clear that the 'inverse gambler's fallacy' is, indeed, a fallacy: that the dice come up double-six this time does not make it in the least bit more likely that the dice have been rolled before. So, analogously, that the relevant parameters take on values that are conducive to life in our universe does not make it in the least bit more likely that there are other universes in which those parameters take on different values.

It seems to me that this objection is clearly right in the case in which we suppose that there is a 'cosmic roll of the dice' that fixes the values of the relevant parameters at some time t in the early history of the universe. Given that we have good reason to suppose that there was a 'cosmic roll of the dice' at some point in the very early history of the universe, we have no reason to infer from the fact that our universe is life-supporting to the conclusion that there are other universes. But, equally, given that we have good reason to suppose that there was a 'cosmic roll of the dice' at some point in the very early universe, we have no reason to infer from the fact that our universe is life-supporting to the conclusion that there is an intelligent designer. For, if there was a 'cosmic roll of the dice' – in the relevant sense – then the objective chance that *any* given universe would result from that 'cosmic roll of the dice' was astronomically small. That our universe arose is no more in need of further explanation than that any other universe should have arisen, given that there was a 'cosmic roll of the dice': after all, *every* universe will have many features that mark it out as very special in the group of universes as a whole.

Alternative Courts of Appeal

Even if I am right to agree with White and Hacking that we can discern "the inverse gambler's fallacy" at work in the inference from the fact that our

universe is life-supporting to the conclusion that there are other universes
(in the case in which we have good reason to suppose that there is a 'cosmic
roll of the dice' that fixes the values of the relevant parameters at some
time t in the early history of the universe), it doesn't follow that there are no
related facts to which we could legitimately appeal to support the conclusion
that there are many universes (in this case). So far, I have followed White in
supposing that, if he could succeed in showing that the probability that our
universe is life-permitting is independent of the truth of the claim that there
are many universes, then he would succeed in undermining the claim that
the cosmic fine-tuning data support the claim that there are many universes.
But, as White himself concedes, I don't merely have the cosmic fine-tuning
data as evidence; for I also have the fact that this cosmic fine-tuning data
are presented to me for consideration. If we ask whether the probability
that I shall be presented with the evidence of cosmic fine-tuning is greater
on the hypothesis that there are many universes, then we do not get an
answer to this question merely by being told that the objective chance that
our universe is life-permitting prior to t is independent of the truth of the
claim that there are many universes.

Indeed, more strongly, we might suppose that there we can make the
following kind of case for the contention that the probability that I shall be
presented with the evidence of cosmic fine-tuning is greater on the hypothesis that there are many universes (even granted the further assumption that
there is 'a cosmic roll of the dice'):

Suppose that I happen across a table upon which there are five dice, each
showing a six on the uppermost face. What hypothesis should I entertain
about how the dice came to be thus arranged? The most plausible hypothesis,
surely, is that the dice were placed with the sixes showing by someone who was
pleased with this arrangement. (Here, I rely on my background knowledge
that there are many games in which sixes have special significance. In the
game Yahtzee, for instance, five sixes is the best of all possible combinations,
at least in most phases of that game.)

However, suppose that we add the further assumption that the arrangement of the dice is the result of a simultaneous rolling of the dice. What
should we then suppose? The most plausible hypothesis, now, is surely that
the dice were rolled many times, until the desired pleasing configuration
arose. (Of course, this reasoning relies upon the same background knowledge adverted to previously.) Even though we see before us the result of a
single roll – the one upon which five sixes resulted – we have resources to
hand that make it reasonable for us to suppose that there were many rolls
of these dice prior to the production of the configuration that we can see.

Suppose that we add the further assumption that there was only one
occasion upon which the dice on the table were rolled. What then? One
hypothesis that we might now adopt is that the fact that there are five sixes on
display is just the result of chance: there was, after all, one chance in 11,376

that that throw would result in five sixes. However, another hypothesis that seems worth considering is that there were many other tables in the vicinity upon which a single roll of dice was performed, and that this table – with its attendant configuration of dice – was preserved for us to see because it was one – perhaps the only one – on which a favourable result was achieved. (Such reasoning is not unfamiliar. I see film of a golfer making a hole in one, and infer that there is much unpresented film of other golfers failing to make a hole in one. I read in the newspaper that there has been at least one winner in the state lottery each week this year, and infer that a vast number of tickets have been sold to non-winners. Etc.)

Now, suppose that we can think of the fine-tuning of the cosmos for life as something like the result of the rolling of some dice. (Perhaps, for example, there was some symmetry-breaking very early in the history of the universe that resulted in values being assigned to various physical parameters.) Could it be reasonable, in the face of this evidence, to infer that there has been the analogue of many rollings of these dice, or of these kinds of dice? If we have reason for thinking that there has been the analogue of only one rolling of the dice on a given table, could it be reasonable to infer that there are the analogues of the many tables upon which there have been the analogues of single rolls of the dice?

At least superficially, the inference to many universes is tempting, and apparently supported by the suggested analogies. When I see the film of the golfer making a hole in one, it seems right for me to reason that my being presented with this particular evidence – that is, the film and its contents – makes it more likely that there were many golfers who were filmed making shots on this hole than that there was just this one golfer whose shot was filmed. But, given that this is so, why isn't it similarly acceptable for me, when presented with the evidence that there was fine-tuned symmetry-breaking early in the history of the universe, to infer that there are many universes in which this kind of symmetry-breaking has occurred? Doesn't my being presented with this particular evidence – the results of the fine-tuned symmetry-breaking – make it more likely that there are many universes in which there is symmetry-breaking?

White's Counter-arguments
In the face of arguments such as the one laid out above, White makes the following suggestion:

What we need is a probabilistic link between my experiences and the hypothesis in question. One way of establishing such a link in the present case is to suppose that I was once an unconscious soul waiting to be embodied in whichever universe produced a hospitable living organism. On this assumption, the more universes there are, the more likely I am to observe one. This is not just a cheap shot. It is an illustration of the kind of story that we need to support the inference to multiple universes. (244)

But why should we think that we need a story of the kind that White proposes? If there is only one universe, and if there is random symmetry-breaking, then – we are supposing – it is extraordinarily unlikely that there will be *anyone* who is presented with the evidence of fine-tuned symmetry-breaking in the subsequent history of that universe. (If only one golf shot is filmed, then it is extraordinarily unlikely that viewers of that film will get to see a hole in one. If few lottery tickets are purchased, then it is extraordinarily unlikely that readers of the newspaper report will learn that there was a winning ticket.) If there are many universes, and if there is random symmetry-breaking, then it is rather more likely that there will be *someone* who has some kinds of experiences somewhere in the multiverse. (If many golf shots are filmed, then it is more likely that viewers of that film will get to see a hole in one. If many lottery tickets are purchased, then it is more likely that readers of the newspaper report will learn that there are winning tickets.) The analogies upon which I have relied do seem to lend *prima facie* support to the suggestion that it is more likely that I shall observe a life-permitting universe if there are many universes in which there is random symmetry-breaking than if there is one universe in which there is random symmetry-breaking.

White suggests at least one line of response to the above argument. First, the argument is really independent of the *fine-tuning* of the universe: provided that there are many possible universes that could "arise from" some chance mechanism, it seems that I have reason to prefer the hypothesis that there are many universes to the hypothesis that there is only one universe. And, second, the discovery that there is fine-tuning surely *diminishes* the case for multiple universes, since increasing the number of universes provides a less rapid increase in the likelihood of my existence if each universe has only a slim chance of producing life than if each universe has a more significant chance of producing life. We can discount the second point immediately: the question is whether there is *any* support for the hypothesis that there are many universes in the observation of a fine-tuned universe; so, even if White's argument here is correct, it is irrelevant. Moreover, the first point is clearly contestable: unless there is fine-tuning, we should not think that the hypothesis that there are many universes is supported by the observation that I observe a life-permitting universe, since, in the absence of fine-tuning, there is no reason to think it unlikely that random symmetry-breaking will issue in a life-supporting universe.

White also suggests – at least *inter alia* – that the line of reasoning that I have sketched relies upon the fallacy of setting aside a specific piece of evidence in favour of a weaker piece of evidence. True enough, White concedes, it is more likely that *someone* should observe a life-permitting universe that issues from random symmetry-breaking if there are many universes than if there is but one universe. But my evidence is that *I* observe that a life-permitting universe has issued from random symmetry-breaking; and this evidence is no more likely if there are many universes than if there is but one universe, since there is but one universe that I *could* observe (namely, the one in which I find myself). I think that this objection is specious – and not supported by the general principle to which White adverts – because, in fact, I also have evidence that there are *many* observers of a life-permitting universe that has issued from random symmetry-breaking, and this further claim is not entailed by the fact that *I* am an observer of a life-permitting universe of the specified kind. On White's own admission, it is more likely that there should be many observers of a life-permitting universe that issues from random symmetry-breaking if there are many universes than if there is but one universe; yet what is the 'more specific' piece of evidence that has been set aside in taking this claim as the one for which one is seeking an explanation?[25]

Concluding Remarks

I take it that the above discussion makes a plausible case for the follow-ing claims: (i) White's *argument* that the probability that our universe is life-permitting is independent of the truth of the claim that there are many universes fails, except in the case in which there is a 'cosmic roll of the dice'; (ii) White's *arguments* that the probability that I observe that our universe is life-permitting is not raised by the claim that there are many universes are, at best, inconclusive; (iii) there is some as yet undefeated intuitive support for the contention that the claim that there are many universes is supported by the claim that there are six billion observers of a life-supporting universe. Moreover – and perhaps more important – I take it that the above discus-sion also shows that it is important not to be too hasty in supposing that arguments, for the conclusion that the claim that there are many universes receives no support from any true claim concerning the fine-tuning data, are arguments that lend support to the claim that our universe is the product of intelligent design.

4.3.5. Concluding Remarks

There are various objections that can be lodged against each of the differ-ent types of formulations of 'cosmic fine-tuning' arguments for intelligent design. Whether one argues from Bayesian considerations, or from consid-eration of likelihoods, or from classical statistical considerations, it seems to

---

[25] I do not suppose that this argument ends here. Consider the claim that there are six billion human observers of a life-permitting universe, a claim for which I have good evidence. Could White argue that my reasons for believing this claim depend upon my believing the more specific claim that there are *these particular* six billion human beings? I don't think so. But, then, what is there in the arguments that he gives to prevent us from supposing that the claim that there are six billion human observers of a life-permitting universe does raise the probability of the claim that there are many universes?

me that there is no reason at all to suppose that one can produce a successful argument from the fine-tuning data to the conclusion that the universe is the product of intelligent design. Moreover, it seems to me that there is no reason at all to suppose that considerations concerning the fine-tuning data give those who are not already persuaded that the universe is the product of the creative activities of an orthodoxly conceived monotheistic god any reason at all to suppose that the universe is the product of the creative activities of an orthodoxly conceived monotheistic god. Finally – though this is less important for present concerns – it seems to me that the jury is still out on the question of whether the fine-tuning data provide less support for the hypothesis that there are many universes than they do for the hypothesis that the universe is the product of intelligent design, even if it is granted that the fine-tuning data do provide some support for the hypothesis that the universe is the product of intelligent design.

4.4. HUME'S CRITICISMS OF ARGUMENTS FOR DESIGN

Here are three characteristic recent passages on the subject of Hume and the argument for design:

Many philosophers now regard David Hume's *Dialogues Concerning Natural Religion* (1779) as the watershed in this argument's career. Before Hume, it was possible for serious people to be persuaded by the argument, but after the onslaught of Hume's corrosive scepticism, the argument was in a shambles and remained that way forever after. Biologists with an interest in the history of this idea often take a different view (Dawkins, 1986), seeing the publication of Darwin's *Origin of Species* as the watershed event. For the first time, a plausible non-theistic explanation of adaptation was on the table.... It is possible to pose the question about the history of the design argument in two ways. The first is sociological: When (if ever) did educated opinion turn against the design argument? With respect to this question, it is quite clear that Hume's *Dialogues* did not put a stop to the argument.... However, this sociological fact leaves unanswered the second historical question we can ask about the design argument. When (if ever) was the argument shown to be fatally flawed? Many philosophers nowadays think that Hume dealt the deathblow.... [Discussion of two Humean objections excised.] Hume produced other criticisms of the design argument, but these fare no better than the two I have described here. Part of the problem is that Hume has no serious alternative explanation of the phenomena he discusses. It is not impossible that the design argument should be refutable without anything being provided to stand in its stead. For example, this could happen if the hypothesis of an intelligent designer were incoherent or self-contradictory. But I see no such defect in the argument. It does not surprise me that intelligent people strongly favoured the design hypothesis when the only alternative available to them was random physical processes. But Darwin entirely altered the dialectical landscape of this problem. His hypothesis of evolution by natural selection is a third possibility; it requires no intelligent design, nor is natural selection properly viewed as a "random physical process". (Sober (1993: 30–6))

I feel more in common with the Reverend William Paley than I do with the distinguished modern philosopher, a well-known atheist, with whom I once discussed the matter at dinner. I said that I could not imagine being an atheist at any time before 1859, when Darwin's *Origin of Species* was published. 'What about Hume?', replied the philosopher. 'How did Hume explain the organised complexity of the living world?', I asked. 'He didn't', said the philosopher. 'Why does it need any special explanation?'. Paley knew that it needed a special explanation; Darwin knew it, and I suspect that in his heart of hearts my philosopher companion knew it too.... As for David Hume himself, it is sometimes said that that great Scottish philosopher disposed of the Argument from Design a century before Darwin. But what Hume did was criticise the logic of using apparent design in nature as positive evidence for the existence of a God. He did not offer any alternative explanation for apparent design, but left the question open. An atheist before Darwin could have said, following Hume: 'I have no explanation for complex biological design. All I know is that God isn't a good explanation, so we must wait and hope that somebody comes up with a better one'. I can't help feeling that such a position, though logically sound, would have left one feeling pretty unsatisfied, and that although atheism might have been logically tenable before Darwin, Darwin made it possible to be an intellectually fulfilled atheist. I like to think that Hume would agree, but some of his writings suggest that he underestimated the complexity and beauty of biological design. (Dawkins (1986: 5–6))

It may be argued that there is still something that calls for further explanation.... There is only one actual universe, with a unique set of basic materials and physical constants, and it is therefore surprising that the elements of this unique set-up are just right for life when they might easily have been wrong. I suspect, however, that this objection also is being presented in a question-begging way. Though some small variation from the actual initial materials and constants would, perhaps, eliminate the possibility of life's having developed as it did, we really have no idea of what other interesting possibilities might have been latent within others of the endless range of possible initial conditions. We are not in a position, therefore, to regard the actual initial materials and constants as a uniquely fruitful set, and as surprising and as specially calling for further explanation on that account. Once these matters are cleared up, we can see that the shift of topic due to the work of Darwin and his successors greatly diminishes the plausibility of the argument for design. The reciprocal adjustments of structures and functions in myriads of different organisms are indeed so delicate and complicated as to be initially surprising in the extreme, and not merely to invite but to require a search for some further explanation; and then the hypothesis of design is at least one to be considered among others. But we find nothing comparable to this in sub-atomic particles or the laws that govern them. Atomic and nuclear physics are, no doubt, intricate enough to be of theoretical as well as practical interest, but we cannot see them as involving reciprocal adjustments which might plausibly be taken as signs of purposiveness. (Mackie (1982: 141–2))

The views expressed in these passages – and the examples could easily be multiplied – seem to me to make various errors. Sober claims (i) that Hume produces no good criticisms of design arguments, (ii) that Hume offers no serious alternative explanations of (biological) design, and (iii) that design was the best explanation available prior to 1859. Dawkins claims, (i) that one could not have been an intellectually fulfilled atheist prior to 1859, (ii) that Hume offered no alternative explanations of (biological) design, and (iii) that Paley *knew* that there must be some non-Humean explanation of apparent biological design. Mackie claims (i) that the work of Darwin greatly diminishes the plausibility of design arguments, and (ii) that there are no reciprocal adjustments in cosmology that are as plausible candidates for evidence of design as cases from biology. None of these claims can withstand scrutiny, as I shall now attempt to demonstrate. More exactly, I shall argue (a) that the claim that Hume offered no (serious) alternative explanations of apparent (biological) design is, perhaps, strictly correct, but that, taken alone, it misrepresents the strength of the resources that Hume provided for developing (serious) alternative explanations of apparent (biological) design, and (b) that all of the other claims are simply false.

4.4.1. Hume's Objections to the Inference to Design

As we noted earlier, arguments for design proceed from certain features of the world – complexity of organisation, complexity of structure, complexity of adaptation – to a conclusion that entails that those features are evidence that the world is a product of intentional design. The features in question can belong to cosmology, or particle physics, or chemistry, or biochemistry, or biology, or any of a number of other disciplines. The eighteenth- and nineteenth-century versions of these arguments focussed heavily – though not exclusively – on (i) the physical structure of the solar system, (ii) the structural organisation of (parts of) plants and animals, and (iii) the providential arrangement of conditions on the surface of the earth. Often, arguments were restricted to examples drawn from biology, (presumably) because it was felt that an overwhelming case could be constructed by considering these alone; but there are numerous examples – for instance, among the Boyle lectures and Bridgewater Treatises – of arguments that are developed entirely from non-biological cases.[26] Also, while the conclusion of the argument might have been taken merely to be that there is at least one designer, the characteristic conclusion of the eighteenth- and nineteenth-century design arguments was that there is a unique, very good, very powerful, very wise designer (or even, that there is a unique, omnibenevolent, omnipotent, omniscient designer).

---

[26] William Derham's 1712 Boyle Lectures were published under the title *Astro-Theology; or, A Demonstration of the Being and Attributes of God, from a Survey of the Heavens*. William Whewell's 1833 Bridgewater Treatise was titled *Astronomy and General Physics Considered with Reference to Natural Theology*. My favourite title amongst the Bridgewater Treatises is William Prout's 1834 *Chemistry, Meteorology, and the Function of Digestion*, which, on *a priori* grounds, one can hardly fail to suspect of being a rather windy tome. But I digress.

The interpretation of Hume's *Dialogues* is extremely controversial. Some scholars think that Hume intended to defend a deistic explanation of apparent design. Others think that he used the dialogue format to disguise the force of the best case that could be made against any hypothesis of design. And there are other positions that might be taken as well. Whatever the truth of the matter, it is clear that one can choose from the materials and techniques that Hume offers to construct a powerful case against any hypothesis of design – that is, it is possible to read the *Dialogues* as a source book for vigorous attacks on the eighteenth- and nineteenth-century design arguments.

Among the powerful objections that an atheist or agnostic (or even, at least for the first two objections, deist) might take from the *Dialogues*, there are at least the following three. (1) It is obviously hopeless to think that the *inference* to a very good, very powerful, and very wise designer is a good one, given just the evidence of apparent design: for there are lots of evils in the world, lots of imperfect adaptations of structure to function, lots of wasted materials, and so on. (*Dialogues*, Parts X and XI: "the inaccurate workmanship of all the springs and principles of the great machine of nature"). (2) Not unrelatedly, there are many alternative hypotheses that account for the evidence of apparent design at least as well as the hypothesis that there is a unique, very good, very powerful, very wise designer: for example, that there is a committee of designers, who couldn't come to unanimous agreement on all matters (hence the imperfections in the final product); that there is a fairly incompetent but very persistent designer, who botches up universe after universe; and so on (*Dialogues*, Parts V–VIII). (3) Even if we restrict ourselves to the conclusion that there is at least one (more or less) intelligent designer, we face the problem of explanatory advance: given that we want to explain the occurrence of certain kinds of complexity in the world, what advantage do we gain by postulating similar kinds of unexplained complexity in some other realm? If we are content to leave the complex intentions, and so on, of the designer(s) unexplained, why shouldn't we have been content to leave the original complexity in the world unexplained? And how could we even pretend to an explanation of those complex intentions, and so on? (Dialogues, Part IV, esp. pp. 34–5).

The examples from the last paragraph serve to refute the first of Sober's claims. Hume produced lots of good criticisms of arguments for design. For, first, he produced compelling criticisms of the typical eighteenth- and nineteenth-century inference to the existence of a unique, very good, very wise, and very powerful designer. And, second, he produced at least one very powerful criticism of the more modest inference to the existence of at least one (more or less) intelligent designer. Note that I don't say that this second objection is decisive: there are hard questions about theoretical virtues and explanatory advance still to be addressed. However, I do think that it is clear that this is a *very* powerful criticism. (There is some irony in the fact that Dawkins twice makes use of this second Humean criticism.

Consider: "[O]f course any God capable of intelligently designing something as complex as the DNA/protein replicating machine must have been at least as complex and organised as the machine itself. . . . To explain the origin of the DNA/protein machine by invoking a supernatural Designer is to explain precisely nothing, for it leaves unexplained the origin of the Designer. You have to say something like 'God was always there', and if you allow yourself that kind of lazy way out, you might as well just say 'DNA was always there' or 'Life was always there', and be done with it" (Dawkins (1986: 141)). And: "If we want to postulate a deity capable of engineering all the organised complexity in the world, either instantaneously or by guiding evolution, that deity must already have been vastly complex in the first place. The creationist, whether a naive Bible-thumper or an educated bishop, simply postulates an already existing being of prodigious intelligence and complexity. If we are going to allow ourselves the luxury of postulating organised complexity without offering an explanation, we might as well make a job of it and simply postulate the existence of life as we know it!" (Dawkins (1986:316)).)

Of course, there are still some subtleties that need to be addressed here. Hume's objection (as I am construing it) is to the *inference* from apparent design, and not necessarily to the idea that the apparent design could be explained by the existence of a designer. If one supposes that one has independent reasons for holding that there is a very intelligent creator – for example, on the basis of an ontological argument – then one will quite rightly think that "Hume's objection" is not very compelling. But that isn't how the dialectic goes: the eighteenth- and nineteenth-century proponents of the design arguments took those arguments to be the best (perhaps even the only) basis for an inference to the existence of an orthodoxly conceived monotheistic god. I claim that Hume's objections to these people were very strong indeed.

4.4.2. Alternative Humean 'Explanations' of Design

Despite the claims of Sober and Dawkins to the contrary, it seems to me that Hume did more than merely criticise the inference from apparent design; that is, it seems to me that he offered alternative explanations of the apparent evidence for design, and moreover that he offered *serious* alternative explanations of this apparent evidence. Perhaps I am wrong about this; but, in any case, all I really need to establish is that Hume *could* have offered alternative explanations of the apparent evidence for design, that is, that he had available to him serious alternative explanations of this apparent evidence. If merely *Humean* alternative explanations are serious competitors to the design hypothesis, then that is enough to defeat the claims of Sober and Dawkins about the logical importance of the publication of *The Origin of Species*. (There are at least four different questions here: (i) What alternative explanations are explicitly offered by Hume? (ii) What alternative explanations are implicitly developed by Hume? (iii) What alternative explanations are natural extensions or analogues of explanations that are developed by Hume? (iv) What alternative explanations were available to Hume, given the state of scientific knowledge at the time? I shall – more or less – grant to Sober and Dawkins that Hume does not explicitly offer serious alternative explanations to design. But this concession leaves open the question of the logical importance of Humean considerations for the pre-1859 argument for design.)

Before I try to defend these claims, there are two important preliminary points to note. First, we need to remind ourselves of what Hume (and Paley) *didn't* know. As Dawkins and Sober emphasise, they knew nothing about the degree of complexity of organisms and (the mechanism of) natural selection. But they also knew nothing (much) about: geology (the age of the earth); thermodynamics (the second law, which concerns the overwhelming statistical likelihood of increases in entropy in isolated systems); the expanding universe (the Hubble shift); and the Big Bang (the cosmic microwave background radiation, the COBE data, the age of the universe). Second, we need to remind ourselves of what Hume (and Paley) took themselves to know (or, at least, could have reasonably allowed themselves to believe, if they were well versed in current scientific ideas). According to the then current Newtonian cosmology, the universe is both spatially and temporally infinite. At any time, it contains infinitely many stars – and, hence, presumably, infinitely many solar systems. (The inference to infinitely many solar systems would probably have been rejected by Newton himself, on the grounds that God must constantly intervene to preserve the stability of our solar system. However, many subsequent Newtonians did not accept this part of Newton's views. In Part VIII of the Dialogues, Philo develops some alternative explanations of apparent design based on the assumption that the universe contains only finitely many particles of matter. These explanations are in conflict with the best physics of the day.)

How, then, did (or could) Hume seek to explain the apparent evidence for design? I suggest that he had (or could have had) a number of strategies, all with a reasonable degree of plausibility.

(1) *First*, one might offer to explain apparent present design in terms of apparent past design: at any time, the order in the world is explained as the product of order that existed at an even earlier time. Given ignorance about the finitude of the past and the second law of thermodynamics, this explanation doesn't seem utterly implausible. (Hume does defend explanatory regresses (Part IX); and he does note, several times, that present apparent design can be explained in terms of immediately past apparent design (e.g., Part III). However, he doesn't actually undertake to explain present apparent design in terms of an infinite temporal regress – that is, this explanation is merely Humean. On the other hand, he does offer to explain present

order in terms of an "eternal inherent principle of order" – Part VI – and this explanation could perhaps be expanded in the way I have suggested.)

(2) *Second*, one might offer to explain apparent design in terms of an infinite regress of increasing levels of 'organised complexity': wherever there is 'organised complexity' in the world, there is even more 'organised complexity' elsewhere that serves to explain the initially observed 'organised complexity'. While, as far as I know, there is no textual support for the claim that Hume ever actually considered a hypothesis of this sort, I do not doubt that he would have smiled upon the suggestion that life came to earth from somewhere else in the cosmos where it exists in more complex and interesting forms. Allowing this kind of explanation to regress – which seems permissible in an infinite cosmos – yields an explanation of why it is that there is 'organised complexity' on the surface of the earth; or so, at any rate, some might be tempted to suppose.

(3) *Third*, one might offer to explain apparent design in terms of an ensemble of worlds: even though it is highly unlikely that apparent design could have arisen by chance, if there are sufficiently many different venues, then apparent design is bound to appear in lots of them. Against the Newtonian background, this looks like a pretty good explanation. (Hume actually gives a temporal version of this argument (Part VIII): if there are only finitely many possible states of the world, then in an infinite amount of time, each will appear infinitely often; and even if there are infinitely many possible states of the world, in an infinite amount of time, highly ordered members amongst the infinitely many possible states of the world are bound to appear. (A tacit assumption that appears to be at work here is that disordered states give rise to later states in a random fashion.) Hume also mentions various hypotheses that involve world ensembles, for example, in Part V ("Many worlds might have been bungled or botched", p. 39).)

(4) *Fourth*, one might offer to explain apparent design in terms of chance. Sure, it seems unlikely that the apparent design that we see arose by chance – but it isn't impossible, and there is no better explanation to be had. True enough, this suggestion may not sound Humean: Philo says (Part VI) that "Chance has no place, on any hypothesis". However, Philo also says here that he prefers the hypothesis of an "eternal inherent principle of order in the world", and this sounds suspiciously like an occult property of the kind lampooned in Part IV. Moreover, the context strongly suggests that Philo would prefer to say that order is just a brute fact, with no further explanation ("Were I obliged to defend any particular system of this nature . . ."). Perhaps there is room for debate about whether this should count as an "explanation"; however, the important point is that the hypothesis of chance is a perfectly respectable competitor, which needs to be taken into account.

(5) *Fifth*, one might offer to 'explain' apparent design in terms of 'brute fact' : perhaps there is simply no explanation of the appearance of design to be given. As we have had occasion to note elsewhere, if there is contingency,

there is bound to be brute contingency: there are features of the world that have no explanation. Moreover, if it is insisted that 'organised complexity' can be explained only in terms of greater 'organised complexity', and if one is opposed to an infinite regress, then one is obliged to postulate a maximum level of 'organised complexity' for which there is simply no explanation. Again, one might worry that this approach is not one that is directly broached by Hume in the *Dialogues*; but, as I insisted above, it is clearly an 'explanation' that is broadly Humean in nature.

In my view, the considerations raised in the last three paragraphs show, *contra* Sober and Dawkins, that Hume did have (or could have had) serious alternative non-supernaturalistic 'explanations' of apparent design available, and moreover these considerations also show that design was not the best explanation prior to 1859. Of course, an atheist or agnostic prior to 1859 ought to have confessed that he didn't know which was the correct explanation of apparent (biological) design. However, the problem should have appeared to be one of embarrassment of riches: there are too many roughly equally good explanations, and no obvious means of choosing between them. (If Dawkins supposes that an intellectually fulfilled atheist needs to know everything, then it is plain that there never have been, and never will be, intellectually fulfilled atheists. Furthermore, given that the alternative hypotheses are plainly no worse than the hypothesis of design, it is also clear that parity of argument will entail that there could have been no intellectually fulfilled theists prior to 1859.)

Moreover, these same considerations show, *contra* Dawkins, that Paley did not *know* that there must be some *other* special explanation of apparent biological design. The problem, prior to 1859, was that no one had hit upon the correct explanation of apparent biological design, namely, the Darwinian explanation, which is manifestly vastly superior to any of the alternatives. However, prior to 1859 – or, at least, prior to Darwin's precursors – no one had even the faintest idea that there was such an explanation to be had. Of course, *ex post facto*, we can see that their situation was manifestly unsatisfactory – there was a much better explanation to be had, if only they could find it. But what reason is there to suppose that they had any awareness of the existence of this better explanation? Often, we can't guess at the form that a good explanation will take until we have it; the case of apparent biological design is, in my view, simply a case in point.

There is a clear tension in the remarks that Dawkins makes about Hume. On the one hand, he claims – on the basis of characteristically Humean reasoning – that the theistic hypothesis isn't even a competitor, let alone a serious competitor, to the hypothesis of natural selection. On the other hand, he claims that, prior to 1859, atheists incurred special liabilities from their failure to hit upon a good explanation for apparent biological design. These two claims could be reconciled only by an argument that showed that the theistic hypothesis is greatly superior to the Humean alternatives – but Dawkins nowhere attempts to produce such an argument. With good reason, in my view: I know of no persuasive argument for this conclusion.

Of course, there are (unpersuasive!) objections that might be offered against my claim that design was not obviously the best explanation prior to 1859. *First*, it may be said that a commitment to one complex system that arises by chance is better than a commitment to many complex systems that arise by chance – better one big mystery than many little mysteries. However, it seems to me that this objection relies upon unfair methods of accounting. There is just one universe, with a level of complexity that is at least equalled by the level of complexity of its designer(s). The universe has many parts that are complex – but, corresponding to these parts, there are parts of the designer(s) that have a corresponding degree of complexity (the particular creative intentions that apply to those parts). To compare one unexplained complex system (the designer(s)) with many unexplained complex systems (the complex parts of the universe) is simply to cheat. *Second*, it might be said that more argument is required to show that the theistic hypothesis is not better than the Humean alternatives. I suppose that the Humean point about explanatory advance – perhaps together with more general considerations about theoretical virtues – constitutes a very powerful *prima facie* case for the claim that the theistic hypothesis is no better than the Humean competitors as an explanation of apparent design. At the very least, the examples show that it is very far from obvious that design was the best explanation of apparent design prior to 1859. (Perhaps, owing to the vagaries of history, prior probabilities were so distributed before 1859 that there is a sense in which design was the best overall explanation prior to 1859. However, even if it were so, this sociological fact would be irrelevant to our investigation of the logical status of the hypothesis of design. Naturalistic explanations *were* especially virtuous even then.) At least *pro tem*, then, I take it that the claim that design was not obviously the best explanation prior to 1859 is in pretty good shape.

4.4.3. Darwin and Arguments for Design

Even if I have managed to show that Sober and Dawkins underestimate the pre-1859 force of Humean objections to design arguments, I have not yet done anything much towards establishing the claim, *contra* Mackie, that Darwin's work didn't greatly diminish the plausibility of design arguments. Here, I can be brief. Apparent biological design is only one kind of apparent design. If there are other apparent kinds of design that seem to be about as much in need of explanation as apparent biological design, and that are untouched by Darwin ian considerations, then the design argument as a whole is undamaged by the Darwinian assault. I claim that there are such cases: cosmology, for one. (I shall return to this topic in the next section.)

Why then did Darwin and his contemporaries suppose that the theory of evolution posed such a threat to the argument for design? I offer a socio-logical conjecture. For more than 150 years, many – perhaps even most – (intelligent) people had supposed that all the proof that one needed for the existence of a very good, very wise, very powerful designer could be found in apparent biological design. Moreover, the apparent design in question was such that anyone could appreciate it – it didn't require any background mathematical or physical knowledge, and so on – and hence it could be readily appealed to from pulpit and editorial. As a result, the argument from biological design came to have a social importance that greatly exceeded its logical importance. Given that it was one of the common, shared assump-tions of the day, that apparent biological design is the best, and all the needed, evidence for the existence of a very good, very wise, very powerful designer, it should not be surprising that Darwin's theory was greeted with considerable consternation. (It is perhaps worth noting that "the argument from the heavens" can't proceed merely from a quick glance at the night sky – the order alleged to be found there can be discerned only from lengthy astronomical observations (albeit observations that were once made solely by the unaided human eye). The "order" that so impressed the Greeks was principally an artefact of the rotation of the earth about its axis; but some reasonable data about the orbits of the planets could have been obtained by naked eye observation. Moreover, the arguments in the eighteenth and nineteenth century were able to draw upon telescopic data as well.)

Of course, the argument of the last paragraph is extremely hypothetical and simplistic. We have no figures to support the claims involved, nor any means of obtaining them. However, it is I think very plausible to hold that some suitably filled out sociological explanation of this form is correct. *Con-tra* Sober, it most certainly was not Darwin who dealt the fatal logical blow to design arguments – though, plausibly, he and his successors did utterly demolish the argument for biological design.

Then again, even the claim that Darwin and his successors did utterly demolish the argument for biological design is not obviously correct. If we suppose that the world is deterministic – or, at least that, given a complete set of data for a single time and a complete set of data for infinity at all subsequent times, the laws determine all the data for all subsequent times – then there is still the improbability of the initial data and conditions at infin-ity, which permit the later development of apparent evidence for biological design, to be accounted for. Obviously, there is no Darwinian explanation of this improbability in the offing – so a Newtonian might well feel justified in maintaining that Darwin didn't demolish *all* versions of the argument for biological design.

More generally, one might cast the current objection as follows: Darwin showed that the process of natural selection could have led to the grad-ual production of certain kinds of complexity from conditions in which those kinds of complexity were completely absent. Biological complexity – complexity of function, structure, and adaptation – did not need to be produced in a single step, whether by chance or special creation. However, the Darwinian argument says nothing about the likelihood of obtaining initial conditions upon which natural selection can plausibly operate to produce biological complexity. Moreover, *contra* Mackie, there seems to be good reason to think that the likelihood of obtaining suitable conditions by chance is actually vanishingly small. At any rate, this is what the argument from cosmology – which turns out not to be entirely independent from the argument from biology – tells us. (Mackie claims that, while life as it developed would have been impossible, we don't know what else might have developed. However, as we shall see, the "suitable conditions" in question are plausibly suitable conditions for anything that might plausibly be called "life". Could there be anything that deserved to be called "life" in a universe that lasted for only a fraction of a second? Could there be anything that deserved to be called "life" in a universe that contained nothing but very dilute radiation? Setting aside very bizarre speculations, the answer seems to be: clearly not. At the very least, it is plain that it isn't just carbon-based life that is at issue here.)

Inspired by the argument of the last two paragraphs – to the correctness of which I make no commitment – one might even suppose that there is a more or less *a priori* argument that entails that current improbability is bound to resist *complete procedural* explanation. Suppose that the current state of the world is improbable. Suppose further that there is a procedure that renders the present state of the world very highly probable given some range of past states of the world. Suppose that the procedure in question is instantiated. Then, the relevant range of past states of the world must be highly improbable – for, if not, then the present state of the world would be highly probable, contrary to our initial assumption. (Of course, if the relevant range of past states is probable, then the conclusion to be drawn is that, despite appearances, the present state of the world is probable too. Perhaps it is this inference that defenders of the logical importance of cumulative selection for the argument for design have in mind. But it should be noted that there is nothing in the theory of cumulative selection that suggests that the relevant past states of the world are probable.)

4.4.4. Hume and Cosmic Fine-Tuning

What should we say in the face of the apparent evidence for "fine-tuning", if we suppose that there is something here that requires explanation? Well, it seems to me that we are pretty much in the same position as Hume was in when he confronted the apparent evidence for biological design. Moreover, we seem to have roughly the same range of options: we can appeal to an infinite regress, of one kind or another; we can appeal to an ensemble of universes; we can appeal to chance; or we can insist that the apparent fine-tuning is a brute fact, and hence not in need of explanation. Perhaps there are options that ought to have been included on this list, but that have been omitted, for example, e.g. Leslie's hypothesis that it is an 'efficacious creative principle' that the world exists because it is good that it should exist. However, it is hard to believe that there are hypotheses to which we might appeal here that do not have parallels to which Hume could have appealed.

At the very least, it seems to me that the recent blooming of arguments for design based on cosmic fine-tuning present a serious difficulty for those who suppose that it was reasonable to accept biological arguments for design prior to Darwin, and yet who insist that Darwinian considerations suffice to utterly demolish those arguments. If Hume could provide no decent alternative explanations for the appearance of biological design, and if it was not sufficient for Hume to point to weaknesses in the inference to design on the basis of the alleged biological evidence, then what is someone like Dawkins to say in the face of the contemporary arguments for design on the basis of alleged cosmic fine-tuning? The work of Lee Smolin and Quentin Smith notwithstanding, it seems to me to be very hard to believe that there is an acceptable evolutionary explanation of apparent cosmic fine-tuning. But if it is not acceptable to object to the inference to intelligent design on the basis of apparent cosmic fine-tuning, and if there are no other 'acceptable' explanations to be had, then how can one avoid coming to the conclusion that apparent cosmic fine-tuning is actually good evidence for intelligent design?

In my view, those who wish to object to arguments from design are bound to pursue a two-part strategy: on the one hand, they will take the view that there are *arguments* for design in which the conclusion of the argument – 'that such and such feature of the world is the product of intelligent design' – is simply not supported by the premises of that argument; and, on the other hand, they will take the view that the *considerations* to which appeal is made in the formulation of arguments for design can be adequately accommodated in a non-supernaturalistic theory of the universe. Consequently, in my view, there is no prospect of an utterly non-Humean response to arguments for design, of the kind apparently envisaged by Dawkins and Sober, that essentially appeals only to the manifest truth of Darwinian evolutionary theory.

Perhaps it is worth noting here – in conclusion – that Sober appears to have moderated his views about biological arguments for design. In Sober (2003: 42), he claims that 'design argument's fatal flaw does not depend upon seeing the merits of Darwinian theory'. Moreover, while he insists that 'Hume's criticisms largely derive from an empiricist epistemology that is too narrow', I do not think that he would disagree with my claim that the proper response to design arguments on the part of non-theists has to be broadly Humean (or, as he might perhaps prefer to say, philosophical).

4.5. CONCLUDING REMARKS

In this very brief tour of teleological arguments, I have argued for the following conclusions: (i) that Paley's argument for design is typically misinterpreted, but when it is properly interpreted, it is clear that it is entirely unpersuasive; (ii) that Behe's argument for design is not very different from Paley's argument, and fails to improve upon that argument in any way; (iii) that there are good reasons not to be persuaded by current formulations of 'cosmic fine-tuning' arguments for design; (iv) that it is not yet absolutely clear that an inference from 'the fine-tuning data' to many universes is worse than an inference to intelligent design from that data; and (v) that it is a mistake to suppose that the various arguments for intelligent design can be defeated simply by appeal to relevant well-supported scientific theories, without any recourse to philosophical considerations of one kind or another. I recognise – of course – that there is much, much more that could be said on each of these topics; perhaps I will be able to provide a more expansive account elsewhere.

There are various places at which considerations about infinity intrude into discussions of teleological arguments. On the one hand, as we noted in our discussion of Paley's argument, there is a question of whether the appearance of design requires any explanation in an infinitely old universe in which order is preserved as time passes: perhaps, prior to advances in geology and physics, it was more reasonable to suppose that the apparent order in the world needed no explanation than to suppose that there is an intelligent designer. On the other hand, as we noted in our discussion of 'cosmic fine tuning' arguments, one of the central issues for the formulation of these arguments turns on considerations about countable additivity for probability functions.

There may be other ways in which concerns about infinity are relevant to teleological arguments that we have not yet discussed. In particular, there are questions about the powers and nature that we must assign to the hypothesised designer if it turns out that there are respects in which the world is (actually) infinite.

5

Pascal's Wager

The following discussion of Pascal's Wager relies upon the discussion of the infinite in Oppy (2006). In particular, I assume familiarity with the discussion of probability and decision theory in that other work.

5.1. THE ARGUMENT

I shall suppose that the label "Pascal's Wager" denotes the following argument:[1]

1. Rationality requires either that you wager for an orthodoxly conceived monotheistic god or that you do not wager for an orthodoxly conceived monotheistic god.
2. Rationality requires that you hold:
   (a) the utility of wagering for an orthodoxly conceived monotheistic god, if an orthodoxly conceived monotheistic god exists, is positive infinity
   (b) the utility of wagering for an orthodoxly conceived monotheistic god, if an orthodoxly conceived monotheistic god does not exist, is less than positive infinity
   (c) the utility of not wagering for an orthodoxly conceived monotheistic god, if an orthodoxly conceived monotheistic god exists, is less than positive infinity

---

[1] For other presentations and discussions of Pascal's Wager, see, e.g.: Ryan (1945), Flew (1960), Penelhum (1964), Cargile (1966), Turner (1968), Swinburne (1969), Landsberg (1971), Hacking (1972), Dalton (1975, 1976), Martin (1975, 1983, 1990), Yarvin (1976), Nicholl (1979), Centore (1980), Mackie (1982), Natoli (1983), Brown (1984), Makinde (1985), Rescher (1985), Duff (1986), Morris (1986), Lycan and Schlesinger (1989), Oppy (1990), Jordan (1991a, 1991b, 1993a, 1993b, 1994a), Taliaferro (1992), Byl (1994), Golding (1994), Mougin and Sober (1994), Anderson (1995), Sobel (1996), and MacIntosh (2000).

(d) the utility of not wagering for an orthodoxly conceived monotheistic god, if an orthodoxly conceived monotheistic god does not exist, is less than positive infinity

3. Rationality requires that the probability that you assign to an orthodoxly conceived monotheistic god's existence is positive, and not infinitesimal.

4. Rationality requires that you perform the act of maximising expected utility (provided that there is one action that maximises expected utility).

5. (Therefore) Rationality requires that you wager for an orthodoxly conceived monotheistic god.

6. (Therefore) You should wager for an orthodoxly conceived monotheistic god.

Moreover, I shall suppose – following standard practice – that the justification for the claim that wagering on an orthodoxly conceived monotheistic god maximises expected utility is most readily conveyed by means of the following table:

	An orthodoxly conceived monotheistic god exists and Pr(an orthodoxly conceived monotheistic god exists)=p	It is not the case that an orthodoxly conceived monotheistic god exists and Pr(it is not the case that an orthodoxly conceived monotheistic god exists)=$1 - p$
Wager for an orthodoxly conceived monotheistic god	Positive Infinite Value	Less than Positive Infinite Value
Do not wager for an orthodoxly conceived monotheistic god	Less than Positive Infinite Value	Less than Positive Infinite Value

Following the standard prescription for the calculation of expected utilities, and performing the calculation in the standard arithmetic on Я, it is readily seen that:

EU(Wager for an orthodoxly conceived monotheistic god)
$= p \times$ (Positive Infinite Value) $+ (1 - p)$
$\times$ (Less than Positive Infinite Value)
$=$ Positive Infinite Value

and that:

EU(Do not wager for an orthodoxly conceived monotheistic god)
$= p \times$ (Less than Positive Infinite Value) $+ (1 - p)$
$\times$ (Less than Positive Infinite Value)
$=$ Less than Positive Infinite Value

So, if the decision situation is properly represented by the table, and if the calculation in Я is acceptable, then it seems that we have shown that wagering on an orthodoxly conceived monotheistic god maximises expected utility. Given the assumptions that we made in setting out our argument, there is at least *prima facie* reason to claim that it does follow from those assumptions that one ought to wager on an orthodoxly conceived monotheistic god.

It is, of course, possible to argue about the extent to which this argument accurately captures the considerations that are presented in Pascal's *Pensées*. However, it seems to me that it is plausible to claim that this argument is no worse than any other clearly stated arguments that have been alleged to be contained in Pascal's scribblings. Moreover, the interesting considerations that have been raised in connection with other formulations of the wager argument also arise in connection with this argument.

There is a certain awkwardness in the formulation of the first premise that is avoided in other formulations. It seems to me that it is simply true that either you wager for an orthodoxly conceived monotheistic god or you do not wager for an orthodoxly conceived monotheistic god; or, at least, this is so provided that some determinate content is given to the notion of 'wagering for an orthodoxly conceived monotheistic god'. Consequently, there is only a trivial sense in which rationality requires that either you wager for an orthodoxly conceived monotheistic god or you do not wager for an orthodoxly conceived monotheistic god: whether or not you conform to the norms of rationality – whatever those may happen to be – you cannot make it false that either you wager for an orthodoxly conceived monotheistic god or you do not wager for an orthodoxly conceived monotheistic god. However, it is clear that no harm is done; and it is also clear that we must have some equivalent means of importing claims within the scope of the 'rationality requires' operator.

5.2. SOME OBJECTIONS TO THE ARGUMENT

There are many points at which this argument can be contested that have no significant involvement in considerations about infinity. I shall mention just a few of the more important points here.

First, the proponent of the wager argument assumes that there are rational requirements that govern the assignment of utilities to outcomes: it is rationally required, for example, that one assign infinite utility to wagering on an orthodoxly conceived monotheistic god if an orthodoxly conceived monotheistic god exists. It is highly controversial whether there are such requirements of rationality on the assignment of utilities to outcomes. Famously, Hume denied that there are any such requirements: in his view, it is not contrary to *reason* to prefer the destruction of the world to the scratching of one's little finger. Moreover, even if one is not prepared to agree with Hume on this point, one might well suppose that it could hardly be contrary to reason to assign some finite utility to wagering on an orthodoxly conceived monotheistic god if an orthodoxly conceived monotheistic god exists. But if one does assign a finite utility to wagering on an orthodoxly conceived monotheistic god if an orthodoxly conceived monotheistic god exists, then there is certainly no good argument to the conclusion that one ought to wager on an orthodoxly conceived monotheistic god that is independent of the details of the calculation of expected utility in this case, that is, the precise values that are assigned to the probabilities and utilities.

It may be said that this objection arises only as an artefact of the form in which I have cast the wager argument. If we suppose that the second premise concerns that which is rationally permissible, rather than that which is rationally required, we can still get out the conclusion that someone who makes the assignments of utilities that are prescribed in the second premise is rationally required to wager on an orthodoxly conceived monotheistic god unless that makes person some change to the assignment of utilities. Rather than think of the argument as a tool that is good for all rational agents, think of it instead as a tool that is good for those rational agents who make the assignment of utilities that is prescribed in the second premise, and who do so robustly or resiliently, so that they will not resile from this assignment in the face of the wager argument.

If we think about the argument in this way, then it seems to me that the assignment of infinite utility to wagering on an orthodoxly conceived monotheistic god if an orthodoxly conceived monotheistic god exists becomes irrelevant: all that can matter is whether an agent assigns a high enough utility to wagering on an orthodoxly conceived monotheistic god if an orthodoxly conceived monotheistic god exists to bring it about that the expected utility of wagering on an orthodoxly conceived monotheistic god is greater than the expected utility of not wagering on an orthodoxly conceived monotheistic god. Moreover, if there were nothing else wrong with the wager argument, then one might have some reason to predict that there would be a large number of cases in which the wager argument is ineffective: reasonable atheists and agnostics would surely assign utilities in such a way that it did not turn out that the expected utility of wagering on an orthodoxly conceived monotheistic god is greater than the expected utility of not wagering on an orthodoxly conceived monotheistic god. However, whether there is any reason to examine this prediction depends upon whether the wager argument survives the many other kinds of objections that can be lodged against it.

Second, there is some *prima facie* reason to suppose that the proponent of the wager argument assumes that we can reasonably adjust the probabilities that we assign to propositions in the light of our preferences (values, utilities, etc.). At least at first glance, it seems that if I initially hold that $\Pr($an orthodoxly conceived monotheistic god exists$) \approx 10^{-100}$, and if the wager argument is good, then after I have gone through the argument, I have reason to hold that $\Pr($an orthodoxly conceived monotheistic god exists$) > 0.5$. So, at least at first glance, it seems that the value that I assign to believing that an orthodoxly conceived monotheistic god exists if an orthodoxly conceived monotheistic god exists is supposed to lead justifiably to a change in the probability that I assign to the proposition that an orthodoxly conceived monotheistic god exists. This looks *suspicious,* to say the least: surely it is just wishful thinking to adjust my probabilities in the light of my preferences in this way.

Whether this is a telling objection plausibly depends upon what we suppose is involved in *wagering for an orthodoxly conceived monotheistic god.* If wagering for an orthodoxly conceived monotheistic god requires believing that an orthodoxly conceived monotheistic god exists, then it does seem that the conclusion of the argument is that you are rationally required to ramp up the probability that you assign to the claim that an orthodoxly conceived monotheistic god exists in the light of your strong preference for believing that an orthodoxly conceived monotheistic god exists if, indeed, an orthodoxly conceived monotheistic god exists. However, if wagering for an orthodoxly conceived monotheistic god does not require believing that an orthodoxly conceived monotheistic god exists, then it is unclear what justification there is for the claim that one should assign infinite utility to wagering for an orthodoxly conceived monotheistic god if an orthodoxly conceived monotheistic god exists. If one supposes that, if an orthodoxly conceived monotheistic god exists, one gets an infinite reward even without believing that an orthodoxly conceived monotheistic god exists, provided only that one wagers for an orthodoxly conceived monotheistic god, then, at the very least, one owes an account of what wagering is and why an orthodoxly conceived monotheistic god attaches such value to it. If, on the other hand, one supposes that one gets the infinite reward only if an orthodoxly conceived monotheistic god exists and one comes to believe that an orthodoxly conceived monotheistic god exists, then it seems that the wager argument requires violation of a plausible "reflection" principle for belief: while you are not required to believe that an orthodoxly conceived monotheistic god exists, you are required to believe that you ought to believe that an orthodoxly conceived monotheistic god exists. But it is doubtful that there is a stable cognitive state of this kind: how can I coherently hold both that the probability that an orthodoxly conceived monotheistic god exists is 10^{-100}, and that I ought to hold that the probability that an orthodoxly conceived monotheistic god exists is > 0.5?

Third, if we suppose that the wager argument only assumes that it is rationally permissible to assign infinite utility to believing in an orthodoxly conceived monotheistic god if an orthodoxly conceived monotheistic god exists – and if we suppose that the aim of the wager is only to persuade those who make the appropriate assignment of utility – then it seems that this style of argument is a double-edged sword. Suppose that – for whatever reasons – I assign high utility to disbelieving in an orthodoxly conceived monotheistic god, and not much utility to believing in an orthodoxly conceived monotheistic god: I find the thought that an orthodoxly conceived monotheistic god exists repulsive; I very much want there to be no orthodoxly conceived monotheistic god, whether or not an orthodoxly conceived monotheistic god exists. Then, even if theists have theoretical arguments that make the existence of an orthodoxly conceived monotheistic god fairly probable, I can still, without violating reason, appeal to my values in order to drive down the probability that an orthodoxly conceived monotheistic god exists to a figure much less than 0.5. Anyone who thinks that the wager argument is good *for those* who assign infinite utility to believing in an orthodoxly conceived monotheistic god if an orthodoxly conceived monotheistic god exists will have to allow that there is a corresponding good argument for atheism *for those* who assign vastly greater utility to disbelieving in an orthodoxly conceived monotheistic god whether or not an orthodoxly conceived monotheistic god exists than to believing in an orthodoxly conceived monotheistic god whether or not an orthodoxly conceived monotheistic god exists.

Fourth, the proponent of the wager argument assumes that it is rationally required that one assign a non-zero probability to the proposition that an orthodoxly conceived monotheistic god exists. Even if we suppose that reasonably systems of belief are *regular* – that is, do not assign zero probability to propositions that are not known *a priori* to be false – it is not clear that we cannot suppose that it is rationally permissible to hold that the probability that an orthodoxly conceived monotheistic god exists is zero. There are various *a priori* arguments against the existence of an orthodoxly conceived monotheistic god. If we can reasonably suppose that one of these arguments is successful, then we can reasonably attribute zero probability to the claim that an orthodoxly conceived monotheistic god exists. Pascal himself began his deliberations about the wager with the observation that reason is powerless to make any judgment about the proposition that an orthodoxly conceived monotheistic god exists. If we take this observation literally, then Pascal himself was not prepared to rule out the possibility that it is *a priori* false that an orthodoxly conceived monotheistic god exists. But it is quite mysterious how one could suppose that the wager argument succeeds unless one is prepared to rule that it is not *a priori* false that an orthodoxly conceived monotheistic god exists. Surely, I ought not to assign a non-zero probability to the claim that an orthodoxly conceived monotheistic god exists if I am not prepared to make any judgment on the claim that it is *a priori* false that an orthodoxly conceived monotheistic god exists.

Here, again, one might try making the response that we considered in connection with the first objection above: whatever Pascal himself may have suggested, it is surely possible for rational agents to assign a non-zero probability to the proposition that an orthodoxly conceived monotheistic god exists. Even if there are rational agents who escape the wager argument because they refuse to assign a non-zero probability to the claim that an orthodoxly conceived monotheistic god exists, it is plausible to suppose that there are rational agents who are unable to escape the wager argument in this way. As before, whether this observation has consequences that are worth pursuing depends upon whether the wager argument survives all of the other objections that can be lodged against it.

Fifth – a point closely related to the previous one – the proponent of the wager argument assumes that both the probabilities that a rational agent assigns to propositions and the utilities that a rational agent assigns to outcomes are always properly modelled using real numbers. If we suppose – as seems plausible – that we often get a better representation of the probabilities and utilities of agents if we assign intervals – or families of intervals – to those agents, then there is another way in which the argument for the wager can break down. We have already seen one example of this: if I'm not prepared to rule out the possibility that it is *a priori* false that an orthodoxly conceived monotheistic god exists, then the probability that I assign to this proposition should be vague over an interval $[0, n]$ or $[0, n)$ – and, in that case, the calculation of expected utility fails to yield any result. In general, if the probability that is assigned to the proposition that an orthodoxly conceived monotheistic god exists is vague over a collection of values that includes 0, or if the utility that is assigned to the outcome of wagering on an orthodoxly conceived monotheistic god if an orthodoxly conceived monotheistic god exists is vague over a collection of values that includes some finite values, then, at the very least, orthodox calculation of maximum expected utility can be stymied. Moreover, while one might think that the case in which 0 probability is assigned to the proposition that an orthodoxly conceived monotheistic god exists and the case in which finite utility is assigned to the outcome of wagering on an orthodoxly conceived monotheistic god if an orthodoxly conceived monotheistic god exists are both cases in which one is not dealing with a rational agent, it is much harder to maintain that one could not reasonably make interval assignments of probabilities and/or utilities that will disarm the wager argument. Indeed, more strongly, one might think that anyone who is moved by the kinds of considerations to which Pascal appeals at the beginning of the wager argument is obliged to make just these kinds of assignments: if reason can tell us nothing about these matters, then the probability that is assigned to the claim that an orthodoxly conceived monotheistic god exists ought to be $[0, 1]$, and the utility that is assigned to wagering on an orthodoxly conceived monotheistic god if an orthodoxly conceived monotheistic god exists ought to be $[\infty, -\infty]$. At the very least, those who suppose that the wager argument can be reinstated in the face of the insistence that the relevant probabilities and utilities are better represented by assignments of intervals than by assignments of precise numerical values clearly have much work to do.

Sixth – as many people have noted – there are theological reasons to be suspicious of the wager argument. On the one hand, if we do not help ourselves to details of the standard monotheistic conceptions of salvation and the afterlife, then it seems doubtful that we have any good reason to suppose that "wagering on an orthodoxly conceived monotheistic god" really does have infinite utility. If the content of my belief in the supernatural can be summed up in the claim that there is a supernatural cause of the universe – and if I am prepared to hazard no further guesses about the nature of that cause – then there seems to be no justification for the claim that "wagering on an orthodoxly conceived monotheistic god" has infinite utility. On the other hand, if we do help ourselves to the details of standard monotheistic conceptions of salvation and the afterlife, then there is at least some reason for suspicion that those ideas are not consistent with the claim that an orthodoxly conceived monotheistic god would reward those who have such venal motives for "wagering on an orthodoxly conceived monotheistic god". There is at least a hint of moral corruption in the reasons that the wager argument presents for "wagering on an orthodoxly conceived monotheistic god" – or so, at least, many religious believers have been prepared to suppose. Pascal himself maintained that if one subsequently ceased to have the venal motive that initially persuaded one to accept the wager argument, then one would qualify for the infinite reward – subsequent genuine faith would trump the grubby considerations that prompted the first steps along the way to that faith. At the very least, there is room for considerable doubt about whether this is really so.

Seventh, there are many other – perhaps lesser – objections that have been raised against the wager argument that have not been hinted at in the discussion to date. For example, there are those who are prepared to repudiate the suggestion that rational decision making requires maximisation of expected utility: if we are not prepared to buy into standard decision theory, then there is no way that the non-standard decision theory embodied in the wager argument can generate conviction. For another example, there are also those who would contest the move from the claim that rationality requires that one wager on an orthodoxly conceived monotheistic god to the all-things-considered claim that one ought to wager on an orthodoxly conceived monotheistic god. If we suppose that there are many different kinds of non-rational requirements that can bear on a decision – for example, moral requirements or aesthetic requirements – then, at the very least, it seems that the move from 5 to 6 in the wager argument stands in need of further justification. I shall not make any attempt to explore these – and other – suggestions here.

Apart from the objections that have been considered thus far, there are also at least four points at which the wager argument can be contested that turn on considerations about infinity.

First, there are various questions that can be raised about the use that is made in the argument of the assumption that it is at least rationally permissible to hold that "wagering on an orthodoxly conceived monotheistic god" has infinite utility if an orthodoxly conceived monotheistic god exists. Unless we are strong actual infinitists, we shall dismiss this claim out of hand: we can't so much as make sense of the assignment of infinite utilities to outcomes. Moreover, even if we are strong infinitists who suppose that we can make sense of the assignment of infinite utilities to outcomes – for example, by way of considerations about access to infinite utility streams – we may still have good reasons to deny that there is any way that we can draw reasonable conclusions about what to do in cases in which we attribute infinite utilities to outcomes. As I note in Oppy (2006), the development of infinite decision theory is fraught with problems: the suggestion that the calculation that supports the wager argument is unproblematic deserves to be treated with the utmost suspicion.

Second, even if we agree that we should not assign zero probability to the claim that an orthodoxly conceived monotheistic god exists, we might nonetheless dispute the claim that we must assign a finite probability to the claim that an orthodoxly conceived monotheistic god exists. Given that the proponent of the wager argument is supposing that we can make sense of the assignment of infinite utilities to outcomes, it is very hard to see how the proponent of the argument could deny that we can make sense of the assignment of infinitesimal probabilities to propositions. But if the probability that is assigned to the claim that an orthodoxly conceived monotheistic god exists is infinitesimal, then the calculation of expected utility is stymied: there is nothing in our arithmetic for extended $\aleph$ that tells us how to compute $\infty \times 1/\infty$. Even if we suppose that we can assign some particular finite value to this computation, it is clear that the result of the calculation of expected utility will now depend on the exact value that is assigned in this case, as well as upon the exact values that are assigned to the other probabilities and utilities.

Given that we are strong actual infinitists, we can give an argument for the conclusion that the proponent of the wager argument should be prepared to countenance rational assignment of infinitesimal probabilities. Consider the hypothesis that there is a source of infinite utility that one will obtain just in case one forms a correct belief about the identity of a natural number that is intimately associated with admission to this source of infinite utility. For example, suppose that the guardian of the source of infinite utility has a favourite natural number – three, perhaps? – and that one secures entry to heaven just in case one forms a correct belief of the form 'the favourite number of the guardian of the source of infinite utility is n'. Given that one is prepared to countenance infinite sources of utility, it seems that considerations of regularity ought to lead one to the conclusion that one cannot assign *zero* probability to any claim of the form 'the favourite number of the guardian of the source of infinite utility is n'. Moreover, given that one has no further information than this, it seems that one could reasonably suppose that there are infinitely many hypotheses, each of which should be attributed some non-zero probability; but the only way that one can conform to this requirement is to suppose that there are infinitely many hypotheses that are assigned infinitesimal probability.

Of course, even if this argument is acceptable, it does not suffice to show that one could reasonably believe that the probability that an orthodoxly conceived monotheistic god exists is infinitesimal. However, at the very least, it seems that there is yet another possible category of non-believers that ought not to be persuaded by the wager argument, even if there is nothing else that is wrong with the argument: it is not merely those who suppose that the probability that an orthodoxly conceived monotheistic god exists is zero who cause the argument to short-circuit in the way described earlier. Whether it is plausible to suppose that there are many – or, indeed, any – actual people who reasonably suppose that the probability that an orthodoxly conceived monotheistic god exists is infinitesimal is an interesting question: perhaps there are some people whose belief state is most plausibly represented in this way, even if they would not themselves acknowledge that this is so. Or perhaps this is a merely theoretical possibility that can be met by the addition to the wager argument of a further premise that explicitly rules out the assignment of infinitesimal probabilities.

Third, there are important questions to ask about the way in which the decision scenario is represented in the table that we constructed. The wager argument assumes that there are just two actions to choose between (wagering on an orthodoxly conceived monotheistic god and not wagering on an orthodoxly conceived monotheistic god) and just two outcomes that we need to consider (an orthodoxly conceived monotheistic god exists or no orthodoxly conceived monotheistic god exists). However – especially in view of the considerations mentioned in the discussion of the previous objection – one might well think that this standard exposition fails to identify the relevant actions and outcomes with sufficient precision.

One of the standard objections – perhaps the standard objection – to the wager argument is that there are many other possible gods that ought to be considered when one enters into the decision theoretic calculation.

Given that we waive all of the other objections that might be lodged against the wager argument, we can insist that there are many other hypotheses concerning the obtainment of infinite utility that ought to be considered when one is deciding whether or not to wager on an orthodoxly conceived monotheistic god.

Here are some suggestions that have been countenanced.

If an orthodoxly conceived monotheistic god does not exist, then there might be an unorthodoxly conceived perverse monotheistic god who infinitely rewards all and only those who do not wager on an orthodoxly conceived monotheistic god. That is, those who wager on an orthodoxly conceived monotheistic god are infinitely rewarded if an orthodoxly conceived monotheistic god exists, and those who do not wager on an orthodoxly conceived monotheistic god are infinitely rewarded if an unorthodoxly conceived perverse monotheistic god exists. Unless we are prepared to set the probability that an unorthodoxly conceived perverse monotheistic god exists to zero – or to an infinitesimal value – then it will turn out that, for us, wagering for an orthodoxly conceived monotheistic god and not wagering for an orthodoxly conceived monotheistic god both have infinite expected utility. So, once we refine our account of the possible outcomes – to allow for the possibility that an unorthodoxly conceived perverse monotheistic god exists as well as for the possibility that neither an orthodoxly conceived monotheistic god nor an unorthodoxly conceived perverse monotheistic god exists – our decision-theoretic calculation breaks down: we have no guidance at all about whether to wager on an orthodoxly conceived monotheistic god or not to wager on an orthodoxly conceived monotheistic god.

If an orthodoxly conceived monotheistic god does not exist, then there might be an unorthodoxly conceived evil monotheistic god who infinitely rewards all and only those who wager on an unorthodoxly conceived evil monotheistic god, and who infinitely punishes all and only those who do not wager on an unorthodoxly conceived evil monotheistic god, including all of those who wager on an orthodoxly conceived monotheistic god. Unless we are prepared to set the probability that an unorthodoxly conceived evil monotheistic god exists to zero – or to an infinitesimal value – then, if we suppose that an orthodoxly conceived monotheistic god infinitely punishes all of those who wager on an unorthodoxly conceived evil monotheistic god if an orthodoxly conceived monotheistic god exists, then we calculate the "value" $\infty - \infty$ for the expected utility of both an orthodoxly conceived monotheistic god and an unorthodoxly conceived evil monotheistic god. Once we refine our account of the possible outcomes – to allow for the possibility that an unorthodoxly conceived evil monotheistic god exists, as well as for the possibility that neither an orthodoxly conceived monotheistic god nor an unorthodoxly conceived evil

monotheistic god exists – our decision-theoretic calculation breaks down:
it provides us with no guidance about whether to wager on an orthodoxly
conceived monotheistic god or to wager on an unorthodoxly conceived evil
monotheistic god.

And so on. Once one sets one's mind to it, there is almost no end to
the competing hypotheses that one can dream up here. Perhaps there is an
unorthodoxly (?) conceived Calvinistic monotheistic god who has predetermined our final destiny, so that what we do in this life has no consequences
for our fortunes in the next life. Perhaps there is an unorthodoxly conceived rational monotheistic god who infinitely rewards all and only those
who proportion their beliefs to the evidence that they have available to
them, and who infinitely punishes all of those who try to follow Pascal's
advice about ways of inculcating belief. Perhaps there is an unorthodoxly
(?) conceived demanding monotheistic god who infinitely rewards all and
only those who subscribe to *all* of the principles of the one true faith –
be it Mormonism, Seventh Day Adventism, Islam, Judaism, Hinduism, or
whatever. Perhaps there is a committee of n unorthodoxly conceived gods
who infinitely reward all and only those who believe that there are exactly n
unorthodoxly conceived gods, where n is some particular natural number.
Taking some – or all – of these competing hypotheses into account causes
the reasoning of the wager argument to fail utterly.

It is sometimes said, in response to this many gods objection, that the
wager argument is intended to apply only to those who suppose that there
is only one possible orthodoxly conceived monotheistic god in whom one
might believe, or that the argument is intended to take account only of
possible orthodoxly conceived monotheistic gods who are serious objects
of belief. Both of these responses seem to me to be inadequate. Certainly,
they cannot be available to Pascal. If we suppose that theoretical reason is
impotent when it comes to the question of the existence of an orthodoxly
conceived monotheistic god, then we simply lack the wherewithal to determine that there is only one possible orthodoxly conceived monotheistic
god in whom one might believe. Given the alleged impotence of theoretical reason, we are in no position to claim that we ought not to take the
hypothesis of an unorthodoxly conceived perverse monotheistic god seriously even though we ought to take the hypothesis of an orthodoxly conceived monotheistic god seriously. Moreover, while it may well be true that
there has never been anyone who has attributed a substantial probability –
say, greater than 10^{-10} – to the truth of any of these alternative hypotheses,
there is no reason at all to suppose that this consideration somehow undermines the many gods objection. After all, we *can* apply Pascal's reasoning to
these other cases; and, if we claim to be able to follow the reasoning where
it seems to lead in the case of the initial wager argument, then we have no
excuse for not following the argument where it leads in these other cases
as well.

To make this point clearer, it may help to consider the following argument:

1. Rationality requires either that you wager for an orthodoxly conceived monotheistic god or that you do not wager for an orthodoxly conceived monotheistic god.
2. Rationality requires that you hold:
   (a) the utility of wagering for an orthodoxly conceived monotheistic god, if an unorthodoxly conceived perverse monotheistic god exists, is less than positive infinity
   (b) the utility of wagering for an orthodoxly conceived monotheistic god, if no unorthodoxly conceived perverse monotheistic god exists, is less than positive infinity[2]
   (c) the utility of not wagering for an orthodoxly conceived monotheistic god, if an unorthodoxly conceived perverse monotheistic god exists, is positive infinity
   (d) the utility of not wagering for an orthodoxly conceived monotheistic god, if no unorthodoxly conceived perverse monotheistic god exists, is less than positive infinity
3. Rationality requires that the probability that you assign to an unorthodoxly conceived perverse monotheistic god's existence is positive, and not infinitesimal.
4. Rationality requires that you perform the act of maximising expected utility (provided that there is one action that maximises expected utility).
5. (Therefore) Rationality requires that you do not wager for an orthodoxly conceived monotheistic god.
6. (Therefore) You should not wager for an orthodoxly conceived monotheistic god.

Clearly, questions about whether anyone seriously believes – or could seriously believe – in the existence of an unorthodoxly conceived perverse monotheistic god are simply irrelevant to the assessment of the merit of this argument. If you accept the third premise – that is, if you are prepared to allow that there is some positive chance, however small, that an unorthodoxly conceived perverse monotheistic god exists – then it is very hard to see how one could claim that this argument fails whereas Pascal's wager argument succeeds. But why should anyone who is not already a believer in an

---

[2] In assigning a finite value to the utility of wagering for an orthodoxly conceived monotheistic god if there is no unorthodoxly conceived perverse monotheistic god, we follow the model of the original wager, and simply *ignore* the thought that there might be an orthodoxly conceived monotheistic god: the only supernatural hypothesis that is being countenanced, when we come to the specification of possible *outcomes*, is that there is an unorthodoxly conceived monotheistic god.

orthodoxly conceived monotheistic god suppose that there is such an enormous divide between the hypothesis that an orthodoxly conceived monotheistic god exists and the hypothesis that an unorthodoxly conceived perverse
monotheistic god exists: why should anyone who is not already a believer
in an orthodoxly conceived monotheistic god suppose that the hypothesis
that an orthodoxly conceived monotheistic god exists gets finite probability
while the hypothesis that an unorthodoxly conceived perverse monotheistic god exists gets zero or infinitesimal probability? (Of course, there are
similar arguments that can be run with any combination of the alternative
hypotheses that we mentioned previously. It seems that the defender of the
wager argument needs to believe that each of these hypotheses is in an
entirely different doxastic category from the hypothesis that an orthodoxly
conceived monotheistic god exists. I think that it is very hard to suppose
that there are significant numbers of non-believers – and, perhaps, that it is
similarly difficult to suppose that there are any *rational* non-believers – who
share this belief.)

   Fourth, there is an argument – due to Duff (1986) – that suggests that
the wager argument is not so much as valid. Suppose we accept that, as
the proponent of the wager argument would have it, the expected utility
of wagering on God is positive infinite. Then, plausibly, there are lots of
other actions other than wagering on an orthodoxly conceived monotheistic
god that will have the same positive infinite expected utility. Suppose, for
example, that I shall toss a fair coin, and, if it comes down heads, I will wager
for an orthodoxly conceived monotheistic god, and if it comes down tails,
I will not wager for an orthodoxly conceived monotheistic god. Obviously,
the expected utility of this course of action is positive infinity. Moreover,
the point generalises: if the expected utility of wagering on an orthodoxly
conceived monotheistic god is positive infinite, then the expected utility of a
vast range of other "mixed" actions that one might do instead is also positive
infinite.

   Indeed, one might think that the point generalises much further: since,
no matter what you do, there is some chance that it will set you on the road
to heaven, aren't we in a position to conclude that more or less every possible action has infinite expected utility? While some might worry that this
objection threatens to violate one of the basic principles of decision theory – namely, that it is possible to assign unique utilities to action/outcome
pairs – the argument in Oppy (2006) shows that this is not so. The point
of Duff's objection is that, in the presence of sources of infinite utility, one
should always stop to think whether one of the consequences of a proposed
course of action will be that one gains entry into an infinite utility stream.
In ordinary cases, one can reasonably ignore distant future consequences of
proposed courses of action in decision-theoretic calculations; but if there are
sources of infinite utility, then the justification for ignoring distant future

consequences breaks down. So, I think, we do indeed get the conclusion that decision-theoretic calculation breaks down entirely in the presence of sources of infinite utility.

A proponent of the wager argument might respond by saying that the proper conclusion of the wager argument is that you should set out on the course of action – whichever that is – that has the greatest probability of leading you to an orthodoxly conceived monotheistic god. But this recommendation is not obviously right, as it stands, since it entirely overlooks the costs involved in following any given course of action. If there is a 1000-ticket lottery for which the payout is positive infinite, and I already hold 900 of the tickets, what grounds are there for insisting that I should be prepared to betray all of my friends and family in order to obtain another ticket? Moreover – and perhaps more important – while this suggestion is staightforwardly applied in the case of simple "mixed" courses of action, it seems unlikely that it will be any use in the general case: amongst all of the things that I might do right now, which is the one that will most likely lead me to wager on an orthodoxly conceived monotheistic god? If, any time I am to make a decision about what to do, I am to choose the action that has the greatest likelihood of leading to a wager on an orthodoxly conceived monotheistic god, then I am not going to be well placed to make very many decisions at all.

5.4. MODIFIED WAGERS

In the face of these objections, one might wonder whether there is some way that Pascal's wager argument can be modified so as to avoid the difficulties that have been raised. There are a number of modifications that might be proposed.

First, one might try suggesting that the utility of wagering for an orthodoxly conceived monotheistic god, if an orthodoxly conceived monotheistic god exists, is large but finite. If one adopts this suggestion, then one certainly avoids any involvement with infinite utilities, and one can also avoid any difficulties that might be raised by infinitesimal probabilities. Whether one avoids Duff-style objections may depend upon just how big the utility that is assigned to wagering on an orthodoxly conceived monotheistic god turns out to be: if one can never ignore this utility when one is deciding what to do, then decision theory may be no less crippled than it would be if there were infinite utilities. However, that's about the end of the good news. This suggestion is no help at all with the many-gods objection, nor with the difficulties raised by the use of intervals in representing degrees of belief and strengths of preference. Furthermore, this suggestion doesn't alleviate the worries about the use of preferences to alter assigned probabilities, nor does it help with doubts about the grubbiness of the motives to

which appeal is made in order to motivate wagering on an orthodoxly conceived monotheistic god. Finally, the suggestion that the utility of wagering
on an orthodoxly conceived monotheistic god is large but finite is only dubi-
ously consistent with the deeper motives for religious belief. If the utility of
wagering on an orthodoxly conceived monotheistic god is N utils, why is
it N utils rather than $N + 1$ utils? The apparent arbitrariness of any such
supposition is at odds with the role that belief in an orthodoxly conceived
monotheistic god is supposed to play in avoiding explanatory regresses and
the acceptance of brute contingencies. Moreover, if the utility of wagering
on an orthodoxly conceived monotheistic god is only N utils, what does this
tell us about the nature of the afterlife? Are we to suppose that life in heaven
is also finite – albeit, perhaps, much more enjoyable and of much greater
extent than life on Earth? For all of these reasons, it seems that a finite wager
is no improvement on the wager that Pascal originally proposed.

   Second, one might try suggesting that the utility of wagering on an orthodoxly conceived monotheistic god, if an orthodoxly conceived monotheistic
god exists, is simply incommensurable with the utilities that one ascribes to
other action/outcome pairs. Following a suggestion due to Alex Byrne –
reported by Alan Hájek – we might suppose that utilities are vector valued,
and take the form $\langle e, h \rangle$, where e is an earthly value and h is a heavenly
value. Add in the assumption that any amount of heavenly value trumps any
amount of earthly value – so that $\langle e, h \rangle$ is smaller than $\langle e', h' \rangle$ exactly when
$h < h'$ or $h = h'$ and $e < e'$ – and we can avoid the difficulties that are raised
by the introduction of infinities and infinitesimals into decision-theoretic
reasoning, provided that we assume that wagering on an orthodoxly conceived monotheistic god gets you some finite amount of heavenly value
(say, one unit). Plainly enough, however, this proposal does not evade the
Duff objection – if anything, it makes it more obvious that this objection
has real bite – and neither does it do anything to meet the problems that
are raised by the many gods. As in the previous case, this suggestion does
not help with the difficulties raised by the use of intervals in representing
degrees of belief; nor does it alleviate the worries about the use of preferences to alter assigned probabilities; and nor does it help with doubts
about the grubbiness of the motives to which appeal is made in order to
motivate wagering on an orthodoxly conceived monotheistic god. For all of
these reasons, it seems that we are justified in concluding that the hypothesis of an incommensurable heavenly value does not give rise to a wager
that is a marked improvement on the wager argument that Pascal originally
proposed.

   Third, perhaps, one might try arguing that the utility of wagering on
an orthodoxly conceived monotheistic god, if an orthodoxly conceived
monotheistic god exists, takes some non-standard infinite value, for example, an infinite value that belongs to **No**, that is, to Conway's field of non-
standard numbers. It is unclear that this suggestion helps with any of the

problems that we have raised for the standard wager argument, and it is plausible that it also adds further problems that were not present initially. While one now has a neat mathematical apparatus for handling infinities and infinitesimals, it is not clear that we have any way of understanding how this apparatus can be applied to the case at hand. If we suppose that there is a limit ordinal that is such that the utility of wagering on an orthodoxly conceived monotheistic god takes on a value above this limit ordinal and the utility of performing any other action lies below this limit ordinal, then we can replicate the reasoning of the standard wager argument – but we get back all of the same difficulties that applied in the case of that argument. On the other hand, if we suppose that there is no limit ordinal that is such that the utility of wagering on an orthodoxly conceived monotheistic god takes on a value above this limit ordinal and the utility of performing any other action lies below this limit ordinal, then we can replicate the reasoning of the finite version of the wager argument – and we get back all of the same difficulties that applied in the case of *that* argument. Either way, it is very hard to believe that a move to non-standard number theory is going to provide any substantial assistance to proponents of Pascal's wager argument.

As Hájek (2003) notes, the value of wagering for an orthodoxly conceived monotheistic god in these modified wagers does not meet all of the conditions that Pascal himself imposed on the value of wagering for an orthodoxly conceived monotheistic god. Pascal supposed that the value of wagering for an orthodoxly conceived monotheistic god is such that it cannot possibly be increased: 'unity joined to infinity adds nothing to it... the addition of a unit can make no change in its nature'. As Hájek notes, it is plausible to suppose that this same condition requires that the value of wagering for an orthodoxly conceived monotheistic god cannot be increased by multiplication by a number greater than one: $\infty + \alpha = \infty$ for all $\alpha > 0$ iff $\infty \times (1 + \alpha) = \infty$ for all $\alpha > 0$. But Duff's objection – and, in particular, the objection from mixed strategies – kicks in if it is true that $\infty \times (1 - \alpha) = \infty$ for any $0 < \alpha < 1$. So Pascal's argument requires a conception of the infinite value of wagering for an orthodoxly conceived monotheistic god that satisfies both the claim that $\infty + \alpha = \infty$ for all $\alpha > 0$ and the claim that $\infty \times (1 - \alpha) < \infty$ for all $0 < \alpha < 1$. Thus, as Hájek says, it is very hard to believe that there is a coherent conception of the infinite value of wagering for an orthodoxly conceived monotheistic god that satisfies both of these claims. But – as we in effect argued above – it is also very hard to believe that there is a cogent non-Pascalian wager argument that does without one – or both – of these assumptions about the infinite value of wagering for an orthodoxly conceived monotheistic god. So it seems that we have very strong reason for supposing that there is no cogent argument – whether Pascalian or non-Pascalian – that turns on the idea that wagering for an orthodoxly conceived monotheistic god has infinite expected utility.

5.5. CONCLUDING REMARKS

There are many compelling objections to Pascal's wager argument. Even if we suppose that the proponent of the argument has only the limited ambition of persuading those who make a series of substantive assumptions – for example, that the probability that an orthodoxly conceived monotheistic god exists is non-zero; that the probability that an orthodoxly conceived monotheistic god exists is not infinitesimal; that there is only one supernatural hypothesis that should be taken seriously, namely, the proposition that an orthodoxly conceived monotheistic god exists; that the utility of wagering on an orthodoxly conceived monotheistic god if an orthodoxly conceived monotheistic god exists is infinite; that one ought to act always so as to maximise expected utility; or that one can simply opt to wager for an orthodoxly conceived monotheistic god – it seems that we shall be justified in declaring that the wager argument is a complete failure. Moreover, the prospects for rehabilitation of the argument by recasting it in some new form seem equally dim: while one may be able to avoid some of the difficulties that arise when one tries to make a decision-theoretic calculation that involves an infinite utility, there is no prospective amendment to the argument that comes close to meeting all of the damaging objections that can be raised against the wager argument.

6

Arguments from Evil

Perhaps it is worth saying at the outset that I do not attach very much importance to arguments from evil. At best, arguments from evil create problems for the hypothesis that there is a *perfect* being, that is, a being that is omnipotent, omniscient, and *perfectly good*. It is a controversial question whether all orthodoxly conceived monotheistic gods have these properties; at the very least, there is clearly a case to be made for the contention that the monotheistic gods that are described in the scriptures of the major monotheistic religions fall far short of perfect goodness. But, in any case, I think that there are no supernatural beings of any kind; and, moreover, I do not think that I need to have special reasons for supposing that there is no omnipotent, omniscient, and perfectly good supernatural being; my reasons for supposing that there are no supernatural beings are, in themselves, good reasons for supposing that there is no omnipotent, omniscient, and perfectly good supernatural being.

Despite the fact that I have no personal investment in the *success* of arguments from evil – at least insofar as we are interested solely in the conclusion of those arguments, that is, in the claim that there is no omnipotent, omniscient, and perfectly good being – I do think that it ought to be possible to make a pretty strong case for the claim that no arguments of this kind are successful. However, I also think that it ought to be possible to make a fairly strong case for the claim that these arguments are no worse than the various arguments that are standardly advanced on behalf of the claim that there is an orthodoxly conceived monotheistic god; and I think that it is worth pointing out that – as is the case for those who reject the various arguments that are standardly advanced on behalf of the claim that there is an orthodoxly conceived monotheistic god – there are substantive commitments that must be drawn upon in the rejection of at least the strongest versions of arguments from evil.

After I discuss some brief introductory matters, there are three topics that I propose to take up in this chapter.

First, I shall consider 'logical' arguments from evil, and, in particular, the dismissive handling of these arguments in many contemporary discussions. I find it somewhat odd that there has been an increased tendency amongst certain schools of philosophers to be highly dismissive of 'logical' arguments from evil at the same time as there has been an increased tendency amongst certain schools of philosophers to take the various traditional arguments on behalf of the existence of orthodoxly conceived monotheistic gods more seriously – particularly when both of these tendencies are realised in the work of the very same authors. Consequently, even though I do not believe that Mackie's argument is successful, I shall focus my attention on pointing out respects in which the virtues of Mackie's argument have been underestimated in contemporary discussions.

Second, I shall consider 'evidential' arguments from evil, and, in particular, the recent debate about Rowe's defence of an argument of this kind. Once again, while I do not wish to claim that Rowe's argument is successful, I want to emphasise that many of the responses to Rowe's argument have involved what I take to be indefensible counter-assertions. In particular, I shall focus my attention on the claim – made by various 'sceptical theists' – that no one can reasonably believe that it is fairly likely that if there were reasons why a perfect being would not non-arbitrarily improve the world if it prevented certain horrendous evils that have actually occurred, then we would be able to identify those reasons. I see no reason at all not to suppose that this probability judgment is just one of the many matters about which theists and non-theists can reasonably disagree.

Third, I shall consider 'the problems of heaven', that is, the problems that arise when one 'adds' to the claim that there is an orthodoxly conceived monotheistic god the further claim that there is an afterlife that is essentially free of moral evil. It is a natural further step to consider whether more general considerations about evil raise difficulties for belief in orthodoxly conceived monotheistic gods that are more pressing than those difficulties that are raised merely by the amounts and kinds of evil that are to be found in the natural universe. Moreover – and more important for present concerns – it is a natural further step to see what bearing considerations about heaven have on free will replies to 'logical' arguments from evil and free will theodicies. While I do not believe that 'the problems of heaven' raise insurmountable difficulties for reasonable monotheists, I do think that they ought to prompt some reconsideration of orthodox presentations of free will replies to 'logical' arguments from evil and free will theodicies.

6.1. PRELIMINARY CONSIDERATIONS

Before I turn to consider the various arguments from evil, I need to say something about the concept of evil. Typical arguments from evil contain premises that claim that there is evil in the world, or that there is such-and-such amount of evil in the world, or that there are so-and-so kinds of evil in the world, or that this particular evil event occurred, and so forth. But there are certain kinds of (non-theistic) meta-ethical views according to which the word 'evil' is a non-referring term – and, on those meta-ethical views, it seems that the relevant premises in arguments from evil must either be false or lacking in truth value. And there are other kinds of (theistic) meta-ethical views according to which there can be evils in the world only if there is an orthodoxly conceived monotheistic god that is the 'ground' for the distinction between good and evil – and, on those meta-ethical views, it seems that there is something incoherent in the attempt to argue from the relevant premises in arguments from evil to the conclusion that there is no orthodoxly conceived monotheistic god.

I take it that the difficulties here are merely apparent. Consider the following – obviously unsuccessful – 'logical' argument from evil:

1. If a perfect being exists, then that being is the omnipotent, omniscient, and perfectly good sole creator of the universe.
2. If a perfect being exists, then it prefers worlds that contain free agents and no moral evil to worlds that contain free agents and moral evil.
3. If a perfect being exists, then, if it chooses to make a world that contains free agents, it can choose to make a world that contains free agents and no moral evil.
4. There is moral evil in the world.
5. (Hence) There is no perfect being.

There are various ways in which one might attempt to rewrite this argument so that the fourth premise does not commit one to the 'unprotected' use of the word 'evil', if one supposes that there is something suspicious about the 'unprotected' use of the word 'evil' in the context of this argument. Since it makes no difference to the virtues of the argument, one can start by making the fourth premise conditional: if there is a perfect being, then there is moral evil in the world. While this move won't satisfy those who think that the word 'evil' is a non-referring term, it does seem that this move might be enough for those who suppose that there can be evils in the world only if there is an orthodoxly conceived monotheistic god that is the 'ground' for the distinction between good and evil. But even if it is not sufficient, it seems that we meet both difficulties by replacing talk of 'evil' with talk of 'state of affairs that orthodox theists would agree are properly called "evil"':

1. If a perfect being exists, then that being is the omnipotent, omniscient, and perfectly good sole creator of the universe.
2. If a perfect being exists, then it prefers worlds that contain free agents and no states of affairs that orthodox theists agree are properly called 'moral evils' to worlds that contain free agents and states of affairs that orthodox theists agree are properly called 'moral evils'.

3. If a perfect being exists, then, if it chooses to make a world that contains free agents, it can choose to make a world that contains free agents and no states of affairs that orthodox theists agree are properly called 'moral evils'.

4. There are both free agents and states of affairs in the world that orthodox theists agree are properly called 'moral evils'.

5. (Hence) There is no perfect being.

Even those who deny that there is anything that is properly called 'moral evil' – and those who assert that nothing can properly be called 'moral evil' unless there is an orthodoxly conceived monotheistic god – will surely concede that there are states of affairs of which it may truly be said that orthodox theists agree that those states of affairs are properly called 'moral evils'. But that is all that arguments from evil require. Since orthodox monotheists agree that rape, murder, killing of the innocent, and so forth, are properly called 'moral evils', we can proceed to an examination of arguments from 'evil' without embroiling ourselves in controversial meta-ethical disputes.

6.2. "LOGICAL" ARGUMENTS FROM EVIL

Many philosophers seem to suppose that the argument of Plantinga (1974) – or a suitably elaborated variant thereof – utterly demolishes the kinds of "logical" arguments from evil developed in Mackie (1955).[1] I am not sure

---

[1] Here are a few examples taken from papers collected together in Howard-Snyder(1996a): "It is now acknowledged on (almost) all sides that *the logical argument is bankrupt.* . . . [The] inductive argument from evil is in no better shape than *its late lamented cousin*" (Alston, 97, 121, emphasis added). "Like logical positivism, Mackie's argument has found its way to the dustbin of philosophical fashions (Howard-Snyder, (1996a), xiii)". "It is widely conceded that there is nothing like straightforward contradiction or necessary falsehood in the joint affirmation of God and evil. And (as I see it) rightly so" (Plantinga (1988/96), 71n3). "It used to be widely held that evil . . . is incompatible with the existence of God: that no possible world contained both God and evil. So far as I am able to tell, this thesis is no longer defended (van Inwagen (1991/6), 151)". For a dissenting voice, compare: "I argue that the logical problem posed by moral evil is still with us (Gale (1996), 206)".

It should be noted that if we are using *alethic* – as opposed to, say, *doxastic* – modalities, then there surely are *many* philosophers who continue to maintain that there is no possible universe made by a perfect being that contains moral evil. However, it is now much harder to find philosophers who are prepared to maintain that one cannot consistently believe that there are possible universes containing evil that are made by a perfect being. And it is no easier to find philosophers who are prepared to maintain that there are demonstrations that establish that there is no possible universe made by a perfect being that contains moral evil. I take it that Alston, Howard-Snyder, Plantinga, van Inwagen, et al. think that there are conclusive arguments that show that there are possible universes containing evil that are made by a perfect being (and that it is simply irrational to suppose that the existence of moral evil is logically incompatible with the existence of a perfect being who created our universe). However, nothing that I go on to argue in the present section depends upon this assumption.

that this is a correct assessment of the current state of play. First, I think that Plantinga's free-will defence involves a hitherto undetected inconsistency. Second, I think that even if Plantinga's free-will defence is consistent, it relies upon some questionable metaphysical assumptions. Third, I think that even if the metaphysical assumptions upon which Plantinga's free-will defence relies are defensible, there are serious questions to be raised about the moral assumptions that are made in that defence. Finally, I think that, even if Plantinga's free-will defence is acceptable, there are arguments closely related to those developed in Mackie (1955) that are not vulnerable to any variant of Plantinga's free-will defence, and yet that are clearly deserving of further examination.

The structure of the section is as follows. In part 6.2.1, I present a standard "logical" argument from moral evil, and give Plantinga's reply to it. In part 6.2.2, I provide my argument in support of the claim that there is an inconsistency in Plantinga's free-will defence. In part 6.2.3, I assess those parts of Plantinga (1974) that might be taken to bear on my claim that there is an inconsistency in Plantinga's free-will defence. In parts 6.2.4 and 5, I identify some of the controversial metaphysical assumptions that are required for Plantinga's reply, and I suggest that at least one of these assumptions is really not acceptable. In part 6.2.6, I consider some assumptions about values that are also required for Plantinga's reply, and argue that here Plantinga is probably on safer ground. In part 6.2.7, I consider an alternative formulation of the free-will defence that avoids both the inconsistency and the unacceptable metaphysical assumptions, but that is subject to the other kinds of worries that can be raised in connection with Plantinga's reply. In part 6.2.8, I turn to consider some probabilistic arguments from moral evil that are natural developments from the standard "logical" argument from moral evil. In the final section, I consider replies that might be made to these probabilistic arguments.

Throughout this section, the aim of my discussion is to show that the assumption that there is nothing further to be said on behalf of arguments from moral evil – and, in particular, on behalf of the kind of argument that is developed in Mackie (1955) – is premature. I don't claim to be able to show that there are successful arguments from moral evil; however, I do think that philosophers ought not to be more readily inclined to dismiss these arguments out of hand than they are to dismiss all of the other familiar theistic arguments for the existence of monotheistic deities out of hand.[2]

---

[2] Perhaps it is worth noting here that I certainly do not think that there are extant arguments from moral evil of such strength that perfect being theists who are not persuaded by these arguments to give up on their perfect being theism are *eo ipso* convicted of irrationality. If good arguments are required to be rationally compelling for all rational people not already disposed to accept their conclusions, then no extant argument from moral evil is good. However, arguments that fail this stringent requirement – and hence that are not successful *qua* arguments – *might* have other virtues.

Moreover – as I shall also go on to argue – I think that it is independently plausible to claim that arguments from moral evil generate serious constraints on positive arguments that can be mounted for the existence of a perfect being.

6.2.1. Plantinga's Free-Will Defence

The standard "logical argument" from moral evil – really, an *assertion* rather than an argument – claims that it is logically impossible for the following set of claims to be jointly true:

1. A perfect being exists.[3]
2. Any perfect being is omnipotent.
3. Any perfect being is omniscient.
4. Any perfect being is perfectly good.
5. If there is a perfect being, then it is the sole creator of the universe.
6. Moral evil exists.[4]

Plantinga's response to this "argument" is, in effect, to describe a logically possible world in which 1–6 are all true.[5] In what follows, I shall try to give a reasonably faithful reconstruction of the kind of possible world that Plantinga envisages, and of the kind of conception of logical space that one must have if one is to suppose that what one has described is, indeed, a logically possible world.

Focus attention on possible worlds in which there are perfect beings. Perhaps it is not logically possible for there to be any such worlds. However,

---

[3] The following premises – 2–5 – can be taken to define implicitly the expression 'perfect being'. Of course, the defining terms – 'omnipotent', 'omniscient', 'perfectly good', etc. – also require explanation; but, for the purposes of the present section, I shall suppose that these terms are sufficiently well understood.

[4] I shall not attempt to provide any analysis of the notion of 'moral evil'. As I noted in the first section of this chapter, there are meta-ethical conceptions on which claim 6 fails to express a proposition. However, on those meta-ethical conceptions, the occurrence of 'perfect goodness' in 4 ensures that it, too, fails to express a proposition (and, hence, given the previous footnote, the expression 'perfect being' fails to be well defined). An argument for the logical impossibility of the joint truth of 1–6 thus ought to proceed in two stages: first, we consider how things stand if one or more of 1–6 fails to be truth-apt; second, we consider how things stand on the assumption – or, if you prefer, under the pretence – that 1–6 are indeed all truth-apt. For the remainder of this section, I shall assume – or, perhaps, pretend – that 1–6 are indeed all truth-apt, and that 6 is true.

[5] It might be said that Plantinga actually argues for a stronger claim, viz., that there is a sense in which the existence of moral evil in the actual world may have been necessitated by the creative activities of the perfect being that made our world. However, it remains true that Plantinga does attempt to describe a logically possible world in which 1–6 are all true; and it is important to bear in mind that Plantinga does not deny that it is logically possible for 1–5 to be true in a world in which there is no moral evil.

if we have good reason to believe this, then we don't need to proceed to an examination of the logical argument that is our current target. Perhaps, too, every possible world is one in which there is a perfect being; if so, then our attention is merely directed to all possible worlds.[6]

Some – that is, at least one – of these worlds will contain nothing but the perfect being, and whatever else, if anything, is necessitated by the existence of the perfect being.[7] Others will contain the perfect being and further things that exist as a result of the free creative activities of the perfect being. Amongst these further possible worlds, there may be some that do not contain any free agents. However, our interest lies in those possible worlds in which there is a perfect being who has created a universe containing free agents. (As a matter of definition, a "universe" will be that part of the possible world that is left over when the perfect being (and whatever else is necessitated by the existence of the perfect being) is "subtracted" away. Within the perhaps restricted class of possible worlds that we are now considering, universes are the products of the free creative activities of perfect beings.[8])

Suppose that freedom is libertarian, that is, suppose that if an agent X acts freely in performing action A in circumstances C at time T in world W, then it is not made true by the truth-making core of the world W prior to T that

---

[6] The "perhaps" in the text should be taken to indicate some kind of doxastic – rather than some kind of alethic – possibility: while the claim in question may not be logically possible, it is a claim that reasonable people can reasonably believe. I do not believe that it is logically possible that every world contains a perfect being; however, I do think that this is something that a reasonable person can believe. There are obvious difficulties that will arise for my discussion if one believes that every possible world contains a perfect being (though I do think that these difficulties can ultimately be finessed by further appeal to the distinction between alethic and doxastic modalities).

Perhaps I should add here that, unlike many philosophers, I do not believe that there is a genuine distinction to be made between (broadly) logical possibility and metaphysical possibility. Those who suppose that there is such a distinction should disambiguate my writings in whatever way maximises the likelihood of truth!

[7] Perhaps there is only one such world. There are tricky questions here about, e.g., the *thoughts* of a perfect being: given that it has libertarian freedom, there is at least some reason to suppose that a perfect being can have different thoughts in situations in which it is the only existent. To pursue this matter further, we would need to worry about whether a perfect being can have *any* thoughts.

[8] To accommodate familiar talk about the possibility that a perfect being might make more than one "universe", we need to introduce a further distinction. The idea that we want to accommodate is that a perfect being might make a universe that consists of more than one (more or less) causally isolated sub-universe. At least roughly speaking, sub-universes are maximal causally connected aggregates of contingent states of affairs. This is rough, in part, because the perfect being's creative activities are excluded from the "maximal" aggregates: the intuitive idea is that there is no causal interaction between sub-universes, and no causal connections other than those that run through the perfect being. For the purposes of the present chapter, no harm will come from adoption of the assumption that perfect beings make no more than one big-bang (sub-)universe.

agent X will do A in circumstances C.[9] Compatibilists reject this conception of freedom; they hold that an agent X can act freely in performing action A in circumstances C at time T in a world W in which the truth-making core of the world prior to T is such that, for any world W′ with exactly the same truth-making core prior to T, the agent X does action A in circumstances C at time T in W′. That is, compatibilists – unlike libertarians – do not require that a free agent is "able to do otherwise in the circumstances of her actions". Note that it is a consequence of this account that, if there are truths about what agents with libertarian freedom will do in a world W at time T, then those truths do not belong to the truth-making core of the world W prior to the time T. Note, too, that it is a consequence of this account that, if a truth does not belong to the truth-making core of a world W at a time T, then that truth does not constrain the actions of agents with libertarian freedom at time T in world W: if nothing prior to T has made it true that the agent does not do A at T in W, then – provided that there is some possible world W′ at which the agent does do A at T[10] – the agent is *able* to do A at T in W.[11]

Suppose that when a perfect being creates a universe containing free agents, we can distinguish two parts of the universe: that part S for which the perfect being has sole responsibility, and that part J whose nature is in part determined by the free choices of the created free agents. Suppose further that, "when" a perfect being "deliberates" about whether or not to create a universe containing free creatures, and – in the circumstances in which it does decide to create a universe containing free creatures – about

---

9 The intuitive picture is something like this. The libertarian conception of freedom requires that we can make sense of the idea that, at the time at which an agent chooses to act, the outcome of the choice is not already fixed but is rather "up to the agent". So, the libertarian conception of freedom requires a distinction between propositions whose truth value at T is already fixed by the world prior to T, and propositions whose truth value at T is not already fixed by the world prior to T. (If, prior to T, it is already *fixed* that the proposition "X does A at T" is true, then – on the libertarian conception of freedom – the agent does not have a genuine choice about whether to do A at T.) Consequently, given that we adopt the libertarian conception of freedom, we must be able to distinguish between those propositions that are true at T that are already fixed – or made true – by the world prior to T and those propositions that are true at T but whose truth value is not fixed by the world prior to T. We call the former set of propositions – or perhaps some specially distinguished subset that suffices to generate the whole set, e.g., by closure under entailment – the *truth-making core* of the world prior to T. (Note that we assume that the laws are part of the truth-making core at any time, and that the laws cannot be different at different times. Without these assumptions, it is very hard to make sense of the dispute between compatibilists and libertarians within the established theoretical framework.)

10 Strictly, the qualification is redundant: if it is impossible for the agent to do A at T in W, then there is something that makes it true that the agent does not do A at T in W.

11 For the purposes of this discussion, I am supposing that it is logically impossible for there to be backwards causation. If this assumption is not made, then there are elaborate epicycles that need to be added – but nothing of any importance for the main argument under consideration is required to be changed.

which universe containing free creatures to create, it begins with a survey of all of the possible universe parts S′ for which it has sole responsibility that it could make.

Thus far, there is no difference between the activities of the perfect being in one possible world, and the activities of the perfect being in any other possible world: the possible universe parts for which it has sole responsibility do not vary from one possible world to the next. However, suppose further that, in any given possible world, there are true counterfactuals about the parts of universes whose nature is in part determined by the free choices of free created agents that *would* ensue were the perfect being to create any given universe part that is entirely up to it. That is, suppose that something like the following is true:

In world w_1, if the perfect being were to make S_1, then J_{11} would ensue; if the perfect being were to make S_2, then J_{12} would ensue; if the perfect being were to make S_3, then J_{13} would ensue; and so on.
In world w_2, if the perfect being were to make S_1, then J_{21} would ensue; if the perfect being were to make S_2, then J_{22} would ensue; if the perfect being were to make S_3, then J_{23} would ensue; and so on.
In world w_3, if the perfect being were to make S_1, then J_{31} would ensue; if the perfect being were to make S_2, then J_{32} would ensue; if the perfect being were to make S_3, then J_{33} would ensue; and so on.
And so on, through all of the possible worlds in question. Note that there is no assumption that, say, $J_{11} \neq J_{21}$; rather, what is assumed is that, for any pair of worlds w_i and w_k, there is at least one of the S_j for which $J_{ij} \neq J_{kj}$.

So, in each possible world, there is some – perhaps not necessarily proper – subset of the possible Js that is available to the perfect being as a result of its creative activities. Some of the S + Js are universes in which there are free creatures who always freely choose the good. Some of the S + Js are universes in which there are free creatures who always freely choose the bad. Many of the S + Js are universes in which there are free creatures who sometimes freely choose the good and sometimes freely choose the bad.[12] Moreover – and this is the crucial point – there are some possible worlds in which the S + Js that are available to the perfect being as a result of its creative activities do not include any universes in which there are free creatures who always

---

[12] Consider worlds that contain only one free creature X that makes N free choices (each of which has two possible outcomes: Right and Wrong). Since the choices are all free, no one choice determines the results of any of the others. Ignoring other features of these worlds, there are 2^N different worlds: one in which X always goes right, one in which X always goes wrong, and 2^{N-1} in which X sometimes goes right and sometimes goes wrong. Of course, this little argument hardly suffices to show that *most* of the S + J are universes in which there are free creatures who sometimes freely choose the good and sometimes freely choose the bad – but it surely does suffice to suggest that there will be *many* such universes.

freely choose the good. As an extreme example, there is at least one possible world in which, no matter which of the S_i the perfect being were to choose, the resulting $S + J$ *would* contain free creatures who *all always* freely choose the bad.

Given this picture of the creative activities of a perfect being – and of the logical space in which that creative activity is embedded – it seems at least *prima facie* plausible to claim that there are possible worlds in which it is true that, if the perfect being creates any universe that contains free agents, then it creates a universe in which it is not true that all free agents always freely choose the good.

Of course – even given the assumptions that we have already made – this is not enough to show that it is *prima facie* plausible to claim that there are possible worlds in which a perfect being makes a universe in which it is not the case that everyone always freely chooses the good. For plainly one might think that, in circumstances in which a perfect being could not make a universe in which everyone always freely chooses the good, the perfect goodness of that being ensures that it will make no universe at all. However, setting this consideration aside – or, what amounts to the same thing, adding the extra assumption that, in at least some circumstances in which it is not possible for a perfect being to make a universe in which everyone always freely chooses the good, it is possible for a perfect being to make universes in which it is not the case that everyone always freely chooses the good – it seems *prima facie* plausible to claim that we do indeed get to the conclusion that there are possible worlds in which 1–6 are all true.

6.2.2. A Dilemma for Counterfactuals of Freedom

I think that, despite appearances, there is an 'inconsistency' in Plantinga's "possibility proof"; that is, I think that he has not succeeded in describing a logically possible world. Consider the counterfactuals of freedom that Plantinga supposes constrain the creative activities of a perfect being "when" it is making universes, and yet that are not inconsistent with the libertarian freedom of creatures in those universes. Either these counterfactuals of freedom are "then" part of the truth-making core for the world, or they are not.

On the one hand, if they are "then" part of the truth-making core for the world, then it follows from the libertarian account of freedom that no one ever acts with libertarian freedom, for there is no other world with the "then" same truth-making core in which agents do anything other than what they do in the world in question. Allowing that the counterfactuals of freedom are part of the truth-making core of the world "when" the perfect being makes its creative decisions entails that there is no libertarian freedom in the world. So, on the assumption that counterfactuals of freedom are part of the truth-making core "when" the perfect being makes its creative decisions, Plantinga's free-will defence does not go through.

On the other hand, if the counterfactuals of freedom are not "then" part of the truth-making core for the world, then it follows from the earlier noted consequences of the libertarian account of freedom that these counterfactuals *cannot* constrain the choices that a perfect being can make, and neither *can* they constrain the actions that that being can perform. Why not? Because the truth of the counterfactuals of freedom is not *fixed* "when" the perfect being deliberates, but rather somehow depends upon "subsequent" features of the universe in question. "Prior" to the creative decision of the perfect being, there just isn't anything that makes the counterfactuals of freedom true; hence, which counterfactuals of freedom are "then" true *depends upon* the creative choice that is made by the perfect being. Allowing that the counterfactuals of freedom are not part of the truth-making core "when" the perfect being makes its creative decisions entails that those counterfactuals of freedom cannot *constrain* the choices that the perfect being makes. So, again, on the assumption that counterfactuals of freedom are not part of the truth-making core "when" the perfect being makes its creative decisions, Plantinga's free-will defence does not go through.

So, no matter how one thinks about the relationship between Plantinga's counterfactuals of freedom and the truth-making core of the world "when" a perfect being deliberates about which universe to make, Plantinga's free-will defence does not go through: it *cannot* be that the truth of those counterfactuals *both* constrains the choice that the perfect being makes and yet also allows that there are creatures in the chosen universe that have libertarian freedom.

Before I turn to consider why Plantinga (1974) misses this objection, it might be worth explaining the argument on each side of the above dilemma in a little more detail. I shall begin with the horn of the dilemma that assumes that counterfactuals of freedom impose a genuine constraint on the creative activities of a perfect being.

(A) Counterfactuals of Freedom in the Truth-Making Core
Recall, again, that one key idea behind Plantinga's free-will defence is that the truth of certain counterfactuals of freedom *constrains* the universe-making activities of a perfect being: given that it is true at w, prior to the creation of any universe, that, if the perfect being were to make S_1, then universe $S_1 + J_{11}$ would ensue, then, at w, the perfect being *cannot* bring about any of the worlds $S_1 + J_{1k}$, for $k \neq 1$.[13] So, "when" the perfect being comes to make universes, the counterfactuals of freedom impose genuine constraints (from which it follows that those counterfactuals of freedom must "then" be part of the truth-making core for the world).

---

[13] In Plantinga's terminology, the perfect being cannot "weakly actualise" any of the $S1 + J1^k$, for $k + 1$.

But now, suppose that the perfect being makes S_1, and consider an allegedly free being X's allegedly free choice of an action A within $S_1 +$ J_{11}. In order for X's doing A at w to be free – on the libertarian account of freedom – there must be a world w' whose truth-making core is identical to the truth-making core of w up until the time of X's acting, but in which X does something other than A. However, given the membership in the truth-making core of the counterfactual of freedom that constrained the universe-making activities of the perfect being, there is no such possible world: a world in which X does something other than A cannot be a world in which it was part of the truth-making core "when" the perfect being engaged in its creative activities that, were the perfect being to make S_1, then $S_1 +$ J_{11} would ensue. If "counterfactuals of freedom" can constrain the universe-making activities of perfect beings, then they cannot fail to constrain the actions of allegedly free agents.

Of course, it is no reply to this argument simply to insist that 'counterfactuals of freedom' are counterfactuals of *freedom*, and hence by definition consistent with the freedom of the agents in question. We have an official account of freedom – the libertarian account mentioned earlier – that holds that nothing in the circumstances of a free choice can *fix* the outcome of that choice. If there is no logically possible world with the same truth-making core in which there is a different outcome for the choice, then the choice is determined by the truth-making core, and hence is not free. In other words, there is no logically possible world in which (1) it is part of the truth-making core prior to T that, were conditions C to obtain, agent A would make choice X at T; (2) conditions C obtain; and (3) agent A does not make choice X at T. Given that the counterfactual is part of the truth-making core prior to the choice, the agent simply does not have libertarian freedom.

But now, suppose that it is part of the truth-making core prior to the creation of any universe that, were a perfect being to make S_1, then agent A would make choice X at time T in circumstances C. (By hypothesis, this is one consequence of the more general claim that it is part of the truth-making core prior to the creation of any universe that, were a perfect being to make S, then universe $S_1 + J_{11}$ would result, given that agent A makes choice X at time T in circumstances C in $S_1 + J_{11}$.) Then, there is no logically possible world in which (1) it is part of the truth-making core prior to the creation of any universe that, were a perfect being to make S_1, agent A would make choice X at time T in circumstance C; (2) a perfect being makes S_1; and (3) agent A makes some choice other than X at time T in circumstance C. So, given that the counterfactual is part of the truth-making core, the agent simply does not have libertarian freedom with respect to this choice.

(B) No Counterfactuals of Freedom in the Truth-Making Core

If we suppose that, "when" the perfect being is deliberating about which universe to make, there are true counterfactuals of freedom that are not part of the truth-making core, then we are supposing that the truth values of these counterfactuals depend upon free decisions that are made "after" the creative deliberations of the perfect being have "commenced". Moreover – and consequently – we are also supposing that the truth values of these counterfactuals depend upon the creative decision that the perfect being makes: which counterfactuals of freedom are true *depends upon* which of the S_i the perfect being chooses to make.

Consider a relevant possible world w_i. In this world, it is true that if the perfect being were to make S_1, then J_{i_1} would result; and it is true that if the perfect being were to make S_2, then J_{i_2} would result; and it is true that if the perfect being were to make S_i, then J_{i_3} would result; and so on. But it is also true in w_i that the perfect being *does* make S_j, say. Moreover, it is also true in w_i that, at the time when the perfect being chose to make S_j, it *had it within its power* to make some other universe, S_k, say. And, crucially, it is also true in w_i that, *had* the perfect being exercised its power to make S_k, then – for at least *some* values of k – a different set of counterfactuals of freedom *would* have obtained in w_i "when" the perfect being made its decision to create. (This is what follows from the assumption that the counterfactuals of freedom are not part of the truth-making core "when" the creative decision is made.)

But if it is true – as we are supposing – that the perfect being has it within its power to choose which universe to make, and if it is also true that which counterfactuals of freedom are true depends upon which universe the perfect being chooses to make, then it cannot be the case that the choice that the perfect being makes is *constrained* by the "prior" truth of those counterfactuals of freedom. If the perfect being's choice to create universe S_j makes it true – or, at any rate, plays an important role in making it true – that every creaturely essence of at the world suffers from transworld depravity, and yet it would not have been true that every creaturely essence suffers from transworld depravity had the perfect being created world S_k instead, then we simply do not end up with a demonstration that there is a possible world in which the perfect being is *unable* to create a universe in which everyone always freely chooses the good.

Clearly, there is a question to ask about the seriousness of this gap in Plantinga's "possibility proof" (on the assumption that counterfactuals of freedom do not belong to the truth-making core). In particular, one might suspect that there must be some way of reinstating Plantinga's argument using nested counterfactuals: if the perfect being were to make S_1, then such-and-such counterfactuals of freedom would be true; if the perfect being were to make S_2, then such-and-such counterfactuals of freedom would be true; if the perfect being were to make S_3, then such-and-such counterfactuals of freedom would be true; and so forth. I do not think that this can be right. For exactly the same question about the truth-making core can be raised for these nested counterfactuals that was raised in connection with the initial counterfactuals of freedom, and exactly the same difficulties will be seen to arise for the two ways in which that question might be answered. In particular, if these nested counterfactuals do not belong to the truth-making core, then they, too, take truth values that depend upon the creative choice that the perfect being makes (and hence we go down exactly the same argumentative path).

So – unless there is some way of repairing Plantinga's construction that I have overlooked – it seems pretty safe to conclude that Plantinga has *not* managed to describe a possible world in which a perfect being is unable to choose to make a universe in which everyone always freely chooses the good. It may be, for all that I have argued, that there is such a possible world; the point is just that no argument has been offered that can reasonably be said to have settled the case.

6.2.3. Plantinga on Analyses of Libertarian Freedom

As far as I know, the objection to Plantinga's argument that I have been developing here has not been raised previously. There is a much-discussed related objection that I will consider in the next section. But first, I want to say something about why Plantinga misses this objection, and to comment on passages in Plantinga (1974) that might be thought to be relevant.

The most important point to note, I think, is that Plantinga does not explicitly address the question of the analysis of libertarian freedom at the level of detail that is required in order to answer the question of whether the truth of a counterfactual of freedom "determines" the subsequent behaviour of agents whose actions are detailed in the consequent of that counterfactual. All that Plantinga says about an agent with (libertarian) freedom is that "no...antecedent conditions determine either that he will perform the action, or that he will not. It is within his power, at the time in question, to perform the action, and within his power to refrain."[14] But this does nothing at all towards providing a clear possible-worlds analysis of the notions of *freedom, determination,* and *the possession of powers* (and this despite the fact that the bulk of the book is concerned with possible-worlds analyses of modal notions). In my view, it is this shortcoming in the discussion that leads Plantinga to overlook the difficulty upon which I have focussed.

Perhaps it is worth noting that Plantinga does give reasons for denying that the proponent of libertarian freedom is committed to the claim that, if agent A acts freely in performing action X in circumstances C at time T in world W, then there is a world W' that is identical to world W up until the time T at which A chooses to act, but in which A does something other than X in circumstances C at time T. According to Plantinga, it is true in W before T that A will do X, and it is true in W' before T that A will not do X – and so the worlds are not identical before T as claimed. But, of course, while this point is fine as far as it goes, the crucial point to note is that the characterisation of libertarian freedom that Plantinga considers pays no attention to the question of whether the worlds W and W' are identical in all respects, or whether they are identical only with respect to their truth-making cores. As we noted earlier, the principle to which the libertarian is committed is that if agent A acts freely in performing action X in circumstances C at time T in world W, then there is a world W′ with the same truth-making core as world W up until the time T at which A chooses to act, but in which A does something other than X in circumstances C at time T. And, of course, it is obvious that truths about what the agent *will* do cannot be part of the truth-making core if the agent is to have libertarian freedom.

6.2.4. Against Ungrounded Counterfactuals

Of course, even if there is some problem with the argument presented in section 6.2.2 of this chapter, there are *further* questions that can be asked about the assumptions that are required for Plantinga's "possibility proof". As I have already indicated, there is a much-discussed objection to Plantinga's argument that is not entirely unrelated to the argument given in the previous section of this chapter. This objection focuses on the assumption that there *are* true counterfactuals of freedom, that is, on the assumption that, in any given possible world, there are true counterfactuals about the parts of universes whose nature is in part determined by the free choices of free created agents that *would* ensue were the perfect being to create any given universe part that is entirely up to it. I shall first give the objection in my own terms, and note some consequences that seem to follow. And then I will (briefly) comment on some other discussions of this objection.

The core of the objection is the observation that the assumption that there are true counterfactuals of freedom seems to be in conflict with the plausible metaphysical claim that counterfactual claims that are true at a given possible world require a categorical grounding in that world. If a counterfactual claim is true at a possible world, then there must be something in that possible world that serves as a truth maker for the counterfactual claim. There are no possible worlds in which counterfactual claims are *bare* truths; there are no pairs of possible worlds with minimal truth-making cores – or minimal supervenience bases – that differ *only* with respect to the truth values of counterfactual claims.[15]

These requirements are plainly violated by the construction described in the first section of this chapter. According to that construction, there are different possible worlds w_1 (= perfect being + S_1 + J_1 + counterfactuals of

---

[15] Suppose that T is an exhaustive list of the truths about a world w. Any subset S of T such that every member of T is entailed by some collection of the truths in S is a supervenience base for w. Any S for which there is no S′ such that S ⊃ S′, where S and S′ are both supervenience bases for w, is a minimal supervenience base for w. (There is an analogous definition of "minimal truth-making core" – cf. the last sentence in note 9.) It is a substantive claim that worlds have minimal supervenience bases or minimal truth-making cores; however, we shall not pursue questions about "turtles all the way down" alternatives here. (Again, the effect of such a pursuit is merely to add epicycles to the discussion.)

freedom C_1) and w_2 (=perfect being $+ S_1 + J_1 +$ counterfactuals of freedom C_2) with minimal supervenience bases that differ only in the counterfactual claims that were true in that world when the perfect being was deliberating about which universe to make. (In each of these worlds, the perfect being chooses the universe $S_1 + J_1$ – because, say, that is the best option that is open to it – but the range of options from which it has to choose differs between the worlds.)

I take it that, even in the absence of the previous argument – and even if one fails to pay any attention to the distinction between counterfactuals that do, and counterfactuals that do not, belong to the truth-making core "when" the perfect being engages in its creative activities – this observation would cast very serious doubt on Plantinga's claim to have described a possible world in which 1–6 are all true. The principle that there are no pairs of possible worlds with minimal supervenience bases that differ *only* with respect to the truth-values of counterfactual claims is, I think, a pretty secure piece of metaphysical doctrine. At the very least, it is worth noting that it hasn't been plucked from the air merely to serve the interests of the current argument. There is a long history – going back at least to the criticisms that Armstrong (1989) and Martin make of Ryle's dispositional theory of mind[16] – of reliance upon this principle that is completely independent of the use that might be made of it in the context of discussion of logical arguments from evil. Many people have thought that Plantinga's counterfactuals of freedom are pretty suspicious entities; if I'm right, there is a strongly principled basis to this suspicion.

Of course, Plantinga does have a reply to those who disagree with his claim that there are true counterfactuals of freedom. He gives the example of offering a small bribe to someone in order to get a good recommendation. When the bribe fails miserably, he wonders what would have happened had the bribe been larger. Plantinga claims that there must be some definite, non-probabilistic answer to the question of whether a larger bribe would have succeeded. However, if I am right, then it is only the *determinist* who is entitled to this claim: the libertarian about freedom has to allow that the size of the bribe cannot determine the response of the agent, and that the agent has "the power to do otherwise" in the very circumstances that obtained when the bribe was offered.[17] (Of course, there are right answers to the question

---

[16] See Bigelow (1988) for defence of the related claim that truth supervenes upon being, and Lewis (1999) for various approving mentions of this idea.

[17] It is perhaps worth noting at this point that Plantinga assumes that the perfect being is *unable* to make a world in which everyone always freely chooses the good if it is true that for any S that it is open to the perfect being to make, were it to make S, not everyone would always freely choose the good in the resulting $S + J$. But if it is true that I *would* choose the bribe *were* I offered it, then surely it follows that I am *unable* to refrain from accepting the bribe in exactly the same sense in which the perfect being is *unable* to make a world in which everyone always freely chooses the good.

about what I would have done – e.g., that my mendacity ensures that the chance that I will take the bribe is >99%. But there is no right answer of the kind that Plantinga supposes there to be, if I have libertarian freedom.)

Consider a different case. Suppose that there were a tiny piece of uranium – a single atom – in the pencil sharpener on my desk as I write. Suppose we ask: would that uranium atom decay within the next thirty seconds? On the assumption that radioactive decay is a genuinely chancy process, I take it that intuition supports the view that there is just no answer to this question. But, as we noted earlier, if we have libertarian freedom, then our choices are chancy: for any decision that we make, there is a possible world that is identical to the actual world up until the instant of decision – that is, involving exactly the same weighing of reasons, exactly the same preferences, and so on – and yet in which a different choice is made. So, we should say exactly the same thing about counterfactuals concerning the choices of agents with libertarian freedom: there is just no right answer to the question of what they would do were they asked to make certain kinds of choices in given circumstances – even though there are right answers to the question of what they would *very likely* do in those circumstances.

Although it is a bit of a digression from the main line of argument, it is perhaps worth pointing out that there is one class of theists who should find the above line of argument particularly disturbing, namely, those theists who are firmly committed to arguments that rely upon a strong version of the principle of sufficient reason. According to strong versions of this principle, any contingent feature of any possible world has a *complete* explanation in that possible world: that is, for any pair of possible worlds w and w', and any contrasting features S and S' of those worlds, there is an explanation in w of why S rather than S', and there is an explanation in w' of why S' rather than S. Given that counterfactuals of freedom are contingent features of worlds, it follows immediately that there cannot be *bare* true counterfactuals of freedom: the theoretical machinery to which Plantinga is committed requires the falsity of strong versions of the principle of sufficient reason.

There is a similar point that can be made about free-will defences more generally. The above criticism turns on the details of Plantinga's chosen method of developing a free-will defence. But it is a non-negotiable part of any free-will defence that it appeals to a libertarian conception of freedom. According to the libertarian conception of freedom, however, when agents act freely, there can be no complete explanation for their acting in the way that they do. Suppose we ask: why did agent A freely choose to do action S rather than action S' in circumstances C (in which agent A was able to do S and S')? According to the libertarian conception of freedom, there are possible worlds W and W' whose truth-making cores are identical in every respect up until the moment of the agent's choice in circumstances C, but that differ with respect to the chosen actions S and S'. Consequently, there is nothing in either world that can serve as a complete explanation of the choice that is made in that world.[18]

If this line of argument is well taken, then it suggests that theists who advocate cosmological arguments for the existence of a perfect being cannot consistently appeal to any kind of free-will defence in order to reply to logical arguments from evil (except in those cases in which the cosmological arguments make no appeal to strong principles of sufficient reason). Moreover, this same line of argument also suggests that non-theists who respond to cosmological arguments by rejecting strong forms of the principle of sufficient reason cannot consistently object to the claim that there are bare true counterfactuals of freedom on the grounds that this claim violates strong versions of the principle of sufficient reason. Of course, there may well be other reasons for rejecting the claim that there are bare true counterfactuals of freedom – and, indeed, it seems to me that there are such reasons. However, the key point that I wish to make here is just that there is a lot of heavy duty metaphysical machinery that is built into Plantinga's free-will defence, and that the use of this machinery has consequences for what one can consistently say and do in other contexts.

Since the digression of the past three paragraphs was fairly lengthy, it may be worth reminding readers of where the main line of argument now stands. I have argued (1) that Plantinga's free-will defence fails because it allows no coherent answer to the question of whether counterfactuals of freedom belong to the truth-making core of a world "when" a perfect being is engaged in universe creation; and (2) that Plantinga's free-will defence is in serious trouble because it relies on the assumption that there are true "ungrounded" counterfactuals of freedom. However, I do not think that the troubles for Plantinga's free-will defence end here.

6.2.5. Truth Makers for Counterfactuals of Freedom?

So far, we have only considered difficulties that follow from the assumption that there *are* counterfactuals of freedom of the kind that Plantinga supposes that there are. But there are more difficulties that follow if we make a definite decision about whether these counterfactuals belong to the truth-making

---

[18] Of course, it doesn't follow that there are no senses of "explanation" in which libertarian choices can be "explained". If Jones likes chocolate more than strawberry, then we can appeal to that in "explaining" why she chooses chocolate. But according to libertarians, there is a possible world in which Jones opts for strawberry, even though she goes through exactly the same process of deliberation, has exactly the same preferences, etc. When we contrast the actual world with this (allegedly) possible world, the libertarian has no resources for explaining why Jones's process of deliberation, preferences, etc. actually resulted in a choice of chocolate and not strawberry (since, *ex hypothesi*, there is no relevant difference to which appeal can be made).

core. In particular, let us suppose that they do not, that is, let us suppose that the counterfactual in question is not a fixed feature of the circumstances of the agent's choice.[19] Then we must be supposing that there is something outside the truth-making core upon which the truth of the counterfactual depends. But what could this be? Could it be, for example, that the truth of the counterfactual depends upon the choice that the agent makes? No, that can't be right. "When" the perfect being is choosing which universe to make, very many counterfactuals of freedom are supposed to be true, including very many that advert to merely possible universes (and, in many cases, merely possible agents). But it makes no sense at all to say that the truth of these counterfactuals depends upon the choices that the agents make – because, *ex hypothesi*, there *are* no such choices. But what else is there for the truth of these counterfactuals to depend upon?

Perhaps it might be said that the truth of these counterfactuals does depend upon the choices that the agents make, but that these choices take place in possible worlds other than the actual world. But, at least *prima facie*, that can't be right either. The true counterfactuals of freedom are truths about free choices made by agents with libertarian freedom. So we know that, for any given choice, there are possible worlds in which the agent takes each of the options available. Appealing *merely* to what happens in other possible worlds cannot hope to deliver truth makers for counterfactuals of freedom.

Perhaps it might be said not only that it is that case that there are other possible worlds, but also that there are fixed relationships of similarity among the worlds that play a crucial role in making counterfactuals of freedom true. What makes a given true counterfactual of freedom true in a given world is what happens in all of the worlds *sufficiently close* to the given world. But now we need to ask: are there fixed relations of similarity among worlds at times, or are there only fixed relations of similarity among worlds? And we also need to ask: are relationships of similarity between worlds primitive, or do they depend upon the intrinsic properties of worlds? If we can suppose that relationships among worlds are primitive – and hence independent of the intrinsic properties of worlds – and if we can suppose that there are only fixed relations of similarity among worlds, then perhaps we *can* claim that we have now found truth makers for counterfactuals of freedom. But if we accept – as we surely should! – that relationships of similarity among worlds *depend only upon* intrinsic properties of worlds, then surely we are in

---

[19] The following discussion has some affinity to the discussion in Gale (1991: 152–68). However, Gale seems content not to challenge the assumption that there can be bare counterfactual truths (see, e.g., p. 144). It is worth asking what Gale would now say about this matter, given his newfound enthusiasm for strong versions of the principle of sufficient reason – cf. Gale and Pruss (1999).

no position to claim that we have found truth makers for counterfactuals of freedom. Truth supervenes upon being. Which counterfactuals are true at a world depends just upon the intrinsic properties of that world. But these intrinsic properties are simply insufficient to make true all of the counterfactuals of freedom that Plantinga supposes to be true "when" the perfect being deliberates about which world to make.[20]

If what I have said here is right, then there is good reason to be suspicious of arguments that claim that analogies between tensed claims and counterfactuals support the suggestion that there are true counterfactuals of freedom of the kind that Plantinga supposes that there are.[21] There are many good reasons – both physical and metaphysical – to support the claim that there *are* past and future times; hence, there are good reasons for claiming that there *are* truth makers in the truth-making core for past tense claims, and that there *are* truth makers outside the truth-making core for future tense claims. Of course, it is controversial to claim that the future exists; but that claim is *nowhere near* as controversial as the battery of assumptions that are required in order to claim that there are truth makers for counterfactuals of freedom.

6.2.6. Grounds for Refusing to Create

As I noted towards the end of the first part of this section, even someone who accepts all of the metaphysical machinery that is required for Plantinga's free-will defence might not accept the claim that Plantinga succeeds in describing a possible world in which 1–6 are all true. For someone who accepts all of Plantinga's metaphysical machinery might perfectly well think that, in circumstances in which a perfect being could not make a universe in which everyone always freely chooses the good, the perfect goodness of that being ensures that it will make no universe at all.

On the picture that we have been given, there will surely be possible worlds in which the perfect being engages in no creative activity involving free moral agents. Consider again a possible world in which, no matter which of the S_i the perfect being were to choose, the resulting $S + J$ *would* contain free creatures who *all always* freely choose the bad. In this possible world, it seems to me that it is just obvious that a perfect being will not make any universe at all containing free creatures: it is just inconsistent with the perfect goodness of a perfect being that it should knowingly make a world in which there is nothing but unrelieved moral evil.

---

[20] Although I have given no argument that there could be no other kinds of truth makers for counterfactuals of freedom – under the assumptions made in the present section – I do think that it is very hard to find plausible suggestions about where such truth makers might be found.

[21] See, e.g., Flint (1998), 121–137, and references therein.

Perhaps there are sceptical theists who might deny the claim that I have made here. Perhaps there are sceptical theists who will say: given our limited knowledge about possible goods, and possible evils, and the possible connections between them – and given the vastly greater knowledge that a perfect being has of possible goods, and possible evils, and the possible connections between them – how can we have any confidence at all in the judgment that a perfect being could not knowingly make a world in which there is nothing but unrelieved moral evil?[22] However, this response seems to me to be unbelievable: what sense can someone who makes this response be giving to the words "perfect goodness"?

Suppose, then, that we agree that there are some possible worlds in which a perfect being engages in no creative activity involving free moral agents *because* of the moral evils that would inevitably be contained in the universes available to the perfect being for creation. Then the following question naturally arises: in *which* possible worlds is the knowledge afforded by counterfactuals of freedom consistent with the creation of a universe containing free agents? (Given the libertarian conception of freedom, and given the assumption that the perfect being has libertarian freedom with respect to the creation of universes containing free agents, there must be possible worlds in which a perfect being engages in no creative activity involving free moral agents *even though* the perfect being is in a position to bring about universes containing free agents who all always freely choose the good. However, our present question need not lead us to make a detour through these further difficulties concerning the freedom of a perfect being with respect to creation: all we want to know here is how good a universe containing free moral agents has to be before it is possible for a perfectly good being to make it.)

It seems plausible to claim that, if a perfect being is able to make a universe containing free creatures that all always freely choose the good, then the creation of such a universe does not conflict with the perfect goodness of the perfect being. But what of the following cases:

(a) universes in which there is at least one free creature that freely chooses the bad on at least one occasion?
(b) universes in which there is at least one free creature that freely chooses the bad on every occasion?
(c) universes in which every free creature freely chooses the bad on at least one occasion?

(Plantinga famously uses the expression "transworld depravity" to describe a situation in which every universe that it is open to the perfect being to make is of kind (c): the possible creatures that the perfect being can make suffer from *transworld depravity* at a given possible world if they go wrong

---

[22] See, e.g., Bergmann (2001). For a partial critique of sceptical theism, see section 6.3 below.

in every possible universe in which they exist that it is open to the perfect being to make at that possible world.)

It seems to me that it is not in the least bit obvious that a perfectly good being *can* make a universe in any of these circumstances. After all, if the perfectly good being does not make a universe, then the possible world is never sullied by any kind of moral evil; on the other hand, if the perfectly good being does make a universe, then moral evil makes an appearance at that possible world. Given the choice between a possible world in which there is no moral evil, and a possible world in which there is moral evil, why shouldn't we suppose that a morally perfect being will inevitably opt for the world in which there is no moral evil?

But – it will be replied – there are goods that are foregone if a universe of free agents is not created; and those goods outweigh the introduction of moral evil into the world.

How confident should we be that this is so? Suppose, for example, we take seriously the sceptical theist claims: (1) that we have very limited knowledge about possible goods, and possible evils, and the possible connections between them; and (2) that a perfect being would have vastly more knowledge about possible goods, and possible evils, and the possible connections between them. Then, it seems to me, we are in no position to judge whether a perfectly good being is able to make a world in which there is even the slightest amount of moral evil. And if that's right, then – in the absence of any other relevant considerations – we are in no position to determine whether 1–6 are logically consistent. (Perhaps this is a victory of sorts for the sceptical theist, even though it requires a substantial step back from the position that Plantinga defends.[23])

Suppose, instead, that we feel comfortable about our ability to determine what a perfect being would do in circumstances in which every universe that it can make contains some moral evil. What would it do? For what it's worth, my intuitive judgment is that it would make no universe at all. However, since I can see no persuasive argument to back up this judgment, the most that I am prepared to say is that there is room for further thought about this aspect of logical arguments from moral evil. If there were nothing else questionable about Plantinga's free-will defence, then it would probably be necessary to concede that there is decent support for the claim that the defence succeeds (where this decent support lies in the intuitive judgments

---

[23] Of course, if we are so irremediably ignorant about perfect beings, then it is hard to see how there could be any kind of argument capable of bringing those not already persuaded that there is a perfect being to accept the claim that there is a perfect being. (If almost any evidence is compatible with the existence or non-existence of a perfect being, then almost no evidence can tell in favour of the existence of a perfect being.) But if there is no chain of reasoning that can lead reasonable non-believers to the conclusion that there is a perfect being, then it surely follows that there can be reasonable non-believers (contrary to the doctrinal commitments of a substantial number of theists).

of those who suppose that a perfect being could make a world that contains moral evil in circumstances in which it can make no other kind of world).

6.2.7. An Alternative Free-Will Defence

Even if the argument in the preceding sections of this chapter is sufficient to cast doubt on Plantinga's free-will defence, it does not follow that there is good reason for theists to be worried about the logical argument from moral evil. Since the difficulty upon which we focussed is due to the metaphysical machinery that is used in constructing Plantinga's response, a natural thought is to look to some other metaphysical framework upon which to hang a response. Perhaps such a framework is not so far to seek.

Focus again on possible worlds in which a perfect being is deliberating about whether or not to create a universe containing free agents. Suppose further that, prior to the actual making of a free decision by a free agent, there is no fact of the matter about what that free agent will do. Suppose, relatedly, that if a perfect being makes a universe in which there are free agents, then the perfect being does not *know* what those free agents will freely choose to do "until" they make the choices in question.[24] Suppose, finally, that there is a universe part S that it is open to the perfect being to make, and that it knows will form part of a universe in which there are free agents who make free choices. (There may well be many such universe parts; however, no harm will come from the pretence that there is only one such universe part.)

Consider all of the possible worlds in which the perfect being exists, and in which it chooses to make a universe that contains S as the part that is entirely up to the creative activities of the perfect being. In some of these possible worlds, all of the free agents will always freely choose the good. In other of these possible worlds, some of the free agents will sometimes freely choose the bad. And in yet other of these possible worlds, the other options described in preceding sections of this chapter will also be realised. By hypothesis, our perfect being has no way of knowing how the universe that contains S as a part will turn out. Hence, while it is clearly *possible* that, in making a universe that contains S as a part, the perfect being will make a universe in which everyone always freely chooses the good, this is not a matter that the perfect being can decide by fiat. If the perfect being makes a universe that contains S as a part, then it is an objectively chancy matter whether the universe ends up containing moral evil.

---

[24] Does this supposition amount to giving up on the assumption that the perfect being is omniscient? No, of course not: at most, omniscience requires only knowledge of that which it is logically possible to know; and, *independent* of the free choices of the free agents, there just isn't anything that it is logically possible to know about these choices.

Plainly enough, we have here the materials for a variant of the free-will defence that avoids the kind of objection that was made against Plantinga's free-will defence in the second section of this chapter. On the assumption that a perfectly good being is able to make a universe that contains S as a part in the circumstances described, it is clear that the mere unfolding of objectively chancy events can then bring about a world in which 1–6 are all true.

However, while this version of the free-will defence does not fall foul of the metaphysical principle concerning the grounding of counterfactuals, it still has to face the other objections that were raised in the preceding parts of this chapter. First, it is clear that any proponent of this defence has to give up on strong versions of the principle of sufficient reason (since, of course, proponents of strong versions of the principle of sufficient reason deny that there can be objectively chancy events). And, second, there is a serious question to ask about whether, in the envisaged circumstances, a perfect being can make a universe that contains S as a part. After all, in the circumstances, it is possible that the perfect being will make a universe in which everyone always freely chooses the bad – and it is not clear that a perfect being would take this kind of risk, however unlikely the awful outcome is.

Although it involves a substantial digression from our main argument, perhaps it is also worth noting that, even in the circumstances envisaged, it *might* be that a perfect being could do something very much like choosing that there should be a world in which everyone always freely chooses the good. Suppose that there is nothing to prevent a perfect being in a given possible world from making more than one "physical universe", that is, more than one maximal spatio-temporally connected sub-part of the larger universe. Then, by making enough physical universes, a perfect being can make it as close to certain as it pleases that there will be at least one physical universe in which everyone always freely chooses the good. Suppose, further – as many theists do – that the perfect being is required to sustain physical universes in existence at every moment at which those physical universes exists. If the perfect being allows any physical universe to pass out of existence as soon as a wrong choice occurs within it, then the perfect being can choose to make an ensemble of physical universes (i.e., a universe) – including, almost certainly, some physical universes that are never allowed to pass out of existence – in which, with vanishingly few exceptions, everyone always freely chooses the good.[25] Perhaps it might be objected that it is

---

[25] Of course, there is *some* moral evil in this setup, and so there are still questions about whether the amount of moral evil is too much for a perfect being to countenance. But – to anticipate considerations to be taken up in the later sections of the current chapter – this setup certainly seems to have a better *probable* ratio of good to evil than the setup in which just one universe is made.

inconsistent with the perfect goodness of a perfect being to allow physical universes to pass out of existence because of the wrong choices made by denizens of those physical universes; it is not *utterly* obvious to me that this is so. In particular, it seems to me that those who are sympathetic to the views that Epicurus and Lucretius take towards the alleged harm of death will be hard pressed to say why a perfect being could not act in the way outlined. Of course, there is much more that could be said here; but this digression would turn into another chapter if we tried to pursue it.

6.2.8. An Argument from Mackie

Mackie (1955) provides the materials for the following argument (which sets out the informal argument of the first section of this chapter in a more systematic fashion). To state the argument, we need to introduce some new vocabulary. We begin with the thought that, amongst possible universes, there is a class of possible universes – the *A-universes* – that are non-arbitrarily better than all of the other universes that contain free agents. The A-universes are some, but by no means all, of the universes in which there are free agents who all always freely chooses the good.

1. Necessarily, a perfect being can just choose to make an A-universe. (Premise)
2. Necessarily, A-universes are better than non-A-universes in which there are free agents. (Premise)
3. Necessarily, if a perfect being chooses between options, and one option is non-arbitrarily better than the other options, then the perfect being chooses that option. (Premise)
4. Hence, necessarily, if a perfect being makes a universe that contains free agents, then it makes an A-universe. (From 1–3)
5. Our universe contains free agents, but it is not an A-universe. (Premise)
6. Hence, it is not the case that a perfect being made our universe. (From 4 and 5)

The strategy behind free-will defences is to deny the first premise of this argument: because of the libertarian nature of freedom, it is not necessarily true that a perfect being can just choose to make a world in which everyone always freely chooses the good. (Plausibly, on a compatibilist analysis of freedom, it would be necessarily true that a perfect being can just choose to make a world in which everyone always freely chooses the good. While this claim is clearly in need of argumentative support, I shall not try to provide such support here.) While the remaining premises in the argument – that is, 2, 3, and 5 – are not incontestable, I think that there is likely to be widespread agreement amongst both theists and non-theists concerning their plausibility; at any rate, I don't propose to examine these premises further in the present chapter. On the assumption that I am right about the status of these further premises, then the success or failure of this argument turns entirely on the debate about the analysis of freedom. Since it is a controversial matter whether freedom can be given a libertarian analysis, it is a controversial matter whether there is a successful reply to this variant of Mackie's argument, *when* the argument is supplemented with subsidiary arguments that support premise 1.[26]

I take it that the above considerations are sufficient to establish that – contrary to the claims of many – there is still genuine life in Mackie's argument. Suppose, though, that we are persuaded that premise 1 renders the argument unsuccessful. Does this mean that all arguments of this kind must be abandoned? I don't think so. For, even if one can defend a metaphysical position according to which it is *possible* that a perfect being is not able to choose to make a universe in which everyone always freely chooses the good, it is much less clear that one can defend a metaphysical position according to which it is at all *likely* that there is a perfect being that was not able to choose to make a universe in which everyone always freely chooses the good.

The intuitive idea here is very simple. Clearly enough, agents who are strongly disposed towards doing good can nonetheless act freely (and, moreover, their freedom can be significant). Indeed, agents who are separately and collectively as strongly disposed as you please towards doing good can nonetheless act freely. Among the universe parts that it is open to a perfect being to make, there are universe parts in which the free agents that arise are collectively as strongly disposed as you please towards doing good. But, on the one hand, if we accept Plantinga's metaphysical picture (outlined in section 1 above), then (arguably) it follows that, if there is a perfect being, then it is as close to certain as you please that that being *was* able to choose to make a universe in which everyone always freely chooses the good; and, on the other hand, if we accept the alternative metaphysical picture (outlined in section 4 above), then (arguably) it follows that, if there is a perfect being, then it *was* able to choose a world in which it was as close to certain as you please that everyone would always freely choose the good and as close to certain as you please that if not everyone always freely chose the good, then these departures from optimal choice would be minimal.[27]

Constructing arguments with these new claims as initial premises is not a straightforward matter. The specimens that I am about to offer are pretty

---

[26] Of course, as things stand, the controversy about Premise 1 is enough to establish that 1–6 is not, itself, a successful argument for the conclusion that our universe was not made by a perfect being.

[27] The need for the second condition here was impressed upon me by Geoff Brennan, with help from Peter Godfrey-Smith. There is subsequent discussion of the need for this condition in the main text.

plainly imperfect; however, I am confident that there is something to be learned even from these imperfect attempts.

On the one hand, if we adopt the metaphysical framework that Plantinga defends, then we can construct arguments such as the following (Argument 1).

1. It is as close to certain as you please that a perfect being can choose to make a universe in which everyone always freely chooses the good. (Premise)
2. Necessarily, universes in which everyone always freely chooses the good are non-arbitrarily better than universes in which someone sometimes freely chooses the bad. (Premise)
3. Necessarily, if a perfect being chooses between options, and one option is non-arbitrarily better than the other options, then the perfect being chooses that option. (Premise)
4. Hence, it is as close to certain as you please that, if a perfect being makes a universe, then it makes a universe in which everyone always freely chooses the good. (From 1–3)
5. It is not the case that everyone always freely chooses the good. (Premise)
6. Hence, it is as close to certain as you please that our universe was not made by a perfect being. (From 4 and 5)

On the other hand, if we adopt the alternative metaphysical framework outlined in section 6.2.4 of this chapter, then – as foreshadowed in note 31 – we need to take account of the following consideration. When deliberating about which universe part to make, a perfect being will be concerned not only with the likelihood that the universe part belongs to a universe in which there are free agents who always freely choose the good, but also with the likelihood that, if the free agents do not always freely choose the good, then they depart from perfect goodness rarely and in relatively unimportant ways. That is, when selecting a universe part, a perfect being will select an A^*-*part*, that is, a universe part that is *both* almost certain to result in a universe in which there are free agents who all always freely choose the good *and* almost certain to result in a universe in which there is only minimal departure from universal choice of good if there is such departure.

Given this consideration, we can go on to construct arguments such as the following (Argument 2).

1. Necessarily, a perfect being can choose to make an A^*-part. (Premise)
2. Necessarily, A^*-parts are preferable to other parts that give rise to universes in which there are free agents. (Premise)
3. Necessarily, if a perfect being chooses between options, and one option is non-arbitrarily better than the other options, then the perfect being chooses that option. (Premise)

4. Hence, necessarily, if a perfect being chooses a universe part, then it will choose an A*-part. (From 1–3)
5. It is not the case that our world involves no more than minimal departure from universal choice of good. (Premise)
6. Hence, it is as close to certain as you please that our universe was not made by a perfect being. (From 4 and 5)

These arguments are pretty natural developments from the argument of Mackie (1955), and so will likely be heir to whatever difficulties are attached to that argument (apart from considerations involving libertarian freedom). Of course, I have suggested that there are no such further difficulties for Mackie's argument. Nonetheless, these arguments are also plainly subject to difficulties of their own; and it is some of these potential difficulties that will be the focus of the final part of this section of the book. (This final part of the section is a digression from the main line of argument of the section. I take it that the argument of the present part is already sufficient to vindicate the claim that discussion of the kinds of considerations raised by Mackie is far from exhausted, *even* if the argument set out at the beginning of this part is vitiated by its reliance upon a compatibilist analysis of freedom.)

6.2.9. Objections to the Preceding Arguments

It seems to me that there is a clear sense in which claim 4 in Argument 1 is correct: if we arbitrarily select a possible world containing a perfect being, then it is as close to certain as you please that, in that world, the perfect being is able to make a universe in which everyone always freely chooses the good. However, the clear sense in which (I take it that) this claim is correct relies upon the fact that our "arbitrarily selecting" a possible world requires that we do not have any other contingent or *a posteriori* information about that world. But once this is recognised, it seems fairly clear that the inference from 4 and 5 to 6 is no good: even given that it is certain that there is moral evil in the world, the fact that, *on the basis of a priori information alone*, it is as close to certain as you please that, in our world, a perfect being would have been able to make a universe in which everyone always freely chooses the good *does not entail that, on the basis of all relevant information,* it is as close to certain as you please that our universe was not made by a perfect being. Taking all of the relevant evidence into account, one might rather believe that our universe was made by a *massively unlucky* perfect being.

A similar kind of point can be made in connection with Argument 2. Again, it seems to me that there is a clear sense in which claim 4 is correct: if a perfect being makes a universe part, then it must make an A*-universe part. However, the clear sense in which (I take it that) this claim is correct relies upon the fact that we are only considering how things stood "when" the creative action occurred. Once this is recognised, it seems fairly clear that the inference from 4 and 5 to 6 is no good: even given that it is now certain that our world involves more than minimal departure from universal choice of good, the fact that, if the creative action occurred, it was "*then*" as close to certain as you please that the universe would involve no more than minimal departure from universal choice of good *does not entail that* it is *now* as close to certain as you please that our universe was not made by a perfect being. Taking all of the relevant information into account, one might rather believe that our universe was made by a *massively unlucky* perfect being.

No doubt most readers will now have guessed where this digression is heading. Even if we are prepared to accept that it is quite all right to believe in the kind of unexplained – and, presumably, unexplainable – bad luck that it seems must be invoked by the perfect being theist, there are consequences of this invocation that perfect being theists must face. In particular, perfect being theists can have no truck with any of the fine-tuning arguments for intelligent design that have received so much attention in recent times (since, by parity of reasoning, they shall have to allow that it is perfectly appropriate to respond to these arguments with the claim that it is just a matter of unexplained, and most likely unexplainable, good luck that our universe turned out to be hospitable to life, and that it turned out to contain the complex kinds of organisms that it in fact contains[28]). As I noted above in connection with the logical argument from moral evil, *defences* against

---

[28] We might suppose that a standard "fine-tuning" argument takes one of the following two forms:

1. It is very close to certain that, if some fundamental parameters in a big-bang universe are fixed arbitrarily, then that universe contains no life.
2. Our big bang universe contains life.
3. (Hence) It is very close to certain that those fundamental parameters of our universe were not fixed arbitrarily.

1. If some fundamental parameters in a big-bang universe are fixed arbitrarily, then it is very close to certain that that universe contains no life.
2. Our big-bang universe contains life.
3. (Hence) It is very close to certain that those fundamental parameters in our universe were not fixed arbitrarily.

We can say against each of these arguments just what was said against each of our probabilistic arguments from moral evil: while the initial premise may very well be plausible when nothing other than *a priori* information is taken into account, it is just illegitimate to infer from this fact that the conclusion is plausible when all relevant information is taken into account. (Of course, I don't say that this is the *only* thing to be said against these fine-tuning arguments. However, it would seem to be a useful response for those non-theists who are unsure of what else to say in response to these arguments when these arguments are propounded by perfect-being theists.)

arguments bring with them commitments that cannot be ignored when one comes to mount positive arguments of one's own.

Doubtless, some theists will claim to be distinctly unimpressed by all of this. Even if it were true that the cost of meeting arguments from moral evil is that all decent *a posteriori* arguments for the existence of a perfect being must be foregone,[29] it might well be insisted that it remains open to theists to follow Plantinga (1979a) in claiming that rational belief in a perfect being does not require any kind of argumentative support. Suppose that's right, that is, suppose that there is some sense in which belief in a perfect being can be properly basic. Nonetheless, it seems that the *kinds* of considerations that we have been developing might well suffice to show that there is no good reason for those who are not already convinced of the truth of perfect-being theism to become perfect-being theists. While arguments from moral evil may not show that perfect-being theists are irrational, there is at least some reason to think that these arguments can form an important plank in a case that shows that rational considerations are insufficient to move anyone to *become* a perfect-being theist.

Of course, I do not think that the brief argument of this part – and the earlier digression about principles of sufficient reason – conclusively establishes the claim that is mentioned at the end of the previous paragraph. However, as I said at the beginning of this section, my main aim is a moderate one, namely, to show that there is more to be learned from arguments concerning moral evil than many philosophers are currently prepared to concede. If there is anything at all to the line of thought developed in the current part of this section, then there is *still* plenty of life left in the kinds of considerations that are appealed to in Mackie (1955).

6.2.10. Concluding Observations

What do I think can be learned from the preceding discussion? *First*, it is highly questionable whether Plantinga (1974) provides a satisfactory response to the standard "logical assertion" about moral evil. *Second*, there is a logical argument from moral evil in Mackie (1955) that (plausibly) stands or falls with a compatibilist analysis of freedom. *Third*, the acceptance of a libertarian analysis of freedom imposes non-trivial constraints on the kinds of principles of sufficient reason that one can endorse (and, hence, on the

---

[29] Of course, the claim that is being entertained here goes far beyond anything that I have tried to argue for: it would take a much more extended argument to show that all *a posteriori* arguments for the existence of a perfect being are neutralised by the defensive measures that must be taken in order to have adequate replies to arguments from evil. Nonetheless, it does seem to me that there is a question here worth asking: not everyone has noticed that there may be more than one way in which arguments from evil can advance the cause of non-theists. (Plainly enough, theists can make similar kinds of points – about, say, responses to arguments for the inadequacy of naturalism – against those non-theists who are naturalists.)

kinds of cosmological arguments that one can promote). *Fourth,* there are probabilistic analogues of the more powerful logical argument from Mackie (1955) that bear serious comparison with currently popular "fine-tuning" arguments for intelligent design. I do not suppose that this exhausts the important points to be established by a serious reconsideration of the arguments in Mackie (1955); I, for one, am keen to retrieve that paper from 'the dustbin of philosophical fashions'. At any rate – and perhaps more modestly – I am keen to defend the contention that there is no more reason to consign Mackie's argument from evil to 'the dustbin' than there is to consign all of the extant arguments for the existence of orthodoxly conceived monotheistic gods to the same resting place.

6.3. EVIDENTIAL ARGUMENTS FROM EVIL (CO-WRITTEN WITH MICHAEL J. ALMEIDA)

The best known recent defence of evidential arguments from evil is due to William Rowe (1979, 1984, 1986, 1988, 1991, 1995, 1996, 2001). Rowe's argument has gone through various modifications since its initial formulation, and each of these formulations has been subject to various kinds of attack.

6.3.1. Sceptical Theism

In recent times, a number of philosophers have championed 'sceptical theist' responses to evidential arguments from evil. (Fitzpatrick (1981), Wykstra (1984, 1996), van Inwagen (1991/6), Plantinga (1979b, 1988/96), Alston (1991/6, 1996), Howard-Snyder (1996a, 1996c), Bergmann (2001)). The core idea behind these responses to evidential arguments from evil is that considerations of human cognitive limitations are *alone* sufficient to undermine those arguments. This core idea is developed in different ways. Some 'sceptical theists' – (Howard-Snyder (1996a, 1996c), Bergmann (2001); – claim that consideration of human cognitive limitations in the realm of value are alone sufficient to undermine evidential arguments from evil. Other 'sceptical theists' – Plantinga (1979b, 1988), Wykstra (1984, 1996), Alston (1991/6, 1996), van Inwagen (1991/6) – claim that consideration of human cognitive limitations in various spheres including the realm of value are alone sufficient to undermine evidential arguments from evil. My response to these 'sceptical theists' is in two parts. First, I argue – against Bergmann (2001), and others – that it isn't true that considerations of human cognitive limitations in the realm of value are *alone* sufficient to undermine evidential arguments from evil. Second, I argue against Alston (1991, 1996), and others – that it isn't true that considerations of human cognitive limitations in various spheres including the realm of values are *alone* sufficient to undermine evidential arguments from evil.

The structure of the section is as follows. In the first part, I provide what I take to be a more or less canonical formulation of an evidential argument from evil. This argument differs in some ways from arguments that have hitherto been presented in the literature, but nothing turns on these differences: the subsequent argument could be developed equally well in connection with William Rowe's more familiar formulations of evidential arguments from evil.[30] What is crucial is that the kind of evidential argument that I consider – and that is the target of 'sceptical theist' critique – contains a key inference that moves from a premise of the form 'We have found no reasons why...' to a conclusion of the form 'There are no reasons why...'. The burden of the 'sceptical theist' critique of the argument is to attack this inference by appeal to nothing more than certain (alleged) human cognitive limitations; I shall argue in reply that the inference in question cannot be undermined merely by appeal to considerations about human cognitive limitations in the realm of value, or by appeal to considerations about human cognitive limitations in a variety of spheres including the realm of value.

In the second part of this section, I discuss Stephen Wykstra's claim that the premise in the key inference does not even weakly support the conclusion of that inference, that is, the claim that our failure to find reasons of a certain kind does not raise the probability that there are no reasons of that kind *at all*.[31] I suggest that this claim is massively implausible: it would require very special circumstances in order for a claim of the form 'We have found no reasons why...' to fail to provide *any* support for the claim that 'There are no reasons why...'; and it is not credible to suppose that our target evidential argument from evil provides such a case.

In the third part of this section, I move on to discuss Michael Bergmann's 'sceptical theist' argument – based on a 'general scepticism about our knowledge of the realm of value' – that the premise in the key inference does not provide substantial support for the conclusion of that inference.[32] I claim that, if the inference from 'We have found no reasons why...' to 'There are no reasons why...' is blocked by the considerations to which Bergmann adverts in the case of evidential arguments from evil, then similar inferences

---

[30] See Rowe (1979) and many subsequent publications. In more recent publications, Rowe has moved away from arguments that involve the kind of inference that will be the main focus of our discussion in this chapter. However, there is a fairly straightforward variant of the sceptical theist response that can be made to Rowe's new arguments, and exactly the same kinds of considerations will arise. So there is no loss of generality in focussing on the particular evidential argument from evil that we set out below.

[31] This claim is made in Wykstra (1984); it is retracted in Wykstra (1996).

[32] Bergmann (2001). Rowe has a reply to Bergmann in the same volume of the journal. However, I shall not discuss this reply, since it takes a quite different tack from the one that I wish to pursue.

will be blocked in cases of ordinary moral reasoning that we all have reason to endorse. Thus, I claim, Bergmann faces a dilemma: either his 'general scepticism about our knowledge of the realm of value' is too benign to save theism from the evidential argument from evil; or else his 'general scepticism about our knowledge of the realm of value' is so strong that it threatens to disrupt our ordinary patterns of moral reasoning.

In the fourth and fifth parts of this section, I turn to consider possible objections to my argument against Bergmann. In particular, I consider the suggestion that my argument fails to pay due attention to the fact that it makes a huge difference that it is not we but rather a perfect being who is the subject of the key inference in our evidential argument from evil; and I also consider the suggestion that I am wrong to think that the moral scepticism that is mandated by the principles that Bergmann endorses is anything other than benign.

In the sixth part of this section, I consider the prospects for extending my critique of Bergmann (2001) to other kinds of 'sceptical theist' responses to evidential argument from evil. In particular, I focus on Alston (1991, 1996). Unlike Bergmann, Alston does not claim that considerations concerning human cognitive limitations in the sphere of value are alone sufficient to undermine evidential arguments from evil. However, it seems to me that Alston is committed to the claim that considerations concerning human cognitive limitations in a range of spheres including the realm of values are alone sufficient to undermine evidential arguments from evil. But – as I shall go on to argue – if the objection that I develop against Bergmann is good, then it carries over to this view as well. Moreover, if we suppose – as I think we should – that it is constitutive of 'sceptical theist' responses to evidential arguments from evil to claim that considerations concerning human cognitive limitations in a range of spheres including the realm of values are alone sufficient to undermine evidential arguments from evil, then my argument carries over to all versions of 'sceptical theist' responses to evidential arguments from evil.[33]

Perhaps it is worth emphasising here that I am not setting out to defend the claim that some evidential arguments are successful pieces of atheological argumentation. Rather, what I am aiming to do is to defend the reasonableness of one kind of judgment that typically features in arguments of this type from one kind of theistic counterattack. I am prepared to allow that, for example, the 'G.E. Moore shift' described by Rowe (1979) provides a

---

[33] Perhaps there is some room for dispute about whether the other writers to whom I have referred conform to this account of 'sceptical theism'. My target in this section is the view that I have just characterised; I'm happy to defer argument about exactly who has defended this kind of view in print to some other occasion. I think that it is clear that this view is defended by Bergmann, Alston, Howard-Snyder, etc.; but I don't propose to argue the remaining cases here.

perfectly satisfactory response to these arguments. (Why shouldn't the theist presented with Rowe's argument infer that it is very likely that there are unknown goods that justify an orthodoxly conceived monotheistic god in permitting certain kinds of evils? Such an inference is entirely compatible with the further claim that we know that there are no unknown goods that bear on our own moral evaluations – not least, perhaps, because we have a guarantee from an orthodoxly conceived monotheistic god that this is so.) However, it is important to note that the 'sceptical theist' response is distinctive because, were it correct, it would establish that no one – theist or non-theist – should make the crucial probability judgment that undergirds evidential arguments from evil. The direction of the 'sceptical theist' argument is from considerations concerning our cognitive limitations – and nothing but our cognitive limitations – to the conclusion that a certain probability judgment is out of bounds. And it is this that I claim to be able to show is wrong.

6.3.2. Formulating the Argument

I begin, then, with the formulation of a more or less canonical version of an evidential argument from evil. The main sub-conclusion of the evidential argument from evil that I shall discuss is that there are evils for which it is true that, were a perfect being to prevent those evils, then the world would be non-arbitrarily improved thereby. It follows from this sub-conclusion that, if there are such evils, then there is no perfect being. It is tempting to call such evils 'gratuitous'; however, it seems doubtful that this usage is in accord with the standard definition(s) in the literature.[34] So let me instead call them 'problematic'.[35]

---

[34] For instance, some people have claimed that God is not *required* to prevent any evil whose existence is logically entailed by some greater overall good. On the assumption that 'evils' are evil states of affairs, and 'goods' are good states of affairs, the further assumption that there are conjunctive states of affairs that are goods, even though they contain conjuncts that are evils, will pretty quickly lead to the conclusion that there are almost all evils are such that God is not required to prevent them. While there are ways of avoiding the trivialisation of this kind of conception of 'gratuitous' evil, it seems to us to be preferable to look for a different way of thinking about the kinds of evils that God would be obliged to prevent.

[35] It should be noted that I have taken no stand on the question of what is required in order for the prevention of an evil to non-arbitrarily improve the world. Perhaps what is required is, at least, that the 'net value' of the world is non-arbitrarily increased; perhaps what is required is, at least, that the 'net value' of the world should not decrease while the 'net evil' is non-arbitrarily decreased; perhaps what is required is, at least, that the 'net evil' in the world is non-arbitrarily decreased sufficiently to justify a corresponding decrease in the 'net value' of the world; perhaps what is required is something else. One suggestion I cannot accept is that what is required is that the 'net value' of the world is maximised; this suggestion is plainly too demanding. The subsequent discussion does not require that I take any stance on this issue.

Evidential arguments from evil – of the kind that I am investigating here – aim to establish that there are problematic evils, or that there is most reason to think that there are problematic evils, or that there is at least some reason to think that there are problematic evils. (Later, I shall fuss more about the strength of the conclusion that is to be drawn in arguments of this kind; for now, I leave the matter open.)

Before I turn to the formulation of our target argument, I should explain what I mean when I insist that problematic evils are evils that are such that, if they were prevented by the actions of a perfect being, then the world would be *non-arbitrarily* improved.

As a first step towards motivating my account of problematic evils, it should be noted that it would not suffice for the purposes of the argument to claim that there are evils for which it is true that, were a perfect being to prevent those evils, then the world would not thereby be made worse. Suppose that there are two worlds, w_1 and w_2, that are in all respects alike except that w_1 contains evil E_1 and w_2 contains E_2, where E_1 and E_2 are of equal (dis)value. If w_1 is actual, then it casts no doubt on the claim that there is a perfect being to point out that a perfect being could have prevented the occurrence of E_1 – by actualising world w_2 instead – without thereby making the world worse. (I assume – what some have denied – that, if a perfect being must choose between w_1 and w_2, then it can do so.)

As a more important step towards motivating my account of problematic evils, it should be noted, too, that it would not suffice for the purposes of the argument to claim that there are evils for which it is true that, were a perfect being to prevent those evils, then the world would be improved. Suppose that there is a sequence of worlds $w_1, w_2, \ldots, w_n, \ldots$ that contain sequences of evils $\{E_1, E_2, \ldots, E_n, \ldots\}, \{E_2, E_3, \ldots, E_n, \ldots\}, \ldots, \{E_k, E_{k+1}, \ldots, E_n, \ldots\}, \ldots,$ and that are otherwise identical. (So, by hypothesis, w_1 is worse than w_2, which is worse than w_3, etc.) Suppose further that any world that contains only a finite number of the E_i is worse than any of the worlds $w_1, w_2, \ldots,$ $w_n, \ldots,$ because a final infinite segment of the sequence of evils $E_1, E_2, \ldots,$ $E_n, \ldots,$ is required in order to ensure some massive 'outweighing' good. If w_k is actual, it casts no doubt on the claim that there is a perfect being to point out that a perfect being could have prevented the obtaining of E_k – by actualising world w_{k+1}, say – and thereby made the world better. (Again, I assume – what some may deny – that if a perfect being has to choose one final infinite section of the sequence $E_1, E_2, \ldots, E_n, \ldots,$ then it can do so.)

The point here is that it is possible that a perfect being may need to make an arbitrary choice, from amongst a set of worlds that it can make, if it is to make any world at all. If, for example, for any world that a perfect being can make, there is a better world, then, if the perfect being is to make any world at all, it must arbitrarily choose one that is good enough. But in these circumstances, it is then no criticism of the activity of the perfect being that it could have made a better world: in the circumstances, the mooted improvement of the world is *arbitrary*. The case that I have described in the previous paragraph is simply meant to show that improvements of the world by the prevention of evils *could* be arbitrary in exactly the same sense: there may be evils that are not required for the obtaining of greater goods, or for the non-obtaining of greater evils, and yet that a perfect being does not have reason to prevent. However, I do assume – what some may perhaps deny – that, if the world would be *non-arbitrarily* improved by the prevention of some evil, then, *a fortiori*, a perfect being would prevent that evil; in other words, if there are problematic evils, then there is no perfect being.

With these preliminaries out of the way, I can now turn to my formulation of an evidential argument from evil. Let E be some candidate – that is, *prima facie* – problematic evil that has occurred, for example, the rape, beating, and murder by strangulation of a five-year-old girl, or the prolonged and painful death of a fawn that has been trapped in a forest fire, or the like. I shall use the following as my representative evidential argument from evil.

(1) We have been unable to find even *pro tanto* reasons why the world would not be non-arbitrarily improved if a perfect being prevented E. (Premise)

(2) (Therefore) There are not even *pro tanto* reasons why the world would not be non-arbitrarily improved if a perfect being prevented E. (From 1)

(3) There are at least *pro tanto* reasons why the world would be non-arbitrarily improved if a perfect being prevented E. (Premise)

(4) (Therefore) There is all-things-considered reason why the world would be non-arbitrarily improved if a perfect being prevented E. (From 2 and 3)

(5) (Therefore) The world would be non-arbitrarily improved if a perfect being prevented E. (From 4)

(6) (Therefore) There is no perfect being. (From 5)

In support of (1), I note that we can point to no greater good that would be lost if E were prevented by a perfect being; no greater evil that would ensue if E were prevented by a perfect being; nothing that suggests that there must be some events like E – violations of young children – if there are to be greater goods that would otherwise be lost; nothing that suggests that there must be some events like E – violations of young children – if there are not to be greater evils that would otherwise ensue.[36]

---

[36] Perhaps the argument in this paragraph is more controversial than I have allowed. For instance, if van Inwagen (1991/6) were right, then we do have some reason to think that, if the world is to be law-governed, then there must be some events like E. I think that van Inwagen is not right; but I don't propose to try to argue the case here.

In support of (3), I note that we all agree that the world could have been non-arbitrarily improved if one of us had intervened to prevent E, other circumstances permitting. Indeed, I note that we all agree that, other circumstances permitting, we would have a moral obligation to intervene: if we could, without risk to ourselves and others, and without extravagant use of resources, prevent E, then that is what we are required to do. (No doubt, our moral obligation runs further than this; however, all we need is the uncontroversial claim that our obligations run at least this far.) The awfulness of E is enough to establish that a perfect being has at least a *pro tanto* reason to prevent it.

The inference from (4) to (5) is uncontroversial. The inference from (2) and (3) to (4) also looks solid: if there are not even *pro tanto* reasons why the world would not be non-arbitrarily improved if a perfect being prevented E, and there are *pro tanto* reasons why the world would be non-arbitrarily improved if a perfect being prevented E, then it surely follows that there is all-things-considered reason why the world would be non-arbitrarily improved if a perfect being prevented E.[37] That leaves the inference from (1) to (2); and here there are many philosophers who will want – and have wanted – to raise objections. In what follows, I shall consider some of the objections that have been made to the inference from (1) to (2).

6.3.3. Wykstra's Critique

The inference from (1) to (2) moves from 'It is not the case that we have found reasons of such-and-such a kind' to 'There are no reasons of such-and-such a kind.'[38] Plainly, this is not in general a good deductive inference: it is perfectly possible for claims of the former kind to be true while the corresponding claims of the latter kind are false. However, it does not follow from this claim alone that the inference from (1) to (2) is not a good inference; it may be that there is some other kind of evidential or probabilistic support that (1) lends to (2). Moreover, it seems natural – at least initially – to suppose that this is the case: surely (1) does lend some kind of evidential or probabilistic support to (2). That I have failed to find reasons of

---

[37] Note that the argument that I offer here is not the argument given by Russell (1989): I am not supposing that it follows, from the fact that (7) there is all-things-considered reason why the world would be non-arbitrarily improved if *we* prevented E, that (4) there is all-things-considered reason why the world would be non-arbitrarily improved if a *perfect being* prevented E. Perhaps it might be argued that (7) is at least weak evidence for (4); however, there are obvious difficulties that confront the claim that (7) is strong evidence for (4). In particular, it could well be that, even though the world would be non-arbitrarily improved by *our* preventing E, the world would not be non-arbitrarily improved by a *perfect being's* preventing E.

[38] In the literature, inferences of this kind are sometimes referred to as 'noseeum inferences', after Wykstra (1996). I shall sometimes make use of this label.

such-and-such kind may well be evidence for the claim – may well make it more likely – that there are no reasons of such-and-such kind.[39]

We need to distinguish at least two different possible claims here. One claim is that (1) provides *strong evidential* support for (2): given (1), we have substantial reason – perhaps even more reason than not – to believe (2). A weaker claim is that (1) provides *weak evidential* support for (2): given (1), we have more reason to believe (2) than we had before we took (1) into account. I shall first briefly consider views that dispute even the weaker claim, before turning to consideration of arguments against the stronger claim.

A clear example of someone who disputes even the weaker claim is Wykstra (1984). In his view: 'Cognisance of suffering ... *should not in the least* reduce our confidence that [perfect-being theism] is true. When cognisance of suffering does have this effect, it is perhaps because we had not understood [what perfect-being theism] proposes for belief in the first place' (Wykstra (1984: 91), emphasis added). Of course, this kind of position is very strong. If cognisance of suffering should not in the least reduce our confidence that perfect being theism is true, then it seems that observations of evils in the world must be completely irrelevant for the question of the assessment of the truth of the claim that there is a perfect being. Suppose, for example, that we were to discover that there are a billion other inhabited planets in our galaxy, and that the trillions of intelligent inhabitants of all those other planets live lives of unrelieved misery. Suppose that we extend our search, and find the same figures reproduced for the millions of other galaxies. Suppose, finally, that we are utterly unable to think of any way in which all of this misery could subserve some greater good. The view in question entails that *none* of this would provide any evidence at all against perfect-being theism. It is very tempting to suppose that this is a *reductio* of the view in question.

What would one need to believe in order to defend the claim that (1) does not even provide weak evidential support for (2)? Well, the claim is that F, the failure to find reasons why the world would not be non-arbitrarily improved if a perfect being prevented E, provides no support at all for the hypothesis, R, that there is no reason why the world would not be non-arbitrarily improved if a perfect being prevented E. Since, by Bayes' theorem, $\Pr(R/F) = \Pr(R) \times \Pr(F/R)/\Pr(F)$, it follows that what needs to be believed is that $\Pr(F/R) \leq \Pr(F)$. (Here, I assume that F weakly supports R exactly if $\Pr(R/F) > \Pr(R)$.) That is, we need to think that it is no less likely that *we shall fail to find reasons why the world would not be non-arbitrarily improved if a perfect being prevented E* than it is that *we shall fail to find reasons why the world*

---

[39] To strengthen the case for this claim, we can add that the investigation has been neither careless nor casual: many people have devoted extensive effort to the search for reasons of the kind in question.

would not be non-arbitrarily improved if a perfect being prevented E given *that there is no reason why the world would not be non-arbitrarily improved if a perfect being prevented E.* But it is *certain* that, if there is no reason why the world would not be non-arbitrarily improved if a perfect being prevented E, then we shall fail to find reasons why the world would not be non-arbitrarily improved if a perfect being prevented E. In other words, the conditional probability that we should assign here is as high as a conditional probability can be. So what is required – in order to defend the position that Wykstra espouses – is that we assign a probability of *no less than one* to the claim that we shall fail to find reasons why the world would not be non-arbitrarily improved if a perfect being prevented E. But that is absurd; none of us should assign a probability of no less than one – that is, of exactly one – to the claim that we shall fail to find reasons why the world would not be non-arbitrarily improved if a perfect being prevented E.[40]

Wykstra himself identified a different condition that he supposed would need to be satisfied in order for (1) to provide weak evidential support for (2). In his view, (1) cannot provide even weak evidential support for (2) unless it is true that, were there a perfect being that had reasons for not preventing E, we would be able to find those reasons. Moreover, Wykstra also holds that, in fact, it isn't true that were there a perfect being that had reasons for not preventing E, we would be able to find those reasons. Why should we accept this claim? Because we should accept that, were there a perfect being that had reasons for not preventing E, we would not even be able to *understand* those reasons.

The discussion in the previous paragraph but one suggests several reasons for dissatisfaction with this argument. As I noted there, what needs to be argued is that it is *very* likely that we shall fail to find reasons why the world would not be non-arbitrarily improved if a perfect being prevented E. Even if we claimed that it is *certain* that, were there a perfect being that had reasons for not preventing E, we would not be able to understand those reasons – something that plainly goes far beyond what it is reasonable to claim – it would not follow that it is *very* likely that we shall fail to find reasons why the

---

[40] Note that, even if we were to suppose that the conditional probability in question is merely *very* high – perhaps because we mistakenly supposed that it is relevant to note that we could mistakenly suppose that there are reasons when in fact there are none – it would still be the case that Wykstra's position should be rejected. Under this revised supposition, it would be the case that what needs to be argued for is the claim that we should assign a more than very high probability to the claim that we shall fail to find reasons why the world would not be non-arbitrarily improved if a perfect being prevented E. But even if one thinks that it is certain that there is a perfect being, it is hard to see how one could be justified in supposing that it is so close to certain that we shall fail to find reasons why the world would not be non-arbitrarily improved if a perfect being prevented E. What justification is there, for instance, for being so very confident that we shall never construct a theodicy that is able to provide such reasons?

world would not be non-arbitrarily improved if a perfect being prevented E.[41] If we give a realistic assessment of the likelihood that, were there a perfect being that had reasons for not preventing E, we would not be able to understand those reasons, then it seems reasonable to suppose that we shall not arrive at the conclusion that it is *very* likely that we shall fail to find reasons why the world would not be non-arbitrarily improved if a perfect being prevented E.[42]

In my view – and, I believe, in the view of most who now write on this topic[43] – our failure to find reasons why the world would not be non-arbitrarily improved if a perfect being prevented E *does* weakly support the claim that there are no such reasons. Thus, in my view – though perhaps not also in the view of most who now write on this topic – our failure to find reasons why the world would not be non-arbitrarily improved if a perfect being prevented E *does* weakly support the claim that there is no perfect being.[44]

---

[41] Here is another way of thinking about these issues. There are two ways in which it could be that there are reasons why a perfect being would not non-arbitrarily improve the world if it prevented E. First, there might be reasons that we are able to comprehend; second, there might be reasons that we are unable to comprehend. If we look for reasons, and are unable to find them, then our confidence in the first of these alternatives should be reduced; in consequence – unless our failure to find reasons should make us more confident that there are reasons that we are unable to comprehend – our confidence that there are reasons *tout court* should also be reduced. This reasoning can be blocked if we suppose that there *could not* be reasons that we are able to comprehend; but that is surely an incredible assumption to make.

[42] It should perhaps be noted that we can't suggest that the reasons that a perfect being would have for not preventing E need not turn on the issue of whether the world would be non-arbitrarily improved by its prevention of E. For, while this suggestion – if cogent – would provide a reason for rejecting Wykstra's contention, there are good reasons for refusing to accept the suggestion. If 'the world' – the entire sphere of contingency – is not made better by the perfect being's prevention of E, then the perfect being simply *does not* have a reason to prevent E. This point – about the logical connection between reasons and the good – cannot be undermined by considerations about the vast gulf between the understanding of a perfect being and our own imperfect understanding.

[43] Several people have suggested to me that Plantinga is one of those who disagrees, and that I really ought to say something about his views in this context. I agree that I ought to say something about Plantinga's views – though I prefer to defer that discussion to some other occasion – but I am not convinced that Plantinga does disagree. At any rate, a careful reading of Plantinga (1988) did not make it obvious to me that Plantinga outright dismisses the suggestion that, other considerations aside, our failure to find reasons why the world would not be non-arbitrarily improved if a perfect being prevented E does make it less likely – however minutely! – that there is a perfect being. Plantinga (1988/96) makes it quite clear that he thinks that he could accept this claim with equanimity; moreover, Plantinga (1988/96) also makes it quite clear that he would reject the corresponding claim about substantial support. But I have not been able to make an accurate determination of his view on the question that is the focus of the present part of this book.

[44] Perhaps those who think otherwise are misled by the thought that we should hardly expect to have insight into the reasons – the reasoning and motivation – of a perfect being. But even

6.3.4. Bergmann's Critique

Even if it is granted that our failure to find reasons why a perfect being would not non-arbitrarily improve the world if it prevented E does provide weak support for the claim that there is no perfect being, it remains to be determined how strong this support is. It seems quite implausible to suppose that, all by itself, this failure is sufficient to establish that it is more likely than not that there is no perfect being. After all, there might be other reasons – perhaps even quite strong reasons – for believing that there is a perfect being. To assess this question, we need to take all of the relevant evidence into account – and that is not a task that anyone should suppose is easily accomplished![45]

However, even if we can't hope to show that our failure to find reasons why a perfect being would not non-arbitrarily improve the world if it prevented E is sufficient to establish that it is more likely than not that there is no perfect being, we might nonetheless hope to show that our failure to find reasons why a perfect being would not non-arbitrarily improve the world if it prevented E does provide *significant* support for the claim that there is no perfect being. While I concede that I might do more to explain what is required in order for one proposition to provide significant support for another, I shall follow the standard practice of hoping that this notion is sufficiently well understood to allow me to proceed.

Given the way in which I have set up the discussion, the central task is to determine whether it is likely that, were there reasons why a perfect being would not non-arbitrarily improve the world if it prevented E, we would be able to find those reasons. If we suppose that it is quite likely – or very likely – that, *were there reasons why a perfect being would not non-arbitrarily improve the world if it prevented E, we would be able to find those reasons*, then we should hold that our failure to find reasons why a perfect being would not non-arbitrarily improve the world if it prevented E does provide significant support for the claim that there is no perfect being. On the other hand, if we deny that it

if it is true that we should think it likely that our insight into the reasoning and motivation of a perfect being is limited, that is not relevant to the assessment of our argument. For the underlying question is whether the world would not be non-arbitrarily improved if a perfect being prevented E; and what we are looking for is reasons for thinking that this question should be answered in the affirmative. Thus – as much of the more recent literature recognises – the central questions really concern limitations on our abilities to recognise goods rather than limitations on our insights into the reasoning and motivation of perfect beings.

[45] Of course, there are questions about the prior probability that is assigned to R that might be raised at this point. If $Pr_{prior}(R)$ is very much less than $Pr_{prior}(\sim R)$, then more than weak support from F would be required to make $Pr_{posterior}(R) > Pr_{posterior}(\sim R)$. But this is not the only way in which 'strong support' might be understood. If, for example, $Pr_{prior}(R)/Pr_{posterior}(R)$ is very much less than one, then there is a sense in which F gives strong support to R, even if it is also the case that $Pr_{posterior}(R)$ is very much less than $Pr_{posterior}(\sim R)$. I shall not need to worry about these kinds of niceties in what follows.

is fairly likely – or very likely – that, *were there reasons why a perfect being would not non-arbitrarily improve the world if it prevented E, we would be able to find those reasons*, then we should hold that our failure to find reasons why a perfect being would not non-arbitrarily improve the world if it prevented E does not provide significant support for the claim that there is no perfect being.[46] Why might we deny that it is quite likely that, were there reasons why a perfect being would not non-arbitrarily improve the world if it prevented E, we would be able to find those reasons?

Well, as Bergmann (2001) argues, this judgment might follow from a more general scepticism about our knowledge of the realm of value. If we pay due attention to our cognitive limitations, and to the vastness and complexity of reality, then it may well seem plausible to suppose that our understanding of the realm of value falls miserably short of capturing all that is true about that realm. More positively, that same due attention might suggest that we are entitled to accept the following kinds of claims:

(ST1) We have no good reason for thinking that the possible goods we know of are representative of the possible goods there are.

(ST2) We have no good reason for thinking that the possible evils we know of are representative of the possible evils there are.

(ST3) We have no good reason for thinking that the entailment relations we know of between possible goods and the permission of possible evils are representative of the entailment relations there are between possible goods and the permission of possible evils.[47]

But if we accept these kinds of claims, then won't we be entitled to claim that we are in no position to judge that it is fairly likely – or very likely – that, were there reasons why a perfect being would not non-arbitrarily improve the world if it prevented E, we would be able to find those reasons?

I think not. Suppose we take seriously the idea that it follows from our acceptance of (ST1)–(ST3) that is not unlikely that there are goods beyond our ken – or relations beyond our ken among goods and evils (which

---

46 Note that the denial in question can take one of two forms. One could insist that it is fairly unlikely – or very unlikely – that, were there reasons why a perfect being would not non-arbitrarily improve the world if it prevented E, we would be able to find those reasons. Alternatively, one could insist that we are in no position to form any judgment at all about the likelihood that, were there reasons why a perfect being would not non-arbitrarily improve the world if it prevented E, we would be able to find those reasons. While either of these positions would suffice for the purposes of sceptical theists, it is the latter that shall be the major focus of my attention.

47 There is potential ambiguity in (ST1)–(ST3). I take it that the right way to read, say, (ST1) is as follows: we have no good reason for thinking that the goods we know of are representative of the goods that there are in the world. It is less controversial that we have no good reason for thinking that the goods we know of are representative of the goods that there are in all possible worlds. But that less controversial claim is of no use to the sceptical theist, since – as Rowe insists – goods in other possible worlds cannot justify God's actions in our world.

themselves may or may not be beyond our ken)[48] – that justify a perfect being in not preventing E. Suppose further that we are, right now, witnesses to E, and that we could intervene to stop it at no personal cost. What we have just conceded is that, merely on the basis of our acceptance of (ST1)–(ST3), we should insist that it is not unlikely that there is some good that, if we were smarter and better equipped, we could recognise as a reason for a perfect being's not intervening to stop E.[49] Plainly, we should also concede – by parity of reason – that, merely on the basis of our acceptance of (ST1)–(ST3), we should insist that it is not unlikely that there is some good that, if we were smarter and better equipped, we could recognise as a reason for our not intervening to stop the event. That is, our previous concession surely forces us to allow that, given our acceptance of (ST1)–(ST3), it is not unlikely that it is for the best, all things considered, if we do not intervene. But if we could easily intervene to stop the heinous crime, then it would be *appalling* for us to allow this consideration to stop us from intervening. Yet if we take the thought seriously, how can we also maintain that we are morally required to intervene? After all, as a result of our acceptance of (ST1)–(ST3), we are allegedly committed to the claim that it is not unlikely that it would be for the best, all things considered, if we did not do so.

Bergmann claims that we should give high probability to (ST1)–(ST3). What seems to follow from this – at least if we follow the model that Bergmann offers in the case of the claim that there are goods that, if we were smarter and better equipped, we would recognise as reasons for *a perfect being* not to prevent E – is that we have no good reason to assign a low probability to the claim that there are goods that, if we were smarter and better equipped, we would recognise as reasons for *us* not to prevent E. Yet if we do not have good reason to assign a low probability to the claim that there are goods that, if we were smarter and better equipped, we would recognise as reasons for us not to prevent E, then how can we have good reason to interfere and to prevent it? True enough, rape and murder are terrible evils; hence, that a particular event is an instance of rape and murder is a *pro tanto* reason to prevent that event. But an event can be many things at once, and even a rape and murder *could* be an event that is a very great good (e.g., the

---

[48] Hereafter, I shall use the shorthand formulation that refers only to goods beyond our ken, and omits reference to the considerations about relations beyond our ken between goods and evils. However, this is only for ease of formulation: it is very important – as Bergmann and Alston both insist – that it is not merely the goods and evils that may be beyond our ken.

[49] Perhaps it might be disputed that I did previously concede this. If we suppose that we are essentially unable to recognise the reasons in question, then – no matter how much smarter and better equipped we were – we would not be able to recognise the reasons for the perfect being's not intervening to stop E. However, there is nothing other than ease of exposition that is lost if we grant this point – parity of reason *will* still get us to the claim that, for all we know, it would be best, all things considered, if we did not intervene.

prevention of the destruction of the world, to take a hackneyed example). If we are not prepared to judge that it is unlikely that a particular instance of rape and murder is not also a very great good – and that is just the kind of judgment that acceptance of (ST1)–(ST3) is supposed to preclude – then we do not have sufficient reason to interfere, and to prevent the rape and murder, no matter how little it would cost us to do so.

The conclusion for which I have argued here is that what Bergmann calls 'sceptical theism' really does involve an unacceptable scepticism if it is strong enough to provide a telling objection to evidential arguments from evil. Bergmann considers some other ways in which one might try to make this case and (rightly) argues that they fail.[50] However, my discussion seems to show *either* that our moral practice implicitly commits us to the assignment of a high probability to the claims that, according to (ST1)–(ST3), we have no good reason for believing; or else that (ST1)–(ST3) are insufficient to license the conclusion that it is not unlikely that there are goods beyond our ken that would justify a perfect being in not preventing E. Perhaps there is some reason to think that (ST1)–(ST3) embody a relatively benign form of scepticism – perhaps it is plausible that the goods we know fail to be representative of the goods there are; that the evils we know fail to be representative of the evils there are; and that the entailment relations we know of between goods and the permission of evils are representative of the entailment relations there are between goods and the permission of evils – but, if so, then there must be some problem with the inference that Bergmann draws. Our moral practice – our ordinary moral behaviour – shows that we do think it unlikely that there are goods beyond our ken that would justify us in not preventing E; so there is plainly room for serious doubt about the suggestion that considerations like (ST1)–(ST3) are sufficient to establish that it is not unlikely that there are goods beyond our ken that would justify a perfect being in not preventing E.

Here is another way of making my key point. Suppose that we try to give a rational reconstruction of the moral reasoning that we undertake when we reach the decision to intervene in the case in which we can easily prevent rape and murder. The reconstruction will have to go something like the following.

(1) There is *pro tanto* reason for me to intervene to prevent E. (Indeed, I have a *pro tanto* duty to intervene to prevent E.) (Premise)

(2) I have found no *pro tanto* reason for me not to intervene to prevent E. (Premise)

(3) (Hence) There is no *pro tanto* reason for me not to intervene to prevent E. (From 2)

(4) (Hence) I have all-things-considered reason to intervene to prevent E. (From 1 and 3)

---

[50] We shall return to some of Bergmann's arguments in section 6.3.5.

If we like, we can make this reconstruction look even more like the evidential argument from evil, by casting it in terms of reasons why the world would not be non-arbitrarily improved if I were to prevent E. However, even the version that we have given makes the point clearly enough: our reasoning from *pro tanto* reasons to all things considered reasons always relies upon a 'noseeum' inference of just the kind that appears in our evidential argument from evil. If sceptical theism is sufficient to block 'noseeum' inferences about values, then we lose our ability to reason to all-things-considered conclusions about what to do.

If the case that I have argued is cogent, then the sceptical theist opponent of the evidential argument from evil has been placed in an uncomfortable position. The sceptical theist wants to be able to claim that it is not unlikely that there are unknown goods that would justify a perfect being in not preventing E. Yet if the considerations to which the sceptical theist appeals can establish this, then they will also suffice to establish that it is not unlikely that there are unknown goods that would justify us in not preventing E. But if we do believe that it is not unlikely that there are unknown goods that would justify us in not preventing E, then it is very hard to see how we could fail to be justified in not preventing E.

The key question, on my view, is not – as sceptical theists have typically supposed – whether there is reason to hold that it is not unlikely that there are goods outside our ken that would justify a perfect being in not preventing E; rather, the key question is whether there is reason to hold that it is not unlikely that there are goods outside our ken that would justify a perfect being in not preventing E *that is not also* reason to hold that it is not unlikely that there are goods outside our ken that would justify us in not preventing E. Perhaps unsurprisingly, most extant discussions in the literature are little help on this point. For instance, Howard-Snyder (1996c) gives two arguments for the claim that it is fairly likely that there are goods outside our ken that would have a role to play in the deliberations of a perfect being. However, even if those arguments – the *Progress* argument and the *Complexity* argument – are good reasons for thinking that there are goods outside our ken that have a role to play in the deliberations of a perfect being, those arguments are plainly of no help at all in establishing the conclusion that, while it is very unlikely that there are *unknown goods* that would be forgone if we were to prevent E, it is fairly likely that there are *unknown goods* that would be forgone if a perfect being were to prevent E. Yes – perhaps! – facts about axiological discoveries and the complexity of moral considerations make it likely that there are goods outside our ken that would not be outside a perfect being's ken; but those facts do not lend *any* significant support to the claim that, while it is very unlikely that there are unknown goods that would be forgone if we were to prevent E, it is not very unlikely that there are unknown goods that would be forgone if a perfect being were to prevent E.

Of course – as I noted at the beginning of this discussion – it might be that perfect-being theists have independent reasons for thinking that it is fairly likely that there are unknown goods that would be forgone if a perfect being were to prevent E; so I do not suppose – even if the considerations that I have urged thus far are cogent – that I have shown that the evidential argument from evil does succeed in establishing, or even in strongly supporting, the claim that there is no perfect being. However – unless I have made a mistake elsewhere in our assessment of the argument – it seems to me that I have now done enough to show that Bergmann's version of 'sceptical theism' does not provide a good response to the claim that the evidential argument from evil provides significant support for the claim that there is no perfect being.

6.3.5. First Possible Reply

Where might we have gone wrong in my argument? Well, one obvious suggestion is that I have not paid due attention to the fact that it makes a huge difference that it is not we but rather the perfect being who fails to prevent E. But what reason is there to believe that this difference is so important? If there are goods utterly beyond our ken – and if the motives and purposes of a perfect being are utterly beyond our ken – then it is hard to see that we have any reason to think that this is a relevant difference. Given that we have no knowledge of the goods at issue, surely it must be an entirely open question whether they can be secured by our failure to prevent E.

Perhaps it might be replied: we know that a perfect being would not make a world like *that*; indeed, we *know* that a perfect being would set things up so that great goods will be secured by our prevention of E. Really? And how is this alleged knowledge supposed to be compatible with our unutterable ignorance about the motives of a perfect being, and the goods that there might be? How do we get to know *these* things, while remaining ignorant about those other things that we are required not to know in order to have a reply to the evidential argument from evil? Surely, given what sceptical theists claim can be made of considerations like (ST1)–(ST3), they are obliged to maintain that we can assign no probability to the judgment that a perfect being would not make a world in which very great goods are secured by our failure to prevent E.

Perhaps it might be replied: there is a perfect being, and that being has revealed to us – by way of personal experience, scripture, and religious tradition – that the world is not set up in that way. By this kind of communication, the perfect being guarantees – or, anyway, makes it overwhelmingly likely – that there are no goods to be secured by our failure to prevent E. (Actually, the alleged commandments are typically stronger than that: we have a guarantee that the perfect being wants us to prevent events like E when they threaten to occur.) *But*, of course, in making this reply, one would be giving up the sceptical theist ambition: it is no longer true that it is merely considerations about our cognitive limitations that yield the desired conclusion.

The whole point of the sceptical theist response is that it is supposed to avoid appeal to the other evidence that theists claim to possess for the existence of a perfect being and the directives that that being makes in connection with our behaviour.

Perhaps it might be replied that there are significant relevant differences between what would be good for our creator to do and what would be good for us to do. Parents have certain rights over their children that other people do not. This arises from their being (to a limited extent) the source of their children's existence and well being. Hence, plausibly, parents have the right to send children to a neighbourhood school at which they will not be totally happy, for the benefit of the community as a whole. Strangers do not have those sorts of rights over our children. Plausibly, the state has certain rights over us that we do not have over each other – again, in virtue of its being a benefactor. If this is right, then a perfect being has far greater rights – in view of being a far greater benefactor – to allow us to suffer for the common good (e.g., to endure rape and murder), whereas we do not have those sorts of rights.

Many variants of this objection can be imagined. All seem to me to suffer from the same difficulty, namely, that the fact that there are differences between us and a perfect being with respect to goods of which we have knowledge is completely beside the point. The sceptical theist claim is that, in light of considerations like (ST1)–(ST3), we have good grounds for holding it not unlikely that there are *unknown* goods that are secured by the failure of a perfect being to prevent E. My claim is that, if this is right, then surely those same considerations give us good grounds for holding it not unlikely that there are unknown goods that will be secured by our failure to prevent E. Of course, I do not claim that it is the same unknown goods in each case (nor, even, do I claim that this is likely); that there are different agents involved may well make this further claim implausible. However, if we accept that – on the grounds given by Bergmann – it is not unlikely that *unknown goods* are secured by a perfect being's failure to prevent E, how can we deny that – on the grounds given by Bergmann – it is not unlikely that *unknown goods* will be secured by our failure to prevent E?

For the reason just given, I think that no appeal to the enormous differences between us and a perfect being can have any effect on our argument. So long as sceptical theists appeal to considerations that rule out all 'noseeum' inferences about values if they rule out any, their position will surely be vulnerable to the kind of reply that I have given.

6.3.6. Second Possible Reply

What else might have gone wrong with my argument? Well, another fairly obvious suggestion is that, while, in fact, (ST1)–(ST3) do justify us in accepting the conclusion that, for all we know, there are unknown goods that would be secured by our failure to prevent E, it does not follow that this is any threat to our ordinary moral practice.

I think that this suggestion is quite implausible: if (ST1)–(ST3) do justify us in accepting the sceptical theist conclusion, then – for the reasons given earlier – there is a massive impediment to our reasoning to the conclusion that we ought to try to prevent E. Of course, it is crucial not to mislocate the difficulty that I diagnose: I am not supposing that the sceptical theist is unable to assert that rape and murder are wrong, nor that the sceptical theist is unable to assert that we have a *pro tanto* duty to prevent rape and murder. Rather – to put the point a little tendentiously – my claim is that if you refuse to make any positive judgments about likelihoods, then you are unable to reason your way to decisions. To explain this contention, I shall begin with a case that has nothing to do with values.

Suppose I am trying to decide whether or not to have Weetbix for breakfast. It is possible that something very momentous – say, the outcome of the next *federal* election – turns on my choice. It is possible, too, that the relevant connections between my choice and the election outcome would be utterly obvious to a smarter and better informed creature while being utterly beyond my ken. However, when I engage in my deliberation, I – rightly – assign negligible probability to this possibility, and, in this way, am able to ignore it. Suppose, however, that I am sceptical about my entitlement to make probability judgments of this kind; suppose, that is, that I am not prepared to assign negligible probability – nor, indeed, any other kind of probability – to the claim that my having Weetbix for breakfast will determine that the Liberals win the next election. Then, it seems to us, I am not able to make a decision about what to do to which I can give first personal endorsement; whatever I do, I take seriously the idea that it might be the choice that determines the outcome of the next election to be the result that I desperately do not want. Of course, I can toss a coin – and, in that way, make a 'decision' – but I cannot use the resources that I have at hand in order to *reason* my way to a choice. (Pretend that we are expected utility maximisers. I can use the utility calculus to arrive at a decision only if I am prepared to assign probabilities – or *proper* probability intervals – to outcomes; if some outcomes are simply assigned the interval [0, 1], then – except in a small number of very special cases – calculation is stymied. Even for those who reject decision theory, this result ought to be suggestive.)

Now, of course, exactly the same point applies to values (and utilities). Suppose I'm trying to decide whether or not to perform a certain action – say, (try to) prevent the occurrence of E. It is possible that there are goods and evils about which I know nothing that attach to my performance or non-performance of the action. (Note that I do not assume that the value of the action is determined by its consequences; the values in question can be of any kind whatsoever.) It is possible, too, that these goods and evils about which I know nothing would be utterly obvious to a smarter and better informed creature. However, when I engage in my deliberation, I – rightly – assign negligible probability to this possibility and, in this way, am able to ignore it. Suppose, however, that I am sceptical about my entitlement to make probability judgments of this kind; suppose, that is, that I am not prepared to assign negligible probability – nor, indeed, any other kind of probability – to the claim that the total value of my permitting E is very high. Then, it seems to us, I am not able to make a decision about what to do to which I can give first personal endorsement; whatever I do, I take seriously the idea that the alternative course of action is the one that has the greater value. Of course, I can toss a coin – and, in that way, make a decision – but I cannot use the resources that I have at hand in order to reason my way to a choice. (Pretend, again, that we are expected utility maximisers. I can use the utility calculus to arrive at a decision only if I am prepared to assign values – or *proper* value intervals – to outcomes; if some outcomes are simply assigned the value interval $[-\infty, \infty]$, then – except in a small number of very special cases – calculation is stymied. Even for those who reject decision theory, this result ought to be suggestive.)[51]

In each case, there are alternatives to tossing a coin that amount to the same thing. I could, for example, 'calculate' by the goods of which I have knowledge, and in that way arrive at a 'decision'. (And, in the former case, I could calculate according to the causal considerations of which I have knowledge.) But, from the standpoint of everything that I believe and have reason to believe, these really are arbitrary choices; for, by hypothesis, I am supposed to be completely agnostic about the probability and value assignments that are assumed in order to make a decision possible.

If the forgoing argument is right, then there is a clear sense in which the sceptical theist argument against the evidential argument from evil, if cogent, does undermine our ordinary moral practice; for, if cogent, it undermines our ability to justify our engagement in perfectly ordinary kinds of moral reasoning. However, before I close this section, I shall consider

---

[51] Given the parenthetical asides at the conclusion of the present paragraph and the preceding paragraph, some readers may be tempted to suppose that my overall argument relies on the unjustified meta-ethical assumption that some version of consequentialism is correct. This supposition would be a mistake. As I noted earlier, my argument does not require me to suppose that the values of courses of action open to us are decided *merely* by the values of the consequences of those actions. I think it plausible that consequences are at least sometimes morally relevant considerations; but nothing in my argument requires me to assume even this much. No matter what view of values one takes, it is possible for one to be faced with a choice between a range of possible actions in circumstances in which one can do no more than attach probabilities to a range of possible future states of the world. To make decisions about what to do, one must then have some way of trading off competing values of actions – conflicting *pro tanto* duties, *pro tanto* rights, and the like – whether or not one thinks that the range of possible future states of the world has any bearing on the ultimate decision that one reaches.

some further claims that have been made on behalf of sceptical theism in connection with the claim that it undermines ordinary moral practice.

Bergmann argues for the claim that the sceptical theist argument poses no threat to ordinary moral practice on the grounds that one can quite consistently refuse to hold that it is unlikely that there are unknown goods secured by our refusal to prevent E, while nonetheless maintaining that our refusal to prevent E is morally wrong. For example, it could be that while goods and evils about which one knows give rise to *pro tanto* duties, unknown goods and evils do not. Hence, a perfect being, which knows all goods and evils, has an all-things-considered duty to permit E, while we have an all-things-considered duty to prevent it.

The particular suggestion plainly won't wash: even if we grant that unknown goods and evils cannot give rise to *pro tanto* duties, it is simply a mistake to suppose that the only factors that must be weighed when we determine what it is that we ought to do are our *pro tanto* duties. After all, apart from our *pro tanto* duties, we also have '*pro tanto* permissions' – rights and so on – that need to be weighed in our deliberations. Moreover – and this is the crucial point – there is always a 'noseeum inference' that is required in order to reach a result from our deliberations: we have to be able to infer from the fact that we can see no other relevant considerations (about duties, rights, interests, etc.) that there are no other considerations that are relevant to our deliberations. If we cannot assign a low probability to the claim that we have missed some relevant considerations, then we cannot claim that our deliberations have resulted in a clear verdict. But, of course, unknown goods – and unknown implicational relations involving goods – can give rise to 'permissions' (rights, etc.): while, perhaps, I cannot have duties that I do not know about, I plainly can have rights about which I am completely in the dark. So, to return to the case at hand, I do not require a competing *pro tanto* duty not to intervene in order to be justified in permitting E; rather, all I require is that I fail to attribute a sufficiently low probability to the claim that I have 'permissions' – rights, etc. – that outweigh my *pro tanto* duty to prevent E. If, for example, I cannot assign any likelihood to the claim that both I and the victim will benefit enormously if I do not attempt to prevent E, then how can I assign any likelihood to the claim that I have a *pro tanto* "permission" not to attempt to prevent E?

The reply that I have given to the particular suggestion carries over to Bergmann's more general argument as well. If there is a person who refrains from intervening in the case of E because they have internalised the sceptical theist's scepticism, and hence are unable to find a justification for intervening to which they can give first personal endorsement, then sceptical theists are simply in no position to say this person's failure to intervene is wrong. Bergmann makes it easy for himself by following Russell (1996) in considering a case in which a person fails to prevent E and merely lacks an appropriate motivating reason for doing so. However, even ignoring the point that, at most, these considerations establish that there is a *pro tanto* case for claiming that what the person does is wrong – after all, by the lights of sceptical theists, we can assign no likelihood to the claim that there are unknown goods that justify what the person does! – the crucial observation to make is that the success of the sceptical theist objection to evidential arguments from evil gives such a person all the motivating reason that they need. Or – more exactly – if the person whom we are considering accepts the sceptical theist objection to evidential arguments from evil, and if we do so as well, then we have no basis for claiming that their inaction is wrong: by their lights and ours, their moral reasoning to the conclusion that they lack sufficient reason to prevent E is impeccable.[52]

In sum, then, the sceptical theist response to evidential arguments to evil, if successful, really would pose a serious threat to ordinary moral practice. In any decision situation, we would be in the position of the person who is 'out of her depth' and who knows that she is 'out of her depth'. What is objectionable about this is not the thought that we might always be 'out of our depth', in the sense that we are unable to fully evaluate the considerations that bear on our decisions: for, of course, none of us can know all of the long-term consequences of any action we perform – no doubt there were all kinds of good deeds that were causally necessary for Hitler to be born – and to this extent we are always 'out of our depth' in deciding what to do. Rather, the problem is that, if we are always 'out of our depth' *and* if we are always aware that we are 'out of our depth', then we can never give first personal endorsement to any of our actions; moral deliberation can never end in anything more than the equivalent of tossing a coin. Unless we can give *sufficient* evaluation of the considerations that bear upon our decisions, we are not capable of reaching any embraceable moral decisions at all.

6.3.7. Alston's Critique

Suppose that my argument against Bergmann (2001) is good. Plainly enough, it doesn't follow immediately that no 'sceptical theist' response to evidential arguments from evil is good. After all, for all that I have argued so far, it could be that Bergmann rather incautiously defends a position more extreme than one that 'sceptical theists' are normally inclined to defend. Perhaps, when we look at the writings of Alston, Howard-Snyder, van

---

[52] Part of our complaint against Bergmann is that he simply assumes that one must have a positive motivating justification in order to perform an action, e.g., permitting E. But one can be justified in performing an action if the outcome of one's deliberation ends in deadlock; Buridan's ass is justified in eating the left bale of hay as a result of an arbitrary choice. Similarly, one influenced by the sceptical theist argument could be justified in permitting E as the result of an arbitrary choice, despite the absence of any more positive justification for the action.

Inwagen, Plantinga, Wykstra, and others, we shall find that the views that they defend are more subtle and nuanced than the extreme position that is defended by Bergmann.

And perhaps not. Since I don't have space to examine all of the remaining 'sceptical theists' here, I shall try to make our case only in connection with Alston (1991, 1996); however, I think that the generalisation from what I have to say about Alston is pretty straightforward. What I propose to argue is that, in fact, the position that Alston defends is open to exactly the same kind of objection that I have levelled at Bergmann.

Alston (1996) claims that it is evidently absurd to suppose that the fact that we cannot see what sufficient justifying reason an omniscient, omnipotent being may have for doing something provides strong support for the supposition that no such reason is available for that being. In support of this claim, he mentions two major kinds of considerations. First, it just seems wrong to take the insights attainable by finite fallible human beings as an adequate indication of what is available in the way of reasons to an omniscient, omnipotent being. Second, when we look for justifying reasons in the kind of case to which Rowe adverts, we are involved in an attempt to determine whether there is a so-and-so in a territory the extent and composition of which is largely unknown to us. (Alston (1991) provides the following further claims about this territory: (i) we lack data; (ii) we face greater complexity than we can handle; (iii) we face difficulties in determining what is possible; (iv) we are ignorant of the full range of possibilities; (v) we are ignorant of the full range of values; and (vi) there are limits to our capacity to make well-considered value judgments. Alston (1996) emphasises that it is not merely that there may be goods and evils that are unknown to us: it may also be that our grasp of the nature of goods known to us is not sufficient for us to properly assess their degree and kinds of value; and it may be that our grasp of the conditions of the realisation of known goods is insufficient for us to properly assess what would be required in order for a perfect being to bring about those goods.)

Alston's view, then, is that when we consider human cognitive limitations in a variety of spheres including the realm of value, we see that we have no reason to attribute substantial credibility to the claim that, if there were reasons why a perfect being would not non-arbitrarily improve the world if it prevented E, we would be able to find those reasons. Hence, in particular, we have no reason to attribute substantial credibility to the claim that, if there were goods – or connections between goods and evils – capable of justifying a perfect being in permitting E, then we would be able to find those goods – or connections between goods and evils. Moreover, Alston is also committed to the claim that, in consequence, this consideration of human cognitive limitations in a variety of human spheres including the realm of value is alone sufficient to block the inference from the claim that we can find no goods – or connections between goods and evils – that would justify a perfect being in permitting E to the conclusion that there are no goods – or connections between goods and evils – that would justify a perfect being in permitting E.

But if that is right, then it is clear that the argument that we deployed against Bergmann can also be deployed here. If those considerations about human cognitive limitations are alone sufficient to block the inference from the claim that we can find no goods – or connections between goods and evils – that would justify a perfect being in permitting E to the conclusion that there are no goods – or connections between goods and evils – that would justify a perfect being in permitting E, then those considerations are also alone sufficient to block the inference from the claim that we can find no goods – or connections between goods and evils – that would justify us in permitting E to the conclusion that there are no goods – or connections between goods and evils – that would justify us in permitting E. (As I noted above, Alston relies on the claim that we are ignorant of the full range of goods and evils; that we are ignorant of the full range of connections between goods and evils; that we lack data; that we face greater complexity than we can handle; that we are ignorant of the full range of possibilities; and that there are limits to our capacity to make well-considered value judgments. But if *these* claims are enough to block the inference in Rowe's argument, then surely they must be enough to block the corresponding inference in the case in which we are deciding whether to intervene to prevent E.)

Perhaps the position that Alston defends can also be attacked from another direction. Suppose that we agree that we can assign no probability to the claim that there is some great good that would be lost if a perfect being were to intervene to prevent the occurrence of E. How then can we pretend to be able to assign any probability to the claim that there is some great good that would be lost if *we* were to intervene to prevent the occurrence of E? Perhaps – for all we know – there are very great agent-centred goods that will be lost if we intervene. (Perhaps, for example, the agent will be denied salvation as a result of our intervention. Given our alleged ignorance about the motives of a perfect being, who can say?) Perhaps – for all we know – there are very great non-agent-centred goods that will be lost if we intervene. (Perhaps, for example, there are outweighing benefits that accrue to the attacker and to bystanders in the next life that will be lost if we intervene.[53] Again, given our alleged ignorance about the motives of a perfect being, who can say?) If we really – seriously! – think that we can assign no probability to the claim that our intervention to prevent E would disbar the victim from entry to heaven, then surely we have no way at all of

---

[53] Of course, were this so, it would be 'just one more instance of evil the reason for permitting which we cannot see' (cf. Alston (1996: 321)).

making a reasoned choice about whether or not to intervene. Yet if we are so ignorant about the motives of perfect beings, then how can we assign any probability to the claim in question?

6.3.8. Concluding Remarks

In conclusion, it may be useful to discuss some of the ways in which my argument may be misunderstood. The comments of an anonymous referee can serve as a useful foil here. The referee writes:

> [The author argues] against Bergmann to the effect that if his sceptical position has the intended force against the argument from evil, it will have a debilitating force on ethical reasoning generally. This argument seems to me to neglect a crucial difference between speculative and practical reasoning. [The author claims] that if we cannot know that God does not have a good reason to prevent a certain horrific evil, then we can't know that there is not a good reason for us to avoid preventing it even if we could. But the former point concerns an argument against the existence of God, a speculative (theoretical) activity in which we have no practical concern. We can't do anything about whether God exists, whether he prevents something, or what reasons he does or doesn't have. But the other point involves reflection on whether we should perform a certain action that is open to us. And here the lack of knowledge has a different bearing. Where we are faced with choice to perform A or not, we are, if we make a rational decision, forced to act on the best relevant knowledge we have. Even if we don't know that there isn't a good reason to abstain, it would be irrational to abstain from preventing the evil because of that epistemic possibility. Here we are forced, if we are rational, to make our decision on the basis of what we know (and rationally believe). Hence it would be foolish to avoid action because of something we don't know not to obtain. Whereas in the question of the existence or goodness of God, we are not called upon to make a practical decision to perform an (overt) action but only to evaluate an argument.

First, what I don't say. I *don't* argue that, if we can't know that there is not a good reason for us to avoid preventing E, then we have a reason not to prevent E. I *don't* argue that, if it is epistemically possible that there are outweighing goods that will be lost if we prevent E, then we have a reason not to prevent E. There are at least two difficulties here. First, the key questions are not particularly questions about knowledge (nor even, perhaps, rational belief). When faced with the decision about whether or not to perform an action, rational people act on the basis of the relevant considerations that are available to them (whether or not those considerations count as knowledge or even, perhaps, rational belief). Second, and more important, we have to be able to factor self-confessed ignorance into our process of deliberation. It need not be 'foolish to avoid action because of something we don't know not to obtain'. Suppose that we don't know that it is not the case that the floor boards are rotten (or, taking account of the previous point, that we are not prepared to make any estimation of whether or not it is the case that the floor boards are rotten). How can we then step with complete confidence onto the floor? In practical considerations – no less than in theoretical considerations – probabilities are the stuff of deliberation. And whereof one is not prepared to assign probabilities, thereof one is simply not able to deliberate. (Perhaps it is also worth noting that I object to the suggestion that 'lack of knowledge' has a different bearing in the case of theoretical reason than it does in the case of practical reason. True enough, in the case of theoretical reason one can suspend belief; whereas, in the case of practical reason, one must end with a 'decision' about what to do. However, the key point is that 'deliberation' can run out in just the same kind of way in both cases: because of the imperative to act, one may perform the equivalent of tossing a coin – something that would be reprehensible in the case of theoretical inquiry – but it should not be supposed that this counts as reasoning one's way to a decision.)

Second, what I do say. My central claim is that, if the considerations to which 'sceptical theists' appeal – considerations of human cognitive limitations in the realm of values (and perhaps elsewhere as well) – were alone sufficient to undermine the 'noseeum' inference in evidential arguments from evil, then those considerations would also be alone sufficient to undermine familiar and ordinary kinds of moral reasoning. If the kinds of considerations to which sceptical theists appeal entail that we can assign no probability to the claim that there are great goods that are secured by the failure of a perfect being to prevent E, then the kinds of considerations to which sceptical theists appeal also entail that we can assign no probability to the claim that there are great goods that are secured by our failure to prevent E. But if we can assign no probability to the claim that there are great goods that are secured by our failure to prevent E, then we cannot arrive at a reasoned view about whether or not to intervene to prevent E. And that's not an acceptable result.

Of course, as I have emphasised already, I do not suppose that these considerations – even if cogent – serve in any way to defend the claim that there are *successful* evidential arguments from evil. If the considerations advanced here are cogent, then – I think – they serve to defeat the sceptical theistic contention that one need only appeal to considerations about human cognitive limitations in the realm of values (and perhaps elsewhere as well) – and not to any further considerations whose standing is contested by non-theists – in order to demonstrate that no one can reasonably evaluate the relevant probabilities in the way that proponents of evidential arguments from evil typically do. Indeed, I would go further than this: I would suggest that it is highly implausible to suppose that there is any set of considerations that can be used to establish the contention that no one can reasonably evaluate the relevant probabilities in the way that proponents of evidential arguments from evil typically do. But defence of this stronger claim must wait for some other occasion.

6.4. THE PROBLEM OF HEAVEN (CO-WRITTEN WITH
YUJIN NAGASAWA AND NICK TRAKAKIS)

Belief in a paradisiacal afterlife is a central plank in orthodox theistic belief. On this view, death does not mark the end of the existence of at least some human beings; rather, for those human beings who are granted entry to heaven, it marks a transition to a new and highly desirable phase of existence. So, for example, Swinburne (1983: 39,43) contends that "Heaven is a place where people enjoy eternally a supremely worthwhile happiness" and that "[a] man in Heaven would be in a situation of supreme value".

However, details about the nature of heaven, and about the nature of the afterlife that its denizens enjoy, are controversial. Among the key questions there are at least the following: (1) Is there time in heaven? If so, is heaven temporally related to our universe? (2) Is there space in heaven? If so, is heaven spatially related to our universe? (3) Is there matter in heaven? If so, is the matter in heaven of the same kind as the matter in our universe? If so, are the laws that govern matter in heaven the same as the laws that govern matter in our universe?

Since heaven is assumed to be a place in which individual human beings continue their existence, it is plausible to suppose that those human beings who enter heaven continue their existence as individual conscious beings. True enough, some have maintained that in heaven there is a "merging" with God in which individual consciousness is lost; but, at least *prima facie*, on this kind of view there is no individual survival of death in an afterlife. For the purposes of the present section, I shall restrict my attention to the orthodox theistic belief that maintains that those human beings who enter heaven continue to exist as individual conscious beings (and, indeed, as individual, conscious *human* beings).

Given that heaven contains a community of individual, conscious, *human* beings, there is good reason to suppose that there is time, space, and matter in heaven.[54] The individuation of these beings requires some kind of space within which they occupy distinct locations; the consciousness of these beings requires a time within which states of consciousness can succeed one another; and the "being" of these beings requires some kind of matter from which they are constituted (and which can mediate communications between them).[55] Of course, even if this much is accepted, there are many

---

54 There are theists who hold that people "in" heaven are incorporeal entities located in neither space nor time. While it does not matter for the purposes of this chapter, I insist that it is very doubtful that one can make sense of the idea that human beings will have an afterlife in which they are incorporeal entities located in neither space nor time, and yet in which they continue to communicate, and to engage in friendly relationships with one another.

55 On the topic of the relationships among individual conscious human beings in heaven, Swinburne (1983: 43–4) writes: "According to Christian tradition, heaven will ... comprise friendship with good finite beings, including those who have been our companions on Earth".

alternative conceptions of heaven that remain open. On one view, heaven is merely a final segment of the universe that we currently inhabit; on a second view, heaven is a spatiotemporally separate "universe" (more or less like the one that we currently inhabit, with more or less similar matter and laws); on a third view, heaven is a distinct realm with "space", "time", and/or "matter" very different from that which is found in our universe.

One might think that, unless one takes the view that heaven is merely a final segment of the universe that we currently inhabit, there is no sense to be made of the idea that a single human being can have a pre-mortem existence on Earth and a post-mortem existence in heaven (cf. Flew (1984) and Martin (1997)). While I think that there are many promising ways of making sense of the idea in question – ranging from views that suppose that all one should care about is that one *survives* as a being in heaven (cf. Parfit (1984)) to views that suppose that God can ensure that there is the kind of causal connection between the stages of a being on earth and a being in heaven that makes it the case that these are all stages of a single being (cf. Lewis (1976)) – I do not propose to take up this interesting issue here. Rather, I propose to explore further problems that arise even if it is granted that there is sense to be made of the idea that a single human being can have a pre-mortem existence on earth and a post-mortem existence in heaven.

The difficulties that I have in mind arise when one tries to take account of the claim that existence in heaven is paradisiacal. According to the orthodox view that we are considering, heaven is a place in which there is no evil, and heaven is also a place that overflows with good. On the one hand, there are neither natural evils nor moral evils in heaven. On the other hand, there are goods in heaven that are very much greater – "incomparably greater", "infinitely greater" – than the goods that are available during life on earth. Moreover, according to the orthodox view, it is not an accidental matter that heaven has these characteristics: it is part of the *essence* of heaven that it should be a place in which there is no evil; and it is also part of the *essence* of heaven that it should be a place that overflows with good.

But – and now I turn to the problem that is the subject matter of the present section – if it is part of the *essence* of heaven that it should be a place in which there is no evil, then there is at least some reason to think that heaven must also be a place in which human beings have severely limited freedom of action. On the assumption that an agent is free to do an action of kind K in circumstances C *only if* it is within the power of the agent to perform such an action in those circumstances, it seems to follow straightforwardly, from the claim that it is necessarily true that there is no moral evil in heaven, that no agents are free to perform evil actions in heaven. Moreover, if heaven is a place that overflows with good – and, in particular, if heaven is as good as any place can possibly be – and if human beings have severely limited freedom of action in heaven, then there is at least some reason to think that morally significant freedom of action cannot be an overwhelmingly weighty good. If morally significant freedom of action really were such an important and weighty good, then surely there should be lots of it in heaven – and yet, if the above argument is cogent, then there is reason to think that there cannot be morally significant freedom of action in heaven.

6.4.1. Setting the Stage

There are various responses that one might make to the "problem of heaven". In particular: (1) one might dispute the claim that it is part of orthodox theism to suppose that heaven is essentially a place in which there is no evil; (2) one might reject the libertarian conception of freedom that we have presupposed; and (3) one might deny the claim that all weighty and important goods must be instantiated in heaven. We shall consider the prospects for each of these kinds of responses in turn.

However, before I turn to consider these responses, there is some more stage setting to be done. In particular, I need to say something more about which kinds of orthodox theists might be expected to be troubled by our "problem of heaven". While it might be thought that there is a general difficulty that is raised by the "problem of heaven", I am particularly interested in the capacity for this "problem" to make difficulties for proponents of free-will defences against logical arguments from moral evil, and for proponents of free-will theodicies.[56]

Consider, *first*, logical arguments from moral evil. There are many different formulations of logical arguments from moral evil; for the purpose of having a definite example before us, I shall work with the version that I developed in the second section of the present chapter:

1. Necessarily, a perfect being can choose to make an A-universe (Premise)
2. Necessarily, A-universes are non-arbitrarily better than other universes that contain free agents. (Premise)
3. Necessarily, if a perfect being chooses among options, and one option is non-arbitrarily better than the other options, then the perfect being chooses that option. (Premise)
4. Hence, necessarily, if a perfect being makes a universe that contains free agents, then it makes an A-universe. (From 1–3)

[56] Even more exactly, I am interested in the difficulties that arise for those who also assume some kind of libertarian *analysis* of freedom. There are those – e.g., Gaine (2003) – who propose that early Christians operated with a different analysis of freedom ("freedom for excellence") that can be employed in solving the general "problem of heaven". While I deny that this strategy is successful, I shall not try to defend this denial in the current chapter.

5. Our universe is not an A-universe. (Premise)
6. Hence, it is not the case that a perfect being made our universe. (From 4 and 5)

As I noted in that earlier section, various replies to this argument are possible. However, perhaps the best-known response is the free-will defence, which rejects the first premise. A perfect being is not necessarily able to choose to make a universe in which everyone always freely chooses the good (and yet a perfect being can nonetheless choose to make a universe that contains free agents).[57] This defence requires the assumption that it is logically impossible for agents to make free choices in a universe whose every contingent detail is chosen by a perfect being (and it also requires the assumption that freedom of choice is such a great good that a perfect being is justified in making a universe that contains free agents who make free choices even if that universe contains moral evils). But – and this is where the problem of heaven intrudes – if it is logically impossible for agents to make free choices in a universe whose every contingent detail is chosen by a perfect being, then it follows that agents have free choices in heaven only if it is not the case that the choices of a perfect being completely determine the nature of heaven. But if the choices of a perfect being fail to completely determine the nature of heaven, then why is it the case that heaven is *essentially* a place in which there is no moral evil? Or, to turn to a closely related point: if a perfect being is unable to choose to make a universe in which everyone always freely chooses the good, then how is it that a perfect being is able to choose to make a heaven in which everyone always freely chooses the good?[58]

Consider, *second*, free-will theodicies. There are different versions of free-will theodicies, but they have in common the ambition to show that it is *possible* (at least for all that we know, or, at any rate, for all that we reasonably believe) that the kinds and amounts of evils that are found in the universe are permitted by a perfect being as a trade-off against the goods that are realised through the existence of a universe in which there are free agents who make morally significant free choices. But if there is no freedom in heaven, then it seems that theists must suppose that it is possible for very great goods – "infinitely great", "incomparably great" – to be realised in a domain in which there is no freedom. Yet if that is right, then it is not entirely

[57] Given the libertarian conception of freedom, it seems to follow that, necessarily, a perfect being is not able to choose to make a universe in which everyone always freely chooses the good. But this claim entails the denial of the first premise in the logical argument from evil given in the text: it is not necessarily that case that a perfect being can choose to make a universe in which everyone always freely chooses the good.
[58] Throughout this paragraph – and, indeed, throughout this section – I use the word "universe" to denote that part of the perfect being's creation that does not overlap with heaven. So, if there is no heaven, then the universe is all of the perfect being's creation; otherwise, the universe is less than all that the perfect being creates.

clear that we still have the right to claim that freedom is a great good, or that it is a sufficiently great good to justify the kinds and amounts of evils that are found in the universe. If there can be an abundance of goods without either freedom or evil, then what justification could a perfect being have for making a universe like ours?

For the sake of definiteness, the "argument from heaven" can be set out as follows:

1. Necessarily, there is no evil in heaven. (Premise, justified by appeal to the orthodox conception of heaven)
2. If there is morally significant freedom in heaven, then it is not the case that, necessarily, there is no evil in heaven. (Premise, justified by appeal to the libertarian conception of freedom)
3. (Therefore) There is no morally significant freedom in heaven. (From 1 and 2)
4. Heaven is a domain in which the greatest goods are realised. (Premise, justified by appeal to the orthodox conception of heaven)
5. (Therefore) The greatest goods can be realised in a domain in which there is no morally significant freedom. (From 3 and 4)
6. (Therefore) A perfect being can just choose to make a domain that contains the greatest goods and no evil. (From 5, appealing to the omnipotence of a perfect being)
7. A world that contains the greatest goods and no evil is non-arbitrarily better than any world that contains the greatest goods, *incomparably* lesser goods, and the amounts and kinds of evils that are found in our universe. (Premise)
8. If a perfect being chooses among options, and one option is non-arbitrarily better than the other options, then the perfect being chooses that option. (Premise)
9. (Therefore) It is not the case that a perfect being made our universe. (From 6–8)

Note that Premise 7 can be justified in the following way. On the one hand, the amounts and kinds of evils to be found in our universe are obviously non-negligible when compared with the amounts and kinds of evils to be found in a universe in which there is no evil. On the other hand, the goods to be found in a world in which there are only the goods of heaven differ only negligibly from the goods to be found in a world in which there are the goods of heaven and the goods of our universe. (Why? Because the goods of heaven are "incomparably" – "infinitely", "immeasurably" – greater than the goods of our universe. When we consider the overall good of our world, the goods of our universe register only infinitesimally.) The inference from 5 to 6 could be strengthened and clarified, but I shall leave this for some other time, since I don't expect that the argument will be open to serious challenge at this point.

6.4.2. There could be Evil in Heaven

It seems plausible to claim that, if one rejects the assumption that heaven is essentially a place in which there is no evil, then the "problem of heaven" evaporates. However, it seems to me that the claim that there is evil in heaven simply runs counter to orthodox belief in these matters.[59] So I conclude that the position to which this suggestion leads is that it is merely a matter of contingent fact that there is no evil in heaven: there could have been evil in heaven, but as a matter of fact there isn't.

There are various reasons why orthodox theists might not be content with this proposal. Perhaps the most pressing problem is that the prospects seem poor for a really satisfying explanation of why it happens *actually* to be the case that there is no evil in heaven, given that it is merely a matter of contingent fact that this is so.[60] Indeed, if we suppose that God and heaven are both in time, and if we suppose that there are no truths about future contingents, then it seems that we cannot claim that it is true that there will be no evil in heaven: there is not yet any fact of the matter about whether there is evil in heaven at some future time.

One option here might be to follow the Molinist version of the free-will defence developed in Plantinga (1974) and discussed above. Suppose that there are true counterfactuals of freedom, and that the truth of these counterfactuals of freedom is not something that can just be chosen by a perfect being. For all we know, it is logically possible that, when a perfect being comes to create contingent things, it has open to it the option of making a universe in which free creatures freely go wrong that is conjoined to a heaven in which free creatures always freely go right, but it does not have open to it the option of making a universe in which free creatures always freely go right. (In Plantinga's terms, even though all of the creaturely essences that the perfect being can instantiate suffer from transworld depravity, at least some of those essences have possible instantiations in which their "final segments" always go right.) It is not clear that this proposal makes any *additional* difficulties for Molinism; however, as I have already argued, I think that there are very good independent reasons not to adopt a Molinist version of the free-will defence.

Perhaps the most promising option for those inclined to the line that it is merely a matter of contingent fact that there is no evil in heaven is this. Suppose that neither God nor heaven is in time (i.e., neither God nor

---

[59] I could find no clear scriptural evidence either way. Consider, for example, Luke 12: 33–4: "heaven is a place where no thief comes and no moth destroys [a treasure]". This passage is neutral on the question of whether what is here described is an essential property of heaven.

[60] Swinburne (1983: 44) writes: "The character needed for the inhabitants of heaven is that of perfect goodness". If this is true, then it is possible in principle that heaven is free from evil actions. However, it is not at all clear what sort of mechanism guarantees that there *can* be no evil in heaven.

heaven is located in the spatio-temporal network within which we are all located). Suppose further that there are true claims to be made about future contingents, and that what makes those claims true (at least in some cases) is what actually happens at those future times. In that case, it could be *true* that there are free agents in heaven, and that those free agents always freely choose the good, but that it is merely a matter of contingent truth that those free agents always freely chose the good. So far, so good. But supposing that there are free agents in heaven, and that they do all always freely choose the good, is there an explanation of why it is that they behave in this way? Given that we are talking about human beings, and given what we know about human nature, the odds that a large group of human beings will all freely choose the good for any extended length of time are astronomical. Indeed, given that moral evils extend to include even the slightest moral peccadilloes, the odds are strongly against even one human being freely choosing nothing but the good for any extended length of time. But if this is right, then the likelihood that free human agents in heaven all always freely choose the good is vanishingly small. (And this is so even if there are very few human agents in heaven.) But if the odds that free human agents in heaven all always freely choose the good are astronomical, then why is it the case that free human agents in heaven do in fact always freely choose the good?

At this point, some theists might be tempted to say that a perfect being can play a helping hand in bringing it about that free human agents in heaven always freely choose the good.[61] (Let's not worry about the details here, since they won't matter for our discussion.[62]) There is an obvious difficulty with any suggestion along these lines. If the perfect being can play a helping hand in bringing it about that free human agents in heaven always freely choose the good, then surely a perfect being can do exactly the same for

---

[61] Others might dig in their heels and insist that one goes to heaven only if, at death, one is a mature person in whom will, intellect, inclination, and nature are all perfectly attuned to the good – i.e., someone who has *zero* probability of making bad choices. There are at least two points to make here. First, as above, I suggest that, if this is what it takes, then there aren't any people in heaven: it is not credible to suppose that there has ever been a mere human being who, at death, was such that their probability of making bad choices was *zero*. Second, given that we are supposing that it is possible for these people to make bad choices even though there is zero probability that the bad choices be made, it seems that we still won't have ruled out evil in heaven: for, given an infinite number of choices, it is very likely that some choices with zero probability will be made. Moreover, given that you have libertarian freedom, the fact that your will, intellect, inclination, and nature are all perfectly attuned to the good will not prevent you from making some bad choices, if you are given enough choices to make.

[62] Perhaps, for example, God removes all sources of temptation in heaven; or perhaps God ensures that the denizens of heaven never have the opportunity to exercise their ability to choose the bad. (According to Gaine(2003), Scotus adopted something like the first of these accounts, and Ockham adopted something like the second.)

free human agents on earth. But, in that case, it seems that free-will defences against logical arguments from evil and free-will theodicies are in serious trouble. So the prospects of allowing the perfect being to extend a helping hand in heaven do not seem bright. But it is hard to see where else to turn in looking for an explanation of the fact that free human agents in heaven all always freely choose the good.

Another suggestion that some theists might be inclined to offer is that the paradisiacal nature of the heavenly environment explains why, as a matter of fact, the human inhabitants of heaven do not sin. Given that heaven is an environment that is free from temptation and filled with the presence of divinity, surely we have the materials for an explanation of why even those with a substantial inclination to wander from the path of righteousness do not in fact wander at all. There seem to be two problems with this approach. First, given what we know about human nature, *even* given the absence of temptation and the presence of divinity, it *still* seems extraordinarily unlikely that *free* human agents will survive an eternity without *ever* straying from the path of righteousness. And second, if the absence of temptation and the presence of divinity are not incompatible with the existence of significant freedom, then what explanation is to be given of the presence of temptation and the absence of divinity in the earthly existence of free human agents? Given these problems, it does not seem plausible to suppose that one can appeal to the nature of the heavenly environment in order to explain the contingent absence of evil from heaven.

Perhaps there is some other way in which theists might seek to defend the thesis that it is merely contingently true that there is no evil in heaven. However, at the very least, it is not easy to see how such a defence would go. In the absence of any further suggestion, it seems to me that we can conclude that the prospects for salvation from the "problem of heaven" along this route are not terribly bright. (Some people – e.g., Martin (1997) – have also wanted to press an epistemological objection against the view that we have been exploring in this section. Given that it is a contingent matter whether there is evil in heaven, what reason do we have for believing that there is no evil in heaven, or indeed, what reason do we have for believing that life in heaven is in any way better than life on earth? It would take me too far away from my main line of inquiry to try to assess this objection here.)

6.4.3. Libertarian Freedom

The problem of heaven that I have developed relies upon the assumption that theists are committed to a particularly simple libertarian analysis of freedom. More generally, it relies on the assumption that there are really only two options when it comes to the analysis of freedom: either one is a libertarian (of the simple kind that we have identified) or one is a compatibilist. If one is a compatibilist, then, I think, one should suppose that, necessarily, a perfect being can choose to make a universe in which everyone always freely chooses the good. And if one accepts this assumption, then the logical argument from evil looks very powerful indeed. (Perhaps one might object that, while a compatibilist is obliged to allow that free choices can be completely determined by prior laws and conditions, the compatibilist can insist that it is not possible for free choices to be completely determined by the prior choices of an agent. So, if we consider two (more or less) duplicates of a deterministic universe, one of which has its laws and initial conditions chosen by a perfect being, and the other of which has uncaused laws and initial conditions, then there are no free choices made by the beings in the former universe, and lots of free choices made by the beings in the latter universe. Perhaps this view can be defended; however, I shan't try to pursue *that* line of thought here.)

Even if I am right that the simple libertarian analysis of freedom leads into the difficulties that I have described, all is not lost. For there may be alternative analyses of freedom that are open to theists to adopt. In particular, the suggestion of Sennett (1999) deserves serious consideration.

According to Sennett, the simple libertarian analysis of freedom should be replaced with a more sophisticated alternative. Recall that the simple libertarian analysis with which I began places the following necessary condition on free action: *an agent is free to do an action of kind K in circumstances C only if it is within the power of the agent to perform such an action in those circumstances.* (Perhaps we can strengthen this necessary condition to a necessary and sufficient condition: *an agent is free to do an action of kind K in circumstances C if and only if it is entirely within the power of the agent whether or not to perform such an action in those circumstances.* Two points should be noted about this suggestion. First, if it is within the power of the agent whether or not to perform the action in "the circumstances", then "the circumstances" cannot determine the action. Second, there may be much in "the circumstances of the action" that is not under the control of the agent; what matters is whether, *given* those "circumstances", it is entirely up to the agent whether or not to perform the action.)

Sennett's proposal begins with the suggestion that we adopt instead the following necessary condition on free action: *an agent is free to do an action of kind K in circumstances C only if either (1) the action is free according to the simple libertarian analysis or (2) somewhere along the causal history that leads the agent to perform that action there is another action that is free according to the simple libertarian analysis.* Given this suggestion, it is not ruled out that agents in heaven have freedom of action even though they do not have simple libertarian freedom of action. But why should we suppose that there can be free actions that are not free according to the simple libertarian analysis and yet are free because, somewhere in the causal history that leads to the performance of that action, there is another action that is free according to the simple libertarian analysis?

Sennett's answer to this question turns on considerations about the formation of character. Suppose that it is the case that certain choices that are free according to the simple libertarian analysis play a decisive role in the formation of (certain aspects of) one's character of a kind that support the claim that one has freely chosen (those aspects of) one's character. In this case – and in this case alone – if one's character then determines the actions that one subsequently goes on to perform, it is not ruled out that those subsequent actions are freely chosen (even though they are fully determined by character and circumstance).

So the picture that emerges is this. The actions that human agents perform in heaven are fully determined by their characters and the circumstances in which they find themselves; consequently, human agents in heaven do not have simple libertarian freedom. Nonetheless, human agents in heaven have characters (aspects of) that are as they are *solely* because of previous choices made by those agents during their lives on earth, where those previous choices did exhibit simple libertarian freedom. Consequently, the choices that are made by human agents in heaven are free, even though it is logically impossible for those choices to be evil choices.[63]

I think that this picture is unbelievable. It is not plausible to think that there are – or ever have been – *any* people whose characters are such that, when they die, it is logically impossible for them to make evil choices. It is also not plausible to think that there are – or ever have been – *any* people whose characters are such that, when they die, the features of those characters that bear on any choice that that person might be called upon to make in heaven are as they are *solely* because of libertarian free choices that that person made during his life. And it is even less plausible to think that there are – or ever have been – any people whose characters are such that, when they die, the features of those characters that bear on any choice that that person might be called upon to make in heaven are as they are *solely* because they were consciously and deliberately (and freely) chosen to be that way by the person in question.

Sennett might object that I have misrepresented his view in insisting that the relevant choices have to be the *sole* determinants of character. Indeed, Sennett himself explicitly denies that this is the case towards the end of his paper: "There is room for some kind of doctrine of sanctification, whereby God supplies upon our deaths whatever is lacking in our character formations to bring us to the state of compatibilist free perfection" (77). But this can't be right. If we can act freely by acting on an aspect of character that has

---

[63] Following Kvanvig (1997), we might say that Sennett relies upon the "reward model" – according to which only those who perform good actions are permitted entry to heaven – in order to resolve "the problem of heaven". However, it is worth noting that that entry requirement seems rather more demanding than versions of the "reward model" that are discussed in other contexts.

been given to us by a perfect being, then we simply do not have a reply to the problem of heaven: the perfect being can after all just give us characters that determine that we will always do the good. Sennett claims that "it is the pattern we establish throughout a life of intentional character building that is critical – not our actually attaining the desired character itself in our lifetimes. By establishing such a pattern we are, in effect, giving God permission to fill in the gap $(77/8)$". But the perfect being doesn't *need* permission from us to "fill in the gaps", that is, to endow us with character traits different from those that we actually possess. On the assumption that it is possible for a perfect being to endow us with character traits different from those that we actually possess without impairing our ability to make free choices, it can hardly make any difference to the perfect being what kind of character it begins to work upon.

Perhaps Sennett might insist that there is an important distinction between cases to be drawn here. While a perfect being can endow us with *some* different character traits without impairing our ability to make free choices, there are limits within which the perfect being is required to work. In particular, the perfect being can remove *all* of our remaining character flaws at the ends of our lives without impairing our (significant) freedom only if there have been the *right kinds* of changes in our character traits over the course of our lifetimes. So, consider a person who is very far from perfect at the moment of death, but who has undergone the right kinds of changes for the perfect being to remove all of his or her character flaws and admit him or her to heaven. Suppose, too, that the perfect being makes a duplicate of the perfected person, and admits this duplicate to heaven. (The duplicate has all of the intrinsic properties of the perfected person, but lacks the relational properties of the perfected person to prior states of the world.) On Sennett's account, the actions of the perfected person in heaven are (significantly) free and yet the actions of the duplicate are not. Surely, that's not right. After all, if we imagine the perfect being duplicating the perfected person at an earlier stage of their earthly existence, and placing the duplicate on earth, we don't have any reason at all to deny that the duplicate is capable of acting freely. Indeed, to take an extreme case, we can imagine this duplication taking place before the (to be) perfected being has made any free decisions at all (i.e., when it is a young infant). Here, it would be more than passing strange to deny that only the duplicate being is incapable of (significant) free actions. Given the – surely very plausible – principle that any (intrinsic) duplicate of a creature that is capable of free actions is itself capable of free actions, the claim that Sennett is making here cannot be defended.

On the basis of these considerations, we can conclude that, even if we were to accept Sennett's modified conception of freedom, we would not have an adequate reply to the problem of heaven in the materials that he supplies.

This is not to say that there are not many other difficulties that confront the suggestion that Sennett makes; that is, I do not suppose that the above discussion is in any way exhaustive, and nor do I suppose that that there is not some other set of considerations that would also support my conclusion. However, I do think that the points that I have made suffice to show that we should not be quick to embrace Sennett's proposed solution to the "problem of heaven". (One question that I can't resist drawing attention to concerns the fate of those who die in infancy. Are they doomed to an eternity of dribbling and drooling, with no opportunity to grow into mature agents? Are they simply excluded from heaven? Are they admitted to heaven, but denied the capacity for free agency (under Sennett's revised conception of freedom)? Or what?)

6.4.4. Great Goods That Are Not Heavenly Goods

The third response to the problem of heaven that I propose to discuss turns on the observation that it is not at all obvious that all weighty and important goods must be instantiated in heaven. (For an intimation of this kind of response, see Taliaferro (1998: 315). For a more fully worked out version of this approach, see Swinburne (1983).) Suppose, for the sake of ease of exposition, that a perfect being has to choose between two alternatives. On the one hand, it can make a realm of contingent things that consists of nothing but heaven (a place in which there is no freedom, but in which various goods are realised and in which there is no evil). On the other hand, it can make a realm of contingent things that has two parts: first, a universe (in which there are free agents that make free choices, and in which there is a considerable quantity and variety of evils); and second, heaven (in which there is no freedom, but in which various great goods are realised in the absence of any evil). At least in the abstract, there seems to be no reason why it is impossible for a perfect being to choose the second alternative over the first: perhaps, for example, freedom is such an important good that the second alternative is better than the first despite the various evils that are present in the second alternative.

An obvious objection to this suggestion is that it appears to run counter to the orthodox view that we described in setting up our problem of heaven. On what I take to be the orthodox conception of heaven, the goods of heaven are supposed to be incommensurably *greater* than the goods that are available on Earth. In particular, then, if there is no freedom in heaven, then there must be goods in heaven that are incommensurably greater than the good of freedom. And if that is so, then it can hardly be the case that freedom is a particularly great good. Moreover, if the goods of heaven can be realised in the absence of the good of freedom, then it is hard to see how the claim that the second alternative that we have described can be better than the first. On the one hand, there is the possibility of making a world in which there is nothing but great goods (and no evil). On the other hand, there is the possibility of making a world that contains the goods of the first world, together with some incommensurably lesser goods, and some evils (whose magnitude is at least comparable to the lesser goods). Since freedom is not a particularly important good – by comparison with the goods of heaven – it seems reasonable to hold that there is a strong case for preferring the first alternative. Why introduce suffering in the pursuit of goods that have no more than the most marginal – indeed, very likely, infinitesimal – utility?[64]

The argument of the preceding paragraph relied on the assumption that the goods of heaven are incommensurably greater than the goods of earth, even if it turns out that there is no freedom in heaven. But perhaps it might be said that this assumption is mistaken. If we suppose that the good of freedom is greater than the goods of heaven, then we might be able to explain why the creation of heaven and earth should be preferred to the creation of heaven alone and to the creation of earth alone. However, this supposition does seem to fly in the face of orthodox assumptions about the goods of heaven. Most theists do not suppose that the possession of libertarian freedom is the greatest good, to which no other goods come near. (Note that it probably won't be enough for the purposes of the present objection to claim that the good of freedom is on a par with the goods of heaven. For, in that case, since the goods of heaven can be had without concomitant evils while (we are supposing) the good of freedom cannot, it still seems that the creation of heaven alone would be best.)

One response that might be made to the argument of the present section is that no theist has ever supposed that there is more than one incommensurable good, namely, eternal fellowship with the perfect being. This good is both incommensurable and intrinsic, that is, it is something that is incommensurably good, and good in and of itself. On the other hand, the good of (significant) freedom is neither incommensurable nor intrinsic: (significant) freedom is merely an extrinsic good that makes possible various other goods, including eternal fellowship with the perfect being. More exactly, the idea is that (significant) freedom makes possible the good of *entering into* eternal fellowship with the perfect being, though it is not required for *continued* fellowship with that being. (If it were required for continued fellowship, then heaven would not be essentially a place in which there is no

---

[64] It might be suggested that I should consider here the possibility that the greatness of goods depends upon that to which the goods are attributed: perhaps freedom is a great good relative to earth, but not a great good relative to heaven. If we were to suppose that freedom is a greater good, relative to the fusion of heaven and earth, than are the goods of heaven relative to that fusion, then we would indeed have the makings of an objection to our argument: but who would want to make that assumption?

evil.) But if continued fellowship with the perfect being is possible without (significant) freedom, then surely there can be beings that have always (or eternally) been in continued fellowship with the perfect being; that is, surely the perfect being can just choose to make creatures that are always (or eternally) in continued fellowship with it.[65] Note that this point needn't rely on a contestable assumption about the possibility of actual infinities: what is proposed is that either the perfect being can just make creatures that are in fellowship with it from the first instant of their creation and hence that have never entered into such fellowship, *or* the perfect being can make creatures with an infinite past who, at each instant, are in continuing fellowship with the perfect being despite never having entered into fellowship with that being.

Perhaps it will be replied that an intrinsic duplicate of the heavenly part of a world won't necessarily contain continuing fellowship between the perfect being and the creatures of heaven: whether there is perfect fellowship between the perfect being and the creatures of heaven depends upon whether those creatures made certain kinds of (significantly) free choices prior to their entry to heaven. But this just seems wrong. Suppose that John and Mary love one another. Suppose that they are about to be sent off into space to begin the task of populating a distant galaxy. At the last moment, John and Mary are duplicated, and their duplicates, John* and Mary* are sent off instead (though, of course, John* and Mary* are not made aware of the fact that they are merely duplicates of John and Mary). It is surely hard to deny that John* and Mary* love one another from the very first moment of their existence when they wake up together on board the spaceship – and yet this seems to be precisely the conclusion that the response that we are now considering would require us to embrace. Moreover, exactly the same point would be true if John* and Mary* were not the products of a process of duplication, but were rather the products of advanced biological engineering: from the moment that they wake up together in the spaceship, they love one another. But what goes for "human fellowship" goes for "perfect fellowship" as well: whether there is perfect fellowship in heaven does *not* depend upon the prior history of the universe.

I conclude that, if significant freedom is supposed to be an incommensurably lesser good than eternal fellowship in heaven, then there is no good reason to suppose that significant freedom is required to be instantiated at some earlier stage in the history of the universe in order to make it possible for the good of eternal fellowship to be instantiated in heaven.

---

[65] It might be wondered whether the argument at this point depends upon the assumption that freely chosen continued fellowship is not better than non–freely chosen continued fellowship. The answer is that it does not. What is assumed is that, *given* that freedom is merely a finite and extrinsic good, if a perfect being can choose between non–freely chosen fellowship without evil and freely chosen fellowship with evil, then it will choose the former.

6.4.5. Concluding Remarks

Stump (1999: 53) claims that "a more promising foundation for a solution to the problem of evil . . . might be found if we consider a broad range of beliefs concerning the relations of God to evil in the world which are specific to a particular monotheism". The beliefs that seem especially relevant to Stump are the following three:

1. Adam fell;
2. Natural evil entered the world as a result of Adam's fall;
3. After death, depending on their state at the time of their death, either (a) human beings go to heaven or (b) human beings go to hell.

Stump's proposal includes more than the suggestion that there is a paradisiacal afterlife – and so there may be other ways in which it can be argued that the set of propositions that she proposes for explicit acceptance is inconsistent. However, it is at any rate clear that Stump's proposal is vulnerable to the problem of heaven that has been the subject matter of our section.

There is a general point here (and it applies to many other recent discussions of arguments from evil). If we take seriously the question of whether (say) the proposition that God exists is consistent with the proposition that there is moral evil in the world, then we shall also take seriously the question of whether any set of propositions that contains these two is consistent. That someone who accepts (1)–(3) will be naturally inclined to accept both that God exists and that there is evil in the world – perhaps because (1)–(3) entail that God exists and that there is evil in the world – gives us no additional reason to suppose that the proposition that God exists is after all consistent with the proposition that there is moral evil in the world, *unless* we have good reason to suppose that (1)–(3) – together with the propositions that God exists and that there is moral evil in the world – themselves form a logically consistent set. But – as our discussion of the problem of heaven is intended to demonstrate – it is quite clearly no more certain that (1)–(3) – together with the propositions that God exists and that there is moral evil in the world – form a logically consistent set than it is that the existence of God is compatible with the existence of moral evil in the world.

While there is much more that can be said about the matters that have been discussed in this section, I think that I have done enough to show that there is serious reason to be doubtful that either proponents of free-will defences against arguments from evil or proponents of free-will theodicies will find salvation in heaven.[66] That is to say, there is serious reason to doubt

---

[66] Historical footnote: Bob Adams has suggested that Augustine is a good example of someone who might be seriously taxed by the "problem of heaven". Augustine seems to have made all of the assumptions that I have claimed are jointly inconsistent. On the one hand, he endorses a free-will theodicy; on the other hand, he also claims that when human beings enter heaven (the Kingdom of God) they are unable to sin (*non posse peccare*), which means that there

that Stump's 'promising foundation for a solution to the problem of evil' really does have the makings of a plausible response to 'logical' arguments from evil. However, of course, that's not to say either that there is no other response that theists can give to 'logical' arguments from evil or that there is no satisfactory response that theists can make to the problem of heaven. Still less is this to say that the problem of heaven poses an insuperable objection to belief in a more or less orthodoxly conceived monotheistic god.

6.5. CONCLUDING REMARKS

As I mentioned at the outset, I see no reason to suppose that there are *successful* arguments from evil, that is, arguments that ought to bring those who suppose that there is an orthodoxly conceived monotheistic god to change their minds on this matter. While I am myself inclined to give very little credence to the suggestion that our universe – with all its miseries and woes – is the creative product of an omnipotent, omniscient, and perfectly good orthodoxly conceived monotheistic god, I see no reason at all to suppose that I can construct an *argument* from evil that ought to persuade those who disagree with me, not only in this judgment, but in numerous related judgments about, for example, the reliability of scripture, the strength of testimony to the miraculous, the import of various kinds of religious experiences, the prospects for explaining the existence of the world and its apparent fine-tuning for life in terms of the creative activities of an orthodoxly conceived monotheistic god, and so on and so forth. How one reasonably assesses the bearing, of the obtaining of states of affairs that orthodox theists suppose are properly said to be instances of 'evil', on the hypothesis that there is an orthodoxly conceived monotheistic god, depends upon the views that one reasonably takes about very many other considerations that one (reasonably) takes to be relevant.

Finally, as I noted in passing, there is really only way important way in which considerations about the infinite bear on the assessment of problems of evil, namely, in the assessment of the claim that there is no best world that an omnipotent, omniscient, and perfectly good creator can make. Those who respond to 'logical' arguments from evil by relying on the claim that there is an infinite sequence of possible worlds, each better than the next – so

---

is no freedom in heaven. However – as two anonymous referees pointed out – it is open to question whether Augustine accepted a libertarian account of freedom. Since a similar question arises in the case of Aquinas, we might do better to point to Scotus, Ockham, and Suarez as good examples of people who are *obviously* seriously taxed by the "problem of heaven". Of course, nothing in the argument that I have been pursuing turns on the issue of whether there actually have been people who have accepted all of the assumptions that create the "problem of heaven": the key point is that proponents of free-will defences against arguments from evil and proponents of free-will theodicies who seek salvation in heaven have work to do to explain how their position does not collapse into inconsistency.

that it cannot be true that an orthodoxly conceived monotheistic god has an obligation to create *the best* possible world that it is capable of creating – cannot suppose there is some *conceptual* problem that militates against the existence of infinite collections: for there actually are, on this view, infinitely many distinct choices that an orthodoxly conceived monotheistic god *could* make.

7

Other Arguments

The arguments discussed in this chapter are a grab-bag. In a truly exhaustive study, there would be no kind of argument for or against the existence of monotheistic gods not examined in preceding chapters that is not examined here.[1] However, there are simply too many different arguments out there in the literature to make it feasible to attempt such a task here. I think that it is important to examine each argument that is proposed on its merits. Even if it is true that there are useful taxonomies of arguments for and against the existence of monotheistic deities, and even if it is true that there are criticisms that can be applied to whole families of these arguments, one needs to look carefully at each argument to determine where it belongs in the taxonomy that one has established.

I divide the arguments to be examined in this chapter into six kinds, the last of which is intended to pick up all of the arguments that fail to fall into the first five categories. In short, we shall consider: arguments from *authority*, arguments from *religious experience*, arguments from *morality*, arguments from *miracles*, arguments from *consciousness*, and arguments from *'puzzling phenomena'*. For each of these categories, we shall discuss a representative selection of arguments that can be found either in the current philosophical literature or in current debate more widely construed.

---

[1] Perhaps this claim is something of an exaggeration. There are, after all, many arguments for and against the existence of monotheistic gods that are nothing more than amusements for first-year philosophy students. For instance:

    1. Nothing is greater than an orthodoxly conceived monotheistic god.
    2. Anything that exists is greater than nothing.
    3. An orthodoxly conceived monotheistic god is not greater than itself.
    4. (Hence) There is no orthodoxly conceived monotheistic god.

    At the very least, it seems reasonable to restrict the scope of our inquiry to arguments for and against the existence of (orthodoxly conceived) monotheistic gods that have been taken seriously by some people who have thought a bit about these matters.

There are many different ways in which appeals to authority have been alleged to provide support for belief in the existence of monotheistic gods. We shall do no more than sample from the range of available arguments in the following discussion.

7.1.1. Common Consensus

There are various different ways in which one might try to argue from common consensus that there is an orthodoxly conceived monotheistic god to the conclusion that there is an orthodoxly conceived monotheistic god. The most flat-footed argument of this kind runs as follows:

1. Everyone believes that such-and-such orthodoxly conceived monotheistic god exists.
2. Propositions that everyone believes must be true.
3. (Therefore) Such-and-such orthodoxly conceived monotheistic god exists.

Both of the premises in this argument are problematic, though the first is clearly much harder to defend than the second. It seems to me that it is impossible to mount a serious defence of the first premise. On their admission, there are millions and millions of people in the world who do not believe in *any* orthodoxly conceived monotheistic gods. Unless we suppose that all of these people are mistaken about the contents of their own beliefs, we have overwhelming evidence that there is nothing like universal consensus about the existence of orthodoxly conceived monotheistic gods. Furthermore, there are millions of people – including millions of children – who do not so much as understand talk about orthodoxly conceived monotheistic gods: it is beyond belief to suppose that there is good reason to suppose that these people are nonetheless believers in orthodoxly conceived monotheistic gods.

In the face of these kinds of objections, one might try to restrict the scope of the quantification in the first premise: while there are people who fail to believe that there is an orthodoxly conceived monotheistic god, there are no people who possess the concept of an orthodoxly conceived monotheistic god, and who have thought seriously about these matters, and yet who fail to believe that there is an orthodoxly conceived monotheistic god.

1. Everyone who possesses the concept of such-and-such orthodoxly conceived monotheistic god, and who has thought seriously about whether or not such-and-such orthodoxly conceived monotheistic god exists, believes that such-and-such orthodoxly conceived monotheistic god exists.

2. If a proposition is such that everyone who thinks seriously about that proposition believes that proposition to be true, then that proposition must be true.
3. (Therefore) Such-and-such orthodoxly conceived monotheistic god exists.

Of course, there are millions and millions of people in the world who claim that they have thought seriously about whether or not such-and-such orthodoxly conceived monotheistic god exists and who have reached the conclusion that there is no such orthodoxly conceived monotheistic god. But there is a long-standing line of thought that claims that the avowals that these people make should not be taken seriously: while it is true that there are *practical atheists* and *practical agnostics* who deny – or, at any rate, fail to affirm – the existence of such-and-such orthodoxly conceived monotheistic god for reasons of ignorance, folly, passion, vice, and the like, there are no *theoretical atheists* or *theoretical agnostics*, that is, no people who deny – or, at any rate, fail to affirm – the existence of such-and-such orthodoxly conceived monotheistic god for reasons based on evidence and reflection.

In the face of the objection that it is just obviously true that there have been people – for example, David Hume and John Mackie, to mention only two – who have denied the existence of all orthodoxly conceived monotheistic gods for reasons based on evidence and reflection, proponents of the thesis that there are no theoretical atheists sometimes retreat to weaker theses: for example, that there has never been a society of confirmed and steadfast theoretical atheists.[2] However, it seems doubtful that this weaker claim is sufficient to sustain an argument that is so much as *prima facie* plausible: for why should anyone suppose that the (alleged) fact, that a proposition

---

[2] As Berman (1988) documents, there is a range of theses that can be attributed to different seventeenth- and eighteenth-century proponents of the claim that there are no theoretical ('speculative') atheists or theoretical ('speculative') agnostics:

1. There could not be speculative atheists.
2. There could not be steadfast speculate atheists.
3. There could not be confirmed and steadfast speculative atheists.
4. There has never been a speculative atheist.
5. There has never been a steadfast speculative atheist.
6. There has never been a confirmed and steadfast speculative atheist.
7. There could not be a society of speculative atheists.
8. There could not be a society of steadfast speculative atheists.
9. There could not be a society of confirmed and steadfast speculative atheists.
10. There has never been a society of speculative atheists.
11. There has never been a society of steadfast speculative atheists.
12. There has never been a society of confirmed and steadfast speculative atheists.

Intuitively, a speculative atheist is 'steadfast' if that person maintains speculative atheism for an extended span of time; and a speculative atheist is 'confirmed' if that person maintains speculative atheism in the face of imminent death and the like.

is such that there has never been a society all of whose members have stead-fastly and resiliently rejected that proposition, provides a compelling reason to suppose that that proposition is true? It is very likely that there has never been a society *all* of whose members have steadfastly and resiliently rejected astrology: should we therefore conclude that astrological claims are true?

At this point, proponents of the argument from common consensus currently under discussion might try suggesting that, while it is obviously true that there have been people who have denied the existence of all orthodoxly conceived monotheistic gods for reasons based on evidence and reflection, there has never been anyone who has denied the existence of all orthodoxly conceived monotheistic gods for *good* reasons based on evidence and reflection. However, while this claim *might* be true, it seems clear that an argument that takes this claim as a premise is no longer plausibly construed as an argument from common consensus: what is now doing all of the work in the argument is the claim that no one has ever had good reasons for denying the existence of orthodoxly conceived monotheistic gods. Moreover, even if there is nothing else wrong with the following argument –

1. No one has ever had good reasons for denying the existence of such-and-such orthodoxly conceived monotheistic god.
2. If no one has ever had good reasons for denying that p, then p.
3. (Hence) Such-and-such orthodoxly conceived monotheistic god exists.

– it seems clear that the first premise is sufficiently controversial to ensure that the argument is unsuccessful.

Of course, there are questions that can be asked about the second premise in each of the arguments that we have examined in this section. That everyone believes a given proposition does not *guarantee* that that proposition is true. (Perhaps there was a time when everyone believed that the earth is flat. Nonetheless, it was not true then that the earth was flat.) That everyone who has thought seriously about a given proposition believes that that proposition is true does not *guarantee* that that proposition is true. (Perhaps there was a time when everyone who thought seriously about the matter believed that the earth is infinitely old. Nonetheless, it was not true then that the earth was infinitely old.) That no one has ever had good reasons for denying a proposition does not *guarantee* that that proposition is true. (Perhaps there was a time when no one had good reasons to deny that the speed of light is infinite. Nonetheless, it was not true then that the speed of light was infinite.) If the second premise in each of the arguments that we are considering is given this kind of strong reading, then we have good reason to suppose that that premise is false.

In the face of this point, it might be thought that a defender of these arguments could respond by reasonably insisting that the truth of a proposition is made *more likely* by its being universally believed, or by its being universally believed by those who have thought seriously about it, or by its never having been rejected on the basis of good reasons (even though many people have thought seriously about it). I think that there is something to this response: *at least for certain classes of propositions*, it is not implausible to claim that the likelihood of their truth is increased by their being universally accepted, or by their being universally accepted by those who have thought seriously about them, or by their never having been rejected on the basis of good reasons (even though many people have thought seriously about them). However, the key question to ask here is about the conditions that must be satisfied in order for a proposition to be of the relevant kind. While it is far beyond the scope of the present inquiry to try to answer this question, it seems to me to be worth noting that, if there is independent reason for supposing that a proposition is likely to be universally accepted – or universally accepted by those who have thought seriously about it, or never rejected on the basis of good reason by those who have thought seriously about it – *whether or not that proposition is true*, then the truth of that proposition is not made more likely by its universal acceptance, and so on. Since many nontheists have offered reasons for thinking that, at least under certain kinds of conditions that (plausibly) have been historically realised, the proposition that there is an orthodoxly conceived monotheistic god is likely to be widely accepted even if there is no orthodoxly conceived monotheistic god, it is at the very least clear that there is much more to be said about the prospects for finding a defensible claim fit to play the role of the second premise in the arguments that we have been considering.

In sum, then, flat-footed forms of arguments from common consensus appear to face overwhelming difficulties. However, there are other kinds of arguments from common concensus that may perhaps avoid some of the difficulties that confront the more flat-footed forms of the argument that we have considered thus far. So, for example, one sometimes encounters arguments like the following.

1. Everyone is naturally inclined to believe that such-and-such orthodoxly conceived monotheistic god exists.
2. Propositions that everyone is naturally inclined to believe are true.
3. (Therefore) Such-and-such orthodoxly conceived monotheistic god exists.

Before we can begin to assess this argument, we need to know more about the key notion of 'natural inclination' that it invokes. What conditions must be satisfied for it to be true that someone is 'naturally inclined' to believe a given proposition? What would count as (uncontroversial) evidence that someone is 'naturally inclined' to believe a given proposition? If one can determine one's 'natural inclinations' with respect to a proposition that p simply by considering the attitude that one takes to that proposition when one reflects upon it, then there is overwhelming evidence that many people are not 'naturally inclined' to believe that there are orthodoxly conceived monotheistic gods. I find within myself no urge or impetus to accept the claim that there are orthodoxly conceived monotheistic gods: when I weigh what I take to be all of the relevant considerations, I come down very firmly on the side of the claim that there are no orthodoxly conceived monotheistic gods. If 'natural inclination' is supposed to be accessible to the person to whom it is ascribed, then I take it that it is simply *obviously* false that everyone has a 'natural inclination' to believe in orthodoxly conceived monotheistic gods.

Suppose, on the other hand, that the proponent of our revised argument from common consensus holds that 'natural inclination' can be simply invisible to the person who possesses it. That is, suppose that the proponent of the argument maintains that it can be true that one is 'naturally inclined' to believe that such-and-such orthodoxly conceived monotheistic god exists, even though, no matter how hard one tries, one is unable to detect any trace of this 'natural inclination' by examining one's beliefs, desires, values, conscious states, actions, behavioural history, and so on. (Perhaps, for example, the proponent of the argument maintains that we have been made by an orthodoxly conceived monotheistic god in such a way that, when our cognitive machinery is functioning properly, we believe that there is an orthodoxly conceived monotheistic god. One is 'naturally inclined' to believe that there is an orthodoxly conceived monotheistic god because, if one's cognitive machinery is functioning properly, then one does believe that there is an orthodoxly conceived monotheistic god.) In this case, I take it that it is just obvious that the argument from common concensus fails to be persuasive: anyone who does not already accept the conclusion of the argument will either reject the first premise of the argument – because they will suppose that the 'natural inclination' appealed to in that premise will be present only if the conclusion of the argument is true – or else they will reject the second premise of the argument on the grounds that, if there is naturalistic explanation to be given of the 'natural inclinations' appealed to in the first premise, then those 'natural inclinations' constitute counter-examples to the claim that is made in the second premise.

I think that the preceding discussion makes it very plausible to suppose that there is no successful argument from common consensus. If we are to find a justification for belief in the existence of orthodoxly conceived monotheistic gods, then we certainly need to look elsewhere.

7.1.2. Historical Tradition

There are various ways in which one might attempt to construct – and construe – arguments from 'historical tradition'. One might suppose, for example, that an argument from historical tradition is simply a generalised form of arguments from general consensus: it is not merely that everyone *now* is naturally disposed to believe that there is an orthodoxly conceived monotheistic god; it has *always* been the case that everyone is naturally disposed to believe that there is an orthodoxly conceived monotheistic god. Understood this way, it is not clear that the argument is really different from the argument from common consensus; and, moreover, it is clear that this form of the argument from 'historical tradition' is hostage to all of the difficulties that face arguments from common consensus.

An alternative argument from 'historical tradition', still based on arguments from common consensus, might start with the claim that, while it is not *now* true that everyone is naturally disposed to believe that there is an orthodoxly conceived monotheistic god – or that everyone believes that such-and-such orthodoxly conceived monotheistic god exists – *there was a time* when it was true that everyone was naturally disposed to believe that there is an orthodoxly conceived monotheistic god – or that everyone believed that such-and-such orthodoxly conceived monotheistic god exists. An argument of this type might be formulated in one of the following ways:

1. There was a time when everyone believed that such-and-such orthodoxly conceived monotheistic god exists.
2. Propositions that were universally believed at some time must be true.
3. (Therefore) Such-and-such orthodoxly conceived monotheistic god exists.
4. There was a time when everyone was naturally inclined to believe that such-and-such orthodoxly conceived monotheistic god exists.
5. Propositions that everyone was naturally inclined to believe at some time are true.
6. (Therefore) Such-and-such orthodoxly conceived monotheistic god exists.

Clearly, these arguments are subject to more or less the same kinds of objections that confronted the analogous arguments from *current* common consensus. No doubt it should be conceded that there is good reason to suppose that belief in orthodoxly conceived monotheistic beings was *far more* widespread in certain parts of the world at certain times in the past than it is now. However, it seems to me that there is no good reason to suppose that belief in orthodoxly conceived monotheistic gods was ever universal, except perhaps in very carefully circumscribed communities, and neither is there good reason to suppose that there was ever a time when 'natural inclinations' to believe in orthodoxly conceived monotheistic gods differed from present 'natural inclinations' on this matter because it was then the case that everyone had a 'natural inclination' to believe in orthodoxly conceived monotheistic gods. Moreover, even if there were times and places at which belief in orthodoxly conceived monotheistic gods – or the 'natural inclination' to believe in orthodoxly conceived monotheistic gods – was universal, it is quite unclear why we should attribute any special significance to this fact. Indeed, one might well suspect that one could not possibly have good reason to accept the second premise in these arguments. It is highly likely that there is a claim that *p* of which it is true that, at one time, it was universally believed that *p*, and at another time, it was universally believed that not *p*. But then the second premise of the first formulation of the argument under consideration collapses into contradiction. Moreover, even if there has been no such claim, it is clear that it is merely a matter of contingent good fortune that this is so: there is no reason at all to suppose that it *could not* be the case that there is a claim that *p* of which it is true that, at one time, it was universally believed that *p*, and at another time, it was universally believed that not *p*.

There may be yet other ways in which one might try to construct an argument from 'historical tradition'. For instance, one might point to the important historical role that has been played by belief in such-and-such orthodoxly conceived monotheistic god. There are very large religions – Christianity, Judaism, Islam – that have, as their foundation, belief in a particular, orthodoxly conceived monotheistic god. An important part of these religions is the very large organisations that they support: the particular churches, the particular missions, and so forth. Is it really credible to suppose that belief in a particular, orthodoxly conceived monotheistic god could have such dramatic historical and organisational consequences if that belief is false?

Perhaps we might formulate the implicit argument here as follows.

1. Belief in such-and-such orthodoxly conceived monotheistic god has played, and continues to play, a pivotal role in the history of humanity, and in the development of support of significant human social organisations and institutions.
2. Any belief that plays such a pivotal role in the history of humanity, and in the development of support of significant human social organisations and institutions, must be true.
3. (Therefore) Such-and-such orthodoxly conceived monotheistic god exists.

There are questions that one might raise about the first premise. It is not completely clear what is sufficient to count as belief in such-and-such orthodoxly conceived monotheistic god. If one is required to have a fully explicit conception of the god in question – for example, of the kind that could be acquired only by a close acquaintance with Aquinas' *Summa theologica* or a similar work – then it is not obviously plausible to hold that belief in orthodoxly conceived monotheistic gods has played the role suggested in premise 1. However, if all that is required is that one believes in the existence of an orthodoxly conceived monotheistic god of a kind that can be more fully described by the appropriate experts in one's community, then it is not clear that it really is the belief in such-and-such orthodoxly conceived monotheistic god that is doing the work that is attributed to it in premise 1.

Whatever one thinks about the standing of the first premise, it is clear that one should think that the second premise is far more dubious. It seems entirely obvious that false beliefs have played a major historical role, and that they have been crucial to the development and support of significant social organisations and institutions. Consider, for example, the construction of the Egyptian pyramids, or the development and support of the Mayan and Incan civilisations. No one who thinks that there is an orthodoxly conceived monotheistic god is going to suppose that the religious beliefs of the ancient Egyptians, the Mayans, and the Incas were true. Yet we hardly lack reason to suppose that those religious beliefs played pivotal roles in the history of humanity, and in the development and support of significant human social organisations and institutions. Consideration of the role of Hindu beliefs in the formation and support of contemporary Indian society supports the same conclusion: those who believe in orthodoxly conceived monotheistic gods typically do not suppose that the fundamental claims of the Hindu religion are true; and yet those beliefs continue to have enormous significance for the course of history, and for the development and support of Indian social organisations and institutions.

Moreover – though it is a slightly different point – there are competing conceptions of orthodoxly conceived monotheistic gods that have played pivotal roles in the history of humanity and in the development and support of significant human social organisations and institutions. No one can coherently suppose that there is a single orthodoxly conceived monotheistic god that conforms to the beliefs of the various different kinds of Christians, and the various different kinds of Muslims, and the various different kinds of Jews. Given that different kinds of Christians, and different kinds of Muslims, and different kinds of Jews, have conflicting conceptions of their monotheistic gods, it cannot be the case that all of their beliefs are true – and, consequently, it cannot be the case that the 'historical and social efficacy' of all of those mutually inconsistent beliefs is somehow evidence of their truth. But, at the very least, we lack compelling reason to suppose that some particular variety of monotheistic belief has a privileged kind of 'historical and social efficacy' that somehow marks it out as an obvious bearer of truth.

As I concluded in my discussion of arguments from common consensus, I think that the preceding discussion makes it very plausible to suppose that there is no successful argument for belief in the existence of orthodoxly conceived monotheistic gods from historical tradition. If we are to find a justification for belief in the existence of orthodoxly conceived monotheistic gods, then we shall plausibly need to look elsewhere.

7.1.3. Expert Testimony

There are many different people who are prepared to claim that there is an orthodoxly conceived monotheistic god, and whose assertions or beliefs might be appealed to as the basis for an argument from (expert) testimony. There are philosophers and theologians who have thought long and hard about these matters, and who are resolute in their conviction that there is an orthodoxly conceived monotheistic god. There are priests – and other kinds of religious leaders – who might be supposed to have some kind of expertise in this matter, and who are evidently prepared to endorse the claim that there is an orthodoxly conceived monotheistic god. There are educators – school teachers, university instructors, and the like – who are engaged in the instruction of the young, and who teach that there is an orthodoxly conceived monotheistic god. There are parents who confidently and willingly instruct their own children that there is an orthodoxly conceived monotheistic god. And so on.

It is an interesting question how best to frame an argument from expert testimony. It seems to me that it is not unreasonable to suppose that there are circumstances in which it is reasonable for someone to come to belief in a particular orthodoxly conceived monotheistic god on the basis of the testimony of another person. If parents confidently and willingly instruct their own children that there is an orthodoxly conceived monotheistic god, then – in a range of conceivable circumstances – it will be perfectly reasonable for those children to form the belief that there is an orthodoxly conceived monotheistic god. If school teachers promulgate the view that there is an orthodoxly conceived monotheistic god, then – in a range of conceivable circumstances – it will be perfectly reasonable for their students to form the belief that there is an orthodoxly conceived monotheistic god. If priests and other religious leaders endorse the claim that there is an orthodoxly conceived monotheistic god, then – in a range of conceivable circumstances – it will be perfectly reasonable for those who belong to their communities to form the belief that there is an orthodoxly conceived monotheistic god. If philosophers and theologians who are known to have thought long and hard about these matters assert that there is an orthodoxly conceived monotheistic god, then – in a range of conceivable circumstances – it will be perfectly reasonable for members of their audiences to form the belief that there is an orthodoxly conceived monotheistic god. Depending upon the circumstances in which one is placed, it can be perfectly reasonable for one to form beliefs on the basis of the testimony of experts; I see no reason why it could not be the case that one is reasonable in forming the belief that there is an orthodoxly conceived monotheistic god on the basis of the testimony of (supposed) experts.

Even if you accept the claims that I have just made about the possible role of expert testimony in the production of reasonable belief in the existence of orthodoxly conceived monotheistic gods, you should not suppose that there is an easy step from here to the construction of a persuasive argument for the existence of orthodoxly conceived monotheistic gods on the basis of expert testimony. For how would such an argument go? Suppose you try something like the following.

1. Such-and-such experts believe in so-and-so orthodoxly conceived monotheistic god.
2. (Therefore) So-and-so orthodoxly conceived monotheistic god exists.

The difficulties that confront an *argument* of this kind are obvious. There are plenty of experts – philosophers, theologians, priests, religious leaders, school teachers, university lecturers, parents – who positively disbelieve in any particular orthodoxly conceived monotheistic god; indeed, there are plenty of experts – philosophers, religious leaders, school teachers, university lecturers, parents – who believe that there is no orthodoxly conceived monotheistic god. Given that a successful argument has to be such that it ought to persuade anyone who is apprised of the relevant facts, it is clear that no argument of this kind can be successful. While it can be reasonable to form a belief on the basis of the assertion of someone whom one takes to be an authority – perhaps even in circumstances in which one realises that there are competing 'authorities' that would dissent from the assertion in question – there is no point in trying to mount an *argument* from authority for a conclusion that all informed people know is hopelessly controversial.

I anticipate that some philosophers may wish to object to the way in which I have separated considerations about persuasion by the assertions of experts from considerations about arguments from the testimony of experts. If it is really true that there is no point in trying to mount an argument from authority for a conclusion that all informed people know is hopelessly controversial, then how could one ever be genuinely justified in coming to believe a claim of the kind in question on the basis of expert testimony, particularly if it is the case that one realises that the claim in question is highly controversial? I take it that the answer to this question is pretty straightforward: when you are persuaded of the truth of a controversial claim on the basis of the assertions of a particular expert, it need not be the case that you are persuaded of the truth of those claims by the *arguments* that are advanced by that expert. In the right kind of circumstances, your telling me that it is the case that p can be sufficient grounds for my coming to believe that p, even in cases in which I recognise that it is a controversial question whether it is the case that p. In those kinds of circumstances, the sufficient grounds that I have for coming to believe that p need have nothing to do with the strength of the arguments that you advanced on behalf of the proposition that p: indeed, it can be the case that you offered me no arguments at all that supported the proposition that p.

Perhaps it might be said that, while it is true that your telling me that it is the case that p can be sufficient grounds for my coming to believe that p, this can be so only in circumstances in which there is an argument that I can reconstruct for myself and of which it is reasonable for me to believe that it is a successful argument for the conclusion that p. But how are we to suppose that such an argument would run? Given that I recognise that the claim that p is highly controversial, I am hardly going to suppose that the argument "I believe you when you say that p; therefore p" is a *successful* argument for the conclusion that p. While I take it that I have good reason to believe you when you tell me that p, I can also see that those who are not inclined to accept that it is the case that p may well be inclined to fail to believe you when you say that p. But what other argument am I to construct on the basis of your assertion that p, and my believing you when you make this assertion?

Perhaps it might be said that, if I am to be justified in believing you when you assert that p, I need to be able to produce an argument that reconstructs my reasons for believing you when you say that p. If I am unable to produce a successful argument that justifies the conclusion that you ought to be believed when you assert that p, then what reason is there to suppose that I am justified in believing you when you say that p? There are various reasons why the standards that are being set here seem to me to be too demanding. On the one hand, by these lights, it will turn out that most people are almost never justified in believing what someone else tells them: for, after all, it is no straightforward matter to set out an argument of the kind demanded. On the other hand, even for one who has the ability to construct arguments of the kind in question, it seems to me that the reasons that one has for accepting the assertions that are made by others can outrun the ability that one has to make those reasons explicit. Even if we can make sense of the idea of a cognitive system that is fully 'transparent' to itself, it is not clear that this is an ideal to which it is reasonable to suppose that human beings ought to aspire.

While there is plainly more to say about the matters that I have been discussing in the past few paragraphs, I take it that it is not obviously seriously problematic to claim that, while expert testimony might serve in some cases as a justified basis for belief in orthodoxly conceived monotheistic gods, there is no prospect of constructing a *successful* argument for belief in orthodoxly conceived monotheistic gods on the basis of appeal to expert testimony. Perhaps I should add that, if there is something wrong with the line that I have been trying to defend – that is, if, surprisingly, it turns out that there can be no justified acceptance of belief on the basis of testimony unless there are successful arguments for the claims that are there testified to – then the obvious failings of arguments from testimony to the existence of orthodoxly conceived monotheistic gods would then serve to show that there could never be justified acceptance of the existence of orthodoxly conceived monotheistic gods on the basis of expert testimony.

Quite generally, arguments from expert testimony for the existence of orthodoxly conceived monotheistic gods need to overcome the difficulties raised by the fact that there is no uncontroversial way of identifying relevant experts, by the fact that purported experts do not agree, by the fact that there are plenty of independent reasons for mistrusting many purported experts, and by the fact that, given the controversial nature of the claims in question, the mere testimony of purported experts – as opposed to any arguments that they might present – simply fails to provide an adequate basis for a successful argument. As I concluded in my discussion of arguments from common consensus and historical tradition, I think that the preceding discussion makes it very plausible to suppose that there is no successful argument for the existence of orthodoxly conceived monotheistic gods from expert testimony. If we are to find a successful argument for belief in the existence of orthodoxly conceived monotheistic gods, then we shall plausibly need to look elsewhere.

7.1.4. Scripture

There are various different ways in which one might try to argue from scripture to the existence of an orthodoxly conceived monotheistic god. A very ambitious argument that one sometimes encounters takes the following form.

1. Everything that such-and-such scripture says is true.
2. Such-and-such scripture says that there is an orthodoxly conceived monotheistic god.
3. (Therefore) There is an orthodoxly conceived monotheistic god.

There are difficulties that confront each of the premises in an argument of this kind.

On the one hand, actual scriptures are often both lacking in precise literal details about the nature of the monotheistic god whose existence they proclaim and inconsistent in the precise claims that they do make about that monotheistic god. If we suppose that actual scripture requires minimal interpretation, then we often end up with a conception of a monotheistic god that is both vague and incoherent; and we end up with the best of reasons for supposing that the first premise in our ambitious argument from scripture is simply false. If, however, we suppose that actual scripture requires significant interpretation, to fill in missing details, to resolve internal contradictions, and to determine which passages ought to be given a literal interpretation and which passages ought to be interpreted metaphorically, then, while we may end up with a conception of a monotheistic god that is neither vague nor incoherent, it will be much harder to defend the claim that the scripture itself says that there is such-and-such orthodoxly conceived monotheistic god.

On the other hand, there are often very good reasons for supposing that what appear to be precise literal claims in actual scriptures are simply false. Sometimes, scriptures make historical claims that are simply not supported by the historical record. Sometimes, scriptures report events – the sun standing still in the sky, the coming back to life of someone who has been dead for three days, the magical transformation of a small amount of food into sufficient to feed a multitude, the parting of a sea that permits citizens to flee from an advancing army, and so forth – that we have the strongest possible *independent* reasons to suppose did not occur. There are *many* different kinds of difficulties that face those who wish to determine which parts of any given scripture are reasonably supposed to be literal reports of events that actually took place; there are *many* different kinds of reasons for supposing that there is no straightforward sense in which scriptures are reliable historical records.

Moreover, there are many different scriptural texts that make conflicting claims about the natures of orthodoxly conceived monotheistic gods, and about many other matters as well. Given that scripture T_A says that tribe A – or those with beliefs $A_1, A_2, \ldots, A_n$ – are the 'favourites' of the one and only orthodoxly conceived monotheistic god, and that scripture T_B says that tribe B – or those with beliefs $B_1, B_2, \ldots, B_n$ – are the 'favourites' of the one and only orthodoxly conceived monotheistic god, where AB, and where $\{A_1, A_2, \ldots, A_n\}$ is inconsistent with $\{B_1, B_2, \ldots, B_n\}$, then it cannot be the case that T_A and T_B are both true. But, in the case, it seems that the first premise in our argument from scripture needs to be supported with a defence of the claims of the scripture there adverted to as against the claims of any of the many competing scriptures that are to be found around the world.

For any scripture that one might choose as the basis for an argument of the kind set out above, it seems plausible to suppose that only (some of) those who already believe in the particular orthodoxly conceived monotheistic god whose existence is adverted to in the pages of the scripture in question will believe that all of the claims that are made in the scripture in question are true. Those who accept the claim of some other scripture – and those who accept the claims of no scripture at all – are hardly going to be persuaded of the existence of the particular orthodoxly conceived monotheistic god in question on the basis of this argument. Consequently – particularly in the light of the criticisms of this argument that we have made in the preceding paragraphs – it seems a straightforward call to insist that no argument of this kind is successful: no one ought to find an argument of this kind *persuasive.*

Perhaps there are other, less ambitious, arguments from scripture that might be constructed. However, when one considers the difficulties that are raised by the existence of *many* scriptures, by the apparent need to justify the contention that (certain) claims that are made in a given scripture can be *trusted,* by the need to *interpret* scriptural text, and by the ready availability of *alternative* – naturalistic – explanations of the existence of a proliferation of scriptural texts, it seems clear that the difficulties that confront the construction of any such argument are severe indeed.

7.1.5. Concluding Observation

Given that arguments from authority divide more or less exhaustively into arguments from general consensus, arguments from historical tradition, arguments from expert testimony, and arguments from scripture, I take it that the above discussion makes it very plausible to conclude that there are no good arguments from authority to the conclusion that there are orthodoxly conceived monotheistic gods. Of course, I do not suppose that this conclusion is particularly controversial; one has to search long and hard to find anyone who supposes otherwise. We shall come back to the question of whether considerations about the deliverances of authorities can play some role in cumulative arguments for belief in orthodoxly conceived monotheistic gods.

7.2. ARGUMENTS FROM RELIGIOUS EXPERIENCE

I take it that the general outline of an argument from religious experience looks like the following.

1. So-and-so has had such-and-such experiences of an orthodoxly conceived monotheistic god.
2. (Therefore) There is an orthodoxly conceived monotheistic god.

While there are different ways of filling out this general outline, I propose to start this discussion by introducing some distinctions that will be important for the subsequent discussion, and then to turn my attention to the version of the argument from religious experience that is defended in Swinburne (1979).

First, arguments may vary depending upon who it is that is said to have had the experiences in question. Sometimes, arguments rely on the experiences of a single individual; sometimes they rely on the experiences of groups of individuals. Sometimes, arguments rely entirely upon third-hand reports of experiences; sometimes, the proponent of an argument claims to be one of those who has had the relevant experiences. Sometimes, arguments that rely on the reported experiences of groups of individuals claim that those reports have independent causal origins; sometimes they do not.

Second, arguments may vary according to the ontological category of experience that is mentioned. Sometimes, the claim is that an orthodoxly conceived monotheistic god has been *directly perceived* ('X saw an orthodoxly conceived monotheistic god'); sometimes, the claim is that an orthodoxly conceived monotheistic god has been *indirectly perceived* ('X saw that there is an orthodoxly conceived monotheistic god' or 'X saw that there is an orthodoxly conceived monotheistic god in virtue of seeing such-and-such'); sometimes the claim is that an orthodoxly conceived monotheistic god has been the subject of *revelation* ('It was revealed to X that there is an orthodoxly conceived monotheistic god').

Third, arguments may vary according to the evidential value of the experience that is reported. Sometimes, it is claimed that experiences provide evidence for the teachings of a particular sect; sometimes, it is claimed that experiences provide evidence for the core doctrines of orthodox monotheism; sometimes, it is claimed that experiences provide evidence that there is a 'higher power', or the like. Of course, not all experiences that are claimed to be evidence for the existence of an orthodoxly conceived monotheistic god are experiences that directly concern an orthodoxly conceived monotheistic god: experiences directly concerning angels, or heaven, or the saints, or whatever, *might* be good indirect evidence of the existence of an orthodoxly conceived monotheistic god.

Fourth, arguments may vary according to the evidential virtues of the reported experiences. Some experiences are claimed to be *publicly available*, while others may be claimed to be essentially private – and, in some cases, available only those who already believe in that which is alleged to be the subject of those experiences. Some experiences are claimed to be *repeatable*, that is, such that they can be enjoyed by anyone who is prepared to make suitable preparation; others are claimed to be such that there is no way that anyone can guarantee to succeed if they set out to experience them. Some experiences are claimed to be *testable*, that is, such that their occurrence is open to examination by the techniques of empirical science; other experiences are claimed not to be testable in these ways.

Fifth, some – but not all – arguments from religious experience claim that the experience in question is *mystical* in character. While it is a controversial question just how mystical experience ought to be characterised, it is often said that mystical experiences are ineffable, noetic, passive, and transitive. Moreover, it is often said that the content of these experiences involves a higher reality, spirituality, unity, and/or perfection. Finally, it is worth noting that mystical experiences seem to have much in common with familiar experiences that occur in doxastically untrustworthy states induced by drugs, tiredness, starvation, and the like – and, indeed, that mystical experiences are often induced by taking drugs, fasting, refusing to sleep, and the like.

Sixth, as Swinburne emphasises, some – but not all – arguments from religious experience have premises in which there is 'epistemic' use of verbs such as 'seems', 'appears', or 'looks'. That is, some arguments from religious experience have premises of the form 'It seemed to X that X saw an orthodoxly conceived monotheistic god', or 'It seemed to X that X saw that there is an orthodoxly conceived monotheistic god', or 'It seemed to X that it was revealed to X that there is an orthodoxly conceived monotheistic god', where the initial operator – 'It seemed that...' – is used in an 'epistemic', rather than in a 'comparative', sense. However, in arguments in which there is explicit mention of reporting – for example, 'X claimed that X saw an orthodoxly conceived monotheistic god' – there is no reason to insert an 'epistemic' verb in order to ward off charges that there are crucial questions being begged.

Seventh, Swinburne proposes a further taxonomy of religious experiences as follows: (i) experiences that seem (epistemically) to the subject to be experiences of an orthodoxly conceived monotheistic god but where he seems to perceive that being in perceiving a perfectly ordinary natural object; (ii) experiences that arise from the perception of very unusual public objects or events; (iii) experiences that are private but that can be described using the same vocabulary that one ordinarily uses to describe familiar inputs from the standard five senses; (iv) experiences that are private and that cannot be described using the same vocabulary that one ordinarily uses to describe familiar inputs from the standard five senses; and (v) experiences that do not rely on the having of sensations. Examples: (i) looking at the night sky, and seeing it as the handiwork of an orthodoxly conceived monotheistic god; (ii) the experiences of those who witnessed the resurrection of Jesus, or the appearance of Mary at Fatima, or other alleged miracles; (iii) Joseph's dream as recorded in Matthew 1:20ff.; (iv) mystical experiences; (v) revelations.

Eighth, as Swinburne notes, many arguments from religious experience appeal to some kind of principle of credulity. In Swinburne's formulation, the principle of credulity says that it is 'a principle of rationality' that, *in the absence of special considerations, if it seems epistemically to a subject that* p, *then probably it is the case that* p, where the 'special considerations' adverted to concern (1) the reliability of the subject and the conditions in which the experience is undergone; (2) defeating cases, for example, reasons for supposing that similar claims in similar conditions have often turned out to be mistaken; (3) background knowledge and beliefs, for example, independent reasons for supposing that there is no entity of the kind that has allegedly been experienced; and (4) alternative causal explanations, for example, plausible justifications for the claim that the experience would have occurred just as it did whether or not there is an entity of the kind that is invoked in the experience. It is important to note that, perhaps despite initial appearances, this principle of credulity is really a principle about what a subject ought to believe on the basis of his or her own experiences: given the absence of special considerations – or, if you prefer a more internalist formulation, given what a subject (justifiably?) takes to be the absence of special considerations – if it seems (epistemically) to a subject that *x* is present, then *that subject* is justified in concluding that it is probable that *x* is present.

Ninth, since it is clear that arguments from religious experience are typically intended to persuade those who have never had religious experiences – or, at any rate, those who take themselves never to have had religious experiences – we need some way of moving from Swinburne's principle of credulity to a principle that makes it plausible to suppose that reports that others make about their experiences make it reasonable for one to suppose that the world is as their reported experiences would have it. To accomplish this task, Swinburne proposed a Principle of Testimony, namely, that *the experiences of others are typically as they report them to be.* He then claims – Swinburne (1979: 273) – that, since the Principle of Testimony gives us that it is likely that others have the experiences that they report, and since the Principle of Credulity gives us that it is probable that things are as a subject's experience suggests them to be, it follows that it is (reasonably) likely that things are as others report them to be. Or more carefully: in the absence of special considerations, it is reasonably likely that things are as others report them to be.

Before we turn to the details of Swinburne's defence of the claim that special considerations are often absent in the case of religious experience – whence, by the argument just given, it follows that it is reasonably likely that things are as those who have religious experiences report them to be – it is worth noting that there are serious holes in Swinburne's defence of the claim that, in the absence of special considerations, it is reasonably likely that things are as others report them to be. For how is this claim supposed to be understood? Is it that, if *I* take it that special considerations are absent, then I should think that it is reasonably likely that things are as others report them to be? Or is it that, if *others* take it that special considerations are absent, then I should think that it is reasonably likely that things are as those others report them to be? Given that the Principle of Credulity says that if one supposes that special considerations are absent, then it is reasonable for one to suppose that things are as they appear, then it seems that what follows, by way of the Principle of Testimony, is only that it is reasonable for other people to suppose that things are as they appear to them; nothing at all follows about whether it is reasonable for you to suppose that things are as they appear to them.

Rather than fuss about how fix up Swinburne's argument, it seems to me to be more profitable to try to formulate the kind of principle that it seems reasonable to suppose ought to have application here. I take it that it is something like this: if I take it that no special considerations apply to your claim that your experience makes it reasonable for you to conclude that p, then it is reasonable for me to conclude that it is the case that p. That is, if I do not have – or, perhaps, take myself to have? – good reasons for supposing that you are unreliable when it comes to these matters, or that the circumstances in which you made the observation may have prevented you from making reliable observations about this matter, or that others who have made similar claims in similar circumstances have typically been mistaken, or that I have good independent reason for supposing that it is not the case that p, or that it is very likely that you would conclude that p on the basis of your experience whether or not it is the case that p, then it is reasonable for me to suppose that it is likely that it is the case that p given that you are inclined to conclude that p on the basis of your experience. Of course, it may perfectly well turn out that I suppose that, while you have violated no canons of reason in concluding that p on the basis of your experience, it would nonetheless be a mistake for me to conclude that p on the basis of your reported experience. But that is not the most important point to note; what is crucially at issue here is whether there is a good *argument* for the existence of orthodoxly conceived monotheistic gods on the basis of reported religious experience, not whether there can be good reason to form the belief that there is an orthodoxly conceived monotheistic god if you are yourself the subject of those experiences.

As I have already noted, the core of Swinburne's argument from religious experience is his argument for the conclusion that there are no good reasons – or, at any rate, no good enough reasons – for supposing that there are special considerations that make it reasonable for non-believers to refuse to believe in the existence of orthodoxly conceived monotheistic gods on the basis of the testimony of those who claim to have had experiences as of an orthodoxly conceived monotheistic god. This argument proceeds by cases, considering each of the types of special considerations that might be thought to apply.

First, non-believers might suppose that there are doubts about the reliability of the subjects and the suitability of the conditions in which experiences of orthodoxly conceived monotheistic gods occur. Swinburne (1979: 265) claims that, while this challenge might defeat some claims, it can hardly be generally available: 'most religious experiences are had by men who normally make reliable perceptual claims and have not recently taken drugs'. But here, it seems to me, we need to recall Swinburne's own taxonomy of religious experiences: it is not obvious that the same kind of considerations apply in each case.[3]

On the one hand, it does seem to me that religious experiences of the *first* kind – for example, looking at the night sky, and seeing it as the handiwork of an orthodoxly conceived monotheistic god – are often undergone by those who are in quite normal sensory states, and in quite normal conditions for observation: you don't need to be drugged, starved, sleep-deprived, and so forth in order to respond to the world in this kind of way. But, of course, it is pretty obviously true that, in almost all cases, those who do have these kinds of religious experiences are *already* believers in the existence of orthodoxly conceived monotheistic gods: those who don't already suppose that there is an orthodoxly conceived monotheistic god very rarely look at the night sky

---

[3] I think that it is curious that Swinburne provides a taxonomy of kinds of religious experience, and then treats the category of religious experience as a unified whole when he turns to the discussion of 'special conditions'. It is not so very hard to believe that 'special conditions' may bear differently on different kinds of religious experiences.

and see it as the handiwork of a god of that kind. So, when it comes to the question of finding evidence for the claim that there is an orthodoxly conceived monotheistic god, there is good reason for non-believers to suppose that this kind of experience doesn't count, since it is so obviously polluted by prior theory. Given that I have no commitment to the claim that there is an orthodoxly conceived monotheistic god, it would plainly be a mistake for me to suppose that a believer's claim to see the handiwork of such a god in the night sky carries more evidential weight than a non-believer's claim to fail to see any such thing. In the context of an argument from religious experience, the first category of religious experiences in Swinburne's taxonomy can be set aside.[4]

On the other hand, religious experiences of the other kinds – revelation, miracles, mystical experience, selective appearance – are, I think, much less frequently undergone by those who are in normal sensory states and normal conditions for making observations. This is not to say that, for instance, it is never the case that mystical experiences are had by those who are in normal sensory states and normal conditions for making observations; however, as I noted above, it is not very controversial to claim that, in the typical case, the sensory states and conditions for making observations of those who have mystical experiences are of a kind that we have independent reason to suppose are unreliable. We have plenty of independent reason to suppose that taking drugs, fasting, doing without sleep, and so on affects the normal functioning of the brain; indeed, we have plenty of independent reason to suppose that 'mystical experiences' are simply cases in which the brain malfunctions as a result of some kind of insult or abuse. Non-believers are surely on pretty firm territory when they refuse to accept that mystical experience is good evidence for the existence of an orthodoxly conceived monotheistic god.

Second, non-believers might suppose that they have independent reason for thinking that similar claims in similar circumstances have turned out to be unreliable or mistaken.[5] Swinburne (1979: 265) says: 'If there were a good proof of the non-existence of God or anything similar, then, of course that could be done. But the point here is that the onus of proof is on the atheist; if he cannot make his case the claim of religious experience stands.' Moreover, Swinburne goes on to claim that arguments from the conflicting contents of reported religious experiences, and from the

---

4 While it may not be true universally, it is clear that similar considerations apply to very many cases of revelation and selective ('private') religious experiences. Since these are so rarely reported by those who are not already religious believers – or by those who are not embedded in a community in which there is considerable religious fervour – there are good reasons for non-believers to suspect that there is pollution by prior theory in these cases as well.

5 Here, I follow Swinburne in collapsing the discussion of the second and third kinds of 'special conditions'.

thought that no experience could have the kind of content that is typically claimed for religious experiences as of orthodoxly conceived monotheistic gods, do no more than to slightly weaken the force of the overall argument from religious experience.

Here, it seems to me that Swinburne just misrepresents the dialectical situation. He is the one who is defending an *argument* from religious experience. So it is up to him to make his case. If non-believers can reasonably take themselves to have independent reasons for thinking that there is no orthodoxly conceived monotheistic god, then that is enough to underwrite the claim that they can have good grounds for rejecting – or, at any rate, giving very little weight to – arguments from religious experience. Of course, considerations about the conflicting contents of reported religious experiences, and scepticism about whether one really could have an experience that is properly described as being as of an orthodoxly conceived monotheistic god might play some role in strengthening the conviction that religious believers don't actually have experiences of orthodoxly conceived monotheistic gods; but there is no reason at all why non-believers should not be able to rely upon *all* of the many reasons that they have for supposing that there are no orthodoxly conceived monotheistic gods.

Finally, non-believers might suppose that there are alternative causal explanations for the reporting of the various kinds of religious experience. Swinburne (1979: 270) claims: 'This is a particularly awkward challenge to apply when we are dealing with a purported experience of God. . . . If there is a God, he is omnipresent and all causal processes only operate because he sustains them. . . . A demonstration that God was not responsible for the processes that caused me to have the religious experience can only be attained by demonstrating that there is no God.'

Once again, it seems to me that this response is simply beside the point. I agree that, if they were to construct an account of the world that is complete in every detail, then non-theists would need to provide an explanation for each report of religious experience; moreover, I agree that, in many cases, the construction of such an account would require the provision of alternative causal explanations of religious experiences. But I don't see that there is any sense in which the provision of these alternative accounts needs to be based in a proof that there is no orthodoxly conceived monotheistic god. I have already noted above that it is not implausible to suppose that, at least in some cases, an alternative causal explanation of mystical experiences will simply advert to brain dysfunctions brought on by drugs, fasting, lack of sleep, and the like. Everyone agrees that at least *some* reports of miraculous religious experiences – seeing statues bleed, observing people rise from the dead, healing people by touch, and so forth – are to be explained in terms of mass hysteria, or wilful deceit, and so on. Of course, in any given case, it might be a difficult matter to determine what are the causes of a report of religious experiences of one kind or another; but it is enough if non-theists can reasonably believe that, at least in principle, there is always a naturalistic causal explanation to be given.

In sum: It seems to me that Swinburne's *argument* from religious experience is very weak; and, moreover, it seems to me that the kinds of difficulties that afflict Swinburne's argument from religious experience carry over to other *arguments* from religious experience that might be constructed. Of course, as I have insisted at various points in my discussion, in claiming that arguments from religious experience fail, I am not claiming that no one could reasonably suppose that particular kinds of religious experience are grounds for, or provide support for, belief in orthodoxly conceived monotheistic gods. Given enough of the network of beliefs that are held by a typical believer in an orthodoxly conceived monotheistic god, it will be easy to find reasons for supposing that some religious experiences as of orthodoxly conceived monotheistic gods are veridical. But this claim is perfectly consistent with the claim that, given enough of the network of beliefs that are held by a typical non-believer in orthodoxly conceived monotheistic gods, it is easy to find various mutually supporting reasons for supposing that no religious experiences as of orthodoxly conceived monotheistic gods are veridical. Explanation of reports of religious experiences is just one of *many* matters on which believers and non-believers disagree.

7.3. ARGUMENTS FROM MORALITY

There are many different ways in which moral considerations have been alleged to support belief in the existence of monotheistic gods. Once again, we shall do no more than sample from the range of available arguments in the following discussion.

7.3.1. Objective Values

There are many people who have supposed that considerations about 'objective values' support the conclusion that there is a monotheistic god. Plainly enough, it won't do to argue that, since morality is absolute and objective, and since it is true that, if there is an orthodoxly conceived monotheistic god, then morality is absolute and objective, it therefore follows that there is an orthodoxly conceived monotheistic god. However, at least some people have been tempted by arguments like the following.

1. Morality is absolute and objective.
2. Necessarily, morality is absolute and objective only if there is an orthodoxly conceived monotheistic god.
3. (Therefore) There is an orthodoxly conceived monotheistic god.

As an example of this kind of argument, consider the presentation in Rashdall (1907). It seems to me to be quite just to provide the following encapsulation of Rashdall's argument.

1. The Moral Law has a real, absolute, objective existence.
2. If the Moral Law has a real, absolute, objective existence, then there must be a Mind from which the Moral Law (and hence all of the rest of Reality) is derived.
3. (Hence) There must be a Mind from which the Moral Law (and hence all of the rest of Reality) is derived.

Both premises in arguments of this kind are open to challenge. I shall consider each kind of premise in turn.

Before we can assess the truth of the first premise, we need to determine how it is to be interpreted. This is not a straightforward matter. Suppose that we think that morality is objective iff there are moral properties and moral facts – for example, properties of rightness and goodness, and facts about which actions are right and which states of affairs are good. Following Mackie, one might suppose that, since metaphysically fundamental moral properties and moral facts would be very queer beasts, there aren't any moral properties and moral facts; however, it seems to me to be more plausible to suppose that the upshot of this supposition ought to be that moral properties and moral facts are not metaphysically fundamental. Since, as many philosophers have noted, there is good reason to suppose that whatever moral properties and moral facts there may be are supervenient upon non-moral properties and non-moral facts, a natural conclusion to reach is that there are no moral properties and moral facts that are not somehow constituted by non-moral properties and non-moral facts. Of course, naturalists and supernaturalists will disagree about the non-moral properties and non-moral facts upon which whatever moral properties and moral facts there are supervene; but there is no reason to suppose that they will disagree about the claim that there is a relation of supervenience of this kind.

Of course, there are many naturalists who are prepared to deny that there are moral properties and/or moral facts: consider, for example, expressivists, projectivists, eliminativists, and the like. Setting those cases aside – that is, focussing only on those naturalists who suppose that there are moral properties and moral facts that supervene upon natural properties and natural facts – we can now turn our attention to the second premise of the argument: is there any reason at all to think that these naturalists ought to revise their beliefs to accommodate the claim that the supervenience base for any moral properties and moral facts must include properties of, and facts concerning, an orthodoxly conceived monotheistic god? I don't think so.

On the one hand, there is no evident reason why it could not be the case that moral properties and moral facts supervene upon natural properties and natural facts, rather than upon supernatural properties and supernatural facts. Both the theists and non-theists currently under consideration agree that any minimal non-moral duplicate of our universe is a moral duplicate of our universe as well – but they disagree about whether a minimal non-moral duplicate of our universe is a minimal natural duplicate of our universe. What non-question-begging reason is there to suppose that, while moral properties cannot supervene upon natural properties, they can supervene upon supernatural properties? At the very least, the argument under consideration provides us with no such reasons. Moreover, I think, it is very hard to see what form such reasons could take.

On the other hand, there is an obvious difficulty for the suggestion that *all* moral properties and moral facts *derive from* an orthodoxly conceived monotheistic god, namely, that this suggestion seems to give the wrong answer to the Euthyphro question. If it is up to an orthodoxly conceived monotheistic god to *establish* the relations that obtain between moral properties or facts and non-moral properties or facts, then it must be that there are other possible worlds in which the relations that obtain between moral properties or facts and non-moral properties or facts differ from the relations that obtain in the actual world. In particular, then, it seems that, if it is up to an orthodoxly conceived monotheistic god to establish the relations that obtain between moral properties or facts and non-moral properties or facts, then there other possible worlds – not themselves worlds in which there is an orthodoxly conceived monotheistic god – in which there is a natural duplicate of our universe in which the moral properties are different, for example, possible worlds in which there are universes that share the natural history of our world, but in which the Nazi death camps are not evil. I do not think that it is very controversial to claim that there are no such possible universes.[6]

---

[6] A more orthodox formulation of the Euthyphro question asks us to decide whether an orthodoxly conceived monotheistic god's approval of certain states of affairs is what makes those states of affairs right and good, or whether it is rather that an orthodoxly conceived monotheistic god approves of certain states of affairs because they are right and good. If we are to suppose that that morality *derives from* an orthodoxly conceived monotheistic god, then it seems that we must be committed to the former answer to the Euthyphro question: it can hardly be the case that morality *derives from* an orthodoxly conceived monotheistic god, if that god's approval of certain states of affairs depends upon the independent rightness and goodness of those states of affairs, which is what is required if that god is to approve of those states of affairs *because* they are right and good. But if it is merely an orthodoxly conceived monotheistic god's approval of certain states of affairs that *determines* whether those states of affairs are right or good, then it seems that there is no way of avoiding the conclusion that, had that god approved of the Nazi death camps, then the Nazi death camps would have been right and good; and, moreover, that there is no way of avoiding the conclusion that there are no moral considerations that stood in the way of that god's approval of the Nazi death camps. In

So far, our discussion has focussed only on the claim that there are objective moral values. But the premises in the argument that we are considering also advert to the suggestion that moral values are 'absolute'. This suggestion can be understood in various ways – for example, as the suggestion that moral values are *universal* in their application; that moral values are not *relative* to individuals or societies; that moral values are not *indexed* to individuals or societies; are that moral values are not a matter of *subjective* preferences. The question of whether moral values are 'absolute' in any of these senses is orthogonal to the question of whether moral values are objective, that is, to the question of whether there are moral properties and moral facts. But so far as I can see, there is nothing that prevents non-theists from supposing that morality is both objective and absolute, in one or more of the above senses – and if the argument already given holds up, there is no prospect of explaining why morality is both objective and absolute in terms of the actions of an orthodoxly conceived monotheistic god since there is no prospect of explaining why morality is objective in terms of the actions of an orthodoxly conceived monotheistic god.[7]

Of course, the above considerations do not *rule out* the possibility that there are compelling arguments to be advanced on behalf of each of the premises in the arguments under consideration. However, at the very least, it is clear that no one ought to suppose that these arguments are persuasive; and, moreover, it seems to me that it ought also to be conceded that there is good *prima facie* reason to suspect that the second premise in each of these arguments is not one that orthodox monotheists should rush to embrace. If we suppose that there are moral properties and moral facts, then we ought to suppose that there is a *logical* connection between the instantiation of natural properties and the instantiation of moral properties, and that there is a *logical* connection between the obtaining of natural facts and the obtaining of moral facts – and, consequently, we should suppose that, if there are moral properties and moral facts, then there is no role for orthodoxly conceived

particular, it can't be that that god couldn't approve of the Nazi death camps, either because it is good or they are evil: for we are supposing that, prior to the approval and disapproval of that god, there are no facts of the matter about what is good or bad. (In response to this argument, some people appeal to the doctrine of divine simplicity: surely the trope of perfect goodness can both be the source of morality and yet also have application to itself, thus avoiding both horns of the Euthyphro dilemma. Perhaps; but, as I shall argue elsewhere, I do not think that one can sensibly suppose that an orthodoxly conceived monotheistic god is a trope. Moreover, even if there is an 'out' here for some theists, it is clear that it would be a major task to develop a persuasive argument from objective morality on the basis of this highly controversial metaphysics. Why should reasonable non-theists see any *prima facie* appeal in the pair of claims that morality is absolute and objective, and that morality is absolute and objective only if there is a trope of perfect goodness that creates the world *ex nihilo*?)

[7] I take it that it is obvious that non-theists can be consequentialists – and, in particular, utilitarians – or deontologists, or virtue theorists.

monotheistic gods in *establishing* the connections that obtain between the natural realm and the moral realm.

7.3.2. Virtue

There are many monotheists who suppose that, other things being equal, belief in orthodoxly conceived monotheistic gods is an indication of moral superiority or virtue. While it is not a straightforward matter to construct an argument for the existence of orthodoxly conceived monotheistic gods on the basis of this kind of consideration, there is plenty of evidence that some monotheists have been tempted by arguments like the following.

1. People who do not believe that there is an orthodoxly conceived monotheistic god are morally inferior to people who do believe that there is an orthodoxly conceived monotheistic god.
2. People should always choose that which is morally superior over that which is morally inferior.
3. (Therefore) People ought to believe that there is an orthodoxly conceived monotheistic god.
4. Anything that one ought to believe is true: one cannot have an obligation to believe falsehoods.
5. (Therefore) There is an orthodoxly conceived monotheistic god.

One evident difficulty with arguments of this kind lies in the formulation of the first premise.

If, on the one hand, the claim is that, quite apart from any other considerations, belief that there is an orthodoxly conceived monotheistic god is *itself* morally virtuous, then it seems to me that one can justly complain that, not only is there no good non-question-begging reason to suppose that this is so, but there are good independent reasons to deny this claim. In general, there is no reason to suppose that one accrues moral virtue as a result of the formation of beliefs about particular matters of non-moral fact: one is not morally better or morally worse merely because one has true or false beliefs about what are plainly merely matters of non-moral fact. But the question of whether there is an orthodoxly conceived monotheistic god is just a question of non-moral fact. So there is no reason to suppose that one is morally better or morally worse merely because one has formed a particular view about whether or not there is an orthodoxly conceived monotheistic god. At the very least, defenders of the argument – on this reading of it – would need to supply a *persuasive* reason for thinking that the question of whether there is an orthodoxly conceived monotheistic god is itself a moral question; it seems to me not to be especially sceptical to suppose that it is unlikely that a *successful* argument for this conclusion is awaiting discovery.

If, on the other hand, the claim is that, when everything is taken into account, those who believe that there is an orthodoxly conceived monotheistic god are more virtuous than those who fail to believe that there is an orthodoxly conceived monotheistic god, then it seems to me that the appropriate response is to ask for justification of this claim. *I* see no evidence at all that people who profess to believe that there is an orthodoxly conceived monotheistic god are more virtuous than those who fail to profess to believe that there is an orthodoxly conceived monotheistic god. History is replete with horrendous crimes committed by professed theists and by professed non-theists: murder, rape, genocide, and so forth are no more the exclusive provenance of the one than the other.[8] Likewise, history records many instances of virtuous acts performed by professed theists and by professed non-theists: acts of courage, self-sacrifice, beneficence, and the like. Given the variation in the proportions of theists and non-theists, and the difficulties that face the 'summation' of goods and evils, I see no prospect of arriving at an uncontroversial answer to the question of whether, on the whole, those who have believed that there is an orthodoxly conceived monotheistic god have been morally better than those who have failed to hold this belief.

Even if it is granted that there are moral considerations that 'favour' belief in an orthodoxly conceived monotheistic god – that is, even if it is true that those who believe that there is an orthodoxly conceived monotheistic god are morally superior to those who fail to believe that there is an

---

[8] I have been told that the proportion of the prison population in the United States that professes belief in an orthodoxly conceived monotheistic god is much higher than the proportion of the total population in the United States that professes belief in an orthodoxly conceived monotheistic god. If this is right, then it seems to me to make difficulty for those who claim that those who profess belief in an orthodoxly conceived monotheistic god are evidently morally superior to those who do not thus profess: how do these people propose to explain this apparently strong correlation between the propensity to violate the criminal law and professed belief in an orthodoxly conceived monotheistic god? Of course, one might try saying that it is one thing to profess belief in an orthodoxly conceived monotheistic god, and another thing to really believe in an orthodoxly conceived monotheistic god, but if one responds in this way, then one loses the ability to point to evidence in support of the claim that believers are morally superior unless one can provide some other reliable means for determining who are the genuine believers. It is a truism that those who are morally superior and who profess belief in an orthodoxly conceived monotheistic god are morally superior – but there is no mileage to be obtained from this truism if one is hoping to run the kind of argument that is currently under examination. If one is to argue from the moral superiority of believers to the truth of their beliefs, then one needs to be able to identify the believers independently of their moral virtues; at the very least, it is unclear how this is to be done if sincere profession of belief is deemed insufficient. (As indicated in Paul(2005), there is interesting data that correlates religiosity with moral and social dysfunction. This data multiplies the difficulties for those who would claim that there is any kind of positive link between religious belief and virtue.)

orthodoxly conceived monotheistic god – it is quite unclear why we should suppose that this establishes that we have a moral obligation to believe that there is an orthodoxly conceived monotheistic god. That a particular property F is correlated with moral superiority does not entail that one has a moral obligation to acquire property F: if one has a moral obligation here, it is an obligation to acquire those moral properties with which property F is correlated. Moreover, even if it is granted that there is a moral obligation to believe that there is an orthodoxly conceived monotheistic god, it is quite unclear why we should suppose that this establishes that we have a doxastic obligation to believe that there is an orthodoxly conceived monotheistic god. While it is, perhaps, plausible to suppose that one cannot have a doxastic obligation to believe falsehoods, it is much less obviously plausible to suppose that one cannot have a moral obligation to believe falsehoods. At the very least, getting from the claim that one is a better person if one believes that there is an orthodoxly conceived monotheistic god to the conclusion that there is an orthodoxly conceived monotheistic god is no straightforward matter: there are many other hypotheses that one might advance to explain the moral superiority of those who believe that there is an orthodoxly conceived monotheistic god, in circumstances in which it is true that these people are morally superior.

I suppose that the conclusion to be drawn here – namely, that arguments from the virtue of believers are unsuccessful – is not very surprising. While there may be good reasons for at least some of those who believe in orthodoxly conceived monotheistic gods to suppose that, at least other things being equal, those who believe in orthodoxly conceived monotheistic gods are morally superior to those who fail to believe in orthodoxly conceived monotheistic gods, it is surely very hard to believe that good reasons of that sort could be turned into an argument that ought to persuade those who do not already suppose that there is an orthodoxly conceived monotheistic god that such a being exists. To have good reasons for believing that at least other things being equal, those who believe in orthodoxly conceived monotheistic gods are morally superior to those who fail to believe in orthodoxly conceived monotheistic gods, one must already be a believer in orthodoxly conceived monotheistic gods. Or so, at any rate, it seems to me to be most plausible to suppose.

7.3.3. Happiness

There are many monotheists who suppose that those who believe in orthodoxly conceived monotheistic gods are happier than those who fail to believe in orthodoxly conceived monotheistic gods. Once again, while it is not a straightforward matter to construct an argument for the existence of orthodoxly conceived monotheistic gods on the basis of this kind of consideration, there is plenty of evidence that some monotheists have been tempted by arguments like the following.

1. People who believe in orthodoxly conceived monotheistic gods are happier than those who do not believe in orthodoxly conceived monotheistic gods.
2. The best explanation for the fact adverted to in the preceding premise is that there is an orthodoxly conceived monotheistic god that rewards the virtuous and the faithful with happiness.
3. (Therefore) There is an orthodoxly conceived monotheistic god.

While there are ways in which the examination of this argument is likely to proceed along similar lines to an examination of the previous argument (from virtue), there are also ways in which the discussion of this argument is more straightforward. We begin, as before, with a question about the interpretation of the first premise.

If, on the one hand, the claim that is made in the first premise is that the belief that there is an orthodoxly conceived monotheistic god is, *in itself,* sufficient to guarantee happiness, then it seems to me that it is just obviously false: there are plenty of believers in orthodoxly conceived monotheistic gods who lead miserable lives, and of whom it is simply absurd to claim that they are happy. (Here, I set aside consideration of *future* happiness. Doubtless, there are plenty of orthodox theists who suppose that, in the long run, believers will be more happy than non-believers, since believers *will be* rewarded with infinite happiness in heaven while non-believers *will be* punished with infinite suffering in hell. But – by stipulation, if necessary – I insist that the argument that I am now considering is concerned only with present happiness, that is, with the happiness that is experienced by people before they die. An argument from future happiness obviously requires further premises that are not even hinted at in the argument currently under consideration.)

If, on the other hand, the claim that is made in the first premise is that there is a correlation between belief in orthodoxly conceived monotheistic gods and happiness, then it seems to me that the appropriate response is to ask for justification of this claim. I am not sure how one would go about trying to establish that, across all human societies throughout history, those who have believed in orthodoxly conceived monotheistic gods have been happier than those who have failed to believe in orthodoxly conceived monotheistic gods. How, for example, are we to compare the happiness of those who live in present-day India or medieval China – societies in which most people do not believe in orthodoxly conceived monotheistic gods – with the happiness of those who live now in the United States? Even if there are studies that show that, in particular communities at particular times, those who believe in orthodoxly conceived monotheistic gods are happier than those who do not believe in orthodoxly conceived monotheistic gods, it is very doubtful that those studies could be taken to reliably support the claim that believers in orthodoxly conceived monotheistic gods are happier than those who do not believe in orthodoxly conceived monotheistic gods. At the very least, one would need to consider and rule out irrelevant explanations of the observations recorded in those studies: for example, that, in some communities, the persecution of non-believers by believers explains why non-believers are less happy than believers in those communities. If one's sample of individuals and communities is not uniform across space and time, then one generalises from it at one's peril.

Even if it is true that there is a strong correlation between happiness and belief in orthodoxly conceived monotheistic gods, it seems doubtful that there is much reason to suppose that the best explanation of this correlation is that there is an orthodoxly conceived monotheistic god that rewards the virtuous and the faithful with happiness. If it is true that there is a strong correlation between happiness and belief in orthodoxly conceived monotheistic gods, then a reasonable first guess is that it is the content of the belief in orthodoxly conceived monotheistic gods that is responsible for the greater happiness of those who hold this belief, whether or not the belief turns out to be true. Perhaps there is some reason to think that those who suppose that they will live forever in eternal bliss are going to be happier than those who fail to have this belief; but, if that is so, then the (alleged) fact that those who believe in orthodoxly conceived monotheistic gods are happier than those who fail to have this belief will be no evidence at all of the truth of that belief. Indeed, some philosophers – Marx, Engels, Freud – have gone so far as to suppose that there is a sense in which the persistence of belief in orthodoxly conceived monotheistic gods can be explained in terms of the 'happiness' that is conferred on believers by the adoption of this belief: at least in a superficial sense, believing that you will be rewarded in heaven can make you feel better about your life. One does not need to agree with everything that Marx et al. insist on in their critiques of religion in order to see that there is enough in the key points that they are picking up on to undermine the kind of argument from happiness that we are currently considering.

Perhaps it might be said that the considerations to which we have just adverted point to a difficulty in the discussion to this point – for, after all, Marx et al. did not endorse the claim that belief in orthodoxly conceived monotheistic gods really makes one happy. Given that we prepared to draw a distinction between 'superficial' happiness – 'feeling good' – and 'genuine happiness', however the latter is properly to be understood, we might insist that the argument from happiness can survive the criticisms that have been launched at it thus far. Given that one can be mistaken about whether or not one is happy – and, more generally, given that 'happiness' is a matter of the objective value of the life that one leads – then maybe it is not so obviously absurd to claim that belief in the existence of an orthodoxly conceived monotheistic god is, *in itself,* sufficient to guarantee happiness, or that belief in the existence of an orthodoxly conceived monotheistic god is correlated with happiness. Maybe; but it seems to me that, if we understand 'happiness' in the way that is now being proposed, then the argument turns out to have some of the same kinds of shortcomings as the argument from virtue that we discussed in the previous section. For now there is no suitably uncontroversial way of determining whether or not people are happy, that is, no way of determining that people are happy that is independent of ways of determining whether or not people are believers in orthodoxly conceived monotheistic gods. While believers in orthodoxly conceived monotheistic gods might suppose that no life that lacks such belief possesses objective value, it is clear that there is no prospect of a successful argument for the existence of orthodoxly conceived monotheistic gods that starts from this kind of consideration: to have good reasons for believing that, at least other things being equal, those who believe in orthodoxly conceived monotheistic gods have lives that are objectively more valuable than the lives of those who fail to believe in orthodoxly conceived monotheistic gods, one must already be a believer in orthodoxly conceived monotheistic gods. Or so, at any rate, it seems to me to be most plausible to suppose.

7.3.4. Scripture

There are many monotheists who suppose that the evident moral excellence of their chosen monotheistic scripture provides them with good reason to suppose that that scripture has a supernatural origin in the inspiration of an orthodoxly conceived monotheistic god. We might suppose that the argument that these monotheists have in mind runs along the following lines.

1. No mere human being is capable of producing anything that has the moral excellences of such-and-such scripture.
2. (Therefore) Such-and-such scripture is the inspired product of the workings of an orthodoxly conceived monotheistic god.
3. (Therefore) There is an orthodoxly conceived monotheistic god.

The difficulties that face an argument of this kind are obvious.

First, it is very hard to believe that there is one amongst the many extant scriptures that it so evidently *morally* superior to all of the others that one ought to expect agreement on this point amongst all sincere, thoughtful, reflective, intelligent, and sufficiently well-informed people. But different scriptures would support inferences to different orthodoxly conceived monotheistic gods. The mere fact that there is no morally pre-eminent monotheistic scripture would suffice to defeat the claim that there is a persuasive argument of the kind that is here being considered.

Second, while it may be true that, for some extant scriptures, it is hard to believe that a single human being, working alone, was responsible for the production of one of those scriptures, it is not nearly so hard to believe that many human beings working together, over a very long period of time, could have produced one of those scriptures. Given what we *know* about the production of extant scriptures, we have good reason to suppose that those scriptures were the work of teams of people working over very long periods of time; I see no reason at all to doubt that mere human beings could have produced any of these works. Moreover, even if I am wrong about this, there certainly seems to be little prospect that anyone will develop a successful argument for the opposite point of view.

Third, and more controversially, it is highly contestable whether any extant scriptures *are* morally excellent. True enough, some extant scriptures contain morally admirable precepts. But, in many cases, these morally admirable precepts are mixed up with other precepts that are morally repugnant. At the very least, I see no reason to suppose that one should be able to secure widespread agreement amongst thoughtful and well-informed persons that stubborn and rebellious sons should be stoned to death; or that the handicapped should not be allowed to enter a place of worship; or that women should not be allowed to speak in church; or that believers should never permit non-believers to enter their homes; or that those who work on the weekend should be stoned to death; or that you should never boil a young goat in its mother's milk; or that it is acceptable for soldiers to sacrifice their own daughters to celebrate their victories; and so on. Most scriptures were written long ago. Consequently, most scriptures contain edicts that, by widespread contemporary moral standards, are barbarous, or strange, or worse.

Even if the all-too-human origins of extant scriptures were not so evident, that is, even if it were plausible to suppose that some extant scripture could not have been produced by mere human beings, it seems very hard to suppose that one could confidently conclude that that scripture is the work of some orthodoxly conceived monotheistic god. For, in that case, the evident reasons that there are to suppose the extant scriptures are the work of human beings would be reasons to suppose that the creator of that scripture is not an orthodoxly conceived monotheistic god. Why would an omnipotent, omniscient, and perfectly good god enjoin the stoning to death of women who are no longer virginal when they marry, or engaged women who are victims of rape? These injunctions make sense if issued by the elders in a strongly patriarchal early human society; they make no sense at all if they are supposed to have been issued by an omnipotent, omniscient, and perfectly good being to regulate social relations in the twenty-first century. Instituting death penalties is barbaric; the more so if those found guilty are to be stoned to death. Instituting death penalties to be imposed on *victims* of crimes is worse than barbaric. Even if one supposes that the presence of these kinds of injunctions in extant scriptures can be explained away, it seems to me to be very hard to deny that their presence undermines *arguments* for the claim that the existence of these scriptures is best explained by appeal to the workings of an orthodoxly conceived monotheistic god.

7.3.5. Justice

Russell (1927) presents the following argument as an encoding of widespread monotheistic intuitions.

1. Virtue is not always rewarded in this life.
2. Justice demands that virtue is always rewarded in the end.
3. (Therefore) There is an afterlife in which an orthodoxly conceived monotheistic god ensures that the virtuous are rewarded.
4. (Therefore) There is an orthodoxly conceived monotheistic god.

Of course, those who are motivated by this argument for a heavenly afterlife for the virtuous that is supervised by an orthodoxly conceived monotheistic god may also be moved by an argument for a hellish afterlife for the less than virtuous that is, in some sense, supervised by the same orthodoxly conceived monotheistic god.

1. Vice is not always punished in this life.
2. Justice demands that vice is always punished in the end.
3. (Therefore) There is an afterlife in which an orthodoxly conceived monotheistic god ensures that the vicious are punished.
4. (Therefore) There is an orthodoxly conceived monotheistic god.

One immediate difficulty with these arguments lies in the second premises: it is not obvious – to me, at any rate – that justice does demand what these premises claim that it demands. Even if we suppose that virtue requires compensation, it is not clear why this compensation could not be in the form of an escape from punishment for vice committed elsewhere. Similarly, even if we suppose that vice requires payment, it is not clear why this payment could not be in the form of a failure to be rewarded for virtue exhibited elsewhere. At the very least, it seems to me that the arguments need to be reworked so that they make claims about the net sum of virtue and vice in a given human life: it isn't true that everyone who maintains a positive balance of virtue over vice is rewarded in this life; it isn't true that everyone who maintains a negative balance of virtue over vice is punished in this life. But then we face the problem of making sense of talk about 'the net sum of virtue and vice in a given human life'; and we also face the difficult task of finding good reason to suppose that there are clear instances in which 'net sums of vice and virtue' are not appropriately correlated with 'happiness'.

Suppose, however, that we agree that it is true that there are cases in which 'net sums of vice and virtue' are not appropriately correlated with 'happiness'. Why should we suppose that those whose lives have exhibited an appropriate surplus of virtue over vice when they close *deserve* to be rewarded (unless, perhaps, they have already enjoyed an appropriate overall amount of 'happiness'), and that those who lives have exhibited an inappropriate surplus of vice over virtue when they close *deserve* to be punished (unless, perhaps, they have already enjoyed an appropriate overall amount of 'unhappiness')? True enough, perhaps, there should be *approval* of those who have exhibited an appropriate surplus of virtue over vice (regardless of the amount of 'happiness' that they have enjoyed), and there should be *disapproval* of those who have exhibited an inappropriate surplus of vice over virtue (regardless of the amount of 'unhappiness' that they have suffered). But there is much more to the demand for reward and punishment in the second premise in these arguments than a mere demand for approval and disapproval: what is being suggested here is that substantial benefits should be conferred on those who have been overall virtuous but insufficiently happy, and that substantial sanctions should be imposed on those who have been overall vicious but insufficiently unhappy. It would require a large discussion to properly explore the claim at issue here; perhaps it will suffice for me to note that I doubt that I will be alone in being unable to muster any intuitions that support it.[9]

Even if we agree that it is true that justice demands that virtue is rewarded and vice punished, we have still to face what is arguably the most serious difficulty that confronts acceptance of the arguments that we are now considering. Given that it is a familiar fact that the interests of justice are not fully served in our universe, what non-question-begging reason is there to suppose that there is some other venue where those interests are fully served? Leaving aside the claims of those who suppose that there is a future life in which the interests of justice are served, it seems to me – as it seemed to Russell – that the evidence that we have simply supports the conclusion that there is not perfect justice in the universe, given that justice demands that the virtuous are rewarded and the wicked punished. While it may be that there are theists who have good reason to suppose that there is an afterlife in which an

---

[9] There is at least some reason to suppose that it is dangerous to link moral considerations to expected rewards, because such links tend to undermine genuine morality. If parents give rewards to children – cash, sweets, and the like – when they engage in morally admirable behaviour, then the upshot is that children develop a diminished tendency to engage in morally admirable behaviour, particular when the rewards stop coming. Indeed, more generally, if parents give rewards to children for engaging in particular kinds of behaviour – e.g., drawing or writing stories – that children are initially drawn towards because of the intrinsic merits of those activities, the upshot is typically the destruction of the initial enthusiasm that the children had for these activities. It seems to me that, if people are to be proper moral agents, then they should not be disposed to say that the reason why one ought to behave morally is that one will secure certain rewards in heaven iff one behaves morally; rather, they should say that one ought to behave morally simply because that is what morality enjoins. One ought not to kill innocent people because it is morally wrong to kill innocent people, not because killing innocent people might lead to *your* suffering eternal damnation.

orthodoxly conceived monotheistic god rewards the virtuous and punishes the vicious, it is very hard to suppose that there is a good argument for the claim that there is an orthodoxly conceived monotheistic god that begins from the observation that there is imperfect justice in the physical universe.

In conclusion, it may perhaps also be worth noting that, even if it is granted that there must be some other venue in which virtue is rewarded and vice punished, it is not obvious that the best conclusion to be drawn is that there is an afterlife in which an orthodoxly conceived monotheistic god ensures that the demands of justice are met. There are competing metaphysical schemes – involving karma and reincarnation, or creative ethical principles, or the like – that will deliver the same result; and there are alternatives to orthodoxly conceived monotheistic gods that will also deliver the specified goods in an appropriately structured afterlife. Even if one accepts the first two premises of the arguments that we are considering, and one agrees that the demands of justice will be met, it is not obvious that one should leap to the hypothesis that there is an afterlife supervised by an orthodoxly conceived monotheistic god.

7.3.6. Costs of Irreligion

I have encountered monotheists who are prepared to argue that the evident costs of irreligion made manifest by recent history provide a good reason to suppose that there is an orthodoxly conceived monotheistic god. I take it that the argument that they have in mind runs in something like the following form.

1. Loss of belief in orthodoxly conceived monotheistic gods has coincided with the rise of all of the ills of the modern world: increased divorce rates; increased incidence of violent crimes; lack of respect for authority; and so forth.
2. (Therefore) Loss of belief in orthodoxly conceived monotheistic gods has caused the rise of all of the ills of the modern world.
3. (Therefore) We should all return to belief in orthodoxly conceived monotheistic gods.
4. One cannot have an obligation to adopt false beliefs.
5. (Therefore) There is an orthodoxly conceived monotheistic god.

I am not sure that we have very secure data about the incidence of belief in orthodoxly conceived monotheistic gods throughout the past millennium. Since there have been times when it was very dangerous to give public expression to doubts about the existence of orthodoxly conceived monotheistic gods, and since there have been many authorities that have publicly taken the position that it is impossible for there to be reasoned doubts about the existence of orthodoxly conceived monotheistic gods, I take it that there is good reason to wonder whether the observed increase in the incidence of professions of doubt about the existence of orthodoxly conceived monotheistic gods really does reflect an increase in doubts about the existence of orthodoxly conceived monotheistic gods. Perhaps falling church attendances in mainstream churches can be taken to be a fairly reliable indicator, but even here, there are reasons for supposing both that presence at church need not be an especially strong sign of belief in an orthodoxly conceived monotheistic god (particularly at times when there are heavy social costs involved in admissions of lack of belief) and that absence from church need not be an especially strong sign of absence of belief in an orthodoxly conceived monotheistic god (particularly at times when the organisational structures of the various churches are being subject to serious scrutiny). Despite these qualifications, there may be good reason to claim that there has been a loss of belief in orthodoxly conceived monotheistic gods in some parts of the world in the recent past; the only point that I am making here is that, if this is so, it is not as obviously so as some might assume.

I am also not at all sure that we have very good evidence that 'the world has been getting worse'. If – perhaps *per impossible* – an omnipotent and perfectly trustworthy god gave me the choice of moving myself and my family to any community at any past time – for example, to Pericles' Athens or to Cicero's Rome – I think that I would choose to stay where I am. I suspect that it is almost universally true that, as a generation ages, it claims that the world is going to hell in a hand basket. While some generations have been right in this assessment – for example, the one that experienced the Black Death, or the one that marched off to the First World War – it is not at all clear to me that those who have lived though the second half of the twentieth century are properly entitled to such a view. There are various reasons why one expects that, on the whole, people will experience nostalgic feelings about their childhoods; these feelings are a very insecure foundation on which to try to mount an argument for the existence of orthodoxly conceived monotheistic gods. Again, of course, it might nonetheless be true that 'the world has been getting worse overall'; but, as before, I think that this is much less obviously so than many people are inclined to assume.

Suppose that it *is* true that the world has been getting worse overall, and that there has been a correlated decrease in the incidence of belief in orthodoxly conceived monotheistic gods. Is there any reason to suppose that the decrease in the incidence of belief in orthodoxly conceived monotheistic gods has played an important causal role in the world's getting worse overall? There are, after all, many other changes that are correlated with the (assumed) deterioration in the overall state of the world: for example, most obviously, there is the vast increase in the number of people, which has led to a vast increase in the number of crowded cities, polluted waterways, and so forth. If, for example, there has been an increase in the incidence of violent crime, then one might suppose that this can be plausibly explained in terms of the environments in which so many people live their lives, without adverting to the incidence of the belief that there are orthodoxly conceived monotheistic gods. It seems to me that, if it is true that the world has been getting worse overall, then there is no non-question-begging reason to suppose that decline in the incidence of belief in orthodoxly conceived monotheistic gods has played an important causal role in this decline. Doubtless, some of those who suppose that decline in orthodoxly conceived monotheistic gods is, *itself*, an important measure of deterioration will disagree with this evaluation; however, it seems to me that even they should recognise that there is no serious prospect of developing a successful argument for belief in the existence of orthodoxly conceived monotheistic gods that relies on such a controversial set of claims.

Perhaps it is worth noting in closing that, even if it were true that loss of belief in orthodoxly conceived monotheistic gods has been an important causal factor in the overall decline of the state of the world, it is not at all obvious that we should conclude from this that we should all adopt belief in orthodoxly conceived monotheistic gods. No one seriously supposes that loss of belief in orthodoxly conceived monotheistic gods is the *sole* cause of the overall decline of the state of the world; at best, that loss of belief has been one among many causal factors. But given where we are now and given the other causal factors that are presently operating, it may be that more widespread adoption of belief in orthodoxly conceived monotheistic gods will make matters even worse. It is, I think, fairly easy to believe that one of the greatest difficulties that the world currently faces lies in the clash of fundamentalist religious beliefs: fundamentalist versions of Islam, fundamentalist versions of Hinduism, fundamentalist versions of Judaism, and fundamentalist versions of Christianity. In the face of these evident religious tensions it is, at the very least, not at all obvious that more widespread belief in orthodoxly conceived monotheistic gods is going to make the world a better place. Of course, again, there is much more to be said about the matters mentioned in the present paragraph; but, at the very least, it seems to me that we find here yet more reasons for supposing that there is no serious prospect of developing a successful *argument* for belief in the existence of orthodoxly conceived monotheistic gods of the kind that is currently under consideration.[10]

---

[10] There are other considerations that would need to be addressed in a full discussion of the argument from the costs of irreligion. I think that it is very doubtful that there can be an obligation to form a particular kind of belief that derives from neither evidential nor theoretical considerations. Belief is not subject to the will in the kind of way that it would need to be in order for it to be possible that one have a moral – or social, or political – obligation to believe that there is an orthodoxly conceived monotheistic god. However, there are sufficiently many other things wrong with the argument from the costs of irreligion that it is not necessary to appeal to these kinds of considerations in order to defeat the argument.

7.3.7. Heavenly Reward

I have also encountered monotheists who are prepared to argue from the danger of missing out on the benefits of heavenly reward to the conclusion that there is an orthodoxly conceived monotheistic god. We might suppose that these adaptations from Pascal's wager argument have something like the following form.

1. People who fail to believe in an orthodoxly conceived monotheistic god are guaranteed to miss out on the benefits of infinite heavenly reward.
2. No sensible person chooses to miss out on the benefits of infinite heavenly reward.
3. (Therefore) Every sensible person believes in an orthodoxly conceived monotheistic god.
4. What every sensible person believes cannot be false.
5. (Therefore) There is an orthodoxly conceived monotheistic god.

This is an interesting argument. It seems to me that the first premise is not obviously true: if there is an orthodoxly conceived monotheistic god, then it is not at all obvious that that god will fail to reward those who do not believe that there are orthodoxly conceived monotheistic gods on the basis of careful, thoughtful, and informed reflection. Moreover, of course, there are many different religions that maintain that one can obtain a reward only if one believes a particular set of claims: given that these sets of claims conflict, and given that one cannot be rewarded if one holds contradictory beliefs, it follows that there is no set of beliefs the adoption of which is *epistemically* guaranteed to secure reward. Our previous discussion of Pascal's wager has already indicated some of the pitfalls that arise here.

It seems to me to be plausible to claim that no sensible person would *knowingly* choose to miss out on the benefits of infinite heavenly reward. In particular, if one is knowingly presented with the choice between eternal felicity and eternal damnation, then it doesn't require much imagination to suppose that more or less any sensible person in your position will opt for eternal felicity. But, of course, the second premise in our argument does not claim that no sensible person *knowingly* chooses to miss out on an infinite heavenly reward; rather, it claims that no sensible person chooses to miss out on an infinite heavenly reward. And, of course, a sensible person might well make a choice that leads to the missing out on an infinite heavenly reward in circumstances in which that person fails to realise that making that choice leads to the missing out on an infinite heavenly reward. Indeed, given the point made in the previous paragraph, namely, that there is no set of beliefs the adoption of which is *epistemically* or *doxastically* guaranteed to secure reward, it seems plausible to suppose that, no matter what choices one makes, it is at least doxastically possible that the making of those choices leads one to miss out on an infinite heavenly reward. But, of course, one needn't accept this further point in order to see that the second premise in the argument is not acceptable.

Apart from the difficulties already noted, one might also suppose that it is not obvious that the final premise in the argument is true: it is not clear that it cannot be the case that all sensible people are wrong on some matter. However, even if there is no satisfactory way of getting from the claim that every sensible person believes that there is an orthodoxly conceived monotheistic god to the conclusion that there is an orthodoxly conceived monotheistic god, it would, I think, be troubling enough if there were a successful argument to the conclusion that every sensible person believes that there is an orthodoxly conceived monotheistic god. It seems to me to be *prima facie* incredible to suppose that this could be true now; but as we have seen, it is pretty clear that the argument from reward comes nowhere near being a successful argument for this conclusion.

7.3.8. Conscience

Newman (1870) provides the materials for the construction of the following argument from conscience. While Newman explicitly claims that he is not offering an argument for the existence of an orthodoxly conceived monotheistic god, it seems to me to be plausible to claim that Newman can have succeeded in the task that he sets for himself – namely, the task of showing how we come to have knowledge of an orthodoxly conceived monotheistic god – only if the following argument is successful.

1. Conscience, as a sanction of right conduct, induces feelings (and experiences) of fear, shame, and responsibility within us.
2. Feelings (or experiences) of fear, shame, and responsibility logically require another person who is their 'focus', that is, a person to whom one is responsible, before whom one is ashamed, of whom one is afraid, and so on.
3. There is no human being who can systematically play the role of 'focus' for the feelings that conscience induces.
4. (Hence) Conscience logically requires a relationship to an orthodoxly conceived monotheistic god.
5. (Hence) There is an orthodoxly conceived monotheistic god.

When one first encounters Newman's argument from conscience, one might be given to wonder whether there really is a faculty – 'conscience' – that 'induces feelings in us'. However, the important point is surely that there are certain feelings and experiences that act as sanctions on our conduct. If we treat 'conscience' as a label for this cluster of experiences, then perhaps we can accept that the first premise in this argument is true as a matter of definition. Most people do have feelings and experiences of fear, shame, and responsibility that are consequent upon some of their actions; and it is this fact that is the primary datum upon which Newman's argument draws.

Perhaps it might be granted that it is true that there is a sense in which feelings (or experiences) of fear, shame, and responsibility logically require an entity – or collection of entities – that is their focus, that is, that it is truly *appropriate* to undergo these feelings (or experiences) of fear, shame, and responsibility only in cases in which there is a separate entity – or collection of entities – that is their focus. But even if this is true, it may not suffice for the purposes of Newman's argument: for it remains to be argued that it is *ever* appropriate to undergo feelings (or experiences) of fear, shame, and responsibility of the kind under consideration except in cases in which there is a human being (or group of human beings) that is evidently the appropriate focus for those feelings. If there is no reason to suppose that conscience is legitimate and authoritative except in cases where there is a human being (or group of human beings) that is the appropriate focus for the feelings in question, then there is no reason at all to suppose that facts about conscience support the claim that there is an orthodoxly conceived monotheistic god.

As we have already noted parenthetically, even if conscience is legitimate and authoritative, it is very doubtful that there is good reason to suppose that the second premise in Newman's argument is true. While we may, perhaps, grant that the relevant feelings of fear, shame, and responsibility do require something before which one is ashamed, of which one is afraid, and to which one is responsible, it is a very large leap to suppose that, in every case, the 'focus' of those feelings must be a single person. I have already noted that one might think that, in some cases, the thing before which one is ashamed, of which one is afraid, and to which one is responsible is a group of people: family, friends, community, and so forth. It does not require a very large leap to suppose that, at least sometimes, the focus of appropriate feelings of fear, shame, and responsibility is one's parents, or one's siblings, or the members of one's sporting team, or the like. But if this is right, then the second premise in Newman's argument is misformulated: the suggestion that, in each case, conscience requires a single person to be its focus seems far too strong.

Furthermore, even if it were granted that, on every occasion, there is a single person who is the 'focus' of appropriate feelings of fear, shame, and responsibility, it is a very big leap from here to the claim that there is a single person who is the 'focus' of appropriate feelings of fear, shame, and responsibility whenever and wherever those feelings are manifested in the universe. While it is very plausible to claim that there is no natural entity or collection of natural entities that is the 'focus' of appropriate feelings of fear, shame, and responsibility whenever and wherever those feelings are manifested in the universe, it seems to me that there is no good reason at all to suppose that appropriate feelings of fear, shame, and responsibility have the same 'focus' whenever and wherever they are manifested in the universe.

The most important point to make, in connection with Newman's argument, is that it is most implausible to suppose that there is a *successful* argument for the claim that the phenomena of conscience are better explained on the assumption that conscience is the 'voice' of an orthodoxly conceived monotheistic god than they are on the assumption that conscience is a natural phenomenon that is susceptible of entirely naturalistic explanation. Perhaps I would not go so far as to agree with Mackie (1982: 105) when he says that 'if we stand back from the experience of conscience and try to understand it, it is overwhelmingly plausible to see it as an introjection into each individual of demands that come from other people; in the first place, perhaps, from his parents and immediate associates, but ultimately from the traditions and institutions of the society in which he has grown up, or some special part of that society that has had the greatest influence upon him'. Perhaps it is not true that everyone should find overwhelmingly plausible what Mackie claims is overwhelmingly plausible. Nonetheless, the fact that Mackie himself finds these considerations overwhelmingly plausible does point to a central difficulty for the argument from conscience: to interpret the phenomenon of conscience in the way that Newman does, one must already suppose that there is an orthodoxly conceived monotheistic god; so one can hardly think that there is a successful argument from that interpretation of the phenomenon of conscience to the conclusion that there is an orthodoxly conceived monotheistic god.

7.3.9. Convergence

Sidgwick (1874) presents – but does not endorse – the following argument.

1. What I have most reason to do is always what will best secure my own happiness in the long run.
2. What I have most reason to do is always what morality requires.
3. If there is no moral government of the universe, what will best secure my own happiness is not always what morality requires.
4. (Therefore) There is a moral government of the universe.
5. (Therefore) There is an orthodoxly conceived monotheistic god.

According to Mackie, Sidgwick accepted all of the premises of this argument, but reasonably refused to accept the conclusion, preferring to think instead that 'there is a fundamental and unresolved chaos in our practical reasoning'. Moreover, according to Mackie, Sidgwick was right to respond to the argument in this way, even though it might be possible to escape the argument by insisting that one or both of the first two premises is true only if it is qualified in some way.

I think that it is more plausible to suppose that there is a serious equivocation in the use of the word 'reason' in the two premises of this argument. On the one hand, it is plausible to suppose that one has most *prudential* reason to do what will secure one's own happiness in the long run; on the other hand, it is also plausible to suppose that one has most *moral* reason to do what morality requires. But there is no reason at all to suppose that the interests of prudence and morality *must* coincide; and, moreover, the fact that the interests of prudence and morality fail to coincide gives us no reason at all to conclude that there is a moral government of the universe. Perhaps the fact that the interests of prudence and morality fail to coincide is evidence of 'a fundamental and unresolved chaos in our practical reasoning'; but even if this is so, we plainly have no good ground at all to suppose that there is a single sense of 'most reason' in which I always have most reason to secure my own happiness in the long run *and* most reason to do what morality dictates.

7.3.10. Practical Reason

Perhaps the best-known moral argument for belief in the existence of an orthodoxly conceived monotheistic god is due to Kant. As we have already had occasion to note, Kant argues in the *Critique of Pure Reason* that there is no good argument from pure reason and sensory evidence to the existence of an orthodoxly conceived monotheistic god. However, in the *Critique of Practical Reason*, Kant goes on to claim that, despite the failure of the traditional arguments for belief in the existence of an orthodoxly conceived monotheistic god, it is nonetheless reasonable – and, indeed, rationally obligatory – to believe that there is an orthodoxly conceived monotheistic god. According to Kant, the source of this rational obligation lies not in theoretical reason, but rather in practical concerns: in his view, one cannot lead a proper moral life unless one believes in an orthodoxly conceived monotheistic god. Since we ought to live proper moral lives, it seems to follow that we are obliged to believe that there is an orthodoxly conceived monotheistic god. And if we are rationally obliged to believe that there is an orthodoxly conceived monotheistic god, then surely we do after all have good reason to claim that there is an orthodoxly conceived monotheistic god. Without too much injustice, it seems to me that this Kantian argument can be encapsulated as follows:

1. It is our moral duty to try to bring about the *summum bonum*.[11] ("The highest good is the necessary highest end of a morally determined will and a true object thereof.")

[11] The *summum bonum* is the best possible state of affairs, in which moral goodness exists and is appropriately correlated with happiness.

2. Since we ought to bring about the *summum bonum*, and since ought implies can, it is possible for the *summum bonum* to come about. ("It is a necessity connected with duty as a requisite to presuppose the possibility of the highest good.")

3. It is not within our power to bring about the *summum bonum*. ("We are free to achieve virtue in ourselves, but not to ensure that happiness is added to virtue, thus realising the *summum bonum*.")

4. (Hence) There must be a rational and moral being who has the power to bring moral desert and happiness into harmony with one another. ("The existence is postulated of a cause of the whole of nature, itself distinct from nature, which contains the ground of the exact coincidence of happiness with morality".)

5. (Hence, also) "Since the apportioning of happiness to virtue does not take place in this life, it must be attained in eternity – and so the postulate of immortality is closely connected to the postulate of divine existence."

Plainly enough, Sidgwick's argument is modelled on the earlier argument that Kant produced. The argument from justice that we discussed earlier also shares some of the features of this Kantian argument. There are many questions that one might ask about the Kantian moral argument; I doubt that I shall examine all of them here.

First, there is a question about the starting point of the argument. In my formulation of the first premise, the claim is that one has a duty *to try* to bring about the *summum bonum*. But, in the second premise, the 'ought implies can' principle will only yield that it is possible to try to bring about the *summum bonum*, if this is where we start. And nothing at all follows from this concerning the possibility of bringing about the *summum bonum*: for people can try to do the impossible, for example, to square the circle and the like. So it is clear that I have not formulated the argument correctly: the first premise of the argument must be that it is our moral duty to bring about the *summum bonum*.

Second, though, given that the first premise of the argument is that it is our moral duty to bring about the *summum bonum*, it is far from clear that we should accept this first premise. Setting certain difficulties aside, it might be plausible to suppose that we have a moral duty to try to bring about the *summum bonum*; but it sounds impossibly daunting and demanding to suppose that we have moral duty to succeed in bringing about the best possible state of affairs.

Third, it is far from clear that there is any such thing as *the summum bonum*, that is, *the* best possible state of affairs, in which moral goodness exists and is appropriately correlated with happiness. It might be, for example, that, for any possible state of affairs, there is a better state of affairs. In that case, there is no such thing as the *summum bonum*, and, hence, given the 'ought implies can' principle, no obligation to bring it about. Alternatively, there might be various different ways of trading off happiness with virtue, each of which is equally good. In that case, too, there is no such thing as the *summum bonum*, and, hence, given the 'ought implies can' principle, no obligation to bring it about.

Fourth, in view of the previously mentioned difficulties, one might think that we ought to look for a more plausible statement of our moral duty. Perhaps, for example, we have a moral duty to promote the maximum sum of virtue and happiness in the world; or perhaps we have a moral duty to increase the sum of virtue and happiness in the world as much as we can. I think that it is highly doubtful that we have even these more moderate duties; they still sound awfully daunting and demanding. But, in any case, with this revised starting point, Kant's argument goes nowhere: given that we do have a duty to increase the sum of virtue and happiness in the world as much as we can, nothing at all follows about the possible moral perfectibility of the world.

Fifth, even if we were to concede that Kant manages to establish that it is possible that the *summum bonum* is brought about, it seems clear that we could be under an obligation to try to bring about the *summum bonum* only if it is possible for us to bring it about. While it might be true that it is not within our power to bring about the *summum bonum* – that is, it is not true that, if we were to try to bring about the *summum bonum*, then the *summum bonum* would ensue – it does not follow from the fact that it is not within our power to bring about the *summum bonum* that it is not possible for us to bring about the *summum bonum*; and, moreover, consistency requires that Kant himself recognised that this is so. But, in that case, the inference from the premises to the conclusion in the Kantian argument is plainly a *non sequitur*: given that it is possible for us to bring about the *summum bonum* and hence possible for the *summum bonum* to be brought about, but that it is not within our power to bring about the *summum bonum*, nothing at all follows about the existence of other beings that have the power to bring about the *summum bonum*.

Sixth, even if we supposed that Kant had somehow managed to show both that it is possible for the *summum bonum* to be brought about, and that it is not possible for us to bring about the *summum bonum*, the most that would follow from these premises is that it is possible for some other being to bring about the *summum bonum*. That is, at best, the conclusion of the Kantian argument would be that it is possible that there is an orthodoxly conceived monotheistic god, and not that there actually is an orthodoxly conceived monotheistic god. Perhaps one might think that this gap in the Kantian argument could be repaired by appeal to a modal ontological argument – but, of course, that is hardly an option that would have appealed to Kant himself.

Seventh, there is an interesting question to raise about the status that Kant supposes should be attributed to his argument. If the argument were successful, what would Kant take it to have established? Is it an argument that allows us to 'enlarge our stock of knowledge'? Or is it rather that what he thinks that he has shown is that, unless one believes in the existence of an orthodoxly conceived monotheistic god, one is obliged to give up 'the moral law' – so that, for all that has been said so far, one could reasonably respond by giving up 'the moral law'? (Although I formulated the conclusion of the argument as the claim that there is an orthodoxly conceived monotheistic god, it is not clear that this really does justice to the Kantian text.)

Eighth, as hinted in the previous comment, there are some large and difficult issues that are raised by Kant's moral argument, and the claims that he makes in connection with it. Should we really suppose that there is a distinction between 'pure reason' and 'practical reason'? Should we really suppose that there is a tension between 'rationality' and 'morality'? Can one have reasons for believing propositions that are not grounded in evidence or reasoning to the truth of those propositions? Is Kantian morality too demanding? Is there a tension between Kant's morality and his theism? If rational beings are, as such, competent to prescribe the moral law, then they do not need an orthodoxly conceived monotheistic god to command or advise them – but, in that case, why do they need the assurance of the possibility of the *summum bonum*? Shouldn't the Kantian recognition of the autonomy of morals lead rather to the Stoic view that one needs no actual happiness beyond the consciousness of right action itself? And so on.

While there is plainly much more that could be said about the Kantian moral argument, it seems to me that we have more than enough reason to say that it is clear that this argument is not successful. Perhaps there are ways in which the argument could be reformulated that would avoid some of the difficulties to which I have pointed; but, as things stand, there is no good reason to suppose that there is a successful argument of this kind.

7.3.11. Concluding Remark

There are doubtless moral arguments for the existence of orthodoxly conceived monotheistic gods that I have not considered. Moreover, there are probably ways in which the discussion of these arguments can be made more systematic. However, it seems to me – as it seems to most people who have considered these kinds of arguments – that it is quite implausible to suppose that there are any *successful* moral arguments for the existence of orthodoxly conceived monotheistic gods.[12] Of course, that's not to say that

---

[12] What if we tried putting together all of the considerations that are appealed to in the separate arguments that we have considered: could we suppose that considerations about the absoluteness and objectivity of morality, the moral superiority of theists, the greater happiness of theists, the moral excellence of scripture, the requirements of justice, the costs of irreligion, the heavenly rewards for moral behaviour, conscience, the coherence

theists cannot reasonably claim that the contentious moral claims upon which moral arguments typically depend fit naturally into their theistic world-views. As elsewhere, the aim of this discussion has not been to persuade theists to give up on their theism, but rather to give up on the idea that there are *successful arguments* for theism.

7.4. ARGUMENTS FROM MIRACLES

In the preceding discussion of Swinburne's argument from religious experience, we already adverted to what might plausibly be supposed to be paradigmatic arguments from miracles, namely, cases in which people claim to have experienced 'very unusual public objects or events' – such as the resurrection of someone from the dead, or the turning of water into wine, or the curing of the lame by touching their afflicted limbs, or the parting of the Red Sea, or a statue of Mary weeping tears of blood – that are alleged to be most plausibly taken to be the results of the actions of an orthodoxly conceived monotheistic god. Examples of arguments of this kind are the following.

1. The Red Sea parted for Moses.
2. Only an orthodoxly conceived monotheistic god could part the Red Sea.
3. (Therefore) There is an orthodoxly conceived monotheistic god.

and

1. There is no (known) scientific explanation of certain miraculous recoveries from near death.
2. These recoveries are (best) explained as the result of the will of an orthodoxly conceived monotheistic god.
3. (Therefore) There is an orthodoxly conceived monotheistic god.

After making some brief remarks about these kinds of arguments, I shall turn my attention to Hume's attempt to argue that no one should ever accept testimony to the miraculous. Perhaps unsurprisingly, I shall argue that Hume's attempt is a failure: while *arguments* from reports of miracles to the existence of orthodoxly conceived monotheistic gods are manifestly

of practical reasoning, and the practical necessity of belief in an orthodoxly conceived monotheistic god jointly give rise to a successful argument for the claim that there is an orthodoxly conceived monotheistic god? I don't think so. We have already seen that there is no reason to suppose that any of these considerations should carry weight with those not already persuaded that there is an orthodoxly conceived monotheistic god. But it seems to me that it is pretty clear that there is no reason to suppose that the joint weight of these considerations exceeds the sum of the individual weights that they carry. Whence it follows that the cumulative argument is essentially no more successful than the individual arguments that have already been examined.

unsuccessful, there are no better arguments for the claim that no one could reasonably believe that an orthodoxly conceived monotheistic god has intervened at various points in the history of our universe.

In the first argument from miracles given above, the first premise is highly controversial. While some of those who suppose that there is an orthodoxly conceived monotheistic god will suppose that the premise is true, it seems plausible to claim that, typically, those who deny that there is an orthodoxly conceived monotheistic god will also deny that the premise is true. But if it is true that only (some of) those who already believe that there is an orthodoxly conceived monotheistic god accept the claim that Moses parted the Red Sea, then it is clear that no argument that takes as a key premise the claim that Moses parted the Red Sea can be successful. Given that non-believers do not accept that Jesus rose from the dead, or that Jesus turned water into wine, there is no point in trying to argue from the alleged occurrence of these events to the existence of an orthodoxly conceived monotheistic god.

Even if we set aside the difficulties that are raised by the first premise of our target argument, it is not clear that we should conclude that the argument is otherwise successful. For even if it were conceded that the parting of the Red Sea occurred, it is not clear that the parting of the Red Sea demands a supernatural explanation; and, more important, even if the parting of the Red Sea does demand a supernatural explanation, it is not clear that the best supernatural explanation is to suppose that it is the result of the actions of an orthodoxly conceived monotheistic god. If you suppose that there is an orthodoxly conceived monotheistic god, then you may find it very natural to suppose that the best explanation of the parting of the Red Sea is that it is the result of the actions of that god. But if you are not antecedently convinced that there is an orthodoxly conceived monotheistic god, then it is much less clear that you are obliged to suppose that the best supernatural explanation of the parting of the Red Sea is that it is the result of the actions of an orthodoxly conceived monotheistic god. It isn't hard to dream up alternative supernatural explanations that those who are not antecedently convinced of the existence of an orthodoxly conceived monotheistic god may well find no less plausible than the hypothesis that the Red Sea was parted by an orthodoxly conceived monotheistic god.

In the second of our pair of arguments, the first premise is much less controversial than the corresponding premise in the first argument. There are cases on record in which people have recovered after being very close to death, and in which there is no detailed naturalistic explanation of how that recovery occurred. However, there are various difficulties that confront the suggestion that everyone ought to agree that the best explanation for the fact that there are such cases is that the recovery is the result of the actions of an orthodoxly conceived monotheistic god. Perhaps the most important point to note is that the mere fact that no one has ever given a detailed naturalistic explanation of a certain event is not a particularly good reason to suppose that that event can only have a supernatural explanation. If we insist on enough details, then it is true that there are (almost?) no events that have been given a detailed naturalistic explanation. But everyone agrees that there is a large class of events for which there are detailed naturalistic explanations, even though – perhaps – we shall never be in a position to give those explanations. If it is antecedently plausible to suppose that, on the hypothesis of naturalism, there will sometimes be cases in which people recover after having come very close to death (in circumstances in which we can't even begin to guess at why it is that those people recovered), then there is no reason at all to suppose that particular cases in which people recover after having come very close to death (in circumstances in which we can't even begin to guess at why it is that those people recovered) are evidence that there is an orthodoxly conceived monotheistic god that intervenes in the course of history. And, of course, it is antecedently plausible to suppose that, on the hypothesis of naturalism, there will be cases like this.

Moreover, there are difficulties in the suggestion that there are cases in which the recovery of people who have been near death is best explained as the result of the intervention of an orthodoxly conceived monotheistic god. At the very least, one might suspect that whatever considerations conspire to make it impossible for an orthodoxly conceived monotheistic god to prevent the rape and murder of a five-year-old child without making the world worse will also conspire to make it impossible for an orthodoxly conceived monotheistic god to intervene to prevent the death of someone who is in the advanced stages of bowel cancer without making the world worse. If justice demands that an orthodoxly conceived monotheistic god could not prevent one rape or murder without preventing them all, then surely justice also demands that an orthodoxly conceived monotheistic god could not prevent one death in the advanced stages of bowel cancer without preventing them all. If the need for rule by natural law demands that an orthodoxly conceived monotheistic god could not prevent one rape or murder without preventing them all, then surely the need for rule by natural law also demands that an orthodoxly conceived monotheistic god could not prevent one death in the advanced stages of bowel cancer without preventing them all. And so on.

Furthermore, even if we suppose that there are no good reasons to hold that an orthodoxly conceived monotheistic god is unable to intervene to prevent a death in the advanced stages of bowel cancer, it still remains the case that there might be better competing supernatural explanations of this recovery. It isn't hard to dream up alternative supernatural explanations that those who are not antecedently convinced of the existence of an orthodoxly conceived monotheistic god may well find no less plausible than the hypothesis that a given patient recovered from near death because of the intervention of an orthodoxly conceived monotheistic god. And, in that case, the argument that we are considering is plainly disabled.

While the discussion of my two sample arguments has been brief, I don't expect that many people are likely to dissent from the judgment that arguments such as these are plainly unsuccessful. Either arguments from miracles appeal to premises, about the occurrence of events, whose truth is too hotly contested by non-theists to make it plausible to suppose that arguments with those premises ought to persuade non-theists, or arguments from miracles appeal to premises, about the best or most likely explanation of events, whose truth is too hotly contested by non-theists to make it plausible to suppose that arguments with those premises ought to persuade non-theists, or both of these claims are true. But, in making this judgment, I do not claim that it could never be reasonable for theists to suppose that some historical events are best explained as the result of the intervention of an orthodoxly conceived monotheistic god: my point is one about the force of arguments from miracles, not about the reasonableness of believing in miracles. If you hold enough of the beliefs that are typically held by those who believe in orthodoxly conceived monotheistic gods, then perhaps it can be reasonable for you to accept that certain historical events are best explained as the result of the intervention of an orthodoxly conceived monotheistic god. At the very least, I have no wish to try to argue against this suggestion.

Famously, of course, Hume does try to argue that belief in miracles – or, at any rate, belief in testimony to miraculous events – is never justified: no one can ever reasonably believe that a miracle has occurred on the basis of testimony to the occurrence of that event. His *a priori* argument for this conclusion may, I think, be fairly summarised as follows.

1. A law of nature is, *inter alia*, a regularity to which no exception has previously been observed.
2. A miracle is a violation of the laws of nature.
3. (Hence) There is absolutely uniform experience against miracles ('as compelling a proof from experience as can be possibly imagined').
4. The proof from experience in favour of testimony of any kind cannot be more compelling (and there is no other form of proof in favour of testimony).
5. Testimony should be believed iff the falsehood of the testimony is more improbable than the event attested to.
6. (Hence) Testimony to miraculous events should never be believed: belief in a miracle report can never be justified.

Hume also goes on to note that, in fact, the testimony in favour of miracles is never the best possible: (i) no miracle reports have ever been made in circumstances that guarantee their trustworthiness; (ii) people have an inclination to believe in miracles on the basis of meagre evidence; (iii) in more civilised nations, there are fewer accounts of miracles; and (iv) reports of miracles in one religion destroy the credibility of reports of miracles in contrary religions. We shall come back later to ask about the significance that is properly attached to these kinds of claims.

There are various difficulties that face the argument that I have set out above.

First, it is not clear that we should accept that the laws of nature are regularities to which no exceptions have been observed. Perhaps it is true that, if there are laws of nature, then laws of nature must be such that there can be no *veridical* observations of exceptions to them. Perhaps it is also true that we cannot take something to be a law of nature unless we take it that there have been no trustworthy claims to observations of exceptions to it. But even if these claims are true, I doubt that there are many theists who will suppose that they are true. If we suppose that the laws of nature are such that they can be countermanded – and, indeed, such that they can only be countermanded – by the intervention of an orthodoxly conceived monotheistic god, then we might suppose, contrary to Hume, that exceptions to laws of nature can be observed. Whether or not non-theists are happy to accept Hume's regularity account of laws of nature, it seems to me that it is most unlikely that this account is acceptable to theists. But, in that case, it is not plausible to suppose that this account can serve as a premise in a *successful* argument for the conclusion that belief in miracle reports can never be justified.

Second, it is not clear that we should accept Hume's account of miracles. If we suppose that miracles are the wilful interventions of supernatural agents in the natural world, then it seems that we can suppose that there are miracles even if we suppose that there are no *laws* of nature. Moreover – in the light of Hume's intention to represent miracles as events that are maximally improbable – it is worth noting that, if we suppose that miracles are the wilful interventions of supernatural agents in the natural world, then we don't need to suppose that it is true that miracles are maximally improbable events. (On the other hand, it is hard to see how one could have reason to suppose that an event is miraculous unless it is improbable in the absence of supernatural intervention: while supernatural agents might intervene to bring about events that would have happened anyway if the course of nature had been left alone, it is hard to see how we could have good reason to suppose that a given event is of this kind, reliable testimony from supernatural sources aside.)

Third, while the balancing principle upon which Hume relies – namely, that testimony should be believed iff the falsehood of the testimony is more improbable than the event attested to – seems to me to be beyond reproach, it is quite unclear how we are to use this principle in arguing for the conclusion that the posterior probability of the truth of any given testimony to a miraculous event must be low. Given Hume's characterisation of miracles and laws of nature, it is plausible to claim that the result of Rutherford's experiment – in which he fired α-particles at gold foil, and some of the α-particles came straight back at him – was a miracle: there was 'absolutely uniform experience' against this experimental result prior to its being carried out. If you'd asked Rutherford prior to the experiment what probability he attributed to this experimental outcome, I take it that he would have said that it is as low as you please: not zero, on grounds of regularity, but certainly of no more than negligible size.[13] Nonetheless, after Rutherford has made his observations and published his results, people reasonably believed him, presumably because they judged it much more likely that the α-particles rebounded from the gold foil than that Rutherford was lying, or otherwise mistaken, about this. So, it seems that we have reason – based on experience! – to claim that the 'proof from experience in favour of testimony' can be more compelling than the 'proof from absolutely uniform prior experience' against the occurrence of a certain kind of event. Since Hume should not want to deny that there can be spectacular scientific discoveries, I take it that he ought to concede that he has no good grounds for claiming that 'the proof from experience in favour of testimony *cannot* be more compelling than the absolutely uniform experience against the occurrence of a given kind of event': there are new things under the sun, and we can come to have knowledge of them.

Even if it is agreed that there is no good *a priori* argument against the claim that there can be believable testimony to the miraculous, one might suppose that the various other considerations to which Hume adverts – concerning the quality of actual testimony to the miraculous – are sufficient to support the claim that there never has been believable testimony to the miraculous. However, while I am inclined to agree with Hume's *judgment* that there has never been believable testimony to the miraculous, I do not think that the considerations to which Hume adverts can serve the needs of an *argument* for the conclusion that there has never been believable testimony to the miraculous. Depending upon what else it is that one believes, one may well act reasonably in believing some miracle reports; in particular, if one believes that there is an orthodoxly conceived monotheistic god, then one may well act reasonably in believing that some of the events recorded in one's scripture of choice were actually the results of wilful interventions in the natural order on the part of the orthodoxly conceived monotheistic god in which one believes.

In sum: Hume's argument against belief in miracle reports fails no less surely than do the various arguments from miracle reports to the existence of an orthodoxly conceived monotheistic god.

---

[13] Famously, Rutherford is supposed to have said that he would have been no less surprised had he fired an artillery shell at a piece of tissue paper, and observed the artillery shell rebounding from the tissue paper. I take it that we should all agree that there is 'absolutely uniform experience' against the occurrence of an event of that kind!

7.5. ARGUMENTS FROM CONSCIOUSNESS

Perhaps the best-known recent defence of an argument from consciousness appears in Swinburne (1979). However, there is a long history of arguments that attempt to derive the conclusion that there is an orthodoxly conceived monotheistic god from the claim that it is otherwise impossible to account for the emergence or presence of conscious beings in our physical universe. So, before we turn to examine Swinburne's argument, we shall begin with a brief examination of an argument of this kind to be found in Locke's *Essay Concerning Human Understanding.*

7.5.1. Locke's Argument

In Book 4 ('Of Knowledge and Opinion'), chapter 10 ('Of Our Knowledge of the Existence of God'), sections 8–10, Locke writes as follows:

There is no truth more evident than that something must be from eternity. I never yet heard of anyone so unreasonable or that could suppose so manifest a contradiction, as a time wherein there was perfectly nothing. This being of all absurdities the greatest, to imagine that pure nothing, the perfect negation and absence of all beings, should ever produce any real existence.

There are but two sorts of beings in the world that man knows or conceives. First, such as are purely material, without sense, perception, or thought, as the clippings of our beards, and parings of our nails. Secondly, sensible, thinking, perceiving beings, such as we find ourselves to be. Which, if you please, we will hereafter call cogitative and incogitative beings; which to our present purpose, if for nothing else, are perhaps better terms than material and immaterial.

If, then, there must be something eternal, let us see what sort of being it must be. And to that it is very obvious to reason that it must necessarily be a cogitative being. For it is as impossible to conceive that ever bare incogitative matter should produce a thinking intelligent being, as that nothing should of itself produce matter. Let us suppose any parcel of matter eternal, great or small, we shall find it, in itself, able to produce nothing. For example: let us suppose the matter of the next pebble we meet with eternal, closely united, and the parts firmly at rest together; if there were no other being in the world, must it not eternally remain so, a dead inactive lump? Is it possible to conceive it can add motion to itself, being purely matter, or produce anything? Matter, then, by its own strength, cannot produce in itself so much as motion; the motion it has must be from eternity, or else be produced, and added to matter by some other being more powerful than matter; matter, as is evident, having not power to produce motion in itself. But let us suppose motion eternal too: yet matter, incogitative matter and motion, whatever changes it might produce of figure and bulk, could never produce thought; knowledge will still be as far beyond the power of motion and matter to produce, as matter is beyond the power of nothing or nonentity to produce. . . . Since, therefore, whatsoever is the first eternal being must necessarily be cogitative; and whatsoever is first of all things must necessarily contain in it, and actually have, at least, all the perfections that can ever after exist; nor can it ever give to another any perfection that it hath not either actually in itself, or, at least, in a higher degree; it necessarily follows, that the first eternal being cannot be matter.

I take it that Locke's argument can be fairly encapsulated as follows.

1. There must always have been something in existence.
2. (Therefore) There must be something that has always existed.
3. Every being is either cogitative or incogitative.
4. There are now cogitative beings.
5. From matter and motion alone, thought could never arise; that is, cogitative beings cannot arise from incogitative beings alone.
6. (Therefore) The being that has always existed must be a cogitative being.

There are some obvious difficulties that confront this argument. In particular, the inference from 1 to 2 is simply invalid: it does not follow from $(\forall t)$ $(\exists x)$ (x exists at t) that $(\exists x)$ $(\forall t)$ (x exists at t). Moreover – as we have already seen in our discussion of cosmological arguments – there are difficulties that confront independent attempts to establish that 2 is true. However, if we suppose that time is internal to the physical universe, and if we suppose that the physical universe lies within the range of the initial quantifier in 2, then we shall certainly be prepared to concede that 2 is true. But if we now follow though the logic of Locke's argument, it seems that we will be led to the conclusion that the physical universe is a cogitative being, that is, we shall be led to pantheism and not to the orthodoxly conceived monotheism that Locke intends to defend. Moreover, Locke's distinction between incogitative (=material) and cogitative (=thinking) beings seems to be not obviously exhaustive: for where do numbers, and propositions, and properties, and states of affairs, and so forth sit in this system of classification? But if this is right, then it seems that premise 3 is false, given the interpretation that Locke intends to give to it. And so on.

I think that, despite the above difficulties, there is an interesting argument that can be salvaged from the wreck of Locke's reasoning. This argument runs as follows.

1. There has always been something in existence.
2. Everything is either cogitative or incogitative.
3. There are now cogitative beings.
4. Cogitative beings cannot be produced by, or arise from, incogitative beings alone.
5. (Therefore) There have always been cogitative beings.

Given the results of modern scientific cosmology, it seems that we have good reason to reject the claim that the physical universe has always contained cogitative beings: there is no good reason to suppose that the physical universe contained cogitative beings at any time in its very early history; and there is very good reason to deny that the physical universe contained cogitative beings at any point in its very early history. At the very least, it seems to me that no physicalist can accept the argument that is set out above. But what is there in this argument to which a physicalist can object?

One option is to reject the claim that there are cogitative beings. In recent times, there have been a number of eliminative materialists – for example, Churchland (1979, 1986) and Stich (1983) – who have been prepared to deny that our ordinary mentalistic talk is true of anything in the world. On this view, understood strictly, there are no 'cogitative' beings: there is nothing that is adequately described by the 'postulates of folk psychology', that is, by our familiar talk of beliefs, desires, thoughts, and the like. I take it that it is quite clear that those who embrace eliminative materialism have nothing to fear from Locke's argument. Moreover, I am inclined to think that eliminative materialism is not *so* obviously mistaken as many of its critics would have us believe. Nonetheless, I think that it is not at all plausible to suppose that our revised version of Locke's argument forces physicalists into acceptance of eliminative materialism. But what other alternative is there?

I suppose that no one will be very surprised to be told that the key question is whether it is really true that cogitative beings cannot be produced by, or arise from, incogitative beings alone, that is, whether premise 4 is true. Much here turns on the question of what is meant by the claim that one kind of being is 'produced by' or 'arises from' another kind of being. Suppose, for example, that we think that 'cogitative beings' are purely physical beings that are distinguished by the kind of organisation that they have: suppose, in particular, that it is metaphysically necessary that any merely physical duplicate of an existing 'cogitative being' would itself be a cogitative being. Would the truth of this kind of constitution claim suffice to establish that cogitative beings can be 'produced by' or 'arise from' incogitative beings alone?

As Mackie (1982: 121) suggests, one might think to interpret premise 4 as a claim about what it is plausible to believe, given the complexity of the 'cogitative' beings that are familiar to us. Given the results of modern neuro-scientific investigations, perhaps we have good reason to believe that 'cogitative' beings must have 'irreducibly complex' or 'specifiably complex' internal arrangements that can plausibly be explained only on the postulation of a 'cogitative' designer of those internal arrangements. However, on the one hand, I take it that it is pretty clear that this is not the kind of argument that Locke has in mind; and, on the other hand, we have already seen – in our discussion of teleological arguments – that there are good reasons to suppose that arguments of this type are unsuccessful. Consequently, it seems to me to be most fruitful to interpret premise 4 as a straightforward denial of materialism or physicalism: what Locke's argument from consciousness assumes is that materialism or physicalism is false.

Perhaps it might be objected – as it is by Mackie (1982: 120f.) – that this interpretation of premise 4 is inconsistent with other claims that Locke makes in the *Essay Concerning Human Understanding*. In book 3 ('Of Words), chapter 4 ('Of the Names of Simple Ideas', section 6, Locke says that we cannot decide 'by the contemplation of our own ideas, without revelation . . . whether omnipotency has not given to some systems of matter fitly disposed, a power to conceive and think'. That is, as Mackie (1982: 120f.) notes, Locke leaves it open that a mere material being might think, since it is not impossible for us to conceive that a standardly conceived monotheistic god might 'superadd to matter a faulty of thinking'. While Mackie claims that, in the making of this claim, Locke abandons the suggestion that we know *a priori* that material structures simply could not be conscious – and hence that we know *a priori* that material structures cannot of themselves give rise to consciousness – it seems to me that Locke can still be firmly wedded to the contention that we know *a priori* that the only way in which material structures could become cogitative is through 'the superaddition of cogitative powers' by an orthodoxly conceived monotheistic god.[14] According to Locke, a merely physical duplicate of an existing 'cogitative being' is not itself guaranteed to be a cogitative being, since either the merely physical duplicate will lack an attached immaterial thinking substance (in case substance dualism is true) or else the merely physical duplicate will lack the 'superadded cogitative powers' (in case Locke's alternative hypothesis is true).

Even if I am right to claim that Locke's argument relies crucially on a premise that denies the truth of materialism or physicalism, it remains the case that we haven't yet developed an argument that has anything more than anti-materialist and anti-physicalist conclusions. Perhaps there is some way of getting from the claim that there have always been cogitative beings to the conclusion that there is an orthodoxly conceived monotheistic god; but, at the very least, it is not clear how such an argument would go. Rather than pursue Locke's argument further, I propose, instead, to turn to an examination of Swinburne's argument from consciousness.

7.5.2. Swinburne's Argument

Swinburne's argument from consciousness is part of his cumulative argument for the existence of an eternal, perfectly free, omnipotent, omniscient, perfectly good person without a body who created the universe *ex nihilo*. To give Swinburne's argument a fair hearing, there are quite a few background assumptions that need to be considered. In particular, we need to say something about (1) Swinburne's distinction between *personal explanation* and *scientific explanation*; (2) his distinction among *full explanation, complete explanation, ultimate explanation,* and *absolute explanation*; and (3) his accounts of *simplicity, prior probability,* and *explanatory power*. After we have

---

[14] As Mackie (1982: 120) emphasises, Locke's suggestion that a faculty of thinking might be 'superadded' to matter is meant to be distinguished from the claim that an immaterial thinking substance might be attached to certain material bodies; i.e., the proposal that Locke is here countenancing is not merely a kind of substance dualism.

briefly discussed these matters, we shall return to a presentation of his argument from consciousness.

A. Personal Explanation and Scientific Explanation
Swinburne claims that there are two radically different sorts of explanations that can be given of phenomena.

On the one hand, there is scientific explanation, which Swinburne – initially – characterises in the following way: a state of affairs or event E is *scientifically explained* iff some state of affairs or event C together with a law of nature L entail that C physically necessitates, or makes it physically probable, that E.

And, on the other hand, there is personal explanation, which Swinburne describes in – more or less – the following way: a state of affairs or event E is *personally explained* iff either (1) a rational agent P has an intention J that E occur, the bringing about of E is among the things that P is able to do at will, that is, it is among P's basic powers, and the bringing about of E is a basic action A of the agent P, or (2) a rational agent P has the intention J that E occur as the result of a basic action A, the performance of A is among the things that P is able to do at will, that is, it is among P's basic powers, and the performance of A can be shown to have E as a consequence. (A *basic action* is something that an agent does, but also something that an agent does not do by doing something else – for example, moving one's hand. A *mediated action* is an action that an agent performs by doing something else – for example, signalling by moving one's hand.)

Swinburne claims (i) that personal explanation is not analysable in terms of scientific explanation, and (ii) that there cannot be two distinct full explanations of a phenomenon E, such that neither explanation explains the occurrence or operation of the causes and reasons involved in the other. Both of these claims are highly controversial. It may be worth digressing briefly to explain why this is so.

1. There is a vast literature on the nature of 'personal' – 'intentional' – explanation and scientific explanation. Among the contending positions are (i) the 'eliminative' view that, in a properly basic sense, personal explanations are not genuinely explanations at all, and (ii) the 'reductive' view that personal explanations fit perfectly well into the model of scientific explanation. As far as I know, Swinburne has nothing to say about (i); it is worth noting, however, that if personal explanation is merely apparent – that is, not genuine – explanation, then, on Swinburne's own account, theism will not be a genuinely explanatory theory. However, Swinburne has quite a bit to say about the suggestion that personal explanation is merely a special kind of scientific explanation.

As Swinburne notes, it is at least initially plausible to suppose that an agent's bringing about an effect intentionally can be analysed in terms of the causing of that effect by some internal state of the agent, together with further causally operative factors. (Perhaps these internal states of the agent are 'brain states', or perhaps they are 'functional' states; we needn't pause here to consider the contenders for the most plausible form of this type of theory.) However, Swinburne claims that any such theory fails because, if an intention I of an agent P to bring about a state of affairs or event E were an occurrent state or event, then I could bring about E without P's having intentionally brought about E. To illustrate this objection, Swinburne cites Taylor:

> Suppose . . . that a member of an audience keenly desires to attract the speaker's attention but, being shy, only fidgets uncomfortably in his seat and blushes. We may suppose, further, that he does attract the speaker's attention by his very fidgeting; but he did not fidget in order to catch the speaker's attention, even though he desired that result and might well have realised that such behaviour was going to produce it.

Curiously enough, Swinburne himself draws attention to the difficulty in this argument before he gives it: for it is clear that the *total* explanation of this person's fidgeting is not merely his keen desire to attract the speaker's attention, but rather a complex set of mental states and dispositions, of which this desire is but one. According to Swinburne's own account of personal explanation, this person's desire to attract the speaker's attention is quite correctly seen not be to be complete personal explanation of his attraction of that attention; but, of course, on any reasonable reductive account, the occurrent mental state that constitutes the person's desire to attract the speaker's attention will also not serve as a complete scientific explanation of his attraction of that attention. So Swinburne's putative counter-example to the claim that personal explanation 'reduces' to scientific explanation fails.

Of course, there might be some other argument – some other kind of counter-example – that does succeed in showing that personal explanation is both (i) unanalysable in terms of scientific explanation and (ii) a perfectly legitimate and fundamental species of explanation. However, it seems to me that there is no good reason to suppose that anyone has ever devised a successful argument for this contention: this is one of those points at which the debate between physicalists and non-physicalists has seen no convergence of informed opinion. Consequently, it seems to me that there is no prospect that Swinburne can construct a successful argument from consciousness on the basis of this evidently controversial distinction. (Perhaps it is worth adding that Swinburne's neo-Hempelian account of scientific explanation is also extremely controversial. However, it would require too much of a digression to take up this issue here; instead, we shall need to rest content with an intuitive understanding of what it is for an explanation to be scientific.)

2. In defence of the claim that there cannot be two distinct full explanations of a phenomenon F, such that neither explanation explains the

occurrence or operation of the causes and reasons involved in the other, Swinburne (1979: 46) offers the following argument:

Suppose that causes and reasons F_1 and causes and reasons F_2 each fully explain E, and neither in any way explains the other. Then F_1 is necessary and sufficient for the occurrence of E. Given F_1, E cannot but occur. Now suppose F_1 not to have occurred; suppose a deity to have intervened suddenly to stop F_1 occurring. Then since F_1 in no way explains the occurrence of F_2, the non-occurrence of F_1 would in no way affect whether or not F_2 occurs. So F_2 will still occur. Since F_2 provides a full explanation of E, it is necessary and sufficient for the occurrence of E. So E will occur. E will occur even though F_1 does not occur. So F_1 cannot be necessary and sufficient for the occurrence of E, and so the causes and reasons involved in F_1 cannot fully explain E – contrary to our original supposition.

This argument must be based on an inadequate conception of the notion of a full explanation. For consider any set of causes and reasons G_1 that ostensibly fully explains a state of affairs or event E. Intuitively, it seems that a deity could intervene to stop G_1 occurring while nonetheless ensuring that E occurs. But then it is not true that G_1 is logically necessary and sufficient for the occurrence of E, that is, G_1 is not, after all, a full explanation of E. To meet this argument, Swinburne might insist that a full explanation of an event or state of affairs E by a set of reasons or causes G_1 requires that G_1 is logically necessary and sufficient for E. But, on Swinburne's own account, 'full explanation' merely requires that G_1 is both underwritten by physical law and physically sufficient for E. Moreover, of course, one could hardly demand more of 'full explanation', unless one were prepared to allow that no scientific explanation is ever a 'full explanation'. So it seems that Swinburne's argument against the possibility of there being two distinct full explanations of a phenomenon E fails.

Furthermore, once it is granted that a full explanation merely requires that G_1 is both underwritten by physical law and physically sufficient for E, then it seems clear that it is perfectly possible for there to be two distinct 'full explanations' of a phenomenon. For example, suppose that two exploding bullets simultaneously enter the head of an unfortunate victim V. Each one of these bullets is alone sufficient to cause the death of V; and, moreover, we may suppose, there are physical laws that ensure that when exploding bullets enter heads, the consequences are inevitably dire. So each of these bullets alone would supply a full explanation for the death of V. At the very least, cases of causal over-determination – such as the one just described – are *prima facie* plausible cases in which there are two full explanations of a given phenomenon. True enough, one might be tempted to say that, in these cases, all of the relevant factors must be mentioned in a 'total' explanation. But surely a 'total' explanation is not the same kind of thing as a 'full' explanation, in the sense that Swinburne intends.

B. Varieties of Explanation

Swinburne offers the following accounts of the various kinds of explanations that he distinguishes:

An explanation of E by F is a *full explanation* iff F includes both a cause C and a reason R that together 'entail' the occurrence of E, that is, for which it is true that it is [logically] necessary that if C and R, then E.

An explanation of E by F is a *complete explanation* iff it is a full explanation in which there is no full – or partial – explanation of the existence or operation of the factors operative in F in terms of factors operative at the time of the existence or operation of those factors.

An explanation of E by F is an *ultimate explanation* iff it is a complete explanation in which the factors C and R cited are such that their existence and operation have no full – or partial – explanation in terms of any other factors.

An explanation of E by F is an *absolute explanation* iff it is an ultimate explanation in which the existence and operation of each of the factors cited is either self-explanatory or logically necessary.

Swinburne's point, in introducing these definitions, is to identify the kind of explanation – of events and states of affairs – that he supposes is afforded by the existence of an orthodoxly conceived monotheistic god. According to Swinburne, it is not very plausible to suppose that there is an absolute explanation for all phenomena, since it is not very plausible to suppose that there could be an absolute explanation for contingent phenomena. Similarly, according to Swinburne, it is not necessary to suppose that the natural theologian is interested in ultimate explanations, since it may be that there is an orthodoxly conceived monotheistic god that keeps itself in existence at each moment of time by its own free choice. However, according to Swinburne, it is plausible to suppose that the natural theologian holds that an orthodoxly conceived monotheistic god provides at least a complete explanation for those phenomena that it is invoked to explain.

C. Simplicity, Prior Probability, and Explanatory Power

Swinburne claims that the basic considerations involved in judging a proposed explanation are the prior probability and explanatory power of that which is proposed to do the explaining (the *explanans*). What Swinburne has in mind is this. Confronted with an event or state of affairs E, we may seek an explanation of E. If we do, then we shall wish to know when it is reasonable for us to believe a given explanation H of E. Swinburne has several observations to make about this.

First, he notes that – according to the account already given – a scientific explanation H will advert to two things: a cause – or set of causal factors – C, and a law – or set of laws – of nature, L. So, a scientific explanation will be plausible if it is plausible that L is a law of nature, plausible that C has occurred, and plausible that H really would be a scientific explanation of E, given C and L. But (i) it will be plausible that L is a law of nature iff it belongs to a scientific theory that has high prior probability and great explanatory power, and (ii) it will be plausible that C occurred iff the supposition that C occurred has great prior probability and explanatory power.

By the *prior probability of a theory*, Swinburne means the probability of the theory prior to the consideration of the evidence – event, state of affairs – that is now under consideration, that is, prior to the occurrence of E.[15] This definition seems not unreasonable: I will now have some reason to think that L is a law of nature if, up until now, I have had good reason to think that it is.

By the *explanatory power of a theory*, Swinburne means the ability of a theory to entail or make probable the occurrence of many diverse phenomena that have all been observed to occur, and the occurrence of which would not otherwise have been expected. This definition also seems not unreasonable, though it should be noted that these considerations would surely be included in the assessment of the prior probability of a theory. That is, it seems to me that there is some reason to think that, on Swinburne's account, the explanatory power of a theory is merely one of the factors that contributes to the prior probability of that theory.

By the *prior probability of a hypothesis* that an event or state of affairs C occurred, Swinburne means the probability of that hypothesis prior to the observation of the event or state of affairs E, that is, the probability of that hypothesis in the light of everything that was known prior to the acquisition of the knowledge that E occurred. Once more, this definition seems reasonable: if it is antecedently unlikely that C should occur, then this will detract from the likelihood that C can be invoked in the explanation of E.

Finally, by the *explanatory power of the hypothesis* that an event or state of affairs C occurred, Swinburne means the extent to which that hypothesis makes the occurrence of the event or state of affairs more probable than it otherwise would have been. This definition also seems reasonable: for clearly I will have some reason to think that H is an explanation of E if H makes the occurrence of E more probable than it would otherwise have been.

At least in broad outline, it seems that these definitions can be combined to provide an account of when it is reasonable to suppose that an hypothesis H – embedded in a theory T – correctly explains an event or state of affairs

[15] Swinburne (1979: 52) writes: 'The prior probability of a theory is its probability before we consider the detailed evidence of observation cited in its support.' But this formulation overlooks the fact that an explanation can rely upon the fact that a theory is already 'strongly confirmed' or 'strongly supported' by previously noted evidence. Of course, we can ask about the prior probability of a theory before any 'detailed evidence of observation' is cited in its support – but that is to raise a different question, to which we shall return in the main text.

E, *given* a prior set of beliefs about that hypothesis, that theory, and that state of affairs. However, it should be noted that this account says nothing about the sorts of explanations that it is outright reasonable to accept: for it only talks about what it is reasonable to believe given certain other beliefs. As Swinburne observes, in order to adapt this framework to address that question, we need to reassess the interpretation that is given to the prior probability of a theory, and the interpretation that is given of the relationship between the prior probability of a theory and the explanatory power of that theory.

What Swinburne proposes is that we can make sense of the notion of the probability that is conferred on a theory or hypothesis by the total (relevant) available evidence. If this is so, then we can adopt the definition of 'prior probability' adverted to in note 4: 'the prior probability of a theory is its probability before we consider the detailed evidence of observation cited in its support', and we can also adopt the independent account of the notion of the explanatory power of a theory that goes along with this account of the prior probability of a theory. But is it plausible to suppose that there are any such prior probabilities?

Swinburne claims that the kind of prior probability to which he adverts depends upon three factors: simplicity, fit with background knowledge , and scope. He says that a theory is *simple* insofar as it postulates few mathematically simple laws holding among entities of an intelligible kind, that is, entities of a kind whose nature and interactions seem natural to us; that a theory *fits with our general background knowledge* of how the world works insofar as the kinds of entities and laws that it postulates are similar to those that we reasonably believe to exist and obtain in other fields; and that a theory has large *scope* iff it purports to apply to a large number of objects, and to attribute many different properties to those objects. Moreover, Swinburne claims (i) that, all other things being equal, a simpler theory is more likely to be true – *simplex sigillum veri*; (ii) that, in general, a theory with smaller scope is less simple, because restrictions of scope are usually arbitrary and complicating; and (iii) that, for theories with very wide scope, the criterion of fitting in with general background knowledge ceases to have much importance, since there is less background knowledge with which those theories are required to comport. Then, given (i)–(iii), Swinburne concludes (iv) that for very large-scale theories, the crucial determinant of prior probability is simplicity.

If simplicity, fit with background knowledge, and scope are all that is relevant to prior probability, and if these notions are understood in the way that Swinburne proposes, then it seems to me that it is plausible to claim that (ii) and (iii) suffice to establish that, for theories with very large scope, the crucial determinant of prior probability is simplicity. However, I take it that there are various difficulties that confront Swinburne's account of prior probability. In particular, it seems to me to be highly doubtful that 'the simple is the sign of the true', in the sense in which Swinburne intends this claim to be taken. Given 'tautological evidence' alone – that is, given no empirical data – I take it that one has no reason at all to suppose that the universe is more likely to be one of the 'simple' universes, that is, one of those universes that is governed by few mathematically simple laws that hold of entities of a kind whose nature and interactions seem natural to us. Indeed, given that there is some reason to suppose that such 'simple' universes are going to be rarities in the space of possible universes, one might think that, on 'tautological evidence' alone, it is much more likely that the universe is *not* one of the 'simple' possible universes!

Of course, the point that I have just made is not meant to count at all against the suggestion that scientific model selection involves some kind of trade-off between considerations of simplicity and considerations of goodness of fit. When one has a bunch of data points, and one is trying to work out how the relevant variables are actually related, there is an important role for considerations of 'simplicity' in one's calculations: the best guess that you can make of the relation that actually holds between the relevant variables is the one that trades off considerations of simplicity with considerations of goodness of fit in the correct way. But these considerations about the role of simplicity in scientific model selection do nothing at all to support Swinburne's claim that, on tautological evidence, it is likely that the universe consists of entities of a kind whose nature and interactions seem natural to us, and whose workings obey a few mathematically simple fundamental laws. (Moreover, this is true even if we suppose that there is justification for the claim that scientific model selection favours the adoption of 'negative entropy' priors, or the like: if one could have a 'flat probability distribution' over the space of possible worlds, then, plausibly, one would distribute very little probability to the claim that the universe consists of entities of a kind whose nature and interactions seem natural to us, and whose workings obey a few mathematically simple fundamental laws.)

Perhaps it is worth mentioning some other ways in which Swinburne's account of prior probabilities is problematic. *First*, as we have seen, Swinburne claims that a theory is more likely to be true if it postulates 'entities of a kind whose nature and interactions seem natural to us'. But why should we suppose that 'what seems natural to us' is a reliable guide to likely truth? Indeed, isn't it one of the lessons of twentieth-century physics that we live in a universe whose fundamental constituents are very plausibly entities whose nature and interactions are not in the least bit natural to us? *Second*, as we have also seen, Swinburne claims that a theory is more likely to be true if it is 'similar' to other true theories. Setting aside worries about unrestricted talk of 'similarity' – that is, supposing that we can attribute content to the claim that Swinburne is making here – it seems to me that there is no good reason to suppose that Swinburne is right about this: there are well-known difficulties that confront those who try to take a model that works well in one field, and try to give it application in very different fields. When scientific psychology has tried to model its theories on those of physics, the result has usually been disastrous. *Third*, it is worth noting that Swinburne claims that it is plausible to suppose that we assume and use a 'principle of charity' – namely, the principle that the intentions and ways of acquiring belief of other human beings are very similar to our own – in our understanding of the behaviour of other people, and that, in doing this, we are making an assumption simpler than we would if we were to suppose that the intentions, and so on, of other human beings are vastly different from our own. Again, one might be sceptical about the ungrounded talk of 'similarity' upon which these claims depend; and if one can overcome this scepticism, one might well be given to wonder whether Swinburne's claim can be supported. After all, one might suppose that one can make sense of what other people do without supposing that they act as one would oneself if one were placed in their circumstances. Moreover, it is quite unclear why we should think that it is more simple to suppose that others would act as one would oneself if one were placed in their circumstances, rather than to make some other assumption, until we have seen the details of alternative hypotheses that might be advanced.

D. Intrinsic Probability

According to Swinburne, the *intrinsic probability* of a theory or hypothesis is the probability of that theory or hypothesis in the light of merely tautological evidence. I have already given reasons for being sceptical of the claim that one can appeal to considerations of simplicity – in the way in which Swinburne supposes that one can – when one is trying to establish intrinsic probabilities. Here, I shall consider the reasons that Swinburne advances for supposing that the hypothesis that there is an eternal, perfectly free, omnipotent, omniscient, perfectly good person without a body who created the universe *ex nihilo* is 'a very simple hypothesis indeed'. If any of Swinburne's 'inductive arguments' is to succeed – and, in particular, if his 'argument from consciousness' is to succeed – then, by his own lights, he needs to be able to establish that the hypothesis that there is an eternal, perfectly free, omnipotent, omniscient, perfectly good person without a body who created the universe *ex nihilo* is simple. For otherwise, the intrinsic probability that there is an eternal, perfectly free, omnipotent, omniscient, perfectly good person without a body who created the universe *ex nihilo* is low, and so it is hard for an 'inductive argument' to make it probable that there is an eternal, perfectly free, omnipotent, omniscient, perfectly good person without a body who created the universe *ex nihilo*.

According to Swinburne, a theistic explanation is a personal explanation, – that is, an explanation that explains phenomena as the results of the action of a person brought about in virtue of the capacities, beliefs, and intentions of that person. Moreover, according to Swinburne, (i) theism postulates the simplest sort of person there could be – that is, a person who has the simplest sorts of capacities, beliefs, and intentions; (ii) theism is simple because it holds that all phenomena that have full explanations have complete personal explanations, so that everything that can be explained can be explained in terms of one type of explanation; and (iii) theism postulates that explanation stops at which is intuitively the simplest and most natural terminus for explanation, namely, personal explanation. Finally, according to Swinburne, (i)–(iii) constitute compelling reasons for holding that theism is a simple hypothesis, and, in particular, that theism is simpler than any rival hypothesis – including, in particular, the rival hypothesis that naturalistic science tells the full story about the world.

In defence of (i), Swinburne claims (a) that it is simpler to postulate a being who has no finite limitations than it is to postulate a being with finite limitations ('A finite limitation cries out for an explanation why there is just that particular limit, in a way that limitlessness does not' (94)), and (b) that it is simpler to suppose that all of the limitless properties – omniscience, omnipotence, and so on – belong essentially together than it is to suppose that they are accidentally instantiated in one or more beings. However, both of these claims can be disputed. *First*, I do not see why finite limitations are especially in need of explanation. Swinburne claims that the hypothesis that a particle has infinite velocity is simpler than the hypothesis that it is has a velocity of 301,000 km/sec. But – on the assumption that we allow that it is possible for a particle to have infinite velocity – surely the fact that the velocity is *that* velocity – rather than some other velocity – would be just as much in need of explanation in either case. *Second*, I don't see any plausibility in the claim that orthodoxly conceived monotheistic gods are simple, at least in the sense in which Swinburne understands this claim. In particular, on Swinburne's own account, the postulation of an orthodoxly conceived monotheistic god would seem to involve the postulation of something that is utterly different from anything that is postulated in other fields of inquiry, and the postulation of something of a kind whose nature and interactions do not seem in any way familiar to us. Consequently, it seems to me that – by Swinburne's own lights – he has considerable reason to allow that the postulates of theism are far from simple (and that's *before* we turn to consider particular doctrines of trinity, incarnation, and the like).

In his defence of (ii), Swinburne relies on the claim that an explanation is simpler if it involves only one kind of explanation. It is not clear that this is right. Suppose, for example, that personal explanations can be reduced to scientific explanations, but that the scientific explanation S that constitutes the reduction of a given personal explanation P is typically much more complicated to state. Then, plausibly, there will be circumstances in which the interaction between a person and the physical environment in which that person is located is most simply explained in terms that advert both to personal explanation and to scientific explanation. In the absence of a clearer account of what makes for simplicity of explanation, it seems to me that there is no way of adjudicating Swinburne's tacit claim that an explanation is simpler if it involves only one kind of explanation.

In defence of (iii), Swinburne observes that, in our experience, we are directly aware of ourselves as sources of explanation, and hence find personal explanations particularly natural. But, of course, this hardly shows that personal explanation is the simplest and most natural terminus for explanation, even in the case in which it is facts about us that we seek to explain. While the alleged fact that we find personal explanations particularly natural might do some real work in explaining why belief in the supernatural is so widespread, I do not think that there is any good reason to suppose that this alleged fact raises the intrinsic probability that theism is true.

If the kinds of claims that I have been making in this section are right, then Swinburne fails to provide good reasons for thinking that the intrinsic probability of the hypothesis that there is an eternal, perfectly free, omnipotent, omniscient, perfectly good person without a body who created the universe *ex nihilo* is high. But if that is right, then, as we shall now go on to see, his 'inductive arguments' for belief in an eternal, perfectly free, omnipotent, omniscient, perfectly good person without a body who created the universe *ex nihilo* are in serious trouble.

E. Argument from Consciousness

As we noted much earlier, Locke tried to argue that the only way in which merely material structures could become cogitative is through the superaddition of cogitative powers by an orthodoxly conceived monotheistic god. By way of contrast, Swinburne aims only to argue that the only way in which we can see how to explain the possession of cogitative properties by merely material structures is through the postulation of the superadditive abilities of an orthodoxly conceived monotheistic god. Bringsjord (1986) suggests that Swinburne's argument may be fairly set out as follows:

h: God exists.
e: There are conscious persons with brains.
k: There is an orderly and beautiful universe.

1. If it is unlikely that there is a complete explanation of *e* not involving the agency of an orthodoxly conceived monotheistic god, and it is unlikely that *e* occurs without explanation, then $\Pr(e/\sim h\&k)$ is low.
2. It is unlikely that there is a complete explanation of *e* not involving the agency of an orthodoxly conceived monotheistic god, and it is unlikely that *e* occurs without explanation.
3. (Therefore) $\Pr(e/\sim h\&k)$ is low.
4. If an orthodoxly conceived monotheistic god is likely to bring about *e*, then $\Pr(e/h\&k)$ is high, or, at any rate, substantial.
5. An orthodoxly conceived monotheistic god is likely to bring about *e*.
6. (Therefore) $\Pr(e/h\&k)$ is high, or, at any rate, substantial.

7. (Therefore) $\Pr(e/h\&k) > \Pr(e/\sim h\&k)$.
8. $\Pr(h/e\&k) > \Pr(h/k)$ iff $\Pr(e/h\&k) > \Pr(e/\sim h\&k)$.
9. (Therefore) $\Pr(h/e\&k) > \Pr(h/k)$.

I am not sure that this is really a fair representation of Swinburne's argument, because I am not convinced that Swinburne argues for 3 on the basis of 1 and 2. After all – as Swinburne is well aware – it seems not unreasonable to suppose that non-theists will maintain that, while there is no complete explanation of e – just as there is no complete explanation of most natural phenomena – there is nonetheless a causal explanation of e: there is an account to be given of the evolution of consciousness in purely naturalistic, causal terms. I take it that Swinburne's case for 3 turns on the contention that, even by the lights of committed naturalists, there is no satisfactory naturalistic account of the existence of consciousness in the universe: there is not even the slightest hint of the possibility of an explanation – never mind a complete explanation – of the cognitive abilities of human beings in terms of the principles of natural science. However, setting this reservation aside, I think that Bringsjord's encapsulation does do justice to Swinburne's argument; and, hence, I think that the key claim that needs to be examined is whether it is more likely that an orthodoxly conceived monotheistic god superadds consciousness to merely material human bodies than it is that consciousness can be properly located in a purely naturalistic or physicalistic conception of the universe.

F. Objections to Naturalism

Swinburne's argument against naturalistic accounts of cognition begins with a division of cases. On the one hand, there is the 'strong thesis' that mental events can just be identified with certain kinds of brain events; on the other hand, there is the 'weaker thesis' that mental events can be shown to be events that are governed by scientific laws.

In arguing against the 'strong thesis', Swinburne identifies two forms of 'mind-brain identity theories' – namely, behaviourism and central state materialism – and argues that neither is satisfactory. Even setting aside the point that philosophical behaviourism is not any kind of 'mind-brain identity theory', it is worth pointing out that there are many more kinds of 'strong' materialist theories than are considered in Swinburne's discussion. Essentially, he mentions just two: Smart's version of central state materialism, and Rorty's eliminative materialism. But even if we were to grant that Swinburne succeeds in knocking over these two theories, there are many more 'strong' materialist theories that remain to be considered. In particular, since Swinburne does not consider the possibility that some kind of supervenience relation might be sufficient to underwrite a 'strong' materialist theory of the relationship between the mental and the physical, we can certainly insist that there is nothing in Swinburne (1979) to perturb those who suppose that consciousness can be properly located in a purely naturalistic or physicalistic conception of the universe in the manner suggested by Jackson (1995). (Roughly, the idea here is this: given that any minimal physical duplicate of our world is a duplicate *simpliciter* of our world, it follows that there is an in-principle reduction of the mental to the physical. But the claim that any minimal physical duplicate of our world is a duplicate *simpliciter* of our world is strongly supported by various considerations – for example, the causal closure of the physical world and the like. So, at the very least, there is no evident barrier to the suggestion that physicalists can reasonably take themselves to have good reason to suppose that there is an in-principle reduction of the mental to the physical, even though – of course – no one has ever been in a position to actually set out an accurate representation of any part of such a reduction.)

In arguing against the 'weaker thesis' that mental events are governed by scientific laws, Swinburne proceeds by setting out conditions that he supposes that a defence of such a thesis would need to achieve, and then arguing that none of these conditions can be met. According to Swinburne, a proponent of the 'weaker thesis' needs a theory that does the following three things: (i) it establishes a one-to-one – or, perhaps, many-to-one – correlation between specifiable kinds of mental events and specifiable kinds of brain events; (ii) it establishes that this correlation is evidence of a genuinely causal connection between mental events and brain events; and (iii) it establishes that this genuine causal connection is a natural, law-like connection.

Swinburne claims that the lack of public observability of mental events casts grave doubts on any alleged correlations between mental events and brain events. But, of course, as we have already in effect noted, what a materialist needs is reasonable commitment to the claim that there is a correlation of the requisite kind, and that kind of commitment need not be grounded in the 'establishment' – or 'exhibition' – of a particular scheme of correlation.

Swinburne provides two objections to the claim that it is possible to 'establish' that a correlation between mental events and brain events is causal. First, he alleges that 'experience of choice' is evidence against any such correlation. And, second, he claims that the indeterminism of quantum mechanics provides reason to doubt that there are law-like correlations between mental events and brain events. I shall consider these objections in turn.

Swinburne writes:

It often seems to [a man] that he is selecting on rational grounds between alternative courses of action, choosing the intentions that he will have. It seems to him that the choice is up to him whether to be influenced by rational considerations or not, his choice not being predetermined for him by his brain, character or environment; and that it is rational considerations, not brain states, that influence him, though not conclusively. Now if a man (at any rate sometimes) chooses his intentions and this choice is not pre-determined, his choices cannot be invariably predicted from prior brain-states, nor can any effects in the brain that they may have.

I find this argument puzzling. How things *seem* to an agent will, on a materialist theory, just be a matter of further brain states of that agent, as will the experiences of rational choices and decisions that that agent makes. Consequently, there can be no argument from the phenomena of experience of rational choice to the conclusion that the materialist theory is false. However, if the argument is supposed to be that rational choices and decisions may have no sufficient causal antecedents, then the materialist is once again not threatened – since, if this is so, then, according to the materialist, there are certain brain states that have no sufficient causal antecedents. And if the argument is supposed to be that one has direct experience of the fact that one makes choices quite independently of the events that are going on in one's brain, then the reply – as noted by Mackie (1982: 125) – is that, at least by the lights of the materialist, there can be no such experience. At best, there can be a lack of awareness of any such goings-on; but that is no positive evidence that one's choices really are independent of the events that are going on in one's brain.

Swinburne also writes:

> The basic physical laws are statistical or probabilistic. They only allow us to infer from one brain event B_1 that it was physically very probable that a subsequent brain event B_2 would occur, not that it was physically necessary. But this would leave open the possibility that the explanation of the occurrence of brain state B_2 correlated with intention I_2 was to be explained fully by the joint action of brain event B_1 and intention I_2.

Among the chief difficulties that face this argument, we might note that there is no good reason to insist that scientific explanations are full explanations – in Swinburne's sense – or, indeed, that every event should have a full explanation. Even if the connections between brain states were merely probabilistic, that need cast no doubt at all on the (alleged) law-likeness of the (alleged) connections between mental events and brain events.

The main burden of Swinburne's argument lies in the challenge to 'establish' that there is a natural, law-like connection between mental events and brain events. Following Bringsjord, we might suppose that the core argument upon which Swinburne relies is the following:

1. Brain events differ in an enormous qualitative way from mental events.
2. If one set of events S_1 differs in an enormous qualitative way from another set of events S_2, then natural scientific laws connecting the events in S_1 with the events in S_2 are not formulable.
3. (Hence) Natural scientific laws connecting brain events and mental events are not formulable.
4. If natural scientific laws connecting brain events and mental events are not formulable, then no full scientific explanation of interaction between brain events and mental events is possible.
5. (Hence) No full scientific explanation of interaction between brain events and mental events is possible.

6. (Hence) It is unlikely that there is a complete explanation of e that does not involve the agency of an orthodoxly conceived monotheistic god.

Among the many difficulties that are faced by this argument, perhaps the most pressing is that premise 2 is not at all plausible. It is surely reasonable to say that there is an enormous qualitative difference between the macroscopic phenomena of the observable world and the microscopic phenomena that are invoked to explain those macroscopic phenomena: consider, for example, the macroscopic phenomenon of heat conduction in an iron bar, and the microscopic phenomenon of this phenomenon in terms of the motion and kinetic energy of microscopic particles in the iron bar. But if this is right, then there can hardly be good reason to accept premise 2. Since premise 2. is not explicitly defended by Swinburne, one might suppose that we have good reason not to follow Bringsjord in attributing this argument to Swinburne. But if this is not how Swinburne's argument goes, then how does it go? It is clear that Swinburne supposes that there is a serious difficulty that confronts the claim that there is a *natural* connection between mental states and brain states; but it is quite unclear wherein he supposes this difficulty consists. Chalmers (1996) provides a nice example of a theory in which there are simple, natural connections between phenomenal states and physical states, even though there is no even in-principle reduction of the one to the other; why should we suppose that this theory is in worse shape than the theory according to which similar kinds of connections are established by a supernatural agent?

In sum, then, it seems to me that Swinburne's arguments against naturalistic accounts of cognition are weak. I do not believe that there is anything in his discussion of naturalistic accounts of cognition that ought to give thoughtful and reflective naturalists and physicalists so much as *prima facie* reason to fear that $\Pr(e/{\sim}h\&k)$ is lower than $\Pr(e/h\&k)$. However, before we can reach a settled verdict on this matter, we still need to consider what Swinburne has to say about the virtues of supernaturalistic accounts of cognition.

G. Support for Supernaturalism

Swinburne's argument in favour of a theistic explanation of the presence of consciousness in the universe has two main components, namely, (i) an argument to the conclusion that theism is a good explanation of the presence of consciousness in the universe, and (ii) an argument to the conclusion that theism is a better explanation of the presence of consciousness in the universe than any competing explanation, including the null explanation – that is, the claim that there is no explanation of the presence of consciousness in the universe. I shall consider each of these sub-arguments in turn.

While Swinburne does offer defences of the claims that an orthodoxly conceived monotheistic god has reason for bringing about *e*, that an orthodoxly conceived monotheistic god has reason for bringing about something close to *e*, and that either *e* itself or something close to *e* is intrinsically good, it is hard to see that Swinburne offers any defence of the claim that it is *likely* that an orthodoxly conceived monotheistic god would create a universe in which there are conscious beings. In particular – as sceptical theists are fond of reminding us in other contexts – it seems a bit of a stretch to suppose that we would have much insight into the likely doings of beings so much stronger, smarter, and better than ourselves. Given our apparent ignorance of the possible goods that might be instantiated in a universe, why should we suppose that consciousness is anywhere near the top of the list? True enough, we might allow, consciousness is one of the best features of our universe: but that does very little towards establishing that it is a good that would likely be selected by an orthodoxly conceived monotheistic god.

Moreover, even if we suppose that we can avoid this kind of worry, there are difficulties that arise as a result of Swinburne's use of personal explanation as a separate category of explanation in hypothesis about mind-brain connections. If it is hard to see how there can be simple, natural connections between mental states and brain states, then it is hard to see how there can be a simple, 'natural' way for an orthodoxly conceived monotheistic god to establish connections between mental states and brain states. Given the alleged difficulties that confront the materialist hypothesis that there are simple and natural connections between mental states and brain states, surely there are equally considerable difficulties that confront the contention that it is simple and natural to suppose that there is an orthodoxly conceived monotheistic god that brings it about that there are connections between mental states and brain states. As Mackie (1982: 131) points out, 'if materialism has difficulty in explaining how even the most elaborate neural structure can give rise to consciousness, then theism – with its personal explanations and direct intention-fulfilments – has at least as great a difficulty in explaining why consciousness is found only in them'. Unless there is something independently 'simple and natural' about the correlation between mental states and neural states, there seems to be no reason at all to hold that it is simple and natural to suppose that there is an orthodoxly conceived monotheistic god who brings it about that there are connections between mental states and brain states.

So much, then, for my discussion of Swinburne's reasons for claiming that orthodox theism provides a good explanation of the presence of consciousness in the universe. I turn now to consideration of Swinburne's reasons for claiming that orthodox theism provides the best explanation of the presence of consciousness in the universe.

To argue that the theistic explanation of consciousness is better than any of its competitors, Swinburne assumes that there are really only two important competing explanations, namely, orthodox theism and materialism. But, of course, there are many supernaturalistic competitors to orthodox theism that Swinburne is not entitled to ignore at this point: committees of gods, morally suspect gods, and the like. Moreover, even if we set this difficulty aside, it is worth noting that it might well be contested that Swinburne's theistic explanation possesses the 'naturalness' and 'simplicity' that he alleges is missing from the competing naturalistic explanation. This brings us back to our earlier discussion of the alleged simplicity of the hypothesis that there is an orthodoxly conceived monotheistic god: if the 'intrinsic probability' of the theistic hypothesis, direct intention-fulfillment, and the like, is sufficiently small, because the requisite simplicity is missing, then we have been given no reason at all to suppose that $\Pr(e/\sim h \& k)$ is lower than $\Pr(e/h \& k)$.

In short, then: there are various reasons why we should be sceptical of Swinburne's claim to have established that the presence of consciousness in the universe is best explained on the hypothesis that there is an orthodoxly conceived monotheistic god. For (i) Swinburne does not provide persuasive reasons for ruling out non-scientific competitors to his favoured theistic hypothesis; (ii) Swinburne does not provide persuasive reasons for supposing that his favoured theistic hypothesis is particularly simple; (iii) Swinburne does not provide persuasive reasons for supposing that, on his own favoured account of simplicity, simple theories are more likely to be true; (iv) because Swinburne does not consider the strongest formulations of materialism – functionalism, various supervenience theses – his case against materialist explanations of the presence of consciousness in the universe is plainly incomplete; and (v) most important, the case that Swinburne makes for the claim that $\Pr(e/\sim h \& k)$ is lower than $\Pr(e/h \& k)$ is undermined by these, and other, objections that have been considered in the course of the preceding discussion.

7.6. ARGUMENTS FROM PUZZLING PHENOMENA

There are still plenty of arguments that we haven't looked at yet. I'll briefly consider a few more arguments here. These arguments are linked only by the fact that they have received no attention earlier in this book.

7.6.1. Providence

I begin with a very short argument from the providential nature of our world. A far more elaborate argument of this kind can be found in Swinburne (1979).

1. Our world is just the kind of world that one would expect an orthodoxly conceived monotheistic god to make.
2. (Hence) There is an orthodoxly conceived monotheistic god.

There are interesting questions to be raised about the premise in this argument. In particular, it is worth noting that those who are inclined to endorse a sceptical theist response to evidential arguments from evil are surely not entitled to advance an argument from providence of the kind here under consideration. If we take seriously the idea that there are many aspects of the world that lie forever beyond our comprehension, then our ignorance of those features surely makes it very difficult to be confident that the world really is of a kind that one would expect an orthodoxly conceived monotheistic god to make. Given the features of our world with which we are acquainted, it seems that sceptical theists ought to allow that, so far as *that* evidence goes, our world is equally the kind of world that one would expect an omnipotent, omniscient, and perfectly evil being to make – and that our lack of access to the features of the world that are forever beyond our ken prevents us from arguing from that evidence either to the existence of an omnipotent, omniscient, and perfectly good being or to the existence of an omnipotent, omniscient, and perfectly evil being.

It seems to me that it is very difficult to provide a successful argument on behalf of the claim that such-and-such is just the kind of universe that one would expect an orthodoxly conceived monotheistic god to make. I have already noted that it seems plausible to me to suppose that, if there were a perfect being, then it would not make any universe at all. Other philosophers have supposed that, if there were a perfect being, it would hardly make a universe that contains the horrendous suffering that is to be found in our universe. One need not be possessed of a particularly sceptical mind to find reasons for doubting that one should be ready to embrace the claim that our universe is just the kind of universe that one should expect an orthodoxly conceived monotheistic god to make. Since reasonable non-theists typically do not rush to embrace the suggestion that our universe is just the kind of universe that one should expect an orthodoxly conceived monotheistic god to make, there is good reason to claim that the kind of argument from providence that we are considering here is unsuccessful.

The difficulties that we have already noted, that are involved in arguing for the premise in our argument from providence, are also plausibly taken to undermine the inference from the premise in the argument to the conclusion. In general, the fact that there is a good fit between a hypothesis and some data does not entail that there is good reason to accept that hypothesis; indeed, in general, the fact that there is better fit between a given hypothesis and some data than between any other hypothesis and that same data does not entail that there is good reason to accept that hypothesis. After all, as we know from consideration of the curve-fitting problem, there has to be a trade-off effected between considerations of goodness of fit to the data and other theoretical desiderata such as simplicity: goodness of fit can always be increased at the expense of simplicity, reduction of prior probability, and the like. Even if it were true that our world is just the kind of world that one should expect an orthodoxly conceived monotheistic god to make, there is no reason at all to suppose that this consideration *alone* provides substantial grounds for supposing that it is likely that our world was made by an orthodoxly conceived monotheistic god.

7.6.2. Efficacy of Prayer

There has been considerable interest recently in the efficacy of prayer in curing diseases, and so on. In particular, there have been papers published in reputable medical journals claiming that there is evidence for the efficacy of petitionary prayer in curing diseases (e.g., Harris et al. (1999); Kwang et al. (2001)). Even without appealing to these contentious studies, there are arguments that can be constructed based on "intuitive" data.

1. People sometimes recover from serious illness when we pray for them.
2. (Therefore) Praying for people to recover from serious illness sometimes causes them to recover.
3. If prayers can cause people to recover from serious illness, then this must be because an orthodoxly conceived monotheistic god hears our prayers and acts on them.
4. (Therefore) There is an orthodoxly conceived monotheistic god.

The first point to make about an argument of this kind is that the mere fact that recovery from serious illness sometimes follows prayer is no evidence at all that there is a causal relationship between the prayer and the recovery from illness. Since there is lots of praying being done on behalf of those who are ill, and since recovery from serious illness is not all that uncommon, it is to be expected that it sometimes happens that those who are prayed for recover from serious illnesses, even if there is no casual connection between the praying and the recovery from illness. In a serious argument of this kind, we would need to have information about rates of praying for those who are ill, rates of recovery of those who are prayed for, and rates of recovery of those who are not prayed for. Moreover, we would need to have details about the kinds of praying that is done: after all, there are lots of *general* prayers on behalf of all of those who are sick that are offered on any given day by religious believers of varied stripes and nationalities: but these prayers are plainly not universally efficacious. It is not plausible to suppose that we shall *ever* be in a position to acquire the kind of data that we would need to have in order to run a serious argument from the medical efficacy of prayer.

The second point to note is that even if it turns out that there is some kind of significant statistical correlation between certain kinds of prayers and recovery from serious illness, it is not at all obvious that the best explanation for this correlation is in terms of the activities of an orthodoxly conceived monotheistic god. One might expect that there is going to be some kind of correlation between praying for oneself and one's recovery from serious ill-ness: there is plenty of anecdotal evidence that a 'positive attitude' can play a significant role in this kind of recovery. But, in this kind of case, there is no reason to suppose that the correlation between praying and recovery from serious illness points to the existence of that to which the prayers are offered: it is, after all, highly plausible to suppose that the efficacy of the praying is quite independent of the existence of the object of the prayer. Similarly, one might expect that there is going to be some kind of correlation between one's having knowledge that others who share one's faith are praying for one and one's recovery from serious illness: there is plenty of anecdotal evidence that support of friends and family can play a significant role in this kind of recovery. But, again, in this kind of case, there is no rea-son at all to suppose that the correlation between praying and recovery from serious illness points to the existence of that to which the prayers are offered: it is, after all, highly plausible to suppose that the efficacy of the praying is quite independent of the existence of the object of the prayer.

Suppose, though, that it turns out that there is a statistically significant correlation between recovery from serious illness and being the unwitting subject of prayers offered on one's behalf by those whose religious beliefs one do not share and perhaps even strenuously reject. While there is no reason at all to suppose that there are statistically significant correlations of this kind, it is worth noting that, even if there were, it is not clear that this would provide significant support for the existence of orthodoxly con-ceived monotheistic gods. If, for example, it turned out that the content of the prayer is irrelevant, that is, that prayer to orthodoxly conceived monothe-istic gods is no more efficacious than prayer to Odin or Kali, then it is not clear what conclusion should be drawn – but it does seem clear that there would not be good reason to conclude that there is an orthodoxly con-ceived monotheistic god. If, on the other hand, it turned out that there is a statistically significant correlation between recovery from serious ill-ness and being the unwitting subject of personalised prayers offered to Kali on one's behalf, then perhaps there would be good reason to con-clude that the universe is a much stranger place than anyone had hitherto supposed.

7.6.3. Mathematical Knowledge

There are various domains in which we have knowledge, but in which it is hard to explain how we have that knowledge if one adopts a causal analysis of knowledge and a naturalistic ontology. I shall consider an argument that is specific to mathematics, but one could appeal to various other domains such as logic, metaphysics, modality, morality, and so forth, in order to make a similar – or, perhaps, stronger – point.

1. There is no (agreed) naturalistic explanation of how we are able to come by knowledge of mathematics.
2. Our knowledge of mathematics is (best) explained as the result of an orthodoxly conceived monotheistic god's so constituting us that we are able to have that knowledge.
3. (Therefore) There is an orthodoxly conceived monotheistic god.

The (alleged) fact that there is no *agreed* naturalistic explanation of how we are able to come by knowledge of mathematics is not a strong ground for drawing conclusions about the existence of orthodoxly conceived monotheistic gods; there are, after all, very few *agreed* explanations of perennially controversial philosophical matters. If there is to be a worthwhile argument from our knowledge of mathematics to the existence of an orthodoxly conceived monotheistic god, then it must be the case that the hypothesis, that an orthodoxly conceived monotheistic god so made us that we are able to obtain mathematical knowledge, is a better explanation of the fact that we are able to come by mathematical knowledge than is any (naturalistic) alternative. But, at the very least, it is highly controversial to suppose that the hypothesis, that an orthodoxly conceived monotheistic god so made us that we are able to obtain mathematical knowledge, is a better explanation of the fact that we are able to come by mathematical knowledge than is any (naturalistic) alternative.

Part of the difficulty here is that the hypothesis, that an orthodoxly conceived monotheistic god so made us that we are able to obtain mathematical knowledge, does not provide us with much in the way of details about what it is in virtue of which we are able to obtain mathematical knowledge. What is it about the way in which we were (allegedly) made by an orthodoxly conceived monotheistic god that makes it possible for us to obtain knowledge of mathematics? Given that our ability to obtain knowledge of mathematics depends upon factors X, Y, and Z, what reason do we have for supposing that we could have come to possess factors X, Y, and Z only if they were given to us by an orthodoxly conceived monotheistic god? In the absence of identification of that in which our ability to obtain mathematical knowledge consists – and this, of course, is the point at which the argument begins – what reason do we have for preferring an explanation in terms of the creative activities of an orthodoxly conceived monotheistic god to the claim that there is a hitherto undiscovered naturalistic explanation of this ability? Perhaps, when we do have a clear and uncontroversial account of that in which our ability to obtain mathematical knowledge consists, we shall see that there is a straightforward naturalistic explanation of this ability. At the very least, there is no reason at all to suppose that appeals to the *controversial* nature of philosophical questions about knowledge of mathematics, or modality, or morality, or the like, lead to successful arguments for the existence of an orthodoxly conceived monotheistic god.

7.6.4. Jesus

Perhaps it is a bit tendentious to include this argument here. However, it is one that has had a lot of currency in introductory philosophy classes in the United States in the recent past, and there are well-known and well-credentialled philosophers who seem to take it seriously.

1. Anyone who claims to be the son of God is either a liar, or a fool, or the son of God.
2. Jesus claimed to be the son of God.
3. Jesus was not a liar, that is, he was not someone who deliberately told untruths.
4. Jesus was not a fool, that is, he was not mentally incompetent.
5. (Therefore) Jesus was the son of God.
6. (Therefore) There is an orthodoxly conceived monotheistic god.

Given that we are supposing that people are liars iff they deliberately – knowingly and consciously – tell untruths, and that people are fools iff they are mentally incompetent, that is, barking mad, it is not clear that we should grant the first premise in this argument. It is not obvious to me – without further argument, at least – that a person who claims to be the 'son of God' must either be a fool or a liar in the senses just specified. In particular, it seems to me that there are many other hypotheses – including, for example, those that advert to the influence of mind-altering drugs, sleep deprivation, severe fasting, extreme psychological stress, brainwashing, childhood indoctrination, and the like – that might be involved to explain sincere avowals of this kind of relationship to an orthodoxly conceived monotheistic god. While many of these alternative explanations might be thought of as 'temporary mental incompetence', it is not clear that all of them should be thought of in this way: in particular, it is not clear that childhood indoctrination *could not* lead to the growth of a person who is not barking mad and yet who believes that he is the earthly manifestation of a particular orthodoxly conceived monotheistic god. At the very least, I don't see why non-theists should suppose that this hypothesis is any less plausible than the hypothesis that there *was* an earthly manifestation of a particular orthodoxly conceived monotheistic god.

Even if we accept the first premise in this argument, there are serious difficulties that face all of the remaining premises in the argument. On the one hand, the scriptural evidence that Jesus took himself to *be* the earthly incarnation of an orthodoxly conceived monotheistic god is actually pretty weak. On the other hand, the idea that one can treat the relevant scriptures as a reliable historical record is even more problematic. Perhaps there was never any such person as Jesus. Perhaps there was such a person as Jesus, but the scriptures that we have provide a very inaccurate record of his life and times. Perhaps there was such a person as Jesus, and perhaps there are many respects in which the scriptures provide a reasonable faithful account of his life and times, except for the bits that could be true only if there were an orthodoxly conceived monotheistic god or if Jesus believed that he was the earthly manifestation of an orthodoxly conceived monotheistic god. Given the kinds of doubts that non-Christians have about the historical reliability of the Christian scriptures, there is no reason at all to suppose that the argument that we are considering here is *successful*.

7.6.5. Unbelief

Just for something different, here is an argument for the conclusion that there is no orthodoxly conceived monotheistic god.

1. If there were an orthodoxly conceived monotheistic god, then it would not remain hidden from people.
2. If an orthodoxly conceived monotheistic god did not remain hidden from people, then there would be no unbelievers.
3. There are lots of unbelievers.
4. (Therefore) There is no orthodoxly conceived monotheistic god.

There are various different ways in which monotheists can respond to this argument.

One approach would be to deny that the orthodoxly conceived monotheistic god in which they believe is hidden, even though there are many unbelievers or, perhaps, whether or not there are any unbelievers. If we suppose that an orthodoxly conceived monotheistic god is hidden iff it is possible for reasonable people to reasonably fail to believe in the existence of such a being on the basis of the evidence that is available to them, then it seems that one can take the former line only if one is prepared to accept the claim that there are no reasonable people whose failure to believe in the existence of an orthodoxly conceived monotheistic god is reasonable. While it seems to me to be evidently mistaken to think that there are no reasonable people whose failure to believe in the existence of an orthodoxly conceived monotheistic god is reasonable, I am doubtful that there is a *successful* argument on behalf of the claim that there are no reasonable people whose failure to believe in the existence of an orthodoxly conceived monotheistic god is reasonable.

Another approach that one might take is to deny the claim that, if there were an orthodoxly conceived monotheistic god, then it would not be possible for reasonable people to reasonably fail to believe in the existence of such a being on the basis of the evidence that was available to them. Why should we suppose that, if there were an orthodoxly conceived monotheistic god, then there would be evidence for the existence of this being of such a kind that no one could reasonably fail to believe in its existence? In particular, if we are moved by the kinds of considerations that move sceptical theists, then we might suppose that we have no reason at all to think that we have the requisite kind of insight into the motives of a perfect being to be at all confident that it would ensure that there is evidence of its own existence of such a kind that none of its creatures could reasonably fail to believe in its existence. Moreover, even if we suppose that we can know what a perfect being would do, it is not obvious – to me, at any rate – that a perfect being would ensure that there is evidence of its own existence of such a kind that none of its creatures could reasonably fail to believe in its existence.

A final approach that one might take is to deny that there are any unbelievers. We have already seen that there have been people who are prepared to take this approach. I do not believe that this approach has anything to seriously recommend it; but, again, I doubt that there is an *argument* for the claim that there are unbelievers that could not be reasonably resisted by those who suppose otherwise.

7.6.6. Mystery

When all else fails, one can always fall back on recourse to mystery as a justification for believing in the supernatural. It is possible to encode considerations that one takes to be relevant in an argument.

1. It is a complete mystery how consciousness could arise in a purely physical world.
2. It is a complete mystery how there could be moral values in a purely physical world.
3. It is a complete mystery how there could be love and understanding in a purely physical world.
4. It is a complete mystery how language could arise in a purely physical world
5. And so on.
6. (Therefore) There is an orthodoxly conceived monotheistic god.

The key point to note about this kind of argument is one that we already noted in connection with an earlier argument in this section: if we grant that it is a complete mystery how there could be consciousness – or moral values, or love, or understanding, or language, or whatever – in a purely physical world, then surely we should grant that it is a no less complete mystery how an orthodoxly conceived monotheistic god could bring it about that there is consciousness – or moral values, or love, or understanding, or language, or whatever – in an at least partly physical world. If we accept – as perhaps we ought not – that it is a complete mystery how there could be consciousness – or moral values, or love, or understanding, or language, or whatever – in a purely physical world, there is no reason at all why we should not suppose that there is some hitherto undiscovered naturalistic explanation for these facts, rather than to suppose that an orthodoxly conceived monotheistic god has brought it about that there is consciousness – or moral values, or love, or understanding, or language, or whatever – in an at least partly physical world. Neither the assumption that there is a hitherto undiscovered natural- istic explanation nor the assumption that there is an orthodoxly conceived monotheistic god enables us to make any progress at all in understanding the detailed working out of consciousness – or moral values, or love, or understanding, or language, or whatever – in our at least partly physical world. In view of this consideration, there is no reason at all to suppose that the argument from mystery is successful.

7.6.7. Information

Cognoscenti will recognise that this argument is closely derived from an argument defended in Taylor (1963).

1. We treat our sense organs as we treat the words 'The British Railways welcomes you to Wales' on a Welsh hillside, namely, as conveyors of information.
2. (Hence) We should regard our sense organs as we regard the words 'The British Railways Welcomes you to Wales' on a Welsh hillside, namely, as the work of an intelligent agent.
3. (Hence) There is an orthodoxly conceived monotheistic god.

It seems right to suppose that, if we treat something as a conveyor of informa- tion *in the way that written words are conveyors of information*, then we ought to regard that thing as the product of intelligent design. For – very roughly – it seems correct to claim that written words are merely – or at least principally – vehicles for the intentional encoding and transmission of information that was originally stored in the minds of intelligent agents. (Of course, there are various ways in which this claim could be disputed. But, rather than make the necessary digression, let's just run with it.) However, if this is so, then the crucial question for the argument from information becomes: do we treat our sense organs as conveyors of information in the way that written words are conveyors of information?

I take it that the answer to this question is: obviously not! In treating a collection of marks or rocks as an instance of a written sentence-token – 'The British Railways welcomes you to Wales' – we suppose that the collection of marks or rocks is an instance of that token precisely because someone wanted to communicate the information that, in the circumstances in question, is – standardly and correctly – encoded by that sentence-token. Moreover, it is important that the physical (syntactic) structure of the sentence-token is crucial to the information that it conveys: even the slightest change can lead to an entirely different message – for example, 'The British Railways welcomes you to Wakes'. Consequently, in supposing that the collection of marks or rocks is an instance of a particular sentence-token, we suppose that the marks or rocks have the very structure that they do because that structure encodes the message that someone wished to communicate.

But now consider the sense in which our sense organs may be said to convey information. *First*, it seems obviously incorrect to say that the information that is conveyed at a particular moment is encoded in the physical structure of the sense organ – for example, the eye – at the moment that the information is conveyed: the physical structure of the eye remains more or less constant during the conveying of the information, at least in the sense that there seems to be nothing in that structure that corresponds to the syntactic structure of sentence-tokens. *Second*, there is a disanalogy between the sorts of systems that can receive informational input from sentence-tokens and from eyes. To obtain information from a sentence-token, one needs to be able to 'read' the sentence-token; but there is no comparable process that needs to – or can – be carried out in the case of eyes.[16] *Third*, the use of the expression 'conveyor of information' is different in the two cases in question. Very roughly: *sentence-tokens* convey information in the sense that, because languages are systems of representation of the world, the communication – production and reception – of a sentence-token can be accompanied by the communication of an encoded piece of information, that is, that which is represented by the sentence-token in question; *eyes* convey information in the sense that they act as channels for the input of certain signals to the brain, where these signals are converted into a three-dimensional of the world. In other words: eyes are conduits for information; sentence-tokens are not.

In short: the key premise in our argument is that we regard our sense organs as we regard sentence-tokens, namely, as conveyors of information. But, in an important sense, this is not so: for we never try to read our eyes or listen to our ears, even though we often try to read (and hear) sentence-tokens. Of course, there is a sense in which our sense organs are conveyors of information; and there is a different sense in which sentence-tokens are conveyors of information. In the sense in which sentence-tokens are conveyors of information, there is good reason to suppose that they are – and perhaps even must be – the product of intelligent design. But, in the sense in which our sense organs are conveyors of information, there doesn't seem to

---

[16] Perhaps it might be objected (i) that it is electrical, or electrochemical, patterns in the eye that are really analogous to sentence-tokens, and (ii) that these can be subjected to a comparable reading process. But what reason is there to suppose that these patterns have anything like the syntactic structure of sentence-tokens? And even if these patterns do have something like the syntactic structure of sentence-tokens, why should we suppose that this is evidence that this structure is the result of intelligent design?

be any uncontroversial reason to suppose that they must have been designed in order to fulfil that function.[17]

7.6.8. Beauty

Once again, the following is an argument that has been seriously defended; more exactly, Tennant (1969) claims that the conclusion of this argument receives not insignificant support from its premises.

1. The natural world is (almost) universally beautiful and sublime.
2. Some objects – for example, the products of human industry – that are not the result of intentional aesthetic design are not beautiful and sublime.
3. The facts adverted to in 1 and 2 are well explained by the hypothesis that an orthodoxly conceived monotheistic god made the natural world, whereas human beings (sometimes) make ugliness.
4. The fact adverted to in 1 is not well explained by a mechanistic (psychological) account of how the natural world elicits aesthetic responses from humans, since the ability of the natural world to elicit this response still requires an explanation.
5. The fact adverted to in 1 is not well explained by the Darwinian hypothesis of evolution, since neither the possession of aesthetic properties (by any natural creatures) nor the possession of aesthetic sentiments (by humanity) has much, if any, survival value.
6. The only remaining possibility is that the presence of beauty in the universe, and the ability of humans to respond to that beauty, is due to a chain of improbable coincidences.
7. (Hence) An orthodoxly conceived monotheistic god made the natural world.
8. (Hence) There is an orthodoxly conceived monotheistic god.

There is much that is controversial in this argument.

First, it seems to me that – given almost any understanding of 'the beautiful and the sublime' – the first premise is simply false. True, there is a vast array of features of the natural world – from galaxies to paramecia, from mountains to molehills – to which it is, or can be, appropriate to respond with aesthetic appreciation, and, indeed, with awe, wonder, and so forth.

---

[17] Hick (1970: 25f) criticises Taylor's argument on the grounds that we do not treat our sense organs as we treat a set of words *because* our reason for treating sentences as the expression of human intelligence is that, in our own cases, we use them thus, while there is no parallel reason for treating our sense organs as the products of an intelligent purpose. It seems to me to be highly doubtful to suppose that our reason for treating sentences as the expression of human intelligence is that, in our own cases, we use them thus: the idea that we *infer* to the existence of other minds on the basis of observation of our own case is no more plausible here than it is anywhere else.

However, there is also a vast array of features of the natural world – from decaying carcasses to pools of vomit and piles of excrement – to which, at least *prima facie*, it is, or can be, inappropriate to respond with aesthetic appreciation. If it is replied that these things can be appropriate foci of aesthetic appreciation, then it must be conceded that the products of human industry are also appropriate foci for aesthetic appreciation. But, in that case, the argument that appropriate foci of aesthetic appreciation mostly need to be designed with an eye to their aesthetic appeal will be severely undermined.

Second, there is room for suspicion that Tennant's argument relies on a controversial construal of the notion of an aesthetic property. In particular, it *seems* from the formulation of premise 4 that Tennant supposes that aesthetic properties are properties that an entity may have *independently* and *over and above* its 'scientific' or 'natural' properties. However, if we rather suppose that aesthetic properties are supervenient upon – and hence 'reducible to' – scientific properties, then it is not clear that there is a good sense in which there is anything especially problematic in the 'ability of the natural world to elicit aesthetic responses from people'. Given that we have an independent explanation of the ability of people to respond to aesthetic properties, why should it be a surprise that there are aesthetic properties instantiated in the natural world?

Third, there are objections to be lodged against Tennant's claim that the Darwinian hypothesis cannot explain the possession of developed aesthetic sensibility by natural organisms. We might agree with Tennant that there is no 'direct survival value' in the possession of a developed aesthetic sensibility, while nonetheless insisting that a developed aesthetic sensibility is a predictable concomitant of the possession of features that do have 'direct survival value'. When Tennant says:

It may further be observed that, in so far as the mechanical stability and the analytic intelligibility of the inorganic world are concerned, beauty is a superfluity. Also that in the organic world aesthetic pleasingness of colour, etc. seems to possess survival value on but a limited scale, and then is not to be identified with the complex and intellectualised aesthetic sentiments of humanity which apparently have no survival value. From the point of view of science, beauty proper is, in both its objective and subjective factors, but a byproduct, an epiphenomenon, a biologically superfluous accompaniment of the cosmic process.

we can agree with him that there is a sense in which beauty is evolutionarily 'superfluous', while nonetheless insisting that there is no mystery about how developed aesthetic sensibilities might arise as the result of Darwinian evolution.

While there is much more to be said here – the nature of aesthetics properties and aesthetic responses is a very puzzling and controversial part of philosophy – I suspect that I have already said enough to make it plausible to conclude that there is no *successful* argument from the instantiation of beauty in the natural world to the conclusion that the natural world is the product of the creative workings of an orthodoxly conceived monotheistic god.

7.6.9. Conclusion

Okay, that's enough! While I haven't waded though all of the arguments that have been advanced for and against the contention that there is an orthodoxly conceived monotheistic god, I think that I have done enough to make it plausible to suppose that there just are no successful arguments for the existence of such a being, and to indicate why I think that it is plausible to suppose that there are no successful arguments against the existence of any such being. Of course, the arguments that have been proposed so far might not be a representative sample of all of the arguments that can be constructed: there might be new arguments for or against the existence of orthodoxly conceived monotheistic gods that carry more weight than those that have been proposed hitherto. But given how rarely genuinely new arguments appear in this area, I would not count on meeting such an argument any time soon.

8

Concluding Remarks

Given the view of arguments that I have developed in chapter 1, it is not surprising that I have arrived at the conclusion that there are no successful arguments that have as their conclusion that there are – or that there are not – orthodoxly conceived monotheistic gods. After all, it is a plausible hypothesis that, wherever there is substantial perennial disagreement about matters of philosophy or religion, there is no prospect that there are successful arguments that settle the matter. It is a plain matter of fact that there are sincere, thoughtful, intelligent, well-informed, and reflective theists, sincere, thoughtful, intelligent, well-informed, and reflective atheists, and sincere, thoughtful, intelligent, well-informed, and reflective agnostics; but this would not be the case if there were successful simple arguments of the kind that have been examined in this book.

Perhaps it is worth emphasising again how I conceive of the position that a theorist faces. Before we turn to consider the arguments, we know that if A is a randomly chosen, sincere, thoughtful, intelligent, well-informed, and reflective believer in an orthodoxly conceived monotheistic god, and B is a randomly chosen, sincere, thoughtful, intelligent, well-informed, and reflective rejector of the supernatural, then there are many propositions that p_i for which it is true that A believes that p_i and that B does not believe that p_i, and there are many propositions that q_i for which it is true that B believes that q_i and that A does not believe that q_i, where the p_i and q_i are not both logically and probabilistically independent of the claim that there is an orthodoxly conceived monotheistic god. Since we are assuming that A and B are sincere, thoughtful, intelligent, well-informed, and reflective, it is predictable that we can find different $\{p_i : i \in I\}$ such that $\{p_i : i \in I\}$ either entails or probabilistically supports the claim that there is an orthodoxly conceived monotheistic god, and that we can find different $\{q_i : i \in I\}$ such that $\{q_i : i \in I\}$ either entails or probabilistically supports the claim that there is no orthodoxly conceived monotheistic god. Moreover, given that we are assuming that A and B are sincere, thoughtful, intelligent, well-informed, and reflective, it is also predictable that, for any of these $\{p_i: i \in I\}$ such that $\{p_i: i \in I\}$ either entails or probabilistically supports the claim that there is an orthodoxly conceived monotheistic god, there is at least one p_i that is such that B does not believe that p_i; and it is also predictable that, for any of these $\{q_i: i \in I\}$ such that $\{q_i: i \in I\}$ either entails or probabilistically supports the claim that there is no orthodoxly conceived monotheistic god, there is at least one q_i that is such that A does not believe that q_i. In my view, given these considerations, we do better to allow that there are no successful arguments on either side.

But, of course, this is not the only option. Strange as it sounds, one might allow that there are successful arguments on both sides. Or one might stamp one's foot, and insist – contrary to what I take to be the plain evidence – that it is not true that there are sincere, thoughtful, intelligent, well-informed, and reflective people on both sides in this dispute. If that is how you see the debate, then, doubtless you will suppose that while you are entitled to your considered judgments, you cannot have any sincere, thoughtful, intelligent, well-informed, and reflective opponents who have genuinely considered judgments on these matters – and you will be likely to go in for the kind of dismissive abuse that characterises so much of the discussion of the question of the existence of orthodoxly conceived monotheistic gods. While it cannot be that those who believe in the existence of orthodoxly conceived monotheistic gods and those who do not believe in the existence of orthodoxly conceived monotheistic gods are both right, I do not see any reason why we need to suppose that all of those who fall into one of these categories are thereby shown to be unreasonable, or culpably ill-informed, or stupid, or . . . , in their assessment of the relevant considerations.

Perhaps it might be said that there are good political reasons for repudiating the kind of position that I wish to endorse. After all, if those to whom one is opposed are such that they are quite properly not disposed to change their minds on the question of your religious beliefs, then there is not much point in trying to argue with them on these matters. So – it might be thought – the cause of religious toleration is hardly advanced by the kind of view that I have been proposing. And, in view of the importance that religious differences seem to have in major human conflicts, it might be said that we thus have reason to seek an alternative conception of the state of the debate.

But, of course, the alternative views that we have considered above do no better on this score. If you suppose that those to whom you are opposed are, *ipso facto*, irrational when it comes to the matter under consideration, then, again, you are hardly going to suppose that there is a point in trying to reason with them on these matters. Since it is plain in advance that religious toleration necessarily requires toleration of views almost all of which are false, there is a sense in which the justification of religious toleration can only be pragmatic or political: however the facts of disagreement are disposed, nothing in those facts mandates tolerance in the face of that disagreement. So, I take it, the view that I have advanced cannot have disastrous political consequences since – as far as I can see – it has no political consequences of any kind.

There are, of course, writers who have been inclined to read other morals into the facts concerning disagreement about religion. While I have already had quite a bit to say about these matters in chapter 1, it may be useful to go over this ground again in the context of a discussion of the dispute between Clifford[1] and James[2] over the matter of our doxastic duties. I shall start with Clifford's views, and then move on to a discussion of James's response to Clifford. I shall then return to the rounding out of the discussion that has been presented in this book.

8.1. CLIFFORD

In a very short essay on the ethics of belief, Clifford defends a principle that he takes to justify his renunciation of Catholicism – to which he had initially subscribed – and his conversion to a very tough-minded kind of agnosticism. Clifford sums up his view in the claim – often referred to as 'Clifford's Principle' – that *it is wrong, always, everywhere, and for anyone, to believe anything upon insufficient evidence.* I suspect that the use of the word 'evidence' here may be misleading; I think that Clifford would have been perfectly happy with the claim that *it is wrong, always, everywhere, and for anyone, to believe anything for which there is insufficient reason* (though perhaps this is how his talk of 'evidence' is meant to be understood). There are many views on which there would be something odd about the claim that we must have *evidence* for the truth of those mathematical theorems, logical theorems, and other principles – that are characteristically said to be knowable *a priori* – that we happen to believe.

---

[1] William Kingdom Clifford (1845–79) was a British mathematician and philosopher. He was educated at King's College (London) and Trinity College (Cambridge). He began giving public lectures when he was appointed Fellow of Trinity in 1868; he was appointed professor of mathematics at University College (London) in 1870. His academic career ended prematurely when he died of tuberculosis. There are two pieces of work for which Clifford is principally remembered: (i) a discussion of the nature of space and time that seems to anticipate Einstein's general theory of relativity in some respects, and about which various eminent physicists have remarked 'if only he had lived longer, we might have learned something', and (ii) his short paper on the ethics of belief, which was published after his death in a very interesting pamphlet that collects together his main philosophical essays.

[2] William James (1842–1910) is much better known than William Clifford. Since I may not have occasion to return to this point, it is worth noting at the outset that James was in many respects a humanist and an empiricist who wanted to preserve a place for religious belief even though he doubted that religious belief could be integrated into a scientific world-view. Given the tensions in his beliefs, it is perhaps not surprising that his endorsements of religious belief are apt to end up sounding like endorsements of wishful thinking.

There are various ways in which one might hope to use Clifford's principle to construct arguments that support atheism, or agnosticism (or even theism). I provide four modest examples here.

A. A 'many gods' objection to theism: There is insufficient reason for – and, in particular, insufficient evidence to support – belief in any particular god. Hence, by Clifford's principle, it is wrong, always, everywhere, and for anyone, to believe in any particular god. At most, in light of the forgoing argument, one might be warranted in believing that there is at least one god; but, beyond that, there is nothing that one can justifiably believe about the nature of whatever gods there happen to be.

B. An argument for theism: There are many possible gods. Grant that they're equally likely, and that the probability that there are no gods is the same. Then it is overwhelmingly likely that there are gods – that is, taking the many gods seriously provides an argument for theism.

C. An argument for agnosticism: There are many incompatible (doxastically possible) gods. In circumstances in which there is no reason to prefer one incompatible hypothesis amongst many, the only reasonable thing to do is to suspend judgment: so one should be agnostic about the existence of gods.

D. An unbeliever's perspective: In the face of the available evidence – and perhaps in the face of pretty much any conceivable evidence – there is no more reason to believe in one particular god than there is to believe in one of the many other gods. (Compare with astrology: in the face of the available evidence, there is no more reason to believe in the astrological predictions of one astrologer that there is to believe in the astrological predictions of any other astrologer.) So, religious belief – astrological belief – has to be abandoned. Following Hume, one might strengthen the inference to the conclusion by observing that the claim that there are gods is, in itself, simply insufficient to form the basis of a religion.

While there are obvious difficulties that face some of these arguments – for example, B is plausibly defeated by the observation that no one should grant that the probability that there are no gods is the same as the probability that some particular god exists; and C is plausibly seriously weakened by the observation that, at most, what we should be agnostic about is conditionals of the form *if there are gods, then there is this particular god* – one plausible line of response to all of them is to note their (implicit) dependence upon Clifford's Principle and then to add that there are good reasons for holding that Clifford's Principle is false. However, before we turn to a direct examination of Clifford's Principle, it is worth examining the considerations that Clifford advances on its behalf.

Clifford rests the case in support of his principle on two examples: (i) the case of a shipowner and his doubts; and (ii) the case of some accusers and their accusations. In the former case, a shipowner 'suppresses' doubts about the seaworthiness of his vessel and is thereby responsible for the deaths of those who perish when the vessel sinks; in the latter case, the reputations of reputable citizens are besmirched by accusations from accusers who are plainly in no position to have good grounds for making the accusations that they do. In each case, there is at least a *prima facie* appearance that the believers who appear not to have conformed to Clifford's Principle have indeed done something that is morally wrong. (Clifford is very clear that he supposes that it is *morally* wrong, always, everywhere, and for anyone, to believe anything upon insufficient evidence.) However, in each case, once we have settled on a psychologically satisfying description of the case, it seems rather implausible to suppose that the moral wrong in question has anything to do with the apparent violation of Clifford's Principle.

Consider the case of the shipowner. Clifford's story requires that the shipowner can obtain 'a sincere and comfortable conviction' by 'dismissing ungenerous suspicions' and so on from his mind. This suggests that Clifford's story requires that the shipowner is able to form beliefs at will. But is it surely much more plausible to suppose that the shipowner's decision to send the ship owes more to his over-riding desire to make money that it does to 'suppression' of doubts about the seaworthiness of the vessel: while it is psychologically implausible to suppose that one can form beliefs at will, it is not psychologically implausible to suppose that doubts can be 'trumped' by strong desires. But if this is right, then the psychologically plausible version of the story does not involve any violation of Clifford's principle: the moral wrong lies in allowing unworthy desires to triumph when one acts. (Of course, the general idea here goes back to Hume. Actions are always the products of both beliefs and desires, and the internal processes by which the former are acquired can never be the subject of *moral* criticism.)

Even though it seems to me to be highly plausible to claim that Clifford's examples do not support his principle, it may nonetheless be the case that Clifford's Principle is correct. On the face of it, there is some appeal in Clifford's Principle, though not, I think, if we suppose that the alleged wrong is a *moral* wrong. As William James notes, Clifford's homilies about the ethics of belief – the moral dangers to self, the moral dangers to others, the moral dangers to society and humanity at large – are completely over the top. However, we might nonetheless suppose that there is nothing unreasonable in the claim that it is always, everywhere, and for anyone, *irrational* – contrary to reason – to believe anything for which there is insufficient evidence or reason. Moreover, this *prima facie* not implausible claim is all that is needed to drive the various arguments that are set out above.

Even if we do treat Clifford's Principle as an injunction about reasonable belief, there are still reasons to be sceptical of it. To see why this is so, we need to distinguish among various different ways in which the principle can be formulated. I shall begin with the following four formulations.

(1) It is irrational, always, everywhere, and for anyone, to believe anything for which *there is* insufficient evidence or reason.

(2) It is irrational, always, everywhere, and for anyone, to believe anything for which *that one has* insufficient evidence or reason.

(3) It is irrational, always, everywhere, and for anyone, to believe anything for which *that one could easily have come to see, by that one's own lights, that that one does not have* sufficient evidence or reason.

(4) It is irrational, always, everywhere, and for anyone, to believe anything for which *that one takes himself or herself to have* insufficient evidence or reason.

Formulation (1) seems clearly wrong: one might as well insist that it is irrational, always, everywhere, and for anyone, to believe anything that is not true, or that is not known to be true, or that is not known by the one in question to be true. If there are considerations of which one is unaware – in circumstances in which that lack of awareness is not culpable – then one might reasonably hold that one has good reason to believe something, even though, if one were apprised of those further considerations, one would no longer take oneself to have good reason to believe that thing. Lack of information need not be a crime against reason.

Formulation (2) seems more plausible, though we need to ask exactly what we mean by 'irrational' here. Consider a case in which there are only very difficult chains of reasoning – of a kind that most people are certain not to discover – that show that you do not have good reason to believe something on the evidence that you have. In these circumstances, we might insist that you are irrational – because an ideal reasoner would not draw your conclusions given your evidence and background assumptions – or we might say that you are reasonable – because you have done all that could reasonably be expected of you.

If we take the latter course, then we might wish only to accept (3). Perhaps the distinction that we might wish to draw here is between culpable irrationality and blameless irrationality: given that Clifford's Principle is supposed to tell us when someone ought to be criticised for doxastic failings, there might be reason to be interested only in (3). On the other hand, when we ask what one ought to believe on the reasons or evidence that one has, what we are principally interested in is what an ideal reasoner would believe on these reasons and evidence (or so it seems to me).

Formulation (4) seems more plausible still, though you might wonder whether it is really possible to believe something for which one takes oneself to have insufficient evidence. There is something very odd about claims of the form 'I believe that p, but, of course, I have no justification for doing so': if I think that my believing that p would be unjustified, then surely I do not really believe that p. Of course, in this kind of case, I might have some other kind of attitude towards the proposition that p – for example, I might hope that it is true – but that other kind of attitude will not be any kind of belief.

All things considered, it seems to me that the principle that Clifford has in mind is something very much like (4). Moreover, I think that the doubts that I raised earlier about Clifford's examples are connected to the worry about whether it is so much as possible to do what the principle says that one ought not to do. However, the principle that we need for the arguments that we introduced earlier is something like (2); so, henceforth, I shall suppose that 'Clifford's Principle' is the claim that *it is irrational, always, everywhere, for anyone to believe anything that is not appropriately proportioned to the reasons and evidence that are possessed by that one.* (This formulation is not quite the one given above. However, a different kind of worry that one might have about that earlier formulation is that it fails to take account of the apparently evident truths that beliefs come in degrees, and with different strengths. Given that belief is not a simple on/off matter, it makes sense to retreat to a formulation that speaks of the 'appropriate proportioning' of beliefs to reasons and evidence.)

Even if we understand Clifford's Principle in the way that I have proposed, there are still doubts that one might have about its acceptability. I shall mention just a few of these doubts here.

First, it seems plausible to think that one must already have beliefs before one can recognise and assess evidence. But if that is right, then it can hardly be a rationality constraint on the earliest beliefs that one forms that they are proportioned to the evidence that one possesses. Moreover, given that it seems unlikely that there is a rationality constraint that requires one to keep track of the grounds that one has for adopting beliefs, one might wonder whether there is any prospect for determining which of your beliefs is *fully* compliant with Clifford's Principle. Foundationalists – such as Descartes – might think that it is at least possible to reconstruct one's beliefs in such a way that all of one's beliefs conform fully to Clifford's strictures. However, holists – such as Neurath and Quine – will insist that there is no such possibility: beliefs form a web that may be *updated* in accordance with Clifford's Principle, but for which there is no sense to be made of the idea that every belief in the web conforms to the principle. In the light of this objection one might suppose that Clifford's Principle should really be reinterpreted as a constraint on the *revision* of belief: *one should not take on a new belief that is not appropriately proportioned to the reasons or evidence that one has already in one's possession.*

Second, one might wonder whether violations of Clifford's Principle should be taken to be bad things that can be outweighed by other

considerations, or whether they should be taken to be bad all things considered. In particular, one might ask: is it really a bad thing that belief seems
to be catching, that is, that beliefs can spread through a population even
if many of the people in the population don't seem to have good reasons
or evidence for taking on those beliefs? Is it really so crucially important
to avoid false beliefs, even (perhaps) at the expense of failing to acquire
true beliefs? If it is important to have agreement, and not so important
to have independence, then one might think that violations of Clifford's
Principle should only be taken to be bad things that can be outweighed
by other considerations. On the other hand, if we generally have reason to
believe what those around us believe, at least in the absence of countervail-
ing reasons to believe otherwise, then perhaps these kinds of considerations
have no particular bearing on Clifford's Principle, whether or not they are
cogent. (My own view is that the virtues of global agreement are vastly over-
rated; a healthy society ought to number at least some sceptics who value
avoidance of falsehood above the acquisition of truth. Even if Clifford's
Principle is false, it sets up a norm to which it is desirable that at least *some*
members in a given society aspire. Thus, for example, the practice of science demands that, in their own area of expertise, experts do not take on
beliefs about their own area of expertise that are not appropriately proportioned to the reasons and evidence that those experts already have in their
possession.)

Third, there are apparent counter-examples to Clifford's Principle, even
when it is cast as the claim that one should not take on a new belief that is not
appropriately proportioned to the reasons or evidence that one has already
in one's possession. Consider, for example, the case of the footballers who
play better if they believe that they will win even though their reasons and evidence do not support the proposition that they will win; or the case of young
children who believe things 'because Mummy said so', even though neither
their reasons nor their evidence supports the belief that what Mummy says
is true; or James's case of the mountaineer who will die unless he forms the
belief that he can leap the crevasse that blocks his descent, even though
neither his reasons nor his evidence supports the claim that he can leap the
crevasse; and so on. I think that it is highly doubtful whether these really are
counterexamples to Clifford's Principle. As I noted above – in connection
with the cases that Clifford introduces in order to try to marshal intuitive
support for his principle – desires are also involved in the production of
actions; the connections between belief and the will are (at best) obscure;
and often the most important thing is merely that one should act in a certain way, quite apart from the beliefs that one is able to form. (In the case
of James's mountaineer, it seems to me to be psychologically plausible to
suppose that what the mountaineer needs to do is to draw on his desires –
and other relevant non-belief-like states – in order to make the best possible
jump that he can. While this might be described, colloquially, as 'forming

the belief that he will succeed in jumping the gap', I see no reason at all to suppose that it must be that he forms the *belief* that he is able to successfully leap the crevasse.)

In the light of the discussion to this point, it seems to me that we have not yet found a good reason to deny the claim that *one should not take on a new belief that is not appropriately proportioned to the reasons or evidence that one has already in one's possession.* However – even if there is not some reason that we have not yet considered for rejecting this principle – it seems clear that the various concessions that have been made in the course of our discussion have resulted in a principle that cannot carry the load that is required in the arguments with which we began. Even if it is true that considerations about the many gods establish that those who do not already believe in a particular god ought not to revise their beliefs so as to come to believe in a particular god, those considerations are insufficient to establish that those who already believe in a particular god ought to give up that belief. Even if it is true that considerations about the many gods establish that those who do not already believe in a particular god ought not to take on any religious beliefs that depend upon the assumption that there is an ortho- doxly conceived monotheistic god, those considerations are insufficient to establish that those who already believe in a particular god ought to give up their religious beliefs (at least insofar as those religious beliefs depend upon the assumption that there is an orthodoxly conceived monotheistic god). If there is an acceptable version of Clifford's Principle of the kind that I have proposed, then that Principle cannot do the work that Clifford supposed that his principle would be able to do.

8.2. JAMES

In his famous essay 'The Will to Believe', William James proposes a quite different kind of response to Clifford. In this section, I shall briefly sum- marise the various considerations that James marshals in order to construct his objection to Clifford.

At the beginning of his essay, James distinguishes among three differ- ent ways of categorising what he calls 'options': (i) 'living' and 'dead'; (ii) 'forced' and 'avoidable'; and (iii) 'momentous' and 'trivial'. Since the thesis that James ultimately defends concerns options that are 'living, forced, and momentous', the defence of his thesis relies upon the conferral of a clear sense upon each of the distinctions that he draws.

The next 'preliminary' that James considers concerns what he calls 'the psychology of opinion'. Here, James argues that the central claim that Clifford makes in his essay – namely, that it is wrong always, everywhere, and for anyone, to believe anything upon insufficient evidence – 'flies directly in the teeth of the facts', even though it may be correct in 'purely intellectual cases'. That is, according to James, an 'honest examination of our own convictions' reveals that we all regularly believe claims for which we have insufficient evidence – and yet it is not plausible to suppose that a survey of the psychology of opinion should lead us to the conclusion that we act irrationally most of the time.

The final 'preliminary' that James introduces concerns 'our duty in the matter of opinion'. In particular, there is the question of whether our sole concern can be the avoidance of error, or whether this very thought demonstrates a kind of pathological hatred of being duped. Unless we give due weight to the importance of obtaining the truth, we are very likely to end up with an unlivable scepticism. In particular, then, James suggests that the adoption of Clifford's Principle would lead to an unlivable scepticism.

The principle that James proposes as a corrective to Clifford's Principle is this: our passional nature not only lawfully may, but must, decide an option between propositions, whenever it is a genuine option that cannot by its nature be decided on intellectual grounds; for to say, under such circumstances, 'Do not decide, but leave the question open', is itself a passional decision – just like deciding no or yes – and is attended with the same risk of losing the truth.

There are particular cases – apart from the religious case – in which James claims that we are obliged to exercise the will to believe; he mentions (i) moral questions, and (ii) 'personal' questions about love, hope, and emotion. However, the most important application that James wants to make of his principle is to the case of religion, about which he has very idiosyncratic views. According to James, the principle claims of religion are (i) that 'the best things are the more eternal things'; and (ii) that 'we are better off even now if we believe'. These are the propositions that James would have us believe – on the basis of his alternative to Clifford's Principle – but which he supposes we should otherwise not be able to accept.

There is much that can be criticised in James's views.

The main reason that he gives for religious belief is that it is conducive to psychic health. However, it seems to me that considerations about psychic health could never be reasons for belief to which one could give first-personal endorsement. There is something very wrong with claims of the form 'I believe that p because I believe that it is good for me to believe that p, even though there is not the slightest reason or evidence that supports the claim that p'. The alternative to Clifford's Principle that James proposes seems merely to be an endorsement of wishful thinking; if it were the case that one were obliged to choose between Clifford's Principle and the alternative that James proposes, then it seems to me that no one could reasonably choose the alternative that James offers.

James's view of religion is not merely idiosyncratic: the characterisation that he offers in 'The Will to Believe' is, I think, manifestly inadequate.

In particular, it is not clear why atheists could not be entitled to the claim that the best things are the more eternal things: why shouldn't atheists have preferences of the kind that one would need to have in order to be in a position to make this claim? But if atheists – materialists, those with no religious inclinations whatsoever – can consistently maintain that the best things are the more eternal things – that is, the things that last longer – and that we do better if we have the preferences that are required in order to make this judgment, then those claims simply do not characterise religious belief.

James's claim about the need to rely on his alternative to Clifford's Principle in other cases is also highly dubious. Consider, for example, the case of friendship. James writes: "Turn now ... to ... questions concerning personal relations. ... 'Do you like me or not?' – for example. Whether you do or not depends, in countless instances, on whether I meet you half-way, am willing to assume that you must like me, and show you trust and expectation. The previous faith on my part in your liking's existence is in such cases what makes your liking come. But if I stand aloof, and refuse to budge an inch until I have objective evidence, until you shall have done something apt ... ten to one your liking never comes." I see no reason at all to suppose that my belief about whether or not you like me should not be proportioned to the reasons and evidence that I possess, nor that, in real life cases, my beliefs about such matters are not proportioned to the reasons and evidence that I possess. Of course, when we first meet, I won't believe that you like me – for, after all, you don't know me – though, perhaps, if your liking is to come, I may need to believe that there is a good chance that you will come to like me when you get to know me. But there is no reason at all why my belief that there is a good chance that you will come to like me when you get to know me cannot be proportioned to the reasons and evidence that I possess. There is nothing in Clifford's Principle that mandates the claim that I should be well-disposed towards you only if you are well-disposed towards me first; on the contrary, that sounds like a crazy claim upon which to base one's social interactions.

More generally, James's claim that a survey of the psychology of opinion reveals that Clifford's Principle flies in the teeth of the facts is highly questionable. James says: "As a matter of fact, we find ourselves believing, we hardly know how or why. ... Here in this room, we all of us believe in molecules and the conservation of energy, in democracy and necessary progress, in Protestant Christianity and the duty of fighting for 'the doctrine of the immortal Monroe', all for no reasons worthy of the name." I do not believe that this is so. Assuming that James was right in his assessment of what those in the room believed, it seems to me that we can explain how those who had those beliefs would have taken them to be appropriately apportioned to their reasons and evidence. The best scientific opinion of the day said that energy is conserved, and that there are molecules; that is good reason to adopt those beliefs. Insofar as the other 'beliefs' that James mentions are expressions of preference, they do not fall within the scope of Clifford's Principle; insofar as they really are beliefs, they are susceptible of assessment in the light of reasons and evidence.

While there is much more that can be said about James's critique of Clifford, it seems to me that it is quite clear that one ought not to accept the principle that James offers as a replacement for Clifford's Principle. Rather than leap to embrace wishful thinking, one ought rather to seek a version of Clifford's Principle that one is prepared to endorse. Moreover, if I am right, one can reasonably reject the conclusions of the arguments that appeal to Clifford's Principle that we set out earlier without adopting the kinds of views that James would have us adopt.

8.3. CONCLUDING REMARKS

There are two different things that I have tried to do in this book. On the one hand, I have tried to articulate a conception of the dialectical context within which argument about orthodoxly conceived monotheistic gods occurs that makes it possible to allow that there is a wide range of *reasonable* views about the existence of orthodoxly conceived monotheistic gods. On the other hand, I have tried to defend the view that no *argument* that has been constructed thus far provides those who have reasonable views about the existence of orthodoxly conceived monotheistic gods with the slightest reason to change their minds.

There are various ways in which the execution of each of the projects upon which I have embarked could be improved. In particular, it is clear that I have not discussed all of the arguments that have been constructed thus far; and, as new arguments come in, they will all need to be assessed on their merits. I do not claim to have a successful transcendental argument for the conclusion that there *cannot* be successful arguments about orthodoxly conceived monotheistic gods; my claim is just that, when you bear in mind what is required of a successful argument, you will find that there *are* no successful arguments that have yet been proposed.

There are also questions that one might ask about the coherence of the view of reason and argument that I have been trying to defend. In particular, I have assumed that all *reasonable* parties to the dispute about the existence of orthodoxly conceived monotheistic gods will agree with me about the way in which reason, argument, and dialectic ought to be understood (even though there is no reason why they must agree with me on the question of the existence of orthodoxly conceived monotheistic gods). So, I discriminate. On the one hand, I allow that there are reasonable believers in the existence of orthodoxly conceived monotheistic gods. On the other hand, I deny that there are reasonable believers in the existence of successful arguments for the conclusion that there are orthodoxly conceived monotheistic gods. While I am 'tolerant' or 'liberal' in my views about what can be reasonably believed, there are limits to my 'tolerance' or 'liberalism': some erroneous religious beliefs are not beyond the rational pale, but other mistaken philosophical beliefs certainly are. Doubtless, I shall have reason to come back to these kinds of considerations again in the future.

References

Adams, R. 1971. "The Logical Structure of Anselm's Argument." *Philosophical Review* 80: 28–54.

Adams, R. 1995. "Introductory Note to *1970." In K. Gödel, *Collected Works*, vol. 3: *Unpublished Essays and Lectures*, Solomon Feferman (ed.). New York: Oxford University Press, 388–402.

Almeida, M., and G. Oppy. 2003. "Sceptical Theism and the Evidential Argument from Evil." *Australasian Journal of Philosophy* 81, no. 4: 496–516.

Alston, W. 1983. "Christian Experience and Christian Belief." In A. Plantinga and N. Wolterstorff (eds.), *Faith and Rationality: Reason and Belief in God*. Notre Dame: University of Notre Dame Press.

Alston, W. 1991/6. "The Inductive Argument from Evil and the Human Cognitive Condition." In Howard-Snyder (1996a), 97–125.

Alston, W. 1996. "Some (Temporarily) Final Thoughts on Evidential Arguments from Evil." In Howard-Snyder (1996a), 311–32.

Anderson, C. 1990. "Some Emendations on Gödel's Ontological Proof." *Faith and Philosophy* 7: 291–303.

Anderson, R. 1995. "Recent Criticisms and Defences of Pascal's Wager." *International Journal for Philosophy of Religion* 37: 45–56.

Annice, M. 1956. "Logic and Mystery in the *Quarta Via* of St. Thomas." *Thomist* 19: 22–58.

Armour, L. 1980. "Ideas, Causes and God." *Sophia* 19: 14–21.

Armstrong, D. 1989. "C. B. Martin, Counterfactuals, Causality, and Conditionals." In J. Heil (ed.), *Cause, Mind and Reality: Essays Honouring C. B. Martin*. Dordrecht: Kluwer, 7–15.

Armstrong, D., and S. McCall. 1989. "God's Lottery." *Analysis* 49: 223–4.

Austin, W. 1985. "Philo's Reversal." *Philosophical Topics* 13: 103–12.

Barbour, I. 1966. *Issues in Philosophy of Religion*. Englewood Cliffs, N.J.: Prentice-Hall.

Barnes, J. 1972. *The Ontological Argument*. London: Macmillan.

Barrow, J., and F. Tipler. 1986. *The Anthropic Cosmological Principle*. Oxford: Blackwell.

Baumer, W. 1969. "Kant on Cosmological Arguments." In L. Beck (ed.), *Kant Studies Today*. LaSalle, Ill.: Open Court.

Behe, M. 1996a. *Darwin's Black Box*. New York: Free Press.

Behe, M. 1996b. "Evidence for Intelligent Design from Biochemistry." Http://www. discovery.org/crsc, accessed May 15, 2004.

Behe, M. 2001. "The Modern Intelligent Design Hypothesis: Breaking Rules." *Philosophia Christi* 3: 165–79.

Benacerraf, P. 1962. "Tasks, Supertasks, and the Modern Eleatics." *Journal of Philosophy* 59: 765–84.

Bergmann, M. 2001. "Sceptical Theism and Rowe's New Evidential Argument from Evil." *Nous* 35, no. 2:278–96.

Berman, D. 1988. *A History of Atheism in Britain: From Hobbes to Russell.* London: CroomHelm.

Bigelow, J. 1988. *The Reality of Numbers.* Oxford: Oxford University Press.

Bobik, J. 1968. "The First Part of the Third Way." *Philosophical Studies (Ireland)* 17: 142–60.

Bobik, J. 1972. "Further Reflections on the First Part of the Third Way." *Philosophical Studies (Ireland)* 20: 166–74.

Bobik, J. 1987. "Aquinas' Fourth Way and the Approximating Relation." *Thomist* 51: 17–36.

Bostrom, N. 2002. *Anthropic Bias: Observation Selection Effects in Science and Philosophy.* New York: Routledge.

Bowler, P. 1984. *Evolution: The History of an Idea.* Los Angeles: University of California Press.

Brady, J. 1974. "Note on the Fourth Way." *New Scholasticism* 48: 219–32.

Brecher, B. 1976. "Descartes' Causal Argument for the Existence of God." *International Journal for Philosophy of Religion* 7: 418–32.

Brewster, L. 1974. "How to Know Enough about the Unknown Faculty." *Journal of the History of Philosophy* 12: 366–71.

Bringsjord, S. 1986. "Swinburne's Argument from Consciousness." *International Journal for Philosophy of Religion* 19: 127–43.

Brown, G. 1984. "A Defence of Pascal's Wager." *Religious Studies* 20: 465–80.

Brown, P. 1965. "A Medieval Analysis of Infinity." *Journal for the History of Philosophy* 3: 242–3.

Brown, R. 1982. "A Reply to Kelly on Aquinas' Third Way." *International Journal for Philosophy of Religion* 13: 225–7.

Burns, R. 1987. "Meynell's Arguments for the Intelligibility of the Universe." *Religious Studies* 23: 183–97.

Byl, J. 1994. "On Pascal's Wager and Infinite Utilities." *Faith and Philosophy* 11: 467–73.

Cahn, S. 1976. "Cacodaemony." *Analysis* 37: 69–73.

Campbell, R. 1976. *From Belief to Understanding.* Canberra: ANU Press.

Caputo, J. 1974. "Kant's Refutation of the Cosmological Argument." *Journal of the American Academy of Religion* 42: 686–91.

Cargile, J. 1966. "Pascal's Wager." *Philosophy* 41: 250–7.

Carnap, R. 1950. "Empiricism, Semantics and Ontology." *Revue Internationale de Philosophie* 4. Reprinted in Carnap (1956).

Carnap, R. 1956. *Meaning and Necessity*, 2nd ed. Chicago: University of Chicago Press.

Centore, F. 1980. "Camus, Pascal, and the Absurd." *New Scholasticism* 54: 46–59.

Chad, A. 1997. "The Principle of Sufficient Reason and the Uncaused Beginning of the Universe." *Dialogue* 36: 555–62.

Chalmers, D. 1996. *The Conscious Mind: In Search of a Fundamental Theory.* New York: Oxford University Press.

Chambers, T. 2000. "On Behalf of the Devil: A Parody of St. Anselm Revisited." *Proceedings of the Aristotelian Society* 100: 93–113.

Charlesworth, M. 1965. *St. Anselm's Proslogion.* Oxford: Oxford University Press.

Churchland, P. M. 1979. *Scientific Realism and the Plasticity of Mind.* Cambridge: Cambridge University Press.

Churchland, P. S. 1986. *Neurophilosophy: Toward a Unified Science of the Mind-Brain.* Cambridge, Mass.: MIT Press.

Clack, B., and B. Clack. 1998. *The Philosophy of Religion.* Oxford: Polity.

Clarke, B. 1974. "The Argument from Design – A Piece of Abductive Reasoning." *International Journal for the Philosophy of Religion* 5: 65–78.

Clarke, B. 1979. "The Argument from Design." *Sophia* 18: 1–13.

Clarke, R. 1988. "Vicious Infinite Regress Arguments." In Tomberlin (1988), 369–80.

Clatterbaugh, K. 1980. "Descartes' Causal Likeness Principle." *Philosophical Review* 89: 379–402.

Clayton, P. 1996. "The Theistic Argument from Infinity in Early Modern Philosophy." *International Philosophical Quarterly* 36: 5–17.

Collins, R. 1999. "The Fine-Tuning Design Argument: A Scientific Argument for the Existence of God." In M. Murray (ed.), *Reason for the Hope Within.* Grand Rapids, Mich.: Eerdmans, 67–72.

Collins, R. 2003. "Evidence for Fine-Tuning." In N. Manson (ed.), *God and Design.* London: Routledge, 178–99.

Connolly, T. 1954. "Basis for the Third Proof of the Existence of God." *Thomist* 17: 281–349.

Conway, D. 1974. "Possibility and Infinite Time: A Logical Paradox in St. Thomas' Third Way." *International Philosophical Quarterly* 14: 201–8.

Conway, D. 1983. "Concerning Infinite Chains, Infinite Trains, and Borrowing a Typewriter." *International Journal for Philosophy of Religion* 14: 71–86.

Conway, D. 1984. "'It Would Have Happened Already': On One Argument for a First Cause." *Analysis* 44: 159–66.

Cornman, J., and K. Lehrer. 1968. *Philosophical Problems and Arguments: An Introduction.* New York: Macmillan.

Cox, H. 1974. "Composition and the Cosmological Argument: A Trivial Issue." *New Scholasticism* 48: 365–8.

Craig, W. 1979a. *The Kalām Cosmological Argument.* London: Macmillan.

Craig, W. 1979b. "Whitrow, Popper, and the Impossibility of an Infinite Past." *British Journal for the Philosophy of Science* 30: 166–70.

Craig, W. 1985. "Professor Mackie and the Kalām Cosmological Argument." *Religious Studies* 20: 367–75.

Craig, W. 1988. "Quentin Smith on Infinity and the Past." *Philosophy of Science* 55: 453–5.

Craig, W. 1991a. "The Kalām Cosmological Argument and the Hypothesis of a Quiescent Universe." *Faith and Philosophy* 8: 104–8.

References

Craig, W. 1991b. "Theism and Big Bang Cosmology." *Australasian Journal of Philosophy* 69: 492–503.

Craig, W. 1991c. "Time and Infinity." *International Philosophical Quarterly* 31: 387–401.

Craig, W. 1992a. "God and the Initial Singularity." *Faith and Philosophy* 9: 238–48.

Craig, W. 1992b. "The Origin and Creation of the Universe: A Reply to Adolf Grünbaum." *British Journal for the Philosophy of Science* 43: 233–40.

Craig, W. 1992c. "Philosophical and Scientific Pointers to Creation *Ex Nihilo*." In D. Geivett and B. Sweetman (eds.), *Contemporary Perspectives on Religious Epistemology*. New York: Oxford University Press.

Craig, W. 1993a. "The Caused Beginning of the Universe: A Response to Quentin Smith." *British Journal for the Philosophy of Science* 44: 623–39.

Craig, W. 1993b. "Graham Oppy on the *Kalām* Cosmological Argument." *Sophia* 32: 1–11.

Craig, W. 1994a. "A Response to Grünbaum on Creation and Big Bang Cosmology." *Philosophia Naturalis* 31: 237–49.

Craig, W. 1994b. "Professor Grünbaum on Creation" *Erkenntnis* 40: 325–41.

Craig, W. 1997a. "In Defence of the *Kalām* Cosmological Argument." *Faith and Philosophy* 14: 236–47.

Craig, W. 1997b. "Hartle-Hawking Cosmology and Atheism." *Analysis* 57: 291–5.

Craig, W. 1998. "Theism and the Origin of the Universe." *Erkenntnis* 48: 47–57.

Craig, W. 1999. "A Swift and Simple Refutation of the *Kalām* Cosmological Argument?" *Religious Studies* 35:57–72.

Craig, W. 2000. "Naturalism and Cosmology." In W. Craig and J. Moreland (eds.), *Naturalism: A Critical Analysis*. London: Routledge, 215–52.

Craig, W. 2003a. "The Cosmological Argument." In P. Copan and P. Moser (eds.), *The Rationality of Theism*. London: Routledge, 112–31.

Craig, W. 2003b. "Design and the Anthropic Fine-Tuning of the Universe." In N. Manson (ed.), *God and Design*. London: Routledge, 155–77.

Craig, W., and M. McLeod, eds. 1990. *Rational Theism: The Logic of a Worldview*. Lewiston: N.Y. Edwin Mellen.

Craig, W., and Q. Smith. 1993. *Theism, Atheism and Big Bang Cosmology*. Oxford: Clarendon.

Crawford, P. 1981. "Is the Cosmological Argument Dependent upon the Ontological Argument?" *Sophia* 20: 27–31.

Dalton, P. 1975. "Pascal's Wager: The Second Argument." *Southern Journal of Religion* 13: 31–46.

Dalton, P. 1976. "Pascal's Wager: The First Argument." *International Journal for Philosophy of Religion* 7: 346–68.

Daniels, C. 1997. "God, Demon, Good, Evil." *Journal of Value Inquiry* 31, no. 2:177–81.

Davey, K., and R. Clifton. 2001. "Insufficient Reason and the 'New Cosmological Argument'." *Religious Studies* 37: 485–90.

Davidson, H. 1987. *Proofs for Eternity, Creation and the Existence of God in Medieval Islamic and Jewish Philosophy*. New York: Oxford University Press.

Davies, B. 1993. *An Introduction to the Philosophy of Religion*. Oxford: Oxford University Press.

Davis, J. 1987. "The Design Argument, Cosmic 'Fine-Tuning', and the Anthropic Principle." *International Journal for Philosophy of Religion* 22: 139–50.

References 431

Davis, S. 1997. *God, Reason and Theistic Proofs*. Edinburgh: Edinburgh University Press.

Dawkins, R. 1986. *The Blind Watchmaker*. New York: Norton.

Day, T. 1987. "Aquinas on Infinite Regress." *International Journal for Philosophy of Religion* 22: 151–64.

Delahunty, R. 1980. "Descartes' Cosmological Argument." *Philosophical Quarterly* 30: 34–46.

Deltete, R. 1998. "Simplicity and Why the Universe Exists: A Reply to Quentin Smith." *Philosophy* 73: 490–4.

Deltete, R., and R. Guy. 1997. "Hartle-Hawking Cosmology and Unconditional Probabilities." *Analysis* 57: 304–15.

Dembski, W. 1998. *The Design Inference: Eliminating Chance through Small Probabilities*. Cambridge: Cambridge University Press.

Dembski, W. 2002. *No Free Lunch: Why Specified Complexity Cannot Be Purchased without Intelligence*. Lanham, Md.: Rowman and Littlefield.

Dennett, D. 1991. *Consciousness Explained*. London: Penguin.

Devine, P. 1975. "The Perfect Island, the Devil, and Existent Unicorns." *American Philosophical Quarterly* 12: 255–60.

Dewan, L. 1982. "The Distinctiveness of St. Thomas' 'Third Way'." *Modern Schoolman* 57: 201–18.

Dewan, L. 1991. "The Interpretation of St. Thomas's Third Way." In *Littera, sensus, sententia, Studi in onore del Prof. Clemente J. Vansteenkiste O.P.*, ed., A. Lobato, O.P. Milan: Massimo, 201–18.

Dilley, F. 1970. "Descartes' Cosmological Argument." *Monist* 54: 427–40.

Dilley, F. 1976. "Misunderstanding the Cosmological Argument of St. Thomas." *New Scholasticism* 50: 96–105.

Doolittle, R. 1997. "A Delicate Balance." *Boston Review* (February/March): 28–9.

Doore, G. 1980. "The Argument from Design: Some Better Reasons for Agreeing with Hume." *Religious Studies* 16: 145–61.

Draper, P. 1997. "The *Kalām* Cosmological Argument." In L. Pojman (ed.), *Philosophy of Religion*, 3rd ed. Belmont: Wadsworth, 42–7.

Duerlinger, J. 1982. "Unspoken Connections in the Design Argument." *Philosophy and Phenomenological Research* 42: 519–29.

Duff, A. 1986. "Pascal's Wager and Infinite Utilities." *Analysis* 46: 107–9.

Duncan, C. 2003. "Do Vague Probabilities Really Scotch Pascal's Wager?" *Philosophical Studies* 112: 279–90.

Dupré, L. 1972. "The Cosmological Argument after Kant." *International Journal for Philosophy of Religion* 3: 131–45.

Durrant, M. 1969. "St. Thomas' Third Way." *Religious Studies* 4: 229–43.

Earman, J. 1995. *Bangs, Crunches, Whimpers and Shrieks: Singularities and Acausalities in Relativistic Spacetimes*. Oxford: Oxford University Press.

Earman, J., and J. Norton. 1996. "Infinite Pains: The Trouble with Supertasks." In A. Morton and S. Stich (eds.), *Benacerraf and His Critics*. Oxford: Blackwell.

Edwards, R. 1968. "Composition and the Cosmological Argument." *Mind* 78: 115–17.

Edwards, R. 1971. "The Validity of Aquinas' Third Way." *New Scholasticism* 45: 117–26.

Edwards, R. 1973. "Another Visit to the Third Way." *New Scholasticism* 47: 100–4.

Eells, E. 1988. "Quentin Smith on Infinity and the Past." *Philosophy of Science* 55: 453–5.

Elliot, R., and M. Smith. 1978. "Descartes, God and the Evil Spirit." *Sophia* 17: 33–6.

Fakhry, M. 1959. "The Classical Islamic Arguments for the Existence of God." *The Muslim World* 49: 133–45.

Faricy, R. 1957. "Establishment of the Basic Principle of the Fifth Way." *New Scholasticism* 31: 189–208.

Feinberg, J., ed. 1989. *Reason and Responsibility*, 7th ed. Belmont, Calif.: Wadsworth.

Ferraiolo, W. 2000. "The Heaven Problem." *Southwest Philosophy Review* 16: 75–81.

Fetzer, J., ed. 1984. *Principles of Philosophical Reasoning*. Totowa, N.J.: Rowman and Allanheld.

Finili, A. 1954. "Recent Works in the *Tertia Via*." *Dominican Studies* 7: 22–47.

Fitelson, B., C. Stephens, and E. Sober. 1999. "How Not to Detect Design – Critical Notice: Dembski (1998)." *Philosophy of Science* 66: 472–88.

Fitzpatrick, F. 1981. "The Onus of Proof in Arguments about the Problem of Evil." *Religious Studies* 17: 19–38.

Flage, D., and C. Bonnen. 1989. "Descartes' Factitious Ideas of God." *Modern Schoolman* 66: 197–208.

Flew, A. 1960. "Is Pascal's Wager the Only Safe Bet?" *Rationalist Annual* 76. Reprinted in Flew (1984).

Flew, A. 1984. *God, Freedom and Immortality*. Buffalo: Prometheus.

Flint, T. 1998. *Divine Providence*. Ithaca, N.Y.: Cornell University Press.

Forrest, P. 1982. "Occam's Razor and Possible Worlds." *Monist* 65: 456–64.

Forrest, P. 1983. "Priest on the Argument for Design." *Australasian Journal of Philosophy* 61: 84–7.

Friquegnon, M. 1975. "God and Other Programs." *Religious Studies* 15: 83–9.

Gaine, S. 2003. *Will There Be Free Will in Heaven?* London: T&T Clark.

Gale, R. 1991. *On the Nature and Existence of God*. Cambridge: Cambridge University Press.

Gale, R. 1996. "Some Difficulties in Theistic Treatments of Evil." In Howard-Snyder (1996a), 206–18.

Gale, R. 1998. "Review of Oppy, *Ontological Arguments and Belief in God*." *Philosophy and Phenomenological Research*, 58: 715–19.

Gale, R., and A. Pruss. 1999. "A New Cosmological Argument." *Religious Studies* 35: 461–76.

Gale, R., and A. Pruss. 2003. "A Response to Oppy, and to Davey and Clifton." *Religious Studies* 38: 89–99.

Gaskin, J. 1976. "The Design Argument: Hume's Critique of Pure Reason." *Religious Studies* 12: 331–45.

Geanakoplos, J., and J. Sebenius. 1983. "Don't Bet on It." *Journal of American Statistical Association* 78: 424–6.

Gellman, J. 1994. "Experiencing God's Infinity." *American Philosophical Quarterly* 31: 53–61.

Gillespie, N. 1979. *Charles Darwin and the Problem of Creation*. Chicago: University of Chicago Press.

Glass, M., and J. Wolfe. 1986. "Paley's Design Argument for God." *Sophia* 25: 17–19.

Goetz, S. 1989. "Craig's *Kalām* Cosmological Argument." *Faith and Philosophy* 6: 99–102.

Golding, J. 1994. "Pascal's Wager." *Modern Schoolman* 71: 115–43.

Goodman, L. 1971. "Ghazāl's Argument from Creation." *International Journal of Middle Eastern Studies* 2: 67–85, 168–88.

Gould, S. 1993. *Eight Little Piggies*. New York: Norton, chapter 8: "Darwin and Paley Meet the Invisible Hand," 138–52.

Grave, S. 1976. "Hume's Criticism of the Argument from Design." *Revue Internationale de Philosophie* 30: 64–78.

Grünbaum, A. 1990. "The Pseudo-Problem of Creation in Physical Cosmology." In J. Leslie (ed.), *Physical Cosmology and Philosophy*. New York: Macmillan, 92–112.

Grünbaum, A. 1991. "Creation as a Pseudo-Explanation in Current Physical Cosmology." *Erkenntnis* 35: 233–54.

Grünbaum, A. 1994. "Some Comments on William Craig's 'Creation and Big Bang Cosmology'." *Philosophia Naturalis* 31: 225–36.

Grünbaum, A. 1996. "Theological Misinterpretations of Current Physical Cosmology." *Foundations of Physics* 26: 523–43.

Grünbaum, A. 2000. "A New Critique of Theological Interpretations of Physical Cosmology." *British Journal for the Philosophy of Science* 51: 1–43.

Hacking, I. 1972. "The Logic of Pascal's Wager." *American Philosophical Quarterly* 9: 186–92.

Hacking, I. 1987. "The Inverse Gambler's Fallacy: The Argument from Design. The Anthropic Principle Applied to Wheeler's Universes." *Mind* 76: 331–40.

Hájek, A. 2000. "Objecting Vaguely to Pascal's Wager." *Philosophical Studies* 98: 1–16.

Hájek, A. 2003. "Waging War on Pascal's Wager." *Philosophical Review* 112: 27–56.

Hájek, A. 2004. "Pascal's Wager." In E. Zalta (ed.), *The Stanford Encyclopedia of Philosophy*. Http://plato.stanford.edu/archives/spr2004/entries/pascal-wager, accessed June 15, 2004.

Haldane, J. 1983. "A Benign Regress." *Analysis* 43: 115–16.

Hardy, A. 1975. *The Biology of God*. London: Cape.

Harman, G. 1986. *Change in View: Principles of Reasoning*. Cambridge, Mass.: MIT Press (Bradford Books).

Harris, W., et al. 1999. "A Randomised, Controlled Trial of the Effects of Remote, Intercessory Prayer on Outcomes of Patients Admitted to a Coronary Unit." *Archives of Internal Medicine* 159: 2273–8.

Harrison, C. 1974. "Totalities and the Logic of First Cause Arguments." *Philosophy and Phenomenological Research* 35: 1–19.

Harrison, F. 1961. "Some Brief Remarks Concerning the *Quinque Via* of St. Thomas." *Franciscan Studies* 21: 80–93.

Hazen, A. 1999. "On Gödel's Ontological Proof." *Australasian Journal of Philosophy* 76, no. 3: 361–77.

Hebblethwaite, B. 1986. "Mellor's 'Bridge-Hand' Argument." *Religious Studies* 22: 473–9.

Hick, J., 1970. *Arguments for the Existence of God*. London: Macmillan.

Hinton, J. and C. Martin. 1953/4. "Achilles and the Tortoise." *Analysis* 14: 56–68.

Holcomb, H. 1995. "To Bet the Impossible Bet." *International Journal of Philosophy of Religion* 35: 65–79.

Holder, R. 2002. "Fine Tuning, Multiple Universes, and Theism." *Nous* 36: 295–312.

Hourani, G. 1958. "The Dialogue between Al Ghazāl and the Philosophers on the Origin of the World." *The Muslim World* 48: 183–91.

Howard-Snyder, D., ed. 1996a. *The Evidential Argument from Evil*. Bloomington: Indiana University Press.

Howard-Snyder, D. 1996b. "Introduction." In Howard-Snyder (1996a), xi–xx.

Howard-Snyder, D. 1996c. "The Argument from Inscrutable Evil." In Howard-Snyder (1996a), 286–310.

Hughes, C. 1989. *On a Complex Theory of a Simple God.* Ithaca, N.Y.: Cornell University Press.

Hughes, G. 1995. *The Nature of God.* London: Routledge.

Humphrey, T. 1974. "How Descartes Avoids the Hidden Faculties Trap." *Journal of the History of Philosophy* 12: 371–7.

Hurlbutt, R. 1965. *Hume, Newton and the Design Argument.* Lincoln: University of Nebraska Press.

Immerwahr, J. 1982. "Descartes' Two Cosmological Proofs." *New Scholasticism* 56: 346–54.

Jack, H. 1964. "A Recent Attempt to Prove God's Existence." *Philosophy and Phenomenological Research* 25: 575–9.

Jackson, F. 1995. *From Metaphysics to Ethics.* Oxford: Clarendon.

Jordan, J. 1991a. "Duff and the Wager." *Analysis* 51: 174–6.

Jordan, J. 1991b. "The Many-Gods Objection and Pascal's Wager." *International Philosophical Quarterly* 31: 309–17.

Jordan, J. 1993a. "Pascal's Wager and the Problem of Infinite Utilities." *Faith and Philosophy* 10: 49–59.

Jordan, J. 1993b. "Pascal's Wager and the Rationality of Devotion to God." *Faith and Philosophy* 10: 49–59.

Jordan, J., ed. 1994a. *Gambling on God: Essays on Pascal's Wager.* Rowman & Littlefield.

Jordan, J. 1994b. "The St. Petersburg Paradox and Pascal's Wager." *Philosophia* 23: 207–22.

Katz, B. 1997. "The Cosmological Argument without the Principle of Sufficient Reason." *Faith and Philosophy* 14: 62–70.

Kelly, C. 1981. "Some Fallacies in the First Movement of Aquinas' Third Way." *International Journal for Philosophy of Religion* 12: 39–54.

Kelly, C. 1982. "The Third Way and the Possible Eternity of the World." *New Scholasticism* 56: 273–91.

Kenny, A. 1968. "The Idea of God." In *Descartes: A Study of His Philosophy.* New York: Random House, 126–45.

Kenny, A. 1969. *The Five Ways: St. Thomas Aquinas' Proofs of God's Existence.* New York: Schocken Books.

King-Farlow, J. 1975. "The First Way in Physical and Moral Space." *Thomist* 39: 349–74.

Knasas, J. 1978. " 'Necessity' in the *Tertia Via.*" *New Scholasticism* 52: 373–94.

Knasas, J. 1980. "Making Sense of the *Tertia Via.*" *New Scholasticism* 54: 476–511.

Kondoleon, T. 1980. "The Third Way: Encore." *Thomist* 44: 325–56.

Koons, R. 1997. "A New Look at the Cosmological Argument." *American Philosophical Quarterly* 34: 193–211.

Koons, R. 2001. "Defeasible Reasoning, Special Pleading and the Cosmological Argument: A Reply to Oppy." *Faith and Philosophy* 18: 192–203.

Kragh, H. 1996. *Cosmology and Controversy: The Historical Development fo Two Theories of the Universe.* Princeton: Princeton University Press.

Kretzmann, N., ed. 1982. *Infinity and Continuity in Ancient and Medieval Thought.* Ithaca, N.Y.: Cornell University Press.

Kvanvig, J. 1997. "Heaven and Hell". In P. Quinn and C. Taliaferro (eds.), *A Companion to the Philosophy of Religion*. Oxford: Blackwell, 562–8.

Kwang, C., D. Wirth, and R. Lobo. 2001. "Does Prayer Influence the Success of in Vitro Fertilisation Transfer? Report of a Masked, Randomised Trial." *Journal of Reproductive Medicine* 46: 781–7.

La Croix, R. 1972. *Proslogion II and III: A Third Interpretation of Anselm's Argument*. Leiden: Brill.

Landsberg, P. 1971. "Gambling on God." *Mind* 80: 100–4.

Langtry, B. 1999. "Review of Oppy, *Ontological Arguments and Belief in God*." *Sophia* 36: 147–50.

Lavine, S. 1994. *Understanding the Infinite*. Cambridge, Mass.: Harvard University Press.

Leslie, J. 1985. "Modern Cosmology and the Creation of Life." In E. McMullin (ed.), *Evolution and Creation*. Notre Dame: University of Notre Dame Press, 91–120.

Leslie, J. 1989. *Universes*. London: Routledge.

Leslie, J., ed. 1990. *Physical Cosmology and Philosophy*. New York: Macmillan.

Lewis, D. 1970. "Anselm and Actuality." *Nous* 4: 175–88.

Lewis, D. 1976. "Survival and Identity." In A. Rorty (ed.), *The Identities of Persons*. Los Angeles: University of California Press, 17–40.

Lewis, D. 1986. *On the Plurality of Worlds*. Oxford: Basil Blackwell.

Lewis, D. 1999. *Papers in Metaphysics and Epistemology*. Cambridge: Cambridge University Press.

Linehan, J. 1959. "Modern Science and the Proof from Motion of the Existence of a Theistic God." *Franciscan Studies* 19: 128–41.

Lorca, D. 1995. "A Critique of Quentin Smith's Atheistic Argument from Big Bang Cosmology." *Philosophy* 70: 39–51.

Lycan, W., and G. Schlesinger. 1989. "You Bet Your Life." In Feinberg (1989), 82–90.

Mabey, R. 1971. "Confusion and the Cosmological Argument." *Mind* 80: 124–6.

MacIntosh, D. 1994. "Could God Have Made the Big Bang? (On Theistic Counterfactuals)." *Dialogue* 33: 3–20.

MacIntosh, J. 2000. "Is Pascal's Wager Self-Defeating?." *Sophia* 39: 1–30.

Mackie, J. 1955. "Evil and Omnipotence." *Mind* 64: 200–12.

Mackie, J. 1982. *The Miracle of Theism*. Oxford: Oxford University Press.

Madden, E., and P. Hare. 1968. *Evil and the Concept of God*. Springfield, Ill.: C. Thomas.

Makinde, M. 1985. "Pascal's Wager and the Atheist's Dilemma." *International Journal for Philosophy of Religion* 17: 115–29.

Malcolm, N. 1960. "Anselm's Ontological Arguments." *Philosophical Review* 69: 41–62.

Mann, W. 1972. "The Ontological Presuppositions of the Ontological Argument." *Review of Metaphysics* 26: 260–77.

Manson, N. 2000a. "Anthropocentrism and the Design Argument." *Religious Studies* 36: 163–76.

Manson, N. 2000b. "There Is No Adequate Definition of 'Fine-Tuned for Life'." *Inquiry* 43: 341–51.

Manson, N., ed. 2003. *God and Design*. London: Routledge.

Manson, N., and M. Thrush. 2003. "Fine-Tuning, Multiple Universes and the 'This Universe' Objection." *Pacific Philosophical Quarterly* 84: 67–83.

Markosian, N. 1995. "On the Argument from Quantum Cosmology against Theism."
    Analysis 55: 247–51.
Marmura, M. 1957. "The Logical Role of the Argument from Time in the Tahāfut's
    Second Proof for the World's Pre-Eternity." *The Muslim World* 47: 306–14.
Martin, C. 1959. *Religious Belief.* Ithaca, N.Y.: Cornell University Press.
Martin, M. 1975. "On Four Critiques of Pascal's Wager." *Sophia* 14: 1–11.
Martin, M. 1983. "Pascal's Wager as an Argument for Not Believing in God." *Religious
    Studies* 19: 57–64.
Martin, M. 1990. *Atheism: A Philosophical Justification.* Philadelphia: Temple University
    Press.
Martin, M. 1997. "Problems with Heaven." Http://www.infidels.org/library/modern/
    michael_martin/heaven.html, accessed June 29, 2004.
Matson, M. 1965. *The Existence of God.* Ithaca, N.Y.: Cornell University Press.
Mautner, T. 1969. "Aquinas' Third Way." *American Philosophical Quarterly* 6: 298–304.
McClelland, R., and R. Deltete. 2000. "Divine Causation." *Faith and Philosophy* 17:
    3–25.
McGrew, T., L. McGrew, and E. Vestrup. 2001. "Probabilities and the Fine-Tuning
    Argument: A Sceptical View." *Mind* 110: 127–37.
McLaughlin, R. 1984. "Necessary Agnosticism?" *Analysis* 44: 198–202.
McPherson, T. 1957. "The Argument from Design." *Philosophy* 32: 219–28.
McPherson, T. 1972. *The Argument from Design.* London: Macmillan.
McQuinn, J. 1978. "The Third Way to God: A New Approach." *Thomist* 42: 50–68.
Mellor, D. 1973. "God and Probability." In K. Yandell (ed.), *God, Man and Religion.*
    New York: McGraw-Hill.
Meyer, R. 1987. "God Exists!" *Nous* 21: 345–61.
Miethe, T. 1979. "The Cosmological Argument: A Research Bibliography." *New
    Scholasticism* 53: 285–305.
Miller, K. 1999. *Finding Darwin's God: A Scientist's Search for Common Ground between
    God and Evolution.* New York: Cliff Street Books.
Miller, K. 2003. "Answering the Biochemical Argument from Design." In N. Manson
    (ed.), *God and Design.* London: Routledge, 292–307.
Monk, N. 1997. "Conceptions of Space-Time: Problems and Possible Solutions."
    Studies in the History and Philosophy of Modern Physics 28, no. 1: 1–34.
Moody, T. 1996. *Does God Exist?* Indianapolis: Hackett.
Moreland, J. 2003. "A Response to a Platonistic and to a Set-Theoretic Objection to
    the Kalam Cosmological Argument." *Religious Studies* 39: 373–90.
Morreall, J. 1979. "Aquinas' Fourth Way." *Sophia* 18: 20–8.
Morris, T. 1986. "Pascalian Wagering." *Canadian Journal of Philosophy* 16: 437–54.
Morriston, W. 1999. "Must the Past Have a Beginning?." *Philo* 2: 5–19.
Morriston, W. 2002a. "Craig on the Actual Infinite." *Religious Studies* 38: 147–66.
Morriston, W. 2002b. "Creation *Ex Nihilo* and the Big Bang." *Philo* 5: 23–33.
Mougin, G., and E. Sober. 1994. "Betting against Pascal's Wager." *Nous* 27:
    382–95.
Nagasawa, Y., G. Oppy, and N. Trakakis. 2004. "Salvation in Heaven?" *Philosophical
    Papers* 33: 1, 97–119.
Narveson, J. 1965. "On a New Argument from Design." *Journal of Philosophy* 62:
    223–8.
Natoli, C. 1983. "The Role of the Wager in Pascal's Apologetics." *New Scholasticism*
    57: 98–106.

Nelson, H. 1993. "Kant on Arguments Cosmological and Ontological." *American Catholic Philosophical Quarterly* 67: 167–84.

Nelson, K. 1978. "Evolution and the Argument from Design." *Religious Studies* 14: 423–43.

New, C. 1993. "Antitheism." *Ratio* 6: 36–43.

Newman, J. 1870. *An Essay in Aid of a Grammar of Assent.* Oxford: Clarendon, 72–83.

Nicholl, L. 1979. "Pascal's Wager: The Bet Is Off." *Philosophy and Phenomenological Research* 39: 274–80.

Norton, D. 1968. "Descartes on Unknown Faculties: An Essential Inconsistency." *Journal of the History of Philosophy* 6: 245–56.

Norton, D. 1974. "Descartes' Inconsistency: A Reply." *Journal of the History of Philosophy* 12: 509–20.

Norton, D. 1978. "A Reply to Professor Stevens." *Journal of the History of Philosophy* 16: 338–41.

Noxon, J. 1964. "Hume's Agnosticism." *Philosophical Review* 73: 248–61.

O'Briant, W. 1967. "A New Argument from Design?" *Sophia* 6: 30–4.

O'Briant, W. 1979. "Is Descartes' Evil Spirit Finite or Infinite?" *Sophia* 18: 28–32.

Oderberg, D. 2002a. "Traversal of the Infinite, the 'Big Bang', and the *Kalām* Cosmological Argument." *Philosophia Christi* 4, no. 2: 303–34.

Oderberg, D. 2002b. "The Tristram Shandy Paradox: A Reply to Graham Oppy." *Philosophia Christi* 4, no. 2: 351–60.

O'Donoghue, D. 1953. "Analysis of the *Tertia Via* of St. Thomas." *Irish Theological Quarterly* 20: 129–57.

O'Donoghue, D. 1969. "The First Part of the Third Way: Reply." *Philosophical Studies (Ireland)* 18: 172–7.

Olding, A. 1971. "The Argument from Design – A Reply to R. G. Swinburne." *Religious Studies* 7: 361–73.

Olding, A. 1973. "Design – A Further Reply to R. G. Swinburne." *Religious Studies* 9: 229–32.

O'Leary-Hawthorne, J., and A. Cortens. 1995. "Towards Ontological Nihilism." *Philosophical Studies* 79, no. 2: 143–65.

Oppenheimer, P., and E. Zalta. 1991. "On the Logic of the Ontological Argument." In J. Tomberlin (ed.), *Philosophical Perspectives*, vol. 5: *The Philosophy of Religion.* Atascadero, Calif.: Ridgeview, 509–29.

Oppy, G. 1990. "On Rescher on Pascal's Wager." *International Journal for Philosophy of Religion* 30: 159–68.

Oppy, G. 1991. "Craig, Mackie and the *Kalām* Cosmological Argument." *Religious Studies* 27: 189–97.

Oppy, G. 1994. "Weak Agnosticism Defended." *International Journal for Philosophy of Religion* 36: 147–67.

Oppy, G. 1995a. "Inverse Operations with Transfinite Numbers and the *Kalām* Cosmological Argument." *International Philosophical Quarterly* 35, no. 2: 219–21.

Oppy, G. 1995b. "*Kalām* Cosmological Arguments: Reply to Professor Craig." *Sophia* 34: 15–29.

Oppy, G. 1995c. *Ontological Arguments and Belief in God.* New York: Cambridge University Press.

Oppy, G. 1995d. "Professor William Craig's Criticisms of Critiques of *Kalām* Cosmological Arguments by Paul Davies, Stephen Hawking, and Adolf Grünbaum." *Faith and Philosophy* 12: 237–50.

Oppy, G. 1996a. "Gödelian Ontological Arguments." *Analysis* 56, no. 4 (October) 1: 226–30.

Oppy, G. 1996b. "Hume and the Argument for Biological Design." *Biology and Philosophy* 11: 519–34.

Oppy, G. 1996c. "Ontological Arguments." *Stanford Electronic Encyclopedia of Philosophy*. Http://plato.stanford.edu/entries/ontological-arguments (revised 2002). Accessed March 2, 2004.

Oppy, G. 1996d. "Pascal's Wager Is a Possible Bet (But Not a Very Good One): Reply to Harmon Holcomb III." *International Journal for Philosophy of Religion* 40: 101–16.

Oppy, G. 1996e. "Review of W. Craig and Q. Smith, *Theism, Atheism and Big Bang Cosmology.*" *Faith and Philosophy* 13: 125–33.

Oppy, G. 1997a. "Countable Fusion Not Yet Proven Guilty: It May Be the Whiteheadian Account of Space Whatdunnit." *Analysis* 57, no. 4: 249–53.

Oppy, G. 1997b. "Pantheism, Quantification, and Mereology." *Monist* 80, no. 2: 320–36.

Oppy, G. 1997c. "Some Questions about 'The Hartle-Hawking Cosmology'." *Sophia* 36, no. 1: 84–95.

Oppy, G. 1999. "Koons' Cosmological Argument." *Faith and Philosophy* 16: 378–89.

Oppy, G. 2000a. "*Humean* Supervenience?" *Philosophical Studies* 101, no. 1: 75–105.

Oppy, G. 2000b. "On 'A New Cosmological Argument'." *Religious Studies* 36: 345–53.

Oppy, G. 2000c. "Response to Gettings." *Analysis* 60: 363–7.

Oppy, G. 2001a. "Reply to Langtry." *Sophia* 40: 73–80.

Oppy, G. 2001b. "Time, Successive Addition, and the *Kalām* Cosmological Argument." *Philosophia Christi* 3: 181–91.

Oppy, G. 2002a. "Arguing about the *Kalām* Cosmological Argument." *Philo* 5, no. 1:34–61.

Oppy, G. 2002b. "More Than a Flesh Wound: Reply to Oderberg." *Ars Disputandi* 2: 1–11. Http://www.ArsDisputandi.org.

Oppy, G. 2002c. "Paley's Argument for Design." *Philo* 5, no. 2: 41–53.

Oppy, G. 2002d. "The Tristram Shandy Paradox: A Response to David S. Oderberg." *Philosophia Christi* 4, no. 2: 335–49.

Oppy, G. 2003a. "From the Tristram Shandy Paradox to the Christmas Shandy Paradox: Reply to Oderberg." *Ars Disputandi* 3: 1–24. Http://www.ArsDisputandi.org.

Oppy, G. 2004a. "Arguments from Moral Evil." *International Journal for Philosophy of Religion* 56: 59–87.

Oppy, G. 2004b. "Faulty Reasoning about Default Principles in Cosmological Arguments." *Faith and Philosophy* 21, no. 2: 242–9.

Oppy, G. 2004c. "God, God* and God'." In A. Fisher and H. Ramsay (eds.), *Faith and Reason: Friends or Foes in the New Millennium?* Hindmarsh: ATF Press, 171–86.

Oppy, G. 2004d. "Review of *God and Design*, edited by Neil Manson." *Sophia* 43, no. 1: 127–31.

Oppy, G. 2006. *Philosophical Perspectives on Infinity*. New York: Cambridge University Press.

Oppy, G. In preparation. *Describing Gods*. Unpublished ms.

Owens, J. 1952/3. "Conclusion of the *Prima Via*." *Modern Schoolman* 30: 33–53, 109–21, 203–15.

Owens, J. 1971. "'Cause of Necessity' in Aquinas' *Tertia Via.*" *Medieval Studies* 33: 21–45.

Owens, J. 1974. "Aquinas and the Five Ways." *Monist* 58: 16–35.

Owens, J. 1980. "'*Quandoque*' and '*Aliquando*' in Aquinas' *Tertia Via.*" *New Scholasticism* 54: 447–75.

Paley, W. 1890/1805. *Natural Theology.* London: Gilbert and Rivington.

Parent, W. 1976. "Philo's Confession." *Philosophical Quarterly* 26: 63–8.

Parfit, D. 1984. *Reasons and Persons.* Oxford: Clarendon.

Paul, G. 2005. "Cross-National Correlations of Quantifiable Societal Health with Popular Religiosity and Secularism in the Prosperous Democracies." *Journal of Religion and Society* 7: 1–17.

Pearl, L. 1970. "Hume's Criticism of the Argument from Design." *Monist* 54: 270–84.

Penelhum, T. 1964. "Pascal's Wager." *Journal of Religion* 44: 32–44.

Plantinga, A. 1967. *God and Other Minds.* Ithaca, N.Y.: Cornell University Press.

Plantinga, A. 1974. *The Nature of Necessity.* Oxford: Clarendon.

Plantinga, A. 1979a. "Is Belief in God Rational?" In C. Delaney (ed.), *Rationality and Religious Belief.* Notre Dame: University of Notre Dame Press, 2–29.

Plantinga, A. 1979b. "The Probabilistic Argument from Evil." *Philosophical Studies* 35: 1–53.

Plantinga, A. 1980. *Does God Have a Nature?* Milwaukee, Minn.: Marquette University Press.

Plantinga, A. 1983. "Reason and Belief in God." In A. Plantinga and N. Wolterstorff (eds.), *Faith and Rationality: Reason and Belief in God.* Notre Dame: University of Notre Dame Press.

Plantinga, A. 1988/96. "Epistemic Probability." In Howard-Snyder (1996a), 69–96.

Pomerlau, W. 1985. "Does Reason Demand That God Be Infinite?" *Sophia* 24: 18–27.

Prado, C. 1971. "The Third Way Revisited." *New Scholasticism* 45: 495–501.

Prevost, R. 1990. "Classical Theism and the Kalam Principle." In W. Craig and M. McLeod (eds.), *Rational Theism: The Logic of a Worldview.* Lewiston, N.Y.: Edwin Mellen, 113–25.

Price, H. 1988. "Review of *Change in View.*" *Philosophical Books* 29: 38–41.

Price, H. 1992. "Metaphysical Pluralism." *Journal of Philosophy* 89, no. 8: 387–409.

Priest, G. 1981. "The Argument from Design." *Australasian Journal of Philosophy* 59: 422–31.

Quine, W. 1953. *From a Logical Point of View.* Cambridge, Mass.: Harvard University Press.

Quinn, J. 1978. "The Third Way to God: A New Approach." *Thomist* 42: 50–68.

Quinn, J. 1982. "A Few Reflections on 'The Third Way: Encore'." *Thomist* 46: 75–91.

Rashdall, H. 1907. "The Moral Argument for the Existence of God." Reprinted in J. Hick (ed.) (1964), *Classical and Contemporary Readings in the Philosophy of Religion.* Englewood Cliffs, N.J.: Prentice-Hall, 268–73.

Reichenbach, B. 1972. *The Cosmological Argument: A Reassessment* Springfield, Ill.: Charles C. Thomas.

Remnant, P. 1959. "Kant and the Cosmological Argument." *Australasian Journal of Philosophy* 37: 152–5.

Rescher, N. 1985. *Pascal's Wager.* South Bend, Ind.: University of Notre Dame Press.

Ross, J. 1969. *Philosophical Theology*. Indianapolis: Bobbs-Merrill.

Rowe, W. 1975. *The Cosmological Argument*. Princeton: Princeton University Press.

Rowe, W. 1979. "The Problem of Evil and Some Varieties of Atheism." *American Philosophical Quarterly* 16: 335–41.

Rowe, W. 1984. "Rationalistic Theology and Some Principles of Explanation." *Faith and Philosophy* 1: 357–69.

Rowe, W. 1986. "Evil and the Theistic Hypothesis." *International Journal for Philosophy of Religion* 16: 95–100.

Rowe, W. 1988. "Response to Dicker." *Faith and Philosophy* 5: 203–5.

Rowe, W. 1991. "Ruminations about Evil." *Noûs*, supp. 5: 69–88.

Rowe, W. 1995. "Religion within the Bounds of Naturalism." *International Journal for Philosophy of Religion* 38: 17–36.

Rowe, W. 1996. "The Evidential Argument from Evil: A Second Look." In Howard-Snyder (1996a), 262–85.

Rowe, W. 2001. "Sceptical Theism: A Response to Bergmann." *Noûs* 35: 297–303.

Ruse, M. 1977. "William Whewell and the Argument for Design." *Monist* 54: 244–68.

Ruse, M. 1979. *The Darwinian Revolution*. Chicago: University of Chicago Press.

Ruse, M. 2003. "Modern Biologists and the Argument from Design." In N. Manson (ed.), *God and Design*. London: Routledge, 308–28.

Russell, Lord B. 1927. "Why I Am Not a Christian." Rationalist Press Association Ltd. London: Watts and Co.

Russell, B. 1989. "The Persistent Problem of Evil." *Faith and Philosophy* 6: 121–39.

Russell, B. 1996. "Defenceless." In Howard-Snyder (1996a), 193–205.

Ryan, J. 1945. "The Wager in Pascal and Others." *New Scholasticism* 19: 233–50. Reprinted in Jordan (1994b).

Sadowsky, J. 1988. "Did Darwin Destroy the Design Argument?" *International Philosophical Quarterly* 28: 95–104.

Salamucha, J. 1958. "The Proof '*Ex Motu*' for the Existence of God: Logical Analysis of St. Thomas' Arguments." *New Scholasticism* 32: 334–72.

Salmon, W. 1978. "Religion and Science: A New Look at Hume's Dialogues." *Philosophical Studies* 33: 143–76.

Sanford, D. 1967. "Degrees of Perfection, Argument for the Existence of God." In P. Edwards (ed.), *Encyclopedia of Philosophy*. New York: Macmillan, 324–6.

Schindler, D. 2002. "Freedom beyond Our Choosing: Augustine on the Will and Its Objects." *Communio: International Catholic Review* 29: 4–12.

Schlesinger, G. 1973. "Probabilistic Arguments for Divine Design." *Philosophia* 3: 1–16.

Schlesinger, G. 1983. "Theism and Confirmation." *Pacific Philosophical Quarterly* 64: 46–56.

Schoen, E. 1990. "The Sensory Presentation of Divine Infinity." *Faith and Philosophy* 7: 3–18.

Sennett, J. 1999. "Is There Freedom in Heaven?" *Faith and Philosophy* 16: 69–82.

Sidgwick, H. 1874. *The Methods of Ethics*. London: Macmillan.

Smart, J. 1955. "The Existence of God." In A. Flew and A. MacIntyre (eds.), *New Essays in Philosophical Theology*. New York: Macmillan.

Smith, Q. 1985. "Kant and the Beginning of the World." *New Scholasticism* 59: 339–48.

Smith, Q. 1987. "Infinity and the Past." *Philosophy of Science* 54: 63–75.

Smith, Q. 1988. "The Uncaused Beginning of the Universe." *Philosophy of Science* 55: 39–57.

Smith, Q. 1991. "Atheism, Theism and Big Bang Cosmology." *Australasian Journal of Philosophy* 69: 48–65.

Smith, Q. 1993a. "A Defence of the Cosmological Argument for God's Non-Existence." In W. Craig and Q. Smith, *Theism, Atheism and Big Bang Cosmology*. Oxford: Clarendon, 232–55.

Smith, Q. 1993b. "The Concept of a Cause of the Universe." *Canadian Journal of Philosophy* 23: 1–24.

Smith, Q. 1993c. "Reply to Craig: The Possible Infinitude of the Past." *International Philosophical Quarterly* 33: 109–15.

Smith, Q. 1994a. "Did the Big Bang Have a Cause?" *British Journal for the Philosophy of Science* 45: 649–68.

Smith, Q. 1994b. "Stephen Hawking's Cosmology and Theism." *Analysis* 54: 236–43.

Smith, Q. 1995a. "A Defence of a Principle of Sufficient Reason." *Metaphilosophy* 26: 97–106.

Smith, Q. 1995b. "Internal and External Causal Explanation of the Universe." *Philosophical Studies* 79: 283–310.

Smith, Q. 1997a. "Quantum Cosmology's Implication of Atheism." *Analysis* 57: 295–304.

Smith, Q. 1997b. "Simplicity and Why the Universe Exists." *Philosophy* 72: 125–32.

Smith, Q. 1999. "The Reason the Universe Exists Is That It Caused Itself to Exist." *Philosophy* 74: 579–86.

Smith, Q. 2000. "Problem's with John Earman's Attempt to Reconcile Theism with General Relativity." *Erkenntnis* 52: 1–27.

Sobel, J. 1987. "Gödel's Ontological Proof." In J. J. Thomson (ed.), *On Being and Saying: Essays for Richard Cartwright*. Cambridge, Mass.: MIT Press, 241–61.

Sobel, J. 1996. "Pascalian Wagers." *Synthese* 108: 11–61.

Sobel, J. 2004. *Logic and Theism*. New York: Cambridge University Press.

Sober, E. 1993. *The Philosophy of Biology*. Boulder, Colo.: Westview.

Sober, E. 2003. "The Design Argument." In N. Manson (ed.), *God and Design*. London: Routledge.

Solon, T. 1973. "The Logic of Aquinas' *Tertia Via*." *Mind* 82: 598–9.

Sorabji, R. 1983. *Time, Creation and the Continuum*. London: Duckworth.

Stainsby, H. 1967. "Descartes' Argument for God." *Sophia* 6: 11–16.

Stein, E. 1990. "God, the Demon, and the Status of Theologies." *American Philosophical Quarterly* 27: 163–7.

Stevens, J. 1978. "Unknown Faculties and Descartes' First Proof of the Existence of God." *Journal of the History of Philosophy* 16: 334–8.

Stich, S. 1983. *From Folk Psychology to Cognitive Science: The Case against Belief*. Cambridge, Mass.: MIT Press.

Stump, E. 1999. "The Problem of Evil." *Faith and Philosophy* 2: 392–418.

Sullivan, T. 1990. "Coming to Be without a Cause." *Philosophy* 65: 261–70.

Sullivan, T. 1994. "On the Alleged Causeless Beginning of the Universe: A Reply to Quentin Smith." *Dialogue* 33: 325–35.

Sweeney, E. 1993. "Thomas Aquinas' Double Metaphysics of Simplicity and Infinity." *International Philosophical Quarterly* 33: 297–317.

Swinburne, R. 1966. "The Beginning of the Universe." *Proceedings of the Aristotelian Society* 40: 125–38.

Swinburne, R. 1968. "The Argument from Design." *Philosophy* 43: 199–211.

Swinburne, R. 1969. "The Christian Wager." *Religious Studies* 4: 217–28.

Swinburne, R. 1972. "The Argument from Design – A Defence." *Religious Studies* 8: 193–205.

Swinburne, R. 1977. *The Coherence of Theism.* Oxford: Clarendon.

Swinburne, R. 1979. *The Existence of God.* Oxford: Clarendon.

Swinburne, R. 1983. "A Theodicy of Heaven and Hell." In A. Freddoso (ed.), *The Existence and Nature of God.* Notre Dame: Notre Dame University Press.

Swinburne, R. 1994. *The Christian God.* Oxford: Clarendon.

Swinburne, R. 1996. *Is There a God?* Oxford: Oxford University Press.

Taliaferro, C. 1992. "Imaginary Evil: A Sceptic's Wager." *Philosophia* 21: 221–33.

Taliaferro, C. 1998. *Contemporary Philosophy of Religion.* Oxford: Blackwell.

Taylor, J. 1997. "*Kalām*: A Swift Argument from Origins to a First Cause?" *Religious Studies* 33: 167–79.

Taylor, R. 1963. *Metaphysics.* Englewood Cliffs, N.J.: Prentice-Hall.

Tennant, F. 1969. *Philosophical Theology*, 2 vols. Cambridge: Cambridge University Press.

Tomberlin, J., ed. 1988. *Philosophical Perspectives* 2. Atascadero, Calif.: Ridgeview.

Tooley, M. 1970. "Does the Cosmological Argument Entail the Ontological Argument?" *Monist* 54: 416–26.

Tooley, M. 1981. "Plantinga's Defence of the Ontological Argument." *Mind* 90: 422–7.

Turner, M. 1968. "Deciding for God – the Bayesian Support of Pascal's Wager." *Philosophy and Phenomenological Research* 29: 84–90.

Urban, L. 1984. "Understanding St. Thomas' Fourth Way." *History of Philosophy Quarterly* 1: 281–95.

Van Fraassen, B. 1995. "'World' Is Not a Count Noun." *Nous* 29, no. 2: 139–57.

Van Inwagen, P. 1991/6. "The Problem of Evil, the Problem of Air, and the Problem of Silence." In Howard-Snyder (1996a), 151–74.

Wainwright, W. 1982. "Critical Notice of *The Kalām Cosmological Argument.*" *Nous* 16: 328–34.

Wallace, W. 1956. "Newtonian Antinomies against the *Prima Via.*" *Thomist* 19: 151–92.

Wallace, W. 1975. "The First Way: A Rejoinder." *Thomist* 39: 375–82.

Walls, J. 2002. *Heaven: The Logic of Eternal Joy.* Oxford: Oxford University Press.

White, R. 2000. "Fine-Tuning and Multiple Universes." *Nous* 34: 260–76.

Williams, B. 1978. "God." In *Descartes: The Project of Pure Enquiry.* Harmondsworth: Penguin, 130–62.

Wilson, P. 1991. "What Is the *Explanandum* of the Anthropic Principle?" *American Philosophical Quarterly* 28: 167–73.

Wolfson, H. 1966. "Patristic Arguments against the Eternity of the World." *Harvard Theological Review* 59: 354–67.

Wolfson, H. 1976. *The Philosophy of the Kalām.* Cambridge, Mass.: Harvard University Press.

Wolterstorff, N. 1983. "Can Belief in God Be Rational If It Has No Foundations?" In A. Plantinga and N. Wolterstorff (eds.), *Faith and Rationality: Reason and Belief in God*. Notre Dame: University of Notre Dame Press.

Wright, T. 1951. "Necessary and Contingent Being in St. Thomas." *New Scholasticism* 25: 439–66.

Wykstra, S. 1984. "The Humean Obstacle to Evidential Arguments from Suffering: On Avoiding the Evils of 'Appearance'." *International Journal for Philosophy of Religion* 16: 73–93.

Wykstra, S. 1996. "Rowe's Noseeum Arguments from Evil." In Howard-Snyder (1996a), 126–50.

Yarvin, H. 1976. "The Will to Come Out All Right." *Religious Studies* 12: 303–9.

Index

absolute value, 355
Adams, Bob, 70, 86, 89, 92, 328
addition, successive, 142
adventitious ideas, 110
agnosticism, 37, 39, 53, 58, 129, 179, 231, 235, 244, 307, 333, 414, 416, 417
Alston, William, 289, 309
Anderson, Tony, 70
Anselm, St., 65, 72, 88
Aquinas, St. Thomas, xvi, 101, 120, 124, 329, 338; Five Ways, 98, 107, 130; The First Way, 102, 103; The Second Way, 99, 102; The Third Way, 103, 107
arguments from evil, xvii, 4, 103, 123, 208, 259, 321, 328, 402; evidential arguments from evil, 4, 289, 313; logical arguments from evil, 4, 262, 289
arguments, minor evidential, 4
arguments, moral, see moral arguments
arguments, successful, 7, 10
arguments, teleological, see teleological arguments
Armstrong, David, 274
atheism, 1, 15, 34, 37, 229, 246, 333
Augustine, 328
axiom of choice, 124

background knowledge, 176, 177, 182, 209, 217, 218, 221, 224, 347, 391
bacterial flagellum, 192, 195
Barbour, Ian, 175
Barcan principle, 125
Barnes, Jonathon, 89
Bayesianism, 8, 38, 202, 203, 204, 208, 209, 212, 227, 296

beauty, 411
begging the question, 5, 11, 30, 51, 52, 57, 58, 64, 67, 91, 101, 102, 106, 125, 142, 182, 229, 347, 354, 356, 364, 367
behaviourism, 396
Behe, Michael, 187
belief: coherence, of, 9; and motivation, 40; web of, 8
Bergmann, Mike, 289, 304, 309
big-bang cosmology, 101, 138, 149, 154, 158, 172
Big Conjunctive Contingent Fact, 130, 132
Bigelow, John, 274
Boyle lectures, 185, 230
Brennan, Geoff, 284
Bridgewater treatises, 185, 230
Bringsjord, Selmer, 395, 398
brute contingency, 120, 134, 136, 160, 234, 239
Bugge, Thomas, 196
Burman, David, 333
Byrne, Alex, 256

Campbell, Richard, 89
Cantor, Georg, 33, 139, 140
Carnap, Rudolf, 67
causation, 3, 97, 98, 99, 100, 101, 102, 170
central state materialism, 396
Chalmers, Dave, 399
Chambers, Timothy, 72, 88
Charlesworth, Max, 89
choice, axiom of, 124
Churchland, Pat, 384
Churchland, Paul, 384
Clark, Romane, 101